Lecture Notes in Computer Science 8544

Commenced Publication in 1973
Founding and Former Series Editors:
Gerhard Goos, Juris Hartmanis, and Jan van Leeuwen

T0236354

Willy Susilo   Yi Mu (Eds.)

Information Security and Privacy

19th Australasian Conference, ACISP 2014
Wollongong, NSW, Australia, July 7-9, 2014
Proceedings

 Springer

Volume Editors

Willy Susilo
University of Wollongong
Centre for Computer and Information Security Research
School of Computer Science and Software Engineering
Northfields Avenue
Wollongong, NSW 2522, Australia
E-mail: wsusilo@uow.edu.au

Yi Mu
University of Wollongong
Centre for Computer and Information Security Research
School of Computer Science and Software Engineering
Northfields Avenue
Wollongong, NSW 2522, Australia
E-mail: ymu@uow.edu.au

ISSN 0302-9743   e-ISSN 1611-3349
ISBN 978-3-319-08343-8   e-ISBN 978-3-319-08344-5
DOI 10.1007/978-3-319-08344-5
Springer Cham Heidelberg New York Dordrecht London

Library of Congress Control Number: 2014941281

LNCS Sublibrary: SL 4 – Security and Cryptology

Typesetting: Camera-ready by author, data conversion by Scientific Publishing Services, Chennai, India

Printed on acid-free paper

Springer is part of Springer Science+Business Media (www.springer.com)

Preface

The 19th Australasian Conference on Information Security and Privacy (ACISP 2014) was held at Wollongong, Australia, during July 7–9, 2014. The conference was sponsored by the Centre for Computer and Information Security of the University of Wollongong. The submission and review process was conducted with Easychair.

There were 91 submissions. Each submission was reviewed by at least 3 Program Committee members. The Program Committee selected 26 full papers and 6 short papers for presentation at the conference after a rigorous review process and thorough discussion. These papers are included in the proceedings. The accepted papers cover a range of topics in information security, including cryptographic protocols, cryptanalysis, key exchange protocols, cryptographic theories, lattices and homomorphic encryption, and cryptographic applications.

The conference proceedings contain revised versions of the selected papers. Since some of them were not checked again for correctness prior to the publication, the authors bear full responsibility for the contents of their papers. We would like to thank the authors of all papers for submitting their papers to the conference.

In addition to the contributed papers, the program comprised two invited talks. The invited speakers were Tatsuaki Okamoto (NTT Laboratory, Japan) with the topic on "Oblivious Functional Search" and Giuseppe Ateniese (Sapienza, Università di Roma) with the topic on "Cloud Storage in the Bitcoin Era". We would like to express our thanks to them.

As in previous years, the Program Committee selected a "best student paper". To be eligible for selection, a paper has to be co-authored by a postgraduate student, whose contribution was more than 50%. The winner was Liang Liu from Xidian University, Xi'an, China for the paper "A Secure Three-Party Computational Protocol for Triangle Area".

We would like to thank all the people who helped with the conference program and organization. In particular, we heartily thank the Program Committee and the sub-reviewers listed on the following pages for the effort and time they contributed to the review process. We would also like to express our thanks to Springer for continuing to support the ACISP conference and for help in the conference proceedings production.

Finally, we would like to thank the general chair, Jennifer Seberry, and the Organizing Committee for their excellent contribution to the conference.

July 2014

Willy Susilo
Yi Mu

Organization

Program Chairs

Willy Susilo   University of Wollongong, Australia
Yi Mu   University of Wollongong, Australia

General Chair

Jennifer Seberry   University of Wollongong, Australia

Program Committee

Man Ho Au	University of Wollongong, Australia
Joonsang Baek	Khalifa University of Science, United Arab Emirates
Lynn Batten	Deakin University, Australia
Alex Biryukov	University of Luxembourg, Luxembourg
Ioana Boureanu	EPFL Lausanne, Switzerland
Xavier Boyen	Queensland University of Technology, Australia
Serdar Boztas	RMIT University, Australia
Liqun Chen	Hewlett-Packard Laboratories, UK
Xiaofeng Chen	Xidian University, China
Kim-Kwang Raymond Choo	University of South Australia, Australia
Nicolas Courtois	UCL, UK
Ed Dawson	Queensland University of Technology, Australia
Qiong Huang	South China Agricultural University, China
Xinyi Huang	Fujian Normal University, China
Xuejia Lai	Shanghai Jiaotong University, China
Jin Li	Guangzhou University, China
Dongdai Lin	Chinese Academy of Sciences, China
Joseph Liu	Institute for infocomm research, Singapore
Chris Mitchell	Royal Holloway, University of London, UK
Atsuko Miyaji	Japan Advanced Institute of Science and Technology, Japan
Tatsuaki Okamoto	NTT, Japan
Udaya Parampalli	The University of Melbourne, Australia
Josef Pieprzyk	Macquarie University, Australia
Reza Reyhanitabar	EPFL Lausanne, Switzerland

Rei Safavi-Naini   University of Calgary, Canada
Pierangela Samarati   Università degli Studi di Milano, Italy
Palash Sarkar   Indian Statistical Institute, India
Douglas Stebila   Queensland University of Technology, Australia
Damien Stehle   CNRS, France
Ron Steinfeld   Monash University, Australia
Douglas Stinson   David R. Cheriton School of Computer Science,
                               Canada
Tsuyoshi Takagi   Kyushu University, Japan
Huaxiong Wang   Nanyang Technological University, Singapore
Duncan Wong   City University of Hong Kong, Hong Kong
Hongjun Wu   Nanyang Technological University, Singapore
Qianhong Wu   Wuhan University, China
Guomin Yang   University of Wollongong, Australia
Kan Yasuda   NTT Corporation, Japan
Xun Yi   Victoria University, Australia
Jianying Zhou   Institute for infocomm research, Singapore

Publication Chairs

Man Ho Au   University of Wollongong, Australia
Yong Yu   University of Wollongong, Australia

Local Organization Committee

Fuchun Guo   University of Wollongong, Australia
Thomas Plantard   University of Wollongong, Australia

External Reviewers

Aoki, Kazumaro	Futa, Yuichi	Liang, Kaitai
Askari, Mina	Gong, Zheng	Libert, Benoit
Bartlett, Harry	Gong, Zhong	Lin, Changlu
Bay, Asli	Guo, Yanfei	Liu, Liang
Boyd, Colin	Henricksen, Matt	Liu, Weiran
Chen, Jiageng	Huang, Jialin	Liu, Zhen
Chen, Jie	Huang, Tao	Livraga, Giovanni
Chun, Guo	Ishiguro, Tsukasa	Lu, Yao
Dalkilic, Gokhan	Jhawar, Mahavir	Luo, Yiyuan
Deng, Hua	Jiang, Tao	Ma, Jiangang
Deng, Yi	Khovratovich, Dmitry	Ma, Sha
Derbez, Patrick	Kojima, Tetsuya	Mandal, Kalikinkar
Duc, Alexandre	Le Corre, Yann	Martini, Ben
El Kaafarani, Ali	Lee, Peter Hyun-Jeen	Meng, Weizhi
Foresti, Sara	Li, Wei	Morozov, Kirill

Mouha, Nicky
Nguyen, Khoa
Omote, Kazumasa
Paulet, Russell
Pelosi, Gerardo
Perret, Ludovic
Perrin, Leo Paul
Pustogarov, Ivan
Quang Dinh, Trung
Radke, Kenneth
Rahman, Sk Md Mizanur
Renault, Guenael
Roy, Arnab
Sasaki, Yu
Schmidt, Desmond
Smith, Ben

Su, Chunhua
Sun, Li
Susil, Petr
Tan, Xiao
Tao, Huang
Tibouchi, Mehdi
Tso, Raylin
Upadhyay, Jalaj
Vadnala, Praveen Kumar
Velichkov, Vesselin
Vizár, Damian
Wang, Jianfeng
Wang, Wenhao
Wang, Yujue
Wei, Lei
Welch, Ian

Wong, Kenneth
Wu, Wei
Xie, Xiang
Xu, Hong
Xue, Weijia
Yang, Anjia
Yang, Yanjiang
Zhang, Hui
Zhang, Huiling
Zhang, Jiang
Zhang, Liang Feng
Zhang, Shiwei
Zhang, Yinghui
Zhao, Xingwen

Table of Contents

Cryptanalysis

Improved Multidimensional Zero-Correlation Linear Cryptanalysis and
Applications to LBlock and TWINE............................... 1
   Yanfeng Wang and Wenling Wu

Differential and Impossible Differential Related-Key Attacks on
Hierocrypt-L1 17
   Bungo Taga, Shiho Moriai, and Kazumaro Aoki

Some Insights into Differential Cryptanalysis of Grain v1.............. 34
   Subhadeep Banik

On Selection of Samples in Algebraic Attacks and a New Technique to
Find Hidden Low Degree Equations 50
   Petr Sušil, Pouyan Sepehrdad, and Serge Vaudenay

Cryptographic Protocols

Strongly Simulation-Extractable Leakage-Resilient NIZK 66
   Yuyu Wang and Keisuke Tanaka

A Secure Three-Party Computational Protocol for Triangle Area 82
   Liang Liu, Xiaofeng Chen, and Wenjing Lou

Universally Composable Efficient Priced Oblivious Transfer from a
Flexible Membership Encryption 98
   Pratish Datta, Ratna Dutta, and Sourav Mukhopadhyay

TMDS: Thin-Model Data Sharing Scheme Supporting Keyword Search
in Cloud Storage... 115
   Zheli Liu, Jin Li, Xiaofeng Chen, Jun Yang, and Chunfu Jia

Cryptanalysis

Low Data Complexity Inversion Attacks on Stream Ciphers via
Truncated Compressed Preimage Sets 131
   Xiao Zhong, Mingsheng Wang, Bin Zhang, and Shengbao Wu

A New Attack against the Selvi-Vivek-Rangan Deterministic Identity
Based Signature Scheme from ACISP 2012 148
    Yanbin Pan and Yingpu Deng

Further Research on N-1 Attack against Exponentiation Algorithms 162
    Zhaojing Ding, Wei Guo, Liangjian Su, Jizeng Wei, and Haihua Gu

Cryptanalysis of RSA with Multiple Small Secret Exponents 176
    Atsushi Takayasu and Noboru Kunihiro

Fine-grain Cryptographic Protocols

New Model and Construction of ABE: Achieving Key Resilient-Leakage
and Attribute Direct-Revocation 192
    Mingwu Zhang

Expressive Bandwidth-Efficient Attribute Based Signature and
Signcryption in Standard Model 209
    Y. Sreenivasa Rao and Ratna Dutta

Incrementally Executable Signcryptions 226
    Dan Yamamoto, Hisayoshi Sato, and Yasuko Fukuzawa

Hierarchical Identity-Based Broadcast Encryption 242
    Weiran Liu, Jianwei Liu, Qianhong Wu, and Bo Qin

Key Exchange

Continuous After-the-Fact Leakage-Resilient Key Exchange 258
    Janaka Alawatugoda, Colin Boyd, and Douglas Stebila

Sakai-Ohgishi-Kasahara Identity-Based Non-Interactive Key Exchange
Scheme, Revisited 274
    Yu Chen, Qiong Huang, and Zongyang Zhang

Fundamentals

On the Impossibility of Proving Security of Strong-RSA Signatures via
the RSA Assumption 290
    Masayuki Fukumitsu, Shingo Hasegawa, Shuji Isobe, and
    Hiroki Shizuya

ELmE : A Misuse Resistant Parallel Authenticated Encryption 306
    Nilanjan Datta and Mridul Nandi

Lattices and Homomorphic Encryption

Lattice Decoding Attacks on Binary LWE 322
  Shi Bai and Steven D. Galbraith

Privacy-Preserving Wildcards Pattern Matching Using Symmetric
Somewhat Homomorphic Encryption 338
  *Masaya Yasuda, Takeshi Shimoyama, Jun Kogure,
  Kazuhiro Yokoyama, and Takeshi Koshiba*

Applications

Once Root Always a Threat: Analyzing the Security Threats of Android
Permission System 354
  *Zhongwen Zhang, Yuewu Wang, Jiwu Jing, Qiongxiao Wang, and
  Lingguang Lei*

A High-Throughput Unrolled ZUC Core for 100Gbps Data
Transmission 370
  Qinglong Zhang, Zongbin Liu, Miao Li, Ji Xiang, and Jiwu Jing

Another Look at Privacy Threats in 3G Mobile Telephony 386
  Mohammed Shafiul Alam Khan and Chris J. Mitchell

ExBLACR: Extending BLACR System 397
  *Weijin Wang, Dengguo Feng, Yu Qin, Jianxiong Shao, Li Xi, and
  Xiaobo Chu*

Short Papers

A Semantics-Aware Classification Approach for Data Leakage
Prevention 413
  *Sultan Alneyadi, Elankayer Sithirasenan, and Vallipuram
  Muthukkumarasamy*

Route 66: Passively Breaking All GSM Channels 422
  Philip S. Vejre and Andrey Bogdanov

An Analysis of Tracking Settings in Blackberry 10 and Windows Phone
8 Smartphones 430
  *Yogachandran Rahulamathavan, Veelasha Moonsamy, Lynn Batten,
  Su Shunliang, and Muttukrishnan Rajarajan*

Running Multiple Androids on One ARM Platform 438
  Zhijiao Zhang, Lei Zhang, Yu Chen, and Yuanchun Shi

CoChecker: Detecting Capability and Sensitive Data Leaks from
Component Chains in Android.................................... 446
    Xingmin Cui, Da Yu, Patrick Chan, Lucas C.K. Hui,
    S.M. Yiu, and Sihan Qing

Integral Zero-Correlation Distinguisher for ARX Block Cipher, with
Application to SHACAL-2 454
    Long Wen and Meiqin Wang

Author Index... 463

Improved Multidimensional Zero-Correlation Linear Cryptanalysis and Applications to LBlock and TWINE

Yanfeng Wang[1,3] and Wenling Wu[1,2]

[1] Trusted Computing and Information Assurance Laboratory, Institute of Software, Chinese Academy of Sciences, Beijing 100190, P.R. China
[2] State Key Laboratory of Computer Science, Institute of Software, Chinese Academy of Sciences, Beijing 100190, P.R. China
[3] Graduate University of Chinese Academy of Sciences, Beijing 100049, P.R. China
{wwl,wangyanfeng}@tca.iscas.ac.cn

Abstract. Zero-correlation linear cryptanalysis is a new method based on the linear approximations with correlation zero. In this paper, we propose a new model of multidimensional zero-correlation linear cryptanalysis by taking the equivalent relations of round keys into consideration. The improved attack model first finds out all the longest multidimensional zero-correlation linear distinguishers, then regards the distinguishers with the least independent guessed keys as the optimal distinguishers and finally chooses one optimal distinguisher to recover the secret key of cipher by using the partial-compression technique. Based on the improved attack model, we extend the original 22-round zero-correlation linear attack on LBlock and first evaluate the security of TWINE against the zero-correlation linear cryptanalysis. There are at least 8×8 classes of multidimensional zero-correlation linear distinguishers for 14-round LBlock and TWINE. After determining the corresponding optimal distinguisher, we carefully choose the order of guessing keys and guess each subkey nibble one after another to achieve an attack on 23-round LBlock, an attack on 23-round TWINE-80 and another attack on 25-round TWINE-128. As far as we know, these results are the currently best results on LBlock and TWINE in the single key scenario except the optimized brute force attack.

Keywords: lightweight block cipher, LBlock, TWINE, multidimensional zero-correlation linear cryptanalysis, partial-compression.

1 Introduction

Zero-correlation cryptanalysis[1] is a novel promising attack technique for block ciphers. The distinguishing property used in zero-correlation cryptanalysis is the existence of zero-correlation linear hulls over a part of the cipher. Those linear approximations hold true with probability p equal to $1/2$ and correlation $c = 2p - 1$ equal to 0. The original scheme had the disadvantage of requiring almost the full codebook of data. Bogdanov et.al proposed a framework which

W. Susilo and Y. Mu (Eds.): ACISP 2014, LNCS 8544, pp. 1–16, 2014.

uses several independent zero-correlation linear approximations to reduce data complexity[2]. In a follow-up work at ASIACRYPT'12[3], a multidimensional distinguisher has been constructed for the zero-correlation property, which removed the unnecessary independency assumptions on the distinguishers.

With the development of communication and electronic applications, the limited-resource devices such as RFID tags and sensor nodes have been used in many aspects of our life. Traditional block cipher is not suitable for this extremely constrained environment. Therefore, research on designing and analyzing lightweight block ciphers has become a hot topic. Recently, several lightweight block ciphers have been proposed, such as PRESENT[4], LED[5], Piccolo[6], LBlock[7], TWINE[8], etc. To reduce the cost of hardware and to decrease key set-up time, the key schedules of the lightweight ciphers are rather simple. As is known to us, the diffusion of the key schedule plays an important role on the security of the block cipher. In contrast to the serious effort spent on the algorithm design, the aspect of key schedules for block ciphers has attracted comparatively little attention.

In order to take advantage of the simple key schedule algorithm, we introduce an improved model of multidimensional zero-correlation linear cryptanalysis in this paper. In the previous basic attack, the adversary partly encrypts the plaintexts and decrypts the ciphertexts to obtain the values of the corresponding positions determined by the zero-correlation distinguisher. During the above process, attackers need to guess internal subkeys and the sizes of guessed keys are various for different zero-correlation distinguishers. In the improved attack model, we first compute the number of guessed round keys for all possible longest zero-correlation distinguishers and choose the one with least guessed key as the optimal distinguisher. After determining the optimal distinguisher, we finally reduce the complexity of the partial computation by guessing each subkey nibble one after another, which is called partial-compression technique.

To demonstrate the practical impact of our attack model, we apply the improved multidimensional zero-correlation linear attack model to LBlock and TWINE. The attacked round of LBlock against zero-correlation linear cryptanalysis is improved from 22-round to 23-round. As shown in [9], there are 8×8 different classes of zero-correlation linear hulls for 14-round LBlock. We evaluate the sizes of guessed keys for all classes of distinguishers and choose one distinguisher with least independent to attack 23-round LBlock. It cost a time complexity of 2^{76} 23-round LBlock encryptions. Similarly, we also apply the above multidimensional zero-correlation linear cryptanalysis to TWINE block cipher. We first find 8×8 different classes of zero-correlation linear hulls for 14-round TWINE. Then, two different zero-correlation linear distinguishers are chosen for TWINE-80 and TWINE-128 because of their different key schedule algorithms. Based on zero-correlation approximations with dimension 8, we carefully apply the partial-compression technique to present an attack on 23-round TWINE-80 and 25-round TWINE-128. Table 1 outlines the results and compares the results with previous attacks under the single-key model. The security of full-round LBlock and TWINE have been evaluated by biclique cryptanalysis[10,11] but the biclique cryptanalysis can be regarded as an optimization of brute-force attack. In this paper, we do not discuss such an optimized brute-force attack with a small advantage of a constant factor.

Table 1. Comparisons of Cryptanalysis Results on LBlock and TWINE

Ciphers	Round	Data	Time	Memory	Attacks	Source
LBlock	22	2^{61} CP	2^{70}	2^{63}	Integral	[12]
LBlock	22	2^{58} CP	$2^{79.28}$	2^{68}	Impossible Differential	[13]
LBlock	22	$2^{62.1}$ KP	$2^{71.27}$	2^{64}	Zero-Correlation Linear	[9]
LBlock	23	$2^{62.1}$ KP	2^{76}	2^{60}	Zero-Correlation Linear	Sec.4
TWINE-80	22	2^{62} CP	$2^{68.43}$	$2^{68.43}$	Saturation	[8]
TWINE-80	23	$2^{61.39}$ CP	$2^{76.88}$	$2^{76.88}$	Impossible Differential	[8]
TWINE-80	23	$2^{62.1}$ KP	$2^{72.15}$	2^{60}	Zero-Correlation Linear	Sec.5.1
TWINE-128	23	$2^{62.81}$ CP	$2^{106.14}$	$2^{106.14}$	Saturation	[8]
TWINE-128	24	$2^{52.21}$ CP	$2^{115.10}$	$2^{115.10}$	Impossible Differential	[8]
TWINE-128	25	2^{48} CP	2^{122}	2^{125}	Multid Meet-in-the-Middle	[14]
TWINE-128	25	$2^{62.1}$ KP	$2^{122.12}$	2^{60}	Zero-Correlation Linear	Sec.5.2

† CP: Chosen Plaintexts, † KP: Known Plaintexts † Multid: Multidimensional

The remainder of this paper is organized as follows. Section 2 presents the general structure of previous multidimensional zero-correlation cryptanalysis. Section 3 proposes the improved model of multidimensional zero-correlation linear cryptanalysis. Section 4 applies the improved zero-correlation linear cryptanalysis to 23-round LBlock. Section 5 shows the key recovery attacks on 23-round TWINE-80 and 25-round TWINE-128. Finally, Section 6 concludes this paper.

2   Notations and Preliminaries

In this section, we introduce the definition of zero-correlation linear approximation[1] and the previous basic methods of multidimensional zero-correlation cryptanalysis.

2.1   Zero-Correlation Linear Approximations

Consider an n-bit block cipher f and let the input of the function be $x \in F_2^n$. A linear approximation (u, v) with an input mask u and an output mask v has probability

$$p(u, v) = Pr_{x \in F_2^n}(u \cdot x \oplus v \cdot f(x) = 0).$$

The value $c_f(u, v) = 2p(u, v) - 1$ is called the correlation of linear approximation (u, v). Note that $p(u, v) = 1/2$ is equivalent to zero correlation $c_f(u, v) = 0$.

Zero-correlation linear cryptanalysis uses linear approximations that the correlations are equal to zero for all keys. The round function of ciphers often makes use of three basic operations: XOR operation, branching operation and a permutation S-box. Linear approximations over these operations obey three major rules(see also [15]):

Lemma 1 *(XOR operation): Either the three linear masks at an XOR $\oplus$ are equal or the correlation over $\oplus$ is exactly zero.*

Lemma 2 *(Branching operation): Either the three linear masks at a branching point • sum up to 0 or the correlation over • is exactly zero.*

Lemma 3 *(S-box permutation): Over an S-box S, if the input and output masks are neither both zero nor both nonzero, the correlation over S is exactly zero.*

In order to find the longest zero-correlation linear approximations, several methods are proposed to find the linear hull with zero-correlation. The matrix method are proposed in [9] by using the miss-in-the-middle technique to establish zero-correlation linear approximations. Given a distinguisher of zero-correlation linear approximation over a part of the cipher, the basic key recovery can be done with a technique similar to that of Matsui's Algorithm 2[15], partially encrypting/decrypting from the plaintext/ciphertext up to the boundaries of the property. This is the key recovery approach used in all zero-correlation attacks so far. In this paper, we aim to improve upon this by exploiting the weakness of the key schedule algorithm and using the partial-compression technique to reduce the computational complexity of attacks.

2.2 Multidimensional Zero-Correlation Linear Cryptanalysis

For most ciphers, a large number of zero-correlation approximations are available. To remove the statistical independence for multiple zero-correlation linear approximations, the zero-correlation linear approximations available are treated as a linear space spanned by m different zero-correlation linear approximations such that all $l = 2^m - 1$ non-zero linear combinations of them have zero correlation[3]. Given m linear approximations

$$\langle u_i, x \rangle + \langle w_i, y \rangle, \quad i = 1, ..., m$$

where x and y are some parts of data in encryption process, one obtains an m-tuples z by evaluating the m linear approximations for a plaintext-ciphertext pair

$$z = (z_1, ..., z_m), \quad z_i = \langle u_i, x \rangle + \langle w_i, y \rangle.$$

For each $z \in \mathbb{F}_2^m$, the attacker allocates a counter $V[z]$ and initializes it to value zero. Then for each distinct plaintext, the attacker computes the corresponding data in $\mathbb{F}_2^m$ and increments the counter $V[z]$ of this data value by one. Then the attacker computes the statistic T:

$$T = \sum_{z=0}^{2^m-1} \frac{(V[z] - N2^{-m})^2}{N2^{-m}(1-2^{-m})} = \frac{N \cdot 2^m}{(1-2^{-m})} \sum_{z=0}^{2^m-1} \left(\frac{V[z]}{N} - \frac{1}{2^m}\right)^2. \quad (1)$$

The statistic T for the right key guess follows a χ^2-distribution with mean $\mu_0 = l\frac{2^n - N}{2^n - 1}$ and variance $\sigma_0^2 = 2l(\frac{2^n - N}{2^n - 1})$, while for the wrong key guess it follows a χ^2-distribution with mean $\mu_1 = l$ and variance $\sigma_1^2 = 2l$.

In order to show the relationships between data complexity and success probability, we first denote the type-I error probability (the probability to wrongfully discard the right key) with α and the type-II error probability (the probability to wrongfully accept a random key as the right key) with β. We consider the decision threshold $\tau = \mu_0 + \sigma_0 z_{1-\alpha} = \mu_1 + \sigma_1 z_{1-\beta}$, then the number of known plaintexts N should be about

$$N = \frac{2^n(z_{1-\alpha} + z_{1-\beta})}{\sqrt{l/2} - z_{1-\beta}}, \tag{2}$$

where $z_p = \Phi^{-1}(p)$ for $0 < p < 1$ and Φ is the cumulative function of the standard normal distribution.

3 Improved Multidimensional Zero-Correlation Linear Cryptanalysis

In contrast to the serious effort spent on the algorithm design, the aspect of key schedules for block ciphers has attracted comparatively little attention. In this section, we give an improved model of multidimensional zero-correlation linear cryptanalysis by taking advantage of the weakness of key schedule algorithms.

Having the zero-correlation linear distinguisher, the adversary partly encrypts the plaintexts and decrypts the ciphertexts to obtain the values of the corresponding positions determined by the distinguisher. Attackers need to guess internal subkeys during the above process. As mentioned above, a large number of zero-correlation hulls are available for a single block cipher. Moreover, the sizes of guessed keys can vary for different key schedule algorithms and different classes of zero-correlation distinguishers. Thus, the choice and position of the zero-correlation linear hull will influence the result of security evaluation. In order to obtain a better attack on the target cipher, we present an improved model of multidimensional zero-correlation linear cryptanalysis.

Specifically, the following steps are processed to reduce the time complexity of attacks on some R-round block cipher.

1. Find all the longest multidimensional zero-correlation linear distinguishers by using the matrix method or other properties of encryption algorithm. We denote the number of different distinguishers by n and the round number of that by R_d. Obviously, we assume that R_d is always smaller than R.
2. Put the R_d-round distinguisher in the middle of the cipher and calculate the number of related round keys during the process of the partial computation.
   (a) The set of possible cases are noted with $\{(i, R_e), 0 \leq i < n, 0 \leq R_e \leq R - R_d\}$ and the pairs are sorted according to the number of related round keys. In each pair, the parameter i means the indexed number of different distinguishers and R_e means the round number of partial encryption.

Meanwhile, the corresponding round number of partial decryption is $R - R_d - R_e$. Thus, different elements in the set represent different attack schemes.

(b) Save the pairs (i, R_e) with least number of keys in a set S.

The above process is determined by the diffusion of the encryption algorithm and has no relation with the key schedule algorithm.

3. Minimize the set S to an optimal set O by taking the key schedule algorithm into consideration. Having known the position of the corresponding distinguisher, we can determine the realistic round keys for every pair in S. Furthermore, the equivalent relations in round keys can be obtained by carefully analyzing the key schedule algorithm.

   (a) For each element in S, update the number of related keys with the number of independent guessed keys.

   (b) Sort S again and only save the pairs with least guessed keys to O.

4. Choose an arbitrary pair from O to recover the secret key of the R-round cipher. Assume that the dimensional number of the distinguisher is m.

   (a) Allocate a counter $V[z]$ for m-bit z. The vector z is the concatenation of evaluations of m zero-correlation linear approximations.

   (b) Update the counter $V[z]$ by guessing subkeys nibble one after another by using the partial-compression technique.

   (c) For each guessing key k, compute $T_k = \frac{N \cdot 2^m}{(1 - 2^{-m})} \sum_{z=0}^{2^m - 1} \left(\frac{V[z]}{N} - \frac{1}{2^m} \right)^2$.

   (d) If $T_k < \tau$, then the guessed subkey values are possible right subkey candidates.

   (e) Do exhaustive search for all right candidates.

In the following sections, these new improvements will be illustrated with applications to block ciphers LBlock and TWINE.

4 Application to LBlock

In this section, we will evaluate the security of LBlock against multidimensional zero-correlation linear cryptanalysis by using the above improved model and give an attack on 23-round LBlock. We first give a brief description of LBlock and then show the properties of zero-correlation linear distinguishers for 14-round LBlock. Finally, a key recovery attack on 23-round LBlock is given.

4.1   A Brief Description of LBlock

Encryption Algorithm. The general structure of LBlock is a variant of Feistel Network, which is depicted in Figure 1. The number of iterative rounds is 32. The round function of LBlock includes three basic functions: AddRoundKey AK, confusion function S and diffusion function P. The confusion function S consists of eight 4×4 S-boxes in parallel. The diffusion function P is defined as a permutation of eight 4-bit words.

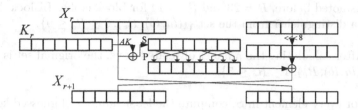

Fig. 1. Round function of LBlock block cipher

Key Schedule Algorithm. To reduce the cost of hardware and to decrease key set-up time, the key schedule of LBlock is rather simple. The 80-bit master key MK is stored in a key register and represented as $MK = k_0k_1...k_{79}$. At round i, the leftmost 32 bits of current contents of register MK are output as the round key K_i, i.e., $K_i = k_0k_1...k_{31}$. The key schedule of LBlock can be shown as follows:

1. $K_0 = MK[0 - 31]$
2. For $i \leftarrow 1$ to 31
   (a) $MK = MK <<< 29$
   (b) $MK[0 - 3] = s_9(MK[0 - 3])$
       $MK[4 - 7] = s_8(MK[4 - 7])$
   (c) $MK[29 - 33] = MK[29 - 33] \oplus [i]_2$
   (d) $K_i = MK[0 - 31]$

4.2 Zero-Correlation Linear Approximations of 14-Round LBlock

If an incompatible pair of linear masks can be shown for each linear trail in a linear hull, the correlation of the linear hull is zero. As studied in [9], there are 8×8 different classes of zero-correlation linear hulls for 14-round LBlock and the characteristics can be summarized as the following property:

Property 1. For 14-round LBlock, if the input mask a of the first round locates at the left branch and the output mask b of the last round locates in the right branch, then the correlation of the linear approximation is zero, where $a, b \in F_2^4$, $a \neq 0$ and $b \neq 0$.

To distinguish the 64 different zero-correlation hulls, we express them with two integers as (la, lb), where $0 \leq la \leq 7$ and $8 \leq lb \leq 15$.

4.3 Key Recovery for 23-Round LBlock

In order to attack 23-round LBlock, we follows the improved attack model of multidimensional zero-correlation cryptanalysis.

Step 1. As noted before, $R = 23$ and $R_d = 14$ for block cipher LBlock. We need to choose a distinguisher from the set $\{((la, lb), R_e), 0 \leq R_e \leq 9\}$.

Step 2. After calculating the number of related keys, the original set is reduced to $S = \{((la, lb), R_e), 4 \leq R_e \leq 5\}$.

Step 3. For every element in S, compute the least number of guessed keys. The least number of guessed keys is 63. Meanwhile, only four choices are left in the optimal set and $O = \{((1, 14), 4), ((2, 14), 4), ((3, 14), 4), ((6, 14), 4)\}$.

Step 4. Finally, we select $((1, 14), 4)$ to give an attack on 23-round LBlock. Because $R_e = 4$, we put the 14-round zero-correlation linear hull in rounds 4 to 17 and attack LBlock from round 0 to round 22 (Figure 2).

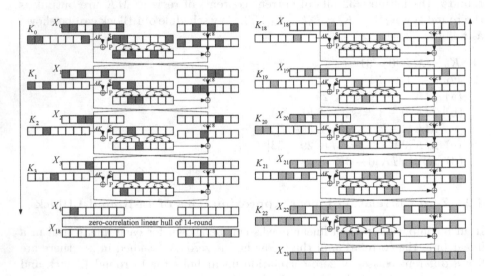

Fig. 2. Attack on 23-Round LBlock

After collecting sufficient plaintext-ciphertext pairs, we guess corresponding subkeys for the first four rounds and the last five rounds to estimate the statistic T. If we directly guess the subkeys bits involved in the key recovery process, then the time complexity will be greater than exhaustive search. Therefore, in order to reduce the time complexity, we first express the two target values by using the related round keys and plaintexts or ciphertexts, then use the partial-compression technique to reduce the time complexity significantly.

As shown in Figure 2, the nibble X_4^1 is affected by 32 bits of plaintext X_0 and 28 bits of round keys and the expression can be shown as:

$$X_4^1 = X_0^5 \oplus S(X_0^{12} \oplus S(X_0^0 \oplus K_0^0) \oplus K_1^2) \oplus S(X_0^{15} \oplus S(X_0^7 \oplus K_0^7) \oplus$$
$$S(X_0^4 \oplus S(X_0^{10} \oplus S(X_0^1 \oplus K_0^1) \oplus K_1^0) \oplus K_2^2) \oplus K_3^3)$$

Similarly, the nibble X_{18}^{14} is affected by 48 bits of ciphertext X_{23} and 48 bits of round keys:

$$X_{18}^{14} = X_{23}^0 \oplus S(X_{23}^9 \oplus K_{22}^1) \oplus S(X_{23}^{14} \oplus S(X_{23}^2 \oplus S(X_{23}^8 \oplus K_{22}^0) \oplus K_{21}^4) \oplus K_{20}^0) \oplus$$
$$S(X_{23}^9 \oplus S(X_{23}^1 \oplus S(X_{23}^{11} \oplus K_{22}^3) \oplus K_{21}^3) \oplus S(X_{23}^6 \oplus S(X_{23}^{12} \oplus K_{22}^4) \oplus$$
$$S(X_{23}^{15} \oplus S(X_{23}^4 \oplus S(X_{23}^{13} \oplus K_{22}^5) \oplus K_{21}^6) \oplus K_{20}^1) \oplus K_{19}^2) \oplus K_{18}^5)$$

After analyzing the key schedule of LBlock, we find the following relations in the round keys:

$$K_0^7 \Rightarrow K_1^0[0-2], \quad K_{21}^3 \Rightarrow K_{18}^5[0-2], \quad K_{21}^4 \Rightarrow K_{18}^5[3], \quad K_{22}^0 \Rightarrow K_{19}^2[0-2],$$
$$K_{22}^1 \Rightarrow K_{19}^2[3] \text{ and } K_{20}^0 \Rightarrow K_{22}^5[2-3].$$

Assuming that N known plaintexts are used, the partial encryption and decryption using the partial-compression technique are proceeded as in Table 2. The second column stands for the subkey nibbles that have to be guessed in each step. The third column denotes the time complexity of corresponding step measured in S-box access. In each step, we save the values of the 'Obtained States' during the encryption and decryption process. For each possible value of $x_i(1 \leq i \leq 13)$, the counter $N_i[x_i]$ will record how many plaintext-ciphertext pairs can produce the corresponding intermediate state x_i. The counter size for each x_i is shown in the last column.

To be more clear, we explain some steps in Table 2 in detail.

Step 4.1. We allocate the 60-bit counter $N_1[x_1]$ and initialize it to zero. We then guess 17-bit keys and partially encrypt N plaintexts to compute x_1, and increment the corresponding counter.

The guessed keys are $K_0^1, K_0^7, K_1^0[3]$ and K_{22}^0, K_{21}^4. Because $K_0^7[1-3]$ are equivalent to $K_1^0[0-2]$, K_1^0 are all known. As shown in Figure 2, the values of $X_4^1|X_{18}^{14}$ are affected by 32 bits of plaintext and 48 bits of ciphertext. They are represented by

$$x_0 = X_0^5|X_0^{12}|X_0^0|X_0^{15}|X_0^7|X_0^4|X_0^{10}|X_0^1|X_{23}^1|X_{23}^9|X_{23}^{14}|X_{23}^2|X_{23}^8|X_{23}^1|X_{23}^{11}|$$
$$X_{23}^6|X_{23}^{12}|X_{23}^{15}|X_{23}^4|X_{23}^{13}.$$

As the following three equations

$$X_1^5 = X_0^{15} \oplus S(X_0^7 \oplus K_0^7)$$
$$X_2^2 = X_0^4 \oplus S(X_0^{10} \oplus S(X_0^1 \oplus K_0^1) \oplus K_1^0)$$
$$X_{21}^8 = X_{23}^{14} \oplus S(X_{23}^2 \oplus S(X_{23}^8 \oplus K_{22}^0) \oplus K_{21}^4)$$

are true for LBlock, the 80-bit x_0 can be reduced to 60-bit x_1 after guessing the 17 bits keys. Update the expressions of X_4^1 and X_{18}^{14}:

$$X_4^1 = X_0^5 \oplus S(X_0^{12} \oplus S(X_0^0 \oplus K_0^0) \oplus K_1^2) \oplus S(X_1^5 \oplus S(X_2^2 \oplus K_2^2) \oplus K_3^3)$$

$$X_{18}^{14} = X_{23}^0 \oplus S(X_{23}^9 \oplus K_{22}^1) \oplus S(X_{21}^8 \oplus K_{20}^0) \oplus S(X_{23}^9 \oplus S(X_{23}^1 \oplus S(X_{23}^{11} \oplus K_{22}^3)$$
$$\oplus K_{21}^3) \oplus S(X_{23}^6 \oplus S(X_{23}^{12} \oplus K_{22}^4) \oplus S(X_{23}^{15} \oplus S(X_{23}^4 \oplus S(X_{23}^{13} \oplus K_{22}^5)$$
$$\oplus K_{21}^6) \oplus K_{20}^1) \oplus K_{19}^2) \oplus K_{18}^5)$$

Step 4.2. We first allocate 56-bit counter $N_2[x_2]$ and initialize them to zero. We then guess 4-bit K_{20}^0 and partially decrypt x_1 to compute x_2 and add the corresponding $N_1[x_1]$ to $N_2[x_2]$. During the above process, A is defined as $X_{23}^0 \oplus S(X_{21}^8 \oplus K_{20}^0)$. Meanwhile, the expression of X_{18}^{14} is update as:

$$X_{18}^{14} = A \oplus S(X_{23}^9 \oplus K_{22}^1) \oplus S(X_{23}^9 \oplus S(X_{23}^1 \oplus S(X_{23}^{11} \oplus K_{22}^3) \oplus K_{21}^3) \oplus S(X_{23}^6 \oplus$$
$$S(X_{23}^{12} \oplus K_{22}^4) \oplus S(X_{23}^{15} \oplus S(X_{23}^4 \oplus S(X_{23}^{13} \oplus K_{22}^5) \oplus K_{21}^6) \oplus K_{20}^1) \oplus K_{19}^2) \oplus K_{18}^5.$$

Table 2. Partial encryption and decryption on 23-round LBlock

Step	Guess	Time	Obtained States	Size
4.1	$K_0^1, K_0^7, K_1^0[3]$ K_{22}^{12}, K_{21}^4	$N \cdot 2^{17} \cdot 5$	$x_1 = X_0^5\|X_0^{12}\|X_0^0\|X_1^5\|X_2^2\|X_{23}^0\|X_{23}^9\|X_{21}^8\|$ $X_{23}^1\|X_{23}^{11}\|X_{23}^6\|X_{23}^{12}\|X_{23}^{15}\|X_{23}^4\|X_{23}^{13}$	2^{60}
4.2	K_{20}^0	$2^{60} \cdot 2^{17+4}$	$x_2 = X_0^5\|X_0^{12}\|X_0^0\|X_1^5\|X_2^2\|A\|X_{23}^9\|X_{23}^1\|$ $X_{23}^{11}\|X_{23}^6\|X_{23}^{12}\|X_{23}^{15}\|X_{23}^4\|X_{23}^{13}$	2^{56}
4.3	$K_{22}^5[0,1]$	$2^{56} \cdot 2^{21+2}$	$x_3 = X_0^5\|X_0^{12}\|X_0^0\|X_1^5\|X_2^2\|A\|X_{23}^9\|$ $X_{23}^1\|X_{23}^{11}\|X_{23}^6\|X_{23}^{12}\|X_{23}^{15}\|X_{22}^{14}$	2^{52}
4.4	K_2^2	$2^{52} \cdot 2^{23+4}$	$x_4 = X_0^5\|X_0^{12}\|X_0^0\|X_3^3\|A\|X_{23}^9\|X_{23}^1\|X_{23}^{11}\|X_{23}^6\|X_{23}^{12}\|X_{23}^{15}\|X_{22}^{14}$	2^{48}
4.5	K_0^0	$2^{48} \cdot 2^{27+4}$	$x_5 = X_0^5\|X_1^2\|X_3^3\|A\|X_{23}^9\|X_{23}^1\|X_{23}^{11}\|X_{23}^6\|X_{23}^{12}\|X_{23}^{15}\|X_{22}^{14}$	2^{44}
4.6	K_1^2	$2^{44} \cdot 2^{31+4}$	$x_6 = X_3^{11}\|X_3^3\|A\|X_{23}^9\|X_{23}^1\|X_{23}^{11}\|X_{23}^6\|X_{23}^{12}\|X_{23}^{15}\|X_{22}^{14}$	2^{40}
4.7	K_3^3	$2^{40} \cdot 2^{35+4}$	$x_7 = X_4^1\|A\|X_{23}^9\|X_{23}^1\|X_{23}^{11}\|X_{23}^6\|X_{23}^{12}\|X_{23}^{15}\|X_{22}^{14}$	2^{36}
4.8	K_{22}^3	$2^{36} \cdot 2^{39+4}$	$x_8 = X_4^1\|A\|X_{23}^9\|X_{22}^1\|X_{23}^{11}\|X_{23}^6\|X_{23}^{12}\|X_{23}^{15}\|X_{22}^{14}$	2^{32}
4.9	K_{22}^4	$2^{32} \cdot 2^{43+4}$	$x_9 = X_4^1\|A\|X_{23}^9\|X_{22}^1\|X_{22}^{11}\|X_{23}^8\|X_{23}^{15}\|X_{22}^{14}$	2^{28}
4.10	K_{21}^6	$2^{28} \cdot 2^{47+4}$	$x_{10} = X_4^1\|A\|X_{23}^9\|X_{22}^{11}\|X_{22}^8\|X_{21}^9$	2^{24}
4.11	K_{20}^1	$2^{24} \cdot 2^{51+4}$	$x_{11} = X_4^1\|A\|X_{23}^9\|X_{22}^{11}\|X_{20}^{10}$	2^{20}
4.12	$K_{22}^1(K_{19}^2)$	$2^{20} \cdot 2^{55+4} \cdot 2$	$x_{12} = X_4^1\|B\|C\|X_{22}^{11}$	2^{16}
4.13	$K_{21}^3(K_{18}^5)$	$2^{16} \cdot 2^{59+4} \cdot 2$	$x_{13} = X_4^1\|X_{18}^{14}$	2^8

† $A = X_{23}^0 \oplus S(X_{21}^8 \oplus K_{20}^0)$ † $B = A \oplus S(X_{23}^9 \oplus K_{22}^1)$ † $C = X_{23}^9 \oplus S(X_{20}^{10} \oplus K_{19}^2)$

Because the following steps are similar to the above two steps, we do not explain in details. Besides, we note that the numbers of guessed keys in Step 12 and Step 13 are both 4-bit. However, the numbers of known keys are both 8 bit, that is because the key in the $'()'$ can be obtained by using the relations of round keys.

To recover the secret key, the following steps are performed:

1. Allocate a counter $V[z]$ for 8-bit z.
2. For 2^8 values of x_{13}:
   (a) Evaluate all 8 basis zero-correlation masks on x_{13} and get z.
   (b) Update the counter $V[z]$ by $V[z] = V[z] + N_{13}[x_{13}]$.
3. For each guessing key k, compute $T_k = \frac{N \cdot 2^8}{(1 - 2^{-8})} \sum_{z=0}^{2^8-1} \left(\frac{V[z]}{N} - \frac{1}{2^8} \right)^2$.
4. If $T_k < \tau$, then the guessed subkey values are possible right subkey candidates.
5. Do exhaustive search for all right candidates.

Complexity. We set $\alpha = 2^{-2.7}, \beta = 2^{-9}$, then $z_{1-\alpha} \approx 1, z_{1-\beta} \approx 2.88$. Since $n = 64$ and $l = 255$, then according to equation 2, the data complexity N is about $2^{62.1}$. Now we evaluate the time complexity of the key recovery on 23-round LBlock. We first sum the cost of step 1 to step 14 in the process of partial computation and the result is about $2^{81} \cdot 6$ S-box access, which is about $2^{81} \cdot 6 \cdot 1/8 \cdot 1/23 \approx 2^{76}$ 23-round LBlock encryptions. The number of remaining key candidates is about $2^{80} \cdot \beta \approx 2^{71}$. The total time complexity is $2^{76} + 2^{71} \approx 2^{76}$ 23-round LBlock encryptions.

All in all, the data complexity of our attack on 23-round LBlock is $2^{62.1}$ known plaintexts, the time complexity is 2^{76} 23-round LBlock encryptions and the memory requirements are about 2^{60} bytes.

5 Application to TWINE

In this section, we apply the improved multidimensional zero-correlation linear attack model to TWINE block cipher and give attacks on 23-round TWINE-80 and 25-round TWINE-128.

5.1 A Brief Description of TWINE

Encryption Algorithm. Round function of TWINE consists of eight identical 4-bit S-boxes and a diffusion layer π, which is depicted in Figure 3. This round function is iterated for 36 times for both TWINE-80 and TWINE-128, where the diffusion layer of the last round is omitted.

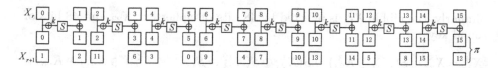

Fig. 3. Round function of TWINE block cipher

Key Schedule Algorithm. The key schedule of TWINE is quite simple. S-boxes, XOR operations and a series of constants are used in the key schedule. Due to the page limit, see the specific key schedule algorithms for both key lengths in Reference [8].

5.2 Zero-Correlation Linear Approximations of 14-Round TWINE

We find that there are at least 8×8 zero-correlation linear hulls for 14-round TWINE and the characteristics can be summarized as the following property:

Property 2. For 14-round TWINE, if the input mask a of the first round locates at the even nibble and the output mask b of the last round locates in the odd nibble, then the correlation of the linear approximation is zero, where $a, b \in F_2^4$, $a \neq 0$ and $b \neq 0$.

To distinguish the 64 different zero-correlation hulls, we express the distinguisher as (l_a, l_b), where $0 \leq l_a \leq 14$ is an even integer and $1 \leq l_b \leq 15$ is an odd integer.

5.3   Key Recovery for 23-Round TWINE-80

Step 1. As noted before, $R = 23$ and $R_d = 14$ for block cipher TWINE-80. The original set is $\{((l_a, l_b), R_e), 0 \leq R_e \leq 9\}$.

Step 2. After analyzing the encryption algorithm, the candidates are reduced to $S = \{((l_a, l_b), R_e), 4 \leq R_e \leq 5\}$.

Step 3. Only one element $\{((2, 9), 4)\}$ is left in the optimal set O. The size of the guessed keys is reduced from 76 bits to 60 bits.

Step 4. We use $((2, 9), 4)$ to give an attack on 23-round TWINE-80. By puting these 14-round zero-correlation linear approximations in rounds 4 to 17, we can attack TWINE-80 from round 0 to round 22. Similarly, we first express the two target values and then guess the keys one nibble after another to reduce the time complexity of partial computation. The nibble X_4^2 is affected by 32 bits of plaintext X_0 and 28 bits of round keys and the expression can be shown as:

$$X_4^2 = X_0^{12} \oplus S(X_0^{15} \oplus S(X_0^{14} \oplus K_0^7) \oplus K_1^7) \oplus S(X_0^7 \oplus S(X_0^6 \oplus K_0^3) \oplus$$
$$S(X_0^0 \oplus S(X_0^3 \oplus S(X_0^2 \oplus K_0^1) \oplus K_1^2) \oplus K_2^6) \oplus K_3^5)$$

Similarly, the nibble X_{18}^9 is affected by 48 bits of ciphertext X_{23} and 48 bits of round keys:

$$X_{18}^9 = X_{23}^8 \oplus S(X_{23}^3 \oplus K_{22}^3) \oplus S(X_{23}^5 \oplus S(X_{23}^{12} \oplus S(X_{23}^7 \oplus K_{22}^2) \oplus K_{21}^0) \oplus K_{20}^1) \oplus$$
$$S(X_{23}^3 \oplus S(X_{23}^{10} \oplus S(X_{23}^{15} \oplus K_{22}^6) \oplus K_{21}^4) \oplus S(X_{23}^2 \oplus S(X_{23}^9 \oplus K_{22}^5) \oplus$$
$$S(X_{23}^1 \oplus S(X_{23}^6 \oplus S(X_{23}^{13} \oplus K_{22}^4) \oplus K_{21}^5) \oplus K_{20}^7) \oplus K_{19}^6) \oplus K_{18}^4)$$

The following relations exist in the related round keys:

$$K_3^5 \Longleftrightarrow K_0^3, K_2^6 \Longleftrightarrow K_0^1, K_{21}^0 \Longleftrightarrow K_{18}^4 \text{ and } K_{20}^1 \Longleftrightarrow K_{22}^6.$$

Assuming that N known plaintexts are used, the partial encryption and decryption using the partial-compression technique are proceeded as in Table 3. Finally, attackers compute the statistic T_k for every guessed k and do exhaustive search for all right candidates. The process can be referred to that of LBlock.

Complexity. We also set $\alpha = 2^{-2.7}, \beta = 2^{-9}$, then $z_{1-\alpha} \approx 1, z_{1-\beta} \approx 2.88$. Since $n = 64$ and $l = 255$, the data complexity N is about $2^{62.1}$. The complexity of partial computation is about $2^{76} \cdot 8$ S-box access, which is about $2^{76} \cdot 8 \cdot 1/8 \cdot$

Table 3. Partial encryption and decryption on 23-round TWINE-80

Step	Guess	Time	Obtained States	Size
4.1	$K_3^5(K_0^3)$, $K_2^6(K_0^1)$, K_1^2	$N \cdot 2^{12} \cdot 5$	$x_1 = A\|X_0^{15}\|X_0^{14}\|X_{23}^8\|X_{23}^3\|X_{23}^5\|X_{23}^{12}\|$ $X_{23}^7\|X_{23}^{10}\|X_{23}^{15}\|X_{23}^2\|X_{23}^9\|X_{23}^1\|X_{23}^6\|X_{23}^{13}$	2^{60}
4.2	K_0^7	$2^{60} \cdot 2^{16}$	$x_2 = A\|X_1^{14}\|X_{23}^8\|X_{23}^3\|X_{23}^5\|X_{23}^{12}\|X_{23}^7\|X_{23}^{10}\|$ $X_{23}^{15}\|X_{23}^2\|X_{23}^9\|X_{23}^1\|X_{23}^6\|X_{23}^{13}$	2^{56}
4.3	K_1^7	2^{76}	$x_3 = X_4^2\|X_{23}^8\|X_{23}^3\|X_{23}^5\|X_{23}^{12}\|X_{23}^7\|X_{23}^{10}\|$ $X_{23}^{15}\|X_{23}^2\|X_{23}^9\|X_{23}^1\|X_{23}^6\|X_{23}^{13}$	2^{52}
4.4	K_{22}^2	2^{76}	$x_4 = X_4^2\|X_{23}^8\|X_{23}^3\|X_{23}^5\|X_{23}^5\|X_{23}^{10}\|X_{23}^{15}\|X_{23}^2\|X_{23}^9\|X_{23}^1\|X_{23}^6\|X_{23}^{13}$	2^{48}
4.5	K_{21}^0	2^{76}	$x_5 = X_4^2\|X_{23}^8\|X_{23}^3\|X_{21}^1\|X_{23}^{10}\|X_{23}^{15}\|X_{23}^2\|X_{23}^9\|X_{23}^1\|X_{23}^6\|X_{23}^{13}$	2^{44}
4.6	$K_{22}^6(K_{20}^1)$	$2^{76} \cdot 2$	$x_6 = X_4^2\|B\|X_{23}^3\|X_{22}^{13}\|X_{23}^2\|X_{23}^9\|X_{23}^1\|X_{23}^6\|X_{23}^{13}$	2^{36}
4.7	K_{22}^5	2^{72}	$x_7 = X_4^2\|B\|X_{23}^3\|X_{22}^{13}\|X_{22}^{11}\|X_{23}^1\|X_{23}^6\|X_{23}^{13}$	2^{32}
4.8	K_{22}^4	2^{72}	$x_8 = X_4^2\|B\|X_{22}^3\|X_{22}^{13}\|X_{22}^{11}\|X_{21}^1\|X_{22}^9$	2^{28}
4.9	K_{21}^5	2^{72}	$x_9 = X_4^2\|B\|X_{23}^3\|X_{22}^{13}\|X_{22}^{11}\|X_{21}^{11}$	2^{24}
4.10	K_{20}^7	2^{72}	$x_{10} = X_4^2\|B\|X_{23}^3\|X_{22}^{13}\|X_{20}^{15}$	2^{20}
4.11	K_{22}^3	2^{72}	$x_{11} = X_4^2\|X_{20}^3\|X_{23}^3\|X_{22}^{13}\|X_{20}^{15}$	2^{20}
4.12	K_{21}^4	2^{76}	$x_{12} = X_4^2\|X_{20}^3\|X_{21}^9\|X_{20}^{15}$	2^{16}
4.13	K_{19}^6	2^{76}	$x_{13} = X_4^2\|X_{18}^9$	2^8

$\dagger$ $A = X_0^{12} \oplus S(X_0^7 \oplus S(X_0^6 \oplus K_0^3) \oplus S(X_0^0 \oplus S(X_0^3 \oplus S(X_0^2 \oplus K_0^1) \oplus K_1^2) \oplus K_2^6) \oplus K_3^5)$
$\dagger$ $B = X_{23}^8 \oplus S(X_{21}^1 \oplus K_{20}^1)$

$1/23 \approx 2^{71.48}$ 23-round TWINE-80 encryptions. The number of remaining key candidates is about $2^{80} \cdot \beta \approx 2^{71}$. Thus, the total time complexity is $2^{71.48} + 2^{71} \approx 2^{72.15}$ 23-round TWINE-80 encryptions. Meanwhile, the memory requirements are about 2^{60} bytes.

5.4 Key Recovery for 25-Round TWINE-128

Step 1. $R = 25$ and $R_d = 14$ for block cipher TWINE-128 and the original set equals to $\{((l_a, l_b), R_e), 0 \le R_e \le 11\}$.

Step 2. When encrypting 5 or 6 rounds, the number of guessed keys is minimal(124 bits) and $S = \{((l_a, l_b), R_e), 5 \le R_e \le 6\}$.

Step 3. After deleting the equivalent keys for every element in S, we find that only the cases in $O = \{((l_a, l_b), 5), ((l_a^*, l_b^*), 6), l_a \in \{0, 4, 12, 14\}, l_b = 9, l_a^* \in \{0, 4, 10, 14\}, l_b^* = 11\}$ needs to guess 112-bit keys.

Step 4. The distinguisher $((4, 9), 5)$ is chosen to attack 25-round TWINE-128. Firstly, express X_5^4 by using subkeys and plaintexts and X_{19}^9 by using subkeys and ciphertexts.

$$X_5^4 = X_0^{13} \oplus S(X_0^{12} \oplus K_0^6) \oplus S(X_0^4 \oplus S(X_0^9 \oplus S(X_0^8 \oplus K_0^4) \oplus K_1^3) \oplus K_2^4) \oplus$$
$$S(X_0^{12} \oplus S(X_0^{15} \oplus S(X_0^{14} \oplus K_0^7) \oplus K_1^7) \oplus S(X_0^7 \oplus S(X_0^6 \oplus K_0^3) \oplus S(X_0^0 \oplus$$
$$S(X_0^3 \oplus S(X_0^2 \oplus K_0^1) \oplus K_1^2) \oplus K_2^6) \oplus K_3^5) \oplus K_4^1)$$

$$X_{19}^9 = X_{25}^{13} \oplus S(X_{25}^4 \oplus S(X_{25}^1 \oplus K_{24}^1) \oplus K_{23}^3) \oplus S(X_{25}^{12} \oplus S(X_{25}^7 \oplus K_{24}^2) \oplus$$
$$S(X_{25}^{15} \oplus S(X_{25}^8 \oplus S(X_{25}^3 \oplus K_{24}^3) \oplus K_{23}^2) \oplus K_{22}^0) \oplus K_{21}^1) \oplus$$
$$S(X_{25}^4 \oplus S(X_{25}^1 \oplus K_{24}^1) \oplus S(X_{25}^9 \oplus S(X_{25}^{14} \oplus S(X_{25}^{11} \oplus K_{24}^7) \oplus K_{23}^6) \oplus K_{22}^4) \oplus$$
$$S(X_{25}^1 \oplus S(X_{25}^6 \oplus S(X_{25}^{13} \oplus K_{24}^4) \oplus K_{23}^5) \oplus S(X_{25}^0 \oplus S(X_{25}^5 \oplus K_{24}^0) \oplus$$
$$S(X_{25}^3 \oplus S(X_{25}^{10} \oplus S(X_{25}^{15} \oplus K_{24}^6) \oplus K_{23}^4) \oplus K_{22}^5) \oplus K_{21}^7) \oplus K_{20}^6) \oplus K_{19}^4)$$

Meanwhile, the following equivalent relations exist in the related round keys of TWINE-128:

$$K_4^1 \Longleftrightarrow K_1^3, K_{24}^2 \Longleftrightarrow K_{20}^6 \text{ and } K_{24}^6 | K_{24}^7 \Rightarrow K_{19}^4.$$

The partial encryption and decryption are similarly proceeded as in Table 4.

Table 4. Partial encryption and decryption on 25-round TWINE-128

Step	Guess	Time	Obtained States	Size
4.1	$K_{24}^{0-4,6,7}, K_{22}^{4,5},$ K_{23}^{2-6}, K_{21}^7	$N \cdot 2^{60} \cdot 17$	$x_1 = A\|X_{23}^5\|X_{23}^0\|X_0^{15}\|X_0^{14}\|X_0^{13}\|X_0^{12}\|$ $X_0^9\|X_0^8\|X_0^7\|X_0^6\|X_0^4\|X_0^3\|X_0^2\|X_0^0$	2^{60}
4.2	K_{22}^0	2^{124}	$x_2 = A\|X_{22}^1\|X_0^{15}\|X_0^{14}\|X_0^{13}\|X_0^{12}\|X_0^9\|$ $X_0^8\|X_0^7\|X_0^6\|X_0^4\|X_0^3\|X_0^2\|X_0^0$	2^{56}
4.3	K_{21}^1	2^{124}	$x_3 = X_{19}^9\|X_0^{15}\|X_0^{14}\|X_0^{13}\|X_0^{12}\|X_0^9\|$ $X_0^8\|X_0^7\|X_0^6\|X_0^4\|X_0^3\|X_0^2\|X_0^0$	2^{52}
4.4	K_0^4	2^{124}	$x_4 = X_{19}^9\|X_0^{15}\|X_0^{14}\|X_0^{13}\|X_0^{12}\|X_1^6\|X_0^7\|X_0^6\|X_0^4\|X_0^3\|X_0^2\|X_0^0$	2^{48}
4.5	K_1^3	2^{124}	$x_5 = X_{19}^9\|X_0^{15}\|X_0^{14}\|X_0^{13}\|X_0^{12}\|X_2^8\|X_0^7\|X_0^6\|X_0^3\|X_0^2\|X_0^0$	2^{44}
4.6	K_0^7	2^{124}	$x_6 = X_{19}^9\|X_1^{14}\|X_0^{13}\|X_0^{12}\|X_2^8\|X_0^7\|X_0^6\|X_0^3\|X_0^2\|X_0^0$	2^{40}
4.7	K_0^3	2^{124}	$x_7 = X_{19}^9\|X_1^{14}\|X_0^{13}\|X_0^{12}\|X_2^8\|X_1^8\|X_0^3\|X_0^2\|X_0^0$	2^{36}
4.8	K_0^1	2^{124}	$x_8 = X_{19}^9\|X_1^{14}\|X_0^{13}\|X_0^{12}\|X_2^8\|X_1^8\|X_1^4\|X_0^0$	2^{32}
4.9	K_1^2	2^{124}	$x_9 = X_{19}^9\|X_1^{14}\|X_0^{13}\|X_0^{12}\|X_2^8\|X_1^8\|X_2^{12}$	2^{28}
4.10	K_2^6	2^{124}	$x_{10} = X_{19}^9\|X_1^{14}\|X_0^{13}\|X_0^{12}\|X_2^8\|X_3^{10}$	2^{24}
4.11	K_2^4	2^{124}	$x_{11} = X_{19}^9\|B\|X_1^{14}\|X_0^{12}\|X_3^{10}$	2^{20}
4.12	K_1^7, K_3^5	$2^{128} \cdot 3$	$x_{12} = X_{19}^9\|C\|X_0^{12}$	2^{12}
4.13	K_0^6	2^{124}	$x_{13} = X_{19}^9\|X_5^4$	2^8

† $A = X_{23}^7 \oplus S(X_{23}^6 \oplus S(X_{23}^{13} \oplus K_{22}^4) \oplus S(X_{23}^{11} \oplus S(X_{23}^2 \oplus S(X_{23}^9 \oplus K_{22}^5) \oplus K_{21}^7) \oplus K_{20}^6) \oplus K_{19}^4)$
† $B = X_0^{13} \oplus S(X_2^8 \oplus K_2^4)$
† $C = B \oplus S(X_0^{12} \oplus S(X_1^{14} \oplus K_1^7) \oplus S(X_3^{10} \oplus K_3^5) \oplus K_4^1)$

Complexity. We set $\alpha = 2^{-2.7}, \beta = 2^{-9}$, then $z_{1-\alpha} \approx 1, z_{1-\beta} \approx 2.88$. Since $n = 64$ and $l = 255$, then according to equation 2, the data complexity N is also about $2^{62.1}$. The total time complexity is $2^{121.95} + 2^{119} \approx 2^{122.12}$ 25-round TWINE-128 encryptions and the memory requirements are about 2^{60} bytes to store counter in Step 4.1.

6 Conclusion

In this paper, we first present an improved model of multidimensional zero-correlation linear cryptanalysis by taking the key schedule algorithm into consideration. Besides, partial-compression technique is used to reduce the time complexity, which is similar to the partial-sum technique of integral attack. In order to illustrate the improved attack model, we evaluate the security of LBlock and TWINE block cipher against zero-correlation linear cryptanalysis. Based on 14-round zero-correlation distinguishers, we presented attacks on 23-round LBlock, 23-round TWINE-80 and 25-round TWINE-128. In terms of the number of attacked rounds, the result on LBlock is better than any previously published results in the single key model up to now. While the previous attack on TWINE-80 and TWINE-128, which can break the same number of rounds, uses chosen plaintexts, our attacks assume only the known plaintexts and the attack on TWINE-80 is of the less time complexity and memory. As discussed above, we conclude that the diffusion of the key schedule algorithms influence the security of block ciphers against zero-correlation linear cryptanalysis. Moreover, the results reveal a criterion of designing the key schedule algorithm. Specifically, designers should avoid equivalent subkeys when partly encrypting or decrypting ciphers to obtain a single nibble.

Acknowledgments. We thank the anonymous reviewers for their useful comments that help to improve the paper. The research presented in this paper is supported by the National Basic Research Program of China (No. 2013CB338002) and National Natural Science Foundation of China (No. 61272476, No.61232009 and No. 61202420).

References

1. Bogdanov, A., Rijmen, V.: Linear Hulls with Correlation Zero and Linear Cryptanalysis of Block Ciphers. Designs, Codes and Cryptography 70(3), 369–383 (2014)
2. Bogdanov, A., Wang, M.Q.: Zero Correlation Linear Cryptanalysis with Reduced Data Complexity. In: Canteaut, A. (ed.) FSE 2012. LNCS, vol. 7549, pp. 29–48. Springer, Heidelberg (2012)
3. Bogdanov, A., Leander, G., Nyberg, K., Wang, M.Q.: Integral and Multidimensional Linear Distinguishers with Correlation Zero. In: Wang, X., Sako, K. (eds.) ASIACRYPT 2012. LNCS, vol. 7658, pp. 244–261. Springer, Heidelberg (2012)
4. Bogdanov, A., Knudsen, L.R., Leander, G., Paar, C., Poschmann, A., Robshaw, M.J.B., Seurin, Y., Vikkelsoe, C.: PRESENT: An Ultra-Lightweight Block Cipher. In: Paillier, P., Verbauwhede, I. (eds.) CHES 2007. LNCS, vol. 4727, pp. 450–466. Springer, Heidelberg (2007)

5. Guo, J., Peyrin, T., Poschmann, A., Robshaw, M.: The LED Block Cipher. In: Preneel, B., Takagi, T. (eds.) CHES 2011. LNCS, vol. 6917, pp. 326–341. Springer, Heidelberg (2011)
6. Shibutani, K., Isobe, T., Hiwatari, H., Mitsuda, A., Akishita, T., Shirai, T.: Piccolo: An Ultra-Lightweight Block Cipher. In: Preneel, B., Takagi, T. (eds.) CHES 2011. LNCS, vol. 6917, pp. 342–357. Springer, Heidelberg (2011)
7. Wu, W., Zhang, L.: LBlock: A Lightweight Block Cipher. In: Lopez, J., Tsudik, G. (eds.) ACNS 2011. LNCS, vol. 6715, pp. 327–344. Springer, Heidelberg (2011)
8. Suzaki, T., Minematsu, K., Morioka, S., Kobayashi, E.: TWINE: A Lightweight Block Cipher for Multiple Platforms. In: Knudsen, L.R., Wu, H. (eds.) SAC 2012. LNCS, vol. 7707, pp. 339–354. Springer, Heidelberg (2013)
9. Soleimany, H., Nyberg, K.: Zero-Correlation Linear Cryptanalysis of Reduced-Round LBlock. Cryptology ePrint Archive, https://eprint.iacr.org/2012/570
10. Wang, Y., Wu, W., Yu, X., Zhang, L.: Security on LBlock against Biclique Cryptanalysis. In: Lee, D.H., Yung, M. (eds.) WISA 2012. LNCS, vol. 7690, pp. 1–14. Springer, Heidelberg (2012)
11. Çoban, M., Karakoç, F., Boztaş, Ö.: Biclique Cryptanalysis of TWINE. In: Pieprzyk, J., Sadeghi, A.-R., Manulis, M. (eds.) CANS 2012. LNCS, vol. 7712, pp. 43–55. Springer, Heidelberg (2012)
12. Sasaki, Y., Wang, L.: Comprehensive Study of Integral Analysis on 22-round LBlock. In: Kwon, T., Lee, M.-K., Kwon, D. (eds.) ICISC 2012. LNCS, vol. 7839, pp. 156–169. Springer, Heidelberg (2013)
13. Karakoç, F., Demirci, H., Harmancı, A.E.: Impossible Differential Cryptanalysis of Reduced-Round LBlock. In: Askoxylakis, I., Pöhls, H.C., Posegga, J. (eds.) WISTP 2012. LNCS, vol. 7322, pp. 179–188. Springer, Heidelberg (2012)
14. Boztaş, Ö., Karakoç, F., Çoban, M.: Multidimensional Meet-in-the-middle Attacks on Reduced-Round TWINE-128. In: Avoine, G., Kara, O. (eds.) LightSec 2013. LNCS, vol. 8162, pp. 55–67. Springer, Heidelberg (2013)
15. Matsui, M.: Linear Cryptanalysis Method for DES Cipher. In: Helleseth, T. (ed.) Advances in Cryptology - EUROCRYPT 1993. LNCS, vol. 765, pp. 386–397. Springer, Heidelberg (1994)

Differential and Impossible Differential Related-Key Attacks on Hierocrypt-L1

Bungo Taga[1,2,*], Shiho Moriai[2], and Kazumaro Aoki[3]

[1] National Police Academy
3-12-1, Asahi-cho, Fuchu-shi, Tokyo, 183-8558, Japan
b.taga@nparc.ac.jp
[2] National Institute of Information and Communications Technology
4-2-1 Nukui-Kitamachi, Koganei, Tokyo, 184-8795, Japan
shiho.moriai@nict.go.jp
[3] NTT Secure Platform Laboratories, Nippon Telegraph and Telephone Corporation
3-9-11 Midoricho, Musashino-shi, Tokyo, 180-8585 Japan
aoki.kazumaro@lab.ntt.co.jp

Abstract. Hierocrypt-L1 is one of the Japanese e-Government Recommended Ciphers listed by CRYPTREC in 2003, and its security was reconfirmed as secure by CRYPTREC in 2013. In this paper we first find differential characteristics with probability 1 in the key scheduling of Hierocrypt-L1. Then, using the above characteristics, we construct related-key differentials and related-key impossible differentials. The impossible differentials are in a new type of impossible differential characteristics in that the S-box impossible differentials are directly utilized. The above related-key differentials and impossible differentials are applied to key recovery attacks on 8 S-function layers of Hierocrypt-L1, which are the best attacks on Hierocrypt-L1 in terms of the number of attackable S-function layers.

Keywords: Cryptanalysis, key scheduling, related-key attacks, impossible differential, Hierocrypt-L1, CRYPTREC.

1 Introduction

Hierocrypt-L1 [21,11,24] is a block cipher developed by Toshiba Corporation in 2000. It was among the final candidates competing to be in the list of portfolio of the NESSIE project [19]. After that it was selected to be one of the Japanese e-Government Recommended Ciphers in 2003, and its security was reconfirmed as secure by CRYPTREC [13] in 2013.

The block size and key size of Hierocrypt-L1 are 64 bits and 128 bits, respectively. The design of the key scheduling part of Hierocrypt-L1 consists of a Feistel structure in the 64-bit left half and a linear diffusion transformation in the 64-bit right half, which is independent of the left half, while the left half is

---

* Most of the work was done when the first author was in National Institute of Information and Communications Technology (NICT).

W. Susilo and Y. Mu (Eds.): ACISP 2014, LNCS 8544, pp. 17–33, 2014.
© Springer International Publishing Switzerland 2014

Table 1. Key-recovery attacks on Hierocrypt-L1

Attack	S-function layers	Data	Time	Memory
SQUARE[1] [9]	6	$6 \cdot 2^{32}$ CP	2^{53}	not given
Impossible differential[1] [23]	6	2^{71} KP	2^{55}	not given
SQUARE[1] [9]	7	$14 \cdot 2^{32}$ CP	2^{118}	not given
Related-key impossible differential (Sect. 5.2)	8	$2^{67.5}/k(k-1)$ CP, k-RK	$2^{122.5}$	2^{120}
Related-key differential (Sect. 5.1)	8	2^{61} CP, 2-RK	2^{117}	2^{120}

- KP: known plaintexts, CP: chosen plaintexts, RK: related keys, k: the number of related keys ($k \geq 4$)
- The unit of time about related-key impossible differential attack is the time for marking an incorrect 120-bit round key.
- The unit of time about related-key differential attack is the time for incrementing a counter for correct 120-bit round key candidates.
- The unit of memory is a counter for 120-bit round keys, which is at most one byte.

---

[1]single-key setting

dependent on the right half. In our analysis, the above properties are exploited to find the particular differential characteristics of the key scheduling part in Section 3 to recover the encryption key of Hierocrypt-L1 more efficiently than a brute force attack.

Regarding full-round Hierocrypt-L1, no theoretical attacks are yet known. The previous best known attack on Hierocrypt-L1 was the SQUARE attack [9] on the last 7 out of the 12 S-function layers in the single-key setting.

Biryukov et al. showed the first attack on full-round AES-192 and AES-256 [14], which recovered an AES encryption key and distinguished AES from a random permutation more efficiently than a brute force attack in the related-key setting [6,7]. A related-key attack is not theoretical, but may be practical in case of careless key generation or distribution.

In this paper we will first analyze the key scheduling part of Hierocrypt-L1 to find differential characteristics with probability 1. Then, using them, we will search for the best related-key differential characteristics of the data randomizing part. As a result, we will show that the encryption key can be recovered more efficiently by a related-key differential attack and a related-key impossible differential attack than by a brute force attack on the 8 S-function layers of Hierocrypt-L1. These are the best attacks in terms of the number of attackable S-function layers. The previous best attack and our attacks are shown in Table 1. Furthermore, we will show a new type of impossible differential characteristics. It is a new point that S-box impossible differentials are utilized directly on impossible differential characteristics.

Table 2. The notation used in this paper

Subscript:$_{(128)}$	Denotes 128-bit data
Subscript:$_{1(64)}$	Denotes the left half 64-bit data of 128-bit data
Subscript:$_{2(64)}$	Denotes the right half 64-bit data of 128-bit data
Subscript:$_{n(32)}$	Denotes the n-th word of 128-bit data ($n = 1, 2, 3, 4$) e.g., $X_{(128)} = X_{1(64)} \| X_{2(64)} = X_{1(32)} \| X_{2(32)} \| X_{3(32)} \| X_{4(32)}$
`Typewriter style`	Hexadecimal notation (e.g., 9a)
$Z^{(r)}_{(128)}$	The r-th round intermediate key, $Z^{(r)}_{(128)} = Z^{(8-r)}_{(128)}$
$K^{(r)}_{(128)}$	The round key used in the r-th round of the data randomizing part
$X^{(r)}_{(64)}$	The intermediate data after the r-th operation of the round function
$I^{(r)}_{K1(64)}$	The intermediate data after the XOR operation of $K^{(r)}_{1(64)}$
$I^{(r)}_{K2(64)}$	The intermediate data after the XOR operation of $K^{(r)}_{2(64)}$
$I^{(r)}_{s1(64)}$	The intermediate data after the 1st S-function operation of the r-th round
$I^{(r)}_{s2(64)}$	The intermediate data after the 2nd S-function operation of the r-th round
$I^{(r)}_{mL(64)}$	The intermediate data after the MDS_L transformation of the r-th round

This paper consists of the following sections: In Section 2 we outline the design of Hierocrypt-L1 and related-key and impossible differential attacks. In Section 3 we analyze the key scheduling part and thereby find differential characteristics with probability 1. In Sections 4 and 5 we describe related-key differential and impossible differential attacks using the above characteristics. In Section 6 we summarize our results.

2 Preliminaries

2.1 Notation

The notation used throughout this paper is as shown in the references [11,24] and Table 2. The position of each data byte is numbered from the left, and 1 word is defined as 32-bit data in this paper.

2.2 Description of Hierocrypt-L1

The algorithm of Hierocrypt-L1 consists of a key scheduling part and a data randomizing part. In the following, we will describe each Hierocrypt-L1 part. In regard to the details of Hierocrypt-L1, see the references [11,24].

Encryption. The data randomizing part is sketched in Fig. 1. It consists of five ρ-functions and one XS-function. The ρ-function consists of two linear transformation layers, which are the MDS_L- and MDS_H-function, and two nonlinear S-function layers. The XS-function is the same structure as the ρ-function without the last MDS_H-function. The S-function consists of 8 parallel S-boxes that is the only nonlinear transformation in Hierocrypt-L1. The maximum differential probability of the S-box is 2^{-6}.

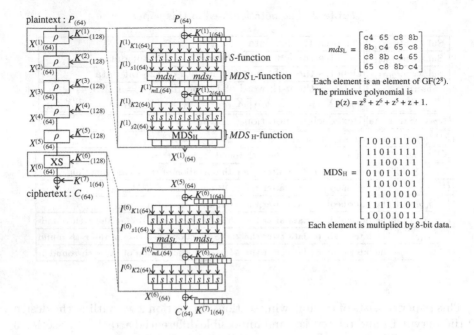

Fig. 1. Data randomizing part of Hierocrypt-L1

Key Scheduling. The key scheduling part is sketched in Fig. 2. It consists of nonlinear Feistel transformations and linear transformations, which operate on the left and right two words of the encryption/intermediate keys, respectively. The input is a 128-bit encryption key denoted by $K_{(128)}$. The output consists of six 128-bit round keys and one 64-bit round key, denoted by $K^{(r)}_{(128)}$ ($1 \leq r \leq 6$) and $K^{(7)}_{1(64)}$. The 128-bit intermediate keys denoted by $Z^{(r)}_{(128)}$ ($0 \leq r \leq 7$) are generated in the process of the key scheduling operation. The 5th to 7th round functions are the inverse of the 2nd to 4th ones; therefore, the following relationships hold: $Z^{(r)}_{(128)} = Z^{(8-r)}_{(128)}$ ($5 \leq r \leq 7$). The right two words of the intermediate keys are independent of the left two words by virtue of the structure of the key scheduling part.

2.3   Related-Key Attacks

Related-key attacks were proposed in the early 1990s [2,15]. In a related-key setting, attackers can obtain pairs of plaintexts and ciphertexts associated with each other by related keys besides the encryption key. Attackers can also discover and control the relationships between the encryption key and related keys, even if they do not know the encryption key itself. In our attack, we consider the

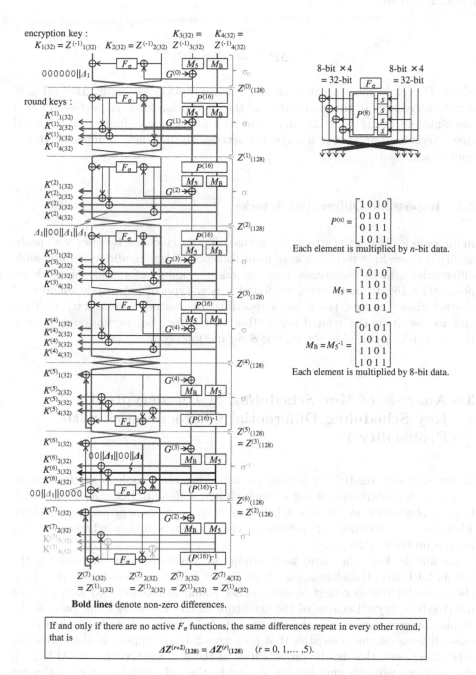

Fig. 2. Key scheduling part of Hierocrypt-L1 and differential characteristics with probability 1

following setting:

$$P \xrightarrow{K} C$$
$$P \oplus \Delta P \xrightarrow{K \oplus \Delta K} C \oplus \Delta C,$$

where P and K denote plaintext and the encryption key, and ΔP and ΔK denote differences in the plaintexts and the encryption keys, respectively. Good combinations of ΔP and ΔK may lead to a greater probability of differential characteristics than that in a single-key setting, so that more number of rounds may be attacked.

2.4   Impossible Differential Attacks

In impossible differential attacks [3], we use differential characteristics with probability 0 to exclude incorrect keys from the correct key candidates. Impossible differential attacks sometimes work on many number of rounds of block ciphers [17,8,16]. In our attack, we found a new type of impossible differential characteristics in that the S-box impossible differentials are directly utilized, and we use it in the related-key setting to recover the encryption key for a Hierocrypt-L1 reduced to the middle 8 S-function layers.

3   Analysis of Key Scheduling of Hierocrypt-L1 –– Key Scheduling Differential Characteristics with Probability 1

In the case of a related-key setting for attacking block ciphers or the Davies-Meyer hash construction using a block cipher, differential characteristics with large probabilities in the key scheduling may be advantageous to attackers. Therefore, we searched for differential characteristics in key scheduling of as large a probability as possible.

As for the key scheduling part, nonlinear transformations are only in the left 64-bit Feistel transformations. If no Feistel round functions are active, then the same differences repeat in every other round of the left two words of the intermediate keys. Because of the structure of the key scheduling part, if the similar property appears in the third word of the intermediate keys, then there exist differential characteristics that no active S-boxes appear in the entire key scheduling part, that is, the probabilities of these characteristics are 1! Even if this property appears only in part of rounds, the differential characteristics are expected to be advantageous to attackers in a related-key setting.

To search for the characteristics that the same differences repeat in every other round of the third word of the intermediate keys, $\Delta Z^{(r)}{}_{3(32)}$, we solved

Table 3. Differences in the encryption key and round keys that lead to differential characteristics with probability 1

$\Delta K_{(128)}$	$000000\|\Delta_1$ 00000000	00000000	$000000\|\Delta_1$
$\Delta K^{(1)}{}_{(128)} = \Delta K^{(3)}{}_{(128)}$	00000000 $000000\|\Delta_1$	$000000\|\Delta_1$	00000000
$\Delta K^{(2)}{}_{(128)} = \Delta K^{(4)}{}_{(128)}$	$000000\|\Delta_1$ 00000000	$\Delta_1\|00\|\Delta_1\|\Delta_1$	$\Delta_1\|00\|\Delta_1\|\Delta_1$
$\Delta K^{(5)}{}_{(128)}$	$000000\|\Delta_1$ 00000000	$000000\|\Delta_1$	$000000\|\Delta_1$
$\Delta K^{(6)}{}_{(128)}$	$000000\|\Delta_1$ $\Delta_1\|00\|\Delta_1\|\Delta_1$	$00\|\Delta_1\|00\|\Delta_1$	$00\|\Delta_1\|0000$
$\Delta K^{(7)}{}_{1(64)}$	$000000\|\Delta_1$ 00000000		
$\Delta K_{(128)}$	00000000 $000000\|\Delta_2$	$\Delta_2\|00\|\Delta_2\|\Delta_2$	$00\|\Delta_2\|00\|\Delta_2$
$\Delta K^{(1)}{}_{(128)} = \Delta K^{(3)}{}_{(128)}$	$000000\|\Delta_2$ 00000000	$\Delta_2\|00\|\Delta_2\|\Delta_2$	$\Delta_2\|00\|\Delta_2\|\Delta_2$
$\Delta K^{(2)}{}_{(128)} = \Delta K^{(4)}{}_{(128)}$	00000000 $000000\|\Delta_2$	$000000\|\Delta_2$	00000000
$\Delta K^{(5)}{}_{(128)}$	$000000\|\Delta_2$ $\Delta_2\|00\|\Delta_2\|\Delta_2$	$00\|\Delta_2\|00\|\Delta_2$	$00\|\Delta_2\|0000$
$\Delta K^{(6)}{}_{(128)}$	$000000\|\Delta_2$ 00000000	$000000\|\Delta_2$	$000000\|\Delta_2$
$\Delta K^{(7)}{}_{1(64)}$	$000000\|\Delta_2$ $\Delta_2\|00\|\Delta_2\|\Delta_2$		

$(\Delta_1, \Delta_2 = 01, 02, \ldots, \mathtt{ff})$

the following linear algebraic equation for $\Delta Z^{(r)}{}_{3(32)}$:

$$\Delta Z^{(r)}{}_{3(32)} \| \Delta Z^{(r+2)}{}_{4(32)} = \left(P^{(16)} \begin{pmatrix} M_5 & O \\ O & M_B \end{pmatrix} \right)^2 \Delta Z^{(r)}{}_{3(32)} \| \Delta Z^{(r)}{}_{4(32)}$$
$$(r = 0,\ 1\ \text{and}\ 2)$$

where

$$\begin{pmatrix} M_5 & O \\ O & M_B \end{pmatrix} X_{3(32)} \| X_{4(32)} := M_5 X_{3(32)} \| M_B X_{4(32)}.$$

Note that $\Delta Z^{(r)}{}_{4(32)}$ and $\Delta Z^{(r+2)}{}_{4(32)}$ are not necessarily equal. Then, we found two different characteristics that

$$\Delta Z^{(2r')}{}_{(128)} = 00000000 \quad 000000\|\Delta_1\ 00000000 \quad \Delta_1\|00\|\Delta_1\|\Delta_1 \qquad (1)$$

$$\Delta Z^{(2r')}{}_{(128)} = 000000\|\Delta_2\ 00000000 \quad 000000\|\Delta_2\ 000000\|\Delta_2 \qquad (2)$$
$$(\Delta_1, \Delta_2 = 01, 02, \ldots, \mathtt{ff},\ r' = 0,\ 1\ \text{and}\ 2).$$

The differences in the encryption key and the round keys are derived from $\Delta Z^{(r)}{}_{(128)}$s. They are shown in Table 3. The positions of active bytes are independent of the values of Δ_1 or Δ_2. Because of linearity, it is easy to make sure that the probabilities of the differential characteristics represented by the linear combinations of (1) and (2) are 1.

Among the 2^{16} encryption keys related to each other by (1) and (2), one round key enables attackers to immediately obtain the other $2^{16} - 1$ round keys. In Fig. 2 the differential characteristics for equation (1) is shown.

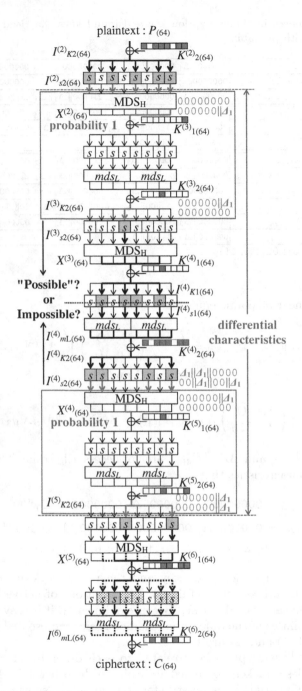

Fig. 3. Related-key possible/impossible differential characteristics on the middle 5 S-function layers of Hierocrypt-L1 with 9 active S-boxes

4 Construction of Related-Key Differentials and Impossible Differentials

In this section, related-key differentials and impossible differentials are constructed using the differential characteristics in the key scheduling that are found in Section 3.

4.1 Truncated Differentials

We searched for truncated differential characteristics in the data randomizing part with the related key in which the number of active S-boxes did not exceed 10. This is because if the number of active S-boxes is more than 10, then the corresponding probability is less than 2^{-64}. As a result, we found that the longest truncated differential characteristic in the middle 5 S-function layers placed between $I^{(2)}{}_{s2(64)}$ and $I^{(5)}{}_{K2(64)}$, with nine active S-boxes in which the related key shown in (1) is used (see also Fig. 3). From $I^{(2)}{}_{s2(64)}$ to $I^{(3)}{}_{K2(64)}$ and from $X^{(4)}{}_{(64)}$ to $I^{(5)}{}_{K2(64)}$, there are no active S-boxes and the corresponding differential probabilities are 1.

For each Δ_1 in equation (1) we investigated whether the truncated differential characteristic in Fig. 3 was impossible or not. As a result, we found that this characteristic is *possible* if and only if Δ_1 in equation (1) is an element of

$$\{06, 13, 34, 3f, 65, 66, 68, 7f, 9a, a6, ac, b2, bd, c6, dc, f0\}. \tag{3}$$

For example, consider the case of $\Delta_1 = 9a$;

- All bytes of $\Delta I^{(3)}{}_{K2(64)}$ are 0 except for the 4th byte, so the 1st, 3rd, 6th and 8th bytes of $\Delta I^{(4)}{}_{s1(64)}$ are 0 and $\Delta I^{(3)}{}_{s2(64)}$, $\Delta X^{(3)}{}_{(64)}$ and $\Delta I^{(4)}{}_{K1(64)}$ are represented as in the 2nd to 4th lines of Table 5.
- The 3rd, 4th, 5th and 7th bytes of $\Delta I^{(4)}{}_{s2(64)}$ are 0, so the same bytes of $\Delta I^{(4)}{}_{mL(64)}$ are all 9a.
- Searching for $\Delta I^{(4)}{}_{s1(64)}$ and $\Delta I^{(4)}{}_{mL(64)}$ that satisfy the above conditions, there is only one pair of $\Delta I^{(4)}{}_{s1(64)}$ and $\Delta I^{(4)}{}_{mL(64)}$
- For the above $\Delta I^{(3)}{}_{K2(64)}$ and $\Delta I^{(4)}{}_{s1(64)}$, ΔI is restricted to be 18 values in Table 5.
- For the above $\Delta I^{(4)}{}_{mL(64)}$ and $\Delta I^{(4)}{}_{s2(64)}$, $\Delta I^{(4)}{}_{K2(64)}$ is restricted to be the only value represented in Table 5.
- The differential probability is equal to the sum of the differential characteristic probabilities for all possible ΔIs.

If Δ_1 is in (3), then, by the same procedure, the differential probabilities are calculated to be those shown in Table 4, which is useful for differential attacks. Otherwise, there are no ΔI and $\Delta I^{(4)}{}_{K2(64)}$ that satisfy both the conditions in 4th and 5th steps of the above procedure, then the differential probabilities are 0, which is useful for impossible differential attacks.

Table 4. Differential probabilities between $I^{(2)}{}_{s2(64)}$ and $I^{(5)}{}_{K2(64)}$ (see also Fig. 3)

Δ_1	06	13	34	3f	65	66	68	7f	9a
Prob.	$2^{-58.75}$	$2^{-58.75}$	$2^{-58.75}$	$2^{-58.68}$	$2^{-59.42}$	$2^{-59.09}$	$2^{-59.00}$	$2^{-59.30}$	$\mathbf{2^{-58.61}}$

Δ_1	a6	ac	b2	bd	c6	dc	f0	others	(00)
Prob.	$2^{-58.91}$	$2^{-59.09}$	$2^{-58.75}$	$2^{-58.83}$	$2^{-59.00}$	$2^{-58.68}$	$2^{-58.91}$	0	(1)

Table 5. Differential characteristics and probabilities for $\Delta_1 = 9a$ illustrated in Fig. 3

$\Delta I^{(3)}{}_{K2(64)}$	0000009a 00000000
$\Delta I^{(3)}{}_{s2(64)}$	$000000\|\Delta I$ 00000000
$\Delta X^{(3)}{}_{(64)}$	$00\|\Delta I\|00\|\Delta I$ $\Delta I\|00\|\Delta I\|00$
$\Delta I^{(4)}{}_{K1(64)}$	$00\|\Delta I\|00\|\Delta I\oplus9a$ $\Delta I\|00\|\Delta I\|00$
$\Delta I^{(4)}{}_{s1(64)}$	003f007b ac00ac00
$\Delta I^{(4)}{}_{mL(64)}$	340f9a9a 9aca9aca
$\Delta I^{(4)}{}_{K2(64)}$	ae0f0000 00ca0050
$\Delta I^{(4)}{}_{s2(64)}$	9a9a0000 009a009a

ΔI	0a,21,3c,53,55,56,8b,8d,9d,a3,ad,ae,ba,ca,ee,f5,fe	fd	others	total
Prob.	2^{-63}	2^{-61}	0	$2^{-58.61}$

Equivalent Transform. For convenience, the positions of the XORing two round keys were changed. As a result, $\Delta K'^{(6)}{}_{1(64)}$ and $\Delta K'^{(6)}{}_{2(64)}$ were also changed, and $X'^{(5)}{}_{(64)}$ and $I'^{(6)}{}_{mL(64)}$ were redefined, simultaneously, as follows (see also Fig. 4):

$$\Delta K'^{(6)}{}_{1(64)} = MDS_{\mathrm{H}}^{-1}(\Delta K^{(6)}{}_{1(64)}) = MDS_{\mathrm{H}}^{-1}(0000009a\ 9a009a9a)$$
$$= 9a9a9a00\ 9a9a0000$$
$$\Delta K'^{(6)}{}_{2(64)} = MDS_{\mathrm{L}}^{-1}(\Delta K^{(6)}{}_{2(64)}) = MDS_{\mathrm{L}}^{-1}(009a009a\ 009a0000).$$
$$= d52ed52e\ 6002b52c$$
$$X'^{(5)}{}_{(64)} = I^{(5)}{}_{s2(64)} \oplus K'^{(6)}{}_{1(64)}$$
$$I'^{(6)}{}_{mL(64)} = I^{(6)}{}_{s1(64)} \oplus K'^{(6)}{}_{2(64)} .$$

4.2 New Type of Impossible Differentials

The truncated differentials derived in Section 4.1 lead to impossible differentials besides "possible" differentials depending on Δ_1. That is, the impossible differentials are directly connected to impossible differentials for S-box at $I^{(4)}{}_{K1(64)}$ and $I^{(4)}{}_{s1(64)}$. In this sense, these are the novel type of impossible differentials as far as we know. Similar studies were done in [5] using a small differential expansion rate, while our construction for an impossible differential directly uses the impossible differentials in S-box when we apply the "miss-in-the-middle" technique [4].

5   Related-Key Attacks on Hierocrypt-L1

By using the differentials constructed in Section 4.1, related-key differential and impossible differential attacks can be done. In this section, the related-key differential attack and the related-key impossible differential attack are shown (See also Fig. 4).

5.1   Related-Key Differential Attack

Attack Procedures. We consider the case of two related keys, one of which is the encryption key itself, and adopt $\Delta_1 = 9a$ in (3) because it leads to the largest differential probability (See Table 4).

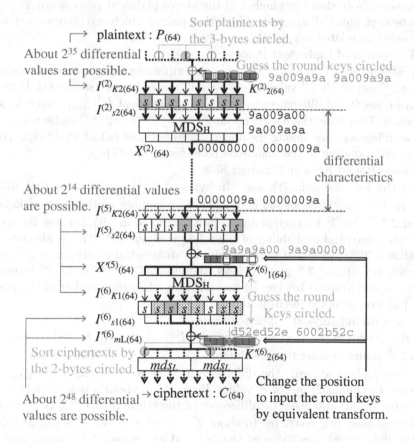

Fig. 4. Procedure for a related-key possible/impossible differential attack on the middle 8 S-function layers of Hierocrypt-L1

(i)   Choice of Plaintexts

First, sort by the 2nd, 4th and 6th bytes of plaintexts, form 2^{24} sets containing 2^{40} plaintexts and choose 2^n ($1 \leq n < 24$) sets so that two sets are chosen simultaneously in which differences in the 2nd and 6th bytes of plaintexts are 0 and difference in the 4th byte of plaintexts is 9a. Then, encrypt all 2^{n+40} plaintexts using the encryption key and the related key, and sort also by the 1st and 6th bytes of $I'^{(6)}{}_{mL(64)}$.

(ii)   Formation of Plaintext Pairs

There are five active bytes at $I^{(2)}{}_{K2(64)}$, and the difference in each active byte at $I^{(2)}{}_{K2(64)}$ is restricted about 2^7 values because the difference in each active byte at $I^{(2)}{}_{s2(64)}$ is restricted to 9a. So, the differences in $I^{(2)}{}_{K2(64)}$ and plaintext are restricted to about $2^{7 \cdot 5} = 2^{35}$ values. Therefore, about $2^{n+40+35} = 2^{n+75}$ plaintext pairs can be formed whose differences are among the above 2^{35} differences. Note that the number of the above plaintext pairs is not 2^{n+75-1} because each pair is distinguished from that pair in which two plaintexts change each other in related key settings.

(iii)   Extraction of Ciphertext Pairs

The differences in $I^{(6)}{}_{s1(64)}$, $I'^{(6)}{}_{mL(64)}$ and ciphertext, are restricted to about $2^{8 \cdot 6} = 2^{48}$ out of all 2^{64} values, because differences in the 1st and 6th bytes of $I^{(6)}{}_{s1(64)}$ are 0 and differences in the other six bytes of $I^{(6)}{}_{s1(64)}$ can take any 2^8 values. Therefore, there exist about $2^{n+75-(64-48)} = 2^{n+59}$ ciphertext pairs whose differences are among the above 2^{48} differences out of 2^{n+75} ciphertext pairs corresponding to the plaintexts pairs formed in (ii).

(iv)   Guess Round Keys at Plaintext Side

Guess the 1st, 3rd, 5th, 7th and 8th bytes of $K^{(2)}{}_{2(64)}$ in order that difference in $I^{(2)}{}_{s2(64)}$ is 9a009a00 9a009a9a. The number of these round keys is about $2^{(8-7) \cdot 5} = 2^5$ for each plaintext pair extracted in (iii), because the mean nonzero differential probability of the S-box is about 2^{-7}. This is also derived as follows: 2^{n+40} plaintext pairs satisfy the differential condition at $I^{(2)}{}_{s2(64)}$ for each key among 2^{40} guessed keys, therefore, $2^{n+40+40} = 2^{n+80}$ tuples of plaintext and guessed key can be constructed, while the number of the plaintext pairs constructed in (ii) is about 2^{n+75}.

(v)   Guess Round Keys at Ciphertext Side

The differences in the 4th and 8th bytes of $I^{(5)}{}_{s2(64)}$ are restricted to about 2^7 out of 2^8 values in order that the difference in $I^{(5)}{}_{K2(64)}$ is 0000009a 0000009a. For each ciphertext pair, the difference in each active byte of $I^{(6)}{}_{K1(64)}$ is restricted to about 2^7 out of 2^8 values. First, think about a pair of ciphertexts extracted in (iii) and guess the difference in the 8th byte of $I^{(5)}{}_{s2(64)}$. For each ciphertext pair, it is restricted to about $2^{7-(8-7) \cdot 2} = 2^5$ out of about 2^7 values by the differential conditions at the 3rd and 8th bytes of $I^{(6)}{}_{K1(64)}$ and for each of them 2^2 out of 2^{16} values of the 3rd and 8th bytes of $I^{(6)}{}_{K1(64)}$ are possible. Then, about $2^{5+2} = 2^7$ values of the 3rd and 8th bytes of $I^{(6)}{}_{K1(64)}$ are possible. Next, guess the difference in the 4th byte of $I^{(5)}{}_{s2(64)}$. It is restricted to about $2^{7-(8-7) \cdot 4} = 2^3$ out of about 2^7 values by the differential conditions at the 2nd, 4th, 5th and 7th bytes of $I^{(6)}{}_{K1(64)}$ and for each of them 2^2 out of 2^{16} values of the 3rd and 8th bytes of $I^{(6)}{}_{K1(64)}$ are possible. Finally, guess the 1st and 6th bytes of $K'^{(6)}{}_{2(64)}$ and the 4th and 8th bytes of $K'^{(6)}{}_{1(64)}$. About $2^{8+8+1+1} = 2^{18}$ out of $2^{8\cdot4} = 2^{32}$ guessed keys satisfy the differential condition at $I^{(5)}{}_{K2(64)}$. After all, about $2^{14+18} = 2^{32}$ guessed keys, the 4th and 8th bytes of $K'^{(6)}{}_{1(64)}$ and all bytes of $K'^{(6)}{}_{2(64)}$, remain for each ciphertext pairs. Note that these procedures are independent of the procedure in (iv).

(vi)   Construction of Tuples of Plaintext Pair, Ciphertext Pair and Round Key
By the argument in (iv) and (v), about $2^{5+32} = 2^{37}$ round keys, which consist of the 1st, 3rd, 5th, 7th and 8th bytes of $K^{(2)}{}_{2(64)}$, the 4th and 8th bytes of $K'^{(6)}{}_{1(64)}$ and all bytes of $K'^{(6)}{}_{2(64)}$, remain for each plaintext pair with corresponding ciphertext pair extracted in (iii). Overall, $2^{n+59+37} = 2^{n+96}$ tuples of plaintext pairs with corresponding ciphertext pairs and round keys satisfy the differential conditions. They suggest the correct key candidates.

(vii)   Extraction from Key Candidates
As mentioned in (iv), 2^{n+40} pairs satisfy the differential conditions at the plaintext side for each key candidate. Among the 2^{n+40} pairs, about $2^{n+40-58.61} = 2^{n-18.61}$ pairs satisfy the conditions of the differences at both plaintext side and ciphertext side for the correct key, while about $2^{n+40-64} = 2^{n-24}$ pairs satisfy those conditions for incorrect keys. By counting the number of votes suggested by the 2^{n+96} tuples mentioned in (vi), we can extract the correct key candidates because of the differences of probabilities between for the correct key and for incorrect keys.

Complexities

(a)   Data Complexity
As mentioned in (i), 2^{n+40} plaintexts with their corresponding ciphertexts and two related keys are necessary, which are the data complexity for this attack.

(b)   Time Complexity
There are four procedures taking large complexities. The first is to choose about 2^{n+59} plaintext pairs with corresponding ciphertext pairs. By sorting plaintexts and ciphertexts appropriately, the time complexity of this procedure become $\mathcal{O}(2^{n+59})$. The second is to construct about 2^{n+96} tuples of plaintext pairs with corresponding ciphertext pairs and guessed keys. This procedure on the plaintext side is independent of that on the ciphertext side. On the plaintext side, it takes $\mathcal{O}(2^{n+59+5}) = \mathcal{O}(2^{n+64})$ times. On the ciphertext side, it takes $\mathcal{O}(2^{n+59+32}) = \mathcal{O}(2^{n+91})$ times, because the key candidates can be efficiently picked up according to the procedure mentioned in (v). The third is to increment and count counters for key candidates. It takes about 2^{n+96} times. Therefore among the first three procedures, the third has dominant time complexity. The last is exhaustive search for remaining keys. Its complexity depends on n and threshold to distinguish the correct key and incorrect keys mentioned later.

(c)   Memory Complexity

As mentioned in (vii), 2^{120} counters for guessed keys are necessary, which is independent of n. It is enough for each counter to have one byte.

For example, consider the case of $n = 21$. The correct key is expected to be suggested about $2^{21-18.61} = 5.25$ times by the $2^{21+96} = 2^{117}$ tuples mentioned in (vi), while incorrect keys are expected to be suggested about $2^{21-24} = 2^{-3}$ times. If key candidates suggested at least four times are regarded as the correct key and remains, then the number of remaining correct key candidates is about $2^{103.3}$ out of 2^{120}, and then the probability of a successful attack is about 0.77. The data, time and memory complexities are $2^{40+21} = 2^{61}$ plaintexts with two related keys, incrementing and counting counter for correct key candidates $2^{21+96} = 2^{117}$ times and enough memory for 2^{120} round keys, respectively. If the above threshold is lowered, then the number of remaining correct key candidates increases, although the probability of success increases.

5.2   Related-Key Impossible Differential Attack

Attack Procedures. In this attack, k (≥ 4) related keys are necessary because of large data complexity to be mentioned later, and Δ_1s must be non-zero values excluding those in (3). We assume that all Δ_1s are neither 0 nor in (3). Then $\binom{k}{2}$ related-key pairs can be formed, though in practice 16 among the 255 non-zero Δ_1s are in (3).

(i)   Choice of Plaintexts

This procedure is same as described in Section 5.1, except for using k related keys.

(ii)   Formation of Plaintext Pairs

This procedure is same as described in Section 5.1. Then about $\binom{k}{2} \cdot 2^{n+75}$ plaintext pairs with their corresponding related-key pairs can be formed.

(iii)   Extraction of Ciphertext Pairs

This procedure is same as described in Section 5.1. Then about $\binom{k}{2} \cdot 2^{n+59}$ plaintext pairs with their corresponding related-keys pairs and ciphertext pairs are extracted.

(iv)   Guess Round Keys at Plaintext Side

This procedure is same as described in Section 5.1.

(v)   Guess Round Keys at Ciphertext Side

This procedure is same as described in Section 5.1.

(vi)   Construction of Tuples of Plaintext Pair, Ciphertext Pair and Round Key

This procedure is same as described in Section 5.1. Then about $\binom{k}{2} \cdot 2^{n+96}$ tuples of plaintext pairs with corresponding ciphertext pairs and guessed keys are constructed.

(vii)   Exclusion of incorrect keys from Key Candidates

The key candidates satisfying the same conditions as those in Section 5.1 are excluded from the correct key candidates in impossible differential attacks, unlike in differential attacks. About 2^{37} among the 2^{120} 120-bit round keys satisfy these conditions for each pair. Therefore, they are excluded by impossible differentials, unlike the case in Section 5.1.

Complexities

(a) Data Complexity
Similar to the argument in Section 5.1, attackers need 2^{n+40} plaintexts with k related keys.

(b) Time Complexity
Similar to the argument in Section 5.1, to mark incorrect keys or search for remaining keys has dominant complexity. The time complexity to mark incorrect keys is about $\binom{k}{2} \cdot 2^{n+96}$ times. In order to reduce the number of 120-bit round key candidates to 2^{120-d}, the following equation holds:

$$2^{120-d} = 2^{120}(1 - 2^{37-120})^{\binom{k}{2} \cdot 2^{n+59}}.$$

(c) Memory Complexity
Similar to the case in Section 5.1, attackers need to have enough memory for 2^{120} 120-bit round keys, which is independent of n. It is enough for each counter to have one byte.

For example, if $d = 8$, then the data complexity is $2^{67.5}/k(k-1)$ with k related keys. k must be at least four, otherwise the data complexity exceeds 2^{64}. The time complexity is marking incorrect keys about $2^{122.5}$ times. As d decreases, the number of remaining key candidates increases, while the data/time complexities decrease, and vice versa.

6 Conclusion

We found particular differential characteristics in key scheduling of Hierocrypt-L1. They have no active S-boxes, that is, their probability is 1. Such characteristics do not exist in many block ciphers [14,1,22,18,10,12], except the trivial example like DES [20] with no S-boxes in its key scheduling part. Using these characteristics, we present two related-key attacks on the middle 8 S-function layers of Hierocrypt-L1. One is an ordinary differential attack, for which the data/memory/time complexities are 2^{61} chosen plaintexts with two related keys/$2^{117}/2^{120}$. The other is an impossible differential attack, for which the data/memory/time complexities are $2^{67.5}/k(k-1)$ chosen plaintexts with k (≥ 4) related keys/$2^{122.5}/2^{120}$. In the impossible differential attack, we use a new type of impossible differential characteristic.

There might be other differential characteristics in the key scheduling that can lead to powerful attacks on more than 8 S-function layers in Hierocrypt-L1, though the probability of differential characteristics in key scheduling is less than 1. There also might be other kinds of attack using those characteristics. These problems remain open.

References

1. Aoki, K., Ichikawa, T., Kanda, M., Matsui, M., Moriai, S., Nakajima, J., Tokita, T.: Camellia: A 128-Bit Block Cipher Suitable for Multiple Platforms - Design and Analysis. In: Stinson, D.R., Tavares, S. (eds.) SAC 2000. LNCS, vol. 2012, pp. 39–56. Springer, Heidelberg (2001)

2. Biham, E.: New types of cryptanalytic attacks using related keys. J. Cryptology 7(4), 229–246 (1994)
3. Biham, E., Biryukov, A., Shamir, A.: Cryptanalysis of Skipjack Reduced to 31 Rounds Using Impossible Differentials. In: Stern, J. (ed.) EUROCRYPT 1999. LNCS, vol. 1592, pp. 12–23. Springer, Heidelberg (1999)
4. Biham, E., Biryukov, A., Shamir, A.: Miss in the Middle Attacks on IDEA and Khufu. In: Knudsen, L.R. (ed.) FSE 1999. LNCS, vol. 1636, pp. 124–138. Springer, Heidelberg (1999)
5. Bouillaguet, C., Dunkelman, O., Fouque, P.-A., Leurent, G.: New Insights on Impossible Differential Cryptanalysis. In: Miri, A., Vaudenay, S. (eds.) SAC 2011. LNCS, vol. 7118, pp. 243–259. Springer, Heidelberg (2012)
6. Biryukov, A., Khovratovich, D.: Related-Key Cryptanalysis of the Full AES-192 and AES-256. In: Matsui, M. (ed.) ASIACRYPT 2009. LNCS, vol. 5912, pp. 1–18. Springer, Heidelberg (2009)
7. Biryukov, A., Khovratovich, D., Nikolić, I.: Distinguisher and Related-Key Attack on the Full AES-256. In: Halevi, S. (ed.) CRYPTO 2009. LNCS, vol. 5677, pp. 231–249. Springer, Heidelberg (2009)
8. Bai, D., Li, L.: New Impossible Differential Attacks on Camellia. In: Ryan, M.D., Smyth, B., Wang, G. (eds.) ISPEC 2012. LNCS, vol. 7232, pp. 80–96. Springer, Heidelberg (2012)
9. Barreto, P.S.L.M., Rijmen, V., Nakahara Jr., J., Preneel, B., Vandewalle, J., Kim, H.Y.: Improved Square Attacks against Reduced-Round Hierocrypt. In: Matsui, M. (ed.) FSE 2001. LNCS, vol. 2355, pp. 165–173. Springer, Heidelberg (2002)
10. CRYPTREC: Cryptographic Techniques Specifications: CIPHERUNICORN-A, http://www.cryptrec.go.jp/cryptrec_03_spec_cypherlist_files/PDF/07_02espec.pdf
11. CRYPTREC: Specification on a Block Cipher: Hierocrypt-L1, http://www.cryptrec.go.jp/cryptrec_03_spec_cypherlist_files/PDF/04_02espec.pdf
12. CRYPTREC: Specification on a Block Cipher: Hierocrypt-3, http://www.cryptrec.go.jp/cryptrec_03_spec_cypherlist_files/PDF/08_02espec.pdf
13. CRYPTREC homepage, http://www.cryptrec.go.jp/english/index.html
14. FIPS-197: Advanced Encryption Standard (November 2001), http://csrc.nist.gov/publications/fips/fips197/fips-197.pdf
15. Knudsen, L.R.: Cryptanalysis of LOKI91. In: Zheng, Y., Seberry, J. (eds.) AUSCRYPT 1992. LNCS, vol. 718, pp. 196–208. Springer, Heidelberg (1993)
16. Liu, Y., Gu, D., Liu, Z., Li, W.: Impossible Differential Attacks on Reduced Round LBlock. In: Ryan, M.D., Smyth, B., Wang, G. (eds.) ISPEC 2012. LNCS, vol. 7232, pp. 97–108. Springer, Heidelberg (2012)
17. Mala, H., Dakhilalian, M., Rijmen, V., Modarres-Hashemi, M.: Improved Impossible Differential Cryptanalysis of 7-Round AES-128. In: Gong, G., Gupta, K.C. (eds.) INDOCRYPT 2010. LNCS, vol. 6498, pp. 282–291. Springer, Heidelberg (2010)
18. Matsui, M.: New block encryption algorithm MISTY. In: Biham, E. (ed.) FSE 1997. LNCS, vol. 1267, pp. 54–68. Springer, Heidelberg (1997)
19. NESSIE project, https://www.cosic.esat.kuleuven.be/nessie/
20. NIST Special Publication 800-67 Revision 1: Recommendation for the Triple Data Encryption Algorithm (TDEA) Block Cipher, http://csrc.nist.gov/publications/nistpubs/800-67-Rev1/SP-800-67-Rev1.pdf

21. Ohkuma, K., Muratani, H., Sano, F., Kawamura, S.: The Block Cipher Hiero-crypt. In: Stinson, D.R., Tavares, S. (eds.) SAC 2000. LNCS, vol. 2012, pp. 72–88. Springer, Heidelberg (2001)
22. Shimoyama, T., Yanami, H., Yokoyama, K., Takenaka, M., Itoh, K., Yajima, J., Torii, N., Tanaka, H.: The Block Cipher SC2000. In: Matsui, M. (ed.) FSE 2001. LNCS, vol. 2355, pp. 312–327. Springer, Heidelberg (2002)
23. Toshiba Co., Ltd.: Self Evaluation: Hierocrypt-L1, http://www.toshiba.co.jp/ rdc/security/hierocrypt/files/hcl1_01eeval.pdf
24. Toshiba Co., Ltd.: Specification on a Block Cipher: Hierocrypt-L1, http://www.toshiba.co.jp/rdc/security/hierocrypt/index.htm

Some Insights into Differential Cryptanalysis of Grain v1

Subhadeep Banik*

Applied Statistics Unit, Indian Statistical Institute Kolkata
s.banik_r@isical.ac.in

Abstract. As far as the Differential Cryptanalysis of reduced round Grain v1 is concerned, the best results were those published by Knellwolf et al. in Asiacrypt 2011. In an extended version of the paper, it was shown that it was possible to retrieve **(i)** 5 expressions in the Secret Key bits for a variant of Grain v1 that employs 97 rounds (in place of 160) in its Key Scheduling process using 2^{27} chosen IVs and **(ii)** 1 expression in Secret Key bits for a variant that employs 104 rounds in its Key Scheduling using 2^{35} chosen IVs. The authors had arrived at the values of these Secret Key expressions by observing certain biases in the keystream bits generated by the chosen IVs. These biases were observed purely experimentally and no theoretical justification was provided for the same. In this paper, we will revisit Knellwolf's attacks on Grain v1 and try to provide a theoretical framework that will serve to prove the correctness of these attacks. We will also look at open problems which may possibly pave way for further research on Differential Cryptanalysis of Grain v1.

Keywords: eStream, Differential Cryptanalysis, Dynamic Cube Attack, Stream Cipher.

1 Introduction

The Grain v1 stream cipher is in the hardware profile of the eStream portfolio [1] that has been designed by Hell, Johansson and Meier in 2005 [15]. It is a synchronous bit oriented cipher, although it is possible to achieve higher throughput at the expense of additional hardware. The physical structure of Grain is simple as well as elegant and it has been designed so as to require low hardware complexity. Following the publication of two attacks [6, 18] on the initial design of the cipher, the modified version Grain v1 [15] was proposed. Later, the designers came up with a second version of Grain, i.e., Grain-128 [16] that uses 128 bit Key. Thereafter, cipher Grain-128a [2] was designed for the dual purpose of message authentication alongside message encryption. For detailed cryptanalytic results related to this family, the reader may refer to [3–5, 7–9, 13, 14, 21] and the references therein.

---

* Supported by Center of Excellence in Cryptography and R.C. Bose Center for Cryptology and Information Security, ISI Kolkata.

W. Susilo and Y. Mu (Eds.): ACISP 2014, LNCS 8544, pp. 34–49, 2014.

Cube attacks was first introduced by Dinur and Shamir in [12] and have been used extensively to attack reduced round variants of the Grain family. In [10, 11], cube attacks have been used to successfully cryptanalyze reduced-round variants as well as full Grain 128. In [17], cube distinguishers were used to distinguish a variant of Grain-128a, that employs 189 out of the 256 rounds in the Key Scheduling process. However, due to the relative complex nature of the component functions used in the design of Grain v1, there have not been many advances in this direction against it. The best published work on Grain v1 is by Knellwolf et al [20], an extended version of which appeared in [19, Chapter 3.4]. The attack, which can be best described as a dynamic cube attack over a single-dimensional cube, achieves the following objectives:

a) It retrieves 5 expressions in the Secret Key bits for a variant of Grain v1 that employs 97 rounds (in place of 160) in its Key Scheduling process using 2^{27} chosen IVs.

b) It retrieves 1 expression in Secret Key bits for a variant that employs 104 rounds in its Key Scheduling using 2^{35} chosen IVs.

The values of these Secret Key expressions by observing certain non-randomness in the keystream bits generated by the chosen IVs. More specifically, the authors could enumerate a set of IVs for which, the sum of the output bits over the single dimensional cube were biased towards 0. These biases were observed purely experimentally and no theoretical justification was provided for the same. Providing a theoretical explanation of these experimental observations has thus been an open problem in this domain.

In this paper we will try to provide some answers to these questions which have thus far remained open. We will first briefly revisit the details of the attacks on Grain v1 described in [19, Chapter 3.4]. We will then describe a Differential Engine that will keep track of the differential trails in the Key Scheduling part of the cipher. Using this tool we will show that biases observed in the output cubes after 97 rounds respectively are due to unbalanced derivatives of the NFSR update function g and output function h used in the design of Grain v1, i.e., there exist differentials α, β for which the Boolean Functions $g(\mathbf{x}) \oplus g(\mathbf{x} \oplus \alpha)$ and $h(\mathbf{x}) \oplus h(\mathbf{x} \oplus \beta)$ are both unbalanced. For the attack on 104 rounds, the author of [19] observes that the bias is observed in only about 50% of the cases, and at this point it is not exactly clear what algebraic conditions the Secret Key needs to satisfy in order to observe the bias and perform the Key recovery.

1.1   Description of Grain v1

Grain v1 consists of an 80-bit LFSR and an 80-bit NFSR. Certain bits of both the shift registers are taken as inputs to a combining Boolean function, whence the key-stream is produced. The update function of the LFSR is given by the equation $y_{t+80} = f(Y_t)$, where $Y_t = [y_t, y_{t+1}, \ldots, y_{t+79}]$ is the 80-bit vector that denotes the LFSR state at the tth clock interval and f is a linear function on the LFSR state bits. The NFSR state is updated as $x_{t+n} = y_t \oplus g(X_t)$.

Here, $X_t = [x_t, x_{t+1}, \ldots, x_{t+n-1}]$ is an n-bit vector that denotes the NFSR state at the tth clock interval and g is a non-linear function of the NFSR state bits. The output key-stream is produced by combining the LFSR and NFSR bits as $z_t = h'(X_t, Y_t) = \bigoplus_{a \in A} x_{t+a} \oplus h(X_t, Y_t)$, where A is some fixed subset of $\{0, 1, 2, \ldots, n-1\}$.

The cipher uses an 80-bit Secret Key and a 64-bit IV. The Key is loaded in the NFSR and the IV is loaded in the 0th to the 63rd bits of the LFSR. The remaining bits of the LFSR are loaded with the $P = $ 0x ffff. After this, the Key-Scheduling Algorithm (KSA) is executed, during which for 160 rounds, the key-stream produced at the output point of the function h' is XOR-ed to both the LFSR and NFSR update functions, i.e., during the first 160 clock intervals, the LFSR and the NFSR bits are updated as $y_{t+80} = z_t \oplus f(Y_t)$, $x_{t+80} = y_t \oplus z_t \oplus g(X_t)$. After the completion of the KSA, the feedback of the keystream bit is discontinued and made available for encryption. For a complete mathematical description of the functions f, g, h please refer to [15].

2   Knellwolf's Attack on Grain v1

The paper [20] by Knellwolf et al. at Asiacrypt 2011 remains the best published result in the field of cryptanalysis of Grain v1 in terms of the number of rounds attacked. We will describe a slightly modified version of the same attack that appeared in [19, Chapter 3.4]. As alluded to earlier, the attack can be described as a dynamic cube attack over a cube of dimension one. Grain v1 employs a 64 bit IV, and the 37th IV bit was chosen as the cube variable. Algebraically, this is equivalent to analyzing two initializations of the Grain v1 cipher, one with the initial state equal to

$$X_0 = [k_0, k_1, \ldots, k_{79}], \quad Y_0 = [v_0, v_1, \ldots, v_{37}, \ldots, v_{63}, 1, 1, \ldots, 1],$$

and the other with the initial state equal to

$$X_0' = [k_0, k_1, \ldots, k_{79}], \quad Y_0' = [v_0, v_1, \ldots, 1 \oplus v_{37}, \ldots, v_{63}, 1, 1, \ldots, 1].$$

where $K = [k_0, k_1, \ldots, k_{79}]$, $V = [v_0, v_1, \ldots, v_{37}, \ldots, v_{63}]$, $V' = [v_0, v_1, \ldots, 1 \oplus v_{37}, \ldots, v_{63}]$ are the formal notations for the Secret Key and the two IVs that differ in the 37th position. Let X_i, Y_i and X_i', Y_i' denote the NFSR, LFSR states at the ith KSA round produced during the evolution of X_0, Y_0 and X_0', Y_0' respectively.

The two initializations by X_0, Y_0 and X_0', Y_0', thus, imply that at the beginning of the Key Scheduling Algorithm (KSA), a differential is introduced in the 37th LFSR bit. It seems inevitable that as more and more KSA rounds are completed the difference would inevitably spread to the NFSR as well, i.e., there exists some i for which X_i and X_i' would no longer be algebraically equal. The strategy of the attackers, in [19], was to delay the inevitable and prevent the diffusion of the differential to the NFSR for as many KSA rounds as possible, by imposing certain algebraic conditions on the IV and Secret Key bits. As a result of this the attacker obtains several algebraic relations between the Secret Key bits and the IV bits that must be satisfied if the differential is to be contained in the LFSR for as long as possible. These relations may be of the following types :

Type 1: A relation of the form $F_1(V) = 0$, i.e., involving only the IV bits.
Type 2: A relation of the form $F_2(K, V) = 0$, i.e., involving both the Secret Key and the IV bits.

Now let the term z_t, z'_t respectively be used describe the output bit produced in the tth KSA round by the Key-IV pair K, V and K, V' (note that when we try to cryptanalyze Grain v1 reduced to r KSA rounds, the values of the output bits z_t, z'_t for all $t < r$ are unavailable to the attacker). The attacker now analyzes the pair of simplified cipher initializations where the the differential originally introduced in the 37th LFSR bit is prevented from propagating into the NFSR by imposing suitable **Type 1, 2** relations between the Key and IV bits. In such a simplified cipher, the attacker now tries to find some i for which the distribution of the sum $z_i \oplus z'_i$ shows some non-randomness. Based on this randomness the attacker tries to guess the values of one or several expressions in the Secret Key bits. We will illustrate this attack paradigm with this concrete example as described below.

1. The attacker begins to analyze the two algebraic systems resulting from the initialization of Grain v1 by the Key-IV pairs K, V and K, V' respectively. Thus the attacker has to analyze the evolution of the difference between the states X_i, Y_i and X'_i, Y'_i for increasing values of i starting from 0, with $X_0 = K, Y_0 = V||\texttt{0x ffff}$ and $X'_0 = K, Y'_0 = V'||\texttt{0x ffff}$ as described above.

2. The attacker then looks at all KSA rounds t during which the differential could propagate to the NFSR. The first such instance occurs at round $t = 12$, when the difference originally introduced at LFSR bit 37 at $t = 0$, now sits in LFSR location 25 which feeds the output function h. Since during the KSA the NFSR is updated as $x_{t+n} = g(X_t) \oplus y_t \oplus z_t$, the difference generated between the updated NFSR bits x_{80+12} and x'_{80+12} is given by

$$x_{80+12} \oplus x'_{80+12} = [\, g(X_{12}) \oplus y_{12} \oplus z_{12} \,] \oplus [\, g(X'_{12}) \oplus y'_{12} \oplus z'_{12} \,]$$
$$= z_{12} \oplus z'_{12} = v_{15}v_{58} \oplus v_{58}k_{75} \oplus 1$$

By algebraic calculation it can be verified that $X_{12} = X'_{12}$ and $y_{12} = y'_{12}$ and hence the above result follows. Now, the attacker must therefore set $x_{80+12} \oplus x'_{80+12} = v_{15}v_{58} \oplus v_{58}k_{75} \oplus 1 = 0$ to prevent the propagation of this differential. This can be achieved by setting $v_{58} \oplus 1 = 0$ and

$$C_1 : \; v_{15} \oplus K_1 = 0, \tag{1}$$

where $K_1 = k_{75} \oplus 1$. Thus we obtain one **Type 1** relation and one **Type 2** relation.

3. The next instance of difference propagation occurs at KSA round $t = 34$. At this round, the difference generated between the updated NFSR bits x_{80+34} and x'_{80+34} is given by

$$x_{80+34} \oplus x'_{80+34} = [\ g(X_{34}) \oplus y_{34} \oplus z_{34}\ ] \oplus [\ g(X'_{34}) \oplus y'_{34} \oplus z'_{34}\ ] = z_{34} \oplus z'_{34}$$
$$= y_{98} \oplus y_{59}y_{80} \oplus y_{80}y_{98} \oplus y_{80}x_{97}$$

This difference can be nullified if we set $y_{98} = y_{80} = 0$. Now, both y_{98} and y_{80} are functions of $k_0, k_1, \ldots, k_{79}$ and $v_0, v_1, \ldots, v_{63}$ and hence $y_{98} = y_{80} = 0$ is satisfied if we impose the following conditions: $v_0 = 0, v_1 = 0, v_3 = 0, v_4 = 0, v_5 = 0, v_{21} = 0, v_{25} = 0, v_{26} = 0, v_{27} = 0, v_{43} = 0, v_{46} = 0, v_{47} = 0, v_{48} = 0$

$$C_2: \quad v_{13} \oplus v_{23} \oplus v_{38} \oplus v_{51} \oplus v_{62} \oplus K_2 = 0, \tag{2}$$

$$C_3: \quad v_2 \oplus v_{18} \oplus v_{31} \oplus v_{40} \oplus v_{41} \oplus v_{53} \oplus v_{56} \oplus K_3 = 0, \tag{3}$$

where

$$K_2 = k_1 \oplus k_2 \oplus k_4 \oplus k_{10} \oplus k_{31} \oplus k_{43} \oplus k_{56},$$

and K_3 is a polynomial expression of degree 7 with 39 monomials and 31 key variables.

4. The next instance is at $t = 40$. Again it can be verified that

$$x_{80+40} \oplus x'_{80+40} = [g(X_{40}) \oplus y_{40} \oplus z_{40}] \oplus [g(X'_{40}) \oplus y'_{40} \oplus z'_{40}] = z_{40} \oplus z'_{40}$$
$$= v_{43}y_{86} \oplus v_{43} \oplus y_{86}x_{103} \oplus y_{86} \oplus x_{103}$$

The difference is nullified if we set $v_{43} = 0, y_{86} = 0$, and $x_{103} = 0$ for which the following conditions are imposed: $v_8 = 0, v_9 = 0, v_{10} = 0, v_{19} = 0, v_{28} = 0, v_{29} = 0, v_{31} = 0, v_{44} = 0, v_{49} = 0, v_{51} = 0, v_{52} = 0, v_{53} = 0, v_{57} = 0$

$$C_4: \quad v_6 \oplus K_4 = 0, \tag{4}$$

$$C_5: \quad v_7 \oplus v_{20} \oplus v_{23} \oplus v_{32} \oplus v_{45} \oplus K_5 = 0, \tag{5}$$

$$K_4 = k_7 \oplus k_8 \oplus k_{10} \oplus k_{16} \oplus k_{37} \oplus k_{49} \oplus k_{62} \oplus 1$$

and K_5 is a polynomial expression of degree 15 with 2365 monomials in 57 key variables.

The five **Type 2** relations $C_1, C_2, \ldots, C_5$ obtained in Equations (1)-(5) are crucial to the Key recovery attack. First note that due to the several **Type 1** relations that assign 27 of the IV bits to 0 or 1, the effective IV space is reduced to $\{0,1\}^{37}$. We will partition this space into 2^5 disjoint sets T_i, $0 \leq i < 32$ as follows. Let $\{v_2, v_6, v_7, v_{13}, v_{15}\}$ be the set of dynamic cube variables. Let $K_1, K_2, \ldots, K_5$ be the unknown key expressions as described above and write $\mathbf{U} = [K_1, K_2, K_3, K_4, K_5]$. Then, for each $\mathbf{U} \in \{0,1\}^5$ the set $T_{\mathbf{U}}$ can be generated as follows:

1. Define the Set

$$T_{\mathbf{U}} \leftarrow \{V \in \{0,1\}^{64} \mid v_{58} = 1, v_0 = 0, v_1 = 0, v_3 = 0, v_4 = 0, v_5 = 0, v_{21} = 0,$$
$$v_{25} = 0, v_{26} = 0, v_{27} = 0, v_{43} = 0, v_{46} = 0, v_{47} = 0,$$
$$v_{48} = 0, v_8 = 0, v_9 = 0, v_{10} = 0, v_{19} = 0, v_{28} = 0,$$
$$v_{29} = 0, v_{31} = 0, v_{44} = 0, v_{49} = 0, v_{51} = 0, v_{52} = 0,$$
$$v_{53} = 0, v_{57} = 0\}$$

2. For all $V \in T_{\mathbf{U}}$, adjust $v_2, v_6, v_7, v_{13}, v_{15}$ according to $\mathbf{U}$:

$$v_{15} \leftarrow K_1, \quad v_{13} \leftarrow v_{23} \oplus v_{38} \oplus v_{51} \oplus v_{62} \oplus K_2,$$
$$v_2 \leftarrow v_{18} \oplus v_{31} \oplus v_{40} \oplus v_{41} \oplus v_{53} \oplus v_{56} \oplus K_3$$
$$v_6 \leftarrow K_4, \quad v_7 \leftarrow v_{20} \oplus v_{23} \oplus v_{32} \oplus v_{45} \oplus K_5$$

The attacker observes that if the conditions C_1 to C_5 are all satisfied then the distributions of $z_{97} \oplus z'_{97}$ and $z_{104} \oplus z'_{104}$ exhibit non-random behavior. More specifically, it was experimentally observed that

$$\Pr\left[z_{97} \oplus z'_{97} = 0 \mid C_i \text{ is satisfied } \forall i \in [1,5]\right] = \frac{1}{2} + \epsilon_1, \tag{6}$$

$$\Pr\left[z_{104} \oplus z'_{104} = 0 \mid C_i \text{ is satisfied } \forall i \in [1,5]\right] = \frac{1}{2} + \epsilon_2, \tag{7}$$

where ϵ_1, ϵ_2 are some positive biases. Note that these biases were observed experimentally and no theoretical proof was provided for them. In this paper, we shall attempt to provide a theoretical framework to prove the bias at round 97. To mount the attack, the attacker tries to compute the distribution of $z_{97} \oplus z'_{97}$ and $z_{104} \oplus z'_{104}$ in each of the 32 sets $T_{\mathbf{U}}$. Observe that all the conditions $C_1, C_2, \ldots, C_5$ are satisfied in only one of these sets $T_{\mathbf{U}_0}$ where $\mathbf{U}_0$ is the correct value of $\mathbf{U}$. The attacker will therefore be able to observe the bias in the set $T_{\mathbf{U}_0}$, and by standard randomness assumptions, fail to observe any bias in the other sets, thereby determining the values of the five expressions $K_1, K_2, \ldots, K_5$. As it turns out, it the attacker may observe bias in three other sets $T_{\mathbf{U}'}$, where the values of $\mathbf{U}'$ are different from the correct $\mathbf{U}_0$. In fact the conditions C_2, C_3 need not be satisfied and thus the bias will be observed in all the other 3 sets where C_1, C_4, C_5 are satisfied but C_2, C_3 are not, and we shall provide a framework to prove this.

3   The Differential Engine $\Delta\mathsf{Grain}_{\mathsf{KSA}}$

In order to prove the biases observed in the distribution of $z_{97} \oplus z'_{97}$ and $z_{104} \oplus z'_{104}$ we will define a tool $\Delta\mathsf{Grain}_{\mathsf{KSA}}$ that will keep track of the differential trails of any cipher in the Grain family during the Key Scheduling process. The tool is a modification of the engine D-GRAIN that appeared in [3]. Note that while D-GRAIN computed the differential trails during the PRGA, our engine will do so during the KSA.

3.1   Generalized Grain Cipher

To begin, let us define a generalized Grain stream cipher which will cover the descriptions of Grain v1, Grain-128 and Grain-128a as well. Any cipher in the Grain family consists of an n-bit LFSR and an n-bit NFSR. The update function of the LFSR is given by the equation

$$y_{t+n} = f(Y_t) = y_t \oplus y_{t+f_1} \oplus y_{t+f_2} \oplus \cdots \oplus y_{t+f_a},$$

where $Y_t = [y_t, y_{t+1}, \ldots, y_{t+n-1}]$ is an n-bit vector that denotes the LFSR state at the tth clock interval and f is a linear function on the LFSR state bits obtained from a primitive polynomial in $GF(2)$ of degree n. The NFSR state is updated as

$$x_{t+n} = y_t \oplus g(X_t) = y_t \oplus g(x_t, x_{t+g_1}, x_{t+g_2}, \ldots, x_{t+g_b})$$
$$= y_t \oplus x_t \oplus x_{t+g_1} \oplus \cdots \oplus x_{t+g_{b_0}} \oplus g'(x_{t+g_{b_0}+1}, x_{t+g_{b_0}+2}, \ldots, x_{t+g_b})$$

Here, $X_t = [x_t, x_{t+1}, \ldots, x_{t+n-1}]$ is an n-bit vector that denotes the NFSR state at the tth clock interval and g is a non-linear function of the NFSR state bits in which the NFSR locations $0, g_1, g_2, \ldots, g_{b_0}$ only contribute linearly. The output key-stream is produced by combining the LFSR and NFSR bits as

$$z_t = x_{t+l_1} \oplus x_{t+l_2} \oplus \cdots \oplus x_{t+l_c} \oplus y_{t+i_1} \oplus y_{t+i_2} \oplus \cdots \oplus y_{t+i_d} \oplus$$
$$h(y_{t+h_1}, y_{t+h_2}, \ldots, y_{t+h_e}, x_{t+j_1}, x_{t+j_2}, \ldots, x_{t+j_w}).$$

Here h is another non-linear combining Boolean function. So it is clear that Grain v1, Grain-128 and Grain-128a are particular instances of the generalized Grain cipher.

3.2 ΔGrain$_{KSA}$

As defined earlier, let $S_0 = [X_0 || Y_0] \in \{0,1\}^{2n}$ be the initial state of the generalized Grain KSA and $S_0^\phi = [X_0^\phi || Y_0^\phi]$ be the initial state which differs from S_0 in some LFSR location $\phi \in [0, m-1]$, where m is the length of the IV. Note that, in the particular case of Grain v1, where we introduce the difference in the 37th IV bit, the notation X_0', Y_0' actually implies X_0^{37}, Y_0^{37} in this context.

The task is to ascertain how the corresponding internal states in the tth round S_t and S_t^ϕ will differ from each other, for some integer $t > 0$. We present the following algorithm which we will call ΔGrain$_{KSA}$ that takes as input the difference location $\phi \in [0, m-1]$ and the value r of the number of rounds, and returns the following: (i) a set of r integer arrays χ_t, for $0 \leq t < r$, each of length $c + d$, (ii) a set of r integer arrays Υ_t, for $0 \leq t < r$, each of length $e + w$ and (iii) an integer array ΔZ of length r. Note that as already defined in the description of generalized Grain, d, c are the number of LFSR, NFSR bits which are linearly added to the output function h. And e, w are the number of LFSR, NFSR bits that are input to the function h.

Now consider the corresponding generalized differential engine Δ_ϕ-Grain$_{KSA}$ with an n-cell LFSR ΔL and an n-cell NFSR ΔN. All the elements of ΔL

and ΔN are integers. We will denote the tth round state of ΔL as $\Delta L_t = [u_t, u_{t+1}, \ldots, u_{t+n-1}]$ and that of ΔN as $\Delta N_t = [v_t, v_{t+1}, \ldots, v_{t+n-1}]$. Initially all the elements of $\Delta N, \Delta L$ are set to 0, with the only exception that – The cell numbered ϕ of ΔL is set to 1. The initial states $\Delta N_0, \Delta L_0$ are indicative of the difference between S_0 and S_0^ϕ and we will show that the tth states $\Delta N_t, \Delta L_t$ are indicative of the difference between S_t and S_t^ϕ. Define the function lin : $\cup_{i=1}^\infty \mathbb{Z}_+^i \to \{0, 1, 2\}$ (where $\mathbb{Z}_+$ is the set of non negative integers)

$$\text{lin}(q_1, q_2, \ldots, q_i) = \begin{cases} q_1 + q_2 + \cdots + q_i \bmod 2 & \text{if } \max(q_1, q_2, \ldots, q_i) \le 1, \\ 2, & \text{otherwise.} \end{cases}$$

Define the intermediate variables ℓ_t, r_t, Ω_t as follows:

$$\ell_t = \text{lin}\,(u_t, u_{t+f_1}, \ldots, u_{t+f_a}), \quad r_t = \text{lin}\,(u_t, v_t, v_{t+g_1}, \cdots, v_{t+g_{b_0}})$$

$$\Omega_t = 2 \cdot \text{OR}(v_{t+g_{b_0}+1}, v_{t+g_{b_0}+2}, \ldots, v_{t+g_b}).$$

Here OR is a map from $\cup_{i=1}^\infty \mathbb{Z}_+^i \to \{0, 1\}$ which roughly represents the logical 'or' operation and is defined as

$$\text{OR}(q_0, q_1, \ldots, q_i) = \begin{cases} 0, \text{ if } q_0 = q_1 = q_2 = \cdots = q_i = 0, \\ 1, \text{ otherwise.} \end{cases}$$

Let $\chi_t = [v_{t+l_1}, v_{t+l_2}, \ldots, v_{t+l_c}, u_{t+i_1}, u_{t+i_2}, \ldots, u_{t+i_d}]$, and also define the vector $\Upsilon_t = [u_{t+h_1}, u_{t+h_2}, \ldots, u_{t+h_e}, v_{t+j_1}, v_{t+j_2}, \ldots, v_{t+j_w}]$. Note that $\chi_t(\Upsilon_t)$ is the set of cells in Δ_ϕ-Grain$_{\text{KSA}}$ which corresponds to the bits which are linearly added to the output function h (input to h) in the tth KSA stage of the actual cipher. The tth key-stream element π_t produced by this engine is given as

$$\pi_t = \text{lin}\,(\text{lin}(\chi_t), 2 \cdot \text{OR}(\Upsilon_t))$$

Here $\mathbf{0}$ denotes the all zero vector. Now ΔL updates itself as $u_{t+n} = \text{lin}(\ell_t, \pi_t)$. And similarly, ΔN updates itself as $v_{t+n} = \text{lin}(r_t, \Omega_t, \pi_t)$. We will now explain the rationale behind choosing the internal variables and then explain clearly the working of the engine:

1. The Keystream element π_t: We will begin with the working hypothesis that if any element in the differential engine is :
   $\to 0$, the difference of the corresponding elements in S_t and S_t^ϕ is always 0.
   $\to 1$, the difference of the corresponding elements in S_t and S_t^ϕ is always 1.
   $\to 2$, the difference of the corresponding elements in S_t and S_t^ϕ is probabilistically either 0 or 1 and the exact value would depend on the exact value of the initial vector S_0 and actual update functions.
   For example if some element u_{t+n} is 0 we can assume that the corresponding LFSR bits y_{t+n} and y_{t+n}^ϕ are always equal, if π_t is 1 for some t, then we can assume that difference of the keystream bits z_t and z_t^ϕ is always unequal etc. We will show that this hypotheses is correct as we go along trying to explain the rationale behind the various elements of the engine.

The function $\mathsf{lin}(\mathbf{\Delta})$ computes the modulo 2 sum of the elements of the vector $\mathbf{\Delta}$ only if all its elements are 0 or 1, otherwise it returns 2. This captures the notion of difference propagation rules over ordinary GF(2) addition. Let $\mathbf{x}$ and $\mathbf{x}^\phi$ be vectors in the original cipher initializations S_0 and S_0^ϕ respectively, whose contents need to be summed for some intermediate cipher operation. Let $\delta = \mathbf{x} \oplus \mathbf{x}^\phi$, then the difference of sums of the bits of $\mathbf{x}$ and $\mathbf{x}^\phi$ is equal to the sum of the contents of δ. Now if the elements of δ are always 0 or 1 (this corresponds to all elements of $\mathbf{\Delta}$ being either 0 or 1 in the differential engine), it implies that the corresponding elements of $\mathbf{x}$ and $\mathbf{x}^\phi$ are respectively always equal or different. Then, the difference of sums of the bits of $\mathbf{x}$ and $\mathbf{x}^\phi$ will either be always 0 or 1 and is given by the sum of elements of δ. In such an event, $\mathsf{lin}(\mathbf{\Delta})$ computes the modulo 2 sum of the elements of $\mathbf{\Delta}$ which is either 0 or 1. If, however, some corresponding elements $\mathbf{x}$ and $\mathbf{x}^\phi$ are only probabilistically equal (this corresponds to some elements of $\mathbf{\Delta}$ being equal to 2), then the difference between the sums of their contents is also probabilistically 0 or 1. and $\mathsf{lin}(\mathbf{\Delta})$ returns 2.

The function $2 \cdot \mathsf{OR}(\mathbf{\Delta})$ returns 0 only if all elements of the vector $\mathbf{\Delta}$ is 0 and returns 2 otherwise. This captures the notion of difference propagation rules over non-linear Boolean functions. Again, let $\mathbf{x}$ and $\mathbf{x}^\phi$ be vectors in the original cipher initializations S_0 and S_0^ϕ respectively, which are fed to some non-linear function F during some intermediate cipher operation. As above, let $\delta = \mathbf{x} \oplus \mathbf{x}^\phi$. Then difference between $F(\mathbf{x})$ and $F(\mathbf{x}^\phi)$ is deterministically 0 only if all elements of δ are also deterministically 0 (this corresponds to all elements of $\mathbf{\Delta}$ being 0). If even one element of δ is not deterministically 0 then the difference between $F(\mathbf{x})$ and $F(\mathbf{x}^\phi)$ becomes probabilistic and depends on the nature of the Boolean Function $F(\mathbf{x}) \oplus F(\mathbf{x}^\phi)$. In such an event, $2 \cdot \mathsf{OR}(\mathbf{\Delta})$ returns 2.

Now observe the equation defining π_t. Note that χ_t consists of tap locations that add linearly to the output function and Υ_t consists of the locations that feed the non-linear h function in the original generalized Grain cipher. Thus the $\mathsf{lin}()$ of $\mathsf{lin}(\chi_t)$ and $2 \cdot \mathsf{OR}(\Upsilon_t)$ will effectively capture the difference between actual t^{th} round keystream bits z_t and z_t^ϕ in the two initializations of the generalized cipher.

2. Update rule of ΔL: In the original cipher, the update to the LFSR is the GF(2) sum of 2 parts: the keystream bit z_t and the linear update function f over the LFSR bits $y_t, y_{t+f_1}, y_{t+f_2}, \ldots, y_{t+f_a}$. The function $\ell_t = \mathsf{lin}(u_t, u_{t+f_1}, \ldots, u_{t+f_a})$ captures the difference propagation over the linear sum. So the definition of u_{t+n} which is $\mathsf{lin}(\ell_t, \pi_t)$ captures the difference between y_{t+n} and y_{t+n}^ϕ.

3. Update rule of ΔN: In the original cipher, the update to the NFSR is the GF(2) sum of 4 parts: the keystream bit z_t, the LFSR bit y_t, the linear function over the NFSR bits $x_t, x_{t+g_1}, \ldots, x_{t+g_{b_0}}$ and the non-linear update function g' over the bits $x_{t+g_{b_0}+1}, \ldots, x_{t+g_b}$. The function $r_t = \mathsf{lin}\,(u_t, v_t, v_{t+g_1}$

$, \cdots, v_{t+g_{b_0}})$ captures the difference propagation over the linear parts, and $\Omega_t = 2 \cdot \mathsf{OR}(v_{t+g_{b_0}+1}, v_{t+g_{b_0}+2}, \ldots, v_{t+g_b})$ captures the difference over the non-linear function g'. And thus the definition of v_{t+n} which is $\mathrm{lin}(r_t, \Omega_t, \pi_t)$ captures the difference between x_{t+n} and x_{t+n}^{ϕ}.

4. An exception to the rule: Our definition of π_t some times fails to capture the exact difference between z_t and z_t^{ϕ}. We will demonstrate this with an example: We go back to our original system in Grain v1 where the differential is introduced via the 37th IV bit and therefore we run the engine $\Delta_{37}\text{-}\mathsf{Grain}_{\mathsf{KSA}}$. At round 30 the values of χ_t and Υ_t are as follows:

$$t = 30: \quad \chi_t = \mathbf{0}, \quad \Upsilon_t = [u_{t+3} = 0, u_{t+25} = 0, u_{t+46} = 0, u_{t+64} = 1, v_{t+63} = 0]$$

Here $\mathbf{0}$ is the all zero vector. This implies that if we introduce an IV differential at location 37 then at KSA round 30 all state bits in S_{30} and S_{30}^{37} involved in the computation of their respective keystream bits are equal except the bits y_{t+64} and y_{t+64}^{37}, which are deterministically unequal, i.e., $y_{t+64} = 1 \oplus y_{t+64}^{37}$ always holds. Then, it follows that

$$z_{30} \oplus z_{30}^{37} = h(y_{33}, y_{55}, y_{76}, y_{94}, x_{93}) \oplus h(y_{33}, y_{55}, y_{76}, 1 \oplus y_{94}, x_{93})$$
$$= y_{33}y_{76} \oplus y_{33} \oplus y_{76}x_{93} \oplus y_{76} \oplus x_{93} = 1.$$

The above follows because y_{76} is initialized to 1 as it is a part of the $\mathtt{0x\ ffff}$ padding that is used in Grain v1. Thus, z_{30} and z_{30}^{37} are deterministically unequal. But according to the definition of π_t, the value of π_{30} would be computed as 2. To prevent a situation like this one must always check if for some t, the values of χ_t and Υ_t throw up an exception. If it does we must assign the value 1 to π_t. Thus the definition of π_t can be rewritten thus:

$$\pi_t = \begin{cases} 1 & \text{if } \chi_t, \Upsilon_t \text{ throws up an exception} \\ \mathrm{lin}\left(\mathrm{lin}(\chi_t), 2 \cdot \mathsf{OR}(\Upsilon_t)\right) & \text{otherwise.} \end{cases}$$

We present an algorithmic description of $\Delta_{\phi}\text{-}\mathsf{Grain}_{\mathsf{KSA}}$ in Algorithm 1.

4   Proving the Biases

We will now provide a theoretical frame work to prove the biases reported in Equations (6), (7) using the differential engine $\Delta_{\phi}\text{-}\mathsf{Grain}_{\mathsf{KSA}}$ that was described in the previous Section. Note that the probability values we shall work out are computed over the randomness due to the Key bits and the those IV bits not assigned by the **Type 1, 2** relations in Section 2. However, these results also hold, even if the Key is fixed, and the randomness comes only from the IV bits. Before we do that let us look at the following Lemma that we will use. As the lemma is quite straightforward, we state it here without proof.

Input: ϕ: An LFSR location $\in [0, m-1]$, an integer $r(> 0)$;

Output: An integer array ΔZ of r elements;

Output: Two integer arrays χ_t, Υ_t for $0 \leq t < r$;

$[u_0, u_1, \ldots, u_{n-1}] \leftarrow \mathbf{0}, [v_0, v_1, \ldots, v_{n-1}] \leftarrow \mathbf{0}, t \leftarrow 0, u_\phi = 1$;

while $t < r$ **do**

    $\Upsilon_t \leftarrow [u_{t+h_1}, u_{t+h_2}, \ldots, u_{t+h_e}, v_{t+j_1}, v_{t+j_2}, \ldots, v_{t+j_w}]$;

    $\chi_t \leftarrow [v_{t+l_1}, v_{t+l_2}, \ldots, v_{t+l_c}, u_{t+i_1}, u_{t+i_2}, \ldots, u_{t+i_d}]$;

    $\ell_t \leftarrow \mathsf{lin}(u_t, u_{t+f_1}, u_{t+f_2}, \ldots, u_{t+f_a})$;

    $r_t \leftarrow \mathsf{lin}(u_t, v_t, v_{t+g_1}, \cdots, v_{t+g_{b_0}})$;

    $\Omega_t \leftarrow 2 \cdot \mathsf{OR}(v_{t+g_{b_0}+1}, v_{t+g_{b_0}+2}, \ldots, v_{t+g_b})$;

    if χ_t, Υ_t *throws up an exception* **then**

    | $\pi_t \leftarrow 1$

    end

    else

    | $\pi_t \leftarrow \mathsf{lin}\,(\mathsf{lin}(\chi_t), 2 \cdot \mathsf{OR}(\Upsilon_t))$

    end

    $u_{t+n} \leftarrow \mathsf{lin}(\pi_t, \ell_t), v_{t+n} \leftarrow \mathsf{lin}(\pi_t, r_t, \Omega_t)$;

0.1   /*Any modification goes here */;

    $t = t + 1$;

end

Return $[\chi_0, \chi_1, \ldots, \chi_{r-1}], [\Upsilon_0, \Upsilon_1, \ldots, \Upsilon_{r-1}], \Delta Z = [\Delta z_0, \Delta z_1, \ldots, \Delta z_{r-1}]$

Algorithm 1: Δ_ϕ-Grain$_{\mathsf{KSA}}$

Lemma 1. *Let F be an i-variable Boolean function, with $wt(F) = \mathsf{w}$. If the vector X is chosen uniformly from $\{0, 1\}^i$ then $\Pr[F(X) = 0] = 1 - \frac{\mathsf{w}}{2^i}$.*

4.1 Δ_ϕ-Grain$_{\mathsf{KSA}}$ with Overrides

The system Δ_ϕ-Grain$_{\mathsf{KSA}}$ works fine to track differential trails produced due to difference introduced in the ϕth IV bit. But notice that, Knellwolf's attack imposes several algebraic conditions among the Secret Key and IV bits in order to prevent the propagation of any difference to the NFSR. So, in order to replicate the difference propagation in Knellwolf's system by using the engine Δ_ϕ-Grain$_{\mathsf{KSA}}$ certain modifications need to be made to it.

Since Knellwolf's system introduces difference at the 37th IV bit, we run Δ_{37}-Grain$_{\mathsf{KSA}}$. Thereafter the propagation of the differential is stopped at $t = 12, 34, 40$. Hence at these rounds u_{t+n}, v_{t+n} need to be manually assigned to 0. This corresponds to inserting the following code snippet at line 0.1 of Algorithm 1.

$$\text{if } t \in \{12, 34, 40\} : u_{t+n} \leftarrow 0, \ v_{t+n} \leftarrow 0$$

Thereafter we look at the output produced by such a system at KSA round 97. The values of χ_{97}, Υ_{97} are as follows:

$$\chi_{97} : [v_{98} = 0, v_{99} = 0, v_{101} = 0, v_{107} = 0, v_{128} = 2, v_{140} = 0, v_{153} = 2]$$

$$\Upsilon_{97} : [u_{100} = 0, u_{122} = 1, u_{143} = 2, u_{161} = 2, v_{160} = 2]$$

This implies that of all the bits S_{97}, S'_{97} involved in the computation of z_{97} and z'_{97} respectively, the relations between only i) x_{128}, x'_{128} ii) x_{153}, x'_{153} iii) y_{143}, y'_{143} iv) y_{161}, y'_{161} v) x_{160}, y'_{160} is probabilistic. Therefore we have

$$z_{97} \oplus z'_{97} = [x_{128} \oplus x'_{128}] \oplus [x_{153} \oplus x'_{153}] \oplus \\ [h(y_{100}, y_{122}, y_{143}, y_{161}, y_{160}) \oplus h(y_{100}, 1 \oplus y_{122}, y'_{143}, y'_{161}, y'_{160})] \tag{8}$$

We begin with the assumption that the random variables $x_{128} \oplus x'_{128}$, $x_{153} \oplus x'_{153}$, $y_{143} \oplus y'_{143}$, $y_{161} \oplus y'_{161}$ and $x_{160} \oplus y'_{160}$ are statistically mutually independent of one another. It is difficult to prove this assumption theoretically but extensive computer simulations have shown that one can make this assumption. We must therefore attempt to find the distributions of these variables, to prove the bias.

A. $x_{128} \oplus x'_{128}$: To find this distribution we need to look at the state of our modified Δ_{37}-Grain$_{KSA}$ at $t = 128 - 80 = 48$. At this round the vectors χ_t, Υ_t are as follows:

$$\chi_{48} : \mathbf{0}, \quad \Upsilon_{48} : [u_{51} = 0, u_{73} = 0, u_{94} = 1, u_{112} = 1, v_{111} = 0]$$

Among, the other state bits used in the computation of v_{128} only $v_{110} = 1$ and the rest are 0.Thus we have

$$x_{128} \oplus x'_{128} = [g(X_{48}) \oplus y_{48} \oplus z_{48}] \oplus [g(X'_{48}) \oplus y'_{48} \oplus z'_{48}] \\ = [g(x_{48}, x_{57}, \dots, x_{110}, x_{111}) \oplus g(x_{48}, x_{57}, \dots, 1 \oplus x_{110}, x_{111})] \oplus \\ [h(y_{51}, y_{73}, y_{94}, y_{112}, x_{111}) \oplus h(y_{51}, y_{73}, 1 \oplus y_{94}, 1 \oplus y_{112}, x_{111})] \\ = x_{111} \oplus y_{94}x_{111} \oplus y_{94} \oplus y_{112}x_{111} \oplus y_{112}$$

The above equations follow because $y_{73} = 1$ as required by the padding rule of Grain v1, and $y_{51} = 0$ as this is one of the **Type 1** conditions imposed on the IV bits. Assuming that the variables y_{94}, x_{111}, y_{112} are uniformly and independently distributed, and since $x_{111} \oplus y_{94}x_{111} \oplus y_{94} \oplus y_{112}x_{111} \oplus y_{112}$ is a Boolean Function of weight 6 we can use Lemma 1 to say:

$$\Pr[x_{128} \oplus x'_{128} = 0] = 1 - \frac{6}{8} = \frac{1}{4}$$

B. $x_{153} \oplus x'_{153}$: To find this distribution we need to look at the state of our modified Δ_{37}-Grain$_{KSA}$ at $t = 153 - 80 = 73$. At this round, it turns out that $\chi_t = \Upsilon_t = \mathbf{0}$. Among the other elements involved in the computation of v_{153} only $v_{110} = v_{135} = 1$ and $v_{133} = 2$ and the rest are zero. Since $v_{133} = 2$, the difference between x_{133} and x'_{133} is still probabilistic. We would need to compute the distribution of $x_{133} \oplus x'_{133}$ before we can compute the distribution of $x_{153} \oplus x'_{153}$.

To find this distribution we look at Δ_{37}-Grain$_{\mathsf{KSA}}$ at $t = 133 - 80 = 53$. At this round among all the elements involved in the computation of v_{153} only $u_{117} = 1$ and the rest are 0. So we have,

$$\begin{aligned}
x_{133} \oplus x'_{133} &= [\, g(X_{53}) \oplus y_{53} \oplus z_{53} \,] \oplus [\, g(X'_{53}) \oplus y'_{53} \oplus z'_{53} \,] \\
&= h(y_{56}, y_{78}, y_{99}, y_{117}, x_{116}) \oplus h(y_{56}, y_{78}, y_{99}, 1 \oplus y_{117}, x_{116}) \\
&= y_{56}y_{99} \oplus y_{56} \oplus y_{99}x_{116} \oplus y_{99} \oplus x_{116}
\end{aligned}$$

Again, assuming independent and uniform distribution of the inputs, and since $y_{56}y_{99} \oplus y_{56} \oplus y_{99}x_{116} \oplus y_{99} \oplus x_{116}$ is Boolean Function of weight 6, we have

$$\Pr[x_{133} \oplus x'_{133} = 0] = 1 - \frac{6}{8} = \frac{1}{4}$$

Now going back to the original problem, we have

$$\begin{aligned}
x_{153} \oplus x'_{153} &= [\, g(X_{73}) \oplus y_{73} \oplus z_{73} \,] \oplus [\, g(X'_{73}) \oplus y'_{73} \oplus z'_{73} \,] \\
&= g(\ldots, x_{110}, \ldots, x_{133}, x_{135}, \ldots) \oplus g(\ldots, 1 \oplus x_{110}, \ldots, x'_{133}, 1 \oplus x_{135}, \ldots)
\end{aligned}$$

Define

$$G_1 = g(\ldots, x_{110}, \ldots, x_{133}, x_{135}, \ldots) \oplus g(\ldots, 1 \oplus x_{110}, \ldots, x_{133}, 1 \oplus x_{135}, \ldots)$$

$$G_2 = g(\ldots, x_{110}, \ldots, x_{133}, x_{135}, \ldots) \oplus g(\ldots, 1 \oplus x_{110}, \ldots, 1 \oplus x_{133}, 1 \oplus x_{135}, \ldots)$$

We have $x_{153} \oplus x'_{153}$ equal to G_1 if $x_{133} \oplus x'_{133} = 0$ and equal to G_2 otherwise. Since, G_1 is a Boolean Function of weight 3456 and weight of G_2 is 3840, under standard assumptions of independence we have

$$\begin{aligned}
\Pr[x_{153} \oplus x'_{153} = 0] &= \sum_{i=0}^{1} \Pr[x_{133} \oplus x'_{133} = i]\Pr[G_1 = i] \\
&= \frac{1}{4}\left[1 - \frac{3456}{2^{13}}\right] + \frac{3}{4}\left[1 - \frac{3840}{2^{13}}\right] = \frac{139}{256}
\end{aligned}$$

C. $y_{143} \oplus y'_{143}$: As before we look at the output of Δ_{37}-Grain$_{\mathsf{KSA}}$ at $t = 143 - 80 = 63$. At this round we have $\chi_{63} = \mathbf{0}$ and

$$\Upsilon_{63} : [u_{66} = 0, u_{88} = 0, u_{109} = 0, u_{127} = 2, v_{126} = 2]$$

All other elements involved in the computation of u_{143} are zero. We therefore need to compute the distributions of $y_{127} \oplus y'_{127}$ and $x_{126} \oplus x'_{126}$.

To compute the distribution of $y_{127} \oplus y'_{127}$ we look at $t = 47$. All elements involved in the computation of u_{127} is 0 except $v_{110} = 1$. So we have

$$\begin{aligned}
y_{127} \oplus y'_{127} &= [\, f(Y_{47}) \oplus z_{47} \,] \oplus [\, f(Y'_{47}) \oplus z'_{47} \,] \\
&= h(y_{50}, y_{72}, y_{93}, y_{111}, x_{110}) \oplus h(y_{50}, y_{72}, y_{93}, y_{111}, 1 \oplus x_{110}) \\
&= y_{50}y_{93} \oplus y_{93} \oplus y_{93}y_{111} \oplus y_{111} \oplus 1
\end{aligned}$$

The above expression represents a balanced Boolean Function and hence we have $\Pr[y_{127} \oplus y'_{127} = 0] = \frac{1}{2}$. To compute the distribution of $x_{126} \oplus x'_{126}$ we look at $t = 46$. At this round all the elements involved in the computation of v_{126} are zero except $u_{110} = 1$. So we have

$$x_{126} \oplus x'_{126} = [\, g(X_{46}) \oplus y_{46} \oplus z_{46} \,] \oplus [\, g(X'_{46}) \oplus y'_{46} \oplus z'_{46} \,]$$
$$= h(y_{49}, y_{71}, y_{92}, y_{110}, x_{109}) \oplus h(y_{49}, y_{71}, y_{92}, 1 \oplus y_{110}, x_{109})$$
$$= y_{92}x_{109} \oplus y_{92} \oplus x_{109}$$

This is an Boolean Function of weight 3 and so we have $\Pr[x_{126} \oplus x'_{126} = 0] = 1 - \frac{3}{4} = \frac{1}{4}$. Now we have

$$y_{143} \oplus y'_{143} = [\, f(Y_{63}) \oplus z_{63} \,] \oplus [\, f(Y'_{63}) \oplus z'_{63} \,]$$
$$= h(y_{66}, y_{88}, y_{109}, y_{127}, x_{126}) \oplus h(y_{66}, y_{88}, y_{109}, y'_{127}, x'_{126})$$
$$= h(1, y_{88}, y_{109}, y_{127}, x_{126}) \oplus h(1, y_{88}, y_{109}, y'_{127}, x'_{126})$$

The above follows since $y_{66} = 1$ is a part of the padding used in Grain v1. For $i, j = 0, 1$, define

$$h_{ij} = h(1, \ldots, y_{127}, x_{126}) \oplus h(1, \ldots, i \oplus y_{127}, j \oplus x_{126})$$

h_{01}, h_{11} are balanced functions and $\Pr[h_{10} = 0] = \frac{1}{4}$. Assuming independence, $\Pr[y_{143} \oplus y'_{143} = 0]$ is given by the expression

$$\sum_{i=0}^{1} \sum_{j=0}^{1} \Pr[y_{127} \oplus y'_{127} = i] \Pr[x_{126} \oplus x'_{126} = j] \cdot \Pr[h_{ij} = 0] = \frac{17}{32}$$

D. $y_{161} \oplus y'_{161}$ **and** $x_{160} \oplus x'_{160}$: To compute the distribution of $y_{161} \oplus y'_{161}$ we need to look at round $t = 81$. At this round both χ_t and Υ_t have many elements equal to 2 and hence at this point we have to delve into several lower KSA rounds, and frankly this exercise becomes a little tedious. Due to lack of space we do not include extensive analysis of these two distributions and simply state the results.

$$\Pr[y_{161} \oplus y'_{161} = 0] = 0.5, \quad \Pr[x_{160} \oplus x'_{160} = 0] = 0.4977$$

E. $h(y_{100}, y_{122}, y_{143}, y_{161}, y_{160}) \oplus h(y_{100}, 1 \oplus y_{122}, y'_{143}, y'_{161}, y'_{160})$: For the sake of conciseness, let this expression be denoted by the symbol H and again for $i, j, k = 0, 1$, let us define the functions

$$H_{ijk} = h(y_{100}, y_{122}, y_{143}, y_{161}, y_{160}) \oplus h(y_{100}, 1 \oplus y_{122}, y_{143} \oplus i, y_{161} \oplus j, y_{160} \oplus k)$$

It turns out that all H_{ijk} are balanced except for H_{000} for which $\Pr[H_{000} = 0] = \frac{1}{4}$. Assuming independence, $\Pr[H = 0]$ is given by the expression:

$$\sum_{i,j,k=0}^{1} \Pr[y_{143} \oplus y'_{143} = i] \, \Pr[y_{161} \oplus y'_{161} = j] \, \Pr[x_{160} \oplus x'_{160} = k] \, \Pr[H_{ijk} = 0]$$
$$= 0.467$$

4.2   Computing $\Pr[z_{97} \oplus z'_{97} = 0]$

Now we know from Equation (8), that $z_{97} \oplus z'_{97}$ is the GF(2) sum of the three expressions $x_{128} \oplus x'_{128}$, $x_{153} \oplus x'_{153}$ and H whose distributions we have just computed. Thus we have

$$\Pr[z_{97} \oplus z'_{97} = 0] = \sum_{i \oplus j \oplus k = 0} \Pr[x_{128} \oplus x'_{128} = i] \cdot \Pr[x_{153} \oplus x'_{153} = j] \cdot \Pr[H = k]$$

$$= 0.5014$$

The above bias has been verified by experiments with over 2^{20} randomly chosen Secret Keys.

4.3   Biases in the Other Sets

In [19], it was observed that bias can be observed in 3 other sets T_U other than the one indexed by the 5 correct Key expressions U_0. These sets are those indexed by sets three T_U where **a)** C_2 is not satisfied but C_1 is, **b)** C_1 is not satisfied but C_2 is and **c)** None of C_1 or C_2 is satisfied. This can be proven in a similar manner by performing the above analysis with Δ_{37}-Grain$_{KSA}$ with a different set of overrides than the ones used in the previous proof. Note that for all the cases **a-c** implies that the differential at KSA round $t = 34$ is not eliminated. So as before we analyze a modified Δ_{37}-Grain$_{KSA}$, i.e., a modified Algorithm 1 in which Line 0.1 is replaced by

$$\text{if } t \in \{12, 40\} : u_{t+n} \leftarrow 0, \quad v_{t+n} \leftarrow 0$$

5   Conclusion and Open Problems

In this paper, we revisited Knellwolf's attacks [19,20], on Grain v1. The attacks, which were the best published on Grain v1, in terms of the number of rounds attacked, were based on certain biases that were observed experimentally in the distribution of the keystream bits. There were however no theoretical proof of these biases. In this work, we have tried to provide a theoretical framework to prove the biases and thus prove correctness of these attacks. One open problem in this area is, of course, to use the engine Δ_ϕ-Grain$_{KSA}$ to attack a higher number rounds of the KSA of Grain v1. Another important open problem in this domain is to prove the bias at round 104. The author of [19] observes that at round 104, a bias is observed in one of the Sets in only about 50 % of the cases. It would be a worthwhile exercise, to determine explicitly, the algebraic conditions the Secret Key bits need to satisfy for the bias to be observed.

References

1. The ECRYPT Stream Cipher Project. eSTREAM Portfolio of Stream Ciphers (revised on September 8, 2008)
2. Ågren, M., Hell, M., Johansson, T., Meier, W.: A New Version of Grain-128 with Authentication. In: Symmetric Key Encryption Workshop 2011, DTU, Denmark (February 2011)

3. Banik, S., Maitra, S., Sarkar, S.: A Differential Fault Attack on the Grain family under reasonable assumptions. In: Galbraith, S., Nandi, M. (eds.) INDOCRYPT 2012. LNCS, vol. 7668, pp. 191–208. Springer, Heidelberg (2012)
4. Banik, S., Maitra, S., Sarkar, S.: A Differential Fault Attack on the Grain Family of Stream Ciphers. In: Prouff, E., Schaumont, P. (eds.) CHES 2012. LNCS, vol. 7428, pp. 122–139. Springer, Heidelberg (2012)
5. Banik, S., Maitra, S., Sarkar, S., Meltem Sönmez, T.: A Chosen IV Related Key Attack on Grain-128a. In: Boyd, C., Simpson, L. (eds.) ACISP. LNCS, vol. 7959, pp. 13–26. Springer, Heidelberg (2013)
6. Berbain, C., Gilbert, H., Maximov, A.: Cryptanalysis of Grain. In: Robshaw, M. (ed.) FSE 2006. LNCS, vol. 4047, pp. 15–29. Springer, Heidelberg (2006)
7. Berzati, A., Canovas, C., Castagnos, G., Debraize, B., Goubin, L., Gouget, A., Paillier, P., Salgado, S.: Fault Analysis of Grain-128. In: IEEE International Workshop on Hardware-Oriented Security and Trust, pp. 7–14 (2009)
8. Bjørstad, T.E.: Cryptanalysis of Grain using Time/Memory/Data tradeoffs (v1.0 / February 25, 2008), http://www.ecrypt.eu.org/stream
9. De Cannière, C., Küçük, Ö., Preneel, B.: Analysis of Grain's Initialization Algorithm. In: Vaudenay, S. (ed.) AFRICACRYPT 2008. LNCS, vol. 5023, pp. 276–289. Springer, Heidelberg (2008)
10. Dinur, I., Güneysu, T., Paar, C., Shamir, A., Zimmermann, R.: An Experimentally Verified Attack on Full Grain-128 Using Dedicated Reconfigurable Hardware. In: Lee, D.H., Wang, X. (eds.) ASIACRYPT 2011. LNCS, vol. 7073, pp. 327–343. Springer, Heidelberg (2011)
11. Dinur, I., Shamir, A.: Breaking Grain-128 with Dynamic Cube Attacks. In: Joux, A. (ed.) FSE 2011. LNCS, vol. 6733, pp. 167–187. Springer, Heidelberg (2011)
12. Dinur, I., Shamir, A.: Cube Attacks on Tweakable Black Box Polynomials. In: Joux, A. (ed.) EUROCRYPT 2009. LNCS, vol. 5479, pp. 278–299. Springer, Heidelberg (2009)
13. Englund, H., Johansson, T., Sönmez Turan, M.: A framework for chosen IV statistical analysis of stream ciphers. In: Srinathan, K., Rangan, C.P., Yung, M. (eds.) INDOCRYPT 2007. LNCS, vol. 4859, pp. 268–281. Springer, Heidelberg (2007)
14. Fischer, S., Khazaei, S., Meier, W.: Chosen IV statistical analysis for key recovery attacks on stream ciphers. In: Vaudenay, S. (ed.) AFRICACRYPT 2008. LNCS, vol. 5023, pp. 236–245. Springer, Heidelberg (2008)
15. Hell, M., Johansson, T., Meier, W.: Grain - A Stream Cipher for Constrained Environments. ECRYPT Stream Cipher Project Report 2005/001 (2005), http://www.ecrypt.eu.org/stream
16. Hell, M., Johansson, T., Meier, W.: A Stream Cipher Proposal: Grain-128. In: IEEE International Symposium on Information Theory, ISIT 2006 (2006)
17. Lehmann, M., Meier, W.: Conditional Differential Cryptanalysis of Grain-128a. In: Pieprzyk, J., Sadeghi, A.-R., Manulis, M. (eds.) CANS 2012. LNCS, vol. 7712, pp. 1–11. Springer, Heidelberg (2012)
18. Khazaei, S., Hassanzadeh, M., Kiaei, M.: Distinguishing Attack on Grain. ECRYPT Stream Cipher Project Report 2005/071 (2005), http://www.ecrypt.eu.org/stream
19. Knellwolf, S.: Cryptanalysis of Hardware-Oriented Ciphers, The Knapsack Generator, and SHA-1. PhD Dissertation (2012), http://e-collection.library.ethz.ch/eserv/eth:5999/eth-5999-02.pdf
20. Knellwolf, S., Meier, W., Naya-Plasencia, M.: Conditional Differential Cryptanalysis of NLFSR-based Cryptosystems. In: Abe, M. (ed.) ASIACRYPT 2010. LNCS, vol. 6477, pp. 130–145. Springer, Heidelberg (2010)
21. Stankovski, P.: Greedy Distinguishers and Nonrandomness Detectors. In: Gong, G., Gupta, K.C. (eds.) INDOCRYPT 2010. LNCS, vol. 6498, pp. 210–226. Springer, Heidelberg (2010)

On Selection of Samples in Algebraic Attacks and a New Technique to Find Hidden Low Degree Equations

Petr Sušil*, Pouyan Sepehrdad, and Serge Vaudenay

EPFL, Switzerland
{petr.susil,pouyan.sepehrdad,serge.vaudenay}@epfl.ch

Abstract. The best way of selecting samples in algebraic attacks against block ciphers is not well explored and understood. We introduce a simple strategy for selecting the plaintexts and demonstrate its strength by breaking reduced-round KATAN32 and LBlock. In both cases, we present a *practical* attack which outperforms previous attempts of algebraic cryptanalysis whose complexities were close to exhaustive search. The attack is based on the selection of samples using cube attack and ElimLin which was presented at FSE'12, and a new technique called Universal Proning. In the case of LBlock, we break 10 out of 32 rounds. In KATAN32, we break 78 out of 254 rounds. Unlike previous attempts which break smaller number of rounds, we do not guess any bit of the key and we only use structural properties of the cipher to be able to break a higher number of rounds with much lower complexity. We show that cube attacks owe their success to the same properties and therefore, can be used as a heuristic for selecting the samples in an algebraic attack. The performance of ElimLin is further enhanced by the new Universal Proning technique, which allows to discover linear equations that are not found by ElimLin.

Keywords: algebraic attacks, LBlock, KATAN32, ElimLin, Gröbner basis, cube attack, universal proning.

1 Introduction

Algebraic attacks is a very powerful method for breaking ciphers in low data complexity attacks. This scenario is the most usual in practice. Algebraic cryptanalysis has brought about several important results (see [1, 14–17, 25]). An algebraic attack can be divided into several steps: building a system of equations and finding the solution to the system using an appropriate algorithm. The methods for finding the solution are, however, not sufficiently adapted for algebraic cryptanalysis, which shed a skeptical light on the entire discipline. The attacks mostly report breaking several rounds of a target cipher, but fail to explore scalable strategies for improvements. In this paper, we start filling this gap.

* Supported by a grant of the Swiss National Science Foundation, 200021‑134860/1.

W. Susilo and Y. Mu (Eds.): ACISP 2014, LNCS 8544, pp. 50–65, 2014.

One approach in algebraic cryptanalysis is building a system of linear equations in the key variables using extensive preprocessing, such as cube attacks [5, 23, 25, 26]. Another approach is building a system of multivariate quadratic equations, and solving the system using Gröbner basis computation (F4/F5, XL/mXL), see [2, 28, 34, 39, 40, 43], using XSL algorithm, see [12, 13, 19, 37], or converting the multivariate system into algebraic normal form and running SAT solvers. such as in [42]. All these methods usually implement a common step called ElimLin [22]. ElimLin is a simple algorithm which uses linear equations from the linear span of a system for elimination of variables by substitution. It works iteratively until no new linear equation can be found. Using this method we can, in some cases, linearize a large multivariate polynomial system. Since this technique is used as the first step by all advanced techniques a proper understanding of ElimLin algorithm is crucial for further advances in algebraic cryptanalysis. In this paper, we present evidence that the success of SAT solvers in algebraic attacks depends on the performance of ElimLin algorithm and we expect similar phenomena to occur in the case of F4 and mXL. We show that the selection of samples based on a cube attack on R round ciphers performs well when breaking $R + \epsilon$ rounds cipher for a small ϵ. We demonstrate this by breaking 10 rounds (out of 32) of LBlock [44] in Section 3.4 and 78 rounds of KATAN32 (out of 254) [10] without guessing any key bits in Section 6, while all previous approaches were guessing $32 - 45$ bits of the key. Therefore, the complexity of their attack is of order $2^{32}T(SAT) - 2^{45}T(SAT)$. We also note that unlike SAT solvers, whenever ElimLin with our extensions, which we introduce in Section 5, was successful to recover one key, it was successful to recover the key in all cases we tested. The running time of our attack was several hours for smaller sets of samples, and up to 10 days for the largest sets of samples. Finally, we introduce a technique called Universal Proning which allows to find additional linear equations of the system which are satisfied for a random key with high probability. The relation between these algebraic methods have been extensively studied. ElimLin is a basic algorithm which is part of every algebraic tool. XSL is an ad-hoc version of XL which was analyzed in [13]. The XL algorithm computes the Gröbner basis in a similar way as F4, but it performs additional unnecessary computations [4]. The mXL variant of XL [40] is equivalent to F4 [3]. The comparison between Gröbner basis computation and performance of SAT solver was shown in [27]. The complexity of SAT was further studied in [38]. The asymptotic estimates of the complexity of XL and Gröbner basis were given in [45]. The multivariate equations representing the cipher are difficult to solve in general. The most general solving technique is to find the Gröbner basis of the ideal generated by the system using algorithms such as F4. Using this technique, the degree of equations in the system is iteratively increased until the first fall appears [32, Section 4.6], and the system is fully solved, when a so-called degree of regularity is reached [8, Definition 3]. This degree is usually high [7] and therefore such computation is often infeasible due to memory requirements. The SAT solving techniques also do not perform very well for complicated systems. The XL algorithm is a variant of the F4 algorithm [3] and therefore, suffers from the same problems. ElimLin algorithm can be seen as iterations of a Gauss elimination and a substitution. It does not increase the degree of the system in any intermediate step, and hence it finds no solution in many cases. We observe that the running time of all the techniques above depends on the selection of plaintext-ciphertext pairs. In this paper, we introduce a technique for the selection of samples which significantly improves the running time for selected ciphers. In Section 2, we recall ElimLin algorithm then, in Section 3, we introduce our method for selecting samples in an algebraic attack and show its performance using reduced round LBlock. In Section 4, we discuss implementation improvements of ElimLin, which allow to parallelize the attack and reduce memory requirements. In Section 5, we introduce a new technique called Universal Proning for recovering linear equations which cannot be found by ElimLin, but which are satisfied for a random key with high probability. We use this technique together with ElimLin in Section 6 to attack reduced round KATAN32. It was previously analysed in [33, 35, 41]. We compare our results to state-of-the-art algebraic attacks on KATAN32 and show that our technique of selecting samples and recovering hidden linear equations outperform previous results.   The recent attack against KATAN32 in [41] achieves similar number of rounds as we do but the authors guess 45 statebits before running the SAT. Hence, the complexity of their attack is $2^{45}T(SAT)$ which is comparable to a previous attack in [6]. We show the effectiveness of our approach on two well-known ciphers as an example and provide evidence to support the hypothesis that this would be the case for other ciphers as well. Our sample selection technique can also be used in attacks based on F4/mXL and SAT solvers. The trade-off between increasing number of samples for ElimLin and increasing degree in F4/mXL still remains an open problem.

2   The ElimLin Algorithm

The ElimLin algorithm is a very simple tool for solving systems of multivariate equations. It is based on iterations of a Gauss elimination and a substitution of variables by linear equations. It is used as a preprocessing tool in most computer algebra systems, e.g., F4/F5 algorithm, XL, or even in cryptominisat. Since this algorithm is a common base of all solvers, it is important to carefully investigate its properties and capabilities. We refer the reader to [22] for additional details. Later in the paper, we discuss a strategy to improve the running time of ElimLin when we consider many samples. It was already shown in [22] that increasing the number of samples helps to find the secret key using ElimLin. We now show that selecting the plaintexts carefully can significantly improve the performance of ElimLin and even outperforms state-of-the-art attacks based on SAT solvers. Since ElimLin performs only substitution by linear terms, the degree of the system cannot increase. Therefore, ElimLin can solve the system and recover the secret key only in very special cases. ElimLin is performed as the first step of Gröbner basis computation and even some SAT solvers, such as cryptominisat, run ElimLin as a preprocessing step. Therefore, we focus on the selection of plaintexts which allows ElimLin to solve the system or eliminate the highest possible number of variables.

3   On the Selection of Samples

In this section, we define our system of equations and give necessary definitions. In part 3.1, we give a new characterization of the system when ElimLin succeeds. In part 3.2, we find a strategy for selection of samples, which allows to satisfy this condition. This selection strategy is based on cube attacks which we recall in part 3.3. In part 3.4, we show the performance of such a technique on LBlock, and compare our results to previous algebraic attacks based on ElimLin. In part 3.5, we give further insight into our method and directions for future testing and improvements.

Notation 1. *We use kln to represent the key length. We use sln to represent the message length and the length of the state vector. We use smpn to represent the number of plaintext/ciphertext pairs. We use rndn to represent the number of rounds of the cipher.*

We represent state bits and key bits by variables. Each state variable $s_{p,r}^j$ corresponds to a plaintext of index p, a round r, and an index j in the state vector. The key is represented by key variables $k_1, \ldots, k_{kln}$. The plaintext p is represented by $s_{p,0}^j$ and ciphertext by $s_{p,rndn}^j$.

Notation 2. *We denote* $V = \bigcup_{t\in[1,kln]} \{k_t\} \cup \bigcup_{p\in[1,smpn]} \bigcup_{r\in[0,rndn]} \bigcup_{j\in[1,sln]} \{s_{p,r}^j\}$ *the set of variables.*

The round function of the cipher is represented by a set of polynomials r_r^j which takes as input all state variables at round r and returns the j-th state variable at round $r+1$, i.e., $s_{p,r+1}^j$ is given by polynomial $r_r^j(s_{p,r}^1, \ldots, s_{p,r}^{sln}, k_1, \ldots, k_{kln})$. We denote corresponding equation[1] $Eq_{j,r}^p = r_r^j(s_{p,r}^1, \ldots, s_{p,r}^{sln}, k_1, \ldots, k_{kln}) - s_{p,r+1}^j$.

Notation 3 (system). *We denote*

$$\mathcal{S} = \left(\bigcup_{p\in[1,smpn]} \bigcup_{r\in[0,rndn]} \bigcup_{j\in[1,sln]} \{Eq_{j,r}^p\} \right) \cup \left(\bigcup_{v\in V} \{v^2 - v\} \right)$$

where the first part represents equations between variables of round r and $r+1$ and the second part represents equations which hold trivially over $\mathbf{F}_2$. We further denote $\mathcal{S}_{\omega,\star,\star} = \mathcal{S} \cup \bigcup_{p\in[1,smpn]} \bigcup_{j\in[1,sln]} (s_{p,0}^j - \omega_p^j)$, $\mathcal{S}_{\star,\star,\kappa} = \mathcal{S} \cup \bigcup_{i\in[1,kln]} \{k_i - \kappa_i\}$

$\mathcal{S}_{\star,\gamma,\star} = \mathcal{S} \cup \bigcup_{p\in[1,smpn]} \bigcup_{j\in[1,sln]} (s_{p,rndn}^j - \gamma_p^j)$,

---

[1] We assume that our equations are sound in the sense being fully "Describing" equations [18] for each component of the encryption process.

We use notation $\mathcal{S}_{\omega,\gamma,\kappa}$ to denote that we set plaintext to ω, ciphertext to γ and key to κ. The symbol $\star$ at any position means that the value is unset. Hence, $\mathcal{S}_{\omega,\star,\star}$ is the system of equations when we fix the plaintexts to χ and $\mathcal{S}_{\star,\gamma,\star}$ is the system when we fix the ciphertexts to γ. We later use $\mathcal{S}_{\omega,\gamma,\star}$ which represents, thus, the system in which we fix both the plaintext and the ciphertext.

Notation 4. *For a system $\mathcal{S}$, we denote $\mathcal{S}_{\omega,\star,\kappa} = \mathcal{S}_{\omega,\star,\star} \cup \mathcal{S}_{\star,\star,\kappa}$, $\mathcal{S}_{\star,\gamma,\kappa} = \mathcal{S}_{\star,\gamma,\star} \cup \mathcal{S}_{\star,\star,\kappa}$, and $\mathcal{S}_{\omega,\gamma,\star} = \mathcal{S}_{\omega,\star,\star} \cup \mathcal{S}_{\star,\gamma,\star}$*

Assumption 5. *We assume that the ideal $\langle \mathcal{S}_{\omega,\gamma,\star} \rangle$ is a maximal ideal.*

We recall that smpn denotes the number of plaintext/ciphertext pairs. For the assumption to be satisfied we require that smpn is large enough to uniquely characterize κ. In our experiments, the equations for KATAN32 are build as in [6] and the equations for LBlock as in [22]. This allows for more accurate comparison of our the method of selection of samples.

3.1   Characterization of Systems when ElimLin Succeeds

We now explore the properties of systems for which ElimLin succeeds to recover the secret key. We use this characterization in Part 3.2 to derive a selection strategy for plaintexts.

Lemma 6. *Consider a system $\mathcal{S}$ such that ElimLin applied to $\mathcal{S}_{\omega,\gamma,\star}$ recovers the key bit k_j as value $c_j \in \mathbf{F}_2$. Let ElimLin' be a variant of ElimLin which treats plaintext and ciphertext variables of the system $\mathcal{S}$ as if they had degree 0. Then, $\exists q \in \textbf{elspan'}(\mathcal{S})$ which has the following form: $q = k_j + c_j + q'$ and q' evaluates to 0 when we set plaintext variables to ω and ciphertext variables to γ.*

Proof. *We perform the same substitution while running ElimLin' and obtain the polynomial q'.*

The polynomial q' will be important in the selection strategy of plaintexts. The existence of such a polynomial is essential for ElimLin to be able to recover the secret key. At the same time, the existence of such polynomials can be guaranteed if we select the samples based on a successful cube attack.

3.2   A Selection Strategy for Plaintexts in ElimLin

Lemma 6 characterizes the span of ElimLin when it recovers the value of the key k_j. We now discuss the strategy to ensure that this condition is satisfied. We now consider the polynomial q' from Lemma 6. Since we cannot choose simultaneously the plaintext and the ciphertext for a single sample, we consider several different scenarios: selecting plaintexts only, ciphertexts only, selecting partly plaintexts and partly ciphertexts. The selection of related plaintexts such that corresponding ciphertexts are also related is considered in [21]. These pairs are constructed using higher order and/or truncated differential cryptanalysis

[36]. In our scenario, we concentrate on the selection of only plaintexts. We found no advantage in the selection of only ciphertexts. The selection of part of plaintexts and part of ciphertexts is yet to be explored. The selection of related plaintexts and corresponding ciphertexts is specific to a chosen cipher. However, our goal is to determine an optimal generic selection of samples. We use Lemma 6 for the selection of plaintexts. It specifies the properties of q' which has to evaluate to 0 when we set plaintext and ciphertext variables, i.e., when we set ω and γ. However, we would like to guarantee that q' evaluates to 0 only when setting the plaintexts since we cannot control both the plaintexts and the ciphertexts. Hence, we are looking for a set of samples that lead to existence of such q' when we set only plaintext variables. Let $\deg_r(p)$ denote the total degree of the polynomial p in variables corresponding to round r, i.e., $s_{1,1}^r, \ldots, s_{smpn,sln}^r$. Provided the $\deg_0(q') < d$, we can build a set of 2^D samples, i.e., find ω, such that q' evaluates to 0. This leads us to setting values ω according to a cube recovered from cube attack.

3.3   Cube Attack

The cube attack [23] can be seen as a tool to analyze a black-box polynomial. Throughout the paper, we represent this polynomial by $f(x, k)$. The aim is to derive a set of equations which is easy to solve and which is satisfied for all keys, i.e., for all values of k. The attacker does this in the offline phase. Afterwards, in the online phase, the attacker finds the evaluation for each equation and solves the system. We query this polynomial in an offline phase for both parameters x and k. In the online phase, we are allowed to use queries only in the first parameter x, since k is set to an unknown value κ. The objective is to recover this κ. To achieve this, we find a hidden structure of $f(x, k)$ in the offline phase and use it to derive κ in the online phase. In the offline phase, we find sets of plaintexts C_i such that $\sum_{x \in C_i} f(x, k)$ behaves like a linear function $\ell_i(k)$ and ℓ_i's are linearly independent. In the online phase, we ask the oracle for encryptions of plaintexts from C_i and solve the system of linear equations. In the following, we derive the algebraic expression of $\sum_{x \in C_i} f(x, k)$ and show that this function can indeed behave like a function $\ell(k)$. Let $f(x, k)$ be a black-box polynomial which can be for some coefficients $a_{IJ} \in \mathbf{F}_2$ expressed as $f(x, k) =$

$$\sum_{\substack{I \subseteq \{0,1\}^{sln} \\ J \subseteq \{0,1\}^{kln}}} a_{IJ} \prod_{i \in I} x_i \prod_{j \in J} k_j.$$

Definition 7. *Let* $m \in \{0, 1\}^{sln}$ *and* $t \in \{0, 1\}^{sln}$ *such that* $t \wedge m = 0$. *We define* $C_{m,t} = \{x : x \wedge \bar{m} = t\}$. *We call* $C_{m,t}$ *a "cube",* m *a "mask", and* t *a "template", and we denote* $I_m = \{i : 2^i \wedge m \neq 0\}$, *where* 2^i *represent the bitstring with 1 at position* i.

Example: Let $m = 00010110$ and $t = 11100001$. Then, we have $|C_{m,t}| = 2^3$. $C_{m,t} = \{11110111, 11100111, 11110101, 11110011, 11100011, 11100001, 11110101, 11100001\}$.

The success of cube attacks is based on finding enough cubes C_{m_i,t_i}, i.e., enough m_is, t_is, such that $\sum_{w \in C_{m_i,t_i}} f(x,k) = \sum_{J \subseteq \{0,1\}^{kln}} a_J^i \prod_{j \in J} k_j$ are linearly independent low degree equations. Even though cube attack may be a powerful tool in algebraic cryptanalysis, it has been successful against only very few ciphers. The reduced round TRIVIUM [9] can be attacked for 784 and 799 rounds [30], and can be distinguished with 2^{30} samples up to 885 rounds [5]. The full round TRIVIUM has 1152 rounds, which means that 70% of the cipher can be broken by this simple algebraic technique. GRAIN128 [31] was broken using so called dynamic cube attack in [25]. KATAN32 was attacked in [6] using so called side-channel cube attack first introduced in [24]. While cube attacks celebrate success in only few cases, we show that they can be used for selection of samples in other algebraic attacks.

3.4   Selection of Plaintexts

In this section, we show that the selection of plaintexts based on the success of cube attack is a good strategy for satisfying the condition from Section 3.1. We give an attack against 10 rounds of LBlock. This attack outperforms the previous attempts of algebraic cryptanalysis [22]. We compare our strategy of using samples for cube attack to the strategy of selecting a random cube or a random set of samples. The strategy of selecting a random cube was previously explored in [29]. The authors were choosing correlated messages based on a algebraic-high order differential.

Breaking 8 rounds of LBlock. The previous result on breaking 8 rounds of LBlock using ElimLin required 8 random plaintexts, and guessing 32 bits of the key (out of 80bits). We found that if we select 8 plaintexts based on cube $C_{m,t}$ for m=0x0000000000000007 and t=0xe84fa78338cd9fb0, we break 8 rounds of LBlock without guessing any key bits. We verified this result for 100 random keys and we were able to recover each of the 100 secret keys we tried using ElimLin.

Breaking 10 rounds of LBlock. We found that if we select 16 plaintexts based on cube $C_{m,t}$ for m=0x0000000000003600 and t=0xe84fa78338cd89b6, we break 10-rounds of LBlock without guessing any key bits. We verified this result for 100 random keys. We were able to recover each of the 100 secret keys we tried using ElimLin. We tried to extend the attack to 11 rounds of LBlock, however we have not found any cube of dimension 5 or 6 which would allow ElimLin to solve the system.

Random vs Non-Random Selection of Plaintexts. We tested the performance of ElimLin applied to 10-round LBlock for the same number of plaintext-ciphertext pairs. Our results show that when ElimLin algorithm is applied to a set of n plaintexts from a cube, the linear span it recovers is larger than for a set of n random samples. We also show that ElimLin behaves better on some cubes, and that this behavior is invariant to affine transformation. The results are summarized in Table 1.

Table 1. Results on 10-round LBlock

10 rounds of LBlock: $C_{m,t}$ system of 2^4 samples	solved	remaining variables
m=0x0000000000003600	t=0xe84fa78338cd89b6	yes	0
m=0x0000000000d00001	t=0x856247de122f7eaa	yes	0
m=0x0000000000003600	random	yes	0
m=0x0000000000d00001	random	yes	0
m=random deg4	random	no	≈ 700
random set		no	≈ 2000

3.5 ElimLin and Cube Attacks

In this section, we explain the intuition behind using a cube attack for selecting samples for ElimLin. We first elaborate on our observations about ElimLin's ability to recover the equation found by cube attack. Later, we compare our approach to classical cube attacks and give additional observations about behavior of ElimLin with our selection of samples.

Structure of the cube. Let E_κ denote the encryption under the key κ, and let consider two samples for the plaintexts ω and $\omega + \Delta$, where Δ has a low Hamming weight. Many statebits in the first rounds of computation $E_\kappa(\omega)$ and $E_\kappa(\omega + \Delta)$ take the same value since they can be expressed by the same low degree polynomial in the key and state variables. This can be detected by ElimLin and used to reduce the total number of variables of the system. Therefore, good candidates for the selection of samples are plaintexts which are pairwise close to each other — in other words, plaintexts from a cube. Let now consider $\omega = (\omega_p : \omega_p \in C_{m,t})$. We consider a blackbox polynomial $f(x, k)$ computing the value of state variable $s_{x,r}^j$ for a key k, a plaintext x, a statebit j and r rounds. The cube attack gives an equation $\sum_{\omega_p \in C_{m,t}} f(\omega_p, k) = \ell(k)$ for a linear function ℓ. We observe that the equation $\sum_{\omega_p \in C_{m,t}} f(\omega_p, k) = \ell(k)$ is found also by ElimLin in a majority of cases. We further found that ElimLin can find many pairs of indices (a, b), such that $s_{a,r}^j$ equals to $s_{b,r}^j$. We assume that this is the fundamental reason for the success of cube attack. Thanks to such simple substitutions, ElimLin can break a higher number of rounds while decreasing the running time.

ElimLin vs. Cube Attacks. The attack based on cube attack consists of an expensive offline phase, where we build the system of equations which is easy to solve, i.e., linear (or low degree) equations in the key bits, and the online phase where we find evaluations for these linear equations and solve the system. The attack based on ElimLin consists of a cheap offline phase, since the system of equations represents the encryption algorithm, and the online phase is therefore more expensive. Our attack can be seen as a mix of these two approaches. We increase the cost of the offline phase to find a good set of samples and run ElimLin on the system without the knowledge of ciphertext. Hence, we simplify the system for the online phase.

Comparison of number of attacked rounds by Cube Attacks and ElimLin with same samples. In our attacks we observed an interesting phenomena which occurs for every cipher we tested. Our first phase consists of finding a cube attack against a R round ciphers. In the next phase, we consider $R + r$ round cipher, build a system of equations, set plaintext bits correspondingly, and run ElimLin to obtain a system P. In the next step, we query the encryption oracle for ciphertexts, build a system of equations corresponding to rounds $[R, R + r]$, and run ElimLin to obtain a system C. We found that the success of ElimLin to recover the secret key of $R + r$ round cipher strongly depends on the selection of plaintexts: random samples perform worse than random cubes and random cubes preform worse than the ones which perform well in cube attack. The plaintexts selected based on a cube allow ElimLin to find more linear relations, which are in many cases of form $s_{a,r}^j = s_{b,r}^j$. Hence, we obtain a system with significantly less variables. This allows us to recover the secret key. In the cases of LBlock and KATAN32 we obtained $r \approx \frac{R}{3}$. These observation suggest a further research in performance of ElimLin against ciphers such as TRIVIUM and GRAIN128, since there already exist cube attacks against a significant number of rounds [30, 25, 5].

4   Optimizing ElimLin

The implementation of ElimLin faces several challenges. For ElimLin to be successful it is necessary to consider a lot of samples. However, a high number of samples leads to an increase in memory requirements. We remind the Theorem 13 from [22] and use the result to split the system into small subsystems corresponding to different plaintext samples and recover most linear equations with small memory requirements.

Definition 8. *Let S be the initial set for ElimLin. Let S_T, S_L be the resulting sets of ElimLin. We call the linear span of $S_T \cup S_L$ ElimLin span and denote it by* $\boldsymbol{elspan}(S) = \boldsymbol{linspan}(S_T \cup S_L)$.

Theorem 9 (ElimLin invariant [22]).
The span $\boldsymbol{elspan}(S)$ is invariant with respect to the order of substitutions and Gauss elimination.

In the next section, we show the performance of our new version of ElimLin algorithm and give examples of reduced round KATAN32 and sets of plaintexts that allow us to derive the key using ElimLin. All our attacks outperform the best known attacks and they can be performed using a standard computer with sufficient RAM. In our case, the limitation was 40GB of RAM memory. We expect that our results can be improved both in terms of time, memory and data. This requires better implementation of ElimLin and finding a better cube for selection of samples. Therefore we mainly concentrate on successes and failures of ElimLin to recover the secret key. Additionally, we use a method called Universal Proning which we describe in Section 5. This method allows to recover equations among state variables corresponding to different plaintexts which are valid for every key. These additional equations further speed up ElimLin and allow to break more rounds in some cases.

5 Universal Proning: Recovering Linear Polynomials not found by ElimLin

We observe that most linear equations which ElimLin recovers are satisfied independent of the secret key, these are the linear equations in $\mathbf{elspan}\,(\mathcal{S}_{\omega,\star,\star})$ and $\mathbf{elspan}\,(\mathcal{S}_{\star,\gamma,\star})$. Therefore we introduce a new method called Universal Proning for finding all linear equations which are satisfied independently of the value of the key.

In this section, we introduce universal polynomials. A universal polynomial is a polynomial $f \in R$, such that $f \in \langle \mathcal{S}_{\omega,\star,\kappa} \rangle$ or $f \in \langle \mathcal{S}_{\star,\gamma,\kappa} \rangle$ for every key κ, hence, the name universal. Intuitively, we can see that a universal polynomial cannot help to recover the secret key but it helps to simplify the polynomial system. The concept of universal polynomials is closely related to concepts earlier studied in [20, slide 118-120]. Let us consider a polynomial $m \in \mathbf{F}_2[V]$ and a function which evaluates m under key κ.

Definition 10. *Let $\mathbf{F}_2[V]$ be the set of all polynomials in variables V over $\mathbf{F}_2$. Let us define the function $e_\omega : \mathbf{F}_2[V] \to \mathsf{Func}\,(\mathbf{F}_2^{kln}, \mathbf{F}_2)$, such that $e_\omega(m)$ is the function mapping κ in F_2^{kln} to the reduction of the polynomial m modulo $\langle \mathcal{S}_{\omega,\star,\kappa} \rangle$. Similarly, let us define the function $d_\gamma : \mathbf{F}_2[V] \to \mathsf{Func}\,(\mathbf{F}_2^{kln}, \mathbf{F}_2)$, such that $d_\gamma(m)$ is the function mapping κ in F_2^{kln} to the reduction of the polynomial m modulo $\langle \mathcal{S}_{\star,\gamma,\kappa} \rangle$.*

We recover universal polynomials from approximation of $\mathsf{ker}\,(e_\omega)$ and $\mathsf{ker}\,(d_\gamma)$.

6 Selection of Samples in KATAN32

We give the results of the attack against KATAN32 in Table 3. The previous best algebraic attack is given by Bard et al. [6]. The authors attack:

- 79 rounds of KATAN32 using SAT solver, 20 chosen plaintexts and guessing 45 key bits.
- 71 and 75 rounds of KATAN32, and guessing 35-bits of the key.

In our attacks, we do not guess any key bit and achieve a comparable number of rounds. However, we need to use more plaintext ciphertext pairs (128 − 1024 instead of 20). The main advantage of our attack is not only the fact that we do not need to guess the key bits but also its determinism. Since the success of other algebraic attacks such as SAT solvers and Gröbner basis depends on the performance of ElimLin, our results may be applied in these scenarios for improving the attacks. In Table 2, we show that the selection of samples is important for KATAN32. The reader can observe that in the case of 69 rounds, the template of the cube is important for ElimLin to succeed. In the case when the template was selected based on cube attack for 55 rounds, the attack using ElimLin is successful to recover the key. However, when we use the same mask but a fixed template, ElimLin cannot recover any key bit. We can also see that when the number is maximal for this set of plaintexts: when we increase the number of rounds, ElimLin fails to recover the key. The reader should also note that the number of linear equations we recover for 70 round KATAN32 in the Universal Proning phase varies for different cubes. In the first case we recover less linear equations by Universal Proning compared to 69 round case, because some linear equations were already recovered by ElimLin. In the second case, ElimLin was unable to recover the new equations appearing in the additional round, but they exist in the ideal, and therefore they can be found by the Universal Proning technique. The reader can also see that an increase in the number of samples allows to break more rounds in some cases. In the case of 71 rounds we extend the mask of the cube by one bit and in one case we can recover the key using ElimLin. In the other case we cannot. In the case of 76 rounds we were unable to break the system for any cube attack for 55 rounds. However, we found a cube attack of 59 rounds, which allowed ElimLin to solve the system for 76 round KATAN32 and 256 samples. In Table 3, we give successful results of attack by ElimLin applied on reduced round KATAN32 for various number of rounds. The previous best algebraic attacks can be found in [6]. The authors guess 35 out of 80 bits of the key and solve the system using SAT solver. We can achieve the same amount of rounds without any key guessing and with a running time within several hours.

Table 2. Attack on KATAN32 using ElimLin: rounds vs. masks

rnd	cube rnd	mask	template	samples	proned lin	success	time
69	55	m=0x00007104	t=0x39d88a02	32	29	10/10	<1 hour
69	55	m=0x00007104	t=0x65f30240	32	29	10/10	<1 hour
69	n.a	m=0x00007104	t=0x00000000	32	35	no	2 hours
69	n.a	m=0x00007104	t=0xf0000000	32	29	no	2 hours
69	n.a	m=0x00007104	t=0x0f000000	32	29	no	2 hours
69	n.a	m=0x00007104	t=0x00f00000	32	29	no	2 hours
70	55	m=0x00007104	t=0x39d88a02	32	27	no	3 hours
70	55	m=0x00007104	t=0x65f30240	32	30	no	3 hours
71	55	m=0x00007105	t=0x23148a40	64	61	10/10	3 hours
71	55	m=0x00007904	t=0x20128242	64	56	no	7 hours
76	59	m=0x0004730c	t=0x21638040	256	572	3/3	3 days

Table 3. Attack on KATAN32 using ElimLin

rnd	cube rnd	mask	template	samples	proned lin	success	time
71	55	m=0x0002700c	t=0xf2b50080	64	116	5/5	<1 hour
70	55	m=0x0c007104	t=0xa2d88a61	128	235	5/5	<1 hour
70	55	m=0x00a07104	t=0x50570043	128	213	5/5	<1 hour
71	55	m=0x00007105	t=0x23148a40	64	61	10/10	3 hours
72	55	m=0x00a07104	t=0x50570043	128	245	20/20	7 hours
72	55	m=0x0c007104	t=0xa2d88a61	128	238	60/60	7 hours
73	55	m=0x0c007104	t=0xa2d88a61	128	217	5/5	7 hours
73	55	m=0x0002d150	t=0x20452820	128	226	20/20	8 hours
73	55	m=0x0002d150	t=0xffd40821	128	231	20/20	8 hours
74	56	m=0x10826048	t=0xca458604	128	212	5/5	9 hours
75	56	m=0x80214630	t=0x76942040	256	538	5/5	23 hours
75	56	m=0x1802d050	t=0x267129a8	256	563	5/5	23 hours
75	56	m=0x908a1840	t=0x6b05c0bd	256	544	5/5	23 hours
75	56	m=0x08030866	t=0x8620f000	256	592	5/5	23 hours
75	56	m=0x52824041	t=0x0d288d08	256	516	5/5	23 hours
75	56	m=0x10027848	t=0xcf758200	256	588	5/5	23 hours
76	59	m=0x0004730c	t=0x21638040	256	572	3/3	3 days
77	59	m=0x03057118	t=0x2cb20001	1024	2376	3/3	8 days
78	59	m=0x03057118	t=0x2cb20001	1024	2381	2/2	9 days

7 Final Remarks on ElimLin

On increasing the degree in F4 and increasing the number of samples in ElimLin

The F4/mXL keeps increasing the degree until the solution is found in the linear span. ElimLin on the other hand requires more plaintext-ciphertext pairs to recover the key. We show that a better selection strategy improves the success of ElimLin, but the question whether the cipher can be broken for a large enough set of well selected samples remains opened. Similarly, we can consider the increase of the number of samples as an alternative to linearization step of F4/mXL. The open problem is whether these strategies are equivalent or if one or the other performs better. However, we believe there is an advantage of considering multiple samples and using a method introduced in Section 5 over increasing the degree and linearization.

Implications for F4/mXL/SAT solvers

Table 2 show that selection of samples influences the degree of regularity of the system. This claim is based on the fact that for some choices of samples (choices of cubes m, t) ElimLin can solve the system. Therefore, the degree of regularity is at most 2. While for other choices it cannot recover the secret key and hence, the degree of regularity is in these cases greater than 2. We compare several strategies for selection of 16 samples for attacking 10-round LBlock.

In the first case we select the samples based on a cube attack of 6 rounds. Then, we run ElimLin which successfully recovers a secret key only for subset of these cubes. Subsequently, whenever ElimLin succeeds to recover the secret key for a cube, we perform additional tests with 100 random secret keys and were able to recover the secret key in all cases. In the second case we select samples based on a random cube and obtain a system of 700 variables after ElimLin. In the third case we select samples randomly and obtain a system of 2000 variables after ElimLin. This example shows the importance of selection of samples. The running time of F4/mXL is proportional to the degree of regularity and the number of variables in the system and, therefore, the proper selection of samples is a crucial step. In the case of SAT solvers, the running time depends on the number of restarts performed by the solver and the number of restarts depends on the number of high degree relations.

8   Conclusion

We showed that the offline phase of the cube attack can be used for the selection of samples in other algebraic techniques and that such selection significantly outperforms the random selection of samples. We used this method against reduced round KATAN32, and showed that 78 rounds can be broken only using ElimLin and 59-round cube of 2^{10} samples. The approach can be seen as an innovative method of turning a single cube from cube attack into a key recovery technique. Our results highlight several open problems. The strategy of selecting more samples can be seen as an alternative to increasing the degree as it is done by F4/mXL. Using more samples leads to more variables in the system, yet the same goal is achieved by increasing the degree and linearization. Hence, the comparison of our selection of samples for ElimLin and state of the art implementations of XL such as [11, 40] is crucial for future directions for algebraic cryptanalysis. During our work we have discovered the existence of exploitable internal low degree relations inside open-ended systems of equations which depend on the plaintext and depend neither on the ciphertext nor the key [20, slide 118]. These additional equations are not always found by ElimLin and we show that our attacks can be enhanced by finding such equations first, which process we call Universal Proning. The fact that the solution is usually found in $\mathbf{linspan}\,(\mathbf{elspan}\,(\mathcal{S}_{\omega,\star,\star}) \cup \mathbf{elspan}\,(\mathcal{S}_{\star,\gamma,\star}))$ and the proper analysis of Universal Proning is a part of an ongoing research.

References

1. Al-Hinai, S.Z., Dawson, E., Henricksen, M., Simpson, L.R.: On the security of the LILI family of stream ciphers against algebraic attacks. In: Pieprzyk, J., Ghodosi, H., Dawson, E. (eds.) ACISP 2007. LNCS, vol. 4586, pp. 11–28. Springer, Heidelberg (2007)
2. Albrecht, M.R., Cid, C., Faugère, J.-C., Perret, L.: On the Relation Between the Mutant Strategy and the Normal Selection Strategy in Gröbner Basis Algorithms. IACR Cryptology ePrint Archive 2011, 164 (2011)

3. Albrecht, M.R., Cid, C., Faugère, J.-C., Perret, L.: On the relation between the MXL family of algorithms and Gröbner basis algorithms. J. Symb. Comput. 47(8), 926–941 (2012)
4. Ars, G., Faugère, J.-C., Imai, H., Kawazoe, M., Sugita, M.: Comparison between XL and Gröbner basis algorithms. In: Lee, P.J. (ed.) ASIACRYPT 2004. LNCS, vol. 3329, pp. 338–353. Springer, Heidelberg (2004)
5. Aumasson, J.-P., Dinur, I., Meier, W., Shamir, A.: Cube testers and key recovery attacks on reduced-round MD6 and Trivium. In: Dunkelman, O. (ed.) FSE 2009. LNCS, vol. 5665, pp. 1–22. Springer, Heidelberg (2009)
6. Bard, G.V., Courtois, N.T., Nakahara Jr, J., Sepehrdad, P., Zhang, B.: Algebraic, aida/cube and side channel analysis of katan family of block ciphers. In: Gong, G., Gupta, K.C. (eds.) INDOCRYPT 2010. LNCS, vol. 6498, pp. 176–196. Springer, Heidelberg (2010)
7. Bardet, M., Faugère, J.-C., Salvy, B., Yang, B.-Y.: Asymptotic behaviour of the degree of regularity of semi-regular polynomial systems. In: Eighth International Symposium on Effective Methods in Algebraic Geometry, MEGA 2005, Porto Conte, Alghero, Sardinia, Italy, May 27-June 1 (2005)
8. Bardet, M., Faugère, J.-C., Salvy, B., Spaenlehauer, P.-J.: On the complexity of solving quadratic boolean systems. J. Complexity 29(1), 53–75 (2013)
9. De Cannière, C.: Trivium: A Stream Cipher Construction Inspired by Block Cipher Design Principles. In: Katsikas, S.K., López, J., Backes, M., Gritzalis, S., Preneel, B. (eds.) ISC 2006. LNCS, vol. 4176, pp. 171–186. Springer, Heidelberg (2006)
10. De Cannière, C., Dunkelman, O., Knežević, M.: KATAN and KTANTAN - a family of small and efficient hardware-oriented block ciphers. In: Clavier, C., Gaj, K. (eds.) CHES 2009. LNCS, vol. 5747, pp. 272–288. Springer, Heidelberg (2009)
11. Cheng, C.-M., Chou, T., Niederhagen, R., Yang, B.-Y.: Solving quadratic equations with XL on parallel architectures. In: Prouff, E., Schaumont, P. (eds.) CHES 2012. LNCS, vol. 7428, pp. 356–373. Springer, Heidelberg (2012)
12. Choy, J., Yap, H., Khoo, K.: An analysis of the compact XSL attack on BES and embedded SMS4. In: Garay, J.A., Miyaji, A., Otsuka, A. (eds.) CANS 2009. LNCS, vol. 5888, pp. 103–118. Springer, Heidelberg (2009)
13. Cid, C., Leurent, G.: An analysis of the XSL algorithm. In: Roy, B. (ed.) ASIACRYPT 2005. LNCS, vol. 3788, pp. 333–352. Springer, Heidelberg (2005)
14. Courtois, N.T.: Higher order correlation attacks, XL algorithm and cryptanalysis of toyocrypt. In: Lee, P.J., Lim, C.H. (eds.) ICISC 2002. LNCS, vol. 2587, pp. 182–199. Springer, Heidelberg (2003)
15. Courtois, N.T.: Algebraic attacks over $GF(2^k)$, application to HFE challenge 2 and Sflash-v2. In: Bao, F., Deng, R., Zhou, J. (eds.) PKC 2004. LNCS, vol. 2947, pp. 201–217. Springer, Heidelberg (2004)
16. Courtois, N.T., Bard, G.V.: Algebraic cryptanalysis of the data encryption standard. In: Galbraith, S.D. (ed.) Cryptography and Coding 2007. LNCS, vol. 4887, pp. 152–169. Springer, Heidelberg (2007)
17. Courtois, N.T., Bard, G.V., Wagner, D.: Algebraic and slide attacks on KeeLoq. In: Nyberg, K. (ed.) FSE 2008. LNCS, vol. 5086, pp. 97–115. Springer, Heidelberg (2008)
18. Courtois, N.T., Debraize, B.: Algebraic description and simultaneous linear approximations of addition in Snow 2.0. In: Chen, L., Ryan, M.D., Wang, G. (eds.) ICICS 2008. LNCS, vol. 5308, pp. 328–344. Springer, Heidelberg (2008)
19. Courtois, N.T., Pieprzyk, J.: Cryptanalysis of block ciphers with overdefined systems of equations. In: Zheng, Y. (ed.) ASIACRYPT 2002. LNCS, vol. 2501, pp. 267–287. Springer, Heidelberg (2002)

20. Courtois, N.T.: A new frontier in symmetric cryptanalysis. Invited talk, Indocrypt (2008), http://www.nicolascourtois.com/papers/front_indocrypt08_2p.pdf
21. Courtois, N.T., Mourouzis, T., Song, G., Sepehrdad, P., Sušil, P.: Combined Algebraic and Truncated Differential Cryptanalysis on Reduced-Round Simon (April 2014) (Preprint)
22. Courtois, N.T., Sepehrdad, P., Sušil, P., Vaudenay, S.: ElimLin algorithm revisited. In: Canteaut, A. (ed.) FSE 2012. LNCS, vol. 7549, pp. 306–325. Springer, Heidelberg (2012)
23. Dinur, I., Shamir, A.: Cube attacks on tweakable black box polynomials. In: Joux, A. (ed.) EUROCRYPT 2009. LNCS, vol. 5479, pp. 278–299. Springer, Heidelberg (2009)
24. Dinur, I., Shamir, A.: Side Channel Cube attacks on Block Ciphers. IACR Cryptology ePrint Archive 2009, 127 (2009)
25. Dinur, I., Shamir, A.: Breaking grain-128 with dynamic cube attacks. In: Joux, A. (ed.) FSE 2011. LNCS, vol. 6733, pp. 167–187. Springer, Heidelberg (2011)
26. Dinur, I., Shamir, A.: Applying cube attacks to stream ciphers in realistic scenarios. Cryptography and Communications 4(3-4), 217–232 (2012)
27. Erickson, J., Ding, J., Christensen, C.: Algebraic cryptanalysis of SMS4: Gröbner basis attack and SAT attack compared. In: Lee, D., Hong, S. (eds.) ICISC 2009. LNCS, vol. 5984, pp. 73–86. Springer, Heidelberg (2010)
28. Faugère, J.-C.: A new efficient algorithm for computing Grobner bases (F4). Journal of Pure and Applied Algebra 139(13), 61–88 (1999)
29. Faugère, J.-C., Perret, L.: Algebraic cryptanalysis of curry and flurry using correlated messages. In: Bao, F., Yung, M., Lin, D., Jing, J. (eds.) Inscrypt 2009. LNCS, vol. 6151, pp. 266–277. Springer, Heidelberg (2010)
30. Fouque, P.A., Vannet, T.: Improving Key Recovery to 784 and 799 rounds of Trivium using Optimized Cube Attacks. In: FSE 2013 (2013)
31. Hell, M., Johansson, T., Meier, W.: Grain; a stream cipher for constrained environments. Int. J. Wire. Mob. Comput. 2(1), 86–93 (2007)
32. Hodges, T., Petit, C., Schlather, J.: Degree of Regularity for Systems arising from Weil Descent. In: YAC 2012 - Yet Another Conference in Cryptography, p. 9 (2012)
33. Isobe, T., Sasaki, Y., Chen, J.: Related-key boomerang attacks on KATAN32/48/64. In: Boyd, C., Simpson, L. (eds.) ACISP. LNCS, vol. 7959, pp. 268–285. Springer, Heidelberg (2013)
34. Faugère, J.-C.: A New Efficient Algorithm for Computing Gröbner Bases Without Reduction to Zero (F5). In: ISSAC 2002: Proceedings of the 2002 International Symposium on Symbolic and Algebraic Computation, pp. 75–83 (2002)
35. Knellwolf, S., Meier, W., Naya-Plasencia, M.: Conditional differential cryptanalysis of Trivium and KATAN. In: Miri, A., Vaudenay, S. (eds.) SAC 2011. LNCS, vol. 7118, pp. 200–212. Springer, Heidelberg (2012)
36. Knudsen, L.R.: Truncated and higher order differentials. In: Preneel, B. (ed.) FSE 1994. LNCS, vol. 1008, pp. 196–211. Springer, Heidelberg (1995)
37. Lim, C.-W., Khoo, K.: An analysis of XSL applied to BES. In: Biryukov, A. (ed.) FSE 2007. LNCS, vol. 4593, pp. 242–253. Springer, Heidelberg (2007)
38. Lipton, R.J., Viglas, A.: On the complexity of SAT. In: 40th FOCS, October 17-19, pp. 459–464. IEEE Computer Society Press, New York (1999)
39. Mohamed, M.S.E., Mohamed, W.S.A.E., Ding, J., Buchmann, J.: MXL2: Solving Polynomial Equations over GF(2) Using an Improved Mutant Strategy. In: Buchmann, J., Ding, J. (eds.) PQCrypto 2008. LNCS, vol. 5299, pp. 203–215. Springer, Heidelberg (2008)

40. Mohamed, M.S.E., Cabarcas, D., Ding, J., Buchmann, J., Bulygin, S.: MXL3: An efficient algorithm for computing Gröbner bases of zero-dimensional ideals. In: Lee, D., Hong, S. (eds.) ICISC 2009. LNCS, vol. 5984, pp. 87–100. Springer, Heidelberg (2010)

41. Song, L., Hu, L.: Improved algebraic and differential fault attacks on the katan block cipher. In: Deng, R.H., Feng, T. (eds.) ISPEC 2013. LNCS, vol. 7863, pp. 372–386. Springer, Heidelberg (2013)

42. Soos, M.: Cryptominisat 2.5.0. In: SAT Race competitive event booklet (July 2010)

43. Stegers, T.: Faugère's F5 Algorithm Revisited. Cryptology ePrint Archive, Report 2006/404 (2006), http://eprint.iacr.org/

44. Wu, W., Zhang, L.: LBlock: A lightweight block cipher. In: Lopez, J., Tsudik, G. (eds.) ACNS 2011. LNCS, vol. 6715, pp. 327–344. Springer, Heidelberg (2011)

45. Yang, B.-Y., Chen, J.-M., Courtois, N.T.: On asymptotic security estimates in XL and Gröbner bases-related algebraic cryptanalysis. In: López, J., Qing, S., Okamoto, E. (eds.) ICICS 2004. LNCS, vol. 3269, pp. 401–413. Springer, Heidelberg (2004)

Strongly Simulation-Extractable Leakage-Resilient NIZK *

Yuyu Wang and Keisuke Tanaka

Tokyo Institute of Technology

Abstract. This paper defines strongly simulation-extractable leakage-resiliency (sSE-LR), which is a new notion for NIZK proof system. Our definition extends the weaker notion called true simulation-extractable leakage-resiliency (tSE-LR) defined by Garg, Jain, and Sahai in CRYPTO 2011. Moreover, improving the construction of tSE-LR-NIZK proof system by Garg et al., we construct an NIZK scheme that satisfies sSE-LR. An sSE-LR-NIZK proof system is applicable to construct a fully leakage resilient signature scheme which is strongly existentially unforgeable. As far as we know, this is the first fully leakage resilient signature scheme that is strongly existentially unforgeable.

Keywords: NIZK, leakage, simulation-extractability, signature.

1 Introduction

1.1 Background

Non-interactive zero knowledge (NIZK) proof system is a variant of zero knowledge (ZK) proof system. In ZK proof system, the prover makes a proof to convince the verifier that there exists a witness, without the verifier being able to learn any information about the witness. In NIZK proof system, the proof is realized without interaction.

Dodis, Haralambiev, López-Alt, and Wichs [5] defined two new notions called true simulation extractable (tSE) NIZK proof system and strongly simulation extractable (sSE) NIZK proof system and gave their constructions. An NIZK proof system is said to be tSE if there exists a probabilistic polynomial time (PPT) extractor that can always extract a correct witness from any valid proof generated by the adversary on a statement-tag pair. The adversary can obtain proofs of true statements previously given by the simulator. There is a limitation that the statement-tag pair used by the adversary to generate the proof must

---

* Department of Mathematical and Computing Sciences, Graduate School of Information Science and Engineering, Tokyo Institute of Technology, W8-55, 2-12-1 Ookayama, Meguro-ku, Tokyo 152-8552, Japan. Supported by the Ministry of Education, Science, Sports and Culture, Grant-in-Aid for Scientific Research (A) No.24240001 and (C) No.23500010, a grant of I-System Co. Ltd., and NTT Secure Platform Laboratories.

W. Susilo and Y. Mu (Eds.): ACISP 2014, LNCS 8544, pp. 66–81, 2014.

be different from all the pairs having been used by the simulator. For sSE-NIZK proof system, this limitation is relaxed, which means even if the adversary outputs a new proof on a statement-tag pair that has been used by the simulator before, the witness can still be extracted.

Garg, Jain, and Sahai [6] extended the notion of tSE-NIZK proof system to true simulation extractable leakage resilient (tSE-LR) NIZK proof system. That is, there exists a PPT extractor that can always extract a correct witness from any valid proof generated by the adversary, who obtains not only proofs of true statements previously given by the simulator, but also leakage on witnesses and randomness which can explain the proofs. The limitation is the same as tSE-NIZK proof system. They gave the construction of tSE-LR-NIZK proof system by exploiting the UC-secure NIZK proof system by Groth, Ostrovsky and Sahai [7].

Simulation extractable NIZK proof system is useful in many applications. Dodis et al. [5] gave a generic construction of LR-signature scheme based on the tSE-NIZK proof system and a generic construction of LR-CCA-secure encryption based on the sSE-NIZK proof system. Following the approach of Dodis et al. [5], Garg et al. [6] made use of the tSE-LR-NIZK proof system to obtain a fully leakage resilient (FLR) signature scheme.

FLR signature prevents forgery of signature while the information of the secret key and the randomness used by the signing algorithm throughout the lifetime of the system is leaked. Note that in the case of LR-signature, only the information of the secret key is leaked. An FLR signature scheme has to satisfy the security of existential unforgeability (EUF) which prevents forgery of signatures on the messages not signed before. However, for some applications, a stronger security called strongly existential unforgeability (sEUF) is required which also prevents forgery of new signatures on possibly the same messages signed before.

1.2 Our Results

In this paper, we give a definition of strongly simulation-extractable leakage-resilient (sSE-LR) NIZK proof system which relaxes the limitation of tSE-LR-NIZK proof system. Furthermore, we provide a construction of sSE-LR-NIZK proof system. We improve the tSE-LR-NIZK construction in [6], which follows the UC-secure NIZK proof system in [7], to satisfy our definition.

By making use of the sSE-LR-NIZK proof system and the technique by Dodis et al. [5], and Garg et al. [6], we obtain an FLR signature scheme that satisfies the security of sEUF immediately.

There exists several general transformations [2,12,11,1,8] to convert EUF signature schemes into sEUF ones. However, since all of the existing transformations have to add new information to the secret key or generate additional random bits during the signing process, there is no evidence that signatures converted by the existing transformations are secure when the additional secret information is leaked. That is, the existing transformations from EUF-FLR signature schemes into sEUF-FLR ones cannot guarantee the security of the resulting schemes in the bounded leakage model.

We show that an sSE-LR-NIZK proof system is applicable to construct an FLR signature scheme which satisfies sEUF. As far as we know, this is the first FLR signature scheme that is sEUF. In this paper, we call an FLR signature scheme which is sEUF a strongly fully leakage-resilient signature (sFLR) scheme. We compare our result with the related works in Table 1.

Table 1. Comparison between our result and the related works

	Dodis et al. [5]	Dodis et al. [5]	Garg et al.[6]	This work
NIZK	tSE-NIZK	sSE-NIZK	tSE-LR-NIZK	sSE-LR-NIZK
Application	LR-Signature	LR-CCA-Encryption	FLR-Signature	sFLR-Signature

2 Preliminaries

2.1 NIZK Proof System

Let $\mathcal{R}$ be an efficiently computable binary relation. For pairs $(x, w) \in \mathcal{R}$ we call x the statement and w the witness. Let $\mathcal{L}$ be the language consisting of statements in $\mathcal{R}$.

A non-interactive proof system for a relation $\mathcal{R}$ consists of a key generation algorithm K, a prover P and a verifier V. The key generation algorithm produces a common reference string (CRS) σ. The prover takes as input (σ, x, w) and checks whether $(x, w) \in \mathcal{R}$. In case of $(x, w) \in \mathcal{R}$, it produces a proof string π, otherwise it outputs **fail**. The verifier takes as input (σ, x, π) and outputs 1 if the proof is acceptable, and 0 otherwise.

Definition 1 (Non-interactive proof system). *A tuple of algorithms* (K, P, V) *is called a* non-interactive proof system *for a language* $\mathcal{L}$ *with a PPT relation* $\mathcal{R}$ *if the following two conditions hold.*

- *Completeness: For any adversary* $\mathcal{A}$, *we have*

$$\Pr[\sigma \leftarrow K(1^k); (x, w) \leftarrow \mathcal{A}(\sigma); \pi \leftarrow P(\sigma, x, w) :$$
$$V(\sigma, x, \pi) = 1 \text{ if } (x, w) \in \mathcal{R}] \geq 1 - negl(k).$$

- *Soundness: For any adversary* $\mathcal{A}$, *we have*

$$\Pr[\sigma \leftarrow K(1^k); (x, \pi) \leftarrow \mathcal{A}(\sigma) : V(\sigma, x, \pi) = 1 \text{ if } x \notin \mathcal{L}] \leq negl(k).$$

Now we introduce the definition of zero knowledge.

Definition 2 (Zero knowledge). *A non-interactive proof system* (K, P, V) *for a relation* $\mathcal{R}$ *is said to be* zero knowledge *if there exists a simulator* $\mathcal{S} = (S_1, S_2)$ *such that for any adversary* $\mathcal{A}$, *we have*

$$\Pr[\sigma \leftarrow K(1^k) : \mathcal{A}^{P(\sigma, \cdot, \cdot)}(\sigma) = 1] \approx \Pr[(\sigma, \tau) \leftarrow S_1(1^k) : \mathcal{A}^{S'(\sigma, \tau, \cdot, \cdot)}(\sigma) = 1],$$

where $S'(\sigma, \tau, x, w) = S_2(\sigma, \tau, x)$ *if* $(x, w) \in \mathcal{R}$ *and outputs* **fail** *otherwise.*

A non-interactive proof system is said to be an NIZK proof system if the zero knowledge property holds. In this paper, we require another property for NIZK proof system called knowledge extraction [7].

Definition 3 (Knowledge extraction). *We call (K, P, V) a proof of knowledge for a relation $\mathcal{R}$ if there exists a knowledge extractor $\mathcal{E} = (E_1, E_2)$ which satisfies the two properties described below.*

– *For any adversary $\mathcal{A}$, we have*

$$\Pr[\sigma \leftarrow K(1^k) : \mathcal{A}(\sigma) = 1] \approx \Pr[(\sigma, \xi) \leftarrow E_1(1^k) : \mathcal{A}(\sigma) = 1].$$

– *For any adversary $\mathcal{A}$, we have*

$$\Pr[(\sigma, \xi) \leftarrow E_1(1^k); (x, \pi) \leftarrow \mathcal{A}(\sigma); w \leftarrow E_2(\sigma, \xi, x, \pi) :$$
$$V(\sigma, x, \pi) = 0 \text{ or } (x, w) \in \mathcal{R}] \geq 1 - negl(k).$$

2.2 Leakage Resilient NIZK

We now state an extension of the zero knowledge property, called *honest prover state reconstruction* [7,6]. Recall that the property of zero knowledge implies the capability of simulating proofs by the honest prover without any witness. With honest prover state reconstruction property, the randomness of the honest prover is also simulatable with the witness.

Definition 4 (Honest prover state reconstruction). *We say that a non-interactive proof system (K, P, V) for a relation $\mathcal{R}$ has* honest prover state reconstruction *property if there exists a simulator $\mathcal{S} = (S_1, S_2, S_3)$ such that for all adversary $\mathcal{A}$, we have*

$$\Pr[\sigma \leftarrow K(1^k) : \mathcal{A}^{PR(\sigma, \cdot, \cdot)}(\sigma) = 1] \approx \Pr[(\sigma, \tau) \leftarrow S_1(1^k) : \mathcal{A}^{SR(\sigma, \tau, \cdot, \cdot)}(\sigma) = 1],$$

where $PR(\sigma, x, w)$ computes $r \leftarrow \{0,1\}^{\ell_P(k)}$; $\pi \leftarrow P(\sigma, x, w; r)$; returns (π, w, r), and $SR(\sigma, \tau, x, w)$ computes $\rho \leftarrow \{0,1\}^{\ell_S(k)}$; $\pi \leftarrow S_2(\sigma, \tau, x; \rho)$; $r \leftarrow S_3(\sigma, \tau, x, w; \rho)$; and returns (π, w, r). Both of the oracles output **fail** *if $(x, w) \notin \mathcal{R}$.*

LR-NIZK proof system was defined by Garg et al. [6]. The simulator of an LR-NIZK proof system can simulate leakage on the witness and randomness used by the honest prover with a leakage oracle.

The simulator $\mathcal{S}$ is a PPT machine that has access to a leakage oracle $L_w^k(\cdot)$ which is parameterized by the honest prover's witness w and the security parameter k. The leakage oracle accepts queries of the form f where $f(\cdot)$ is an efficiently computable function and outputs $f(w)$. If the verifier obtains ℓ bits of total leakage from the honest prover, then the total leakage obtained by the simulator from the leakage oracle must be bounded by ℓ bits.

Definition 5 (LR-NIZK). *A non-interactive proof system* (K, P, V) *for a PPT relation* $\mathcal{R}$ *is said to be* LR-NIZK *if there exists a simulator* $\mathcal{S} = (S_1, S_2, S_3)$ *such that for any adversary* $\mathcal{A}$, *we have*

$$\Pr[(\sigma) \leftarrow K(1^k) : \mathcal{A}^{PR(\sigma, \cdot, \cdot, \cdot)}(\sigma) = 1]$$
$$\approx \Pr[(\sigma, \tau) \leftarrow S_1(1^k) : \mathcal{A}^{SR^{L_w^k(\cdot)}(\sigma, \tau, \cdot, \cdot, \cdot)}(\sigma) = 1].$$

Here, $PR(\sigma, w, x, f)$ *computes* $r \leftarrow \{0, 1\}^{\ell_P(k)}$; $\pi \leftarrow P(\sigma, x, w; r)$; $y = f(w\|r)$; *and returns* (π, y), *and* $SR^{L_w^k(\cdot)}(\sigma, \tau, x, w, f)$ *computes* $\rho \leftarrow \{0, 1\}^{\ell_S(k)}$; $\pi \leftarrow S_2(\sigma, \tau, x; \rho)$; $f' \leftarrow S_3(\sigma, \tau, x, \rho, f)$; $y \leftarrow L_w^k(f')$; *and returns* (π, y). *The output length of the leakage query* f' *to* $L_w^k(\cdot)$ *is no more than the output length of* f. *Both the oracles* PR *and* SR *output* **fail** *if* $(x, w) \notin \mathcal{R}$.

Garg et al. [6] proved that every NIZK proof system for a relation $\mathcal{R}$ with the honest prover state reconstruction property is an LR-NIZK proof system for $\mathcal{R}$.

2.3 Encryption with Pseudorandom Ciphertexts

A public-key cryptosystem (K_{pseudo}, E, D) has *pseudorandom ciphertexts* of length $\ell_E(k)$ if for any PPT adversary $\mathcal{A}$, we have

$$\Pr[(pk, dk) \leftarrow K_{pseudo} : \mathcal{A}^{E_{pk}(\cdot)}(pk) = 1]$$
$$\approx \Pr[(pk, dk) \leftarrow K_{pseudo} : \mathcal{A}^{R_{pk}(\cdot)}(pk) = 1],$$

where $R_{pk}(m)$ returns $c \leftarrow \{0, 1\}^{\ell_E(k)}$ every time. We require that the cryptosystem has errorless decryption. The existence of public-key cryptosystem with pseudorandom ciphertexts is implied by the existence of trapdoor permutations. We refer the reader to [7] for details of the constructions.

2.4 Simulation-Sound Trapdoor Commitment

A *simulation-sound trapdoor commitment (SSTC) scheme* [9,7] consists of four algorithms $(K_{com}, com, Tcom, Topen)$. K_{com} takes as input 1^k and outputs (ck, tk) where ck is a commitment key and tk is a trapdoor key. com takes as input ck, a message m, a tag **tag**, and randomness r, and outputs the commitment c. To open the commitment c with tag **tag**, we reveal m and r and verify $c = com_{ck}(m, \textbf{tag}; r)$. The commitment scheme must satisfy both hiding and binding properties.

$Tcom$ takes as input tk and **tag** and outputs (c, ek) where c is an equivocal commitment and ek is an equivocal key. $Topen$ takes as input an equivocal ek, an equivocal commitment c, a message m, and a tag **tag**, and outputs r, such that $c = com_{ck}(m, \textbf{tag}; r)$.

The SSTC commitment must satisfy two properties, which are *trapdoor property* and *simulation-soundness property*. The *trapdoor property* is satisfied if for any PPT adversary $\mathcal{A}$, we have

$$\Pr[(ck, tk) \leftarrow K_{com} : \mathcal{A}^{\mathcal{R}(\cdot, \cdot)}(ck) = 1] \approx \Pr[(ck, tk) \leftarrow K_{com} : \mathcal{A}^{\mathcal{O}(\cdot, \cdot)}(ck) = 1].$$

Here, $\mathcal{R}(m, \mathbf{tag})$ chooses r at random and returns $(r, com_{ck}(m, \mathbf{tag}; r))$, $\mathcal{O}(m, \mathbf{tag})$ computes $(c, ek) \leftarrow com_{tk}(\mathbf{tag})$; $r \leftarrow Topen_{ek}(c, m, \mathbf{tag})$; and returns (r, c). In [7,6], the limitation was made that $\mathcal{A}$ does not submit the same tag twice to the oracle. However, according to the definition of trapdoor property and the DSA-based construction of SSTC in [9], this limitation should be removed.

The *simulation-soundness* property is satisfied if for any PPT adversary $\mathcal{A}$, we have

$$\Pr[(ck, tk) \leftarrow K_{com}(1^k); (c, \mathbf{tag}, m, r, m', r') \leftarrow \mathcal{A}^{\mathcal{O}(\cdot)}(ck) :$$
$$\mathbf{tag} \notin Q \text{ and } c = com_{ck}(m, \mathbf{tag}; r) = com_{ck}(m', \mathbf{tag}; r') \text{ and } m \neq m'] \leq negl(k),$$

where $\mathcal{O}$ operates as follows, with Q initially set to $\emptyset$.

- On input $(\mathbf{commit}, \mathbf{tag})$, computes $(c, ek) \leftarrow Tcom_{tk}(\mathbf{tag})$, stores $(c, \mathbf{tag}, ek)$, adds $\mathbf{tag}$ to Q, and returns c.
- On input $(\mathbf{open}, c, m, \mathbf{tag})$, if $(c, \mathbf{tag}, ek)$ has been stored, returns $r \leftarrow Topen_{ek}(c, m, \mathbf{tag})$.

3   sSE-LR-NIZK

In this section we give a definition and a construction of *tag-based sSE-LR-NIZK proof system* which is an extension of sSE-NIZK proof system in [5]. Although the original definition of LR-NIZK (c.f. Definition 5) does not include tags, it can be easily extended to do so [6].

3.1   Definition

Here, we define sSE-LR-NIZK proof system. Our definition is the same as tSE-LR-NIZK proof system in [6], except for the winning condition. For tSE-LR-NIZK, the adversary is not allowed to generate an NIZK proof on the statement-tag pair which was queried to the simulator before. But in our definition, the adversary only needs to generate a new tuple of statement, tag, and proof to win the game, which means it is allowed to generate a different NIZK proof on the statement-tag pair queried before.

Definition 6 (sSE-LR-NIZK proof system). *Let (K, P, V) be an LR-NIZK proof system for a relation $\mathcal{R}$ with a simulator $\mathcal{S} = (S_1, S_2, S_3)$ and a leakage oracle $L_w^k(\cdot)$. We say that (K, P, V) is a tag-based sSE-LR-NIZK proof system if there exists a PPT extractor algorithm Ext such that for any adversary $\mathcal{A}$, we have $\Pr[\mathcal{A} \text{ wins}] \leq negl(k)$ in the following experiment:*

1. *$(\sigma, \tau) \leftarrow S_1(1^k)$.*
2. *$(x^*, \mathbf{tag}^*, \pi^*) \leftarrow \mathcal{A}^{SR^{L_w^k(\cdot)}(\sigma, \tau, \cdot, \cdot, \cdot, \cdot)}$, where $SR^{L_w^k(\cdot)}(\sigma, \tau, x, w, \mathbf{tag}, f)$ computes $r \leftarrow \{0, 1\}^{\ell_S(k)}$; $\pi \leftarrow S_2(\sigma, \tau, x, \mathbf{tag}, r)$; $f' \leftarrow S_3(\sigma, \tau, x, r, f)$; $y \leftarrow L_w^k(f')$; and returns (π, y) (or **fail** if $x \notin \mathcal{L}$). Note that $\mathcal{A}$ can query $SR^{L_w^k(\cdot)}$ multiple times adaptively.*

3. $w^* \leftarrow Ext(\sigma, \tau, x^*, \mathbf{tag}^*, \pi^*)$.
4. $\mathcal{A}$ *wins if: (a) The tuple* $(x^*, \mathbf{tag}^*, \pi^*)$ *is new, that is, either the pair* $(x^*, \mathbf{tag}^*)$ *was not a part of a simulator query or if it was,* π^* *is different from the one(s) generated as the proof(s) of* x^* *with* $\mathbf{tag}^*$ *by the simulator.* *(b)* $V(\sigma, x^*, \mathbf{tag}^*, \pi^*) = 1$. *(c)* $\mathcal{R}(x^*, w^*) = 0$.

3.2 NIZK Proof for Circuit Satisfiability

Before giving the construction of sSE-LR-NIZK proof system, we modify the construction of the NIZK proof system for circuit satisfiability presented in [7]. We use this modified construction as a tool to achieve our goal later. The generation of an NIZK proof by this modified construction is separated into two parts. The first part is to generate two sets c_c and c_p. The second part is to generate the proof π corresponding to the two sets. No fresh randomness is chosen in the second part. For this NIZK proof system, when sampling $c_c\|c_p$, the prover has to know the witness but does not need to see the statement circuit. Furthermore, if there are two different proofs produced with the same $c_c\|c_p$ for the same statement, then at least one of them is invalid.

Let $\mathcal{G}$ be an algorithm which takes a security parameter as input and outputs $(p, q, \mathbb{G}, \mathbb{G}_1, e)$ such that p, q are primes, $n = pq$ and $\mathbb{G}, \mathbb{G}_1$ are descriptions of groups of order n and $e: \mathbb{G} \times \mathbb{G} \rightarrow \mathbb{G}_1$ is a bilinear map. Let $\mathbb{G}_q$ be the subgroup of $\mathbb{G}$ of order q. The construction of NIZK proof system for circuit satisfiability [7] is given in Figure 2 which uses the NIZK proof system in Figure 1 as a tool (we refer the reader to [7] for more details on this NIZK proof system). We also show how we modify this construction to achieve our goal.

Our modification. We modify the NIZK proof system in Figure 2 as follows.

Assume that the length of witness is ℓ' (i.e., let m_i be the ith bit of m and w_i the ith bit of witness, we have $(m_1, ..., m_{\ell'}) = (w_1, ..., w_{\ell'})$.) and the number of the wires in circuit C cannot be larger than ℓ. Every time before starting to generate a proof, the prover randomly chooses r_{i,m_i} from $\mathbb{Z}_n^*$ for $i = 1, ..., \ell'$, randomly chooses $r_{i,b}$ from $\mathbb{Z}_n^*$ for $i = \ell' + 1, ..., \ell$ and $b = 0$ to 1 and lets $c_c = (g^{m_1} h^{r_{1,m_1}}, ..., g^{m_{\ell'}} h^{r_{\ell',m_{\ell'}}}, \{h^{r_{\ell'+1,0}}, gh^{r_{\ell'+1,1}}\}, ..., \{h^{r_{\ell,0}}, gh^{r_{\ell,1}}\})$. For $i = \ell' + 1, ..., \ell$, $\{h^{r_{i,0}}, gh^{r_{i,1}}\}$ has 1/2 chance to be $(h^{r_{i,0}}, gh^{r_{i,1}})$ and 1/2 chance to be $(gh^{r_{i,1}}, h^{r_{i,0}})$. The prover also chooses r_i' randomly from $\mathbb{Z}_n^*$ for $i = 0, ..., 2\ell$ and lets $c_p = (h^{r_1'}, ..., h^{r_{2\ell}'})$. Apparently, to sample c_c and c_p, the prover only needs to know the witness, without seeing the statement.

Instead of encrypting each bit m_i as $c_i = g^{m_i} h^{r_i}$ with $r_i \leftarrow \mathbb{Z}_n^*$ (in Step 2 of **Proof**, Figure 2), the prover uses $g^{m_i} h^{r_{i,m_i}}$ in c_c as the ciphertext of m_i (which is also a commitment for m_i). Furthermore, for the ith NIZK proof, instead of choosing a fresh randomizer r from $\mathbb{Z}_n^*$ and computing π_1, π_2, π_3 with r (in Step 2, 3 of **Proof**, Figure 1), the prover uses $h^{r_i'}$ in c_p as π_1 and uses r_i' to generate π_2 and π_3. In Step 6, Figure 2, the prover returns c_c, c_p, and π as the proof.

Before checking the proof π, the verifier checks whether each ciphertext c_i is the same as $g^{m_i} h^{r_{i,m_i}}$ in c_c for $i \leq \ell'$, whether c_i is from $\{h^{r_{i,0}}, gh^{r_{i,1}}\}$ in c_c for $i > \ell'$, and whether each π_1 for the ith NIZK proof is the same as $h^{r_i'}$ in c_p.

CRS generation:

1. $(p, q, \mathbb{G}, \mathbb{G}_1, e) \leftarrow \mathcal{G}(1^k)$.
2. $n = pq$.
3. Choose a random generator g from $\mathbb{G}$.
4. Choose a random generator h from $\mathbb{G}_q$.
5. Return $\sigma = (n, \mathbb{G}, \mathbb{G}_1, e, g, h)$.

Proof: On input $(\sigma, c, (w, m))$ such that $c \in \mathbb{G}$, $(m, w) \in \mathbb{Z}^2$, $m \in \{0, 1\}$, and $c = g^m h^w$.

1. Check $m \in \{0, 1\}$ and $c = g^m h^w$. Return **failure** if check fails.
2. $r \leftarrow \mathbb{Z}_n^*$.
3. $\pi_1 = h^r$, $\pi_2 = (g^{2m-1} h^w)^{wr^{-1}}$, $\pi_3 = g^r$.
4. Return $\pi = (\pi_1, \pi_2, \pi_3)$.

Verification: On input $(\sigma, c, \pi = (\pi_1, \pi_2, \pi_3))$.

1. Check $c \in \mathbb{G}$ and $\pi \in \mathbb{G}^3$.
2. Check $e(c, cg^{-1}) = e(\pi_1, \pi_2)$ and $e(\pi_1, g) = e(h, \pi_3)$.
3. Return 1 if the check works out, else return 0.

Fig. 1. NIZK proof system of plaintext being zero or one in [7]

If this check works out, the verifier continues to check whether π is a valid proof. Otherwise, the verifier returns 0.

By the modification described above, the properties of completeness, soundness, knowledge extraction, zero knowledge, and honest prover reconstruction can be shown with similar arguments of [7]. The proof is appeared in the full version of this paper.

Additional property. For some statement C, if $c_c \| c_p$ is produced honestly, the ciphertexts are determined by c_c and all the NIZK proofs (Step 6 of **Proof**, Figure 2) are determined by c_p and the ciphertexts. We argue that if two different proofs are generated with the same $c_c \| c_p$ for the same statement, then there must be at least one proof that is invalid. The reason is that there must exist at least one NAND-gate for which, the ciphertext of the output is not the commitment to the right bit. This means a valid NIZK proof cannot be produced for that gate.

In fact, for that gate, we have $c_{i_0} c_{i_1} c_{i_2}^2 g^{-2} = g^m h^r$ where $m \notin \{0, 1\}$, depending on the fact that $b_0 + b_1 + b_2 - 2 \in \{0, 1\}$ if and only if $b_2 = \neg(b_0 \wedge b_1)$ when $b_0, b_1, b_2 \in \{0, 1\}$. If there exists $g^{m^*} h^{r^*}$ such that $m^* \in \{0, 1\}$ and $g^{m^*} h^{r^*} = g^m h^r$, we have $g^{qm^*} = g^{qm}$, equivalently, $mq \equiv q \pmod{n}$ or $mq \equiv 0 \pmod{n}$. However, since both p and q are large prime numbers and $m \in \{-2, -1, 2\}$, none of the equations holds. According to the soundness of the NIZK proof of plaintext being zero or one (Figure 1), a valid NIZK proof cannot be produced.

CRS generation: The same as in Figure 1.

Proof: On input (σ, C, w) such that C is a circuit built from NAND-gates and $C(w) = 1$.

1. Extend w to m which contains the bits of all wires in the circuit.
2. Encrypt each bit m_i as $c_i = g^{m_i} h^{r_i}$, with $r_i \leftarrow \mathbb{Z}_n^*$.
3. For all c_i make an NIZK proof of existence of m_i, r_i, so $m_i = \{0, 1\}$ and $c_i = g^{m_i} h^{r_i}$ (c.f., Figure 1).
4. For the output of the circuit we let the ciphertext be $c_{output} = g$, i.e., an easily verifiable encryption of 1.
5. For all NAND-gates, we do the following. We have input ciphertexts c_{i_0}, c_{i_1} and output ciphertexts c_{i_2}. We wish to prove the existence of $m_{i_0}, m_{i_1}, m_{i_2} \in \{0, 1\}$ and $r_{i_0}, r_{i_1}, r_{i_2}$ so $m_{i_2} = \neg(m_{i_0} \wedge m_{i,1})$ and $c_{i_j} = g^{m_{i_j}} h^{r_{i_j}}$. To do so we make an NIZK proof that there exist m, r with $m \in \{0, 1\}$ so $c_{i_0} c_{i_1} c_{i_2} g^{-2} = g^m h^r$ (c.f., Figure 1).
6. Return π consisting of all the ciphertexts and NIZK proofs.

Verification: The verifier given a circuit C and a proof π.

1. Check that all wires have a corresponding ciphertext and that the output wire's ciphertext is g.
2. Check that all ciphertexts have an NIZK proof of the plaintext being 0 or 1.
3. Check that all NAND-gates have a valid NIZK proof of compliance.
4. Return 1 if all checks work out, else return 0.

Fig. 2. NIZK proof system for circuit satisfiability in [7]

Remark on common random string. As noted in [7], we can choose h to be a random generator of $\mathbb{G}$ instead of choosing h of order q when generating the CRS, i.e., we can use the CRS generated by S_1 instead of the CRS generated by the honest prover. It is clear that the CRS generated by S_1 can be chosen to be a common random string without learning the trapdoor information (p, q, γ). The completeness, soundness, zero-knowledge, honest prover reconstruction, and the additional property do not change since no adversary can distinguish h of order n from h of order q. The property of knowledge extraction does not change as well when $E_1(1^k)$ generates the $\xi = (p, q)$ and the original σ, in which, the h is still of order q.

3.3 Construction of sSE-LR-NIZK Proof System

To obtain the construction, there are two key hurdles as noted in [6]. The first one is that the simulator has to be able to simulate the CRS Σ and proof Π without the witness. It also has to simulate the randomness to explain the proofs, given the witness. The second one is that the simulator has to extract a correct witness from a valid proof Π generated by the adversary for a statement C.

The same as [6], a prover commits to all the bits of witness w and encrypts the openings (while the simulator creates equivocal commitments to do the simulating) and then makes an NIZK proof with the honest prover reconstruction property so that the leakage queries can be simulated.

However, different from [6], we use the NIZK proof system introduced in Section 3.2 as the underlying NIZK proof system. Furthermore, instead of committing to the bits of witness with the tag **tag** directly, we use a new tag which is a concatenation of C, **tag**, and c_{rand}, while c_{rand} is a concatenation of a commitment to witness, commitments to the randomizers and a part of the NIZK proof $c_c \| c_p$.

Intuitively, if the adversary uses a tag which has been used by the simulator, it is difficult to generate a different proof. To generate a different proof, the adversary has to either find other witness or randomizers to explain the commitments than the ones obtained from the leakage, or generate a new proof for the underlying NIZK while the statement and $c_c \| c_p$ are the same as the one(s) used by the simulator, breaking the simulation-soundness property of the SSTC scheme or the additional property of the underlying NIZK described in Section 3.2.

We give the construction of sSE-LR-NIZK in Figure 3 (using the notation from Section 2).

Theorem 1. *The NIZK proof system described in Figure 3 is an sSE-LR-NIZK proof system if (K_{pseudo}, E, D) is a public-key cryptosystem having pseudorandom ciphertexts, $(K_{com}, com, Tcom, Topen)$ is an SSTC scheme, and the underlying NIZK proof system is the one described in Section 3.2.*

Proof. We prove the protocol is an LR-NIZK proof system at first. Then we prove that our construction satisfies the property of strong simulation extractability. We denote the simulator of the sSE-LR-NIZK proof system as S and the simulator of the underlying NIZK proof system as (S_1, S_2, S_3).

Soundness and completeness follow from the soundness and completeness of the underlying NIZK.

Simulating proofs and randomness. S simulates a proof as described in Figure 4.

Now we describe how S simulates the convincing randomness which can explain the proof Π with witness. According to the trapdoor property, for $i = 1, ..., \ell$, S pretends that ρ_{i,w_i} is the randomness r_i used to compute commitment c_i, that r_{i,w_i} is the randomness R_{w_i} used to encrypt r_i, and that $E_{pk}(\rho_{i,1-w_i}, r_{i,1-w_i})$ is the randomness R_i (which is equivalent to $c_{i,1-w_i}$). Furthermore, the randomness used to commit to r_i, R_{w_i}, R_i, and w can be all simulated correctly since the commitments are equivocal and can be opened by S with the equivocation key generated in Step 1 of **proof**, Figure 4. S also runs the simulator algorithm S_3 to obtain the randomness that would lead a honest prover to produce the same proof $c_c \| c_p \| \pi$. With all the randomness being simulated successfully so far, S can transform all the leakage queries made on witness and randomness into queries made only on the witness. Hence, S can use the leakage oracle $L_w^k(\cdot)$ to answer the leakage queries correctly.

CRS generation:

1. $(ck, tk) \leftarrow K_{com}(1^k)$.
2. $(pk, dk) \leftarrow K_{pseudo}(1^k)$.
3. $(\sigma, \tau) \leftarrow S_1(1^k)$.
4. Return $\Sigma = (ck, pk, \sigma)$.

Proof: On input $(\Sigma, C, w, \mathbf{tag})$ such that $C(w) = 1$ do.

1. For $i = 1$ to ℓ choose r_i, r_i', R_{w_i}, R_{w_i}', R_i, R_i' respectively at random and let $c_{r_i} := com_{ck}(r_i, \mathbf{tag}; r_i')$, $c_{R_{w_i}} := com_{ck}(R_{w_i}, \mathbf{tag}, R_{w_i}')$, $c_{R_i} := com_{ck}(R_i, \mathbf{tag}; R_i')$. Choose r_w at random and let $c_w := com_{ck}(w, \mathbf{tag}; r_w)$.
2. Choose randomizer r to generate two sets c_c and c_p (c.f., Section 3.2) with the witness $(w, r_w, \{r_i, r_i', R_{w_i}, R_{w_i}', R_i, R_i'\}_{i=1,\dots,\ell})$.
3. Let $c_{rand} := (c_{r_1}, c_{r_2}, \dots, c_{r_\ell}, c_{R_{w_1}}, c_{R_{w_2}}, \dots, c_{R_{w_\ell}}, c_{R_1}, c_{R_2}, \dots, c_{R_\ell}, c_c, c_p, c_w)$.
4. For $i = 1$ to ℓ, let $c_i := com_{ck}(w_i, C||\mathbf{tag}||c_{rand}; r_i)$.
5. For $i = 1$ to ℓ, set $c_{i,w_i} := E_{pk}(r_i, R_{w_i})$ and $c_{i,1-w_i} := R_i$.
6. Let $c := (c_1, c_{1,0}, c_{1,1}, \dots, c_\ell, c_{\ell,0}, c_{\ell,1}, c_{rand})$.
7. Create an NIZK proof π with c_c and c_p for the statement that there exists w and randomness such that c has been produced as described in Step 1, 3, 4, 5, and 6 and $C(w) = 1$.
8. Return $\Pi = (\mathbf{tag}, c, c_c||c_p||\pi)$.

Verification: On input (Σ, C, Π).

1. Parse $\Pi = (\mathbf{tag}, c, c_c||c_p||\pi)$.
2. Verify the NIZK proof $c_c||c_p||\pi$.
3. Return 1 if the check works out, else return 0.

Fig. 3. sSE-LR-NIZK proof system

To argue that no PPT adversary $\mathcal{A}$ can distinguish its interaction with a real prover from its interaction with a simulator $\mathcal{S}$, we create hybrid games and show the indistinguishability of them.

Game0: $\mathcal{S}$ owns the witness and works as an honest prover.

Game1: Instead of committing to the witness and randomness honestly (Step 1, **proof**, Figure 3), $\mathcal{S}$ creates the commitments equivocally and opens them by computing $r_i' \leftarrow Topen_{ek_{r_i}}(c_{r_i}, r_i, \mathbf{tag})$, $R_{w_i}' \leftarrow Topen_{ek_{R_{w_i}}}(c_{R_{w_i}}, R_{w_i}, \mathbf{tag})$, $R_i' \leftarrow Topen_{ek_{R_i}}(c_{R_i}, R_i, \mathbf{tag})$, $r_w \leftarrow Topen_{ek_w}(c_w, w, \mathbf{tag})$ to make the proof and answer the leakage queries.

Since it is hard to distinguish the normal commitments and openings from the equivocal commitments and openings, it is hard to distinguish **Game0** and **Game1** for $\mathcal{A}$.

After showing that the above two games are indistinguishable, we argue that **Game1** is distinguishable from the interaction between $\mathcal{A}$ and $\mathcal{S}$ which works

---

CRS generation:

1. $(ck, tk) \leftarrow K_{com}(1^k)$.
2. $(pk, dk) \leftarrow K_{pseudo}(1^k)$.
3. $(\sigma, \tau) \leftarrow S_1(1^k)$.
4. Return $\Sigma = (ck, pk, \sigma)$ and $T = (tk, dk, \tau)$.

Proof: On input $(\Sigma, T, C, w, \mathbf{tag})$ such that $C(w)=1$ do.

1. For $i = 1$ to ℓ, let $(c_{r_i}, ek_{r_i}) \leftarrow Tcom_{tk}(\mathbf{tag})$, $(c_{R_{w_i}}, ek_{R_{w_i}}) \leftarrow Tcom_{tk}(\mathbf{tag})$ and $(c_{R_i}, ek_{R_i}) \leftarrow Tcom_{tk}(\mathbf{tag})$. Let $(c_w, ek_w) \leftarrow Tcom_{tk}(\mathbf{tag})$.
2. Choose ρ at random to simulate c_c and c_p.
3. Let $c_{rand} := (c_{r_1}, c_{r_2}, ..., c_{r_\ell}, c_{R_{w_1}}, c_{R_{w_2}}, ..., c_{R_{w_\ell}}, c_{R_1}, c_{R_2}, ..., c_{R_\ell}, c_c, c_p, c_w)$.
4. For $i = 1$ to ℓ, let $(c_i, ek_i) \leftarrow Tcom_{tk}(C||\mathbf{tag}||c_{rand})$.
5. For $i = 1$ to ℓ, and $b = 0$ to 1, choose $r_{i,b}$ at random and set $\rho_{i,b} \leftarrow Topen_{ek_i}(c_i, b, C||\mathbf{tag}||c_{rand})$, $c_{i,b} \leftarrow E_{pk}(\rho_{i,b}; r_{i,b})$.
6. Let $c := (c_1, c_{1,0}, c_{1,1}, ..., c_\ell, c_{\ell,0}, c_{\ell,1}, c_{rand})$.
7. Simulate the NIZK proof for the statement of Step 7, Figure 3 with c_c and c_p.
8. Return $\Pi = (\mathbf{tag}, c, c_c||c_p||\pi)$.

Fig. 4. Simulating proofs

in the way of Figure 4. This part of proof is similar to the proof in [6] except the tag is different.

Game2: Instead of computing $c_i := com_{ck}(w_i, C||\mathbf{tag}||c_{rand}; r_i)$ in Step 4 of **Proof**, Figure 3, $\mathcal{S}$ computes $(c_i, ek_i) \leftarrow Tcom_{tk}(C||\mathbf{tag}||c_{rand})$, and $\rho_{i,w_i} \leftarrow Topen_{ek_i}(c_i, w_i, C||\mathbf{tag}||c_{rand})$, and uses ρ_{i,w_i} instead of r_i in the whole proof.

Since it is hard to distinguish the normal commitments and openings from the equivocal commitments and openings, it is hard to distinguish **Game1** and **Game2** for $\mathcal{A}$.

Game3: Instead of choosing R_i at random, $\mathcal{S}$ computes $\rho_{i,1-w_i} \leftarrow Topen_{ek_i}(c_i, 1-w_i; C||\mathbf{tag}||c_{rand})$ and $R_i := E_{pk}(\rho_{i,1-w_i}; r_{i,1-w_i})$ for a randomly chosen $r_{i,1-w_i}$.

Since it is hard to distinguish the pseudorandom ciphertexts from the real randomizers, it is hard to distinguish **Game2** and **Game3** for $\mathcal{A}$.

Game4: Instead of making NIZK proofs in the same way as an honest prover, $\mathcal{S}$ chooses ρ at random and uses S_2 to simulate $c_c||c_p$ and the NIZK proof π. On input the witness, $\mathcal{S}$ uses $S_3(\sigma, \tau, x, c_c||c_p||\pi, \cdot, \rho)$ to create convincing randomness that would lead the prover to output the same $c_c||c_p||\pi$. Therefore any leakage query on the randomness and witness is reduced to a leakage query only on the witness.

It is hard to distinguish **Game3** and **Game4** for $\mathcal{A}$ according to the properties of NIZK and honest prover reconstruction.

Extraction. Now we prove that for a valid proof Π generated by the adversary $\mathcal{A}$ in the strong simulation extractability experiment, the witness can be extracted.

The proof of strong simulation extractability is divided into two parts. In the first part, we consider the situation that the tuple $(C, \mathbf{tag}, c_{rand})$ produced by $\mathcal{A}$ is not a part of an answer from $\mathcal{S}$. In the second part, we argue that in the contrast situation, namely, when $\mathcal{A}$ creates an proof with a triplet $(C, \mathbf{tag}, c_{rand})$ that has been used by $\mathcal{S}$, the proof is either invalid or the same as the one(s) produced by $\mathcal{S}$.

When it comes to the first situation, $\mathcal{S}$ can definitely extract the witness according to the simulation-soundness property of SSTC schemes and the soundness property of NIZK proof. The proof follows directly from [6]. The details are as follows.

For an NIZK proof $\Pi = (\mathbf{tag}, c, \pi)$ generated by $\mathcal{A}$, the extractor parses c as $(c_1, c_{1,0}, c_{1,1}, ..., c_\ell, c_{\ell,0}, c_{\ell,1}, c_{rand})$ and decrypts $c_{i,b}$'s to get $\rho_{i,b}$'s. Then it checks whether $c_{i,b} = com_{ck}(b, C||\mathbf{tag}||c_{rand}; \rho_{i,b})$ for $i = 1, ..., \ell$ and $b = 0, 1$. If the check works out for some i and b, then the ith bit of w is b, otherwise, $1 - b$.

According to the simulation-soundness property, the probability that $c_i = com_{ck}(0, C||\mathbf{tag}||c_{rand}, \rho_{i,0}) = com_{ck}(1, C||\mathbf{tag}||c_{rand}, \rho_{i,1})$ for some i is negligible since the simulator has never produced any equivocal commitment with the tag $C||\mathbf{tag}||c_{rand}$ before.

According to the soundness property of NIZK, the probability that $c_i \neq com_{ck}(0, C||\mathbf{tag}||c_{rand}, \rho_{i,0})$ and $c_i \neq com_{ck}(1, C||\mathbf{tag}||c_{rand}, \rho_{i,1})$ for some i is negligible, too.

As a result, $\mathcal{S}$ can extract the witness with overwhelming probability in this situation if the proof is valid.

Now we argue that if $\mathcal{A}$ uses $(C, \mathbf{tag}, c_{rand})$ created by $\mathcal{S}$ before, it cannot produce a new valid proof. To prove this, we give a hybrid experiment by substituting $(\sigma, \tau) \leftarrow S_1(1^k)$ (in Step 3 of **CRS generation**, Figure 3) with $(\sigma, \xi) \leftarrow E_1(1^k)$ (c.f., Definition 3) and $SR^{L_w^k(\cdot)}$ with PR (c.f., Definition 5) in the experiment of sSE-LR-NIZK proof system (c.f., Definition 6). According to the property of LR-NIZK proof of knowledge, $\mathcal{A}$ cannot distinguish this hybrid experiment from the original one, i.e., the probabilities that $\mathcal{A}$ produces a new valid proof while $C||\mathbf{tag}||c_{rand}$ is a part of an answer from $\mathcal{S}$ in the two experiments are the same.

When $\mathcal{A}$ outputs the statement, tag, and proof at some point, $\mathcal{S}$ gives ξ to $\mathcal{A}$. Then $\mathcal{A}$ runs algorithm E_2 to extract the witness and randomness from the proof $c_c||c_p||\pi$ if it is valid. Since all the queries are answered by PR which provides no information about the trapdoor string, the witness and randomness which are committed to can be extracted with overwhelming probability.

If c produced by $\mathcal{A}$ is a new one for the same $C||\mathbf{tag}||c_{rand}$ used by simulator, the extracted witness and randomness (committed to in the first step of **Proof**, Figure 3) must be new but lead to the same c_{rand}, breaking the simulation-soundness property of the underlying SSTC.

Now we consider the situation that π produced by $\mathcal{A}$ is new for the same pair $(C\|\mathbf{tag}\|c_{rand}, c)$ used by the simulator. Since the statement described in Step 7 (Figure 3) is determined by $(C\|\mathbf{tag}\|c_{rand}, c)$ and there cannot be two valid proofs for the same statement and the same $c_c\|c_p$ (contained in c_{rand}), the new proof produced by $\mathcal{A}$ is invalid.

Remark on statement circuit. To make use of the underlying NIZK proof system (in Section 3.2), the circuit for the statement described in Step 7 of **proof** (Figure 3) has to be built from NAND-gates. The adversary may have a chance to produce different proof(s) for the same statement and $c_c\|c_p$ if it constructs the circuit in different ways. We rule out this probability by making the prover construct the statement circuit and transform it to a circuit built from NAND-gates in some fixed way. The verifier will check whether the circuit is constructed in that way and return 0 if it is not. By doing this, we make sure that for one statement, there is only one statement circuit.

Remark on the number of circuit wires. As noted in Section 3.2, the elements in c_c and c_p are candidates for the ciphertexts of the wires in the statement circuit. The number of these elements is linear with a number ℓ, which should be larger than the number of the wires. However, since the statement described in Step 7 of **proof** (Figure 3) contains information of c_{rand} which contains $c_c\|c_p$, the number of wires will increase while the number of elements in $c_c\|c_p$ increases. As a result, the number of elements in $c_c\|c_p$ may be not enough for the wires. We can solve this problem by using the hashing of $c_c\|c_p$ instead of $c_c\|c_p$ as a part of c_{rand} and let the verifier check the correctness of the hashing. By doing this, the statement circuit will not become too large when the number of elements in $c_c\|c_p$ increases.

Remark on common random string. According to Garg et al. [6], the public key of the pseudorandom encryption scheme and the SSTC scheme can be chosen randomly without learning the associated secret parameters. Furthermore, as we noted in Section 3.2, the CRS of the underlying NIZK can also be chosen randomly without learning the trapdoor information.

4   sFLR Signature

In this section, we first give the definition of sFLR signature which extends the notion of FLR signature [3,6]. A signature scheme is said to be sFLR if it satisfies sEUF property while the information of the secret key and the randomness used by the signing algorithm throughout the lifetime of the system is leaked. As the same as [6], for convenience, we do not consider the leakage on the randomness used in the key generation algorithm in the definition. However, our construction can tolerate leakage during key generation as discussed later.

We describe only the idea of the construction of the sFLR signature in this section. We give a complete description in the full version of the paper.

The sFLR signature scheme is defined as follows.

Definition 7 (sFLR signature scheme). *A signature scheme* (*KeyGen, Sign, Verify*) *is called an ℓ-sFLR signature scheme in the bounded leakage model if for all PPT adversary $\mathcal{A}$, we have that $\Pr[\mathcal{A} \ wins] \leq negl(k)$ in the following experiment:*

1. *Compute* $(pk, sk) \leftarrow KeyGen(1^k, \ell)$, *and set state* $:= sk$.
2. *Run the adversary $\mathcal{A}$ on input tuple $(1^k, pk, \ell)$. The adversary may make adaptive queries to the signing oracle and the leakage oracle, defined as follows.*
   - *Signature oracle: On receiving a query m_i, the signing oracle samples $r_i \leftarrow \{0,1\}^*$, and computes $\Phi_i \leftarrow Sign_{sk}(m_i; r_i)$. It updates state $:=$ state$\|r_i$ and outputs Φ_i.*
   - *Leakage oracle: On receiving the description of a polynomial-time computable function $f_j : \{0,1\}^* \rightarrow \{0,1\}^{\ell_j}$, the leakage oracle outputs $f(state)$.*
3. *At some point, $\mathcal{A}$ stops and outputs (m^*, Φ^*).*
4. *$\mathcal{A}$ wins in the experiment if : (a) $Verify_{pk}(m^*, \Phi^*) = 1$. (b) The pair (m^*, Φ^*) is new, that is, either m^* was not queried to the signing oracle or it was, Φ^* is not the one(s) generated as the signature(s) of m^* by the signing oracle. (c) $\sum_j \ell_j \leq \ell$.*

By substituting the underlying tSE-LR-NIZK proof system of the FLR signature scheme in [6] with an sSE-LR-NIZK proof system, we can obtain an sFLR signature scheme. By using the sSE-LR-NIZK proof system, the security of the sFLR signature scheme is reduced to the security of a leakage resilient primitive called leakage resilient hard relation (LR-hard relation) defined by Dodis et al. [5], who provided a generic approach to construct an LR-signature scheme by using the LR-hard relation.

Leakage during key generation. As the same as [6], since the CRS of the sSE-LR-NIZK can be sampled without learning the associated secret parameters (as discussed in Section 3.3), this scheme can tolerate leakage during key generation, which makes it satisfy the original definition of [3]. Furthermore, by substituting the LR-hard relation with a continual LR-hard relation [4], we can obtain an sFLR signature scheme in the continual leakage model [4]. In the same way, by instantiating of a hard relation secure in the noisy leakage model [10], we can obtain a scheme secure in the noisy leakage model as well. We refer the reader to [6] for details.

References

1. Bellare, M., Shoup, S.: Two-tier signatures, strongly unforgeable signatures, and Fiat-Shamir without random oracles. In: Okamoto, T., Wang, X. (eds.) PKC 2007. LNCS, vol. 4450, pp. 201–216. Springer, Heidelberg (2007)
2. Boneh, D., Shen, E., Waters, B.: Strongly unforgeable signatures based on computational Diffie-Hellman. In: Yung, M., Dodis, Y., Kiayias, A., Malkin, T. (eds.) PKC 2006. LNCS, vol. 3958, pp. 229–240. Springer, Heidelberg (2006)
3. Boyle, E., Segev, G., Wichs, D.: Fully leakage-resilient signatures. In: Paterson, K.G. (ed.) EUROCRYPT 2011. LNCS, vol. 6632, pp. 89–108. Springer, Heidelberg (2011)
4. Dodis, Y., Haralambiev, K., López-Alt, A., Wichs, D.: Cryptography against continuous memory attacks. In: Proceedings of the 2010 IEEE 51st Annual Symposium on Foundations of Computer Science, FOCS 2010, pp. 511–520. IEEE Computer Society (2010)
5. Dodis, Y., Haralambiev, K., López-Alt, A., Wichs, D.: Efficient public-key cryptography in the presence of key leakage. In: Abe, M. (ed.) ASIACRYPT 2010. LNCS, vol. 6477, pp. 613–631. Springer, Heidelberg (2010)
6. Garg, S., Jain, A., Sahai, A.: Leakage-resilient zero knowledge. In: Rogaway, P. (ed.) CRYPTO 2011. LNCS, vol. 6841, pp. 297–315. Springer, Heidelberg (2011)
7. Groth, J., Ostrovsky, R., Sahai, A.: Perfect non-interactive zero knowledge for np. In: Vaudenay, S. (ed.) EUROCRYPT 2006. LNCS, vol. 4004, pp. 339–358. Springer, Heidelberg (2006)
8. Huang, Q., Wong, D.S., Zhao, Y.: Generic transformation to strongly unforgeable signatures. In: Katz, J., Yung, M. (eds.) ACNS 2007. LNCS, vol. 4521, pp. 1–17. Springer, Heidelberg (2007)
9. MacKenzie, P.D., Yang, K.: On simulation-sound trapdoor commitments. In: Cachin, C., Camenisch, J.L. (eds.) EUROCRYPT 2004. LNCS, vol. 3027, pp. 382–400. Springer, Heidelberg (2004)
10. Naor, M., Segev, G.: Public-key cryptosystems resilient to key leakage. In: Halevi, S. (ed.) CRYPTO 2009. LNCS, vol. 5677, pp. 18–35. Springer, Heidelberg (2009)
11. Steinfeld, R., Pieprzyk, J., Wang, H.: How to strengthen any weakly unforgeable signature into a strongly unforgeable signature. In: Abe, M. (ed.) CT-RSA 2007. LNCS, vol. 4377, pp. 357–371. Springer, Heidelberg (2006)
12. Teranishi, I., Oyama, T., Ogata, W.: General conversion for obtaining strongly existentially unforgeable signatures. In: Barua, R., Lange, T. (eds.) INDOCRYPT 2006. LNCS, vol. 4329, pp. 191–205. Springer, Heidelberg (2006)

A Secure Three-Party Computational Protocol
for Triangle Area*

Liang Liu[1], Xiaofeng Chen[1], and Wenjing Lou[2]

[1] State Key Laboratory of Integrated Service Networks (ISN),
Xidian University, Xi'an 710071, China
liu.liang.xidian@gmail.com, xfchen@xidian.edu.cn
[2] Department of Computer Science,
Virginia Tech, Falls Church 22043, USA
wjlou@vt.edu

Abstract. We address a concrete secure multi-party computational (MPC) problem related to a triangle, of which the coordinates of the three vertexes are confidentially kept by the three participants, respectively. The three parties wish to collaboratively compute the area of this triangle while preserving their own coordinate privacy. As one of the merits, our protocol employs weaker assumptions of the existence of pseudorandom generators. Especially, unlike massive secure MPC protocols that mainly rely on the primitive of oblivious transfer (OT), ours utilizes a new computing idea named round summation to avoid this burdensome obstacle. Finally, we provide a proof of the protocol by a series of security reductions of our newly-defined games, which seems somewhat stronger than the previous simulation-based proofs.

1 Introduction

Secure multi-party computation (a.k.a. SMC) is of great importance in modern cryptography and communication. As one of the most significant cryptographic primitives, it has received much attention from international cryptographic community since its birth. It is created to solve a category of problems, involving n distributed and mutually distrustful parties in evaluating a pre-determined n-ary function $f(x_1, x_2, \ldots, x_n)$, where x_i is the i-th party's private input. After the protocol execution, no more than the output $f_i(x_1, x_2, \ldots, x_n)$ can the i-th party obtain. From its notion, besides a diversity of real-life applications, e.g., secret voting, electronic auction, we can learn that the most appealing feature of MPC may be its theoretical nature that we can treat plenty of other cryptographic protocols as a special case of it.

Similar to our protocol w.r.t. both MPC and geometry, there are some prior works closely related to the two themes, thus several keen-minded researchers have summed up this kind of MPC problems to be in a new subclass, secure multi-party computational geometry (MPCG), or referred to as privacy-preserving computational geometry (PPCG) [1]. It represents a certain kind of MPC problems in which the objective

---

* This work is done when the first two authors were visiting Virginia Polytechnic Institute and State University.

W. Susilo and Y. Mu (Eds.): ACISP 2014, LNCS 8544, pp. 82–97, 2014.

function $f(\cdot)$ relates closely to geometry. These problems has extensive application prospects. For instance, a real estate speculator has learned a fiscal plan made by policymakers that a region will be rebuilt into a commercial center and a trunk road will pass through it, meaning that the storefronts there will soon rise in value. Therefore, he intends to purchase some in advance and wait for their increment. Nevertheless, there are (mainly) two barriers hinder him from making a fortune – one is that he cannot learn the precise locality of the road that may have tremendous influence on the future price of the storefronts now at the same price level, and the other is he is not willing to leak his intention to others. Appreciation of the storefronts differs from each other in terms of their location relations with the road, e.g., the closer the storefront is to the road, the more increment in value it will gain; or the one on the north side of the road (it can be modeled as a point above the curve) will increase more than that on the south side [2]. So of course, the ones have the most potential should be at the top of his priority list. In a nutshell, all above can be ascribed to privately determining the geometrical relation or evaluating the distance between a point (storefront) and a curve (road), which are typical PPCG problems. Beyond that, for the triangle area problem which we target to address, one can imagine such a scenario. Three countries have planned to conduct a joint terrain exploration. Each of them do not want disclose their starting point whereas all of them need to know the area of the triangle consisted by the three points since they must have some (at least approximate) workload assessment before execution.

Apart from the scenarios above, there are also other considerable applications in real life. In the cloud computing era, on one hand a myriad of new applications are springing up in every minute, and on the other hand the security and privacy issues rising along with have unprecedentedly troubled people that much. For instance, location based service (LBS) [3,4], a burgeoning service at present mainly oriented to smart phone users and vehicle drivers, is becoming more and more popular in daily life. It provides us with excellent social activities, economical products, high-quality services as well as other convenience. Nevertheless, at the meantime, privacy concerns that have accompanied with its rapid development are also increasing. Taking the prevailing smart phone chatting software as an example, they usually comprise one or more modules, making use of the application requesters' location data and in turn supplying them for some LBS-related services, e.g., "restaurant recommendation" and "people nearby". This kind of behavior sometimes harms the interest of the application users due to the sensitivity of their private location data. However, secure multi-party computation, especially PPCG when in the settings that the function of the protocol is relevant to geometrical problems, offers us a good solution to this tricky situation. It is possible for the users to both reap the benefit of the services and prevent leakage of their privacy by taking advantage of an appropriate secure MPC protocol.

In this paper, we have addressed a new secure three-party computational problem with respect to triangle area. Our contribution can be concluded as follows:

- Our protocol is constructed under simpler assumption, namely, only assuming the existence of pseudo-random generator. A highlighted point worth mentioning is that ours avoids the usage of oblivious transfer, which is a basic tool in secure multi-party computation.

- Our work addresses this kind of problems in a more complex situation compared with former literatures, especially to the one addresses this issue in the two-party case[27]. Besides, our solution can also be deemed as a beginning as well as a basis for some more complex problems, e.g., how to decide other metrics when given more participants.
- We provide a stronger proof for our protocol. Our proof allows for adaptively-chosen output of the function/protocol and arbitrary knowledge of other parties' inputs in the interactive games (not in the protocol itself, otherwise it breaches the principles of SMC).

2 Preliminaries

The main building block of our protocol is Heron's Formula.

Theorem 1. Heron's Formula. *In a triangle $\triangle_{ABC}$, given the length of the three edges and the semiperimeter, the area of $\triangle_{ABC}$ can be calculated as:*

$$S_{area_{ABC}} = \sqrt{P \cdot (P - E_a) \cdot (P - E_b) \cdot (P - E_c)},$$

where E_i is the opposite side of the i-th ($i \in \{a, b, c\}$) vertex, and $P = (E_a + E_b + E_c)/2$ is the semiperimeter of this triangle.

There is a truth about evaluating the summation sum of a certain set of numbers n_i's ($i \in \mathbb{Z}$, $i \geq 3$), where each of the numbers is secretly held by only one participant. And after the execution, every party should not be able to learn more than all the other parties' summation, namely, $sum - n_i$. Here, we referred this process as *summation protocol* (or *round summation protocol*). We make use of a developed version of this protocol several times in our protocol.

Claim 1. *As stated above, in the context of a round summation protocol, the participants can achieve the goal by the following steps: Party 1 launches the protocol by sending to Party 2 the sum of his private number n_1 and a random number r. At this point, they have $s = n_1 + r$. Party 2 then adds up her private number n_2 to s and sends the updated s to the next participant. The protocol proceeds in this manner one by one until the last participant sends back s to the first participant, at which point it satisfies that $s = sum + r$. Finally, Party 1 broadcasts the result $s - r$ to all the other parties within this protocol execution.*

Theorem 2. Single-Message Security Implies Multiple-Message Security. *A public-key encryption scheme $\mathcal{E}$ has indistinguishable encryptions for multiple messages if and only if it has indistinguishable encryptions for a single message, say, for any PPT adversary $\mathcal{A}$, any security parameter n, there exists a negligible function $\mathrm{negl}(\cdot)$ such that,*

$$\mathbf{Adv}_{\mathcal{A},\mathcal{E}}^{\text{ind-cpa}}(n) = \Pr\left[\mathbf{Exp}_{\mathcal{A},\mathcal{E}}^{\text{ind-cpa}}(n) = 1\right] - \frac{1}{2} \leq \mathrm{negl}(n)$$

$$\Longleftrightarrow \mathbf{Adv}_{\mathcal{A},\mathcal{E}}^{\text{ind-cpa-mult}}(n) = \Pr\left[\mathbf{Exp}_{\mathcal{A},\mathcal{E}}^{\text{ind-cpa-mult}}(n) = 1\right] - \frac{1}{2} \leq \mathrm{negl}(n)$$

The ind-cpa-mult experiment is the same as the ind-cpa experiment except that in the Step 2 of the ind-cpa experiment, the adversary $\mathcal{A}$ chooses a pair of message vectors M_0 and M_1 rather than a pair of single messages. For the sake of simplicity, we do not repeat the experiment again.

Theorem 3. Pseudorandom Generators Imply Indistinguishable Encryption Schemes. *There are several ways to bridge these two notions, e.g., pseudorandom generators imply pseudorandom functions and pseudorandom functions imply pseudorandom permutations, which along with an efficient trapdoor generation algorithm imply indistinguishable encryption schemes; or pseudorandom generators imply one-way functions, which along with an efficient trapdoor generation algorithm imply indistinguishable encryption schemes. For simplicity, we do not give constructions here. Readers can refer to revelent books and articles.*

Theorem 2 is used to simplify our proof of the indistinguishability between some adjacence game sequences, e.g., **Game**$_1$ and **Game**$_2$. Theorem 3 speaks to the soundness of our statement that our protocol relies only on the existence of pseudorandom generators.

3 Evaluating the Area of a Triangle While Preserving the Coordinate Privacy

Without loss of generality, we suppose that Alice, Bob and Carol each has a point $P_i = (x_i, y_i) \in \mathbb{Z}^* \times \mathbb{Z}^*, i \in \{a, b, c\}$. Denote as Π the protocol, the aim of which is to engage the three in calculating the area of the triangle composed of their points without leaking any private information more than the area. Next we give our protocol intuition first and then the solution to address this problem.

3.1 Protocol Intuition

Let us recall Heron's Formula. The main idea behind our protocol is that firstly the three participants interactively and privately calculate the three edges E_a, E_b and E_c (E_i is the length of the opposite edge of the point P_i) of the triangle by randomization and modified summation protocol. Note that on account of the changes in the round summation protocol, by which each of the three participants obtains the *product* (with the form of $G(\cdot)E_i$) of its opposite edge and a pseudorandom number rather than trivially obtains the edge, we can achieve the goal of protecting the value of E_i's. And then for the same reason, they can obtain some pseudo-randomized version of semiperimeter P and $(P - E_i)$'s of this triangle by using the modified round summation protocol in nearly the same manner (but not exactly the same). After all these steps, by making use of Heron Formula and derandomization, the correct output of the protocol, namely the area of this triangle, can be obtained.

Intuitively, the difficulty of preserving privacy lies in privately evaluating P and E_i's, which is also one of our highlights. Aiming to solve it, we put forth our protocol Π. Besides, to offer convenience to readers in reading our work, we make some of the symbols more visual and meaningful. For instance, ciphertext $CT_{c \leftarrow a, 1}$ indicates the first ciphertext Alice sends to Carol – the meaning can more or less be learnt by the index.

3.2　Formal Specification of Our Protocol Π

1. Alice and Bob agree on two random numbers, denoted as r_c, r_{c_1} that should be kept secret to Carol. The two then get $G(r_c)$ and $G(r_{c_1})$ respectively.
2. Alice encrypts $G(r_c)x_a + G(r_{c_1})$, $G(r_c)y_a + G(r_{c_1})$ under Carol's public key PK_c and then sends to Carol the ciphertexts $Enc_{PK_c}(G(r_c)x_a + G(r_{c_1}))$ and $Enc_{PK_c}(G(r_c)y_a + G(r_{c_1}))$. Bob uses his point (x_b, y_b) to do the same procedures as Alice does. Thus, after this step, Carol receives

$$CT_{c \leftarrow a,1} = Enc_{PK_c}(G(r_c)x_a + G(r_{c_1})), CT_{c \leftarrow a,2} = Enc_{PK_c}(G(r_c)y_a + G(r_{c_1}))$$

and

$$CT_{c \leftarrow b,1} = Enc_{PK_c}(G(r_c)x_b + G(r_{c_1})), CT_{c \leftarrow b,2} = Enc_{PK_c}(G(r_c)y_b + G(r_{c_1}))$$

3. Carol calculates

$$\sqrt{(Dec_{SK_c}(CT_{c \leftarrow b,1}) - Dec_{SK_c}(CT_{c \leftarrow a,1}))^2 + (Dec_{SK_c}(CT_{c \leftarrow b,2}) - Dec_{SK_c}(CT_{c \leftarrow a,2}))^2}$$

and obtains $G(r_c) \cdot E_c$.
4. The three parties execute Step 1-3 as a whole subprotocol twice, with the exception that Bob and Alice in turn play the computing role as Carol does in the first round execution and the random numbers needed are denoted as r_b, r_{b1} and r_a, r_{a1}. Note that, after this step, Bob and Alice respectively obtain $G(r_b) \cdot E_b$ and $G(r_a) \cdot E_a$.
5. Alice, Bob and Carol respectively calculate their corresponding components,

$$Com_a = \frac{1}{2}G(r_a)E_a \cdot G(r_b) \cdot G(r_c)$$

$$Com_b = \frac{1}{2}G(r_b)E_b \cdot G(r_c) \cdot G(r_a)$$

$$Com_c = \frac{1}{2}G(r_c)E_c \cdot G(r_a) \cdot G(r_b)$$

6. Alice chooses a random number r_{com_a} and sends $Enc_{PK_b}(G(r_{com_a}) - Com_a)$ to Bob; Bob decrypts it and sends $Enc_{PK_c}(G(r_{com_a}) - Com_a + Com_b)$ to Carol; Carol uses her private key SK_c to recover the plaintext $G(r_{com_a}) - Com_a + Com_b$, and then sends $Enc_{PK_a}(G(r_{com_a}) - Com_a + Com_b + Com_c)$ to Alice; after decryption and subtracting $G(r_{com_a})$ from the plaintext, Alice finally obtains

$$Com_b + Com_c - Com_a = G(r_a)G(r_b)G(r_c)(P - E_a) = Mul_a$$

7. Again, they repeat Step 6 twice, with the exception that Bob and Carol in turn play the role as Alice does, viz., one who launches an execution round generates a random number r_{com_i}, $(i \in \{b, c\})$ to hide the corresponding Com_i before starting the modified summation protocol. After this step, Bob and Carol obtain $Mul_b = G(r_a)G(r_b)G(r_c)(P - E_b)$ and $Mul_c = G(r_a)G(r_b)G(r_c)(P - E_c)$, respectively.

8. Alice chooses a random number r_{mul_+}, then she and the other two execute the same procedure except that each of them uses $G(r_a)G(r_b)G(r_c)(P - E_i)$ instead of Com_i, where $i \in \{a, b, c\}$. After this step, Alice obtains

$$Mul_p = Mul_a + Mul_b + Mul_c = G(r_a)G(r_b)G(r_c)P$$

9. Bob chooses a random number $r_{mul_\times}$ and then sends $\text{Enc}_{PK_c}(Mul_b \cdot G(r_{mul_\times}))$ to Carol; Carol multiplies the plaintext $Mul_b \cdot G(r_{mul_\times})$ by $Mul_c/(G(r_a)G(r_b))^4$, and then she sends to Alice the encryption of it, i.e., Alice will receive such message, $\text{Enc}_{PK_a}((Mul_b Mul_c \cdot G(r_{mul_\times}))/(G(r_a)G(r_b))^4)$; Then Alice multiplies $Mul_a Mul_p$ to the plaintext product and after her execution, Bob receives $\text{Enc}_{PK_b}(S)$, a shorthand for $\text{Enc}_{PK_b}((Mul_p Mul_a Mul_b Mul_c \cdot G(r_{mul_\times}))/(G(r_a)G(r_b))^4)$.

10. Bob decrypts $\text{Enc}_{PK_b}(S)$ and sends the other two $\sqrt{S/(G(r_{mul_\times}) \cdot G(r_c)^4)}$, which is exactly the area of the triangle.

3.3 Correctness

We argue that the deduction below guarantees the correctness of our protocol.

$$
\begin{aligned}
S/(G(r_{mul_\times}) \cdot G(r_c)^4) &= \frac{(Mul_p Mul_a Mul_b Mul_c \cdot G(r_{mul_\times}))/(G(r_a)G(r_b))^4}{(G(r_{mul_\times}) \cdot G(r_c)^4)} \\
&= \frac{Mul_p Mul_a Mul_b Mul_c}{G(r_a)^4 G(r_b)^4 G(r_c)^4} \\
&= \frac{(G(r_a)G(r_b)G(r_c)P) \cdot \prod_i^{a,b,c} G(r_a)G(r_b)G(r_c)(P - E_i)}{G(r_a)^4 G(r_b)^4 G(r_c)^4} \\
&= P(P - E_a)(P - E_b)(P - E_b) = S_{area}^2
\end{aligned}
$$

4 Proof of Security

When it comes to security proof for a secure multi-party computational protocol, simulation-based method is always the first (sometimes even the only) avenue one can think of, e.g., the famous UC (Universal Composition) security model. However, we develop a new proof paradigm grounded upon game-based proof methodology, which captures the nature that if a protocol π is secure, none of the participants is able to obtain extra information beyond the protocol's provision even when she knows arbitrary number of inputs belonging to other parties. In addition to providing a new vision for MPC security, we have demonstrated that the novel proof below is "somewhat adaptive", meaning that it can prove security in the manner that the adversary can even choose an (reasonable) output for the function. Due to the similarity of the proof for each of the three participants, we only provide a proof from Alice's stance.

4.1   Definition of the Original Game

Game (Selective Area) IND-PointPairs $\textbf{Game}_{\mathcal{A},\Pi}^{\text{ind-pps}}(n, \kappa)$

- The adversary chooses an area S_{area} which she wants to be challenged upon and sends it to the challenger.
- The challenger generates a collection $\mathcal{P}$ of point pairs, i.e.

$$\mathcal{P} = \{pair_1, pair_2, \ldots, pair_{l(\kappa)}\},$$

  where $pair_i = \{(x_{b,i}, y_{b,i}), (x_{c,i}, y_{c,i})\}$, κ is a security parameter and $l(\cdot)$ is a polynomial.
- The adversary chooses two point pairs from $\mathcal{P}$, say

$$pair_i = \{(x_{b,i}, y_{b,i}), (x_{c,i}, y_{c,i})\} \text{ and } pair_j = \{(x_{b,j}, y_{b,j}), (x_{c,j}, y_{c,j})\}$$

  as the challenging point pairs which are subject to those two restrictions:
  a) the area of the triangle consisting by the adversary's point and every pair of the points from the collection $\mathcal{P}$ must be equal to S_{area}. This requirement is for the correctness. Informally speaking, the triangles must at least have same area so as to prevent the trivial distinction.
  b) the two pairs $pair_i$ and $pair_j$ must have the same slope, namely,

$$\frac{y_{c,i} - y_{b,i}}{x_{c,i} - x_{b,i}} = \frac{y_{c,j} - y_{b,j}}{x_{c,j} - x_{b,j}}$$

  We state that restriction **b)** is only required in our proof. We delay explaining the reason in the appendix. In addition, to be well coincident with the traditional expression of game-based proof, we ignore the index difference, namely, we always denote adversary's choice as $pair_0$ and $pair_1$. After that, She sends them to the challenger.

- The challenger flips a coin $b \in \{0,1\}$ as challenge bit, and executes the protocol with $\mathcal{O}_{\text{IDEAL}_{\text{Bob}}}(\cdot)$ and $\mathcal{O}_{\text{IDEAL}_{\text{Carol}}}(\cdot)$. It records the sequence (denoted as $sequence_b$) it has received, and then sends the sequence to the adversary.
- The adversary returns a guess b', and if $b' = b$, she wins the game.

The advantage of the adversary in this game is,

$$\textbf{Adv}_{\mathcal{A},\text{Game}}^{\text{ind-pps}}(n, \kappa) = \Pr\left[b = b' | sequence_b \leftarrow \textbf{Game}_{\mathcal{A},\Pi}^{\text{ind-pps}}(n, \kappa)\right] - \frac{1}{2}$$

Remark 1.   There are two points worth mentioning. First, note that we ignore the details on by what means the challenger gets $sequence_b$. Second, in our game-based proof the adversary *does* know the private information whereas that should be replaced by one produced by the simulation in the simulation-based proof.

We now specify $sequence_b$ Alice receives[1] in this game. Note that in some literature terminology "sequence" can also be named as "view" or others. Again for readers'

---

[1] Actually, only the content one party cannot obtain by direct deductions can be seen as parts of the *sequence*.

convenience, we make use of meaningful denotations. The front index with the form of "i." of the sequence indicates the step number, viz., i-th step of our protocol Π, and the rear index with the form of "$\textcircled{j}$" of the sequence indicates the game number, viz., j-th game $\mathbf{Game}_j$.

$$
\left\{
\begin{array}{ll}
1.\, r_c,\ r_{c_1},\ G(r_c),\ G(r_{c_1}) & \textcircled{1} \\[4pt]
4.\, r_b,\ r_{b1},\ G(r_b),\ G(r_{b_1});\ CT_{a\leftarrow b,1}, CT_{a\leftarrow b,2}, CT_{a\leftarrow c,1}, CT_{a\leftarrow c,2},\ G(r_a)E_a & \textcircled{2} \\[4pt]
5.\, Com_a = \dfrac{1}{2}G(r_a)E_a \cdot G(r_b) \cdot G(r_c) & \textcircled{3} \\[4pt]
6.\, r_{com_a},\ \mathrm{Enc}_{PK_a}(G(r_{com_a}) - Com_a + Com_b + Com_c),\ Mul_a & \textcircled{4} \\[4pt]
7.\, G(r_{com_b}) - Com_b + Com_c,\ G(r_{com_c}) - Com_c & \textcircled{5} \\[4pt]
8.\, r_{mul_+},\ G(r_{mul_+}),\ Mul_p & \textcircled{6} \\[4pt]
9.\, \mathrm{Enc}_{PK_a}(Mul_b \cdot Mul_c \cdot G(r_{mul_\times})/(G(r_a)G(r_b))^4) & \textcircled{7} \\[4pt]
10.\, S_{area} & \textcircled{8}
\end{array}
\right\}
$$

Let ε_1 be the advantage that the adversary can successfully distinguish a random string r from a string $G(x)$ generated by $G(\cdot)$, which is uniformly chosen from a family of PRGs. According to the widely-adopted assumption, ε_1 is negligible. Likewise, let ε_2 be the advantage that the adversary can successfully distinguish two ciphertexts produced by an IND-CPA secure public-key encryption scheme $\mathcal{E}$. Due to the same reason, we deem ε_2 as a negligible function, too.

4.2 Proof Intuition

It is akin to the classical game-based methodology that we try to change some participants' behavior during the execution of our protocol to turn the current game into a new one, where the two games are indistinguishable from the adversary's stance. And finally, after a set of these transformations, the game moves into a final game which is easy to be proven secure. More specifically, in our design mechanism, $\mathbf{Game}_0$ actually is the real game which is interactively played by the challenger and the adversary. For $\mathbf{Game}_i$, we state that in each $\mathbf{Game}_i$, usually we replace the outputs of $G(\cdot)$ by those equal-length string r's chosen uniformly at random, and/or replace the encryption parts in the distribution (namely, in the $\textcircled{1}$-th part of the sequence) by other ones generated from the same encryption algorithm with the same parameters. After those step-by-step alternations, the final game $\mathbf{Game}_{final}$ is easy to prove secure (in our case, the advantage of the adversary for the final game is 0), and each couple of $\mathbf{Game}_i$ and $\mathbf{Game}_{i+1}$ are proven indistinguishable. Thus, the protocol is proven secure by the set of games.

4.3 Security Games

$\mathbf{Game}_0$. Actually, $\mathbf{Game}_0$ is the original game (namely, $\mathbf{Game}_{A,\Pi}^{\mathrm{ind\text{-}pps}}$) in which the sequence of the adversary (here for Alice) is denoted as $sequence_{g_0}$. It is obvious that $sequence_{g_0} = sequence_b$.

$\mathbf{Game}_1$. In this game, all the steps are executed in the same way as those have been executed in $\mathbf{Game}_0$ expect that:

- We change the randomness in Step 1 of the protocol, that is, replace r_c and r_{c_1} by $\tilde{r}_c$ and $\tilde{r}_{c_1}$. This change will result in the corresponding changes in the sequence of this game. Formally, the ① part of $sequence_{g_1}$ turns into $\{\tilde{r}_c, \tilde{r}_{c_1}, G(\tilde{r}_c), G(\tilde{r}_{c_1})\}$.
- The ciphertexts generated afterwards are a little different from that in the standard protocol. The outputs of the PRG $G(\cdot)$ which are used for randomization will be replaced by random ones, e.g., the ciphertext $CT_{c\leftarrow a,1} = Enc_{PK_c}(G(r_c)x_a + G(r_{c_1}))$ in Step 2 should be replaced by $\widetilde{CT}_{c\leftarrow a,1} = Enc_{PK_c}(\tilde{r}_c x_a + \tilde{r}_{c_1})$

Game$_2$. As stated above, in this game we change Step 4 in the protocol s.t. no more than the (circled) second part of the $sequence_{g_2}$ is different from $sequence_{g_1}$. To achieve this, the random numbers r_b and r_{b_1} Alice and Carol have agreed on during the execution are replaced by $\tilde{r}_b$ and $\tilde{r_{b_1}}$, so do the corresponding outputs of the pseudorandom generator $G(\cdot)$. In addition, the four CT's in this sequence are also changed in the same manner as in **Game$_1$**, namely, four new ciphertexts produced by $\mathcal{E}$ with the same parameters are used to substitute for the four ciphertexts in this sequence. At last, $G(r_a)E_a$ will be changed to $\tilde{r_a}E_a$ where pseudorandom output $G(r_a)$ is replaced by random $\tilde{r}_a$.

Game$_3$. Only one small change should be made, namely, replace $Com_a = \frac{1}{2}G(r_a)E_a \cdot G(r_b) \cdot G(r_c)$ by $\widetilde{Com}_a = \frac{1}{2}\tilde{r_a}E_a \cdot \tilde{r}_b \cdot \tilde{r}_c$. To this end, the players taking part in this game should substitute their corresponding pseudorandom variables by equal-length uniformly random strings.

Game$_4$. In this part, like the changes in the previous games, the changes introduce new identically distributed randomness $\widetilde{r_{com_a}}$ to replace the former one, $G(r_{com_a})$. The encrypted part $Enc_{PK_a}(G(r_{com_a}) - Com_a + Com_b + Com_c)$ is also taken place by $Enc_{PK_a}(\tilde{r}_{com_a} - Com_a + Com_b + Com_c)$. The last part Mul_a is as well changed to $\widetilde{Mul}_a$ along with the changes happened in Com_i's.

Game$_5$. This game, corresponding to Step 7 in our protocol, touches upon two substeps. In each step of the original protocol, the round launcher $i \in \{b, c\}$ subtracts their corresponding component Com_i from the output of $G(\cdot)$ in the randomness r_{com_i}. Here in the proof game, analogous to previous changes, those $G(r_{com_i})$ are replaced by corresponding $\tilde{r}_{com_i}$.

Game$_6$. In this game, a new random variable $\widetilde{r_{mul_+}}$ with the same distribution as $G(r_{mul_+})$ has been selected, which is then used to replace $G(r_{mul_+})$ during this game. The last component Mul_p of this game in $sequence_{g_6}$ will vary following the variations of those Mul_i's where $i \in \{a, b, c\}$.

Game$_7$. This is the last game which needs alternations. From the adversary's (here Alice's) point of view, she receives an encryption of $Mul_b \cdot Mul_c \cdot G(r_{mul_\times})/(G(r_a)G(r_b))^4$. In order to make the final game a random one, the changes in this game must resemble to the former. That is, we replace $Enc_{PK_a}(Mul_b \cdot Mul_c \cdot G(r_{mul_\times})/(G(r_a)G(r_b))^4)$ by $Enc_{PK_a}(\widetilde{Mul}_b \cdot \widetilde{Mul}_c \cdot \tilde{r}_{mul_\times}/(\tilde{r}_a\tilde{r}_b)^4)$.

Game$_8$. There is no change needs to be made in this game due to the restriction that for either $pair_0$ or $pair_1$, the value of the area is a constant chosen in advance.

Game$_{\text{final}}$. As previously mentioned, **Game$_{\text{final}}$** is the ultimate game. Since all the (pseudo) randomness are changed (and replaced), all the IND-CPA secure encryptions are replaced, and all the intermediate variables are correspondingly changed, the protocol becomes unconditionally secure. Moreover, the sequence of this game is identical to the one of **Game$_8$**, namely $sequence_{g_f} = sequence_{g_8}$ as we do not make any change in this game comparing with **Game$_8$**.

4.4 Indistinguishability of Game$_i$ and Game$_{i+1}$

To begin with, we set **Game$_0$** to be the same game as original game **Game$_{A,\Pi}^{\text{ind-pps}}$**. Therefore, as aforementioned, it holds that $sequence_b = sequence_{g_0}$ and the advantage for the adversary to successfully distinguish **Game$_{A,\Pi}^{\text{ind-pps}}$** and **Game$_0$** is 0.

Note that r_c, r_{c_1}, $\tilde{r}_c$ and $\tilde{r}_{c_1}$ are all uniformly chosen in the same domain and all the other parts of $sequence_{g_0}$ and $sequence_{g_1}$ are the same. The advantage of an adversary to distinguish the two sequence is equivalent to that of the same adversary to distinguish two identically distributed variables RV_1 and RV_2 (The output of $G(\cdot)$ is determined, so they cannot provide any useful information for distinguishing). Therefore, the advantage of the adversary to distinguish **Game$_0$** and **Game$_1$** is 0.

For **Game$_1$** and **Game$_2$**, only the second part of each game sequence is different. Therefore, the advantage of the adversary to successfully distinguish the two sequences comes from the advantage over the distinctions between $CT_{a\leftarrow b,1}$, $CT_{a\leftarrow b,2}$, $CT_{a\leftarrow c,1}$, $CT_{a\leftarrow c,2}$, $G(r_a)E_a$ of $sequence_{g_1}$ and $CT_{a\leftarrow b,1}$, $CT_{a\leftarrow b,2}$, $CT_{a\leftarrow c,1}$, $CT_{a\leftarrow c,2}$, $\tilde{r}_a E_a$ of $sequence_{g_2}$. In terms of Theorem 2, we just need to prove that two simplified sequences with the form of $\{CT, G(r_a)E_a\}$ and $\{\widetilde{CT}, \tilde{r}_a E_a\}$. The proof is given as follow:

Proof. For simplicity, denote as $subseq_0$ the subsequence $\{CT, G(r_a)E_a\}$ and $subseq_1$ the subsequence $\{\widetilde{CT}, \tilde{r}_a E_a\}$. Suppose an adversary $\mathcal{A}$ can successfully distinguish the two games, namely, $\mathcal{A}$ can successfully distinguish $subseq_0$ and $subseq_1$ with a non-negligible advantage p. We can construct an adversary $\mathcal{A}'$ to either successfully attack the pseudorandom generator $G(\cdot)$ or the IND-CPA encryption scheme $\mathcal{E}$ (or both) with a non-negligible probability $\frac{1}{2}p$.

Adversary $\mathcal{A}'$ involves in two challenge-response games with the two corresponding challengers, which we respectively denote as $G(\cdot)$-challenger and $\mathcal{E}$-challenger for the sake of clear expressiveness. After setups and other preparation steps, adversary $\mathcal{A}'$ can:

- Directly receive string R's which may be random or pseudorandom from $G(\cdot)$-challenger.
- Receive challenge ciphertext that is the encryption to her chosen plaintexts from $\mathcal{E}$-challenger.

Then $\mathcal{A}'$ combines those elements to form a challenge subsequence $subseq_b = \{CT^{(b)}, R^{(b)}E_a\}$, which then will be sent to $\mathcal{A}$. $\mathcal{A}$ will response in two manners. First, it returns a bit b' to $\mathcal{A}'$ if the subsequence is well-formed. Second, it rejects $subseq_b$ if the subsequence is not well-formed. Say well-formed, we mean that the first part is the encryption of random (or pseudorandom) element with the form of $\tilde{r}_1 \cdot t + \tilde{r}_2$

(or $G(r_1) \cdot t + G(r_2)$) and the second part is the multiplication of a random (or pseudo-random) number and E_a. Note that $R^{(b)}$ is either random or pseudorandom and $CT^{(b)}$ is either an encryption of $\tilde{r_1} \cdot t + \tilde{r_2}$ or $G(r_1) \cdot t + G(r_2)$. The probability of the well-formed subsequence is $\frac{1}{2}$ and in this condition, $\mathcal{A}'$ can win the game by just sending the bit b' to the challenger. Thus the advantage for $\mathcal{A}'$ to win is $\frac{1}{2}p$, which is non-negligible. It is contradictory to the assumption that either ε_1 or ε_2 is negligible. Therefore, the advantage p should be negligible and that is to say, **Game**$_1$ and **Game**$_2$ are indistinguishable.

For **Game**$_2$ and **Game**$_3$, the only difference lies in the third circled part of the two sequences. Therefore, to successfully distinguish these two games, the adversary must successfully distinguish Com_a and $\widetilde{Com_a}$. Recall that $Com_a = \frac{1}{2}G(r_a)E_a \cdot G(r_b) \cdot G(r_c)$ and $\widetilde{Com_a} = \frac{1}{2}\tilde{r_a}E_a \cdot \tilde{r_b} \cdot \tilde{r_c}$. Distinguishing Com_a and $\widetilde{Com_a}$ is identical to distinguishing an output of $G(\cdot)$ and an equal-length uniformly random variable r and thus the advantage for the adversary to successfully distinguish **Game**$_2$ and **Game**$_3$ is ε_1, a negligible function. The reason is that if there exists an adversary $\mathcal{A}$ can successfully distinguish Com_a and $\widetilde{Com_a}$, then an adversary $\mathcal{A}'$ is able to invoke $\mathcal{A}$ as a subprogram to distinguish pseudorandom and true random variables. Adversary $\mathcal{A}'$ taking part in a indistinguishability game can ask for challenge inputs three times and multiples them by a proper E_a to obtain a challenge $Com_a^{(b)}$ which is sent to $\mathcal{A}$. $\mathcal{A}'$ will send the same bit b' it receives from $\mathcal{A}$ to the challenger, meaning that if $\mathcal{A}$ makes a claim that $Com_a^{(b)}$ is product of three random (or pseudorandom) number and E_a, $\mathcal{A}'$ then asserts that the challenge string is random (or pseudorandom). It is obvious that the two advantages are equal. Since the outputs of pseudorandom generators can not be distinguished with a non-negligible advantage from the random strings, **Game**$_2$ and **Game**$_3$ are indistinguishable.

For **Game**$_3$ and **Game**$_4$, it is analogous to the proof for indistinguishability of **Game**$_1$ and **Game**$_2$. At first, we extract the different parts and abbreviate it as $subseq_0 = \{r_{com_a}, CT, Mul_a\}$ and $subseq_1 = \{\widetilde{r_{com_a}}, \widetilde{CT}, \widetilde{Mul_a}\}$. Thus, the slightly different part is that there is a third component in each of the two subsequences which are needed to be distinguished. Recall the form of Mul_a and $\widetilde{Mul_a}$, it is evident that they are a pseudorandom variable and a random variable, respectively. Then for an adversary $\mathcal{A}$ whom is given the task to distinguish the two subsequences with the form of $\{RV_1, CT, psRV_2\}$ and $\{\widetilde{RV}_1, \widetilde{CT}, \widetilde{RV}_2\}$, we can proceed a similar proof to the one for indistinguishability of **Game**$_1$ and **Game**$_2$ following the same methodology: When adversary $\mathcal{A}'$ receives challenge texts, namely CT's and (pseudo)random strings, she can combine them to form a challenge subsequence $subseq_b$ which will be sent to subprogram $\mathcal{A}$. $\mathcal{A}'$ then takes the guess bit b' from $\mathcal{A}$ as her guess. If adversary $\mathcal{A}$ can successfully distinguish the two subsequences with a non-negligible advantage, $\mathcal{A}'$ can also successfully break the pseudorandom generator or the IND-CPA encryption scheme with a non-negligible advantage, which according to the assumption is impossible. Therefore, we have proven that **Game**$_3$ and **Game**$_4$ are indistinguishable.

For the sake of simplicity, we only give the constructions of subsequences for the rest of games which have analogous indistinguishability proofs to the former.

For **Game**$_4$ and **Game**$_5$, it is identical to proving the indistinguishability of $subseq_0$ with the form of two pseudorandom variables $\{psRV_1, psRV_2\}$ and $subseq_1$ with the form of random variables $\{\widetilde{RV}_1, \ \widetilde{RV}_2\}$. For **Game$_5$** and **Game$_6$**, the two subsequences have the form of $\{RV_1, \ psRV_1, \ psRV_2\}$ and $\{\widetilde{RV}_1, \ ps\widetilde{RV}_1, \ \widetilde{RV}_2\}$, respectively. All the two can be proved using the same method stated above. For **Game$_6$** and **Game$_7$**, the only different point is the circled seventh part, namely the ciphertext. So their indistinguishability can be directly proved by the assumption that the encryption scheme is IND-CPA secure. For **Game$_7$** and **Game$_8$**, due to the game restriction that either the triangle $\triangle_0$ consisting of point A and points $pair_0$ or the triangle $\triangle_1$ consisting of point A and points $pair_1$ must have the same area S_{area}, the two game sequences $sequence_{g_7}$ and $sequence_{g_8}$ are in fact the same. For **Game$_8$** and **Game$_{final}$**, as exhibited in game construction, they are the same games that cannot be distinguished with a probability more than $\frac{1}{2}$. And for **Game$_{final}$**, it is a unconditionally secure game in which all the elements are randomized elements or the encryptions of randomized elements. Therefore, up to this point, we finish all the parts of our proof.

5 Related Work

After Yao's seminal work [5] in 1982, which has introduced secure multiparty computation (two-party situation) to the research community via a vivid example named as Millionaires' Problem, the researches to promote it have never ceased. Regarding the question of the existence of general solution to MPC problem, Yao's work has solved this problem in the two-party conditions [6] and Goldreich et al. have given a construction in the multi-party case [7]. Then numerous literatures came out, investigating in every respect of secure multi-party computation. In the early days, research on realizations in the presence of malicious adversary is one of the highlighted directions [8,9,10], which is still an active branch in present research community. In addition, there are also substantial works on other different aspects of security. In reality, one protocol would merely be executed in the isolation setting, where a great deal of secure multi-party computational protocols are traditionally analyzed. Due to the insufficiency of the stand-alone security, concurrent security [11] of the analyzed protocol which may be executed with arbitrarily many other protocols simultaneously are developed and probed. To make progress in promoting the efficiency of secure MPC protocols, some works explore the possibility and methods to improve upon performance in several respects [12,13,14], e.g. round complexity, interactivity. Furthermore, Secure multi-party computation has close connection to other cryptographic tools, such as zero knowledge proof [15,16,17], oblivious transfer [18], secret sharing scheme [19] and it can also be realized by other primitives like (fully) homomorphic encryption [20,21], and so forth. There are also a lot of researches on the practical implementations of secure multi-party computational protocols, e.g. Fairplay [22] system and its enhanced followup FairplayMP [23] system, TASTY [24] and the widely investigated ones by means of cut-and-choose technique based on garbled circuit [25].

Besides those studies on secure multi-party computation regarding *general* problem/function, another important area of secure MPC is to research on the secure MPC protocols with respect to *concrete* problem/function. We emphasize that although study on general secure multi-party computation facilitates rapid progress in lots of aspects of SMC, e.g., solvability in principle, generic design mechanism, lower bounds, it cannot be well competent for all the tasks especially the ones related closely to real life applications. For example, using a general protocol to solve privacy-preserving data mining [26] is impractical. Therefore, constructing different concrete protocols for different problems is of independent interest. In this direction, there are also an amount of works. The most relevant work to our paper by Li et al. [27] solves the same triangle area problem in the two-party case, a little simpler than ours. Moreover, aiming at other geometrical issues and practical applications, investigators probe into areas like privately determining relations between geometrical objects [28], location test. In addition to aforementioned PPCG protocols, the research community, likewise, makes progress in protocol design for other concrete problems, e.g. secure database/set operation [29,30], privacy-preserving data mining, secure clustering [31], scientific computation , approximation [32], private information retrieve [33,34], privacy-preserving auction [35], delegation computation, and so on. Recently, secure two-party computation finds out a fit place in big data scenario [36]. A comprehensive survey offers a summarization of those problems [37]. In particular, in the context of the omnipresent cloud computing that features distributed computing, the study on concrete protocols plays more significant role than ever.

6 Conclusion

In this paper, we first solve a concrete secure three-party computational problem regarding triangle area, in which three participants respectively owning their private point intend to securely evaluate the area without any leakage of their point privacy. More specifically, we employ Heron's Formula and round summation protocol to successfully construct our protocol with weak assumption. Besides, we provide a novel and plausibly stronger proof for our protocol and exhibit the reason why our proof seems to fit better than the traditional simulation-based one. Furthermore, we would like to make a short discussion with respect to the future directions of secure multi-party computation, especially its relation with the emerging primitives and applications. Secure multi-party computation seems to have some connection with functional encryption (FE), while maybe the most different point is that functional encryption requires no interactivity. Although to date, typical functional encryption only involves two participants, we do not consider it as a clear distinction. Secure multi-party computation seems closely related to delegation schemes (a.k.a verifiable delegation, outsourced computation or others), in which circumstances the participants usually has unbalanced computational ability/resources. In our opinion, future secure MPC will have new models related to uneven participants and additional requirements in the computation tasks.

Acknowledgement. We are grateful to the anonymous referees for their invaluable suggestions. This work is supported by the National Natural Science Foundation of China (Nos. 61272455), China 111 Project (No. B08038), Doctoral Fund of Ministry of Education of China (No.20130203110004), and Program for New Century Excellent Talents in University (No. NCET-13-0946). Besides, Lou's work is supported by US National Science Foundation under grant (CNS-1217889).

References

1. Atallah, M.J., Du, W.: Secure multi-party computational geometry. In: Dehne, F., Sack, J.-R., Tamassia, R. (eds.) WADS 2001. LNCS, vol. 2125, pp. 165–179. Springer, Heidelberg (2001)
2. Liu, L., Wu, C., Li, S.: Two privacy-preserving protocols for point-curve relation. Journal of Electronics (China) 29(5), 422–430 (2012)
3. Junglas, I.A., Watson, R.T.: Location-based services. Commun. ACM 51(3), 65–69 (2008)
4. Lien, I.T., Lin, Y.H., Shieh, J.R., Wu, J.L.: A novel privacy preserving location-based service protocol with secret circular shift for k-nn search. IEEE Transactions on Information Forensics and Security 8(6), 863–873 (2013)
5. Yao, A.C.C.: Protocols for secure computations. In: Proc. 23rd Ann. Symp. on Foudations of Computer Science, FOCS 1982, pp. 160–164 (1982)
6. Yao, A.C.C.: How to generate and exchange secrets. In: 27th Annual Symposium on Foundations of Computer Science, vol. 1986, pp. 162–167 (1986)
7. Goldreich, O., Micali, S., Wigderson, A.: How to play any mental game or a completeness theorem for protocols with honest majority. In: Proceedings of the Nineteenth Annual ACM Symposium on Theory of Computing, STOC 1987, pp. 218–229. ACM, New York (1987)
8. Mohassel, P., Franklin, M.K.: Efficiency tradeoffs for malicious two-party computation. In: Yung, M., Dodis, Y., Kiayias, A., Malkin, T. (eds.) PKC 2006. LNCS, vol. 3958, pp. 458–473. Springer, Heidelberg (2006)
9. Lindell, Y., Pinkas, B.: An efficient protocol for secure two-party computation in the presence of malicious adversaries. In: Naor, M. (ed.) EUROCRYPT 2007. LNCS, vol. 4515, pp. 52–78. Springer, Heidelberg (2007)
10. Woodruff, D.P.: Revisiting the efficiency of malicious two-party computation. In: Naor, M. (ed.) EUROCRYPT 2007. LNCS, vol. 4515, pp. 79–96. Springer, Heidelberg (2007)
11. Canetti, R.: Universally composable security: a new paradigm for cryptographic protocols. In: Proceedings of the 42nd IEEE Symposium on Foundations of Computer Science, 2001, pp. 136–145 (2001)
12. Horvitz, O., Katz, J.: Universally-composable two-party computation in two rounds. In: Menezes, A. (ed.) CRYPTO 2007. LNCS, vol. 4622, pp. 111–129. Springer, Heidelberg (2007)
13. Harnik, D., Ishai, Y., Kushilevitz, E.: How many oblivious transfers are needed for secure multiparty computation? In: Menezes, A. (ed.) CRYPTO 2007. LNCS, vol. 4622, pp. 284–302. Springer, Heidelberg (2007)
14. Ishai, Y., Kushilevitz, E., Paskin, A.: Secure multiparty computation with minimal interaction. In: Rabin, T. (ed.) CRYPTO 2010. LNCS, vol. 6223, pp. 577–594. Springer, Heidelberg (2010)
15. Ishai, Y., Kushilevitz, E., Ostrovsky, R., Sahai, A.: Zero-knowledge from secure multiparty computation. In: Proceedings of the Thirty-ninth Annual ACM Symposium on Theory of Computing, STOC 20707, pp. 21–30. ACM, New York (2007)
16. Ishai, Y., Kushilevitz, E., Ostrovsky, R., Sahai, A.: Zero-knowledge proofs from secure multiparty computation. SIAM Journal on Computing 39(3), 1121–1152 (2009)
17. Choi, S.G., Elbaz, A., Malkin, T., Yung, M.: Secure multi-party computation minimizing online rounds. In: Matsui, M. (ed.) ASIACRYPT 2009. LNCS, vol. 5912, pp. 268–286. Springer, Heidelberg (2009)
18. Asharov, G., Lindell, Y., Schneider, T., Zohner, M.: More efficient oblivious transfer and extensions for faster secure computation. In: Proceedings of the 2013 ACM SIGSAC Conference on Computer & Communications Security. CCS 2013, pp. 535–548. ACM, New York (2013)

19. Cramer, R., Damgård, I.B., Ishai, Y.: Share conversion, pseudorandom secret-sharing and applications to secure computation. In: Kilian, J. (ed.) TCC 2005. LNCS, vol. 3378, pp. 342–362. Springer, Heidelberg (2005)
20. Cramer, R., Damgård, I.B., Nielsen, J.B.: Multiparty computation from threshold homomorphic encryption. In: Pfitzmann, B. (ed.) EUROCRYPT 2001. LNCS, vol. 2045, pp. 280–300. Springer, Heidelberg (2001)
21. Damgård, I., Pastro, V., Smart, N., Zakarias, S.: Multiparty computation from somewhat homomorphic encryption. In: Safavi-Naini, R., Canetti, R. (eds.) CRYPTO 2012. LNCS, vol. 7417, pp. 643–662. Springer, Heidelberg (2012)
22. Malkhi, D., Nisan, N., Pinkas, B., Sella, Y.: Fairplay-secure two-party computation system. In: USENIX Security Symposium, pp. 287–302 (2004)
23. Ben-David, A., Nisan, N., Pinkas, B.: Fairplaymp: A system for secure multi-party computation. In: Proceedings of the 15th ACM Conference on Computer and Communications Security, pp. 257–266. ACM (2008)
24. Henecka, W., Kögl, S., Sadeghi, A.R., Schneider, T., Wehrenberg, I.: Tasty: Tool for automating secure two-party computations. In: Proceedings of the 17th ACM Conference on Computer and Communications Security, CCS 2010, pp. 451–462. ACM, New York (2010)
25. Huang, Y., Katz, J., Evans, D.: Efficient secure two-party computation using symmetric cut-and-choose. In: Canetti, R., Garay, J.A. (eds.) CRYPTO 2013, Part II. LNCS, vol. 8043, pp. 18–35. Springer, Heidelberg (2013)
26. Lindell, P.: Privacy preserving data mining. Journal of Cryptology 15(3), 177–206 (2002)
27. Li, S., Wang, D., Dai, Y.: Efficient secure multiparty computational geometry. Chinese Journal of Electronics 19(2), 324–328 (2010)
28. Luo, Y.L., Huang, L.S., Zhong, H.: Secure two-party point-circle inclusion problem. Journal of Computer Science and Technology 22(1), 88–91 (2007)
29. Hazay, C., Lindell, Y.: Efficient protocols for set intersection and pattern matching with security against malicious and covert adversaries. In: Canetti, R. (ed.) TCC 2008. LNCS, vol. 4948, pp. 155–175. Springer, Heidelberg (2008)
30. Hazay, C., Nissim, K.: Efficient set operations in the presence of malicious adversaries. Journal of Cryptology 25(3), 383–433 (2012)
31. Bunn, P., Ostrovsky, R.: Secure two-party k-means clustering. In: Proceedings of the 14th ACM Conference on Computer and Communications Security, CCS 2007, pp. 486–497. ACM, New York (2007)
32. Feigenbaum, J., Ishai, Y., Malkin, T., Nissim, K., Strauss, M.J., Wright, R.N.: Secure multiparty computation of approximations. ACM Trans. Algorithms 2(3), 435–472 (2006)
33. Chor, B., Kushilevitz, E., Goldreich, O., Sudan, M.: Private information retrieval. J. ACM 45(6), 965–981 (1998)
34. Yekhanin, S.: Private information retrieval. Commun. ACM 53(4), 68–73 (2010)
35. Naor, M., Pinkas, B., Sumner, R.: Privacy preserving auctions and mechanism design. In: Proceedings of the 1st ACM Conference on Electronic Commerce, EC 1999, pp. 129–139. ACM, New York (1999)
36. Dong, C., Chen, L., Wen, Z.: When private set intersection meets big data: An efficient and scalable protocol. In: Proceedings of the 2013 ACM SIGSAC Conference on Computer and Communications Security, CCS 2013, pp. 789–800. ACM, New York (2013)
37. Du, W., Atallah, M.J.: Secure multi-party computation problems and their applications: A review and open problems. In: Proceedings of the 2001 Workshop on New Security Paradigms, NSPW 2001, pp. 13–22. ACM, New York (2001)

Appendix

A Brief Note on the Simulation-Based Proof

The traditional simulation-based proofs take advantage of a simulator S to build a (computational indistinguishable) relationship between the real execution and the emulated execution. We now illustrate the major differences between the simulation-based proof and ours in order to indicate the reason why ours seems stronger. For the sake of simplicity, we just prove in Alice's stance as before.

To this end, assume that there are two simulator (resp. S_b and S_c) that execute the protocol with Alice. In simulation-based proof, we should prove that Alice's real view sequence $view_{real}$ is computationally indistinguishable from the ideal view sequence $view_{ideal}$. In the simulation procedures, the adversary is only given the output of the protocol function and access to simulators. For our proof, the most remarkable difference from the simulation-based proof is that we permit the access to the private inputs of others (only in proof, not in protocol). That is why restriction b) in $\mathbf{Game}_{A,\Pi}^{\text{ind-pps}}(n,\kappa)$ is needed. Otherwise, the adversary can win the game by directly comparing the two value

$$slope_0 = \frac{y_{c,0} - y_{b,0}}{x_{c,0} - x_{b,0}} \text{ and } slope_1 = \frac{y_{c,1} - y_{b,1}}{x_{c,1} - x_{b,1}}$$

from the computation of

$$slope_i = \frac{\text{Dec}_{SK_a}(CT_{a \leftarrow b,2}) - \text{Dec}_{SK_a}(CT_{a \leftarrow c,2})}{\text{Dec}_{SK_a}(CT_{a \leftarrow b,1}) - \text{Dec}_{SK_a}(CT_{a \leftarrow c,1})}$$

Besides, our proof supports another stronger change that the adversary can choose the protocol's output while the simulation-based ones do not have such ability. Moreover, due to the different game design mechanism, we prove security in different manner. For instance, some sequences in our proof are different from that in traditional proof which would result in different proofs. Take the third part Com_a in $sequence_{g_3}$ of $\mathbf{Game}_3$ as an example. In our proof, we replace the pseudorandom strings by random ones. It is on contrary to the simulation-based proof in which they prove indistinguishability without those changes.

Universally Composable Efficient Priced Oblivious Transfer from a Flexible Membership Encryption

Pratish Datta, Ratna Dutta, and Sourav Mukhopadhyay

Department of Mathematics
Indian Institute of Technology Kharagpur
Kharagpur-721302, India
{pratishdatta,ratna,sourav}@maths.iitkgp.ernet.in

Abstract. Membership encryption is a newly developed cryptographic primitive that combines membership proof and encryption into an unified setting. This paper presents a new flexible membership encryption scheme which is provably secure and significantly more efficient than the previous scheme. Further we apply our proposed membership encryption to construct a round optimal 1-out-of-n priced oblivious transfer (POT) protocol which, unlike the existing 1-out-of-n POT schemes, is proven secure under the universally composable (UC) security model and thus preserves security when it is executed with multiple protocol instances that run concurrently in an adversarily controlled way. Moreover, using our membership encryption, the POT protocol exhibits constant communication complexity on the buyer's side and $O(n)$ communication cost on the vendor's side, which is so far the best known in the literature.

Keywords: membership encryption, priced oblivious transfer, universally composable security, bilinear maps, non-interactive proof of knowledge, P-Signature, non-interactive range proof.

1   Introduction

Membership proof and *membership encryption* are two important cryptographic primitives of which membership encryption has been developed very recently. Membership proof [7], [2] is useful and nontrivial particularly when protecting the privacy is at prime concern. Membership encryption combines encryption and membership proof into a unified setting, thereby improving the communication efficiency. Further, while a membership proof cannot be converted to a membership encryption, a successful decryption of the ciphertext in membership encryption naturally serves as a proof of membership. The idea of membership encryption is that, if a message is encrypted using an attribute and a privacy preserving token for a group attribute, decryption of the ciphertext is possible if and only if the used attribute is a member of the used group attribute. The concept of membership encryption has been introduced by Guo et al. [12] and, to the best of our knowledge, is so far the only membership encryption available in

W. Susilo and Y. Mu (Eds.): ACISP 2014, LNCS 8544, pp. 98–114, 2014.
© Springer International Publishing Switzerland 2014

the literature. Membership encryption is applicable in advanced cryptographic protocols where privacy protection is important, e.g., priced oblivious transfer.

Priced oblivious transfer (POT) protocol aims at protecting the privacy of customers purchasing digital goods. More specifically, POT allows a buyer to purchase digital goods from a vendor without letting the vendor learn what it is buying. Usually after making a pre-payment to the vendor, the buyer engages in an unlimited number of transactions such that, as long as the buyer's balance contains sufficient funds it will successfully retrieve the selected item and its balance will be debited by the item's price. However, the buyer should be unable to retrieve an item whose cost exceeds its remaining balance.

The first 1-out-of-n priced oblivious transfer scheme [1], as well as subsequent works [15] analyse security in the half-simulation model, where simulation security is required against the buyer only and stand-alone privacy is needed against the vendor. Afterwards, a number of k-out-of-n priced oblivious transfer protocols have been proposed [13], [8], [14] of which only the scheme of [13] is proven secure in the universally composable (UC) security model. The UC-security paradigm [9] provides a framework for representing cryptographic protocols and analysing their security. Protocols that are proven UC-secure maintain their security even when they are run concurrently with an unbounded number of arbitrary protocol instances controlled by an adversary.

Our Contributions: Our contribution in this paper is two fold:
First, we introduce a cost-effective flexible membership encryption scheme secure in the standard model that outperforms the existing one [12]. To be precise, our membership encryption scheme is built on a prime order bilinear group setup. Our scheme is proven to be secure in the selective security model of [12] without using random oracles under the **Square Decisional Bilinear Diffie-Hellman** and **Simultaneous Square Decisional Bilinear Diffie-Hellman** assumptions. Unlike [12], our scheme is flexible in the sense that the universe of attributes can be changed at any time keeping the setup unaltered. This property is crucial for an application such as priced oblivious transfer where item prices may change with time. Further, our membership encryption has smaller (constant) group token and ciphertext sizes, as well as, lesser number of exponentiation and pairing computations compared to [12]. On a more positive note, our scheme, when applied with a fixed universe of attributes, results in constant computational cost.

Next, we apply our proposed membership encryption scheme to construct an 1-out-of-n priced oblivious transfer protocol that is UC-secure under the assumption that there is an honestly generated common reference string, employing Groth-Sahai non-interactive proof techniques [11], P-Signatures [3] and non-interactive range proof [13]. Security is proven in a static corruption model without relying on random oracles. Our protocol allows more than one item to have the same price. After an initialization of complexity $O(n)$, each transfer phase is optimal in terms of rounds of communication. Moreover, the complexities of computation and communication are constant on the buyer's side whereas $O(n)$ on the vendor's side – the best known in the literature for 1-out-of-n POT.

2   Preliminaries

2.1   Bilinear Maps and Complexity Assumptions

Let $\mathbb{G}$ and $\mathbb{G}_T$ be multiplicative groups of prime order p. A bilinear map $e : \mathbb{G} \times \mathbb{G} \to \mathbb{G}_T$ must satisfy the following properties:

(a) *Bilinearity* : A map $e : \mathbb{G} \times \mathbb{G} \to \mathbb{G}_T$ is bilinear if $e(a^x, b^y) = e(a, b)^{xy}$ for all $a, b \in \mathbb{G}$ and $x, y \in \mathbb{Z}_p$;

(b) *Non-degeneracy*: For all generators $g \in \mathbb{G}$, $e(g, g)$ generates $\mathbb{G}_T$;

(c) *Efficiency*: There exists an efficient algorithm that outputs the pairing group setup $(p, \mathbb{G}, \mathbb{G}_T, e, g)$ and an efficient algorithm to compute $e(a, b)$ for any $a, b \in \mathbb{G}$.

Definition 1. [Hidden Strong DH (HSDH)]: *On input $(g, g^\alpha) \in \mathbb{G}^2, u \in \mathbb{G}$, and a set of tuples $(g^{1/(\alpha + c_i)}, g^{c_i}, u^{c_i})_{i=1}^l$ for random exponents $\alpha \in \mathbb{Z}_p^*$, $c_1, \ldots, c_l \in \mathbb{Z}_p$, the l-**HSDH** assumption holds if it is computationally hard to output a new tuple $(g^{1/(\alpha + c)}, g^c, u^c)$ for $c \in \mathbb{Z}_p$.*

Definition 2. [Triple DH (TDH)]: *On input $(g, g^x, g^y) \in \mathbb{G}^3$ and a set of tuples $(c_i, g^{1/(x + c_i)})_{i=1}^l$ for random exponents $x, y \in \mathbb{Z}_p^*$, $c_1, \ldots, c_l \in \mathbb{Z}_p$, the l-**TDH** assumption holds if it is computationally hard to output a tuple $(g^{\mu x}, g^{\mu y}, g^{\mu x y})$ for $\mu \in \mathbb{Z}_p^*$.*

Definition 3. [Decisional Linear (DLIN)]: *On input $(g, g^a, g^b, g^{ac}, g^{bd}, z) \in \mathbb{G}^6$ for random exponents $a, b \in \mathbb{Z}_p^*$, $c, d \in \mathbb{Z}_p$, the **DLIN** assumption holds if it computationally hard to decide whether $z = g^{c+d}$.*

The validity of the **HSDH** assumption in the generic group model is proven by Boyen and Waters [6] and that of the **DLIN** assumption by Boneh et al. [4]. The **TDH** assumption has been introduced by Belenkiy et al. [3]. We introduce two new assumptions, viz., the **Square Decisional Bilinear DH** assumption, which is a derived version of the well-known **Decisional Bilinear DH (DBDH)** assumption introduced by Boneh and Francklin [5], and an extended version of that, namely, the **Simultaneous Square Decisional Bilinear DH** assumption.

Definition 4. [Square Decisional Bilinear DH (SqDBDH)]: *On input $(g, g^a, g^b, z) \in \mathbb{G}^3 \times \mathbb{G}_T$ for random exponents $a, b \in \mathbb{Z}_p^*$, the **SqDBDH** assumption holds if it computationally hard to decide whether $z = e(g, g)^{a^2 b}$.*

Definition 5. [Simultaneous Square Decisional Bilinear DH (SimSqD-BDH)]: *On input $(g, g^a, g^b, z_1, z_2) \in \mathbb{G}^3 \times \mathbb{G}_T^2$ for random exponents $a, b \in \mathbb{Z}_p^*$, the **SimSqDBDH** assumption holds if it is computationally hard to decide whether $z_1 = e(g, g)^{a^2 b}$ and $z_2 = e(g, g)^{ab^2}$.*

The **SqDBDH** problem and the **SimSqDBDH** problem in $(\mathbb{G}, \mathbb{G}_T, e)$ are no harder than the **DBDH** problem in $(\mathbb{G}, \mathbb{G}_T, e)$. However, in both cases, the converse is currently an open problem. Nonetheless, one can easily establish that the computational version of both of our new problems are exactly equivalent to the **Bilinear DH (BDH)** problem. We believe the **SqDBDH** and the **Sim-SqDBDH** assumptions hold in certain bilinear groups of prime order.

2.2 Non-interactive Zero-Knowledge Proofs of Knowledge of [11]

Let R be an efficiently computable relation and $L = \{y : R(y, w) = \text{accept for some } w\}$ be an NP-language. For tuples $(y, w) \in R$, we call y the instance and w the witness. A non-interactive proof of knowledge system consists of algorithms PoKSetup, PoKProve and PoKVerify. PoKSetup(1^λ) outputs a common reference string crs_{PoK}, PoKProve(crs_{PoK}, y, w) computes a proof of knowledge pok of instance y by using witness w and PoKVerify(crs_{PoK}, y, pok) outputs accept if pok is correct.

Zero-knowledge captures the notion that a verifier learns nothing from the proof except the truth of the statement. *Witness-indistinguishability* is a weaker property that guarantees that the verifier learns nothing about the witness that was used in the proof. In either case, we will also require *soundness*, meaning that an adversarial prover cannot convince an honest verifier of a false statement, and *completeness*, meaning that all correctly computed proofs are accepted by the honest verification algorithm.

In addition, a proof of knowledge needs to be extractable. *Extractability* means that $\exists$ a polynomial time extractor (PoKExtractSetup, PoKExtract). Algorithm PoKExtractSetup(1^λ) generates parameters crs_{PoK} that are identically distributed to the ones generated by algorithm PoKSetup and an extraction trapdoor td_{ext}. PoKExtract($crs_{PoK}, td_{ext}, y, pok$) extracts the witness w with all but negligible probability when PoKVerify(crs_{PoK}, y, pok) outputs accept.

We recall the notion of f-*extractability* defined by Belenkiy et al. [3]. In an f-extractable proof system the extractor PoKExtract extracts a value z such that $z = f(w) \wedge (y, w) \in R$ for some w. If $f(\cdot)$ is the identity function, we get the usual notion of extractability.

Commitment schemes: A non-interactive commitment scheme consists of algorithms ComSetup and Commit. ComSetup(1^λ) generates the parameters of the commitment scheme $params_{Com}$. The algorithm Commit($params_{Com}, x, open$) outputs a commitment C to x using auxiliary information $open$. A commitment C is opened by revealing $(x, open)$ and checking Commit($params_{Com}, x, open$) = C. A commitment scheme has a *hiding* property and a *binding* property. Informally speaking, the hiding property ensures that a commitment C to x does not reveal any information about x, whereas the binding property ensures that C cannot be opened to another value x'. When it is clear from the context, we omit the commitment parameters $params_{Com}$.

A notation for f-extractable non-interactive proofs of knowledge (NIPK): We are interested in NIPK about (unconditionally binding) commitments. By 'x in C' we denote that there exists *open* such that $C = \mathsf{Commit}(params_{Com}, x, open)$. After Belenkiy et al. [3], we use the following notation for an f-extractable NIPK *pok*, on the instance $(C_1, \ldots, C_m, \mathsf{Condition})$ with witness $(x_1, open_1, \ldots, x_m, open_m, s)$ that allows to extract all the witnesses except the openings of the commitments. Here Condition stands for a constraint on crs, $x_1, \ldots, x_m$, s.

$$\mathsf{NIPK}\{(x_1, \ldots, x_m, s) : \mathsf{Condition}(crs, x_1, \ldots, x_m, s) \wedge x_1 \text{ in } C_1 \wedge \ldots \wedge x_m \text{ in } C_m\}$$

The f-extractability of a NIPK ensures that, with overwhelming probability over the choice of crs, we can extract $(x_1, \ldots, x_m, s)$ from *pok*, when PoKVerify accepts, x_i is contained in commitment C_i, where $1 \le i \le m$, and $\mathsf{Condition}(crs, x_1, \ldots, x_m, s)$ is satisfied. To further abbreviate this notation, we omit crs when it is understood from the context.

Applying the notation to Groth-Sahai proofs: We now illustrate below the above equation by applying the notation to Groth-Sahai proofs [11] which allow proving statements about pairing product equations. The pairing group setup $(p, \mathbb{G}, \mathbb{G}_T, e, g)$ is part of the common reference string crs_{PoK} output by $\mathsf{PoKSetup}(1^\lambda)$ and the instance consists of the constants $\{\mathcal{A}_i\}_{i=1}^m \in \mathbb{G}$, $t_T \in \mathbb{G}_T$, $\{\gamma_{i,j}\}_{i,j=1}^m \in \mathbb{Z}_p$ of the pairing product equation: $\prod_{i=1}^m e(\mathcal{A}_i, \mathcal{Y}_i) \prod_{i=1}^m \prod_{j=1}^m e(\mathcal{Y}_i, \mathcal{Y}_j)^{\gamma_{i,j}} = t_T$. The prover knows $\{\mathcal{Y}_i\}_{i=1}^m$ satisfying this equation.

Internally, Groth-Sahai proofs prove relations between commitments. A homomorphism guarantees that the same relations also hold for the committed values. Normally, as the first step in creating the proof, the prover prepares commitments $\{C_i\}_{i=1}^m$ for all values $\mathcal{Y}_i$ in $\mathbb{G}$. Then, the instance, known to the prover and the verifier, is the pairing product equation alone, i.e., its constants.

In addition, it is possible to add pre-existing Groth-Sahai commitments $\{C_i\}_{i=1}^n, n \le m$, to the instance for some of the $\mathcal{Y}_i$ values. The corresponding openings $open_{\mathcal{Y}_i}$ become part of the witness. The proof will be computed in the same way, except that for values with existing commitments no fresh commitments need to be computed. We will write $C_i = \mathsf{Commit}(\mathcal{Y}_i, open_{\mathcal{Y}_i})$ to create Groth-Sahai commitments. Note that here Commit uses parameters contained in the crs_{PoK} of the Groth-Sahai proof systems. This proof system generates f-extractable witness indistinguishable[1] NIPK *pok* of the form

$$\mathsf{NIPK}\{(\mathcal{Y}_1, \ldots, \mathcal{Y}_n, \mathcal{Y}_{n+1}, \ldots, \mathcal{Y}_m) : \prod_{i=1}^m e(\mathcal{A}_i, \mathcal{Y}_i) \prod_{i=1}^m \prod_{j=1}^m e(\mathcal{Y}_i, \mathcal{Y}_j)^{\gamma_{i,j}} = t_T \wedge \mathcal{Y}_1 \text{ in }$$

$C_1 \wedge \ldots \wedge \mathcal{Y}_m \text{ in } C_m\}$. In order to construct NIPK for a system of pairing product equations, a separate proof is to be computed for each equation. In [11], Groth and Sahai have given three different instantiations of their proof system. (In fact, their proposed proof system also works in asymmetric pairing groups.) Groth-Sahai proofs are extractable, composable witness-indistinguishable and composable zero-knowledge (given certain conditions). For definitions of these notions the reader is referred to [11]. Out of the three instantiations presented

---

[1] Some classes of pairing product equations also admit zero-knowledge proofs.

in [11], we will consider the one based on the **DLIN** assumption for constructing our POT protocol.

2.3 P-Signature Scheme of [3]

P-Signatures introduced by Belenkiy et al. [3] are signatures equipped with a common reference string crs_{Sig} and a NIPK that allows proving possession of a signature of a committed message. Belenkiy et al. show in [3] how to use the Groth-Sahai proof system to build this proof. Since in their construction $M \in \mathbb{Z}_p$ and Groth-Sahai proofs prove knowledge of a witness in $\mathbb{G}$, they need to compute a bijection $F(M) \in \mathbb{G}$ and prove knowledge of $F(M)$. The P-Signature scheme is said to be F-unforgeable if no p.p.t. adversary can output $(F(M), s)$ without previously obtaining a signature on M.

Below we present the P-Signature scheme of [3]. This P-Signature scheme is employed in the range proof discussed in Section 2.4 and in our POT scheme.

PSetup: Taking as input a security parameter 1^λ, a trusted authority runs the Groth-Sahai PoKSetup under **DLIN** instance with input 1^λ to obtain crs_{PoK} for pairing groups $(p, \mathbb{G}, \mathbb{G}_T, e, g)$, picks random $u \in \mathbb{G}$, and publishes $crs_{Sig} = (crs_{PoK}, u)$.

PKeygen: On input crs_{Sig}, the signer picks a secret key $sk = (\alpha, \beta) \xleftarrow{\$} \mathbb{Z}_p$ and computes a public key $pk = (v, w) = (g^\alpha, g^\beta)$. Note that '$\xleftarrow{\$}$' stands for random selection.

PSign: The signer takes as input $(crs_{Sig}, sk, M \in \mathbb{Z}_p)$, picks random $r \xleftarrow{\$} \mathbb{Z}_p/\{\frac{\alpha - M}{\beta}\}$ and computes $s = (s_1, s_2, s_3) = (g^{1/(\alpha + M + \beta r)}, w^r, u^r)$.

PVerifySig: On input (crs_{Sig}, pk, M, s), verifier outputs accept if $e(s_1, vg^M s_2) = e(g, g)$, $e(u, s_2) = e(s_3, w)$. Otherwise, it outputs reject.

Using Groth-Sahai proofs, a NIPK of such a signature is constructed as follows. This is a proof of a pairing product equation of the form

$$\mathsf{NIPK}\{(g^M, u^M, s_1, s_2, s_3) : e(s_1, vg^M s_2) = e(g, g) \ \wedge e(u, s_2) = e(s_3, w) \ \wedge$$
$$e(u, g^M) = e(u^M, g)\}. \tag{1}$$

We abbreviate this expression as $\mathsf{NIPK}\{(g^M, u^M, s) : \mathsf{PVerifySig}(pk, s, M) = \mathsf{accept}\}$. We would like to highlight the fact that to construct this NIPK the knowledge of g^M and u^M is sufficient, no need to know M explicitly. This scheme is F-unforgeable $(F(M) = (g^M, u^M))$ under the **HSDH** and the **TDH** assumption.

2.4 Non-Interactive Range Proof of [13]

We use the efficient non-interactive range proof proposed by Rial et al. [13] to prove that a committed value $\sigma \in \mathbb{Z}_p$ lies in an interval $[0, d^a)$ by representing σ in base d and employing P-Signature of [3] discussed in Section 2.3.

RPSetup(1^λ): Given a security parameter 1^λ, a trusted third party executes **PSetup**(1^λ) to generate $crs_{Sig} = (crs_{PoK}, u)$.

RPInitVerifier(crs_{Sig}, A): The verifier takes as input $A = d^a$, and runs **PKeygen**(crs_{Sig}) to get (sk, pk). Then $\forall i \in \mathbb{Z}_d$, it computes $S_i = $ **PSign**(crs_{Sig}, sk, i). It outputs $params_{Range} = (pk, \{S_i\}_{i \in \mathbb{Z}_d})$.

RPInitProver($crs_{Sig}, params_{Range}$): Prover parses $params_{Range}$ as $(pk, \{S_i\}_{i \in \mathbb{Z}_d})$. It verifies the signatures by running **PVerifySig**(crs_{Sig}, pk, S_i, i), for all $i \in \mathbb{Z}_d$. If these verifications succeed, it outputs accept. Otherwise it outputs reject.

RangeProve($crs_{Sig}, params_{Range}, g, \sigma, open_\sigma$): The prover computes the following proof for a commitment $C_\sigma = $ Commit($g^\sigma, open_\sigma$):

$$\mathsf{NIPK}\{(g^\sigma, \{g^{\sigma_j}, u^{\sigma_j}, S_{\sigma_j}\}_{j=0}^{a-1}) : \{\mathbf{PVerifySig}(pk, S_{\sigma_j}, \sigma_j) = \mathsf{accept}\}_{j=0}^{a-1} \wedge$$

$$e(g, g^\sigma) \prod_{j=0}^{a-1} e(g^{-d^j}, g^{\sigma_j}) = 1 \wedge g^\sigma \text{ in } C_\sigma\}.$$

The short form $\mathsf{NIPK}\{(g^\sigma) : 0 \leq \sigma < A \wedge g^\sigma \text{ in } C_\sigma\}$ is used to refer to this proof. This proof is only witness indistinguishable. While this is sufficient for our application, it is possible to make the proof zero-knowledge using techniques described in [11].

3 Our Membership Encryption

As defined in [12], a membership encryption consists of four algorithms, viz., **MSetup**, **MGroupGen**, **MEncrypt** and **MDecrypt**, which for our scheme are described as follows.

MSetup: On input a security parameter 1^λ and universe of attributes $\mathbb{A} = \{A_1, \ldots, A_n\} \subseteq \mathbb{Z}_p$, a trusted authority runs the MSetup algorithm that works as follows:

- Choose a pairing group $\mathbb{PG} = (p, \mathbb{G}, \mathbb{G}_T, e, g)$.
- Select distinct $z_1, \ldots, z_n \xleftarrow{\$} \mathbb{Z}_p^*$ such that for all $i \neq j$, $z_i A_i \neq z_j A_j \mod p$ or equivalently $g^{z_i A_i} \neq g^{z_j A_j}$, and compute $u_i = g^{z_i}$, $u_{i,j} = g^{z_i z_j}$, $i, j = 1, 2, \ldots, n, i \neq j$.
- Publish the system parameter $\mathsf{SP} = (\mathbb{PG}, \{u_i\}_{i=1}^n, \{u_{i,j}\}_{i,j=1}^n)$.
$ i \neq j$

MGroupGen: The decryptor takes input a group attribute $\mathbf{G} = \{A_{i_1}, \ldots, A_{i_k}\} \subseteq \{A_1, \ldots, A_n\}$ for any $k \leq n$, the system parameter SP, and computes the group token $\mathcal{P}(\mathbf{G}) = (\prod_{l=1}^k u_{i_l}^{A_{i_l}})g^r = w$ (say), where $r \xleftarrow{\$} \mathbb{Z}_p$ is the secret key of the group token. The decryptor sends $\mathcal{P}(\mathbf{G})$ to the encryptor and keeps r secret to itself.

MEncrypt ($\mathcal{ME}$): Taking as input an attribute $A_{i^*} \in \mathbb{A}$, a group token $\mathcal{P}(\mathbf{G}) = w$, a message $M \in \mathbb{G}_T$ and the system parameter SP, the encryptor prepares the ciphertext as follows:

- Choose $S \xleftarrow{\$} \mathbb{Z}_p$.
- Compute the ciphertext $C = (C_1, C_2) = (e(w/u_{i^*}^{A_{i^*}}, u_{i^*}^S)M, g^S)$ and send C to the decryptor.

MDecrypt ($\mathcal{MD}$): On input the ciphertext $C = (C_1, C_2)$, the secret key r, the attribute A_{i^*}, the group attribute $\mathbf{G} = \{A_{i_1}, \ldots, A_{i_k}\}$ and the system parameter SP, the decryptor proceeds as follows:

- Compute $\Lambda = (\prod\limits_{\substack{l=1 \\ i_l \neq i^*}}^{k} u_{i^*, i_l}^{A_{i_l}})u_{i^*}^r$.

- Retrieve the message as $M = C_1/e(\Lambda, C_2)$.

• **Security Properties:** We adopt the security model of [12] to analyse security of our membership encryption. The security properties of our scheme are summarized in the following theorems. Due to space consideration we omit the proofs of Theorems 1 and 3 which can be found in the full version.

Theorem 1 (Indistinguishability against Secret Key). *The above membership encryption scheme is (t', q_k, ϵ')-selectively secure against secret key under the assumption that the **SimSqDBDH** problem is (t, ϵ)-hard. Here, $t' = t - O(q_k n t_e)$, q_k is number of group token query made by the adversary and $\epsilon' = \frac{\epsilon}{q_k}$, where t_e denotes the average time of an exponentiation in $\mathbb{G}$.*

Theorem 2 (Indistinguishability against Membership). *The membership encryption scheme introduced above is (t', ϵ')-selectively secure against membership under the assumption that the **SqDBDH** problem is (t, ϵ)-hard. Here, $t' = t - O(n^2 t_e)$ and $\epsilon' = \epsilon$, where t_e denotes the average time of an exponentiation in $\mathbb{G}$.*

Proof. Indistinguishability against membership is formally defined by the following game:

Setup: The challenger runs the MSetup algorithm to generate the system parameter SP and sends it to the adversary.

Challenge: The adversary gives the challenger an attribute A_{i^*}, a group token $\mathcal{P}(\mathbf{G}^*)$, group attribute $\mathbf{G}^*$, secret key $\mathbf{S}$ and two messages M_0, M_1. The challenger first verifies that $A_{i^*} \notin \mathcal{P}(\mathbf{G}^*)$ with $\mathbf{G}^*$ and $\mathbf{S}$. Then, the challenger responds by randomly choosing a coin $c \in \{0, 1\}$, generating a ciphertext $C^* \leftarrow \mathcal{ME}[A_{i^*}, \mathcal{P}(\mathbf{G}^*), M_c]$, and sending the challenge ciphertext to the adversary.

Win: The adversary outputs a guess c' of c and wins the game if $c' = c$.
A membership encryption is (t', ϵ')-selectively secure against membership if for all adversaries, whose running time is at most t' and who outputs A_{i^*}, $\mathbf{G}^*$ before

setup of the system parameter, the probability of winning the above game is at most ϵ' better than $1/2$.

Now, suppose there exist an adversary who can (t', ϵ') break the membership encryption against membership under selective security model. We construct an algorithm $\mathcal{B}$ that solves the **SqDBDH** problem in time t with advantage ϵ. $\mathcal{B}$ interacts with the adversary as follows:

Initialization: Let $\mathbb{PG} = (p, \mathbb{G}, \mathbb{G}_T, e, g)$ be the pairing group and $\mathbb{A} = \{A_1, \ldots, A_n\}$ be the attribute universe. The adversary outputs $(A_{i^*}, \mathbf{G}^*)$ for challenge where $A_{i^*} \notin \mathbf{G}^*$.

Setup: Let $(g^a, g^b, e(g, g)^{c_1})$ be the given instance of the **SqDBDH** problem. For $i = i^*$, $\mathcal{B}$ sets $u_{i^*} = g^a$. For $i \neq i^*$, $\mathcal{B}$ randomly chooses distinct $z_i \leftarrow \mathbb{Z}_p^*$ such that $g^{z_i A_i} \neq g^{z_j A_j} \neq g^{a A_{i^*}}$ for all $i \neq j \neq i^*$, and computes $u_i = g^{z_i}$. Also $\mathcal{B}$ sets $u_{i^*,j} = (g^a)^{z_j}, j \neq i^*$. For $i \neq i^*$, $\mathcal{B}$ computes $u_{i,j} = g^{z_i z_j}, i \neq j$. $\mathcal{B}$ sends the system parameter $\mathsf{SP} = (\mathbb{PG}, \{u_i\}_{i=1}^n, \{u_{i,j}\}_{\substack{i,j=1 \\ i \neq j}}^n)$ to the adversary.

Challenge: The adversary returns $(\mathcal{P}(\mathbf{G}^*), \mathbf{S}^*, M_0, M_1)$ for challenge. Let the secret randomness or the secret key in computation of $\mathcal{P}(\mathbf{G}^*)$ as sent by the adversary be $\mathbf{S}^* = r$ and $\mathbf{G}^* = \{A_{i_1}, \ldots, A_{i_k}\}$. $\mathcal{B}$ randomly chooses a coin $c \in \{0, 1\}$ and simulates the challenge ciphertext C^* as follows: $C^* = (C_1^*, C_2^*)$

$$= (M_c e((\prod_{l=1}^k u_{i^*,i_l}^{A_{i_l}}) u_{i^*}^r, g^b) e(g, g)^{-c_1 A_{i^*}}, g^b). \text{ If } c_1 = a^2 b \text{ then } C_1^* = M_c e(g, g)^{\eta},$$

where $\eta = a(\sum_{l=1}^k z_{i_l} A_{i_l} + r - a A_{i^*})b$, which implies that C^* is a valid ciphertext on M_c for $(A_{i^*}, \mathcal{P}(\mathbf{G}^*))$. $\mathcal{B}$ sends the ciphertext C^* to the adversary.

Win: The adversary outputs $c' \in \{0, 1\}$, and the algorithm $\mathcal{B}$ outputs 1 if $c' = c$, i.e., the adversary wins, and outputs 0 otherwise.

This completes the description of our simulation. If $c_1 = a^2 b$, the challenge ciphertext is valid and the adversary will output $c' = c$ with probability $(\frac{1}{2} + \epsilon')$; otherwise, the challenge ciphertext is universally random and the adversary outputs $c' = c$ with probability $\frac{1}{2}$. In order to see the relationship between t and t', note that the simulation time is mainly dominated by the $u_{i,j}$ simulation each of which takes 1 exponentiation and there are $O(n^2)$ such $u_{i,j}$'s.   □

Theorem 3 (Privacy). $\mathcal{P}(\mathbf{G})$ *unconditionally preserves the privacy of all attributes in* $\mathbf{G}$.

Remark 1. As in [12], the membership encryption described above is secure against chosen-plaintext attack (CPA). Using the Fujisaki-Okamoto approach [10] in the random oracle model, our scheme can also be extended to the security against chosen-ciphertext attack (CCA).

• **Efficiency:** Table 1 presents the computation and communication complexities of our membership encryption in comparison with that of [12]. Our construction has significantly less cost than [12] both in terms of computation and communication. In Particular, the number of exponentiations is much smaller in our scheme.

Table 1: Comparison Summary

Membership encryption	$\#E$	$\#P$	Public key size	Group token size	Ciphertext size
[12]	$(n^2 + 3n + 4k + 10)$ in $\mathbb{G}$, 2 in $\mathbb{G}_T$	3	$(n^2 + 3n + 3)$ in $\mathbb{G}$, 1 in $\mathbb{G}_T$	3 in $\mathbb{G}$	2 in $\mathbb{G}$, 1 in $\mathbb{G}_T$
Ours	$((n^2 + n)/2 + 2k + 3)$ in $\mathbb{G}$	2	$((n^2 + n)/2)$ in $\mathbb{G}$	1 in $\mathbb{G}$	1 in $\mathbb{G}$, 1 in $\mathbb{G}_T$

Here, $\#E$, $\#P$ and k denote respectively number of exponentiation, number of pairing and size of group attribute.

Note 1. Our membership encryption scheme has the advantage that, unlike [12] our scheme does not involve the attributes explicitly in the setup parameter. As a result, the same setup can be used for performing the operation using different universe of attributes $\mathbb{A}$ with the only restriction that $|\mathbb{A}| = n$ and A_i's are such that for all $i \neq j$, $g^{z_i A_i} \neq g^{z_j A_j}$ holds. In this sense our scheme is more flexible than that of [12] which can be applied only with an universe of attributes fixed before generation of the system parameters. This property makes our scheme particularly suitable for application in POT where item prices may change with time. Further, in case of our membership encryption, if the attribute universe $\mathbb{A}$ is fixed for the entire operation, then the **MGroupGen, MEncrypt** and **MDecrypt** algorithms will each require only a single exponentiation resulting in a scheme with constant computation complexity.

4   Our Priced Oblivious Transfer

In this section, we show how to construct an efficient 1-out-of-n priced oblivious transfer protocol (POT) from our membership encryption. Our 1-out-of-n POT scheme is inspired from the k-out-of-n POT scheme of [13]. To construct the POT we employ the Groth-Sahai proof system [11] for the **DLIN** instance (Section 2.2), the P-Signature scheme [3] (Section 2.3) and the range proof [13] (Section 2.4) with our membership encryption. In our scheme, each transaction (a single 'buy' operation) requires two passes of communication: (1) a message from the buyer; (2) the vendor's reply. Note that this is optimal. Also our scheme *allows more than one items to have the same price*.

Protocol requirements: Our scheme is parameterized with integers (n, l) (for the number of messages and their length), p_{max} (the upper bound for the prices) and $A = d^a$ (the upper bound for the deposit). This scheme is built on a pairing group setup $(p, \mathbb{G}, \mathbb{G}_T, e, g)$ such that $p_{max} < A \pmod{p}$ holds. As in [1], [13], we develop a prepaid scheme, where in the initialization phase the buyer $\mathcal{B}$ pays an initial deposit ac_0 to the vendor $\mathcal{V}$ and in subsequent transfer phases this deposit is subtracted by the price p_{σ_t} of the message M_{σ_t} that is being bought. The message space is $\{0,1\}^l$, but we abuse notation and write M_i to denote the corresponding group element in $\mathbb{G}_T$ assuming the existence of some efficient and invertible mapping. Also the prices p_i and the deposit ac_0 are considered as elements of $\mathbb{Z}_p$.

A secure POT scheme must ensure that $\mathcal{V}$ learns neither the price of the message being queried nor the new value of the account, while $\mathcal{B}$ pays the correct price for the message updating the balance honestly and that it has enough funds to buy it. Our POT scheme is proven secure in the universally composable security model of [9] with static corruption assuming the existence of an honestly generated common reference string. We formally describe our POT scheme below.

Initialization Phase: At time $t = 0$, on input $(sid, \mathcal{V}, n)$ for the vendor $\mathcal{V}$ and $(sid, \mathcal{B}, n, \mathsf{ac}_0)$ for the buyer $\mathcal{B}$, where sid is the session id of the particular instance of the POT protocol,

1. $\mathcal{V}$ queries $\mathcal{F}_{\mathsf{CRS}}$, the trusted third party or ideal functionality for generating common reference string crs, with $(sid, \mathcal{V}, \mathcal{B}, n)$. $\mathcal{F}_{\mathsf{CRS}}$ generates crs by running $\mathsf{POTGenCRS}(1^\lambda, p_{max}, A, n)$, as discussed below, and sends (sid, crs) to $\mathcal{V}$.

   $\mathsf{POTGenCRS}(1^\lambda, p_{max}, A, n)$: Given security parameter 1^λ and the total number of messages n,
   - $\mathcal{F}_{\mathsf{CRS}}$ generates a Groth-Sahai reference string crs_{PoK} under DLIN instance for the pairing group setup $(p, \mathbb{G}, \mathbb{G}_T, e, g)$ such that $p_{max} < A \pmod{p}$ holds, i.e., $crs_{PoK} = (t_1, t_2, t_3)$, where $t_1 = (g^\alpha, 1, g), t_2 = (1, g^\beta, g), t_3 = (g^{r\alpha}, g^{s\beta}, g^{r+s}) = (y_1, y_2, y_3)$, say, where $\alpha, \beta \xleftarrow{\$} \mathbb{Z}_p^*$ and $r, s \xleftarrow{\$} \mathbb{Z}_p$.
   - $\mathcal{F}_{\mathsf{CRS}}$ picks distinct random $z_1, \ldots, z_n \in \mathbb{Z}_p^*$ and computes $u_i = g^{z_i}, u_{i,j} = g^{z_i z_j}, i, j = 1, 2, \ldots, n, i \neq j$. $\mathcal{F}_{\mathsf{CRS}}$ also computes $v_i = y_3^{z_i}, i = 1, 2, \ldots, n$.
   - $\mathcal{F}_{\mathsf{CRS}}$ chooses random $u \leftarrow \mathbb{G}$ and computes $q_i = u^{z_i}, i = 1, \ldots, n$.
   - $\mathcal{F}_{\mathsf{CRS}}$ runs $\mathbf{PKeyGen}(crs_{Sig})$ of the **P**-Signature scheme, discussed in Section 2.3, where $crs_{Sig} = (crs_{PoK}, u)$ to get a signing-verification key pair $(sk = (\gamma, \delta), pk = (g^\gamma, g^\delta))$, $\gamma, \delta \xleftarrow{\$} \mathbb{Z}_p$, and for all $i \in \{1, \ldots, n\}$, it computes $s_i = \mathbf{PSign}(crs_{Sig}, sk, z_i)$.
   - $\mathcal{F}_{\mathsf{CRS}}$ sets $crs = (crs_{PoK}, \{u_i\}_{i=1}^n, \{u_{i,j}\}_{\substack{i,j=1 \\ i \neq j}}^n, \{v_i\}_{i=1}^n, u, pk, \{(q_i, s_i)\}_{i=1}^n)$.

   We mention that v_i's help $\mathcal{B}$ to decrypt the ciphertext sent by $\mathcal{V}$ and (u_i, q_i, s_i) is used to construct a non-interactive proof of possession of the P-Signature s_i on z_i by $\mathcal{B}$ without knowing z_i, as explained in Section 2.3, in the transfer phase.
2. $\mathcal{B}$ queries $\mathcal{F}_{\mathsf{CRS}}$ with $(sid, \mathcal{V}, \mathcal{B}, n)$. $\mathcal{F}_{\mathsf{CRS}}$ sends (sid, crs) to $\mathcal{B}$. This crs is the same as that generated by $\mathcal{F}_{\mathsf{CRS}}$ following the procedure $\mathsf{POTGenCRS}$.
3. $\mathcal{V}$ runs the following procedure $\mathsf{POTInitVendor}(crs, A)$ to obtain $params_{Range}$ and sends $(sid, params_{Range})$ to $\mathcal{B}$.

   $\mathsf{POTInitVendor}(crs, A)$: Taking input crs and A, $\mathcal{V}$ works as follows:
   - $\mathcal{V}$ parses the crs to obtain $crs_{Sig} = (crs_{PoK}, u)$.
   - $\mathcal{V}$ runs $\mathsf{RPInitVerifier}(crs_{Sig}, A)$, as per Section 2.4, to get $params_{Range}$.

4. Upon receiving $(sid, params_{Range})$ from $\mathcal{V}$, the buyer $\mathcal{B}$ computes $(P, D_0^{(Priv)})$ by invoking POTInitBuyer on input $(crs, params_{Range}, \mathsf{ac}_0)$ as follows. POTInitBuyer$(crs, params_{Range}, \mathsf{ac}_0)$: On input $params_{Range}$ and a deposit $\mathsf{ac}_0 \in [0, \ldots, A)$;

   - $\mathcal{B}$ parses crs to obtain $crs_{Sig} = (crs_{PoK}, u)$.
   - $\mathcal{B}$ runs RPInitProver$(crs_{Sig}, params_{Range})$, discussed in Section 2.4 , to verify $params_{Range}$.
   - If the above check fails, $\mathcal{B}$ outputs reject. Otherwise, $\mathcal{B}$ sets $P = \mathsf{ac}_0$ and $D_0^{(Priv)} = (\mathsf{ac}_0, open_{\mathsf{ac}_0} = (0,0,0))$.

   $\mathcal{B}$ aborts if the output is reject. Otherwise, $\mathcal{B}$ sends (sid, P) to $\mathcal{V}$ and keeps $D_0^{(Priv)}$. Note that, $\mathcal{B}$ also needs to pay an amount of ac_0 to $\mathcal{V}$ through an arbitrary payment channel.

5. After getting the initial deposit money, $\mathcal{V}$ runs POTGetDeposit(crs, P, A) described below to check that ac_0 corresponds to amount of money received. POTGetDeposit(crs, P, A): Receiving P from $\mathcal{B}$, $\mathcal{V}$ works as follows:

   - $\mathcal{V}$ checks that $\mathsf{ac}_0 \in [0, \ldots, A)$
   - $\mathcal{V}$ sets $D_0 = \mathsf{Commit}(g^{\mathsf{ac}_0}, open_{\mathsf{ac}_0} = (0,0,0)) = (1, 1, g^{\mathsf{ac}_0})$.

6. $\mathcal{V}$ stores state information $V_0 = (params_{Range}, D_0)$ and $\mathcal{B}$ stores state information $B_0 = (params_{Range}, D_0^{(Priv)})$.

Transfer Phase: At time $t > 0$ $(t = 1, 2, \ldots)$, $\mathcal{V}$ with state information V_{t-1} and input $(sid, \mathcal{V}, \{M_1, M_2, \ldots, M_n\}, \{p_1, p_2, \ldots, p_n\})$ and $\mathcal{B}$ with state information B_{t-1} and input $(sid, \mathcal{B}, \{p_1, p_2, \ldots, p_n\}, \sigma_t)$ interact as follows. Here M_i's and p_i's are the messages for sale and their corresponding prices such that, for all $i \neq j$, $g^{z_i p_i} \neq g^{z_j p_j}$. Note that this can always be done while selecting p_i's. For instance, if it is found that $g^{z_i p_i} = g^{z_j p_j}$ for some $i \neq j$, then one can choose $p_i = p_i + 1$ etc.

1. $\mathcal{B}$ invokes POTRequest$(crs, params_{Range}, \{p_1, \ldots, p_n\}, D_{t-1}^{(Priv)}, \sigma_t)$ to set a request Q and to generate private state $(Q^{(Priv)}, D_t^{(Priv)})$ as detailed below. $\mathcal{B}$ sends (sid, Q) to $\mathcal{V}$ and stores $(sid, Q^{(Priv)}, D_t^{(Priv)})$ as private information. POTRequest$(crs, params_{Range}, \{p_1, \ldots, p_n\}, D_{t-1}^{(Priv)}, \sigma_t)$: Taking input set of prices $\{p_1, \ldots, p_n\}$ and a selection value $\sigma_t \in \{1, \ldots, n\}$, $\mathcal{B}$ proceeds as follows:

   - $\mathcal{B}$ parses crs to obtain $crs_{PoK}, u, \{u_i\}_{i=1}^n, pk, \{(q_i, s_i)\}_{i=1}^n$.
   - $\mathcal{B}$ parses $D_{t-1}^{(Priv)}$ as $(\mathsf{ac}_{t-1}, open_{\mathsf{ac}_{t-1}} = (l_{t-1,1}, l_{t-1,2}, l_{t-1,3}))$, where $(l_{t-1,1}, l_{t-1,2}, l_{t-1,3}) \in \mathbb{Z}_p^3$, and obtains $D_{t-1} = \mathsf{Commit}(g^{\mathsf{ac}_{t-1}}, open_{\mathsf{ac}_{t-1}})$ $= (g^{\alpha(l_{t-1,1}+rl_{t-1,3})}, g^{\beta(l_{t-1,2}+sl_{t-1,3})}, g^{l_{t-1,1}+l_{t-1,2}+(r+s)l_{t-1,3}} g^{\mathsf{ac}_{t-1}})$.
   - $\mathcal{B}$ also picks fresh $open_{p_{\sigma_t}} = (a_1, a_2, a_3)$, $open_{z_{\sigma_t}} = (b_1, b_2, b_3)$, $open_{z_{\sigma_t} p_{\sigma_t}} = (r_1, r_2, r_3)$, $open_{\mathsf{ac}_t} = (l_{t,1}, l_{t,2}, l_{t,3})$ randomly from $\mathbb{Z}_p^3$, where $\mathsf{ac}_t = \mathsf{ac}_{t-1} - p_{\sigma_t}$ and computes $D_t = \mathsf{Commit}(g^{\mathsf{ac}_t}, open_{\mathsf{ac}_t})$, $h_1 = \mathsf{Commit}(g^{p_{\sigma_t}}, open_{p_{\sigma_t}})$, $h_2 = \mathsf{Commit}(u_{\sigma_t}, open_{z_{\sigma_t}})$, $h_3 = \mathsf{Commit}(g^{z_{\sigma_t} p_{\sigma_t}}, open_{z_{\sigma_t} p_{\sigma_t}})$ as above for D_{t-1}.

- $\mathcal{B}$ runs PoKProve on input crs_{PoK} to compute a witness indistinguishable proof pok_t following approaches discussed in Section 2.2:

$$\mathsf{NIPK}\{(g^{\mathsf{ac}_t}, g^{\mathsf{ac}_t-1}, g^{p_{\sigma_t}}, u_{\sigma_t}, g^{z_{\sigma_t}p_{\sigma_t}}, q_{\sigma_t}, s_{\sigma_t}) : 0 \le \mathsf{ac}_t < A \wedge$$
$$e(g, g^{\mathsf{ac}_t-1})e(g^{-1}, g^{\mathsf{ac}_t})e(g^{-1}, g^{p_{\sigma_t}}) = 1 \wedge$$
$$e(g, g^{z_{\sigma_t}p_{\sigma_t}})e(u_{\sigma_t}, g^{p_{\sigma_t}})^{-1} = 1 \wedge$$
$$\mathbf{PVerifySig}(pk, s_{\sigma_t}, z_{\sigma_t}) = \text{accept} \wedge \mathsf{ac}_t \text{ in } D_t \wedge$$
$$\mathsf{ac}_{t-1} \text{ in } D_{t-1} \wedge p_{\sigma_t} \text{ in } h_1 \wedge u_{\sigma_t} \text{ in } h_2 \wedge g^{z_{\sigma_t}p_{\sigma_t}} \text{ in } h_3\} \quad (2)$$

Note that pok_t includes range proof $\mathsf{NIPK}\{(g^{\mathsf{ac}_t}) : 0 \le \mathsf{ac}_t < A\} = \mathsf{NIPK}\{(g^{\mathsf{ac}_t}, \{g^{\alpha_j}, u^{\alpha_j}, s'_{\alpha_j}\}_{j=0}^{a-1}) : \{\mathbf{PVerifySig}(pk', s'_{\alpha_j}, \alpha_j) = \text{accept}\}_{j=0}^{a-1}$
$$\wedge \, e(g, g^{\mathsf{ac}_t}) \prod_{j=0}^{a-1} e(g^{-d^j}, g^{\alpha_j}) = 1 \wedge g^{\mathsf{ac}_t} \text{ in } D_t\}, \text{ for } \mathsf{ac}_t \text{ committed in } D_t,$$

where pk' and $\{g^{\alpha_j}, u^{\alpha_j}, s'_{\alpha_j}\}_{j=0}^{a-1}$ are contained in $params_{Range}$ sent by $\mathcal{V}$ during the initialization phase and $\mathsf{ac}_t = \sum_{j=0}^{a-1} \alpha_j d^j$. Also pok_t contains a non-interactive proof of possession of the P-Signature s_{σ_t} on z_{σ_t} using u_{σ_t} and q_{σ_t} following equation 1 of Section 2.3.

- $\mathcal{B}$ sets $Q = (h_1, h_2, h_3, pok_t, D_t)$, $Q^{(Priv)} = (\sigma_t, open_{z_{\sigma_t}p_{\sigma_t}})$ and $D_t^{(Priv)} = (\mathsf{ac}_t, open_{\mathsf{ac}_t})$.

2. Upon receiving (sid, Q) from $\mathcal{B}$, $\mathcal{V}$ runs POTRespond on input $(crs, \{M_1, \ldots, M_n\}, \{p_1, \ldots, p_n\}, D_{t-1}, Q)$ to obtain a response R and state D_t as explained below. $\mathcal{V}$ sends (sid, R) to $\mathcal{B}$ and stores (sid, D_t).
POTRespond$(crs, \{M_1, \ldots, M_n\}, \{p_1, \ldots, p_n\}, parms_{Range}, D_{t-1}, Q)$: Taking input $params_{Range}$, a set of messages $\{M_1, \ldots, M_n\}$ with prices $\{p_1, \ldots, p_n\}$, state information D_{t-1} and a request Q, $\mathcal{V}$ works as follows:

- $\mathcal{V}$ parses crs to get $(crs_{PK}, u, \{u_i\}_{i=1}^n, pk)$, Q to get $(h_1, h_2, h_3, pok_t, D_t)$.
- $\mathcal{V}$ verifies pok_t by running PoKVarify on input crs_{PoK} and it aborts if the output is reject. For this verification, $\mathcal{V}$ uses the commitments $(h_1, h_2, h_3, D_{t-1}, D_t)$. For a clear insight regarding such verifications the reader is refer to [11].
- $\mathcal{V}$ parses $h_3 = (w_1, w_2, w_3) = (g^{\alpha(r_1+rr_3)}, g^{\beta(r_2+sr_3)}, g^{z_{\sigma_t}p_{\sigma_t}} g^{r_1+r_2+(r+s)r_3})$ where $open_{z_{\sigma_t}p_{\sigma_t}} = (r_1, r_2, r_3) \in \mathbb{Z}_p^3$ is not known to $\mathcal{V}$. Note that w_3 can be written as $w_3 = g^{z_{\sigma_t}p_{\sigma_t}} g^b$, where $b = r_1 + r_2 + (r+s)r_3 \in \mathbb{Z}_p$ is random since $open_{z_{\sigma_t}p_{\sigma_t}} = (r_1, r_2, r_3) \in \mathbb{Z}_p^3$ is random. Thus w_3 can be viewed as a group token $\mathcal{P}(\mathbf{G})$ for group attribute $\mathbf{G} = \{p_{\sigma_t}\}$ according to our membership encryption introduced in Section 3. However, in this case we are only able to guarantee computational privacy of the group token since the group token in this case is actually part of a commitment of the Groth-Sahai proof system which has computational witness indistinguishability, whereas, in the original membership encryption scheme, the privacy of group tokens is unconditional.

- For $i = 1, \ldots, n$, $\mathcal{V}$ selects random $S_i \leftarrow \mathbb{Z}_p$ and computes $C_i = (C_i^{(1)}, C_i^{(2)}) = (e(w_3/u_i^{p_i}, u_i^{S_i})M_i, g^{S_i})$. Note that, C_i is essentially the membership encryption of M_i using p_i and the group token w_3 for $\{p_{\sigma_t}\}$.
- $\mathcal{V}$ sets $R = (C_1, \ldots, C_n)$.

3. $\mathcal{B}$, upon receiving (sid, R) from $\mathcal{V}$, runs the following procedure POTComplete on input $crs, R, Q^{(Priv)}$ to obtain M_{σ_t}.

   POTComplete$(crs, R, Q^{(Priv)})$: Taking input R and private state $Q^{(Priv)}$,

   - $\mathcal{B}$ extracts $(crs_{PoK}, \{u_i\}_{i=1}^{n}, \{v_i\}_{i=1}^{n}, \{u_{i,j}\}_{\substack{i,j=1 \\ i \neq j}}^{n})$ from crs, parses R as $(C_1, \ldots, C_n)$, $Q^{(Priv)}$ as $(\sigma_t, open_{z_{\sigma_t}p_{\sigma_t}})$ where $open_{z_{\sigma_t}p_{\sigma_t}} = (r_1, r_2, r_3) \in \mathbb{Z}_p^3$ is known to $\mathcal{B}$.

   - $\mathcal{B}$ parses C_{σ_t} as $(C_{\sigma_t}^{(1)}, C_{\sigma_t}^{(2)})$ and it retrieves the message $M_{\sigma_t} = C_{\sigma_t}^{(1)}/e(u_{\sigma_t}^{r_1+r_2}v_{\sigma_t}^{r_3}, C_{\sigma_t}^{(2)})$.

4. $\mathcal{V}$ stores state information $V_t = (params_{Range}, D_t)$ and $\mathcal{B}$ stores state information $B_t = (params_{range}, D_t^{(Priv)})$ and outputs (sid, M_{σ_t}).

Theorem 4. *The priced oblivious transfer protocol described above securely realizes $\mathcal{F}_{POT}$, the ideal functionality for POT, under $\{max\{n, d\}\}$-**HSDH**, $\{max\{n, d\}\}$-**TDH**, **DLIN** and **SqDBDH** assumptions, where $n = $ number of messages and $A = d^a$ is the upper bound of the buyer's account.*

The proof of Theorem 4 is available in the full version.

• **A note on efficiency:** The common reference string of our POT protocol consists of $n^2 + 6n + 12$ group elements. Regarding the communication complexity of this scheme, we note that, in the initialization phase $\mathcal{V}$'s message contains $3d + 2$ group elements, which is the size of $params_{Range}$, and that of $\mathcal{B}$ involves a single element of $\mathbb{Z}_p$. In each transfer phase $\mathcal{B}$'s request Q is composed of $30a + 57$ group elements and $\mathcal{V}$'s response R has $2n$ group elements. For the computational complexity of our POT scheme, observe that the initialization phase requires $n^2 + 6n + 7$ exponentiations for $\mathcal{F}_{CRS}$, $3d + 3$ exponentiations for $\mathcal{V}$ and d exponentiations along with $3d$ pairings for $\mathcal{B}$. Further, each transfer phase involves 2 exponentiations, 1 pairings plus the complexity of constructing the NIPK (2), which involves the cost of generating a range proof, a non-interactive proof of a P-Signature possession and Groth-Sahai non-interactive proof of knowledge for two additional pairing product equations, for $\mathcal{B}$ and $3n$ exponentiations, $n + 87a + 174$ pairings for $\mathcal{V}$. We note that $A = d^a$ is the upper bound of buyer's account.

Remark 2. Observe that, since in our POT construction the membership encryption discussed in Section 3 is applied for singleton group attributes $\{p_{\sigma_t}\}$, $u_{i,j}$'s are not required for decrypting the ciphertext C_{σ_t}. Thus we can omit $\{u_{i,j}\}_{i \neq j}$ from the crs resulting in further reduction in crs size as well as the number of exponentiations computed by $\mathcal{F}_{CRS}$ by n^2. This modification will not affect the security argument.

5   Extending Our Priced Oblivious Transfer to Subscription Setting

The motivation of a subscription is to allow efficient one-way communication from the vendor to the buyer. By subscribing to a particular index, the buyer indicates that it wishes to continue buying the item with that chosen index until overriding the subscription with a new request, provided its balance contains sufficient funds, or unsubscribing, i.e., terminating a previous 'subscribe' request. Here we will briefly sketch how our proposed POT can be modified to fit in a 'subscription' setting. We assume that for subscription a buyer $\mathcal{B}$ is charged the same price p_i for the i-th message effective at time of subscription even if prices may change over time. To initialize the protocol first both the vendor $\mathcal{V}$ and the buyer $\mathcal{B}$ takes crs from $\mathcal{F}_{\mathsf{CRS}}$ and $\mathcal{V}$ sends $(sid, params_{Range})$ to $\mathcal{B}$ by executing POTInitVendor as in the POT of Section 4. In the subscription scenario we have the following operations:

Subscribing: The buyer $\mathcal{B}$ computes $(P, D_0^{(Priv)})$ by running POTInitBuyer on input $(crs, params_{Range}, \mathsf{ac}_0)$, chooses an index σ to subscribe and a time period τ to subscribe. Now $\mathcal{B}$ picks $open_{p_\sigma}, open_{z_\sigma}, open_{z_\sigma p_\sigma}, \{open_{ac_t}\}_{t=1}^{\tau}$ randomly from $\mathbb{Z}_p^3$ and computes $h_1 = \mathsf{Commit}(g^{p_\sigma}, open_{p_\sigma}), h_2 = \mathsf{Commit}(u_\sigma, open_{z_\sigma}), h_3 = \mathsf{Commit}(g^{z_\sigma p_\sigma}, open_{z_\sigma p_\sigma}), D_t = \mathsf{Commit}(g^{ac_t}, open_{ac_t}), t = 1, \ldots, \tau$. Also for $t = 1, \ldots, \tau$, $\mathcal{B}$ runs PoKProve introduced in Section 2.2 on input crs_{PoK} to obtain non-interactive proof of knowledge pok_t:

$\mathsf{NIPK}\{(g^{\mathsf{ac}_t}, g^{\mathsf{ac}_{t-1}}, g^{p_\sigma}, u_\sigma, g^{z_\sigma p_\sigma}, q_\sigma, s_\sigma) : 0 \leq \mathsf{ac}_t < A \wedge$

$$e(g, g^{\mathsf{ac}_{t-1}})e(g^{-1}, g^{\mathsf{ac}_t})e(g^{-1}, g^{p_\sigma}) = 1 \wedge e(g, g^{z_\sigma p_\sigma})e(u_\sigma, g^{p_\sigma})^{-1} = 1 \wedge$$

PVerifySig$(pk, s_\sigma, z_\sigma) = \mathsf{accept} \wedge \mathsf{ac}_t$ in $D_t \wedge \mathsf{ac}_{t-1}$ in $D_{t-1} \wedge$

p_σ in $h_1 \wedge u_\sigma$ in $h_2 \wedge g^{z_\sigma p_\sigma}$ in $h_3\}$.

$\mathcal{B}$ sets $Q = (h_1, h_2, h_3, \{(pok_t, D_t)\}_{t=1}^{\tau})$, $Q^{(Priv)} = (\sigma, open_{z_\sigma p_\sigma})$ and $\{D_t^{(Priv)} = (\mathsf{ac}_t, open_{\mathsf{ac}_t})\}_{t=0}^{\tau}$. $\mathcal{B}$ sends (sid, P, Q, τ) to $\mathcal{V}$ and stores $(Q^{(Priv)}, \{D_t^{(priv)}\}_{t=0}^{\tau})$.

The vendor $\mathcal{V}$ runs $D_0 \leftarrow$ POTGetDeposit(crs, P, A) as in our POT protocol of Section 4. $\mathcal{V}$ sets $D = (Q, \tau)$ after checking whether it really has received τ number of (pok_t, D_t)'s.

Maintaining a Subscription: At time $t > 0$ following a subscription, $\mathcal{V}$ runs POTRespond on input D_{t-1}, Q_t where $Q_t = (h_1, h_2, h_3, pok_t, D_t)$, sends response (sid, R_t) to $\mathcal{B}$ and sets $D = (h_1, h_2, h_3, \{pok_j\}_{j=t+1}^{\tau}, \{D_j\}_{j=t}^{\tau}, \tau - t)$.

Upon receiving (sid, R_t), $\mathcal{B}$ executes POTComplete$(crs, R_t, Q^{(Priv)})$ to obtain $M_\sigma^{(t)}$. Also $\mathcal{B}$ updates $D_t^{(Priv)} = \{(\mathsf{ac}_j, open_{\mathsf{ac}_j})\}_{j=t}^{\tau}$.

Unsubscribing: After time τ (for which $\mathcal{B}$ has subscribed), $\mathcal{V}$ finds $D = (h_1, h_2, h_3, \phi, \{D_\tau\}, 0)$ and hence, $\mathcal{V}$ automatically unsubscribes $\mathcal{B}$. However, if $\mathcal{B}$ wants to unsubscribe after l transfers, where $l < \tau$, then $\mathcal{V}$ sends $(sid, \{D_t\}_{t=l}^{\tau})$ to $\mathcal{B}$. Here D_l contains $\mathcal{B}$'s remaining balance after l-th transaction. $\mathcal{B}$ can open the commitment D_l to any trusted third party or the court of law to claim his remaining balance from $\mathcal{V}$. Note that, since Groth-Sahai commitments are perfectly binding, $\mathcal{B}$ cannot open D_l to any value other than ac_l.

6   Conclusion

In this paper we have constructed a new efficient, provably secure membership encryption scheme and have applied it to develop an efficient 1-out-of-n POT protocol. Our proposed membership encryption has constant length group token and constant ciphertext size both of which is shorter than that of [12], as well as, it computationally outperforms [12]. Also unlike [12], our scheme is flexible in the sense that the same setup can be used with different universe of attributes. This property is important for applications such as POT where item prices may change with time. Our developed POT protocol is secure under universally composable framework and thus, unlike the existing 1-out-of-n schemes [1], [15] available in the literature, preserves security when it is executed with multiple protocol instances that run concurrently in an adversarily controlled way. Further, the protocol is round optimal having constant computation and communication cost on the buyer's side and $O(n)$ complexity on the vendor's side, which is so far the best known for 1-out-of-n POT.

References

1. Aiello, B., Ishai, Y., Reingold, O.: Priced oblivious transfer: How to sell digital goods. In: Pfitzmann, B. (ed.) EUROCRYPT 2001. LNCS, vol. 2045, pp. 119–135. Springer, Heidelberg (2001)
2. Au, M.H., Tsang, P.P., Susilo, W., Mu, Y.: Dynamic universal accumulators for ddh groups and their application to attribute-based anonymous credential systems. In: Fischlin, M. (ed.) CT-RSA 2009. LNCS, vol. 5473, pp. 295–308. Springer, Heidelberg (2009)
3. Belenkiy, M., Chase, M., Kohlweiss, M., Lysyanskaya, A.: P-signatures and noninteractive anonymous credentials. In: Canetti, R. (ed.) TCC 2008. LNCS, vol. 4948, pp. 356–374. Springer, Heidelberg (2008)
4. Boneh, D., Boyen, X., Shacham, H.: Short group signatures. In: Franklin, M. (ed.) CRYPTO 2004. LNCS, vol. 3152, pp. 41–55. Springer, Heidelberg (2004)
5. Boneh, D., Franklin, M.: Identity-based encryption from the weil pairing. In: Kilian, J. (ed.) CRYPTO 2001. LNCS, vol. 2139, pp. 213–229. Springer, Heidelberg (2001)
6. Boyen, X., Waters, B.: Full-domain subgroup hiding and constant-size group signatures. In: Okamoto, T., Wang, X. (eds.) PKC 2007. LNCS, vol. 4450, pp. 1–15. Springer, Heidelberg (2007)
7. Camenisch, J.L., Chaabouni, R., Shelat, A.: Efficient protocols for set membership and range proofs. In: Pieprzyk, J. (ed.) ASIACRYPT 2008. LNCS, vol. 5350, pp. 234–252. Springer, Heidelberg (2008)
8. Camenisch, J., Dubovitskaya, M., Neven, G.: Unlinkable priced oblivious transfer with rechargeable wallets. In: Sion, R. (ed.) FC 2010. LNCS, vol. 6052, pp. 66–81. Springer, Heidelberg (2010)
9. Canetti, R.: Universally composable security: A new paradigm for cryptographic protocols. In: Proceedings of the 42nd IEEE Symposium on Foundations of Computer Science, 2001, pp. 136–145. IEEE (2001)

10. Fujisaki, E., Okamoto, T.: Secure integration of asymmetric and symmetric encryption schemes. In: Wiener, M. (ed.) CRYPTO 1999. LNCS, vol. 1666, pp. 537–554. Springer, Heidelberg (1999)
11. Groth, J., Sahai, A.: Efficient non-interactive proof systems for bilinear groups. In: Smart, N. (ed.) EUROCRYPT 2008. LNCS, vol. 4965, pp. 415–432. Springer, Heidelberg (2008)
12. Guo, F., Mu, Y., Susilo, W., Varadharajan, V.: Membership encryption and its applications. In: Boyd, C., Simpson, L. (eds.) ACISP. LNCS, vol. 7959, pp. 219–234. Springer, Heidelberg (2013)
13. Rial, A., Kohlweiss, M., Preneel, B.: Universally composable adaptive priced oblivious transfer. In: Shacham, H., Waters, B. (eds.) Pairing 2009. LNCS, vol. 5671, pp. 231–247. Springer, Heidelberg (2009)
14. Rial, A., Preneel, B.: Optimistic fair priced oblivious transfer. In: Bernstein, D.J., Lange, T. (eds.) AFRICACRYPT 2010. LNCS, vol. 6055, pp. 131–147. Springer, Heidelberg (2010)
15. Tobias, C.: Practical oblivious transfer protocols. In: Petitcolas, F.A.P. (ed.) IH 2002. LNCS, vol. 2578, pp. 415–426. Springer, Heidelberg (2003)

TMDS: Thin-Model Data Sharing Scheme Supporting Keyword Search in Cloud Storage

Zheli Liu[1], Jin Li[2], Xiaofeng Chen[3], Jun Yang[1], and Chunfu Jia[1,*]

[1] College of Computer and Control Engineering, Nankai University, China
{liuzheli,junyang,cfjia}@nankai.edu.cn
[2] School of Computer Science, Guangzhou University, China
lijin@gzhu.edu.cn
[3] State Key Laboratory of Integrated Service Networks, Xidian University, China
xfchen@xidian.edu.cn

Abstract. Data sharing systems based on cloud storage have attracted much attention recently. In such systems, encryption techniques are usually utilized to protect the privacy of outsourced sensitive data. However, to support data sharing while keeping data confidentiality, encryption keys should be shared by authorized users. As a result, many keys have to be stored and shared by the users in the data sharing system, which would be a bottleneck for users. To tackle the challenges above, we propose a secure thin-model data sharing scheme supporting a keyword search scheme called *TMDS*, where only a user's master key is utilized and the keys used for keyword search are not required to be stored at the user side. Furthermore, the cloud server is assumed to be an honest-but-curious entity in our construction. TMDS offers many attractive features as follows: 1) users are able to encrypt and share data without distributing shared encryption keys; 2) each user can flexibly retrieve and decrypt data from the cloud with only a master key; 3) secure data sharing and keyword search are both supported in a single system. Furthermore, we explain how to construct a data sharing system based on TMDS. Security analysis and performance evaluation show that our scheme is secure and practical.

Keywords: cloud storage, data sharing, searchable encryption, access control.

1 Introduction

With the development of cloud storage, data sharing becomes an important functionality. By migrating the local data management systems into cloud servers, users can enjoy high-quality services and save significant investments on their local infrastructures. For example, an organization (such as company, school, association, etc.) allows its members to store and share files in the cloud. By utilizing the cloud, the members can retrieve data by any device (such as mobile

---

* Corresponding author.

W. Susilo and Y. Mu (Eds.): ACISP 2014, LNCS 8544, pp. 115–130, 2014.

phone, computer, etc) at any time and any place. Thus, they can be completely released from the troublesome local data storage and maintenance.

However, data files stored in the cloud, such as business plans, may be sensitive, while cloud servers are not fully trusted by users. To preserve data privacy, a basic solution is to encrypt data files and upload the ciphertexts into the cloud, but this leads to the challenge of how to retrieve encrypted files containing a given keyword. Searchable encryption (SE) can provide a solution for this challenge, but it has the drawback of requiring a user to provide the cloud server with a keyword trapdoor, which will be used to search over ciphertexts in the cloud.

Considering a data sharing system supporting keyword search in cloud, 1) each member of organization can upload encrypted files and share them with the other users by sending the SE keys and encryption keys to them. For security considerations, different SE keys and data encryption keys are always used for different files, so that the number of keys for each member scales with the number of files shared by others. These keys should be stored in the user's device and it would increase the system complexity on key management. *Even these keys are stored in the USB device, to achieve the goal of retrieving data from cloud by any device at any time, the user must carry the USB device all the time, which would be impractical and inflexible*; 2) access control for verifying user's permission of shared files always needs a trusted center to store the necessary information. Some recently proposed fine-grained access control mechanisms based on ciphertext-policy attribute based encryption (CP-ABE) all require a trusted attribute authority. To construct such a trusted center, one choice is to deploy it in a private cloud, which can be constructed by host trusteeship in cloud service provider, however, *it is impractical for lots of small-scale organizations, because the private cloud construction is expensive for the investment of server and management.*

To implement a practical data sharing system supporting keyword search for an organization, it would be a major contribution if (1) users are not required to send searchable keys to other users while allowing them to perform keyword search, and (2) access control can be supported outside cloud control to save on investment. Compared with the existing data sharing systems, such a system will be more lightweight, simple and flexible because there is no need to carry the shared keys for data sharing all the time. We call it as *"thin-model"* data sharing system.

Our contributions. We propose TMDS, a secure thin-model data sharing scheme supporting keyword search in the cloud, and discuss how to implement such a data sharing system using TMDS. The main contributions include:

1. Our scheme is built on the public cloud to realize secure access control or key management. The group manager (maybe CEO or HR Officer of this organization) will act as the role of system manager, that is to say, he is responsible for user management, maintaining the public system parameters stored in the cloud server.
2. Each member in the group can flexibly share his files to an arbitrary group of members without distributing SE keys and data encryption keys to them.

The user can flexibly retrieve the encrypted files by any device without these sharing keys.

3. Our scheme is very efficient because that the cryptographic operations are based on symmetric encryption, including generation of keyword ciphertext and trapdoors.

2 Related Works

2.1 Data Sharing Scheme

In 2003, Kallahalla et al. [1] proposed a secure file sharing system named Plutus on untrusted servers. In Plutus, data owner must deliver encryption keys to others and brings about a heavy key distribution overhead. Later, Ateniese et al. [2] leveraged proxy re-encryptions to secure distributed storage in 2005. In this system, a trusted cloud is required for encryption and access control.

Recently, attribute-based encryption (ABE) has been widely used in the fine-grained access control [4]. In 2010, Yu et al. [3] presented a data sharing system based on the key-policy ABE (KP-ABE) technique. However, a trusted attribute authority for ABE is need to manage attributes in both systems.

In 2013, Liu et al. [6] proposed a secure multi-owner data sharing scheme named Mona, for dynamic groups in the cloud. By leveraging group signature and dynamic broadcast encryption (BE) techniques, any cloud user can anonymously share data with others. Mona is suitable for sharing files to all members except revoked ones without a trusted cloud, but it is not practical for flexibly sharing files to a group of arbitrary members. *In fact, Mona inspires us to build a flexible data sharing system without a trusted cloud on the basis of broadcast encryption.*

In general, in order to share several files having different encryption keys with the same user, the data owner will normally distribute all these keys to the user, leading to a key management problem. Aiming at tackling this challenge, in 2014, Chu et al. [7] developed the key-aggregate cryptosystem to generate an aggregated key for the user. *The motivation of reducing data encryption keys also inspired us to construct a flexible data sharing system in which encryption keys do not need to be distributed but, nevertheless, the user can decrypt the data.*

2.2 Searchable Encryption

Keyword search is an important functionality of data sharing system. Lots of researches about searchable encryption have been proposed, including searchable symmetric encryption (SSE) [8–10, 13] and public key encryption with keyword search (PEKS) [11, 12, 14–16]. Compared with PEKS, SSE is more efficient, but it is not flexible enough to design schemes supporting complexity query, such as fuzzy keyword search [14], conjunctive wildcard search [15], and so on.

Recently, keyword search under multi-user setting (usually in data sharing scenarios) gets the attention of researchers. In 2006, Curtmola et al. [9] firstly proposed such a scheme using SSE and BE by sharing the SE key. In this scheme,

BE is used to implement access control by encrypting a random number for a group of users. *The implementation of access control based on BE inspires us to build a flexible data sharing system without a trusted cloud.*

In 2012, fine-grained access control based on ABE is applied in multi-user keyword search in [16]. However, in their schemes, trusted attribute authorities are used to manage users' attribute and trusted third parties to verify user's identity. In 2013, Liu et al. [17] proposed the concept of "coarse-grained access control" based on BE, but they didn't give the concrete scheme. Moreover, in their scheme, a trusted cloud is used to perform two-phase encryption to against the collusion attack from revoked users and cloud server.

3   Preliminaries

In this section, we will review some cryptographic tools used in this paper.

3.1   Bilinear Maps

Let $\mathcal{G}$ and $\mathcal{G}_1$ be two cyclic groups of prime order p, and g be a generator of $\mathcal{G}$. A bilinear map is a map $e : \mathcal{G} \times \mathcal{G} \to \mathcal{G}_1$ with the following properties:
1. Bilinearity: for all $u, v \in \mathcal{G}$ and $a, b \in \mathcal{Z}_p^*$, we have $e(u^a, v^b) = e(u, v)^{ab}$.
2. Non-degeneracy: $e(g, g) \neq 1$.
3. Computable: for any $u, v \in \mathcal{G}$, $e(u, v)$ can be efficiently computed.

3.2   Complexity Assumptions

Definition 1 (Computational co-Diffie-Hellman (co-CDH) Assumption on $(\mathcal{G},\mathcal{G}_1)$). *Let $\mathcal{G}$ and $\mathcal{G}_1$ be bilinear groups of prime order p, given $g, g^a \in \mathcal{G}$ and $h \in \mathcal{G}_1$ as input, it is infeasible to compute $h^a \in \mathcal{G}_1$, where $a \in \mathcal{Z}_p^*$.*

Definition 2 (Computational Diffie-Hellman (CDH) Assumption). *If $\mathcal{G} = \mathcal{G}_1$, the co-CDH problem can be reduced to standard CDH problem.*

Definition 3 (Bilinear Diffie-Hellman (BDH) Assumption). *Given a bilinear group $\mathcal{G}$ of prime order p, a tuple $g, g^a, g^b, g^c \in \mathcal{G}$ as input, it is infeasible to compute $e(g, g)^{abc} \in \mathcal{G}$, where $a, b, c \in \mathcal{Z}_p^*$.*

Definition 4 (Bilinear Diffie-Hellman Exponent (BDHE) Assumption). *Given a bilinear group $\mathcal{G}$ of prime order p, a tuple $(h, g, g^a, g^{a^2}, ..., g^{a^n}, g^{a^{n+2}}, g^{a^{n+3}}, ..., g^{a^{2n}} \in \mathcal{G}^{2n+1})$, it is infeasible to compute $e(g, h)^{a^{n+1}}$, where $a, n \in \mathcal{Z}_p^*$.*

4   System Model

We consider a thin-model data sharing system based on cloud storage with an example that an organization uses a public cloud to enable its members or staffs to share files. Each user can freely upload file and specify a group of members to retrieve it. The shared file can be retrieved by the authorized users in the specified group, and it can be searched by the given keywords.

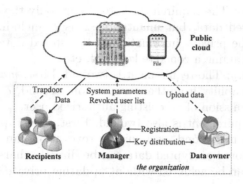

Fig. 1. Thin-model data sharing system in cloud storage

4.1 Role Definitions

As shown in Fig.1, there are four different roles defined as follows:

1. *Public cloud* is operated by cloud service providers (CSPs) and provides priced abundant storage services. Similar to [3], we assume that the cloud server is **"honest but curious"**. That is, the cloud server will provide the right service according to the pre-given scheme, and it will not maliciously delete or modify user data due to the protection of data auditing schemes [18], but will try to learn the content of the stored data.
2. *Manager* takes charge of system parameters generation, user registration, user revocation, and so on. The *Manager* can be acted by the administrator of the organization, such as CEO, HR Officer, etc. Therefore, the manager is fully trusted by the other parties.
3. *Owner* is a registered user that will store his private data into the public cloud and share them with other members or staffs of his organization.
4. *Recipients* are registered users who can query and retrieve the enciphered data with the permission to access.

4.2 Design Goals

In the thin-model data sharing system: 1) the trusted cloud will be removed; 2) SE key and data encryption key will not be distributed to recipients, and these keys are not necessary to be stored in user's device, so that user can flexibly retrieve data from cloud by any device at any time; 3) but its main design goals remain unchanged, including access control, data confidentiality, revocation capability, and efficiency as follows.

Access control: The requirement is to verify the access permission of target data with no help of trusted cloud. Unauthorized users cannot access the cloud resource at any time, and revoked users will be incapable of using the cloud again once they are revoked.

Data confidentiality: The requirement is to ensure only the authorized users can retrieve the shared data, but unauthorized users including cloud are incapable of learning the privacy information of the stored data, including data content, whether containing a concrete keyword, etc.

Revocation capability: The requirement is twofold. First, *manager* can delete a user and revoke his ability from the organization. Second, *owner* can flexibly revoke the access permission of an existing authorized user.

Efficiency: The requirement is also twofold. First, the cryptographic operations should be efficient; second, user join or revocation can be achieved efficiently, that is, the stored encrypted data can be directly shared to a new user, but user revocation can be achieved without updating private keys of others.

5   The Proposed Scheme: TMDS

Our goal is to design a complete cryptography scheme for privacy-preserving data sharing system supporting keyword search without trusted cloud. The design of TMDS is inspired from short signatures scheme named BLS [21], BE schemes [19, 20] and SSE scheme [8]. In this section, we will first describe our scheme TMDS, and then introduce how to use it to construct a concrete thin-model data sharing system in details, which achieves our design goals.

5.1   Scheme Description

1. **Setup(1^λ, n).** The *manager* will use this algorithm to initialize system parameters as follows:
   - Generate a bilinear map group system $\mathcal{B}=(p, \mathcal{G}, \mathcal{G}_1, e(\cdot, \cdot))$, where p is the order of $\mathcal{G}$ and $2^\lambda \leq p \leq 2^{\lambda+1}$.
   - Set n as the maximum number of members in the organization.
   - Pick a random generator $g \in \mathcal{G}$ and a random $\alpha \in Z_p$, and computes $g_i = g^{(\alpha^i)} \in \mathcal{G}$ for $i = \{1, 2, \cdots, n, n+1, \cdots, 2n\}$.
   - Pick a random $\gamma \in Z_p^*$ and set $v = g^\gamma \in \mathcal{G}$.

   Finally, *manager* publishes the system parameters $PK = (\mathcal{B}, PubK, v, H, H_1, E, F)$, where $PubK = (g, g_1, ..., g_n, g_{n+2}, ..., g_{2n}, v) \in \mathcal{G}^{2n+1}$, H is a one-way hash function: $\mathcal{G} \to \{0, 1\}^*$, H_1 is also a one-way hash function: $\{0, 1\}^* \to \mathcal{G}$, E is a pseudo random permutation (a block cipher, such as AES) which is used to encrypt the keyword, and F is a one-way hash function (such as MD5, SHA1):$\{0, 1\}^* \to \{0, 1\}^*$.

2. **Keygen(i).** The *manager* will use this algorithm to generate the key pair for a new user with sequence number of i, where $i \in \{1, ..., n\}$:
   - Pick a random $x \in Z_p^*$ and compute $GX = g^x \in \mathcal{G}$.
   - Compute $d_i = g_i^\gamma \in \mathcal{G}$, note that $d_i = v^{(\alpha^i)}$.

   Finally, *manager* will dispatch the public key $pk_u=(i, GX)$ and private key $sk_u=(x, d_i)$ to this user. Note that: $< x, GX >$ will be used to compute signature for identity authentication based on BLS scheme [21]; $< i, d_i >$ will be used to encrypt the shared keys, which will be stored in the cloud.

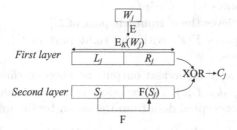

Fig. 2. Computation of the keyword ciphertexts

3. **Encrypt**($PubK$, S, m): The *owner* will use this algorithm to encrypt the data m and generate keyword ciphertexts of m as follows:
   - Let DK be the key for data encryption. The *owner* randomly selects a $d \in Z_p^*$ and computes
   $$DK = H(e(g_{n+1}, g)^d).$$
   Then, *owner* will use E to encrypt data m by DK: $E_{DK}(m)$. In general, data encryption process should be under ECB (Electronic Codebook)or CBC (Cipher Block Chaining) mode.
   - Let SEK be the key for searchable encryption. The *owner* randomly selects a $k \in Z_p^*$ and computes
   $$SEK = H(e(g_{n+1}, g)^k).$$
   Then, *owner* uses E and F to generate keyword ciphertexts: as shown in figure 2, for the given j-th keyword W_j, randomly selects $s \in_R \{0,1\}^*$ and then computes its corresponding keyword ciphertext C_j as:
   $$C_j = E_{SEK}(W_j) \oplus s || F(s).$$
   Finally, *owner* will store both encrypted results into the cloud.
4. **Share**(S, DK, SEK): To make the members in set S can retrieve the keys, the *owner* will use this algorithm to encrypt the data encryption key and SE key, compute $Hdr_{DK} = (D_0, D_1)$, $Hdr_{SE} = (S_0, S_1)$ and store (S, Hdr_{DK}, Hdr_{SE}) to the cloud, where:
   $$D_0 = g^d, D_1 = (v \cdot \Pi_{j \in s} g_{n+1-j})^d$$
   $$S_0 = g^k, S_1 = (v \cdot \Pi_{j \in s} g_{n+1-j})^k$$
5. **Trapdoor**($PubK$, S, W, sk_u): The *recipient* will use this algorithm to generate the trapdoor for a keyword W by the following steps:
   - Step 1. Download the S, Hdr_{SE} from the cloud and compute:
   $$SEK = H(e(g_i, S_1)/e(d_i \cdot \Pi_{j \in s, j \neq i} g_{n+1-j+i}, S_0)).$$
   - Step 2. Generate the trapdoor as: $Tr = E_{SEK}(W)$.

   Finally, *recipient* will send Tr to cloud server.
   In particular, the *recipient* can only run step 1 for the first time to extract the searchable encryption key SEK by a new device.
6. **Match**(Tr, C): After receiving the trapdoor Tr, *cloud* will use this algorithm to test whether the stored encrypted keyword ciphertexts C contains this keyword. For each keyword ciphertext C_j in C, *cloud* :

- Firstly, computes $C'_j = C_j \oplus T_r$.
- Secondly, retrieves the s' from left part of C'_j.
- Finally, compares $F(s')$ with the right part of C'_j. If they are equal, outputs success.

If there is no keyword ciphertext outputting success, *cloud* outputs failure.

7. **Decrypt**($PubK$, sk_u, C_m): The *recipient* will use this algorithm to retrieve and decrypt the encrypted data from the cloud by the following steps:

   - Step 1. Download the S, Hdr_{DK} from the cloud and get DK by computing:
   $$DK = H(e(g_i, D_1)/e(d_i \cdot \Pi_{j \in s, j \neq i} g_{n+1-j+i}, D_0)).$$
   - Step 2. Download the encrypted data C_m and decrypt it by DK.

   In particular, the *recipient* can only run step 1 for the first time to extract the encryption key DK by a new device.

8. **Sign**(sk_u, msg): The user will use this algorithm to generate a signature σ of message msg by computing: $\sigma = H_1(msg)^x$.

9. **Verify**(pk_u, σ): The cloud will use this algorithm to verify the signature σ of msg using user's public key pk_u by testing whether $e(g, \sigma)$ is equal to $e(GX, H_1(msg))$.

5.2   Concrete Data Sharing System

In this section, we will describe the implementation of a concrete thin-model file sharing system constructed by TMDS in details.

Table Definitions. In order to facilitate data management, we assume that the cloud will use database to manage the necessary information. Any type of database can be applied and we define four tables as follows:

- Table **company**<*companyID, companyName, parameters*> is to store the system information, including public parameters of TMDS.
- Table **userinfo**<*userID, userName, password, publicKey*> is to store members information, including user's public key.
- Table **fileinfo**<*fileID, fileName, ownerUserid, HdrDK, HdrSEK, userSet, filePath*> is to store file information of owner with identity *ownerUserid*, including encrypted keys and users who can access this file.
- Table **revokeusers**<*userID, revokeDate*> is to store revoked user information.

When an organization submits an apply for using the file sharing service, the *cloud* will create a database containing above four tables and assign a *companyID* for this organization. Moreover, it will assign an administrator account for the *manager* and insert a record into table **company**. Then, the file sharing system will work under the control of *manager*.

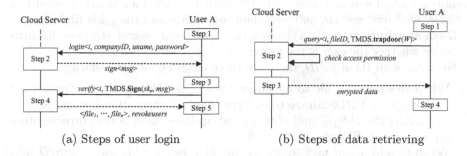

(a) Steps of user login   (b) Steps of data retrieving

Fig. 3. Work flows

Work Flows. To further describe this system in details, we describe its main work flows in this section.

System setup. The *manager* must firstly authorize his identity by the assigned administrator account (we assume this process will be provided by CSPs). Then, *manager* runs the algorithm TMDS.**Setup** to generate the system public parameters PK, and updates the field *parameters* in table **company** as PK.

User registration. When to add the i-th member, the *manager* firstly assigns a *uname* (name, email, etc) as user's identity, sets user's *userID* as i, generates a *password* and runs the algorithm TMDS.**Keygen** to generate the key pair for him. Then, *manager* securely distributes private key sk_u, i, *uname*, *password* and *companyID* to this user, inserts a new record $< i$, *uname*, *companyID*, $pk_u >$ into the table **userinfo**, and appends $< i, pk_u >$ into the PK.

User login. To upload or retrieve file, the user must firstly authorize his identity. As shown in Fig. 3(a), *cloud* can verify his identity by following steps:

- Step 1. User submits a request as *login*<*userID*, *companyID*, *uname*, *password*> to the cloud.
- Step 2. The *cloud* queries the table **userinfo** to verify user's identity. If succeed, *cloud* randomly generates a *msg* $\in \{0, 1\}^*$ and responses *sign*< *msg* > to user to require the signature of this random value.
- Step 3. User runs the algorithm TMDS.**Sign** to generate the signature and sends the request *verify*< i, TMDS.**Sign**(sk_u, *msg*)> to the cloud.
- Step 4. After receiving the *verify* request, *cloud* obtains i-th user's public key from table **userinfo** and runs the algorithm TMDS.**Verify** to verify the signature. If succeed, *cloud* will sends the file list which i-th user can access and revoked user list to this user.
- Step 5. User synchronizes his local file list with the *cloud* (this process is similar with that of other data sharing softwares based on cloud like **dropbox**). If the *revokeusers* is not null, user may update his encrypted files which the revoked user can access by the way of changing keys.

Data uploading. To upload data, *owner* runs the algorithm TMDS.**Encrypt** to encrypt the data and generate keyword ciphertexts, then uploads the encrypted data, his identity *userID* and file information to the cloud. The *cloud*

assigns a *fileID* for it and stores it in the path *filePath*, then inserts a record as
<*fileID*, *fileName*, *userID*, null, null, null, *filePath*> into the table **fileinfo**.

Data sharing. Before data sharing, the *cloud* would search the table **fileinfo**
to verify whether the user is the owner.

For a file with ID of *fileID*, there are three cases about data sharing:

- When to share this file to members whose *userID* is in set S, *owner* runs
  the algorithm TMDS.**Share** to encrypt the data encryption key and SE key
  to conduct the Hdr_{DK} and Hdr_{SE}, and updates them in the corresponding
  record of table **fileinfo**.
- When to add a new user to access this file, *owner* adds user's *userID* into
  the original set S and runs the algorithm TMDS.**Share** to re-encrypt the
  Hdr_{DK} and Hdr_{SE}, then updates the corresponding record as new <S,
  Hdr_{DK}, Hdr_{SE}>.
- When to revoke a user's access permission, *owner* removes user's *userID*
  from the original set S, then re-encrypts and updates the corresponding
  record as new <S, Hdr_{DK}, Hdr_{SE}>.

Data retrieving. As shown in Fig.3(b), for an authorized *recipient* whose
userID is i, there are four steps to retrieve data of file with ID of *fileID*:

- Step 1. The *recipient* uses the algorithm TMDS.**Trapdoor** to generate a
  trapdoor Tr for keyword W and submits a request as *query*< i, *fileID*, Tr>
  to the cloud. In the request, the null value of Tr means that the *recipient*
  wants to download file without keyword search.
- Step 2. The *cloud* checks whether the user is in the set S of this file, if not,
  abort interactive process.
- Step 3. If Tr is not null, *cloud* runs the algorithm TMDS.**Match** to test
  whether file contains the submitted keyword. If contains or Tr is null, *cloud*
  sends the encrypted data to the user.
- Step 4. The *recipient* runs algorithm TMDS.**Decrypt** to get the plaintext.

User revocation. To remove a user with ID of *userID* from the organization,
manager deletes the record of this user in the table **userinfo**, inserts a new record
as <*userID*, current date> into the table **revokeusers** and further notices all
the members to update set S and re-encrypt the keys (if necessary, re-encrypt
file content and re-generate keyword ciphertexts by changing keys).

Analysis. The above system can achieve the design goals:

- User's identity is authorized by password authentication and cryptography
  method without trusted cloud. Thus, the goal of *access control* is achieved.
- Security analysis in 5.3 shows that the system is secure, even if cloud server
  colludes with the revoked user. So, the goals of *data confidentiality* and
  revocation capability are achieved.
- Section 6 evaluates the performance and shows that the goal of *efficiency* can
  be achieved because: 1) data encryption and keyword ciphertexts generation
  are based on symmetric encryption; 2) user can only perform once decryption
  of the Hdr_{DK} and Hdr_{SE} and store them for future use.

5.3   Security Analysis

In this section, we prove the security of our system in terms of access control and data confidentiality.

Theorem 1. Based on the TMDS, the system can achieve secure access control.

Proof: To upload or retrieve data from the cloud, 1) a user must firstly authorize his identity by submitting a signature of random value from the cloud; 2) an authorized user must decrypt the Hdr_{DK} and Hdr_{SE} to get the keys. TMDS.**Sign** can be regarded as a variant of BLS signature scheme [21], and TMDS.**Share** can be regarded as a variant of broadcast encryption scheme [19], and thus they both have a provable security. The demonstration of Theorem 1 can be derived from the following lemmas: □

Lemma 1. An attacker is unable to access the cloud server based on the assumption of the intractability of CDH problem in $\mathcal{G}$.

Proof: If attacker $\mathcal{A}$ wants to pass the authentication of the cloud, he must submit the signature of random value from the cloud. Because attacker $\mathcal{A}$ has no right key, he may attack a real user's private key or generate a correct signature. However, 1) to retrieve the private key x from a real user's public key g^x, $\mathcal{A}$ must resolve the discrete logarithm problem; 2) to conduct a correct signature with the knowledge of g and public key g^x, $\mathcal{A}$ must output the result as the form of h^x, obviously, this contradicts with CDH assumption. □

Lemma 2. Unrevoked users are able to retrieve the encrypted file.

Proof: Lemma 2 is equivalent to the correctness of decryption of the encrypted keys. For correctness, we can see that the i-th user in the set S can get the shared key SEK (the same as DK) by computing:

$$
\begin{aligned}
SEK' &= \frac{e(g_i, S_1)}{e(d_i \cdot \Pi_{j \in s, j \neq i} g_{n+1-j+i}, S_0)} = \frac{e(g^{\alpha^i}, (v \cdot \Pi_{j \in s} g_{n+1-j})^k)}{e(v^{\alpha^i} \cdot \Pi_{j \in s, j \neq i} g_{n+1-j+i}, g^k)} \\
&= \frac{e(g^{\alpha^i}, g^k_{n+1-i}) \cdot e(g^{\alpha^i}, (v \cdot \Pi_{j \in s, j \neq i} g_{n+1-j})^k)}{e(v^{\alpha^i} \cdot \Pi_{j \in s, j \neq i} g_{n+1-j+i}, g^k)} \\
&= \frac{e(g_i, g_{n+1-i})^k \cdot e(g^{\alpha^i}, (v \cdot \Pi_{j \in s, j \neq i} g_{n+1-j})^k)}{e(v^{\alpha^i} \cdot \Pi_{j \in s, j \neq i} g_{n+1-j+i}, g^k)} \\
&= \frac{e(g_{n+1}, g)^k \cdot e(g^{\alpha^i}, (v \cdot \Pi_{j \in s, j \neq i} g_{n+1-j})^k)}{e(v^{\alpha^i} \cdot \Pi_{j \in s, j \neq i} g_{n+1-j+i}, g^k)} \\
&= \frac{e(g_{n+1}, g)^k \cdot e(g, (v^{\alpha^i} \cdot \Pi_{j \in s, j \neq i} g_{n+1-j}))^k}{e(v^{\alpha^i} \cdot \Pi_{j \in s, j \neq i} g_{n+1-j+i}, g)^k} \\
&= e(g_{n+1}, g)^k
\end{aligned}
$$

So, unrevoked user can get $SEK = H(SEK')$ and use it to retrieve data. □

Theorem 2. Based on the TMDS, the system supports data confidentiality.

Proof: Theorem 2 can be deduced from the following lemmas: □

Lemma 3. The cloud server is unable to learn the content of the stored files.

Proof: There are two things to check. First, cloud server has no ability to decrypt the encrypted keys on the basis of its knowledge. With the knowledge of g and g^a in PK, cloud server must resolve the discrete logarithm problem to get the a; with the knowledge of $D_0 = g^d$ and $S_0 = g^k$ in Hdr_{DK} and Hdr_{SE}, cloud server must resolve the discrete logarithm problem to get the d or k, too. As a result, cloud server is incapable of getting the key $e(g_{n+1}, g)^d$ or $e(g_{n+1}, g)^k$. In fact, this result is ensured by the assumption of the intractability of BDHE problem. Second, with the knowledge of $Tr = E_{SEK}(W)$, but without SEK, cloud server has no ability to learn keyword information from the trapdoor. This result is ensured by the adopted pseudo random permutation with proved security like AES. Thus, the correctness of Lemma 3 can be ensured.   □

Lemma 4. Even cloud server colludes with revoked users, the cloud is also incapable of learning the content of the files stored after their revocation.

Proof: With the knowledge of revoke user, the cloud server can know PK, $Hdr_{DK} = (D_0, D_1)$, key pair $< i, d_i = g_i^\gamma >$ and the set S, where $i \notin S$. The equation $e(g_i, D_1)/e(d_i \cdot \Pi_{j \in s, j \neq i} g_{n+1-j+i}, D_0)$ can be used to compute DK by the key pair of revoked user. However, because PK is missing the term $g_{n+1} = g^{a^{n+1}}$, the cloud server cannot finish the computation, so that it is incapable of learning the content.   □

6 Performance Evaluation

Considering that: 1) the user can retrieve data by any possible device in a practical file sharing system based on the cloud, and the mobile devices are widely used now; 2) the cryptographic techniques are adopted to protect data privacy, and the performance of the data sharing system is highly dependent on the basic cryptography operations including symmetric encryption and pairing computation. So, to evaluate TMDS scheme's performance, we focus on whether its cryptography operations can be quickly executed in both computer and mobile device.

6.1 Implementation Details

Block cipher AES is selected as pseudo random permutation E, SHA1 is selected as one-way hash function F. The cryptography operations based on pairing computation are implemented by type A pairing.

In our implementation, some source libraries are used: 1) *polarssl* library is used to implement AES and SHA1 in computer; 2) *jpbc* library is used to implement cryptography operations based on pairing computation running in mobile smartphone; 3) *pbc* library is used to implement cryptography operations based on pairing computation running in computer.

6.2   Evaluation

Each cryptographic operation involved in our construction will be evaluated in
two different platforms: one is in Java on *Samsung G3502U* phone with Android
OS 4.2, the other is in C++ on Computer of Intel(R) Core(TM)i5-3337U CPU
@ 1.80GHZ with Windows7 OS.

Pairing Computation. In 2007, Oliveira et al. [22] shows that the pairing
computation needs $5s$ in mobile phone. In 2010, Li et al. [23] shows that the
pairing computation only need $1.5s$ in sensor node and $0.5s$ in PDA.

Table 1. Execution time of type A pairing computation (ms)

Device	Pairing(in1, in2)	Pow/mul (in $\mathcal{G}$)	Pow/mul (in $\mathcal{G}_1$)	Pow/mul (in Z_p)
Mobile	487	246/251	73/75	0.8/0
Computer	9	13/11	1.7/1.6	0.05/0

A bilinear map $e : \mathcal{G} \times \mathcal{G} \to \mathcal{G}_1$ is tested in our experiments, and let p be the
order of $\mathcal{G}$ and $\mathcal{G}_1$, Z_p be the ring of integers modulo p. As shown in Table 1,
the average time of pairing computation (two different element in $\mathcal{G}$ as input, for
example, $e(g, h)$) is $487ms$ in mobile device, which has the same result in PDA.
Table 1 also shows the results of *pow* and *mul* computation in different groups.

Table 2. Execution time of key extraction in TMDS.**Decrypt** (ms)

Device \ Number of recipients	1	2	3	4	5	10	20	50	500
Mobile	971	1223	1462	1723	1959	3134	5842	13953	129970
Computer	18	29	40	50	63	120	231	576	5634

Data Retrieving. Considering that the recipient always uses smartphone to
retrieve data but not upload them, the cryptography operations of TMDS running in the mobile device mainly include key extraction (i.e, the step 1 of
TMDS.**Decrypt** or TMDS.**Trapdoor**), data decryption and trapdoor generation:

- Key extraction. Table 2 shows the results of key extraction in TMDS.**Decrypt**,
  and we can see that the execution time is linear with the number of recipients.
  When the recipient numbers increase to 500, the decryption time in smartphone will be 2 *minute*, but that in computer will be only 5 *second*.
- Data decryption. Two kinds of AES implementation are evaluated, one is
  android API of *javax.crypto.Cipher*, the other is Java Native Interface (JNI)
  to call the native implementation of *polarssl*. The average time of AES encryption of android API is about $0.5ms$, but that of JNI is only $0.002ms$. So,
  for a file with size of $1M$, the time of decryption by JNI will be only $0.13s$.

– Trapdoor generation. The cryptography operation in trapdoor generation is an AES encryption, whose average time can be only $0.002ms$ in smartphone.

We can see that key extraction is much lower than data decryption or trapdoor generation. Even so, TMDS can be regarded as efficient, because key extraction is only run when the recipient uses his smartphone to retrieve data for the first time. To evaluate it, we test the cost to a single user of running keyword search by his smartphone. In the simulation, we assume that the searchable encryption key will be shared by 5 users, and the recipient will use the same smartphone, that is to say, he will extract the searchable encryption key for the first time and store it for the future use. Table 3 shows the execution time of keyword search at different sequence. From Table 3, we can see that the first keyword search is lowest, because pairing computations in key extraction are executed, but others are all efficient for executing an AES encryption.

Table 3. Execution time of keyword search on a mobile phone (ms)

Sequence number Implementation	1st	2nd	3rd	4th	5th	6th
Android API	1959.002	0.0021	0.0019	0.002	0.0021	0.002
JNI	1959.5	0.51	0.51	0.49	0.5	0.51

Comparison. In this section, we describe the brief comparisons with other data sharing schemes as follows:

– The other data sharing schemes have not considered how to distribute keys, that is to say, they assume that these keys will be distributed through secure channel. So, the key extraction is not considered as the cost of system. In TMDS, the key distribution is viewed as one of important factors to make the system be flexible. Although its cost is included in the TMDS, as described in the above, TMDS can be also regarded as efficient.
– TMDS can support both data sharing and keyword search, especially it provides the keyword search function based on symmetric encryption. However, most of the other data sharing schemes have not considered the searchable encryption. In particular, to realize fine grained access control, public key encryption with keyword search may be used here. In this sense, we think TMDS has a good efficiency for keyword search.

7   Conclusion

We consider building flexible, practical and privacy-preserving data sharing system which supports keyword search based on cloud storage. We observe that there are rare researches focusing on the fact that shared keys stored in user side will increase the complexity of key management, and lead to impracticability and inflexibility when user changes the device. In this paper, we proposed the concept of "thin-model" data sharing system, which needn't carry the shared keys for data sharing all the time and without trusted cloud, and presented such a scheme called "TMDS", in which: 1) each member never sends searchable keys to others, but allows them to perform keyword search; 2) trusted cloud is removed but access control for shared files can be worked normally. Furthermore, we constructed a concrete file sharing system based on TMDS, analyzed its security and evaluated its performance in both computer and mobile device. The analysis and evaluation show that the proposed system is both secure and efficient.

Acknowledgment. This work is supported by the National Key Basic Research Program of China (No. 2013CB834204), the National Natural Science Foundation of China (Nos. 61272423, 61100224, 61272455 and 61300241), National Natural Science Foundation of Tianjin (No. 13JCQNJC00300), Specialized Research Fund for the Doctoral Program of Higher Education of China (No. 20120031120036), Natural Science Foundation of Guangdong Province (Grant No. S2013010013671), the Guangzhou Zhujiang Science and Technology Future Fellow Fund (Grant No.2012J2200094), Distinguished Young Scholars Fund of Department of Education(No. Yq2013126), Guangdong Province, China 111 Project (No. B08038), Doctoral Fund of Ministry of Education of China (No.20130203110004), Program for New Century Excellent Talents in University (No. NCET-13-0946), the Fundamental Research Funds for the Central Universities (BDY15).

References

1. Kallahalla, M., Riedel, E., Swaminathan, R., Wang, Q., Fu, K.: Plutus: Scalable Secure File Sharing on Untrusted Storage. In: Proc. USENIX Conf. File and Storage Technologies, pp. 29–42 (2003)
2. Ateniese, G., Fu, K., Green, M., Hohenberger, S.: Improved Proxy Re-Encryption Schemes with Applications to Secure Distributed Storage. In: Proc. Network and Distributed Systems Security Symp (NDSS), pp. 29–43 (2005)
3. Yu, S., Wang, C., Ren, K., Lou, W.: Achieving Secure, Scalable, and Fine-Grained Data Access Control in Cloud Computing. In: Proc. IEEE INFOCOM, pp. 534–542 (2010)
4. Li, J., Chen, X., Li, J., Jia, C., Ma, J., Lou, W.: Fine-grained Access Control based on Outsourced Attribute-based Encryption. In: Crampton, J., Jajodia, S., Mayes, K. (eds.) ESORICS 2013. LNCS, vol. 8134, pp. 592–609. Springer, Heidelberg (2013)
5. Li, J., Chen, X., Huang, Q., Wong, D.S.: Digital Provenance Enabling Secure Data Forensics in Cloud Computing. In: Future Generation Computer Systems. Elsevier (2013), http://dx.doi.org/10.1016/j.future.2013.10.006
6. Liu, X., Zhang, Y., Wang, B., Yan, J.: Mona: secure multi-owner data sharing for dynamic groups in the cloud. IEEE Transactions on Parallel and Distributed Systems 24(6), 1182–1191 (2013)

7. Chu, C., Chow, S., Tzeng, W., et al.: Key-Aggregate Cryptosystem for Scalable Data Sharing in Cloud Storage. IEEE Transactions on Parallel and Distributed Systems 25(2), 468–477 (2014)
8. Song, X., Wagner, D., Perrig, A.: Practical techniques for searches on encrypted data. In: IEEE Symposium on Security and Privacy, pp. 44–55. IEEE Press (2000)
9. Curtmola, R., Garay, J., Kamara, S., Ostrovsky, R.: Searchable symmetric encryption: improved definitions and efficient constructions. In: Proceedings of the 13th ACM conference on Computer and Communications Security, pp. 79–88. ACM Press (2006)
10. Kamara, S., Papamanthou, C., Roeder, T.: Dynamic searchable symmetric encryption. In: Proceedings of the 2012 ACM Conference on Computer and Communications Security (CCS), pp. 965–976. ACM (2012)
11. Boneh, D., Di Crescenzo, G., Ostrovsky, R., Persiano, G.: Public Key Encryption with Keyword Search. In: Cachin, C., Camenisch, J.L. (eds.) EUROCRYPT 2004. LNCS, vol. 3027, pp. 506–522. Springer, Heidelberg (2004)
12. Hwang, Y.-H., Lee, P.J.: Public Key Encryption with Conjunctive Keyword Search and Its Extension to a Multi-user System. In: Takagi, T., Okamoto, T., Okamoto, E., Okamoto, T. (eds.) Pairing 2007. LNCS, vol. 4575, pp. 2–22. Springer, Heidelberg (2007)
13. Li, J., Chen, X.: Efficient Multi-user Keyword Search Over Encrypted Data in Cloud Computing. Computing and Informatics 32(4), 723–738 (2013)
14. Li, J., Wang, Q., Wang, C.: Fuzzy keyword search over encrypted data in cloud computing. In: Proc. IEEE INFOCOM, pp. 1–5 (2010)
15. Bösch, C., Brinkman, R., Hartel, P., Jonker, W.: Conjunctive wildcard search over encrypted data. In: Jonker, W., Petković, M. (eds.) SDM 2011. LNCS, vol. 6933, pp. 114–127. Springer, Heidelberg (2011)
16. Zhao, F., Nishide, T., Sakurai, K.: Multi-User Keyword Search Scheme for Secure Data Sharing with Fine-Grained Access Control. In: Kim, H. (ed.) ICISC 2011. LNCS, vol. 7259, pp. 406–418. Springer, Heidelberg (2012)
17. Liu, Z., Wang, Z., Cheng, X., et al.: Multi-user Searchable Encryption with Coarser-Grained Access Control in Hybrid Cloud. In: Fourth International Conference on Emerging Intelligent Data and Web Technologies (EIDWT), pp. 249–255. IEEE (2013)
18. Wang, C., Wang, Q., Ren, K., Lou, W.: Privacy-Preserving Public Auditing for Data Storage Security in Cloud Computing. In: Proc. IEEE INFOCOM, pp. 525–533 (2010)
19. Boneh, D., Gentry, C., Waters, B.: Collusion resistant broadcast encryption with short ciphertexts and private keys. In: Shoup, V. (ed.) CRYPTO 2005. LNCS, vol. 3621, pp. 258–275. Springer, Heidelberg (2005)
20. Phan, D.H., Pointcheval, D., Shahandashti, S.F., et al.: Adaptive CCA broadcast encryption with constant-size secret keys and ciphertexts. International Journal of Information Security 12(4), 251–265 (2013)
21. Boneh, D., Lynn, B., Shacham, H.: Short signatures from the Weil pairing. In: Boyd, C. (ed.) ASIACRYPT 2001. LNCS, vol. 2248, pp. 514–532. Springer, Heidelberg (2001)
22. Oliveira, L.B., Aranha, D.F., Morais, E., et al.: Tinytate: Computing the tate pairing in resource-constrained sensor nodes. In: IEEE Sixth IEEE International Symposium on Network Computing and Applications, pp. 318–323 (2007)
23. Li, M., Lou, W., Ren, K.: Data security and privacy in wireless body area networks. IEEE Wireless Communications 17(1), 51–58 (2010)

Low Data Complexity Inversion Attacks on Stream Ciphers via Truncated Compressed Preimage Sets

Xiao Zhong[1,2], Mingsheng Wang[3], Bin Zhang[1,4], and Shengbao Wu[1,2]

[1] Trusted Computing and Information Assurance Laboratory, Institute of Software, Chinese Academy of Sciences, Beijing, China
[2] Graduate School of Chinese Academy of Sciences, Beijing, China
[3] State Key Laboratory of Information Security, Institute of Information Engineering, Chinese Academy of Sciences, Beijing, China
[4] State Key Laboratory of Computer Science, Institute of Software, Chinese Academy of Sciences, Beijing, China
zhongxiao456@163.com, mingsheng_wang@aliyun.com,
{zhangbin,wushengbao}@tca.iscas.ac.cn

Abstract. This paper focuses on the analysis of LFSR-based stream ciphers with low data complexity. We introduce a novel parameter called the k-th truncated compressed preimage set (TCP set), and propose a low data complexity attack to recover the initial LFSR state via the TCP sets. Our method costs very few keystream bits and less time than the brute force under some condition. We apply our method to a 90-stage LFSR-based keystream generator with filter Boolean function which can resist the algebraic attack and inversion attack given by Golić to the greatest extent. It needs only 10-bit keystream to recover the 90-bit initial state, costing less time and data than the algebraic attack. The time complexity is also less than that of the inversion attack. Moreover, we recover the 128-bit initial state of the stream cipher LILI-128 with our method. The data cost is just 9 keystream bits along with a memory cost of $O(2^{8.5})$, which is the minimum data cost to theoretically break LILI-128 so far as we know. The time complexity is $O(2^{122.4})$, better than the brute force. We also define a new security parameter called T_{comp} and suggest a design criterion for the LFSR-based stream ciphers.

Keywords: LFSR-based stream ciphers, k-th truncated compressed preimage set, algebraic attack, inversion attack, LILI-128.

1 Introduction

Last decades have witnessed the fast development of stream ciphers. As a key component of many stream ciphers, LFSR-based keystream generator is often fused with nonlinear filter generator for better performance. There are many stream ciphers which adopt the LFSR-based nonlinear filter generator, such as Grain v1 [8], SNOW 3G [5], WG-7 [9] and LILI-128 [4].

W. Susilo and Y. Mu (Eds.): ACISP 2014, LNCS 8544, pp. 131–147, 2014.
© Springer International Publishing Switzerland 2014

There are many classical analytical methods on LFSR-based stream ciphers, such as algebraic attack [2,1] and inversion attack [6,7]. For LFSR-based generators with nonlinear filter Boolean function, the algebraic immunity [10] of the Boolean function should be large enough to resist the algebraic attack. To resist the inversion attack, the memory size of the stream cipher should be close or equal to the length of the LFSR. We need to note that what is called "memory" has nothing to do with filters or combiners with memory and refers to a specific inversion attack [6,7] in which the attacker guesses as many consecutive bits of the LFSR as spanned by the taps of the filter function. What is called "memory" in these attacks is the span of the filter function. Designers often choose keystream generators filtered by Boolean functions of optimum algebraic immunity along with large memory size.

Analysts value attacks on stream ciphers which cost less time than the brute force or the declared security level. To sufficiently understand the security of the analyzed stream cipher, we should pay attention to the fact that sometimes the amount of the data available to the adversary is extremely small due to the practical restrictions. Then it is necessary to pursue the research of attacks costing small amount of data, along with a time complexity less than the brute force or the declared security level.

In this paper, we propose a low data complexity attack on the LFSR-based keystream generators with nonlinear filter. Our method can recover the initial LFSR state with very few keystream bits faster than the brute force under some condition. It also shows that although the filter Boolean function is of optimum algebraic immunity and the memory size is equal to the length of the LFSR, our method may recover the initial state in less time and data than that of the algebraic attack or inversion attack given by Golić, J.D. et al.

For the model of LFSR-based keystream generator with nonlinear filter Boolean function $f \in B_n$, where B_n is the ring of Boolean functions in n variables, we introduce two parameters called the k-th compressed preimage set (CP set) and k-th truncated compressed preimage set (TCP set). We propose a low data complexity attack to recover the initial LFSR state via the k-th TCP sets. Our method costs very few keystream bits to recover the initial state when the number of the k-th TCP sets for the filter Boolean function is large enough. When the algebraic immunity of the filter function is optimum, people can try our method to see whether they can recover the initial state with less time and data than that of the algebraic attack.

Our method can recover the initial LFSR state with time complexity less than the exhaustive search on condition that at least one k-th appropriate TCP set (ATCP set) exists. We define a new security parameter called T_{comp} when there exists at least one k-th ATCP set. To resist our attack, we suggest that T_{comp} should be larger than 2^{l-1}, where l is the length of the LFSR, which is another design criterion for the LFSR-based stream ciphers.

Furthermore, we apply our method to a 90-stage LFSR-based keystream generator with a 9-variable Carlet-Feng Boolean function as its filter, and its memory size is 90, which indicates that it can resist the algebraic attack given in [2] and inversion attack [6,7] to the greatest extent. The time complexity of our method to recover the 90-bit initial state is $T_{comp} = O(2^{75.1})$, and the data complexity is $D_{comp} = 10$ bits. The time complexity of the algebraic attack is $T_{AA} = O(2^{76.2})$ with a data complexity of $D_{AA} = O(2^{25.4})$. Moreover, the time complexity of the inversion attack [6,7] is close to $O(2^{90})$, which is larger than that of our method. We also recover the 128-bit initial state of the stream cipher LILI-128 with our method. The data cost is just 9 keystream bits along with a memory cost of $O(2^{8.5})$, which is the minimum data cost to theoretically break LILI-128 so far as we know. It highlights the advantage of the low data cost for our method. The time complexity is $O(2^{122.4})$, better than the brute force.

This paper is organized as follows: Section 2 introduces some preliminaries related to our work. In Section 3, we introduce two novel parameters called the k-th compressed preimage set and k-th truncated compressed preimage set and give an algorithm to compute the k-th ATCP sets. In Section 4, for LFSR-based keystream generators with nonlinear filter Boolean function, we propose a low data complexity attack to recover the initial state via the k-th TCP sets. An example is given in Section 5, along with the analysis of the time and data complexity. We also apply our method to the stream cipher LILI-128 in Section 6. Section 7 concludes this paper.

2 Preliminaries

2.1 Brief Description of the LFSR-Based Keystream Generator with Nonlinear Filter

Denote the ring of Boolean functions in n variables as B_n. Let f be any Boolean function in B_n, denote $S_1(f) = \{x \in F_2^n | f(x) = 1\}$, $S_0(f) = \{x \in F_2^n | f(x) = 0\}$.

In this paper, we focus on the model of LFSR-based keystream generator with nonlinear filter Boolean function, which is a common component of the stream ciphers. Figure 1 shows the general model.

keystream

Fig. 1. LFSR-based keystream generator with nonlinear filter

First, we give a brief description for this model. Let the length of the linear feedback shift register be l. L is the "connection function" of the LFSR, and it is linear. The LFSR generator polynomial is a primitive polynomial $p(x) = p_0 + p_1 x + ... + p_{l-1} x^{l-1} + x^l$. Let the initial state of the LFSR be $s^0 = (s_0, s_1, ..., s_{l-1})$, and it generates a m-sequence $s_0, s_1, s_2, ...$ For sake of narrative convenience, we call this m-sequence as LFSR sequence. The state of the LFSR at time t is

$$s^t = (s_t, s_{t+1}, ..., s_{t+l-1}) = L^t(s_0, s_1, ..., s_{l-1}),$$

which is filtered by a balanced nonlinear Boolean function $f \in B_n$ and outputs one bit c_t at time t. For any c_t, there are 2^{n-1} possible preimage tuples $(s_t^1, s_t^2, ..., s_t^n)$. Define the corresponding preimage set as

$$S_{c_t} = \{s \in F_2^n | f(s) = c_t\}.$$

Our goal is to recover the l initial state bits of the LFSR. Suppose we observe $m = \lceil \frac{l}{n} \rceil$ keystream bits $c_{t_1}, c_{t_2}, ..., c_{t_m}$ at time $t_1, t_2..., t_m$, then we can build an equation system.

$$c_{t_i} = f(s^{t_i}) = f(L^{t_i}(s_0, ..., s_{l-1})) = \sum_{j=0}^{l-1} a_{i,j} s_j, i = 1, 2, ..., m. \qquad (1)$$

Notice that the "connection function" of the LFSR is linear, so the coefficient $a_{i,j}$ can be derived from the "connection function" L. Moreover, if the coefficient matrix of the equation system (1) is full rank, then its solution is unique, resulted to the initial state bits of the LFSR.

2.2   Algebraic Attack and Inversion Attack

In this section, we would like to review two classical methods: algebraic attack [2] and inversion attack [6,7], which are efficient analytical methods on LFSR-based keystream generators.

Algebraic Attack
With the same notation in Section 2.1, for each c_t, we can construct an equation involving some key bits and initial value as its variables. Denote the output of the filter generator by $c_0, c_1, c_2, ...$, where $c_i \in F_2$, then we can get the following equation system:

$$\begin{cases} c_0 = f \quad (s_0, s_1, ..., s_{l-1}) \\ c_1 = f(L \ (s_0, s_1, ..., s_{l-1})) \\ c_2 = f(L^2(s_0, s_1, ..., s_{l-1})) \\ \vdots \end{cases} \qquad (2)$$

Then the problem of recovering the l initial state bits of the LFSR is reduced to solving the equation system (2).

The main idea of the algebraic attack proposed in [2] is to decrease the degree of the equation system (2) by using the annihilators of f or $f + 1$.

Algebraic attack motivated the research of the annihilators and algebraic immunity for Boolean functions.

Definition 1. *[10] For $f \in B_n$, define $AN(f) = \{g \in B_n | fg = 0\}$. Any function $g \in AN(f)$ is called an annihilator of f. The algebraic immunity of f, denoted by $AI(f)$, is the minimum degree of all the nonzero annihilators for f or $f + 1$.*

By Courtois and Meier's theorem [2], $AI(f) \leq \lceil \frac{n}{2} \rceil$. In general $AI(f)$ should be as large as possible in order to resist the algebraic attack.

Table 1 shows the complexity of the algebraic attack on the LFSR-based keystream generator in Figure 1, where $N = \binom{l}{AI(f)}$, ω is the parameter of the Gaussian elimination and in theory $\omega \leq 2.376$ [3].

Table 1. Complexity of AA for the Model in Figure 1

Time	Data	Memory
N^{ω}	N	N^2

While as the authors of [2] declare, the (neglected) constant factor in that algorithm is expected to be very big and they regard Strassen's algorithm [12] as the fastest practical algorithm. Then they evaluate the complexity of the Gaussian reduction to be $7 \cdot N^{log_2 7}/64$ CPU clocks. Many scholars adopt $\omega = 3$ when they use Table 1 to evaluate the time and data complexity of the algebraic attack. In this paper, we also adopt $\omega = 3$ in Table 1 to estimate the complexity of the algebraic attack.

Inversion Attack

The main idea of the inversion attack is proposed in [6,7]. With the above notations, let $\gamma = (\gamma_i)_{i=1}^n$ denote the tapping sequence specifying the inputs to the filter Boolean function f, and let $M = \gamma_n - \gamma_1$ denote the input memory size of the nonlinear filter generator regarded as the finite input memory combiner with one input and one output.

The inversion attack in [6] targets to the case when the filter function is linear in the first or the last input variable, and runs forwards or backwards accordingly. The attack guesses M-bit unknown initial LFSR bits first and then recover the initial LFSR state by taking advantage of the property of the filter function and the recursion of the LFSR.

It takes 2^{M-1} trials on average to find a correct initial memory state. One may as well examine all 2^M initial memory states.

Golić, J.D. et al. generalized the inversion attack in [7]. Unlike the inversion attack which requires that the filter function be linear in the first or the last input variable, the attack in [7] can be applied for any filter function. The time complexity remains close to 2^M.

Remark 1. In fact, since algebraic attack and inversion attack are powerful tools for the LFSR-based stream ciphers with nonlinear filter generators, designers often adopt Boolean functions of optimum algebraic immunity, with a memory size close or equal to the length of the LFSR.

3   k-th Truncated Compressed Preimage Sets

In this section, we propose two novel parameters called the k-th compressed preimage set (CP set) and k-th truncated compressed preimage set (TCP set), which helps to recover the l-bit initial LFSR state. To begin with, we give the following definition.

Definition 2. *For a balanced Boolean function $f(x_1, x_2, ..., x_n) \in B_n$, we can get the preimage set $S_u(f)$ for $f(x) = u$, $u \in \{0, 1\}$. For a fixed $k \in [1, n]$, for some fixed set of indexes $I = \{i_1, i_2, ..., i_k\} \subseteq \{1, 2, ..., n\}$ and a certain k-dimensional vector $b = (b_1, b_2, ..., b_k) \in F_2^k$, define the k-th compressed preimage sets of $S_u(f)$ as:*

$$e_{k,b} = \{a \in S_u(f) | a_{i_j} = b_j \text{ for } j = 1, 2, ..., k\}.$$

Denote

$$N_{k,b} = |e_{k,b}|,$$

here $|.|$ denotes the number of the elements in a set.
Define the k-th truncated compressed preimage set $E_{k,b}$ corresponding to $N_{k,b}$ as

$$E_{k,b} = \{b\} = \{(b_1, b_2, ..., b_k)\}.$$

Then we can get that for $f(x_1, x_2, ..., x_n) = u$, the probability that $p(x_{i_1} = b_1, x_{i_2} = b_2, ..., x_{i_k} = b_k)$ is

$$p_k = \frac{N_{k,b}}{2^{n-1}}.$$

Notice that there may exist another k-dimensional vector $b' = (b_1', b_2', ..., b_k') \in F_2^k$ such that $|e_{k,b'}| = N_{k,b}$.

For $f(x) = u$, given a k-th TCP set of $S_u(f)$, $E_{k,b} = \{(b_1, b_2, ..., b_k)\}$, we can get that $p(f(x_1, x_2, ..., x_n) = u | x_{i_1} = b_1, x_{i_2} = b_2, ..., x_{i_k} = b_k) = \frac{N_{k,b}}{2^{n-1}}$. We use the method called "guess and determine" to solve this nonlinear equation at an expected cost of $\frac{2^{n-k} + 2^{n-k-1}}{2} = 2^{n-k-1} + 2^{n-k-2}$, for the worst complexity is the exhaustive search of the 2^{n-k} possible bit-strings for the left $n-k$ unknown bits, and the best case is that one of the left $n-k$ unknown bits can be uniquely determined by guessing the other $n-k-1$ bits. The probability that the solution is the right one is $p = \frac{N_{k,b}}{2^{n-1}}$.

Then we are expected to do the above operation $\frac{1}{p}$ times to get the right solution, we can make it by choosing $\frac{1}{p}$ keystream bits.

The time complexity that we recover the right solution is

$$T = \frac{1}{p} \cdot (2^{n-k-1} + 2^{n-k-2}) = \frac{2^{2n-k-2} + 2^{2n-k-3}}{N_{k,b}}.$$

The data complexity is

$$D = \frac{1}{p}.$$

We can derive that when $2^{n-k-1} + 2^{n-k-2} < N_{k,b} < 2^{n-k}$, then $T < 2^{n-1}$, which means that it is less than the complexity of exhaustive search. We call the k-th TCP sets which satisfy the condition $2^{n-k-1} + 2^{n-k-2} < N_{k,b} < 2^{n-k}$ as the k-th appropriate TCP sets (ATCP sets). The following example shows that we can make the complexity strictly less than the exhaustive search with our idea.

Example 1. Given a 5-variable Carlet-Feng Boolean function $f = x_1x_2x_3x_5 + x_1x_2x_5 + x_1x_2 + x_1x_3x_4x_5 + x_1x_3x_4 + x_1x_3x_5 + x_1x_4x_5 + x_1x_4 + x_2x_3 + x_2x_4x_5 + x_2x_5 + x_3x_4 + x_4x_5 + 1$. $|S_0(f)| = |S_1(f)| = 16$. Table 2 shows some k-th ATCP sets of $S_0(f)$ and $S_1(f)$. Here we choose to compute the sets for $k = 2$.

Table 2. Compute the k-th appropriate TCP sets of $S_0(f)$ and $S_1(f)$

(a) ATCP sets of $S_0(f)$

k	Indexes	$N_{k,b}$	b
2	$\{4,5\}$	7	$\{1,1\}$
2	$\{1,4\}$	7	$\{1,1\}$

(b) ATCP sets of $S_1(f)$

k	Indexes	$N_{k,b}$	b
2	$\{2,4\}$	7	$\{0,0\}$

From Table 2, for $f(x) = 0$, the time complexity to recover the right solution is

$$T_0 = \frac{2^{2n-k-2} + 2^{2n-k-3}}{N_k} = \frac{2^6 + 2^5}{7} = 2^{3.77} < 2^4.$$

For $f(x) = 1$, the complexity to recover the right solution is

$$T_1 = \frac{2^{2n-k-2} + 2^{2n-k-3}}{N_k} = \frac{2^6 + 2^5}{7} = 2^{3.77} < 2^4.$$

We give an algorithm to compute the k-th appropriate TCP sets which satisfy $2^{n-k-1} + 2^{n-k-2} < N_{k,b} < 2^{n-k}$.

Algorithm 1. Compute the k-th ATCP sets of $S_u(f)$ (**ATCP Algorithm**)

Input: Boolean function f, $u \in \{0, 1\}$.
Set $E = \emptyset$, $E_0 = S_u(f)$, $k = 1$.
while $k \leq n$ **do**
    for $\{i_1, i_2, ..., i_k\} \subseteq \{1, 2, ..., n\}$, $b = (b_1, b_2, ..., b_k) \in F_2^k$ **do**
        Compute $E_{k,b}$ defined in Definition 2 and the corresponding $N_{k,b}$;
        if $2^{n-k-1} + 2^{n-k-2} < N_{k,b} < 2^{n-k}$ **then**
            $E = E \bigcup \{((i_1, i_2, ..., i_k), N_{k,b}, E_{k,b})\}$;
    $k = k + 1$;
Output E.

---

4 Low Data Complexity Inversion Attack to Recover the Initial LFSR State via the k-th ATCP Sets

According to Section 2, we can reduce the problem of recovering the initial state of LFSR to solving an equation system whose coefficient matrix is full rank.

With the same model introduced in Figure 1, let the length of the LFSR be l. The LFSR sequence is $s_0, s_1, s_2, \ldots$. The nonlinear filter Boolean function is $f \in B_n$, which is balanced. The keystream bits generated by the LFSR-based nonlinear filter generator are $c_0, c_1, c_2, \ldots$.

In this section, we give a method to recover the initial LFSR state via the k-th ATCP sets. We divide the process into two parts. One is the precomputation phase, the other is the online phase.

Precomputation Phase: For Boolean function $f \in B_n$, for a fixed $k \in [1, n]$, compute the k-th ATCP sets of $S_0(f)$ and $S_1(f)$ respectively, and denote them as group G_0 and group G_1. Choose one set from each group and denote them as E_0 and E_1 respectively. Compute the corresponding probability $p_0 = \frac{N_{k,b}}{2^{n-1}}$ and $p_1 = \frac{N_{k,b'}}{2^{n-1}}$, where $N_{k,b}$ and $N_{k,b'}$ can be derived from the output of the ATCP algorithm.

Online Phase: Denote $m = \lceil \frac{l}{n} \rceil$.

Step 1: According to the specific tap positions of the filter Boolean function f, choose m-bit keystream $c_{t_1}, c_{t_2} \ldots, c_{t_m}$ (continuous or not) which satisfy the following condition:
(1)Denote the set of the tap positions corresponding to c_{t_i} as $A_{t_i} = \{s_{t_i}^1, s_{t_i}^2, \ldots, s_{t_i}^n\}$. Require that A_{t_i}, $i = 1, 2, \ldots, m$ are pairwise disjoint.
(2)The coefficient matrix of the corresponding equation system $c_{t_i} = f(s^{t_i}) = f(L^{t_i}(s_0, \ldots, s_{l-1})) = \sum_{j=0}^{l-1} a_{i,j} s_j$, $i = 1, 2, \ldots, m$ should be full rank.

Step 2: For each c_{t_i}, we can get the k-th ATCP sets of $S_{c_{t_i}}(f)$ from the precomputation phase directly. Choose one set and denote it as E_{t_i}, and then we can get a nonlinear equation with probability of $p_{c_{t_i}}$. Solve this nonlinear equation with "guess and determine" method, we can get a candidate solution $\hat{E}_{t_i}$ for $f(x) = c_{t_i}$ with an expected cost of $2^{n-k-1} + 2^{n-k-2}$. Then we can get a candidate vector $E = \hat{E}_{t_1} || \hat{E}_{t_2} || \cdots || \hat{E}_{t_m}$ for l bits of the LFSR sequence, where "$||$" denotes a concatenation of two vectors. Because A_{t_i}, $i = 1, 2, \ldots, m$ are pairwise disjoint and the coefficient matrix of the corresponding linear equation system is full rank, the probability that E is the right solution for the l-bit LFSR sequence is $P = p_{c_{t_1}} \cdot p_{c_{t_2}} \cdots \cdots p_{c_{t_m}}$.

Step 3: Test the candidate vector E and check that if it is the right one. If it is, then we can derive the initial LFSR state bits, otherwise back to Step 2.
We can also choose the other sets in group G_0 and group G_1 to do the operation.

With the similar analysis in Section 3, the time complexity of the online phase is

$$T = (2^{n-k-1} + 2^{n-k-2})^m \cdot \frac{1}{P}. \tag{3}$$

According to Algorithm 1, we know that $\frac{1}{P} < (\frac{2^{n-1}}{2^{n-k-1} + 2^{n-k-2}})^m$, then $T < 2^{l-1}$.

In the precomputation phase, compute all the k-th ATCP sets of $S_0(f)$: E_0^1, E_0^2,..., and denote the number of them as l_0. Also, compute all the k-th TCP sets of $S_1(f)$: E_1^1, E_1^2,..., and denote the number of them as l_1.

For the keystream bits chosen in Step 1: $c_{t_1}, c_{t_2}, ..., c_{t_m}$, denote

$$n_0 = |\{c_{t_i}|c_{t_i} = 0, i = 1, ..., m\}|, n_1 = |\{c_{t_i}|c_{t_i} = 1, i = 1, ..., m\}|.$$

Then for each m-bit keystream chosen in Step 1, the number of the candidate vectors for the l LFSR sequence bits in Step 2 is

$$l_0^{n_0} \cdot l_1^{n_1}.$$

Then the data complexity of our method is

$$D = m \cdot \frac{\frac{1}{P}}{l_0^{n_0} \cdot l_1^{n_1}}. \tag{4}$$

When the parameters l_0 and l_1 are large enough such that

$$\frac{\frac{1}{P}}{l_0^{n_0} \cdot l_1^{n_1}} \leq 1, \tag{5}$$

then the data complexity of our method would become very small, that is, we need only m keystream bits to recover the initial state of the LFSR. In fact, the values of l_0 and l_1 can satisfy the condition (5) in most cases.

For a fixed $k \in [1, n]$, when there exists at least one k-th ATCP set, we give the following definition.

Definition 3. *For a fixed $k \in [1, n]$, denote the time complexity and data complexity to recover the initial LFSR state via the k-th ATCP sets as T_k and D_k respectively, define*

$$T_{comp} = min\{T_k | k \in [1, n]\}.$$

Denote the data complexity corresponding to T_{comp} as D_{comp}.

Remark 2. Our method suggests a new design criterion for the LFSR-based stream ciphers with nonlinear filter. Suppose the time complexity of our method to recover the l-bit initial LFSR state is T_{comp} given in Definition 3, and the corresponding data complexity D_{comp} is acceptable, then the stream cipher should satisfy the following condition to resist our attack:

$$2^{l-1} < T_{comp}. \tag{6}$$

In the next section, we would like to give an example to show how to apply our method to the LFSR-based nonlinear filter keystream generators.

5   Analysis on a Keystream Generator with a Filter Boolean Function of Optimum Algebraic Immunity

In this section, we choose a model of keystream generator with nonlinear filter Boolean function which can resist the algebraic attack [2] and the inversion attack [6,7] to the greatest extent. Let the length of the LFSR be 90. The filter Boolean function f is a 9-variable Carlet-Feng Boolean function which is listed in Appendix A. The input memory size of the filter function is 90, which is the length of the LFSR. We can see that the stream cipher possesses two advantages: optimum algebraic immunity and large input memory size. The keystream generator outputs one bit each clock. In the following, we apply our method to the above keystream generator.

First of all, we compute the k-th ATCP sets of $S_0(f)$ and $S_1(f)$ using the ATCP algorithm. Practically, we usually choose the k-th ATCP sets whose $N_{k,b}$ is large, which helps to decrease the time and data complexity. Table 3 shows some k-th ATCP sets of $S_0(f)$ and $S_1(f)$.

Table 3. Compute the k-th appropriate TCP sets of $S_0(f)$ and $S_1(f)$

(a) ATCP sets of $S_0(f)$

k	Indexes	$N_{k,b}$	b	k	Indexes	$N_{k,b}$	b
5	$\{1,2,6,7,8\}$	13	[0, 0, 1, 1, 1]	5	$\{1,5,6,7,9\}$	13	[0, 1, 1, 1, 0]
5	$\{2,3,5,7,9\}$	13	[1, 1, 0, 0, 0]	5	$\{1,2,3,5,6\}$	13	[1, 1, 1, 0, 1]
5	$\{2,3,4,6,7\}$	13	[1, 0, 0, 0, 1]	5	$\{3,4,5,6,8\}$	13	[0, 1, 1, 1, 0]
5	$\{4,5,6,8,9\}$	13	[1, 1, 1, 0, 0]	5	$\{1,3,5,7,9\}$	13	[1, 0, 1, 0, 1]
5	$\{1,3,5,6,8\}$	13	[0, 0, 1, 1, 0]	5	$\{3,4,5,7,8\}$	13	[1, 0, 0, 0, 1]
5	$\{2,4,5,7,9\}$	13	[0, 1, 1, 0, 0]	5	$\{1,3,4,8,9\}$	13	[1, 0, 0, 1, 1]
5	$\{2,3,7,8,9\}$	13	[0, 0, 1, 1, 1]	5	$\{1,3,4,6,8\}$	13	[0, 1, 1, 0, 0]
5	$\{1,2,4,6,8\}$	13	[1, 1, 0, 0, 0]	5	$\{1,2,4,5,9\}$	13	[1, 1, 0, 0, 1]
5	$\{2,4,6,8,9\}$	13	[0, 1, 0, 1, 1]	6	159 groups of indexes	7	many

(b) ATCP sets of $S_1(f)$

k	Indexes	$N_{k,b}$	b	k	Indexes	$N_{k,b}$	b
5	$\{1,3,4,5,6\}$	14	[0, 0, 1, 1, 0]	5	$\{1,2,3,7,9\}$	14	[1, 1, 0, 0, 0]
5	$\{1,2,3,4,8\}$	14	[0, 1, 1, 0, 0]	5	$\{4,6,7,8,9\}$	14	[1, 0, 1, 1, 0]
5	$\{1,2,6,8,9\}$	14	[1, 0, 0, 0, 1]	5	$\{2,3,4,5,9\}$	14	[0, 1, 1, 0, 0]
5	$\{1,5,7,8,9\}$	14	[0, 1, 0, 1, 1]	6	130 groups of indexes	7	many

We choose $\lceil \frac{90}{9} \rceil = 10$ keystream bits which obey the two conditions in Step 1 given in Section 4, and denote them as $c_{t_1}, c_{t_2}, , ..., c_{t_{10}}$. Then we follow Step 2, here we choose $k = 6$. Denote $n_0 = |\{c_{t_i}|c_{t_i} = 0, i = 0, 1, ..., 10\}|$ and $n_1 = |\{c_{t_i}|c_{t_i} = 1, i = 0, 1, ..., 10\}|$. Then the time and data complexity of recovering the 90-bit initial LFSR state by the low data complexity attack are

$$T_{LDA} = (2^{9-6-1} + 2^{9-6-2})^{10} \cdot (\frac{256}{7})^{10} = 2^{75.1}.$$

$$D_{LDA} = 10 \cdot \frac{(\frac{256}{7})^{10}}{159^{n_0} \cdot 130^{n_1}}.$$

Because $\frac{(\frac{256}{7})^{10}}{159^{n_0} \cdot 130^{n_1}} < 1$, we just need 10 bits to recover the 90-bit initial LFSR state, then

$$D_{LDA} = 10.$$

The successful probability that we can recover the right 90-bit initial state is

$$P = 1 - (1 - (\frac{7}{256})^{10})^{(\frac{256}{7})^{10}} \approx 1 - e^{-1} \approx 0.63.$$

According to Table 1, the time and data complexity of the algebraic attack on this model are

$$T_{AA} = \binom{90}{AI(f)}^3 = \binom{90}{5}^3 = 2^{76.2}, D_{AA} = \binom{90}{AI(f)} = \binom{90}{5} = 2^{25.4}.$$

If we adopt inversion attack [6,7] to analyze this model, the time complexity T_{IA} is close to 2^{90}.

Table 4 shows the comparison among our method (LDA), algebraic attack (AA) and inversion attack (IA) on the above model.

Table 4. Comparison among LDA, AA and IA

T_{LDA}	D_{LDA}	T_{AA}	D_{AA}	T_{IA}
$O(2^{75.1})$	10	$O(2^{76.2})$	$O(2^{25.4})$	near $O(2^{90})$

We can see that our method costs less time and data than the algebraic attack [2] in this case. The time complexity is also less than that of the inversion attack [6,7].

Remark 3. For the LFSR-based keystream generator model given in Section 2, when the filter Boolean function is of optimum algebraic immunity, people can try our method to see whether the cost of time and data can be less than that of the algebraic attack.

6   Low Data Complexity Attack on LILI-128 via the k-th TCP Sets

In this section, we apply our method to the stream cipher LILI-128 [4] to show the advantage of the low data complexity for our method. The structure of the LILI-128 generator is illustrated in Figure 2. It contains two subsystems: clock control and data generation.

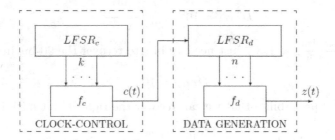

Fig. 2. Structure of LILI-128 Keystream Generator

The clock-control subsystem of LILI-128 adopts a pseudorandom binary sequence produced by a regularly clocked LFSR, $LFSR_c$, of length 39 and a function, f_c, operating on the contents of $k = 2$ stages of $LFSR_c$ to produce a pseudorandom integer sequence, $c = c(t)_{t=1}^{\infty}$. The feedback polynomial of $LFSR_c$ is chosen to be the primitive polynomial

$$x^{39} + x^{35} + x^{33} + x^{31} + x^{17} + x^{15} + x^{14} + x^2 + 1.$$

The data-generation subsystem of LILI-128 uses the integer sequence c produced by the clock subsystem to control the clocking of a binary LFSR, $LFSR_d$, of length $L_d = 89$. The contents of a fixed set of $n = 10$ stages of $LFSR_d$ are input to a specially chosen Boolean function, f_d. The binary output of f_d is the keystream bit $z(t)$. After $z(t)$ is produced, the two LFSRs are clocked and the process repeated to generate the keystream $z = z(t)_{t=1}^{\infty}$.
The feedback polynomial of $LFSR_d$ is chosen to be the primitive polynomial

$$x^{89} + x^{83} + x^{80} + x^{55} + x^{53} + x^{42} + x^{39} + x + 1.$$

The initial state of $LFSR_d$ is never the all zero state. Let the stages of $LFSR_d$ be labeled $\alpha[0], \alpha[1], ..., \alpha[88]$ from left to right. Let the LFSR shift left. Then at time t, we have the following formula to calculate the feedback bit:

$$\alpha[89+t] = \alpha[88+t] \oplus \alpha[50+t] \oplus \alpha[47+t] \oplus \alpha[36+t] \oplus \alpha[34+t] \oplus \alpha[9+t] \oplus \alpha[6+t] \oplus \alpha[t],$$

where $\oplus$ indicates the exclusive-or operation on bits(equivalent to addition modulo 2).

The 10 inputs to f_d are taken from $LFSR_d$ according to this full positive difference set: (0,1,3,7,12,20,30,44,65,80). The following is the expression of f_d:

$f_d = x_4 x_6 x_7 x_8 x_9 x_{10} + x_5 x_6 x_7 x_8 x_9 x_{10} + x_4 x_6 x_7 x_9 x_{10} + x_5 x_6 x_7 x_9 x_{10} + x_3 x_7 x_8 x_9 x_{10}$
$+ x_4 x_7 x_8 x_9 x_{10} + x_4 x_6 x_7 x_8 x_9 + x_5 x_6 x_7 x_8 x_9 + x_4 x_8 x_9 x_{10} + x_6 x_8 x_9 x_{10} + x_4 x_6 x_7 x_9 +$
$x_5 x_6 x_7 x_9 + x_2 x_7 x_8 x_9 + x_4 x_7 x_8 x_9 + x_3 x_7 x_8 x_{10} + x_5 x_7 x_8 x_{10} + x_2 x_7 x_9 x_{10} + x_4 x_7 x_9 x_{10}$
$+ x_6 x_7 x_9 x_{10} + x_1 x_8 x_9 x_{10} + x_3 x_8 x_9 x_{10} + x_6 x_7 x_{10} + x_3 x_8 x_{10} + x_4 x_8 x_{10} + x_2 x_9 x_{10} +$
$x_3 x_9 x_{10} + x_4 x_9 x_{10} + x_5 x_9 x_{10} + x_3 x_7 x_9 + x_6 x_7 x_9 + x_3 x_8 x_9 + x_6 x_8 x_9 + x_4 x_7 x_{10} + x_5 x_7 x_{10} +$
$x_6 x_7 + x_1 x_8 + x_2 x_8 + x_1 x_9 + x_3 x_9 + x_4 x_{10} + x_6 x_{10} + x_2 + x_3 + x_4 + x_5.$

To begin with, we first guess the 39-bit internal state of $LFSR_c$ and attack the second component $LFSR_d$ alone. The total time complexity should be multiplied by 2^{39}. In the following, we recover the internal state of $LFSR_d$ by using our method given in Section 4.

In the case of LILI-128, for $k = 5$, even the parameter $N_{k,b}$ defined in Definition 2 is less than $2^{n-k-1} + 2^{n-k-2}$, the time complexity of recovering the initial state is better than the brute force, which highlights the power of the TCP sets. To comprehensively consider the requirements of less time complexity than the brute force and low data complexity, we choose the 5-th TCP sets whose $N_{k,b}$ satisfy the condition of $20 \leq N_{k,b} < 32$. Table 5 shows the 5-th TCP sets which would be adopted.

We choose $\lceil \frac{89}{10} \rceil = 9$ keystream bits which obey the two conditions in Step 1 given in Section 4, and denote them as $c_{t_1}, c_{t_2}, , ..., c_{t_9}$. Denote $n_0 = |\{c_{t_i}|c_{t_i} = 0, i = 0, 1, ..., 9\}|$ and $n_1 = |\{c_{t_i}|c_{t_i} = 1, i = 0, 1, ..., 9\}|$.

Then the time and data complexity of recovering the 128-bit internal state of LILI-128 are about

$$T_{LDA} = 2^{39} \cdot (2^{10-5-1} + 2^{10-5-2})^9 \cdot (\frac{512}{20})^{n_0} \cdot (\frac{512}{20})^{n_1} = 2^{39} \cdot 24^9 \cdot (\frac{512}{20})^9 = 2^{122.4}.$$

$$D_{LDA} = 9 \cdot \frac{(\frac{512}{20})^{n_0} \cdot (\frac{512}{20})^{n_1}}{36^{n_0} \cdot 35^{n_1}}.$$

Notice that $\frac{(\frac{512}{20})^{n_0} \cdot (\frac{512}{20})^{n_1}}{36^{n_0} \cdot 35^{n_1}} < 1$, then the data complexity is

$$D_{LDA} = 9.$$

We need to store the k-th TCP sets of $S_0(f)$ and $S_1(f)$ shown in Table 5. Then the required memory is

$$M_{LDA} = (36 + 35) \cdot 5 = 2^{8.5}.$$

The successful probability that we can recover the right 89-bit $LFSR_c$ internal state is

$$P = 1 - (1 - (\frac{20}{512})^9)^{(\frac{512}{20})^9} \approx 1 - e^{-1} \approx 0.63.$$

If we apply algebraic attack to LILI-128, the time and data complexity are about

$$T_{AA} = 2^{39} \cdot \binom{89}{AI(f)}^3 = 2^{39} \cdot \binom{89}{4}^3 = 2^{102.7}, D_{AA} = \binom{89}{AI(f)} = \binom{89}{4} = 2^{21.2}.$$

The required memory is about

$$M_{AA} = \binom{89}{AI(f)}^2 = \binom{89}{4}^2 = 2^{42.4}.$$

As related research we note that Tsunoo, Y. et al. proposed an attack which recovers the internal state of LILI-128 by using 2^7 keystream bits and $2^{99.1}$ computations, along with $2^{28.6}$-bit memory [11].

Table 6 shows the comparison among our method (LDA), algebraic attack (AA) and the method in [11] on LILI-128.

Table 5. Compute the 5-th TCP sets of $S_0(f)$ and $S_1(f)$

(a) TCP sets of $S_0(f)$

k	Indexes	$N_{k,b}$	b	k	Indexes	$N_{k,b}$	b
5	$\{1,3,4,5,6\}$	22	[0, 0, 0, 0, 0]	5	$\{2,3,4,5,6\}$	22	[0, 0, 0, 0, 0]
5	$\{1,2,4,5,6\}$	21	[0, 0, 0, 0, 0]	5	$\{1,2,4,5,6\}$	21	[1, 0, 1, 0, 0]
5	$\{1,2,3,4,6\}$	21	[0, 0, 0, 1, 1]	5	$\{1,2,3,4,5\}$	20	[0, 0, 0, 1, 1]
5	$\{1,2,3,4,5\}$	20	[0, 0, 0, 0, 0]	5	$\{2,5,6,7,9\}$	20	[0, 1, 1, 1, 1]
5	$\{2,5,6,7,10\}$	20	[0, 1, 1, 1, 0]	5	$\{2,5,6,9,10\}$	20	[0, 0, 0, 1, 0]
5	$\{2,5,6,8,9\}$	20	[0, 1, 1, 1, 1]	5	$\{2,5,6,8,10\}$	20	[0, 1, 1, 1, 0]
5	$\{2,5,6,8,9\}$	20	[0, 0, 0, 1, 1]	5	$\{2,5,6,9,10\}$	20	[1, 1, 0, 1, 0]
5	$\{2,3,4,5,6\}$	20	[0, 1, 1, 0, 0]	5	$\{2,5,6,8,9\}$	20	[1, 1, 0, 1, 1]
5	$\{2,5,6,9,10\}$	20	[1, 0, 1, 1, 0]	5	$\{1,3,4,5,6\}$	20	[1, 1, 1, 1, 1]
5	$\{2,5,6,7,9\}$	20	[0, 0, 0, 1, 1]	5	$\{2,5,6,7,8\}$	20	[0, 1, 1, 1, 1]
5	$\{2,5,6,8,10\}$	20	[1, 0, 1, 1, 0]	5	$\{2,5,6,7,10\}$	20	[1, 0, 1, 1, 0]
5	$\{2,5,6,7,10\}$	20	[0, 0, 0, 1, 0]	5	$\{2,5,6,8,9\}$	20	[1, 0, 1, 1, 1]
5	$\{1,2,3,4,6\}$	20	[0, 0, 0, 0, 0]	5	$\{2,5,6,8,10\}$	20	[0, 0, 0, 1, 0]
5	$\{1,2,3,5,6\}$	20	[0, 0, 0, 1, 1]	5	$\{2,5,6,8,10\}$	20	[1, 1, 0, 1, 0]
5	$\{2,5,6,7,10\}$	20	[1, 1, 0, 1, 0]	5	$\{2,5,6,7,8\}$	20	[1, 1, 0, 1, 1]
5	$\{2,5,6,7,8\}$	20	[0, 0, 0, 1, 1]	5	$\{1,2,3,5,6\}$	20	[1, 1, 0, 0, 1]
5	$\{2,5,6,7,8\}$	20	[1, 0, 1, 1, 1]	5	$\{2,5,6,9,10\}$	20	[0, 1, 1, 1, 0]
5	$\{2,5,6,7,9\}$	20	[1, 0, 1, 1, 1]	5	$\{2,5,6,7,9\}$	20	[1, 1, 0, 1, 1]

(b) TCP sets of $S_1(f)$

k	Indexes	$N_{k,b}$	b	k	Indexes	$N_{k,b}$	b
5	$\{1,3,4,5,6\}$	20	[0, 0, 0, 1, 0]	5	$\{1,3,4,5,6\}$	20	[0, 0, 0, 0, 1]
5	$\{1,3,4,5,6\}$	20	[0, 0, 1, 0, 0]	5	$\{1,3,4,5,6\}$	20	[0, 0, 0, 1, 0]
5	$\{2,5,6,7,9\}$	20	[1, 1, 1, 1, 1]	5	$\{2,5,6,7,8\}$	20	[1, 0, 0, 1, 1]
5	$\{2,5,6,8,9\}$	20	[0, 0, 1, 1, 1]	5	$\{2,5,6,7,10\}$	20	[0, 1, 0, 1, 0]
5	$\{2,5,6,7,8\}$	20	[0, 0, 1, 1, 1]	5	$\{2,5,6,8,10\}$	20	[1, 1, 1, 1, 0]
5	$\{2,5,6,9,10\}$	20	[1, 0, 0, 1, 0]	5	$\{2,5,6,7,8\}$	20	[0, 1, 0, 1, 1]
5	$\{2,5,6,7,10\}$	20	[1, 1, 1, 1, 0]	5	$\{2,5,6,8,10\}$	20	[0, 1, 0, 1, 0]
5	$\{2,5,6,8,10\}$	20	[1, 0, 0, 1, 0]	5	$\{2,5,6,7,9\}$	20	[0, 0, 1, 1, 1]
5	$\{2,5,6,9,10\}$	20	[0, 1, 0, 1, 0]	5	$\{2,3,4,5,6\}$	20	[0, 0, 0, 0, 1]
5	$\{1,3,4,5,6\}$	20	[0, 1, 0, 0, 0]	5	$\{1,3,4,5,6\}$	20	[1, 0, 0, 0, 0]
5	$\{2,5,6,9,10\}$	20	[0, 0, 1, 1, 0]	5	$\{2,5,6,7,9\}$	20	[0, 1, 0, 1, 1]
5	$\{2,5,6,7,9\}$	20	[1, 0, 0, 1, 1]	5	$\{2,5,6,7,8\}$	20	[1, 1, 1, 1, 1]
5	$\{2,5,6,8,9\}$	20	[1, 0, 0, 1, 1]	5	$\{2,3,4,5,6\}$	20	[1, 0, 1, 1, 1]
5	$\{2,5,6,7,10\}$	20	[1, 0, 0, 1, 0]	5	$\{2,5,6,8,9\}$	20	[0, 1, 0, 1, 1]
5	$\{2,3,4,5,6\}$	20	[1, 0, 0, 0, 0]	5	$\{2,5,6,7,10\}$	20	[0, 0, 1, 1, 0]
5	$\{2,5,6,8,10\}$	20	[0, 0, 1, 1, 0]	5	$\{2,3,4,5,6\}$	20	[0, 1, 0, 0, 0]
5	$\{2,5,6,9,10\}$	20	[1, 1, 1, 1, 0]	5	$\{1,2,3,4,6\}$	20	[0, 0, 0, 1, 0]
5	$\{2,5,6,8,9\}$	20	[1, 1, 1, 1, 1]				

Table 6. Comparison among LDA, AA and method in [11]

	T	D	M
Our method	$O(2^{122.4})$	9	$O(2^{8.5})$
Algebraic attack	$O(2^{102.7})$	$O(2^{21.2})$	$O(2^{42.4})$
Method in [11]	$O(2^{99.1})$	$O(2^7)$	$O(2^{28.6})$

7 Conclusion

This paper introduces two novel parameters for Boolean functions called the k-th compressed preimage set (CP set) and k-th truncated compressed preimage set (TCP set). We give an algorithm to compute the k-th appropriate TCP sets and propose a low data complexity attack to recover the initial LFSR state via the k-th TCP sets. Our method costs very few keystream bits to recover the initial state when the number of the k-th TCP sets is large enough. We apply our method to a 90-stage LFSR-based keystream generator with a 9-variable filter Boolean function of optimum algebraic immunity. The time complexity and data complexity are both less than that of the algebraic attack [2]. The time complexity is also less than that of the inversion attack [6,7]. Moreover, we recover the 128-bit initial state of the stream cipher LILI-128 by using our method. The data cost is just 9 keystream bits along with a memory cost of $O(2^{8.5})$, which is the minimum data cost to theoretically break LILI-128 so far as we know. It highlights the advantage of the low data cost for our method. The time complexity is $O(2^{122.4})$, better than the brute force. Our method also suggests a new design criterion for the LFSR-based stream ciphers with nonlinear filter: with an acceptable data cost, the parameter T_{comp} should be larger than 2^{l-1}, where l is the length of the LFSR.

Acknowledgements. We are grateful to the anonymous reviewers for their valuable comments on this paper. This work was supported by the National Basic Research Program of China (Grant No. 2013CB834203, Grant No. 2013CB338002) and the National Natural Science Foundation of China (Grant No. 61379142, Grant No. 11171323, Grant No. 60833008, Grant No. 60603018, Grant No. 61173134, Grant No. 91118006, Grant No. 61272476), the Strategic Priority Research Program of the Chinese Academy of Sciences (Grant No. XDA06010701), IIEs Research Project on Cryptography (Grant No. Y3Z0016102).

References

1. Armknecht, F., Krause, M.: Algebraic attacks on Combiners with Memory. In: Boneh, D. (ed.) CRYPTO 2003. LNCS, vol. 2729, pp. 162–175. Springer, Heidelberg (2003)
2. Courtois, N.T., Meier, W.: Algebraic attacks on stream ciphers with linear feedback. In: Biham, E. (ed.) EUROCRYPT 2003. LNCS, vol. 2656, pp. 345–359. Springer, Heidelberg (2003)

3. Coppersmith, D., Winograd, S.: Matrix multiplication via arithmetic progressions. J. Symbolic Computation 9, 251–280 (1990)
4. Dawson, E., Clark, A., Golic, J., Millan, W., Penna, L., Simpson, L.: The LILI-128 Keystream Generator, NESSIE submission. In: The Proceedings of the First Open NESSIE Workshop (2000)
5. ETSI/SAGE. Specification of the 3GPP Confidentiality and Integrity Algorithms UEA2 & UIA2. Document 2: SNOW3G Specification, version 1.1 (2006), http://www.3gpp.org/ftp/
6. Golić, J.D.: On the security of nonlinear filter generators. In: Gollmann, D. (ed.) FSE 1996. LNCS, vol. 1039, pp. 173–188. Springer, Heidelberg (1996)
7. Golić, J.D., Clark, A., Dawson, E.: Inversion Attack and Branching. In: Pieprzyk, J., Safavi-Naini, R., Seberry, J. (eds.) ACISP 1999. LNCS, vol. 1587, pp. 88–102. Springer, Heidelberg (1999)
8. Hell, M., Johansson, T., Meier, W.: Grain-A Stream Cipher for Constrained Environments. eStream Project, http://www.ecrypt.eu.org/stream/p3ciphers/grain/Grain-p3.pdf
9. Luo, Y., Chai, Q., Gong, G., Lai, X.: A lightweight stream cipher wg-7 for RFID encryption and authentication. In: GLOBECOM, pp. 1–6 (2010)
10. Meier, W., Pasalic, E., Carlet, C.: Algebraic attacks and decomposition of boolean functions. In: Cachin, C., Camenisch, J.L. (eds.) EUROCRYPT 2004. LNCS, vol. 3027, pp. 474–491. Springer, Heidelberg (2004)
11. Tsunoo, Y., Saito, T., Shigeri, M., Kubo, H., Minematsu, K.: Shorter bit sequnence is enough to break stream cipher LILI-128. Trans. Inf. Theory 51(12), 4312–4319 (2008)
12. Strassen, V.: Gaussian Elimination is Not Optimal. Numerische Mathematik 13, 354–356 (1969)

A   Appendix: 9-variable Carlet-Feng Boolean Function

$f = x_1x_2x_3x_4x_5x_6x_7x_8 + x_1x_2x_3x_4x_5x_6x_8 + x_1x_2x_3x_4x_5x_6x_9 + x_1x_2x_3x_4x_5x_6 +$
$x_1x_2x_3x_4x_5x_7x_8x_9 + x_1x_2x_3x_4x_5x_8 + x_1x_2x_3x_4x_6x_7 + x_1x_2x_3x_4x_6x_8x_9 + x_1x_2x_3x_4$
$x_7x_8x_9 + x_1x_2x_3x_4x_7x_9 + x_1x_2x_3x_4x_8x_9 + x_1x_2x_3x_5x_6x_7x_9 + x_1x_2x_3x_5x_6x_8 +$
$x_1x_2x_3x_5x_7x_8 + x_1x_2x_3x_5x_7x_9 + x_1x_2x_3x_5x_7 + x_1x_2x_3x_5x_8x_9 + x_1x_2x_3x_5x_8 +$
$x_1x_2x_3x_5x_9 + x_1x_2x_3x_6x_7x_8x_9 + x_1x_2x_3x_6x_7x_8 + x_1x_2x_3x_6x_7x_9 + x_1x_2x_3x_6x_7 +$
$x_1x_2x_3x_6x_8 + x_1x_2x_3x_7x_8 + x_1x_2x_3x_8 + x_1x_2x_3x_9 + x_1x_2x_4x_5x_6x_7x_8x_9 + x_1x_2x_4x_5$
$x_6x_7x_9 + x_1x_2x_4x_5x_6x_9 + x_1x_2x_4x_5x_7x_8x_9 + x_1x_2x_4x_5x_8x_9 + x_1x_2x_4x_5x_9 + x_1x_2x_4$
$x_6x_7x_8x_9 + x_1x_2x_4x_6x_7x_8 + x_1x_2x_4x_6x_7 + x_1x_2x_4x_6x_8x_9 + x_1x_2x_4x_6x_8 + x_1x_2x_4x_6$
$+ x_1x_2x_4x_7x_8 + x_1x_2x_4x_7x_9 + x_1x_2x_4x_8 + x_1x_2x_4x_9 + x_1x_2x_5x_6x_7x_8 + x_1x_2x_5x_6x_7 +$
$x_1x_2x_5x_6x_8 + x_1x_2x_5x_7x_8x_9 + x_1x_2x_5x_7x_8 + x_1x_2x_5x_8x_9 + x_1x_2x_5x_9 + x_1x_2x_6$
$x_7x_8x_9 + x_1x_2x_6x_8x_9 + x_1x_2x_6x_8 + x_1x_2x_6 + x_1x_2x_7x_8 + x_1x_2x_7x_9 + x_1x_2x_7 +$
$x_1x_2x_8 + x_1x_2x_9 + x_1x_3x_4x_5x_6x_7x_8x_9 + x_1x_3x_4x_5x_6x_7x_8 + x_1x_3x_4x_5x_6x_7x_9 +$
$x_1x_3x_4x_5x_6x_8x_9 + x_1x_3x_4x_5x_6x_8 + x_1x_3x_4x_5x_6x_9 + x_1x_3x_4x_5x_6 + x_1x_3x_4x_5x_7x_8x_9$
$+ x_1x_3x_4x_5x_7x_8 + x_1x_3x_4x_5x_7x_9 + x_1x_3x_4x_5x_8 + x_1x_3x_4x_5x_9 + x_1x_3x_4x_5 + x_1x_3x_4$
$x_6x_7x_8x_9 + x_1x_3x_4x_6x_7x_8 + x_1x_3x_4x_6x_7x_9 + x_1x_3x_4x_6x_7 + x_1x_3x_4x_7x_8x_9 + x_1x_3x_4$
$x_7x_8 + x_1x_3x_4x_7x_9 + x_1x_3x_4x_8 + x_1x_3x_5x_6x_7x_8x_9 + x_1x_3x_5x_6x_7x_8 + x_1x_3x_5x_6x_8 +$
$x_1x_3x_5x_7x_8 + x_1x_3x_5x_7 + x_1x_3x_5x_8x_9 + x_1x_3x_5x_8 + x_1x_3x_6x_7x_8 + x_1x_3x_6x_7x_9 +$
$x_1x_3x_6x_8 + x_1x_3x_6 + x_1x_3x_7x_8x_9 + x_1x_3x_7x_8 + x_1x_3x_7 + x_1x_3x_8x_9 + x_1x_3x_8 +$
$x_1x_3 + x_1x_4x_5x_6x_7x_8x_9 + x_1x_4x_5x_6x_7x_8 + x_1x_4x_5x_6x_7 + x_1x_4x_5x_6x_8x_9 + x_1x_4x_5x_6$
$+ x_1x_4x_5x_7x_8x_9 + x_1x_4x_5x_8x_9 + x_1x_4x_5x_8 + x_1x_4x_5x_9 + x_1x_4x_5 + x_1x_4x_6x_7x_8x_9 +$
$x_1x_4x_6x_7x_8 + x_1x_4x_6x_7 + x_1x_4x_6x_8x_9 + x_1x_4x_6x_9 + x_1x_4x_7x_8 + x_1x_4x_7 + x_1x_4x_8x_9 +$
$x_1x_4 + x_1x_5x_6x_7x_8 + x_1x_5x_6x_7x_9 + x_1x_5x_6x_7 + x_1x_5x_6x_8x_9 + x_1x_5x_6x_9 + x_1x_5x_7 +$
$x_1x_5x_8x_9 + x_1x_5x_8 + x_1x_6x_7x_8x_9 + x_1x_6x_7x_8 + x_1x_6x_7x_9 + x_1x_6x_7 + x_1x_6x_8 +$
$x_1x_6 + x_1x_7 + x_1x_8x_9 + x_2x_3x_4x_5x_6x_7 + x_2x_3x_4x_5x_6x_9 + x_2x_3x_4x_5x_7x_8 + x_2x_3x_4x_6$
$x_7x_8x_9 + x_2x_3x_4x_6x_8x_9 + x_2x_3x_4x_6x_8 + x_2x_3x_4x_6x_9 + x_2x_3x_4x_7x_8x_9 + x_2x_3x_4x_7x_8$
$+ x_2x_3x_4x_7x_9 + x_2x_3x_4x_8x_9 + x_2x_3x_4x_9 + x_2x_3x_5x_7x_8x_9 + x_2x_3x_5x_7x_8 + x_2x_3x_5x_7$
$x_9 + x_2x_3x_5x_7 + x_2x_3x_5x_8x_9 + x_2x_3x_5x_9 + x_2x_3x_6x_7x_8x_9 + x_2x_3x_6x_7x_8 + x_2x_3x_6x_7$
$x_9 + x_2x_3x_6x_8x_9 + x_2x_3x_7x_9 + x_2x_3x_7 + x_2x_3x_8x_9 + x_2x_3x_8 + x_2x_3x_9 + x_2x_4x_5x_6x_7 +$
$x_2x_4x_5x_6x_8x_9 + x_2x_4x_5x_6x_9 + x_2x_4x_5x_6 + x_2x_4x_5x_7x_8x_9 + x_2x_4x_5x_7x_8 + x_2x_4x_5x_8$
$x_9 + x_2x_4x_5x_9 + x_2x_4x_6x_8x_9 + x_2x_4x_6x_8 + x_2x_4x_6x_9 + x_2x_4x_7x_8x_9 + x_2x_4x_7x_9 +$
$x_2x_4x_7 + x_2x_4x_8x_9 + x_2x_4x_8 + x_2x_4x_9 + x_2x_4 + x_2x_5x_6x_7x_8x_9 + x_2x_5x_6x_7x_8 +$
$x_2x_5x_6x_7 + x_2x_5x_6x_9 + x_2x_5x_6 + x_2x_5x_7x_8x_9 + x_2x_5x_7x_8 + x_2x_5x_8x_9 + x_2x_5x_8 +$
$x_2x_5 + x_2x_6x_7x_8x_9 + x_2x_6x_7x_8 + x_2x_6x_8 + x_2x_6x_9 + x_2x_7x_8x_9 + x_2x_7x_8 + x_2x_7x_9 +$
$x_2x_7 + x_2x_8 + x_3x_4x_5x_6x_7x_8 + x_3x_4x_5x_6x_8x_9 + x_3x_4x_5x_7x_9 + x_3x_4x_5x_8x_9 +$
$x_3x_4x_6x_8x_9 + x_3x_4x_6x_8 + x_3x_4x_7x_8x_9 + x_3x_4x_8 + x_3x_4x_9 + x_3x_5x_6x_7x_8 + x_3x_5x_6x_7 +$
$x_3x_5x_6x_8x_9 + x_3x_5x_7x_9 + x_3x_5x_8 + x_3x_5x_9 + x_3x_5 + x_3x_6x_7x_8x_9 + x_3x_6x_7x_8 +$
$x_3x_6x_7 + x_3x_6x_8x_9 + x_3x_6x_9 + x_3x_6 + x_3x_7x_8x_9 + x_3x_7x_9 + x_3x_8x_9 + x_3x_8 +$
$x_3x_9 + x_4x_5x_6x_7x_8x_9 + x_4x_5x_7x_9 + x_4x_5x_9 + x_4x_6x_7x_8x_9 + x_4x_6x_7x_8 + x_4x_6x_9 +$
$x_4x_6 + x_4x_7x_8x_9 + x_4x_7x_8 + x_4x_7 + x_4x_9 + x_5x_7x_8x_9 + x_5x_7 + x_5x_8x_9 + x_5x_8 +$
$x_6x_8 + x_6x_9 + x_7x_9 + 1.$

A New Attack against the Selvi-Vivek-Rangan Deterministic Identity Based Signature Scheme from ACISP 2012*

Yanbin Pan and Yingpu Deng

Key Laboratory of Mathematics Mechanization, NCMIS,
Academy of Mathematics and Systems Science, Chinese Academy of Sciences
Beijing 100190, China
{panyanbin,dengyp}@amss.ac.cn

Abstract. In ACISP 2012, Selvi, Vivek and Rangan claimed that they proposed the first fully deterministic identity based signature scheme, based on which they also proposed the first fully aggregate identity based signature scheme with no prior communication among different signers. Under the strong RSA assumption, they showed their schemes could resist the adaptive chosen message and adaptive chosen identity attack in the random oracle model. However, Nose gave a universal attack to recover the private key successfully recently. In this paper, we independently present a new universal attack to show there is an alternative way to forge a valid signature on any message instead of using the legal signing procedure with the original private key. The new attack appears more simple, and efficient both in theory and practice. What's more, with our attack, the mistake in the original security proof can be easily pointed out. Such mistake should be avoided in other similar security proofs.

Keywords: Cryptanalysis, Identity Based Deterministic Signature, Aggregate Signature, Full Aggregation.

1 Introduction

To simplify the key management procedures of certificate-based public key infrastructures (PKIs), Shamir [15] first proposed the concept of identity based cryptography in 1984, both identity based encryption and identity based signature (IBS) schemes, by allowing any user to use his identity as the public key. The corresponding secret key is generated by a trusted Private Key Generator (PKG), who derives it from a secret master secret that only the PKG knows.

Since then, a lot of identity based signature schemes have been proposed. Among them, many schemes, like [3,7,5,12], have probabilistic key generation

---

* This work was supported in part by the NNSF of China (No.11201458, and No.61121062), in part by 973 Project (No. 2011CB302401) and in part by the National Center for Mathematics and Interdisciplinary Sciences, CAS.

W. Susilo and Y. Mu (Eds.): ACISP 2014, LNCS 8544, pp. 148–161, 2014.

algorithm and signing algorithm, whereas some others [9,13] have the deterministic signing algorithm but probabilistic key generation algorithm. In ACISP 2012, Selvi, Vivek and Rangan [14] proposed the first fully deterministic IBS scheme which has both the deterministic key generation and deterministic signing algorithms. A fully deterministic IBS scheme has many advantages. For example, the forking lemma is not necessary to analyze its security and the security reduction will be tight due to the determinism, whereas the former IBS schemes usually employ the forking lemma to prove their security. What's more, the Selvi-Vivek-Rangan IBS scheme is shown to be more efficient in practice since it contains just one component, while the former schemes often involve at least two or more components.

Based on the fully deterministic IBS scheme, they also proposed the first full aggregate identity based signature scheme with no prior communication among different signers. An aggregate signature scheme consists of finding a more compact signature to replace a list of signatures produced by different signers. More precisely, suppose there are some signatures $\sigma_1, \cdots, \sigma_t$ on messages $m_1, \cdots, m_t$ by users $ID_1, \cdots, ID_t$, then the aggregate signature scheme generates a single signature σ_{agg} to take place of those σ_i's. It is expected that the size of σ_{agg} is substantially smaller than sum of the sizes of σ_i's, so one can transmit or store σ_{agg} instead of $\sigma_1, \cdots, \sigma_t$, and the communication cost or storage requirements can be significantly reduced. An aggregate signature scheme is called partial aggregation if $|\sigma_{agg}|$ depends on the number of signatures or number of messages (or both) and called full aggregation if $|\sigma_{agg}|$ is independent of both the number of messages and signatures.

Since the public key is just the ID of users, identity based aggregate signature scheme is shown to be more efficient in practice for it does not need transmit the users' public keys and the corresponding signatures from the certification authority. Meanwhile, transmitting or storing fewer data also accords with the original intention to design an aggregate signature scheme.

There are some full aggregate identity based signature schemes that are provably secure in the random oracle model, like [6,8,4,2]. However, these schemes require some communication among users to produce the aggregate signatures, which decreases the efficiency and involves some risks. Selvi, Vivek and Rangan [14] claimed that their aggregate signature scheme does not require any communication among users since the basic IBS scheme is fully deterministic, which settles the open problem proposed in [10].

The security of the Selvi-Vivek-Rangan schemes is related to the strong RSA problem, which asks to write an integer as a non-trivial power in a residue class ring defined by an RSA modulus. Selvi, Vivek and Rangan showed that if the strong RSA problem is hard, both of their schemes are secure against the adaptive chosen message and adaptive chosen identity attack.

However, Nose [11] very recently gave a universal attack against the Selvi-Vivek-Rangan signature scheme. More precisely, it can be shown that the private key of a user can be recovered efficiently by eight genuine signatures on average. Hence, the adversary can then use it to generate forged signatures on any messages. Nevertheless, Nose did not discuss why the original security proof in [14] is not correct.

In this paper, we independently present a new universal chosen message attack against the Selvi-Vivek-Rangan fully deterministic IBS scheme. Instead of recovering the private key of some user, we find there is another way to generate a valid signature on any message besides the original signing procedure. The new attack looks more simple and much easier to understand. Both the theory and experiments show that the attack is very efficient. Since the basic IBS scheme is not secure, the corresponding aggregate signature scheme is not as secure as they claimed.

What's more, our attack reveals the mistake in the original security proof in [14] easily. It can be shown by the fact that the corresponding strong RSA problem can not be solved with our attack by following the idea in the security proof. Simply speaking, we need to find an invertible matrix by querying the signing oracle to complete our attack. However, such an invertible matrix can never be found in their proof since the challenger always returns two dependent hash values in the training phase, but in the random oracle model or the real life we show that such an invertible matrix can be found efficiently with very high probability. Hence, the oracles to replace the hash functions provided by the challenger can be easily distinguished from random oracles, which shows that the proof in [14] was not given in the *real* random oracle model. Such mistake should be avoided in the security proof of any scheme.

Roadmap: The remainder of the paper is organized as follows. In Section 2, we give some preliminaries needed. We describe the Selvi-Vivek-Rangan schemes in Section 3, and present our attack in Section 4. In Section 5, we explain why the original security proof is not correct. Finally, a short conclusion is given in Section 6.

2   Preliminaries

We denote by $\mathbb{Z}$ the integer ring, by $\mathbb{Z}_n$ the residue class ring $\mathbb{Z}/n\mathbb{Z}$ and by $\mathbb{Z}_n^*$ the group of all the invertible elements in $\mathbb{Z}_n$. Let $GL(2,\mathbb{Z}_n)$ be the general linear group that consists of all the invertible matrices over $\mathbb{Z}_n^{2\times 2}$, and $\log(\cdot)$ be the natural logarithm.

2.1   Computational Assumption

The security of the Selvi-Vivek-Rangan deterministic IBS scheme and the corresponding aggregate signature scheme is based on the hardness of the strong RSA problem.

Definition 1 (Strong RSA Problem). *Given a randomly chosen RSA modulus n and a random $c \in \mathbb{Z}_n^*$, the strong RSA problem asks to find $b > 1$ and $a \in \mathbb{Z}_n^*$, such that $c = a^b \bmod n$.*

Roughly speaking, the strong RSA assumption supposes that the strong RSA problem is hard. Formally,

Definition 2 (Strong RSA Assumption). *For any probabilistic polynomial time algorithm $\mathcal{F}$ to solve the strong RSA problem in $\mathbb{Z}_n^*$, the advantage $Adv_{\mathcal{F}}^{sRSA}$ is negligibly small, where*

$$Adv_{\mathcal{F}}^{sRSA} = \boldsymbol{Pr}[\mathcal{F}(n,c) \rightarrow \{a,b\}|(a \in \mathbb{Z}_n^*, b > 1) \wedge (c = a^b \bmod n)].$$

2.2 Generic Framework

Generally, an identity based signature scheme consists of the first four polynomial-time algorithms described below, and the corresponding identity based aggregate signature scheme consists of all the six polynomial-time algorithms below.

- **Setup:** With the security parameter κ, the private key generator (PKG) generates the system parameters *params* and the master private key *msk*. Then, PKG publishes *params* and keeps *msk* secret.
- **Extract:** Given a user's identity ID, the PKG generates the corresponding private key D, and sends it to user ID through a secure channel.
- **Sign:** The user uses his identity ID, his private key D, and the system parameters *params* to produce a signature σ on a message m.
- **Verify:** The verifier checks whether σ is a valid signature on message m by ID or not.
- **AggregateSign:** On receiving the signatures $(\sigma_i)_{i=1}$ to t on message $(m_i)_{i=1}$ to t from different users $(ID_i)_{i=1}$ to t, any third party or one of the signers can generate the aggregate signature σ_{agg} for the set of $(m_i, ID_i)_{i=1}$ to t.
- **AggregateVerify:** Checks whether σ_{agg} is a valid aggregate signature on $(m_i, ID_i)_{i=1}$ to t or not.

Definition 3 (Fully Deterministic IBS Scheme). *An identity based signature scheme is said to be fully deterministic if both the key generation and signing algorithms are deterministic, or equivalently, the signature for a message by a fixed user is always the same.*

2.3 Security Model

An IBS scheme is said to be secure against existential forgery under adaptive chosen identity and message attack if for any probabilistic polynomial time algorithm forger $\mathcal{F}$, its advantage to win the following game is negligibly small.
Game:
Setup Phase: The challenger C runs the setup algorithm, publishes *params* and keeps *msk* secret.
Training Phase: $\mathcal{F}$ can query the two oracles provided by C:

- **Extract Oracle:** C will send $\mathcal{F}$ the private key D of user with identity ID, when $\mathcal{F}$ makes an extract query with ID.

- **Signing Oracle:** C will send $\mathcal{F}$ a valid signature σ on m by ID, when $\mathcal{F}$ makes a signing query with ID and message m.

Forgery Phase: $\mathcal{F}$ outputs a signature σ on a message m, with ID_S as the signer, without querying the extract oracle with ID_S and without querying the signing oracle with (ID_S, m).

$\mathcal{F}$ wins the game if σ is a valid signature. The probability of $\mathcal{F}$ succeeding is called its advantage.

Similarly, for the identity based aggregate signature scheme, we say $\mathcal{F}$ wins the game if $\mathcal{F}$ outputs a valid aggregate signature σ_{agg} for signatures $(\sigma_i)_{i=1}$ to t from the users $(ID_i)_{i=1}$ to t on messages $(m_i)_{i=1}$ to t, where at least one identity in the list of identities, for example ID_S, is not queried by $\mathcal{F}$ to the extract oracle and the corresponding pair (ID_S, m_S) is not queried to the signing oracle. If there is no probabilistic polynomial time algorithm $\mathcal{F}$ has non-negligible advantage to win the game, the identity based aggregate signature scheme is called secure against existential forgery under adaptive chosen identity and message attack.

3   Description of the Selvi-Vivek-Rangan Schemes

3.1   A Simple Description of the Selvi-Vivek-Rangan Schemes

We first describe the deterministic IBS scheme as in [14].

- **Setup(κ):** Given security parameter κ, the PKG generates *params* and *msk* as follows:
  - Chooses two primes p and q with κ bits, such that $(p-1)/2$ and $(q-1)/2$ are also primes.
  - Computes the RSA modulus $n = pq$ and the Euler's totient function $\varphi(n) = (p-1)(q-1)$.
  - Chooses e with $\kappa/4$ bits such that there is a d with $ed = 1 \bmod \varphi(n)$.
  - Chooses three hash functions

  $$H_0 : \{0,1\}^* \times \{0,1\} \to \mathbb{Z}_n^*,$$
  $$H_1 : \{0,1\}^{l_m} \times \{0,1\}^{l_1} \times \{0,1\} \to \{0,1\}^{\kappa/2},$$
  $$H_2 : \{0,1\}^{l_m} \times \{0,1\}^{l_1} \times \{0,1\} \to \{0,1\}^{\kappa/2},$$

  where l_m is the size of message and l_1 is the size of identity of a user. The system parameters published by PKG is

  $$params = (\kappa, n, e, H_0, H_1, H_2)$$

  and the unpublished master secret key is

  $$msk = (p, q, d).$$

- **Extract(ID):** After receiving some user's identity ID, the PKG performs the following to generate the private key D of the corresponding user:

- Compute $g_0 = H_0(ID, 0)$ and $g_1 = H_0(ID, 1)$.
- Compute $d_0 = (g_0)^d \bmod n$ and $d_1 = (g_1)^d \bmod n$.

The private key sent to the corresponding user through a secure and authenticated channel is

$$D = (d_0, d_1).$$

- **Sign**(m, ID, D): To generate a deterministic signature on a message m, the user with identity ID does the following:
  - Picks $\beta \in_R \{0, 1\}$,
  - Computes $h_1 = H_1(m, ID, \beta)$ and $h_2 = H_2(m, ID, \beta)$.
  - Computes $\sigma = (d_0)^{h_1}(d_1)^{h_2} \bmod n$.

Selvi *et al.* suggested picking $\beta = PRF(D, ID, m)$, where $PRF()$ is a private random function (private to the signer). Thus, β is random from others' view but fixed with respect to the signer. Now the signature is

$$S = (\sigma, \beta).$$

- **Verify**(m, σ, β, ID): In order to verify the validity of a signature (σ, β) with respect to the identity ID and message m, the verifier:
  - Computes $g_0 = H_0(ID, 0)$ and $g_1 = H_0(ID, 1)$.
  - Computes $h'_1 = H_1(m, ID, \beta)$ and $h'_2 = H_2(m, ID, \beta)$.
  - Checks whether

$$\sigma^e \bmod n \stackrel{?}{=} (g_0)^{h'_1}(g_1)^{h'_2} \bmod n.$$

  - If the above check holds, outputs "Valid", otherwise outputs "Invalid".

It is easy to see that the verification is correct since

$$\sigma^e = ((d_0)^{h'_1}(d_1)^{h'_2})^e = ((g_0^d)^{h'_1}(g_1^d)^{h'_2})^e = (g_0)^{h'_1}(g_1)^{h'_2} \bmod n.$$

Based on the deterministic IBS scheme, Selvi *et al.* also proposed a deterministic full aggregation identity based signature scheme as below:

- **AggregateSign:** Given a set of t signatures $\{(\sigma_i, \beta_i)\}_{i=1 \text{ to } t}$ and the corresponding message identity pair $\{(m_i, ID_i)\}_{i=1 \text{ to } t}$, such that (σ_i, β_i) is the valid signature on m_i by ID_i, the identity based aggregate signature on the corresponding list of messages, identities is

$$\left(\sigma_{agg} = \prod_{i=1}^{t} \sigma_i \bmod n, \{m_i, ID_i, \beta_i\}_{i=1 \text{ to } t}\right).$$

- **AggregateVerify:** To verify an aggregate signature, check whether

$$\sigma_{agg}^e = \prod_{i=1}^{t} ((g_{i0})^{h'_{i1}}(g_{i1})^{h'_{i2}}) \bmod n$$

holds or not, where $g_{i0} = H_0(ID_i, 0)$, $g_{i1} = H_0(ID_i, 1)$, $h'_{i1} = H_1(m_i, ID_i, \beta_i)$ and $h'_{i2} = H_2(m_i, ID_i, \beta_i)$.

3.2   Security of the Selvi-Vivek-Rangan Schemes

Selvi *et al.* claimed that if the strong RSA problem is assumed to be hard in $\mathbb{Z}_n^*$, where $n = pq$, and p, q, $(p-1)/2$ and $(q-1)/2$ are large prime numbers, then

- their identity based signature scheme (D-IBS) is secure in the random oracle model under adaptive chosen message and adaptive chosen identity attack.
- their identity based aggregate signature scheme (IBAS) is secure in the random oracle model under adaptive chosen message and adaptive chosen identity attack.

4   Our New Chosen Message Attack

In this section, we will present a new chosen message attack against the Selvi-Vivek-Rangan identity based signature scheme and show that it is efficient for $\mathcal{F}$ to forge a valid signature on any message. Hence the IBS scheme is not secure. As a corollary, the corresponding identity based aggregate signature scheme is not secure either.

4.1   Another Way to Sign

After challenger C runs the setup algorithm with parameter κ, generates

$$params = (\kappa, n, e, H_0, H_1, H_2)$$

and secret msk, the forger $\mathcal{F}$ can do the following to forge a valid signature S^* on any message m^* with identity ID.

For every signing query in the training phase, $\mathcal{F}$ queries C with identity ID, message m_i ($m_i \neq m^*$) randomly uniformly independently chosen from $\mathbb{Z}_n^*$ and gets the corresponding valid signatures

$$S_i = (\sigma_i, \beta_i).$$

We denote

$$h_1^{(i)} = H_1(m_i, ID, \beta_i), h_2^{(i)} = H_2(m_i, ID, \beta_i).$$

$\mathcal{F}$ makes K signing queries until one can find a β^* such that there are two signatures with $\beta = \beta^*$, for simplicity,

$$S_1 = (\sigma_1, \beta^*), S_2 = (\sigma_2, \beta^*)$$

satisfying the corresponding matrix defined by

$$\begin{pmatrix} h_1^{(1)} & h_1^{(2)} \\ h_2^{(1)} & h_2^{(2)} \end{pmatrix}$$

is invertible in $\mathbb{Z}_e^{2\times 2}$, where e is contained in the public system parameters *params*. We will show later for K polynomial in κ, such matrix can be found with high probability.

Once the invertible matrix is obtained, $\mathcal{F}$ can forge a valid signature S^* on any message m^* with identity ID efficiently.

- For any m^*, $\mathcal{F}$ first computes

$$h_1^* = H_1(m^*, ID, \beta^*), h_2^* = H_2(m^*, ID, \beta^*).$$

Solving the following linear equation, $\mathcal{F}$ can easily find $x_1, x_2 \in \mathbb{Z}$ such that

$$\begin{pmatrix} h_1^{(1)} & h_1^{(2)} \\ h_2^{(1)} & h_2^{(2)} \end{pmatrix} \begin{pmatrix} x_1 \\ x_2 \end{pmatrix} = \begin{pmatrix} h_1^* \\ h_2^* \end{pmatrix} \mod e,$$

since the matrix is invertible in $\mathbb{Z}_e^{2 \times 2}$. Moreover, $\mathcal{F}$ can also find $w_1, w_2 \in \mathbb{Z}$ efficiently such that

$$\begin{cases} x_1 h_1^{(1)} + x_2 h_1^{(2)} + ew_1 = h_1^* \\ x_1 h_2^{(1)} + x_2 h_2^{(2)} + ew_2 = h_2^*. \end{cases}$$

- $\mathcal{F}$ then computes

$$g_0 = H_0(ID, 0), g_1 = H_0(ID, 1),$$

and

$$\sigma^* = \sigma_1^{x_1} \sigma_2^{x_2} g_0^{w_1} g_1^{w_2} \mod n,$$

and finally outputs the signature on m^* by ID

$$S^* = (\sigma^*, \beta^*).$$

We next show that S^* is a valid signature on m^* by ID. To verify the validity of the signature S^*, the verifier

- Computes $g_0 = H_0(ID, 0)$ and $g_1 = H_0(ID, 1)$.
- Computes $h_1^* = H_1(m^*, ID, \beta^*)$ and $h_2^* = H_2(m^*, ID, \beta^*)$.
- Checks whether

$$(\sigma^*)^e \mod n \overset{?}{=} (g_0)^{h_1^*} (g_1)^{h_2^*} \mod n.$$

Since S_1 and S_2 are valid signatures, we have

$$\begin{cases} \sigma_1^e = g_0^{h_1^{(1)}} g_1^{h_2^{(1)}} \mod n, \\ \sigma_2^e = g_0^{h_1^{(2)}} g_1^{h_2^{(2)}} \mod n. \end{cases}$$

Hence,

$$\begin{aligned} (\sigma^*)^e &= (\sigma_1^{x_1} \sigma_2^{x_2} g_0^{w_1} g_1^{w_2})^e \mod n \\ &= \sigma_1^{ex_1} \sigma_2^{ex_2} g_0^{ew_1} g_1^{ew_2} \mod n \\ &= g_0^{x_1 h_1^{(1)}} g_1^{x_1 h_2^{(1)}} g_0^{x_2 h_1^{(2)}} g_1^{x_2 h_2^{(2)}} g_0^{ew_1} g_1^{ew_2} \mod n \\ &= g_0^{x_1 h_1^{(1)} + x_2 h_1^{(2)} + ew_1} g_1^{x_1 h_2^{(1)} + x_2 h_2^{(2)} + ew_2} \mod n \\ &= g_0^{h_1^*} g_1^{h_2^*} \mod n \end{aligned}$$

- Hence, $\mathcal{F}$ succeeds to construct a "Valid" signature S^* on m^* with ID.

Remark 1. It is obvious that once the invertible matrix in $\mathbb{Z}_e^{2 \times 2}$ is found, the attack can succeed on any message m^*. Taking the procedures of finding the invertible matrix and computing its inverse as precomputation, the attack can be completed in $O(\kappa^3)$ regardless of the computation of the hash values.

4.2   A Theoretical Estimation on K

We next estimate the size of K, which is very important to analyze the time complexity of the attack.

A Rough Bound. We first give a lemma to compute the probability that a uniformly random matrix is invertible in $\mathbb{Z}_e^{2\times 2}$. The proof can be found in Appendix A.

Lemma 1. *Given a positive integer $e = p_1^{s_1} p_2^{s_2} \cdots p_t^{s_t}$, where p_i's are different primes, the probability that a matrix A uniformly randomly chosen from $\mathbb{Z}_e^{2\times 2}$ is invertible is exactly*

$$P(e) = \prod_{i=1}^{t}(1 - \frac{1}{p_i})(1 - \frac{1}{p_i^2}).$$

As suggested in [14], e has $\kappa/4$ bits and is odd (since $\gcd(e, \varphi(n)) = 1$). We next give a lower bound of $P(e)$.

Denote by $p^{(k)}$ the k-th prime, then $p^{(1)} = 2$, $p^{(2)} = 3$, $p^{(3)} = 5, \cdots$. Let e_w be the product of the first t primes except 2 , that is,

$$e_w = 3 \cdot 5 \cdot 7 \cdots p^{(t)}$$

where t is the least number s.t. $\prod_{i=2}^{t} p^{(i)} \geq 2^{\kappa/4}$. By [1], we know that asymptotically,

$$e_w = \exp((1 + o(1))t \log t).$$

Hence, for

$$t = \kappa/4 - 1$$

with κ large enough, $e_w \geq 2^{\kappa/4}$.

Notice that the function $r(p) = (1-\frac{1}{p})(1-\frac{1}{p^2})$ increases when prime p increases and $r(p) < 1$ holds for every prime p. Together with the fact that $P(e)$ is related to the number of e's distinct prime factors, it is easy to conclude that for any odd e with $\kappa/4$ bits,

$$
\begin{aligned}
P(e) \geq &P(e_w) \\
= &(1 - \frac{1}{3})(1 - \frac{1}{9}) \cdot (1 - \frac{1}{5})(1 - \frac{1}{25}) \cdots (1 - \frac{1}{p^{(t)}})(1 - \frac{1}{(p^{(t)})^2}) \\
> &(1 - \frac{1}{3})^2 \cdot (1 - \frac{1}{5})^2 \cdots (1 - \frac{1}{p^{(t)}})^2 \\
> &((1 - \frac{1}{3}) \cdot (1 - \frac{1}{4}) \cdots (1 - \frac{1}{t+1}))^2 \\
= &(\frac{2}{t+1})^2 \\
= &(\frac{8}{\kappa})^2.
\end{aligned}
$$

If we query the signing oracle for $K = \frac{\kappa^2}{16}$ times, then there must exists β^* such the number of signatures with $\beta = \beta^*$ is no less than $\frac{K}{2} = \frac{\kappa^2}{32}$. Taking every two signatures as a pair to generate a matrix in $\mathbb{Z}_e^{2\times 2}$, we have $\frac{K}{4} = (\frac{\kappa}{8})^2$ corresponding matrices, then the probability of that there exists an invertible matrix is greater than

$$1 - (1 - (\frac{8}{\kappa})^2)^{(\frac{\kappa}{8})^2} \approx 1 - \exp(-1) \approx 0.6321,$$

which leads to

Proposition 1. *Under the assumption that the outputs of the hash functions H_1 and H_2 are independently uniformly distributed over $\{0,1\}^{\kappa/2}$, when $K = \frac{\kappa^2}{16}$, $\mathcal{F}$ will output a valid forged signature on m^* by ID with probability greater than 0.6321, and the total time complexity is bounded by $O(\kappa^4)$ regardless of the computation of the hash values.*

Exact Value of $P(e_w)$. In fact, the estimation of K above is very loose due to the loose estimation of the lower bound of $P(e_w)$. We list the exact values of $P(e_w)$ for κ from 512 to 4098 in Table 1. It can be easily concluded that even for $\kappa = 4096$, we just query the signing oracle for at most $4 \cdot \lceil 7.31 \rceil = 32$ times to make sure the probability of success is greater than 0.6321.

Table 1. The Real $P(e_w)$

κ	512	1024	1536	2048	2560	3072	3584	4096
t	27	45	61	76	91	105	119	132
$p^{(t)}$	103	197	283	383	467	571	653	743
$P(e_w)$	0.1916	0.1694	0.1586	0.1517	0.1465	0.1426	0.1394	0.1368
$\frac{1}{P(e_w)}$	5.22	5.90	6.30	6.59	6.83	7.01	7.17	7.31

4.3 Experimental Results

We implemented the attack on an Inter(R)Core(TM) i7 Processor, 2.93 GHz PC with Windows 7 operating system. We did not implement any concrete hash functions, but randomly uniformly independently chose an integer in $\{0,1\}^{\kappa/2}$ as the output of those hash functions. We either did not choose a random $\beta \in \{0,1\}$ for every signing query but fixed a β^*. This would not affect the results since at most $2u$ signatures contains u signatures with the same β^*. Notice that we did not have to take every two signatures as a pair to generate a matrix in $\mathbb{Z}_e^{2\times 2}$ as in the theoretical analysis, since the analysis asks the matrices to be independent whereas the experiments did not need. In our experiments, we checked all the possible $\frac{K(K-1)}{2}$ pairs for K signatures.

For every κ from 512 to 4096 by 512, we tested 100 instances. The attack always succeeded when an invertible matrix was found. We list the average number of K for every κ in Table 2. It can be seen that the invertible matrix can be found efficiently in the average case.

Table 2. The Average Number of K in Our Experiments

κ	512	1024	1536	2048	2560	3072	3584	4096
Average(K)	2.28	2.29	2.26	2.44	2.37	2.18	2.16	2.31

5 Why the Original Security Proof Is Incorrect?

To prove a signature scheme is secure in the random oracle model, every hash function used in the scheme is always replaced by a random oracle. Although the random oracle is often programmable, the distribution of its outputs must be, at least extremely close to, uniform. When there are more random oracles than one, it is reasonable to ask them to be independent and the joint distribution to be uniform. However, we can show that the oracles provided by the challenger in the original security proof are dependent and the joint distribution is far from uniform. Hence, these oracles can be easily distinguished from the random oracles, which implies the original security proof is not completed in a random oracle model.

As seen in our attack, the key point is to find an invertible matrix over $\mathbb{Z}_e^{2\times 2}$ from some legally obtained signatures. However, such an invertible matrix can never been found in the original security proof. More precisely, in the proof, the challenger in the training phase will output a signature of m_i with identity ID, in which the two hash values are set to be:

$$h_1^{(m_i)} = v^{(m_i)} + s_1^{(m_i)}e + t_1^{(m_i)}y$$
$$h_2^{(m_i)} = -v^{(m_i)}w + s_2^{(m_i)}e + t_2^{(m_i)}y$$

where y is a factor of e with $\kappa/8$ bits, w is a fixed $\kappa/8$ bits integer, and $v^{(m_i)}, s_1^{(m_i)}, t_1^{(m_i)}, t_2^{(m_i)} \in_R \{0,1\}^{\kappa/4}$.

For any two messages m_1 and m_2, the corresponding matrix in our attack turns out to be

$$\begin{pmatrix} h_1^{(m_1)} & h_1^{(m_2)} \\ h_2^{(m_1)} & h_2^{(m_2)} \end{pmatrix}.$$

Notice that the matrix can not be invertible in $\mathbb{Z}_e^{2 \times 2}$, since y is a factor of e and

$$\det \begin{pmatrix} h_1^{(m_1)} & h_1^{(m_2)} \\ h_2^{(m_1)} & h_2^{(m_2)} \end{pmatrix} \bmod y$$

$$= \det \begin{pmatrix} v^{(m_1)} + s_1^{(m_1)}e + t_1^{(m_1)}y & v^{(m_2)} + s_1^{(m_2)}e + t_1^{(m_2)}y \\ -v^{(m_1)}w + s_2^{(m_1)}e + t_2^{(m_1)}y & -v^{(m_2)}w + s_2^{(m_2)}e + t_2^{(m_2)}y \end{pmatrix} \bmod y$$

$$= \det \begin{pmatrix} v^{(m_1)} & v^{(m_2)} \\ -v^{(m_1)}w & -v^{(m_2)}w \end{pmatrix} \bmod y$$

$$= v^{(m_1)} \cdot (-v^{(m_2)}w) - v^{(m_2)} \cdot (-v^{(m_1)}w) \bmod y$$

$$= 0 \bmod y.$$

This means that in their proof, although each individual hash value $h_1^{(m_i)}$ and $h_2^{(m_i)}$ returned by the challenger seems random, the two values are never independent again. Moreover, the distribution of $(h_1^{(m_i)}, h_2^{(m_i)})$ over $\{0,1\}^{\kappa/2} \times \{0,1\}^{\kappa/2}$ is far from uniform, since we have proved that an invertible matrix can be found with very high probability for random oracles with the uniform distribution. Hence, it is possible to distinguish the oracles provided by the challenger from random oracles by checking whether such a matrix is invertible or not.

6   Conclusion

In this paper, we present a new universal chosen message attack against the Selvi-Vivek-Rangan schemes to show that they are not secure both in theory and practice. The new attack appears more simple, and easy to understand. Moreover, due to our attack, the mistake in the original proof becomes possible to understand.

Acknowledgement. We very thank the anonymous referees for their valuable suggestions on how to improve the presentation of this paper.

References

1. Tom, M.: Apostol: Introduction to Analytic Number Theory. Springer (1976)
2. Bagherzandi, A., Jarecki, S.: Identity-Based Aggregate and Multi-Signature Schemes Based on RSA. In: Nguyen, P.Q., Pointcheval, D. (eds.) PKC 2010. LNCS, vol. 6056, pp. 480–498. Springer, Heidelberg (2010)
3. Barreto, P.S.L.M., Libert, B., McCullagh, N., Quisquater, J.-J.: Efficient and Provably-Secure Identity-Based Signatures and Signcryption from Bilinear Maps. In: Roy, B. (ed.) ASIACRYPT 2005. LNCS, vol. 3788, pp. 515–532. Springer, Heidelberg (2005)
4. Boldyreva, A., Gentry, C., ONeill, A., Yum, D.H.: Ordered multisignatures and identity-based sequential aggregate signatures, with applications to secure routing, http://eprint.iacr.org/

5. Cha, J.C., Cheon, J.H.: An Identity-Based Signature from Gap Diffie-Hellman Groups. In: Desmedt, Y.G. (ed.) PKC 2003. LNCS, vol. 2567, pp. 18–30. Springer, Heidelberg (2002)

6. Cheng, X., Liu, J., Wang, X.: Identity-Based Aggregate and Verifiably Encrypted Signatures from Bilinear Pairing. In: Gervasi, O., Gavrilova, M.L., Kumar, V., Laganá, A., Lee, H.P., Mun, Y., Taniar, D., Tan, C.J.K. (eds.) ICCSA 2005, Part IV. LNCS, vol. 3483, pp. 1046–1054. Springer, Heidelberg (2005)

7. Galindo, D., Garcia, F.D.: A Schnorr-Like Lightweight Identity-Based Signature Scheme. In: Preneel, B. (ed.) AFRICACRYPT 2009. LNCS, vol. 5580, pp. 135–148. Springer, Heidelberg (2009)

8. Gentry, C., Ramzan, Z.: Identity-Based Aggregate Signatures. In: Yung, M., Dodis, Y., Kiayias, A., Malkin, T. (eds.) PKC 2006. LNCS, vol. 3958, pp. 257–273. Springer, Heidelberg (2006)

9. Herranz, J.: Deterministic identity-based signatures for partial aggregation. The Computer Journal 49(3), 322–330 (2006)

10. Hwang, J.Y., Lee, D.H., Yung, M.: Universal forgery of the identity-based sequential aggregate signature scheme. In: Computer and Communications Security, ASIACCS 2009, pp. 157–160. ACM (2009)

11. Nose, P.: Security weaknesses of a signature scheme and authenticated key agreement protocols. Information Processing Letters 114, 107–115 (2014)

12. Sakai, R., Ohgishi, K., Kasahara, M.: Cryptosystems based on pairing. In: The 2000 Symposium on Cryptography and Information Security, Okinawa, Japan, pp. 135–148 (2000)

13. Sharmila Deva Selvi, S., Sree Vivek, S., Pandu Rangan, C.: Identity-Based Deterministic Signature Scheme without Forking-Lemma. In: Iwata, T., Nishigaki, M. (eds.) IWSEC 2011. LNCS, vol. 7038, pp. 79–95. Springer, Heidelberg (2011)

14. Sharmila Deva Selvi, S., Sree Vivek, S., Pandu Rangan, C.: Deterministic Identity Based Signature Scheme and Its Application for Aggregate Signatures. In: Susilo, W., Mu, Y., Seberry, J. (eds.) ACISP 2012. LNCS, vol. 7372, pp. 280–293. Springer, Heidelberg (2012)

15. Shamir, A.: Identity-Based Cryptosystems and Signature Schemes. In: Blakely, G.R., Chaum, D. (eds.) Advances in Cryptology - CRYPTO 1984. LNCS, vol. 196, pp. 47–53. Springer, Heidelberg (1985)

A   Proof for Lemma 1

Lemma 1. *Given a positive integer $e = p_1^{s_1} p_2^{s_2} \cdots p_t^{s_t}$, where p_i's are different primes, the probability that a matrix A uniformly randomly chosen from $\mathbb{Z}_e^{2\times 2}$ is invertible is exactly*

$$P(e) = \prod_{i=1}^{t}(1 - \frac{1}{p_i})(1 - \frac{1}{p_i^2}).$$

Proof. i) For $e = p$ where p is a prime, there are $p^2 - 1$ choices to pick the first column of A to make A a candidate invertible matrix. After getting the first column, we only have $p^2 - p$ choices for the second column. So the probability is

$$P(e) = \frac{(p^2 - 1)(p^2 - p)}{p^4} = (1 - \frac{1}{p})(1 - \frac{1}{p^2}).$$

ii) For $e = p^s$, notice that $A \in GL(2, \mathbb{Z}_{p^s})$ is equivalent to $A \in GL(2, \mathbb{Z}_p)$ since the determinant of A must be coprime with p. That is, $A = A_0 + pB$ is invertible in $\mathbb{Z}_{p^e}^{2 \times 2}$ is equivalent to A_0 is invertible in $\mathbb{Z}_p^{2 \times 2}$. Hence, the probability becomes

$$P(e) = \frac{(p^2 - 1)(p^2 - p)(p^{4(s-1)})}{p^{4s}} = (1 - \frac{1}{p})(1 - \frac{1}{p^2}).$$

iii) For $e = p_1^{s_1} p_2^{s_2} \cdots p_t^{s_t}$, by the Chinese Remainder Theorem, it is easy to conclude that the probability is

$$P(e) = \prod_{i=1}^{t} (1 - \frac{1}{p_i})(1 - \frac{1}{p_i^2}).$$

So the lemma follows.

Further Research on N-1 Attack against Exponentiation Algorithms

Zhaojing Ding[1], Wei Guo[1,2], Liangjian Su[1], Jizeng Wei[1], and Haihua Gu[3]

[1] School of Computer Science and Technology,
Tianjin University, 300072 Tianjin, P.R. China
[2] State Key Laboratory of Computer Architecture, Institute of Computing
Technology, Chinese Academy of Sciences, 100190 Beijing, P.R. China
{dingzhaojing,weiguo,weijizeng}@tju.edu.cn
[3] Shanghai Huahong Integrated Circuit Co., Ltd., 201203 Shanghai, P.R. China
guhaihua@shhic.com

Abstract. In 2005, Yen et al. firstly proposed the $N-1$ attack against cryptosystems implemented based on BRIP and square-multiply-always algorithms. This attack uses the input message $N-1$ to obtain relevant side-channel information from the attacked cryptosystem. In this paper we conduct an in-depth study on the $N-1$ attack and find that two more special values taken as the input message also can be exploited by an attacker. According to this, we present our chosen-message attack against Boscher's right-to-left exponentiation algorithm which is a side-channel resistant exponentiation algorithm. Furthermore, immunity of the Montgomery Powering Ladder against the $N-1$ attack is investigated. The result is that the Montgomery Powering Ladder is subjected to the $N-1$ attack. But a different approach to retrieve the key is used which derives from the relative doubling attack. To validate our ideas, we implement the two algorithms in hardware and carry out the attacks on them. The experiment results show that our attacks are powerful attacks against these two algorithms and can be easily implemented with one power consumption curve.

Keywords: simple power analysis (SPA), $N-1$ attack, chosen-message attack, modular exponentiation, power collision.

1 Introduction

Although most cryptosystems are theoretically secure, their implementation on embedded devices, such as smart cards and Trusted Platform Modules, can easily be attacked by using side-channel information. The information includes runtime, power consumption, and electromagnetic radiation generated during data processing, which are correlated with the secret key of the cryptosystem. This kind of attack is called Side Channel Attacks (SCA).

The power analysis attacks are a powerful type of SCA. In 1999, Kocher et al.[1] firstly proposed Simple Power Analysis (SPA) and Differential Power Analysis (DPA). Considering modular exponentiation is the core operation of

W. Susilo and Y. Mu (Eds.): ACISP 2014, LNCS 8544, pp. 162–175, 2014.

many cryptosystems, such as the RSA scheme (for example, generating a digital signature or decrypting ciphertext) and the ElGamal encryption scheme, it is necessary to defense it against the power analysis attacks. In the year 2002, Joye and Yen[2] proposed a novel modular exponentiation algorithm which is called Montgomery Powering Ladder. Due to its highly regular execution and no redundant computation, it resists against the classical SPA and the safe-error attacks. As more SCAs were discovered, a blinded Montgomery Powering Ladder was proposed by Fumaroli and Vigilant [3]. This countermeasure will cost more hardware and longer process time than the original Montgomery Powering Ladder. And later it was found that it is vulnerable to the Jacobi Symbol Attack[4]. Based on the blinded Montgomery Powering Ladder, Boscher et al.[5] introduced a random value into the classical right-to-left binary exponentiation algorithm and proposed a side-channel resistant exponentiation algorithm which resists to SPA, DPA and DFA (Differential Fault Attack) at FDTC09. This algorithm is also 33% faster than the blinded Montgomery Powering Ladder.

In order to recover secret information from SPA and some DPA resistant algorithms, the SPA attacks with adaptively chosen messages which are categorized as chosen-message SPA have been proposed recently. Adopting particular message as input, some recognizable characteristics of power consumption that leak the secret information in the execution can be observed. In addition, this type of attacks uses a new power analysis technique to analyze the power traces. By comparing two segments of power trace in one or two executions, this technique can determine whether the data processed are the same. This is so called the power collision. Compared with the classical DPA which uses statistical-based techniques, the chosen-message SPA collects very few amounts of power traces for analysis, thus is more cost-efficient in data acquisition and processing. One of the simplest attacks of chosen-message SPA is the $N - 1$ attack proposed by Yen et al.[6]. They use the particular message $N - 1$ as an input for modular exponentiation where N is the modulus. Theoretically, they defeat the left-to-right square-multiply-always algorithm[7] and BRIP (Binary expansion with Random Initial Point/value) algorithm[8] which both are in left-to-right form. In 2008, Miyamoto et al.[9] implemented some RSA processors on an FPGA platform and demonstrated that the $N - 1$ attack clearly reveals the secret key information in the actual power waveforms. There are also some new development on chosen-message power analysis recently [10][11][12][13].

The motivation of our study comes from the exploration of the $N - 1$ attack on the Boscher's right-to-left binary exponentiation algorithm and the widely used Montgomery Powering Ladder algorithm in the embedded system due to its simplicity. In this paper, we conduct an in-depth study on the $N - 1$ attack proposed by Yen et al. and realize the attacks based on the $N - 1$ attack on Boscher's[5] right-to-left binary exponentiation algorithm and the Montgomery Powering Ladder algorithm. The reminder of this paper is organized as follows: Section 2 gives an overview of modular exponentiation algorithms and describes the $N-1$ attack. Section 3 analyzes our attacks based on the $N-1$ attack against Boscher's right-to-left exponentiation algorithm and the Montgomery Powering

Ladder algorithm. Section 4 presents the practical experimental results using our RSA hardware designs and software simulation. Finally, conclusions are given in Section 5.

2 Preliminary

2.1 Modular Exponentiation Algorithm

Our focus is principally on the security problem of computing modular exponentiation. The modular exponentiation is denoted as $S = M^d \ mod \ n$. Here, M, d and n denotes the input message, the secret key, and the modulus, respectively. The exponent d can be written in its binary form as $\sum_{i=0}^{m-1} d_i 2^i$ where m indicates the bit length of d. In addition, m is also the bit width of the multiplier in embedded device. For embedded devices with limited computation and storage capabilities, exponentiation operation is normally done by classical square-and-multiply algorithm, which is the simplest among all the exponentiation methods in the literature. It has two variations the left-to-right binary form and the right-to-left binary form. The left-to-right form implementation is more widely used since it requires only one variable.

2.2 N-1 Attack

The $N - 1$ attack was proposed by Yen et al. in 2005[6]. It was a type of chosen-message SPA similar to the doubling attack. They are both based on the power collision of two identical operations. For example, an attacker can detect the power collision of two computations $A^2 \ mod \ n$ and $B^2 \ mod \ n$ if $A = B$, even if he does not know the values of A and/or B. However, the $N - 1$ attack can recover the secret key from a single power trace, while the doubling attack needs at least two power traces of a modular exponentiation with the same secret key. The left-to-right square-multiply-always algorithm and BRIP algorithm have proven to be subjected to such attack. To simplify the explanation of the attack, we take one of them (Algorithm 1) as an example below.

Algorithm 1. left-to-right Square-multiply-always algorithm

Input: M, $d = (d_{m-1} \cdots d_i)_2$, n
Output: $M^d \ mod \ n$
 1: $R[2] = 1$
 2: **for** i *from* $(m-1)$ *downto* 0 *do*
 3:     $R[0] = R[2]^2 \ mod \ n$
 4:     $R[1] = R[0] \times M \ mod \ n$
 5:     $R[2] = R[d_i]$
 6: **return** $R[2]$

The $N - 1$ attack is based on the observation that $(n - 1)^2 \equiv 1 \ (mod \ n)$. This observation can be extended to obtain $(n - 1)^j \equiv 1 \ (mod \ n)$ for any even integer j and $(n-1)^k \equiv n-1 \pmod{n}$ for any odd integer k. Given $M = n-1$, Algorithm 1 will have $S = (n-1)^{(d_{m-1} \cdots d_i)_2} \bmod n$ after step 5 of iteration i. If $S = 1$, then $(d_{m-1} \cdots d_i)_2$ is an even integer and $d_i = 0$. Otherwise, $S = n-1$ and $(d_{m-1} \cdots d_i)_2$ is an odd integer and $d_i = 1$. Given the two possible values of S at the iteration i, there will be only two possible computations of the iteration $(i-1)$ shown below.

- If d_i is equal to 0, step 3 of the iteration $(i-1)$ performs:
  $R[0] = 1^2 \bmod n$,
- If d_i is equal to 1, step 3 of the iteration $(i-1)$ performs:
  $R[0] = (n-1)^2 \bmod n$.

Only two possible private keys will be derived and a trial-and-error approach can be used to select the correct d among the two possibilities. For example, if the most significant bit (MSB) is assumed to be one, then one of the two possible keys can be selected easily. For brevity, we write $1^2 \bmod n$, $(n-1)^2 \bmod n$, and $1 \times (n-1) \bmod n$ as 1^2, $(n-1)^2$ and $1 \times (n-1)$ and denote them as **S1**, **S2** and **M** respectively in the following.

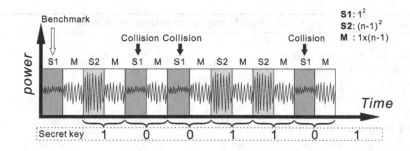

Fig. 1. $N-1$ attack on Algorithm 1 when $M = n-1$

For a more detailed description of the $N-1$ attack, an example against Algorithm 1 is illustrated in Fig.1. Here, we assume $M = n-1$ and $d = 77 = (1001101)_2$. In the figure, the power segment of the first **S1** is recorded as a benchmark. Actually, the **S1** will always be calculated firstly in Algorithm 1 regardless of the value of MSB. Then if another **S1** is detected in the remaining power trace, the corresponding key bit can be determined as 0, otherwise, the key bit is 1. Bit by bit, we can derive the whole key gradually except the least significant bit (LSB). The LSB can be determined by detecting whether the result of $M^d \bmod n$ is 1.

3 Proposed Attack

Previously, the $N-1$ attack is only applied to left-to-right square-multiply-always algorithm and BRIP algorithm. They are both the left-to-right form modular exponentiations. In this section, we point out that the $N-1$ attack is not only applicable to the left-to-right form modular exponentiation algorithm but also the right-to-left form modular exponentiation algorithm described in Algorithm 2 and the high regular Montgomery Powering Ladder algorithm without dummy or redundant operations described in Algorithm 3. To the authors' best knowledge, the attack proposed here is the first successful attempt to crack down Algorithm 2.

3.1   Attack on Boscher's Right-to-left Exponentiation Algorithm

At FDTC09, Boscher et al.[5] proposed a exponentiation method that is immune to almost all the side channel attacks (SPA, DPA, and DFA) with high efficiency described in Algorithm 2. They claimed in their paper that the $N-1$ attack and chosen-message attack that taking advantage of some specific values are inefficient to their algorithm due to the randomization of the registers $R[0]$ and $R[1]$. However, we notice that if the algorithm is used in the embedded device without any modification, it will be vulnerable to chosen-message SPA though it resists against almost all the other side channel attacks.

Algorithm 2. Boscher's right-to-left exponentiation algorithm

---

Input: M, $d = (d_{m-1} \cdots d_i)_2$, n
Output: $M^d \bmod n$ or *"Error"*
 1: *select a random integer r*
 2: $R[0] = r$
 3: $R[1] = r^{-1} \bmod n$
 4: $R[2] = M$
 5: *for i from* 0 *to* $(m-1)$ *do*
 6:     $R[1 - d_i] = R[1 - d_i] \times R[2] \bmod n$
 7:     $R[2] = R[2]^2 \bmod n$
 8: *if* $(R[0] \times R[1] \times M = R[2])$ *then*
 9:     *return* $(r^{-1} \times R[0] \bmod n)$
10: *else*
11:     *return* *("Error")*

By observing Algorithm 2 we can find that the bit value of the private key is only associated with the modular multiplication operation in step 6.

 − If d_i is equal to 0, step 6 of the iteration (i) performs:
   $R[1] = R[1] \times R[2] \bmod n$,
 − If d_i is equal to 1, step 6 of the iteration (i) performs:
   $R[0] = R[0] \times R[2] \bmod n$.

Therefore, the private key can be easily retrieved if we can distinguish which operation is performed. Furthermore, one should notice that register $R[1]$ and $R[0]$ are mutually independent. Consequently, their values do not affect each other and are only reused by themselves. Then, if $R[2]$ is supposed to be 1 in the iteration (i), register $R[1]$ and $R[0]$ will maintain the current value unchanged in subsequent iterations, which is described below.

- If d_i is equal to 0, step 6 of the iterations from (i) to $(m-1)$ performs:
  $R[1] = R[1] \times 1 \bmod n$,
  Here, $R[1]$ is a fixed value, that is $r^{-1} \bmod n$ when $M = 1$.
- If d_i is equal to 1, step 6 of the iterations from (i) to $(m-1)$ performs:
  $R[0] = R[0] \times 1 \bmod n$.
  Here, $R[0]$ is a fixed value, that is r when $M = 1$.

When these two patterns are found, it is easy to derive the secret key. To begin with, a randomly chosen power segment of step 6 in a single power trace is recorded as a benchmark. More accurately, this benchmark indicates the power consumption of step 6 when the current key bit (either 0 or 1) is being processed. Then we compare this benchmark with other power segments of step 6. If a noticeable difference between the tested and the benchmark is observed, it verifies that the key bit under test is different from the one in the benchmark. Otherwise, it means these two key bits are exactly the same. After each power segment is examined, the secret key is also retrieved bit by bit. One should notice that by this way, two possible key candidates, d and its binary inverse $\bar{d}$ are derived as it is unable to confirm whether the benchmark we set is related to 1 or 0. Finally, a trial-and-error approach can be employed to find the correct d between these two possibilities. For example, if $d = (1001101)_2$, then $\bar{d} = (0110010)_2$.

Table 1. Computation of Algorithm 2 when $M = n - 1$, $M = 1$ and $M = n + 1$

i	d_i	Intermediate Steps	Collision Operations		
			$M = n - 1$	$M = 1$	$M = n + 1$
0	1	$R[0] = R[0] \times R[2]$ $R[2] = R[2]^2$	$r \times (n - 1)$	$r \times 1$	$r \times (n + 1)$
1	0	$R[1] = R[1] \times R[2]$ $R[2] = R[2]^2$	$r^{-1} \times 1$	$r^{-1} \times 1$	$r^{-1} \times 1$
2	1	$R[0] = R[0] \times R[2]$ $R[2] = R[2]^2$	$(r \times (n - 1)) \times 1$	$r \times 1$	$r \times 1$
3	1	$R[0] = R[0] \times R[2]$ $R[2] = R[2]^2$	$(r \times (n - 1)) \times 1$	$r \times 1$	$r \times 1$
4	0	$R[1] = R[1] \times R[2]$ $R[2] = R[2]^2$	$r^{-1} \times 1$	$r^{-1} \times 1$	$r^{-1} \times 1$
5	0	$R[1] = R[1] \times R[2]$ $R[2] = R[2]^2$	$r^{-1} \times 1$	$r^{-1} \times 1$	$r^{-1} \times 1$
6	1	$R[0] = R[0] \times R[2]$ $R[2] = R[2]^2$	$(r \times (n - 1)) \times 1$	$r \times 1$	$r \times 1$

Obviously, the countermeasure by introducing a random r in Algorithm 2 does not protect against our attack, worse still, it even facilitates the chance to reveal the secret key.

Two methods would possibly be exploited to set register $R[2]$ to 1. The first method is to assign value 1 to $R[2]$ at the initial time, in other words, to make value 1 as the input message of Algorithm 2. The whole secret key can be derived using this value. Another approach is to make the value of $R[2]^2 \ mod \ n$ equal to 1. We notice that $(n-1)^2 \ mod \ n = 1$ and $(n+1)^2 \ mod \ n = 1$ (Usually, n is m bit length and $n+1 < 2^m$). If the input message of the Algorithm 2 is $n-1$ or $n+1$, the value of register $R[2]$ will be equal to 1 after the first iteration. Then, two patterns will be found and we can use the method mentioned above to retrieve the secret key. However, using these two values all the secret key bits can be derived except d_0. When $n-1$ is used as the input message, d_0 can be known by detecting whether the final result is $M^d = 1$. When $n+1$ is used, four candidates of the secret key must be tested through trial-and-error approach.

For a better understanding of the attack against Algorithm 2, its behavior is illustrated in Table 1 when M is equal to 1, $n-1$ or $n+1$. Here, it is also assumed that $d = 77 = (1001101)_2$. Table 1 shows that the step 6 in the first iteration is different from the other iterations when $M = n-1$ and $M = n+1$. As they have no collisions with other operations, d_0 cannot be retrieved directly as mentioned above. In addition, collision operations are shown in the table too. The secret key can be retrieved easily using power collisions. Fig.2 shows our attack on Algorithm 2 when $M = 1$. It is obvious that when **M1** is calculated, the current key bit is 1 and when **M2** is calculated, the current key bit is 0.

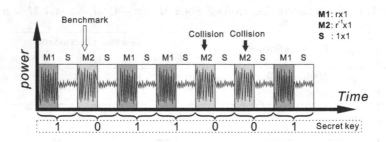

Fig. 2. Proposed attack on Algorithm 2 when $M = 1$

It is noted that some exponentiation algorithms perform a modular reduction before exponentiation to ensure that M is between 0 and N, in which case $N+1$ would be reduced to 1 and the $N+1$ attack would be equivalent to the 1 attack.

3.2   Attack on Montgomery Powering Ladder Algorithm

Montgomery Powering Ladder described in Algorithm 3 was proposed by Joye and Yen[2]. This algorithm can resist some side-channel attacks, such as classical SPA, timing attack and safe-error attacks. In this section, we show in the following this algorithm is vulnerable to the $N - 1$ attack and its extended version. Here, a different approach to retrieve the key which derives from relative doubling attack[14] is exploited.

Algorithm 3. Montgomery powering ladder algorithm

Input: M, $d = (d_{m-1} \cdots d_i)_2$, n
Output: $M^d \bmod n$
1: $R[0] = r$
2: $R[1] = M$
3: **for** i *from* $(m - 1)$ *downto* 0 *do*
4:     $b = \neg d_i$
5:     $R[b] = R[b] \times R[k_i] \bmod n$
6:     $R[k_i] = R[k_i]^2 \bmod n$
7: **return** $R[0]$

Carefully observing Algorithm 3, we can find that it is different from the algorithms mentioned earlier. It behaves very regularly without any padding. In other words, a modular multiplication operation is always followed up by a modular squaring in one loop iteration and the two operations are both associated with the secret key.

- If d_i is equal to 0, step 5 and step 6 of the iterations (i) performs:
  $R[1] = R[1] \times R[0] \bmod n$, $R[0] = R[0]^2 \bmod n$.
- If d_i is equal to 1, step 5 and step 6 of the iterations (i) performs:
  $R[0] = R[0] \times R[1] \bmod n$, $R[1] = R[1]^2 \bmod n$.

It can be seen that if we can distinguish which modular squaring operation is working on, the secret key will be retrieved easily. Observing the association we find that if two consecutive secret key bits, d_i and d_{i-1}, are the same, the step 6 will take the result of step 6 in iteration i as the operand in iteration $i - 1$. That is to say the value of register is reused. While if the two consecutive secret key bits are different, the result of step 5 in iteration i will be taken as the operand of step 6 in iteration $i - 1$. So if an attacker can judge when the operand of the step 6 is changed, he can deduce that d_i is different from d_{i-1}. Otherwise, d_i is the same as d_{i-1}. To retrieve the secret key, MSB (which is usually binary one) of the secret key should be supposed as 1 or 0, and then the other bits (except d_0) can be deduced bit by bit using the characteristic mentioned before. Similarly, d_0 can be known by detecting whether the final result is $M^d = 1$. Finally, since the uncertainty of the MSB, two possible secret key can be got and trial-and-error approach should be used to get the correct secret key.

In order to determine whether the operand of step 6 is changed, $n - 1$ can be used as the input message. Then the characteristic described below can be received $(i \neq m - 1)$. If $d_{m-1} = 1$ or $d_{m-1} = 0$, the operation $(n - 1)^2$ or 1^2 will be calculated respectively.

- If $d_i = d_{i-1}$, step 6 of the iterations $(i - 1)$ performs:$1^2 \ mod \ n$.
- If $d_i \neq d_{i-1}$, step 6 of the iterations $(i - 1)$ performs:$(n - 1)^2 \ mod \ n$.

Furthermore, the extended method of $N - 1$ attack with two input messages m_1 and $m_2 = m_1 \times (n - 1)$ is also applicable to Algorithm 3. To carry out this attack, two executions should be done. Then two patterns described below will be obtained $(i \neq m - 1)$.

- If $d_i = d_{i-1}$, step 6 of the iterations $(i - 1)$ of two executions are the same.
- If $d_i \neq d_{i-1}$, step 6 of the iterations $(i - 1)$ of two executions are different.

Table 2 shows the process to calculate Algorithm 3 and displays the collision operations. In this example, it is assumed that $M = n - 1$ and $d = 77 = (1001101)_2$. It is obvious that when d_i is changed from 0 to 1 or 1 to 0, the operation $(n - 1)^2$ has been calculated. When d_i is the same as d_{i-1}, i.e. $(11)_2$ or $(00)_2$, the operation 1^2 has been calculated. We described the attack when $M = n-1$ in Fig. 3. The first **S2** is chosen as the benchmark. It can be seen that when **S1** is calculated, the corresponding key bit is equal to previous one and when collision operation **S2** is calculated, the corresponding key bit is different from the previous. The conversions are donated by arrows in Fig. 3.

Table 2. Computation of M^d in the Algorithm 3

i	d_i	Intermediate Steps	Collision Operations		
			$M = n - 1$	$M = m_1$	$M = m_1 \times (n - 1)$
6	1	$R[0] = R[0] \times R[1]$ $R[1] = R[1]^2$	$(n - 1)^2$	$m_1{}^2$	$(m_1 \times (n - 1))^2$
5	0	$R[1] = R[1] \times R[0]$ $R[0] = R[0]^2$	$(n - 1)^2$	$m_1{}^2$	$(m_1 \times (n - 1))^2$
4	0	$R[1] = R[1] \times R[0]$ $R[0] = R[0]^2$	1^2	$(m_1{}^2)^2$	$(m_1{}^2)^2$
3	1	$R[0] = R[0] \times R[1]$ $R[1] = R[1]^2$	$(n - 1)^2$	$(m_1{}^5)^2$	$(m_1{}^5 \times (n - 1))^2$
2	1	$R[0] = R[0] \times R[1]$ $R[1] = R[1]^2$	1^2	$(m_1{}^{10})^2$	$(m_1{}^{10})^2$
1	0	$R[1] = R[1] \times R[0]$ $R[0] = R[0]^2$	$(n - 1)^2$	$(m_1{}^{19})^2$	$(m_1{}^{19} \times (n - 1))^2$
0	1	$R[0] = R[0] \times R[1]$ $R[1] = R[1]^2$	$(n - 1)^2$	$(m_1{}^{39})^2$	$(m_1{}^{39} \times (n - 1))^2$

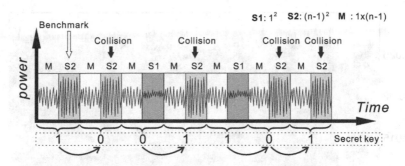

Fig. 3. Proposed attack on Algorithm 3 when $M = n - 1$

4   Experiment Results

In order to verify the effectiveness of our attack, we designed two 1024-bit RSA processors based on Algorithm 2 and Algorithm 3, respectively, using Verilog HDL. The design was synthesized with 0.13 um CMOS standard cell library by Synopsys Design Complier. Then the power consumption waveform was obtained by simulation. And the waveform segments were aligned precisely using the phase-based wave-form matching technique. Finally, the difference between the waveforms was calculated to evaluate the equality of the operations.

The modular multiplication algorithm which we employed is the widely used high-radix Montgomery multiplication called finely integrated operand scanning (FIOS) method i.e. the Type-I algorithm[15]. The multiplier used is 64-bit. The secret key and modulus are chosen randomly.

Given two integers x and y, Montgomery modular multiplication algorithm computes:

$$MontMul(x, y, n) = x \times y \times R^{-1} \ mod \ n \ (R = 2^{\lceil log_2(n) \rceil})$$

Therefore, initialization of the values of registers should be done at the beginning of modular exponentiation algorithms, to transform the operands into the Montgomery form. And at the end of the modular exponentiation the result should also be converted into the normal form. Thus, the operations 1^2 and $(n - 1)^2$ have been changed into $R^2 \ mod \ n$ and $(n - 1) \times R^2 \ mod \ n$. Therefore, the discrimination between the power traces of 1^2 and $(n - 1)^2$ which is described in [10] are unable to be perceived by visual observation. Power collision method can be used to determine whether two operations are the same or different. To simplify the description, we will just intercept the power consumption of the first 12 bits of the key begins from MSB or LSB in the following.

Fig.4 shows a single power trace of Algorithm 2 using the chosen message 1. Its actual first 12 bits of the key are $(101111101101)_2$. By observing the figure, we cannot retrieve the secret key. The reason is that the power traces of every operation are almost the same which cannot be distinguished just by visual observation. Therefore, we chose the power segment of the first **M2** as the

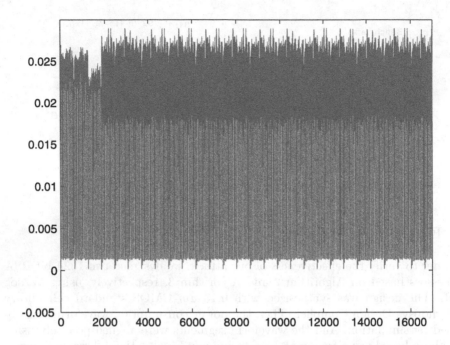

Fig. 4. Power trace of Algorithm 2

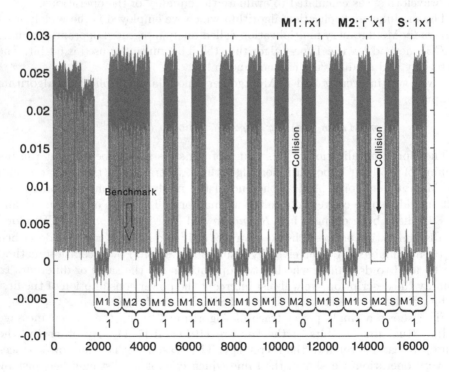

Fig. 5. Power collision result of Algorithm 2

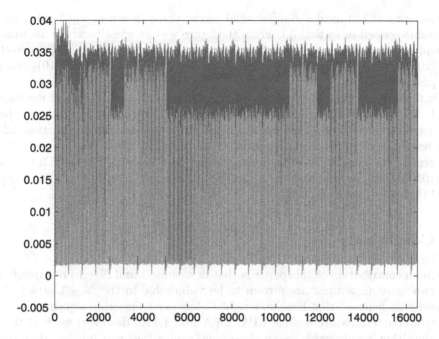

Fig. 6. Power trace of Algorithm 3

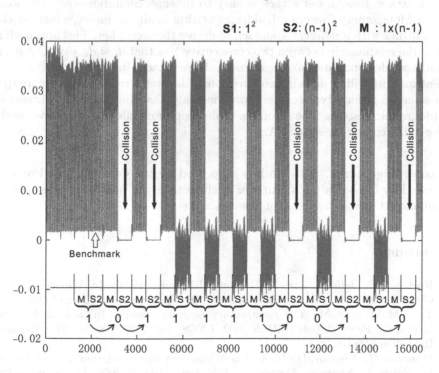

Fig. 7. Power collision result of Algorithm 3

benchmark and obtained the differential power trace shown in Fig.5 using the method described in section 3.1. From the figure we can identify which modular multiplication are the same as the benchmark easily. Then we derived the correct key $(101111101101)_2$ easily regardless of the wrong one $(010000010010)_2$ from two possibilities.

Fig.6 shows a single power trace of Algorithm 3 using the chosen message $n - 1$. Its actual first 12 bits of the key are $(101111100110)_2$. Fig.7 shows the power collision result of Algorithm 3 using the method described in section 3.2. The benchmark is the power segment of the first **S2**. From the power collision result, two possible result can be obtained, which are $(101111100110)_2$ and $(000101001100)_2$. A trial-and-error approach were used to select the correct key $(101111100110)_2$ by us finally.

5 Conclusions

The main contribution of this paper is that new value 1 and $N + 1$ are exploited and two more algorithms are proven to be vulnerable to the $N - 1$ attack. It is previously believed that Boscher's right-to-left exponentiation algorithm is an effective countermeasure against SPA, DPA and DFA. However, we find that this algorithm is vulnerable to our chosen-message attack which is based on the $N - 1$ attack, though our attack is easy to defense. Simultaneously, the well-known Montgomery Powering Ladder algorithm is shown insecure against the $N - 1$ attack with a different approach to derive the secret key. This approach is to use the relationship between two consecutive bits that $d_i = d_{i-1}$ or $d_i \neq d_{i-1}$. Finally, we demonstrate the effectiveness of the attacks in experiments.

Future work will be done in two directions. The first is to investigate more special values in general types of the chosen-message that have potential threats to cryptographic systems. The second is to develop more effective defensive methods against chosen-message SPA.

Acknowledgements. This work is supported by the Open Project Program of State Key Laboratory of Computer Architecture, the Institute of Computing Technology, Chinese Academy of Sciences.

References

1. Kocher, P.C., Jaffe, J., Jun, B.: Differential Power Analysis. In: Wiener, M. (ed.) CRYPTO 1999. LNCS, vol. 1666, pp. 388–397. Springer, Heidelberg (1999)
2. Joye, M., Yen, S.-M.: The montgomery powering ladder. In: Kaliski Jr, B.S., Koç, Ç.K., Paar, C. (eds.) CHES 2002. LNCS, vol. 2523, pp. 291–302. Springer, Heidelberg (2003)
3. Fumaroli, G., Vigilant, D.: Blinded fault resistant exponentiation. In: Breveglieri, L., Koren, I., Naccache, D., Seifert, J.-P. (eds.) FDTC 2006. LNCS, vol. 4236, pp. 62–70. Springer, Heidelberg (2006)

4. Schmidt, J.-M., Medwed, M.: Fault attacks on the montgomery powering ladder. In: Rhee, K.-H., Nyang, D. (eds.) ICISC 2010. LNCS, vol. 6829, pp. 396–406. Springer, Heidelberg (2011)
5. Boscher, A., Handschuh, H., Trichina, E.: Blinded fault resistant exponentiation revisited. In: Breveglieri, L., et al. (eds.) Fault Diagnosis and Tolerance in Cryptography - FDTC 2009, pp. 3–9. IEEE Computer Society (2009)
6. Yen S.-M., Lien W.-C., Moon S., Ha J.: Power analysis by exploiting chosen message and internal collisions-vulnerability of checking mechanism for RSA-decryption. In: Dawson, E., Vaudenay, S. (eds.) Mycrypt 2005. LNCS, vol. 3715, pp. 183-195. Springer, Heidelberg (2005)
7. Coron, J.-S.: Resistance against differential power analysis for elliptic curve cryptosystems. In: Koç, Ç.K., Paar, C. (eds.) CHES 1999. LNCS, vol. 1717, pp. 292–302. Springer, Heidelberg (1999)
8. Mamiya, H., Miyaji, A., Morimoto, H.: Efficient countermeasures against RPA, DPA, and SPA. In: Joye, M., Quisquater, J.-J. (eds.) CHES 2004. LNCS, vol. 3156, pp. 343–356. Springer, Heidelberg (2004)
9. Miyamoto, A., Homma, N., Aoki, T., Satoh, A.: Enhanced power analysis attack using chosen message against RSA hardware implementations. In: ISCAS, pp. 3282–3285 (2008)
10. Courrège, J.-C., Feix, B., Roussellet, M.: Simple power analysis on exponentiation revisited. In: Gollmann, D., Lanet, J.-L., Iguchi-Cartigny, J. (eds.) CARDIS 2010. LNCS, vol. 6035, pp. 65–79. Springer, Heidelberg (2010)
11. Homma, N., Miyamoto, A., Aoki, T., Satoh, A., Samir, A.: Comparative power analysis of modular exponentiation algorithms. IEEE Trans. Comput. 59(6), 795–807 (2010)
12. Clavier, C., Feix, B.: Updated recommendations for blinded exponentiation vs. single trace analysis. In: Prouff, E. (ed.) COSADE 2013. LNCS, vol. 7864, pp. 80–98. Springer, Heidelberg (2013)
13. Aidong, C., Sen, X., Yun, C., Zhiguang, Q.: Collision-based chosen-message simple power clustering attack algorithm. Communications, China, 114–119 (2013)
14. Yen, S.-M., Ko, L.-C., Moon, S.-J., Ha, J.C.: Relative doubling attack against montgomery ladder. In: Won, D.H., Kim, S. (eds.) ICISC 2005. LNCS, vol. 3935, pp. 117–128. Springer, Heidelberg (2006)
15. Miyamoto, A., Homma, N., Aoki, T., Satoh, A.: Systematic design of RSA processors based on high-radix Montgomery multipliers. In: IEEE Transactions on Very Large Scale Integration (VLSI) Systems, pp. 1136–1146 (2011)

Cryptanalysis of RSA with Multiple Small Secret Exponents

Atsushi Takayasu and Noboru Kunihiro

The University of Tokyo, Japan
{a-takayasu@it.,kunihiro@}k.u-tokyo.ac.jp

Abstract. In this paper, we study the security of RSA when there are multiple public/secret exponents $(e_1, d_1), \ldots, (e_n, d_n)$ with the same public modulus N. We assume that all secret exponents are smaller than N^β. When $n = 1$, Boneh and Durfee proposed a polynomial time algorithm to factor the public modulus N. The algorithm works provided that $\beta < 1 - 1/\sqrt{2}$. So far, several generalizations of the attacks for arbitrary n have been proposed. However, these attacks do not achieve Boneh and Durfee's bound for $n = 1$. In this paper, we propose an algorithm which is the exact generalization of Boneh and Durfee's algorithm. Our algorithm works when $\beta < 1 - \sqrt{2/(3n + 1)}$. Our bound is better than all previous results for all $n \geq 2$. We construct the lattices by collecting as many helpful polynomials as possible. The collections reduce the volume of the lattices and enable us to improve the bound.

Keywords: Cryptanalysis, RSA, Lattices, Coppersmith's method.

1 Introduction

1.1 Background

Small Secret Exponent RSA. Small secret exponent RSA is efficient for its low cost decryption and signature generation, but is known to be insecure. We assume that decryption exponent is smaller than N^β. Wiener [Wie90] proposed the polynomial time algorithm to factor public modulus N. The algorithm works when $\beta < 0.25$. The algorithm is constructed by computing the diophantine approximation of rational number.

Boneh and Durfee [BD00] revisited the Wiener's attack. They constucted improved algorithm by using lattice based method to solve modular equations proposed by Coppersmith [Cop96a]. At first, they constructed the lattices which provide Wiener's bound, $\beta < 0.25$. They improved the bound to $\beta < (7 - 2\sqrt{7})/6 = 0.28474\cdots$ by adding some extra polynomials in the lattice bases. Finally, they achieved the stronger bound $\beta < 1 - 1/\sqrt{2} = 0.29289\cdots$ by extracting sublattices from the previous lattices. Though several papers revisited the work [BM01, HM10, Kun11, KSI11, Kun12], none of them improved Boneh and Durfee's stronger bound. Boneh and Durfee's attack has also been applied to the variants of RSA [DN00, IKK08a, May04].

W. Susilo and Y. Mu (Eds.): ACISP 2014, LNCS 8544, pp. 176–191, 2014.
© Springer International Publishing Switzerland 2014

Multiple Small Secret Exponents RSA. Generalizations of small secret exponent attack on RSA have also been considered when there are multiple public/secret key pairs $(e_1, d_1), \ldots, (e_n, d_n)$ for the same public modulus N. All secret keys $d_1, \ldots, d_n$ are smaller than N^β. Howgrave-Graham and Seifert [HS99] generalized Wiener's attack and achieved the bound

$$\beta < \frac{(2n+1) \cdot 2^n - (2n+1)\binom{n}{n/2}}{(2n-2) \cdot 2^n + (4n+2)\binom{n}{n/2}} \text{ when } n \text{ is even,}$$

$$\beta < \frac{(2n+1) \cdot 2^n - 4n\binom{n-1}{(n-1)/2}}{(2n-2) \cdot 2^n + 8n\binom{n-1}{(n-1)/2}} \text{ when } n \text{ is odd.}$$

The bound converges to full size secret exponents, $\beta = 1$.

Sarkar and Maitra [SM10b] used the Coppersmith's method to find small roots of polynomials over the integers [Cop96b] and improved the bound. They constructed the lattices based on Jochemsz and May's strategy [JM06]. The algorithm works when

$$\beta < \frac{3}{4} - \frac{1}{n+1}.$$

The algorithm improved Howgrave-Graham and Seifert's bound for $2 \le n \le 42$. In the same work [SM10b], Sarkar and Maitra achieved ad-hoc improvement, $\beta < 0.422$ for $n = 2$. See also [SM10a].

Aono [Aon13] used the Coppersmith's method to solve modular equations [Cop96a] and improved the bound. Aono's algorithm works when

$$\beta < \frac{3}{4} - \frac{2}{3n+1}.$$

The algorithm improved Sarkar and Maitra's algorithm. The bound is better than Howgrave-Graham and Seifert's bound for $2 \le n \le 46$. In the same work [Aon13], Aono heurisically considered ad-hoc improvement for $n \ge 3$, though no exact conditions are given.

All these algorithms run in polynomial time in $\log N$ and exponential in n. It is clear that these algorithms have the room to be improved. All algorithms only achieve Wiener's bound [Wie90] for $n = 1$. In addition, we should consider the case when there are infinitely many public/secret key pairs. In this case, Aono [Aon13] counted the number of solutions and claimed that public modulus N can be factored with full size secret exponents. Howgrave-Graham and Seifert's bound [HS99] converges to $\beta < 1$. However, Sarkar and Maitra's bound [SM10b] and Aono's bound [Aon13] converge to $\beta < 3/4$. Therefore, we should construct the algorithm which achieves Boneh and Durfee's bound [BD00] and converges to $\beta < 1$.

Lattice Constructions for the Coppersmith's Methods. At Eurocrypt 1996, Coppersmith introduced celebrated lattice based methods. One method is to solve modular univariate equations which have small solutions [Cop96a].

The other method is to find small roots of bivariate polynomials over the integers [Cop96b]. Both methods can be heuristically generalized to more multivariate cases with reasonable assumption. The former method was reformulated by Howgrave-Graham [How97], and the latter method was reformulated by Coron [Cor04, Cor07]. The Coppersmith's methods have been used to reveal the vulnerabilites of several cryptosystems, especially RSA cryptosystem [Cop97, Cop01, NS01, May10].

The Coppersmith's methods have improved several algorithms which compute diophantine approximation of rational numbers. Boneh and Durfee [BD00] improved Winer's small secret exponent attack on RSA [Wie90]. Howgrave-Graham [How01] considered approximate common divisor problems and constructed two types of algorithms. The first algorithm computes diophantine approximation. The second algorithm uses the Coppersmith's method. Since the second algorithm is better than the first algorithm, Howgrave-Graham's results imply that the Coppersmith's method is superior to the other method. Therefore, Howgrave-Graham and Seifert's result [HS99] is expected to be improved by using the Coppersmith's method.

To maximize the solvable root bounds using the Coppersmith's methods, we should select appropriate lattice bases which reduce the volume. At Asiacrypt 2006, Jochemsz and May [JM06] proposed the strategy for lattice constructions. The strategy can automatically decide the selections of lattice bases. The strategy covers several former results [BD00, Weg02, May04, EJMW05], and later some algorithms [JM07] have been proposed based on the strategy including Sarkar and Maitra's work [SM10a, SM10b]. However, it is widely known that Jochemsz and May's strategy does not always select the appropriate lattice bases. In fact, for small secret exponent attacks on RSA, we only obtain Boneh and Durfee's weaker bound $\beta < (7 - 2\sqrt{7})/6$ based on the strategy. The strategy cannot tell us the selections of lattice bases which provide Boneh and Durfee's stronger bound [BD00]. Therefore, Sarkar and Maitra's results [SM10a, SM10b] are expected to be improved by selecting appropriate lattice bases.

For $n \geq 2$, Aono solved simultaneous modular equations. Each single equation is the same one which Boneh and Durfee [BD00] solve. Aono combined Boneh and Durfee's n lattices based on Minkowski sum. However, Aono used Boneh and Durfee's lattices which only achieve Wiener's bound $\beta < 0.25$. Therefore, it is clear that the algorithm cannot achieve Boneh and Durfee's stronger bound for $n = 1$ and is expected to be improved.

What makes the problems difficult is that we should change the selections of lattice bases with respect to the sizes of root bounds. Sarkar and Maitra's ad-hoc improvement [SM10b] for $n = 2$ is achieved based on the condition $\beta < 1/2$. They selected extra polynomials in the lattice bases to reduce the volume. Boneh and Durfee's improvement [BD00] from the Wiener's bound [Wie90] is also based on the condition $\beta < 1/2$ by adding extra polynomials. Conversely, though heuristic, Aono's ad-hoc improvement [Aon13] for $n \geq 3$ is based on the fact that $\beta > 1/2$. Aono claimed that some polynomials in the lattice bases should be eliminated to reduce the volume. Therefore, we should work out the selections of lattice bases which take into account the sizes of root bounds in general.

Collecting Helpful Polynomials. Recently, Takayasu and Kunihiro [TK13] proposed simple and useful strategy for lattice constructions. In their strategy, the notion of *helpful polynomials* is essential. The notion was firstly noted by May [May10]. Helpful polynomials can reduce the volume of the lattices and contribute to the conditions for modular equations to be solved. If each polynomial is helpful or not is decided by comparing the sizes of diagonals and the size of modulus. Takayasu and Kunihiro claimed that as many helpful polynomials as possible should be selected, and as few unhelpful polynomials as possible should be selected in the lattice bases. Based on the strategy, they improved the algorithms to solve two forms of modular multivariate linear equations [HM08, CH12] when each root bound becomes extremely large or small.

1.2 Our Results

In this paper, we solve the same simultaneous modular equations as Aono [Aon13]. However, we change the selections of lattice bases and improve the previous bounds. Based on Takayasu and Kunihiro's strategy for lattice constructions [TK13], we reveal that there are some helpful polynomials which were not selected or there are some unhelpful polynomials which were selected in Aono's lattice bases. This analysis enables us to select as many helpful polynomials as possible and as few unhelpful polynomials as possible. Our algorithm works provided that

$$\beta < 1 - \sqrt{\frac{2}{3n+1}}.$$

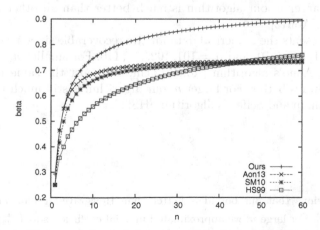

Fig. 1. The comparison of the recoverable sizes of secret exponents

Table 1. Numerical data for the recoverable sizes of secret exponents

n	Ours	[Aon13]	[SM10b]	[HS99]
1	0.292893219	0.25	0.25	0.25
2	0.465477516	0.464285714	0.416666667	0.357142857
3	0.552786405	0.55	0.5	0.4
4	0.60776773	0.596153846	0.55	0.441176471
5	0.646446609	0.625	0.583333333	0.467741935
6	0.675557158	0.644736842	0.607142857	0.493103448
7	0.698488655	0.659090909	0.625	0.512048193
8	0.717157288	0.67	0.638888889	0.530181087
9	0.732738758	0.678571429	0.65	0.544740024
10	0.745999746	0.685483871	0.659090909	0.55872622
⋮	⋮	⋮	⋮	⋮
101	0.918889289	0.743421053	0.740196078	0.805167829
102	0.919286569	0.743485342	0.740291262	0.80595288
103	0.919678067	0.743548387	0.740384615	0.806723605
104	0.920063923	0.743610224	0.74047619	0.807488696
105	0.920444272	0.743670886	0.740566038	0.808240085
106	0.920819242	0.743730408	0.740654206	0.808986071
107	0.921188959	0.74378882	0.740740741	0.809718942
108	0.921553546	0.743846154	0.740825688	0.810446627
109	0.921913119	0.743902439	0.740909091	0.811161748
110	0.922267793	0.743957704	0.740990991	0.811871889

Our algorithm achieves Boneh and Durfee's bound $\beta < 1 - 1/\sqrt{2}$ for $n = 1$, and converges to $\beta < 1$ with infinitely many exponents. The bound[1] is better than all known algorithms [HS99, SM10a, SM10b, Aon13].

Figure 1 compares the recoverable sizes of secret exponents for $n = 1, 2, \ldots, 60$. For smaller n, our algorithm is slightly better than Aono's algorithm [Aon13]. However, for larger n, our algorithm is much better than all other algorithms [HS99, SM10b, Aon13].

Table 1 represents the numerical data for the recoverable sizes of secret exponents for $n = 1, 2, \ldots, 10$, and $n = 101, 102, \ldots, 110$. For smaller n, though our algorithm and Aono's algorithm [Aon13] achieve almost the same bound, our algorithm is always better. For larger n, our algorithm is still much better than Howgrave-Graham and Seifert's algorithm [HS99].

---

[1] It is not obvious that our bound is better than Howgrave-Graham and Seifert's bound [HS99]. For large n, we approximate binomial coefficients as $\binom{n}{n/2} \approx \sqrt{\frac{2}{\pi n}} 2^n$ (see [OLBC10] in detail). The approximation suggests that our bound is better than the previous bound. The detailed analysis is written in the full version.

1.3 Organizations

In Section 2, we introduce the lattice based Coppersmith's method to solve modular equations [Cop96a], and the lattice construction strategy proposed by Takayasu and Kunihiro [TK13]. In Section 3, we recall the Boneh and Durfee's algorithm [BD00] and Aono's algorithm [Aon13]. In Section 4, we analyze the previous lattice constructions [BD00, Aon13] based on Takayasu and Kunihiro's strategy [TK13]. In Section 5, we propose our improved algorithm. In Section 6, we discuss the security of multiple exponents RSA in partial key exposure situations.

2 Preliminaries

In this section, we introduce the Coppersmith's method to solve modular equations which have small solutions [Cop96a]. First, we explain Howgrave-Graham's reformulation of the method [How97], and the LLL algorithm [LLL82]. After that, we introduce the strategy for lattice constructions proposed by Takayasu and Kunihiro [TK13].

Consider the modular equations, $h(x_1, \ldots, x_n) = 0 \pmod{W}$. All sizes of the solutions $(\tilde{x}_1, \ldots, \tilde{x}_n)$ are bounded by $X_1, \ldots, X_n$. When $\prod_{j=1}^{n} X_j$ is much smaller than W, the Coppersmith's method can find all the solutions in polynomial time. We write the norm of polynomials as $\|h(x_1, \ldots, x_n)\|$, which represents the Euclidean norm of the coefficeint vector. The following Howgrave-Graham's Lemma reduces the modular equations into integer equations.

Lemma 1 (Howgrave-Graham's Lemma [How97]). *Let $\tilde{h}(x_1, \ldots, x_n) \in \mathbb{Z}[x_1, \ldots, x_n]$ be a polynomial with at most w monomials. Let $m, W, X_1, \ldots, X_n$ be positive integers. Consider the case when*
1. $\tilde{h}(\tilde{x}_1, \ldots, \tilde{x}_n) = 0 \pmod{W^m}$, where $|\tilde{x}_1| < X_1, \ldots, |\tilde{x}_n| < X_n$,
2. $\|\tilde{h}(x_1 X_1, \ldots, x_n X_n)\| < W^m / \sqrt{w}$.
Then $\tilde{h}(\tilde{x}_1, \ldots, \tilde{x}_n) = 0$ holds over the integers.

To solve n-variate modular equations $h(x_1, \ldots, x_n) = 0 \pmod{W}$, it is suffice to find n new polynomials $\tilde{h}_1(x_1, \ldots, x_n), \ldots, \tilde{h}_n(x_1, \ldots, x_n)$ whose roots are the same as the solutions $(\tilde{x}_1, \ldots, \tilde{x}_n)$ and whose norms are small enough to satisfy Hograve-Graham's Lemma.

To find such polynomials from the original polynomial $h(x_1, \ldots, x_n)$, lattices and the LLL algorithm are often used. Lattices represent the integer linear combinations of the basis vectors. All vectors are row representation. For the basis vectors $\mathbf{b}_1, \ldots, \mathbf{b}_w$, which are all v dimensional vectors in $\mathbb{R}^v$, the lattice spanned by these vectors is defined as

$$L(\mathbf{b}_1, \ldots, \mathbf{b}_w) := \{\sum_{j=1}^{w} c_j \mathbf{b}_j : c_j \in \mathbb{Z} \text{ for all } j = 1, \ldots, w\}.$$

We also use the matrix representation for the basis. We define the basis matrix B as $w \times v$ matrix which has the basis vectors $\mathbf{b}_1, \ldots, \mathbf{b}_w$ in each row. In the same way, the lattice can be rewritten as $L(B)$. We call the lattice full-rank when $w = v$. The volume of the lattice $\text{vol}(L(B))$ is defined as the w-dimensional volume of the parallelpiped $\mathcal{P}(B) := \{xB : x \in \mathbb{R}^w, 0 \le x_j < 1, \text{for all } j = 1, \ldots, w\}$. The volume can be computed as $\text{vol}(L(B)) = \sqrt{\det(BB^T)}$. It is clear that the volume of full-rank lattice can be computed as $\text{vol}(L(B)) = |\det(B)|$.

Lattice is used in many places in cryptography. See [NS01, nv10] in detail. In cryptanalysis, it is very important to find non-zero short lattice vectors. In this paper, we introduce the LLL algorithm [LLL82] which outputs non-zero short lattice vectors in polynomial time.

Proposition 1 (LLL algorithm [LLL82]). *Given basis vectors* $\mathbf{b}_1, \ldots, \mathbf{b}_w$ *in* $\mathbb{R}^k$, *the LLL algorithm finds LLL-reduced bases* $\tilde{\mathbf{b}}_1, \ldots, \tilde{\mathbf{b}}_w$ *that satisfy*

$$\|\tilde{\mathbf{b}}_n\| \le 2^{w(w-1)/4(w-n+1)}(\text{vol}(L(B)))^{1/(w-n+1)} \quad \text{for } 1 \le n \le w,$$

in polynomial time in w, v, *and the maximum input length.*

Again, we consider how to solve modular equations $h(x_1, \ldots, x_n) = 0$ (mod W). First, we construct w polynomials $h_1(x_1, \ldots, x_n), \ldots, h_w(x_1, \ldots, x_n)$, which have the roots $(\tilde{x}_1, \ldots, \tilde{x}_n)$ modulo W^m with positive integer m. We convert these polynomials to the vectors $\mathbf{b}_1, \ldots, \mathbf{b}_w$ in $\mathbb{Z}^v$, and construct the matrix B. The elements of each vector $\mathbf{b}_j$ are the same as the coefficients of $h_j(x_1 X_1, \ldots, x_n X_n)$. All i-th elements of the vectors $\mathbf{b}_1, \ldots, \mathbf{b}_w$ are the coefficients of the same variables $x_1^{i_1} \cdots x_n^{i_n}$ for all $1 \le i \le k$. The vectors can be converted to the polynomials in the opposite way. We span the lattice $L(B)$. Since all the lattice vectors are the integer linear combinations of the basis vectors, the polynomials which are conversions of the lattice vectors have the roots $(\tilde{x}_1, \ldots, \tilde{x}_n)$ modulo W^m. We apply the LLL algorithm to the lattice bases and obtain n LLL-reduced bases $\tilde{\mathbf{b}}_1, \ldots, \tilde{\mathbf{b}}_n$. Finally, we can get the polynomials $\tilde{h}_1(x_1, \ldots, x_n), \ldots, \tilde{h}_n(x_1, \ldots, x_n)$ by converting the LLL-reduced bases. The norm of these polynomials are small. These polynomials satisfy Howgrave-Graham's Lemma provided that

$$(\text{vol}(L(B)))^{1/w} < W^m.$$

We omit the small terms.

When we obtain the polynomials $\tilde{h}_1(x_1, \ldots, x_n), \ldots, \tilde{h}_n(x_1, \ldots, x_n)$, it is easy to solve the modular equation $h(x_1, \ldots, x_n) = 0$ (mod W). What we should do is to find the roots of the polynomials over the integers by computing resultant or Gröbner basis. We should note that the method needs heuristic argument if we consider multivariate problems. Since the polynomials $\tilde{h}_1(x_1, \ldots, x_n), \ldots, \tilde{h}_n(x_1, \ldots, x_n)$ have no assurance of algebraic independency. In this paper, we assume that the polynomials are algebraic independence as the previous works [BD00, SM10a, SM10b, Aon13]. In fact, there are few negative cases reported.

The solvable sizes of small solutions depend on the lattice constructions. To maximize the sizes, we should select appropriate lattice bases which reduce the volume. Recently, Takayasu and Kunihiro [TK13] proposed the strategy for the selections. To construct the triangular basis matrix, we define helpful polynomials whose diagonals are smaller than the modulus W^m. Since helpful polynomials contribute to the conditions for modular equations to be solved, we should select as many helpful polynomials as possible in the lattice bases. Conversely, unhelpful polynomials whose diagonals are larger than the modulus do not contribute to the conditions. We should select as few unhelpful polynomials as possible. The selections should be done with the constraint for the basis matrix to be triangular. The strategy clarifies which polynomials to be selected and which polynomials not to be selected in the lattice bases. To improve the previous bounds, we should add helpful polynomials or eliminate unhelpful polynomials in the lattice bases. When we counstruct the basis matrix which is not triangular, we should transform the basis matrix to be triangular by using unravelled linearization [HM09].

3   Previous Works

In this section, we introduce the lattice constructions in previous works [BD00, Aon13], which used the Coppersmith's method to solve modular equations [Cop96a, How97].

3.1   Boneh and Durfee's Lattice Construction

We recall the RSA key generation,

$$ed = 1 + k\phi(N), \text{ where } \phi(N) = (p-1)(q-1).$$

Boneh and Durfee [BD00] considered the modular polynomial

$$f(x,y) = 1 + x(N+y) \pmod{e}.$$

The polynomial has the roots $(x,y) = (k, 1 - p - q)$. The sizes of the roots are bounded by $X := N^\beta, Y := 3N^{1/2}$. If we can find the roots, we can easily factor RSA modulus N.

To solve the modular equation $f(x,y) = 0$, Boneh and Durfee constructed the basis matrix with polynomials which have the roots $(x,y) = (k, 1 - p - q)$ modulo e^m. At first, Boneh and Durfee used the shift-polynomials,

$$x^i f(x,y)^j e^{m-j}, \text{ with } j = 0, 1, \ldots, m, i = 0, 1, \ldots, m - j,$$

in the lattice bases. The shift-polynomials modulo e^m have the roots $(x,y) = (k, 1 - p - q)$. The shift-polynomials generate the triangular basis matrix with diagonals $X^{i+j}Y^j e^{m-j}$ for all i, j. Ignoring low order terms of m, we can compute the dimension $w = \frac{1}{2}m^2$ and the volume of the lattice $\text{vol}(L(B)) = X^{\frac{1}{6}m^3} Y^{\frac{1}{6}m^3} e^{\frac{1}{3}m^3}$. The lattice provides Wiener's bound $\beta < 0.25$.

To improve the bound, Boneh and Durfee added extra shifts,

$$y^l f(x,y)^u e^{m-u}, \text{ with } u = 0, 1, \ldots, m, l = 1, \ldots, t,$$

in the lattice bases. The shift-polynomials modulo e^m have the roots $(x, y) = (k, 1-p-q)$. We should optimize the parameter $\tau := t/u$. Though the extra shifts do not generate the tirangular basis matrix, we can transform it to be triangular using unravelled linearization [HM09]. The detailed analysis is written in [HM10]. After the transformation, the sizes of the diagonals become $X^u Y^{u+l} e^{m-u}$. Ignoring low order terms of m, we can compute the dimension $w = (\frac{1}{2} + \frac{\tau}{2})m^2$ and the volume of the lattice $\mathrm{vol}(L(B)) = X^{(\frac{1}{3}+\frac{\tau}{3})m^3} Y^{(\frac{1}{6}+\frac{\tau}{3}+\frac{\tau^2}{6})m^3} e^{(\frac{1}{3}+\frac{\tau}{6})m^3}$. We can solve the modular equation $f(x, y) = 0$ provided that $(\mathrm{vol}(L(B)))^{1/w} < e^m$, that is,

$$\beta(\frac{1}{3} + \frac{\tau}{3}) + \frac{1}{2}(\frac{1}{6} + \frac{\tau}{3} + \frac{\tau^2}{6}) + \frac{1}{3} + \frac{\tau}{6} < \frac{1}{2} + \frac{\tau}{2}.$$

To maximize the solvable bound β, we optimize $\tau = 1 - 2\beta$ and obtain the stronger bound $\beta < 1 - 1/\sqrt{2}$.

3.2 Aono's Lattice Construction

For the multiple key setting, the attackers have multiple public exponents $e_1, \ldots, e_n$ that satisfy

$$e_j d_j = 1 + k_j \phi(N), \text{ for } j = 1, 2, \ldots, n.$$

Aono [Aon13] considered n modular polynomials

$$f_j(x_j, y) = 1 + x_j(N + y) \pmod{e_j}, \text{ for } j = 1, 2, \ldots, n.$$

The polynomials have the roots $(x_1, \ldots, x_n, y) = (k_1, \ldots, k_n, 1-p-q)$. The sizes of the roots are bounded by $X_j := N^\beta$ for $j = 1, 2, \ldots, n$, $Y := 3N^{1/2}$. We also write $X := N^\beta$ for simplicity. If we can find the roots, we can easily factor RSA modulus N.

To solve simultaneous modular equations $f_j(x_j, y) = 0$ for $j = 1, 2, \ldots, n$, Aono constructed the basis matrix with polynomials which have the same roots as the solutions of the modular equation modulo $(e_1 \cdots e_n)^m$. Aono combined n lattices, each of which is the lattice to solve a single equation. To solve each single equation, Aono selected the shift-polynoials

$$x_j^{i_j} f_j(x_j, y)^{u_j} e_j^{m-u_j}, \text{ with } u_j = 0, 1, \ldots, m, i_j = 0, 1, \ldots, m - u_j,$$
$$\text{for } j = 1, 2, \ldots, n.$$

The selection for each single equation generates the triangular basis matrix. Aono combined the n lattices based on Minkowski sum. Aono proved that the combined lattices based on Minkowski sum are also triangular, if each basis matrix is triangular. The combined basis matrix has diagonals $X_1^{i_1'} \cdots X_n^{i_n'} Y^{u'} e_1^{m-\min\{i_1', u'\}} \cdots e_n^{m-\min\{i_n', u'\}}$, for $0 \le u' \le \sum_{j=1}^n i_j'$, $0 \le i_j' \le m$ for $j = 1, 2, \ldots, n$. Each polynomial of the row is the integer linear combination of shift-polynomials that have the corresponding diagonals. This operation reduce the powers of $e_1, \ldots, e_n$. The detailed discussion is written in [Aon13].

Ignoring low order terms of m, we can compute the dimension $w = \frac{n}{2}m^{n+1}$, and the volume of the lattice $\text{vol}(L(B)) = X_1^{s_{X_1}} \cdots X_n^{s_{X_n}} Y^{s_Y} e_1^{s_{e_1}} \cdots e_n^{s_{e_n}}$, where $s_{X_j} = (\frac{n}{4} + \frac{1}{12})m^{n+2}, s_Y = (\frac{n^2}{8} + \frac{n}{24})m^{n+2}, s_{e_j} = (\frac{n}{4} + \frac{1}{12})m^{n+2}$, for $j = 1, 2, \ldots, n$. The lattice provides the bound

$$\beta < \frac{3}{4} - \frac{2}{3n+1}.$$

4   Another Look at Previous Lattice Constructions

In this section, we analyze the previous lattice constructions [BD00, Aon13] based on Takayasu and Kunihiro's strategy [TK13]. What we should mention is that if there are as many helpful polynomials as possible or as few unhelpful polynomials as possible in the lattice bases.

4.1   The Analysis of Boneh and Durfee's Lattices

We can rewrite the sizes of diagonals in Boneh and Durfee's basis matrix as $X^{i'} Y^{u'} e^{m-\min\{i',u'\}}$ for $0 \leq u' \leq 2(1 - \beta)i'$, $0 \leq i' \leq m$. We consider the shift-polynomials for $i' < u' \leq 2(1 - \beta)i'$, $0 \leq i' \leq m$. To examine if the shift-polynomials are helpful or not, we compare the sizes of diagonals and the size of the modulus e^m. For easy comparison, we rewrite the sizes as the powers of N. The sizes of diagonals are $N^{\beta i' + \frac{1}{2}u' + m - i'}$, and the size of the modulus is N^m. The shift-polynomials are helpful when $\beta i' + \frac{1}{2}u' + m - i' \leq m$, that is, $u' \leq 2(1-\beta)i'$. Therefore, the shift-polynomials which Boneh and Dufee selected for $i' < u'$ are all helpful polynomials. Moreover, the condition is tight. That means when $2(1 - \beta)i' < u'$, all shift-polynomials are unhelpful. For the basis matrix to be triangular, we have to select the shift-polynomials for $0 \leq u' \leq i', 0 \leq i' \leq m$. This analysis implies that Boneh and Durfee selected as many helpful polynomials as possible and as few unhelpful polynomials as possible.

4.2   The Analysis of Aono's Lattices

Next, we consider the Aono's lattices. We can rewrite the sizes of diagonals in Aono's basis matrix as $X_1^{i_1'} \cdots X_n^{i_n'} Y^{u'} e_1^{m-\min\{i_1',u'\}} \cdots e_n^{m-\min\{i_n',u'\}}$ for $0 \leq u' \leq \sum_{j=1}^{n} i_j'$, and $0 \leq i_j' \leq m$ for $j = 1, 2, \ldots, n$. We show that Aono selected unhelpful polynomials or the selections are not tight. To examine if the shift-polynomials are helpful or not, we compare the sizes of diagonals and the size of the modulus $(e_1 \cdots e_n)^m$. We consider the diagonal $X_1^m \cdots X_n^m Y^{nm}$, which is the case $i_1' = \cdots = i_n' = m, u' = nm$. The size of the diagonal is $(XY)^{nm}$. For easy comparison, we rewrite the sizes as the powers of N. The sizes of the diagonal is $N^{nm\beta + \frac{nm}{2}}$, and the size of the modulus is N^{nm}. The shift-polynomial is helpful when $nm\beta + \frac{nm}{2} \leq nm$, that is, $\beta \leq \frac{1}{2}$. We recall that Aono's lattice provides the bound $\beta < \frac{3}{4} - \frac{2}{3n+1}$. Therefore, Aono selected unhelpful polynomials for $n \geq 3$, and the selections are not tight for $n = 1, 2$.

Aono also pointed out the issue in his paper [Aon13]. They proposed the heuristic improvement in appendix of their paper. They claimed that to improve the bound, some polynomials with highr powers of Y should be omit for $n \geq 3$. However, no exact conditions are given in the paper.

5   Our Improvements

In this section, we show the improved lattice constructions. To improve the bound, we select as many helpful polynomials as possible and as few unhelpful polynomials as possible in the lattice bases. We consider the same simultaneous modular equations as Aono [Aon13], $f_j(x_j, y) = 1 + x_j(N + y) \pmod{e_j} = 0$, for $j = 1, 2, \ldots, n$. We use shift-polynomials $x_j^{i_j} f_j(x_j, y)^{u_j} e_j^{m-u_j}, y^{l_j} f_j(x_j, y)^{u_j} e_j^{m-u_j}$ for $j = 1, 2, \ldots, n$. Aono's analysis suggests that we can construct the triangular basis matrix[2] with diagonals $X_1^{i'_1} \cdots X_n^{i'_n} Y^{u'} e_1^{m-\min\{i'_1, u'\}} \cdots e_n^{m-\min\{i'_n, u'\}}$. We reveal the condition when each lattice basis becomes helpful. We consider the polynomials with $\max\{i'_1, \ldots, i'_n\} \leq u'$. To examine if the shift-polynomials are helpful or not, we compare the sizes of diagonals and the size of modulus $(e_1 \cdots e_n)^m$. The polynomials have the diagonals $X_1^{i'_1} \cdots X_n^{i'_n} Y^{u'} e_1^{m-i'_1} \cdots e_n^{m-i'_n}$. For easy comparison, we rewrite the sizes as the powers of N. The sizes of the diagonals are $N^{\beta \sum_{j=1}^n i'_j + \frac{u'}{2} + nm - \sum_{j=1}^n i'_j}$, and the size of the modulus is N^{nm}. The shift-polynomials are helpful when

$$\beta \sum_{j=1}^n i'_j + \frac{u'}{2} + nm - \sum_{j=1}^n i'_j \leq nm,$$

that is,

$$u' \leq 2(1 - \beta) \sum_{j=1}^n i'_j.$$

Therefore, we select the shift-polynomials $x_j^{i_j} f_j(x_j, y)^{u_j} e_j^{m-u_j}, y^{l_j} f_j(x_j, y)^{u_j} e_j^{m-u_j}$ for $j = 1, 2, \ldots, n$, which generate the diagonals $X_1^{i'_1} \cdots X_n^{i'_n} Y^{u'} e_1^{m-\min\{i'_1, u'\}} \cdots e_n^{m-\min\{i'_n, u'\}}$ for $0 \leq u' \leq 2(1 - \beta) \sum_{j=1}^n i'_j, 0 \leq i'_j \leq m$ for $j = 1, 2, \ldots, n$. It is clear that our selection becomes identical to Boneh and Durfee's selection for $n = 1$. The selection provides the better bound than previous works including Aono's heuristically improved lattices[3].

---

[2] For $n = 1, 2$ we should use unravelled linearization and transform the basis matrix which is not triangular to be triangular. See [HM10] for $n = 1$ and the full version of this paper for $n = 2$ in detail.

[3] Compared with Aono's heuristically improved lattice bases [Aon13], there are less unhelpful polynomials and as many helpful polynomials in our lattice bases. See the full version of this paper in detail.

Ignoring low order terms of m, we can compute the dimension

$$w = \sum_{i'_n=0}^{m} \cdots \sum_{i'_1=0}^{m} \sum_{u'=0}^{\lfloor 2(1-\beta)(i'_1+\cdots+i'_n)\rfloor} 1 = n(1-\beta)m^{n+1},$$

and the volume of the lattice $\mathrm{vol}(L(B)) = X_1^{s_{X_1}} \cdots X_n^{s_{X_n}} Y^{s_Y} e_1^{s_{e_1}} \cdots e_n^{s_{e_n}}$, where

$$s_{X_j} = \sum_{i'_n=0}^{m} \cdots \sum_{i'_1=0}^{m} \sum_{u'=0}^{\lfloor 2(1-\beta)(i'_1+\cdots+i'_n)\rfloor} i'_j = \frac{(3n+1)(1-\beta)}{6}m^{n+2},$$

$$s_Y = \sum_{i'_n=0}^{m} \cdots \sum_{i'_1=0}^{m} \sum_{u'=0}^{\lfloor 2(1-\beta)(i'_1+\cdots+i'_n)\rfloor} u' = \frac{n(3n+1)}{6}(1-\beta)^2 m^{n+2},$$

$$s_{e_j} = \sum_{i'_n=0}^{m} \cdots \sum_{i'_1=0}^{m} \sum_{u'=0}^{\lfloor 2(1-\beta)(i'_1+\cdots+i'_n)\rfloor} (m-\min\{u',i'_j\}) = \frac{1+(3n-1)(1-\beta)}{6}m^{n+2}.$$

We can solve the simultaneous modular equations $f_j(x_j,y) = 1 + x_j(N+y)$ $(\mathrm{mod}\ e_j) = 0$, for $j = 1,2,\ldots,n$, when $(\mathrm{vol}(L(B)))^{1/w} < (e_1 \cdots e_n)^m$,

$$n\beta\frac{(3n+1)(1-\beta)}{6} + \frac{1}{2}\frac{n(3n+1)}{6}(1-\beta)^2 + n\frac{1+(3n-1)(1-\beta)}{6} < n^2(1-\beta),$$

$$(3n+1)\beta^2 - 2(3n+1)\beta + 3n - 1 > 0,$$

that is,

$$\beta < 1 - \sqrt{\frac{2}{3n+1}}.$$

The bound is superior to all known algorithms [HS99, SM10a, SM10b, Aon13].

6   Partial Key Exposure Attacks on RSA

In the context of the security evaluations of RSA, partial key exposure attacks [BDF98, BM03, EJMW05, Aon09, SGM10] have been considered. In the partial key exposure situauion, the attackers know the partial information of secret exponent d. In the work [Aon13], Aono also considered partial key exposure attacks on RSA with multiple key settings. In this case, the attackers know public modulus N and multiple public exonents $e_1,\ldots,e_n$, whose corresponding secret exponents $d_1,\ldots,d_n$ are smaller than N^β, and the least significant $\delta \log N$ bits of secret exponents, $\tilde{d}_1,\ldots,\tilde{d}_n$. Aono proposed the algorithm with Minkowski sum based lattices, which works provided that

$$\beta < \frac{\delta}{2} + \frac{3}{4} - \frac{2}{3n+1}.$$

Based on Takayasu and Kunihiro's strategy [TK13], we propose the improved algorithm for partial key exposure attacks on RSA. Our algorithm works provided that

$$\beta < 1 - \sqrt{\frac{2(1 - 2\delta)}{3n + 1}}, \delta < \frac{1}{2} - \frac{4}{3n + 1}.$$

Our algorithm is the same as Aono's algorithm for $n = 1, 2$, and is superior to Aono's algorithm for $n \geq 3$. The detailed analysis is written in the full version of the paper.

7   Concluding Remarks

In this paper, we analyzed the security of RSA when the attackers have multiple public exponents $e_1, \ldots, e_n$ for the same public modulus N. We proposed improved algorithm for small secret exponent attacks. All secret exponents $d_1, \ldots, d_n$ are smaller than N^β. Our algorithm factors public modulus N provided that $\beta < 1 - \sqrt{2/(3n + 1)}$. To the best of our knowledge, this is the first result that covers Boneh and Durfee's bound $\beta < 1 - 1/\sqrt{2}$ for $n = 1$, and converge to $\beta < 1$ for infinitely large n, simultaneously. Our bound is better than all known previous ones [HS99, SM10a, SM10b, Aon13].

Our lattice construction is based on Takayasu and Kunihiro's strategy [TK13] to collect helpful polynomials. The strategy enables us to determine the selections of polynomials in the lattice bases while taking into account the sizes of root bounds. That is the main difficulty in previous works [SM10b, Aon13].

Acknowledgement. This work was supported by JSPS KAKENHI Grant Number 25280001.

References

[Aon09]   Aono, Y.: A new lattice construction for partial key exposure attack for RSA. In: Jarecki, S., Tsudik, G. (eds.) PKC 2009. LNCS, vol. 5443, pp. 34–53. Springer, Heidelberg (2009)

[Aon13]   Aono, Y.: Minkowski Sum Based Lattice Construction for Multivariate Simultaneous Coppersmith's Technique and Applications to RSA. In: Boyd, C., Simpson, L. (eds.) ACISP. LNCS, vol. 7959, pp. 88–103. Springer, Heidelberg (2013), http://eprint.iacr.org/2012/675

[BM01]   Blömer, J., May, A.: Low secret exponent RSA revisited. In: Silverman, J.H. (ed.) CaLC 2001. LNCS, vol. 2146, pp. 4–19. Springer, Heidelberg (2001)

[BM03]   Blömer, J., May, A.: New partial key exposure attacks on RSA. In: Boneh, D. (ed.) CRYPTO 2003. LNCS, vol. 2729, pp. 27–43. Springer, Heidelberg (2003)

[BD00]   Boneh, D., Durfee, G.: Cryptanalysis of RSA with private key d less than
             $N^{0.292}$. In: Stern, J. (ed.) EUROCRYPT 1999. LNCS, vol. 1592, pp. 1–11.
             Springer, Heidelberg (1999)
[BDF98]   Boneh, D., Durfee, G., Frankel, Y.: Exposing an RSA private key given
             a small fraction of its bits. In: ASIACRYPT 1998. LNCS, vol. 1514,
             pp. 25–34. Springer, Heidelberg (1998)
[CH12]   Cohn, H., Heninger, N.: Approximate common divisors via lattices. In: 10th
             Algorithmic Number Theory Symposium ANTS-X, 2012. Longer version
             available as IACR Cryptology ePrint Archive, Report 2011/437 (2011),
             http://eprint.iacr.org/2011/437
[Cop96a]   Coppersmith, D.: Finding a Small Root of a univariate modular Equation.
             In: Maurer, U.M. (ed.) Advances in Cryptology - EUROCRYPT 1996.
             LNCS, vol. 1070, pp. 155–165. Springer, Heidelberg (1996)
[Cop96b]   Coppersmith, D.: Finding a Small Root of a Bivariate Integer Equation;
             Factoring with High Bits Known. In: Maurer, U. (ed.) Advances in Cryp-
             tology - EUROCRYPT 1996. LNCS, vol. 1070, pp. 178–189. Springer,
             Heidelberg (1996)
[Cop97]   Coppersmith, D.: Small solutions to polynomial equations, and low expo-
             nent RSA vulnerabilities. Journal of Cryptology 10(4), 233–260 (1997)
[Cop01]   Coppersmith, D.: Finding small solutions to small degree polynomials. In:
             Silverman, J.H. (ed.) CaLC 2001. LNCS, vol. 2146, pp. 20–31. Springer,
             Heidelberg (2001)
[Cor04]   Coron, J.-S.: Finding Small Roots of Bivariate Integer Equations Revis-
             ited. In: Cachin, C., Camenisch, J.L. (eds.) EUROCRYPT 2004. LNCS,
             vol. 3027, pp. 492–505. Springer, Heidelberg (2004)
[Cor07]   Coron, J.-S.: Finding Small Roots of Bivariate Integer Equations: A Direct
             Approach. In: Menezes, A. (ed.) CRYPTO 2007. LNCS, vol. 4622, pp.
             379–394. Springer, Heidelberg (2007)
[DN00]   Durfee, G., Nguyên, P.Q.: Cryptanalysis of the RSA Schemes with Short
             Secret Exponent from Asiacrypt '99. In: Okamoto, T. (ed.) ASIACRYPT
             2000. LNCS, vol. 1976, pp. 14–29. Springer, Heidelberg (2000)
[EJMW05]   Ernst, M., Jochemsz, E., May, A., de Weger, B.: Partial key exposure at-
             tacks on RSA up to full size exponents. In: Cramer, R. (ed.) EUROCRYPT
             2005. LNCS, vol. 3494, pp. 371–386. Springer, Heidelberg (2005)
[HM08]   Herrmann, M., May, A.: Solving Linear Equations modulo Divisors: On
             factoring given any bits. In: Pieprzyk, J. (ed.) ASIACRYPT 2008. LNCS,
             vol. 5350, pp. 406–424. Springer, Heidelberg (2008)
[HM09]   Herrmann, M., May, A.: Attacking power generators using unravelled lin-
             earization: When do we output too much? In: Matsui, M. (ed.) ASI-
             ACRYPT 2009. LNCS, vol. 5912, pp. 487–504. Springer, Heidelberg (2009)
[HM10]   Herrmann, M., May, A.: Maximizing Small Root Bounds by Lineariza-
             tion and Applications to Small Secret Exponent RSA. In: Nguyen, P.Q.,
             Pointcheval, D. (eds.) PKC 2010. LNCS, vol. 6056, pp. 53–69. Springer,
             Heidelberg (2010)
[How97]   Howgrave-Graham, N.: Finding small roots of univariate modular equa-
             tions revisited. In: Darnell, M. (ed.) Cryptography and Coding 1997.
             LNCS, vol. 1355, pp. 131–142. Springer, Heidelberg (1997)
[How01]   Howgrave-Graham, N.: Approximate integer common divisors. In: Sil-
             verman, J.H. (ed.) CaLC 2001. LNCS, vol. 2146, pp. 51–66. Springer,
             Heidelberg (2001)

[HS99]   Howgrave-Graham, N., Seifert, J.-P.: Extending Wiener's attack in the presence of many decrypting exponents. In: Baumgart, R. (ed.) CQRE 1999. LNCS, vol. 1740, pp. 153–166. Springer, Heidelberg (1999)

[IKK08a]   Itoh, K., Kunihiro, N., Kurosawa, K.: Small Secret Key Attack on a Variant of RSA (due to Takagi). In: Malkin, T. (ed.) CT-RSA 2008. LNCS, vol. 4964, pp. 387–406. Springer, Heidelberg (2008)

[IKK08b]   Itoh, K., Kunihiro, N., Kurosawa, K.: Small Secret Key Attack on a Takagi's Variant of RSA. IEICE Transactions on Fundamentals of Electronics, Communications and Computer Sceiences E92-A(1), 33–41 (2008)

[JM06]   Jochemsz, E., May, A.: A Strategy for Finding Roots of Multivariate Polynomials. In: Lai, X., Chen, K. (eds.) ASIACRYPT 2006. LNCS, vol. 4284, pp. 267–282. Springer, Heidelberg (2006)

[JM07]   Jochemsz, E., May, A.: A Polynomial Time Attack on RSA with Private CRT-Exponents Smaller Than $N^{0.073}$. In: Menezes, A. (ed.) CRYPTO 2007. LNCS, vol. 4622, pp. 395–411. Springer, Heidelberg (2007)

[Kun11]   Kunihiro, N.: Solving Generalized Small Inverse Problems. In: Steinfeld, R., Hawkes, P. (eds.) ACISP 2010. LNCS, vol. 6168, pp. 248–263. Springer, Heidelberg (2010)

[Kun12]   Kunihiro, N.: On Optimal Bounds of Small Inverse Problems and Approximate GCD Problems with Higher Degree. In: Gollmann, D., Freiling, F.C. (eds.) ISC 2012. LNCS, vol. 7483, pp. 55–69. Springer, Heidelberg (2012)

[KSI11]   Kunihiro, N., Shinohara, N., Izu, T.: A Unified Framework for Small Secret Exponent Attack on RSA. In: Miri, A., Vaudenay, S. (eds.) SAC 2011. LNCS, vol. 7118, pp. 260–277. Springer, Heidelberg (2012)

[LLL82]   Lenstra, A.K., Lenstra Jr., H.W., Lovász, L.: Factoring polynomials with rational coefficients. Mathematische Annalen 261, 515–534 (1982)

[May04]   May, A.: Secret Exponent Attacks on RSA-type Schemes with Moduli $N = p^r q$. In: Bao, F., Deng, R., Zhou, J. (eds.) PKC 2004. LNCS, vol. 2947, pp. 218–230. Springer, Heidelberg (2004)

[May10]   May, A.: Using LLL-reduction for solving RSA and factorization problems: A survey. In: NV10 (2007), http://www.cits.rub.de/permonen/may.html

[MR09]   May, A., Ritzenhofen, M.: Implicit Factoring: On Polynomial Time Factoring Given Only an Implicit Hint. In: Jarecki, S., Tsudik, G. (eds.) PKC 2009. LNCS, vol. 5443, pp. 1–14. Springer, Heidelberg (2009)

[NS01]   Nguyên, P.Q., Stern, J.: The Two Faces of Lattices in Cryptology. In: Silverman, J.H. (ed.) CaLC 2001. LNCS, vol. 2146, pp. 146–180. Springer, Heidelberg (2001)

[nv10]   Nguyen, P.Q., Vallée, B. (eds.): The LLL Algorithm: Survey and Applications. Information Security and Cryptography. Springer, Heidelberg (2007)

[OLBC10]   Olver, F.W.J., Lozier, D.W., Boisvert, R.F., Clark, C.W.: NIST handbook of mathematical functions. Cambridge University Press, Cambridge (2010)

[SGM10]   Sarkar, S., Sen Gupta, S., Maitra, S.: Partial Key Exposure Attack on RSA - Improvements for Limited Lattice Dimensions. In: Gong, G., Gupta, K.C. (eds.) INDOCRYPT 2010. LNCS, vol. 6498, pp. 2–16. Springer, Heidelberg (2010)

[SM10a]   Sarkar, S., Maitra, S.: Cryptanalysis of RSA with two decryption exponents. Information Processing Letter 110, 178–181 (2010)

[SM10b]   Sarkar, S., Maitra, S.: Cryptanalysis of RSA with more than one decryption
           exponents. Information Processing Letter 110, 336–340 (2010)
[TK13]   Takayasu, A., Kunihiro, N.: Better Lattice Constructions for Solving Mul-
           tivariate Linear Equations Modulo Unknown Divisors. In: Boyd, C., Simp-
           son, L. (eds.) ACISP. LNCS, vol. 7959, pp. 118–135. Springer, Heidelberg
           (2013)
[Weg02]   de Weger, B.: Cryptanalysis of RSA with Small Prime Difference, Appli-
           cable Algebra in Engineering. Communication and Computing 13, 17–28
           (2002)
[Wie90]   Wiener, M.J.: Cryptanalysis of Short RSA Secret Exponents. IEEE Trans-
           actions on Information Theory 36(3), 553–558 (1990); Firstly appeared
           In: Quisquater, J.-J., Vandewalle, J. (eds.) EUROCRYPT 1989. LNCS,
           vol. 434, p. 372. Springer, Heidelberg (1990)

New Model and Construction of ABE: Achieving Key Resilient-Leakage and Attribute Direct-Revocation

Mingwu Zhang[1,2,*]

[1] School of Computer Sciences, Hubei University of Technology,
Wuhan 430068, China
[2] State Key Laboratory of Information Security, Institute of Information
Engineering, Chinese Academy of Sciences, Beijing 100093, China
csmwzhang@gmail.com

Abstract. Attribute-Based Encryption allows for implementing fine-grained decentralized access control based on properties or attributes a user has, which has drawn attention for realizing decentralized access control in large and dynamic networks such as Mesh network, Internet of Things and cloud computing. However, in open networks, the attacker can blow the concrete implementation of cryptosystems, and then gain the internal secret states such as pseudo-random number, internal result and secret key to break the system. In this work, we first model a fine-grained attribute revocable (ciphertext-policy) attribute-based encryption in the presence of key leakage, and then give a concrete construction with security and resilient-leakage performance analysis. Our scheme is the first designing enjoying at the same time the following properties: (*i*) Support *attribute direct revocation* that does not affect any other user's secret key. (*ii*) Tolerate the key of matching the challenge ciphertext to be partially revealed. (*iii*) Provide a key update mechanism to support *continual leakage tolerance.*

Keywords: Attribute-based encryption, key leakage, attribute revocation, leakage rate.

1 Introduction

Attribute-Based Encryption (ABE) [3,12,15,24] is a public-key cryptographic primitive in resolving the exact issue of fine-grained access control on shared data in one-to-many communications, which has drawn attention for realizing decentralized access control in large and dynamic networks such as Mesh network, Internet of Things (IoT), and cloud computing [13,25]. Being different from an (hierarchical) identity-based encryption (H-/IBE) [9,18], ABE provides a sound and flexible solution to securely encrypt a message for all users who hold the required attributes, without any knowledge of their exact identities, which

---

* Supported by the National Natural Science Foundation of China (#61370224), the Key Program of Natural Science Foundation of Hubei Province (#2013CFA046).

W. Susilo and Y. Mu (Eds.): ACISP 2014, LNCS 8544, pp. 192–208, 2014.

provides fine-grained controls over the properties or attributes a user has [25]. Especially, in cryptographic operations, attributes map to users' credential, i.e., the attributes represent components of the secret keys. Taking access control in cloud computing as an example, ABE provides means for designing flexible and scalable access control systems without the need of monitoring large access control policies since it is inefficient to make access control rule for each user in large scale cloud environments. For example, we may allow any user, who is an adult and obtains a Phd degree (i.e., Policy $\triangleq$ (AGE $\geq$ 18 AND DPL $= Phd$)), to gain access to the cloud data. In this case, ID card and doctoral diploma can act as the elements of attribute set.

In ciphertext-policy ABE (CP-ABE), attributes are associated to the users' secret keys and access policies are attached to the ciphertexts. Users are able to decrypt a ciphertext if and only if their attributes satisfy the access policies associated to the ciphertexts. An ABE scheme is secure against collusion attacks: if multiple users collude, they can only decrypt the ciphertext those of them can decrypt by himself. Nevertheless, in ABE systems, it needs a Private-Key Generator (PKG) to produce and distribute the secret keys for all users. To obtain a more secure ABE system, we consider the following two aspects:

- SECRET KEY LEAKAGE. Traditional cryptographic technologies are faced with an additional challenge that frequently arises in practical situations in the side-channel attacks. In classical security models, an adversary has access to only the inputs and outputs of cryptographic algorithms, but can not gain any information about the secret keys or internal states. Can we construct a secure ABE in the sense that an adversary is able to obtain partial decryption keys?
- ATTRIBUTE REVOCATION. Attribute revocation is a challenge issue in ABE systems, since each attribute is conceivably shared by multiple users. Attribute revocation of any single user would affect the others who share that attribute. Especially in key leakage situation, a key associated with some revocable attributes will lead to the key vulnerability of the others who have the same attributes.

To withhold leakage attacks, we take into account the amount of leakage that the scheme can tolerate. Typically, this is formalized by introducing a leakage rate parameter γ ($0 < \gamma < 1$) or a leakage bound parameter L, i.e., $\gamma = \frac{L}{|\mathsf{SK}|}$, where SK is the allowable leakage key. Key leakage attacks are formalized by allowing the adversary to submit leakage functions to a leakage oracle with an adaptive manner, that is, the adversary can choose different leakage functions at different points according to its view and prior leakage knowledge.

Motivation and Challenge. In this work, we focus on the above two issues and design a leakage-resilient secure ABE with fine-grained attribute revocation to achieve the semantic security in the continual key leakage model. There are two kinds of revocation techniques in ABEs: *indirect revocation* and *direct revocation* [5]. Indirect revocation enforces revocation by the key *authority* who releases a key update token periodically so that only non-revoked users can update their keys and revoked keys are implicitly rendered useless. Direct revocation is launched by the *encrypter* who specifies the revocation list and embeds the list into the ciphertext. Obviously, indirect revocation is less efficient than direct revocation. However, an efficient direct revocation mechanism in ABE is a challenging issue, since an attribute may distribute in multiple users and the revocation of an attribute will impact all key holders of that attribute.

In an ABE system, there exists a PKG that create and distributes the keys for all users. Thus, between PKG and every user there is always an assumption of secure channels to perform the key distribution. However, this is very difficult in large scale decentralized systems such as wireless sensor networks and cloud computing. Traditionally, provable security will lose if any information about the key is leaked. Recent research shows that such unintended leakages are easily obtained by side-channel attacks [2,8], and thus constructing schemes to resist broad class of leakage attacks are very important in practical applications. We must ensure that the semantic security should guarantee in the presence of combining all key leakage corresponding to some attribute sets from different users.

Our Results and Approach. Our main result is a connection among attribute-based encryption, attribute direct revocation mechanism and key leakage resilience. In particular, we show how to construct an attribute directly revocable CP-ABE in the sense that the secret key might be partially revealed. We also give the performance analysis such as leakage bound, leakage rate and allowable probability in the sense that the direct attribute revocation list is implicitly embedded into the ciphertext.

To demonstrate the benefit of leakage-resilience, we show that in some cases it can be used to obtain no more than L-bit leaked semantic security, even in the presence of key leakage. Conceivably, no construction can provide meaningful security unless one further restricts the leakage function. The restriction imposed is that the overall size of the output of the leakage function f is upper bounded by a leakage parameter. We have to limit the type of leakage functions that the adversary provides. More concretely, the adversary is given access to the bounded leak that performs the leakage attack defined in the output shrinking model (OSM) [2,7,17,27].

In order to obtain leakage resilience in ABE systems, we allow the adversary to handle all key extraction queries and key leakage queries. As there is no need for a separate technique to achieve leakage resilience within the dual system encryption (DSE) framework [17,15,27], we obtain the continual leakage tolerance by allowing key leakage from multiple keys of decrypting the challenge ciphertext. We also extend the semi-functional space to form multiple dimensional vectors and achieve the leakage resilience to fitting the structure in Theorem 2. Because the leakage function on the key must be provided before the production of challenge ciphertext, an adversary whose leakage is suitably bounded can not distinguish orthogonal vectors from uniformly random vectors.

A crucial ingredient in the scheme against continual leakage is designing a mechanism for periodically refreshing the key, that is, replacing the secret key by a new key while maintaining the same public key. We also employ a key refresh algorithm and bound the leakage to provide continual leakage tolerance.

We demonstrate this by providing a leakage-resilient construction of ABE system which retains all of the desirable features of DSE [18,15].

In order to guarantee that attribute revocation does not affect any other user's secret key, we construct the scheme that supports fine-grained attribute revocation under direct revocation mechanism, in which in the key generation algorithm a user's identity is associated with a set of attributes, and in the encryption procedure the valid receivers are associated with an access structure Γ and an additional revocation attribute set $\mathcal{R}$. We employ the access structure as a linear secret sharing scheme (an LSSS) that is explicitly described as (A, ρ), in which function ρ associates rows of A to attributes.

In the security proof, different from the partition techniques [3], we use DSE mechanism [17,18,27] to prove the security such that the simulator can construct any key and any challenge ciphertext, in which there have two kinds of keys and ciphertexts: *normal* and *semi-functional*. In the real construction, the key and the ciphertext are normal, but they will be transformed into semi-functional in the security proof. In the view of adversary, it only has a negligible advantage in distinguishing these transformations. Finally, all keys and ciphertexts are semi-functional, and we also prove that, even the adversary gains partial leakage from the match key, s/he has a negligible advantage in decrypting the challenge ciphertext. Thus the security is concluded by the incapable decryption between a semi-functional key and a semi-functional challenge ciphertext.

Related Works. Sahai and Waters [21] first presented a notion of ABE, in which the sender can specify access to the message as a boolean formula over a set of attributes. Goyal, Pandey and Sahai et al. [12] formulated two complimentary forms of ABE: key-policy ABE and ciphertext-policy ABE. To obtain the fine-grained access, there have been a number of constructions for various classes of functions [13,12,16,17,24,15]. In particular, Goyal, Pandey and Sahai et al. [12] employed access tree to describe the access structure in ABE. Actually, an access structure such as a boolean formula (or a tree structure) can be expressed in terms of an LSSS [3,16,24]. Waters [24] proposed ABE constructions that can work for any access policy in terms of LSSS. Lewko, Okamoto and Sahai et al. [16] presented a (weak) fully secure ABE scheme by extending the dual system encryption methodology in composite-order groups. Nevertheless, these schemes do not support attribute revocation.

Attribute revocation is inevitable and also important in practice [22,23,25]. Boldyreva, Goyal and Kumar [6] proposed a revocable ABE scheme that is derived from a revocable identity-based encryption, which is based on an indirect revocation model that requires the authority to periodically re-issue the keys. Later, Attrapadung and Imai [5] indicated that an ABE scheme can provide direct revocation and indirect revocation. They summarized two modes which are helpful for designing revocation in ABE, and gave two direct/indirect revocation schemes. In [4], Attrapadung and Imai demonstrated that a directly revocable ABE scheme can be converted from the combination of a broadcast encryption mechanism and an ABE scheme.

Akavia Goldwasser and Vaikuntanathan [2] and Naor and Segev [20] provided the security definition against leakage attacks in the public key setting, respectively. Naor and Segev [20] also showed that the variety of public key encryption systems can support different leakage bound in different mathematical assumption, for example, quadratic residuosity (QR) assumption, Paillier assumption, Diffie-Hellman (DH) assumption, and the existence of hash-proof system (HPS). Later, bounded leakage-resilient schemes are proposed in [9,10,17,26]. Chow, Dodis and Rouselakis et al. [9] proposed three leakage-resilient identity-based encryptions that are based on (identity-based) hash proof systems, but their schemes do not allow key update and then do not support *continual leakage* [8,17]. Lewko, Rouselakis and Waters [17] showed that a bounded leakage-resilient encryption against memory leakage attacks can be constructed from the extension of dual system mechanism in the extension of composite order bilinear groups. Zhang, Shi and Wang et al. [26] gave two leakage-resilient ABE constructions in which the access structures are encoded into their minimal sets.

2   Preliminaries

We let $[d]$ denote the set $\{1, \cdots, d\}$ for any $d \in \mathbb{Z}^+$. For a finite set $\mathcal{S}$, $|\mathcal{S}|$ denotes the number of elements in S (i.e., cardinality). Let $\mathbb{G}$ be a finite group of order p, we denote the bits of an element in $\mathbb{G}$ by $\|\mathbb{G}\|$ and denote the bits of order p by $\|p\|$. We let x be chosen uniformly from $\mathbb{Z}_N$ denote by $x \xleftarrow{\$} \mathbb{Z}_N$, and $X \leftarrow Y$ denotes assignment. For a vector $\boldsymbol{x} = (x_1, \cdots, x_d) \in \mathbb{Z}_N^d$, we use $g^{\boldsymbol{x}}$ to denote the vector of group elements $g^{\boldsymbol{x}} \triangleq (g^{x_1}, \cdots, g^{x_d}) \in \mathbb{G}^d$, and denote $\langle \boldsymbol{\rho}, \boldsymbol{\sigma} \rangle$ as a scalar product of vectors $\boldsymbol{\rho}$ and $\boldsymbol{\sigma}$, i.e., $\langle \boldsymbol{\rho}, \boldsymbol{\sigma} \rangle = \sum_i \rho_i \sigma_i$. Similarly, $\langle g^{\boldsymbol{\rho}}, g^{\boldsymbol{\sigma}} \rangle = g^{\sum_i \rho_i \sigma_i} = g^{\langle \boldsymbol{\rho}, \boldsymbol{\sigma} \rangle}$ and $\hat{e}(g^{\boldsymbol{\rho}}, g^{\boldsymbol{\sigma}}) = \hat{e}(g, g)^{\langle \boldsymbol{\rho}, \boldsymbol{\sigma} \rangle}$. We use the term $X_3^{\theta+k}$ to denote the vector X_3 with $\theta + k$ elements.

In order to guarantee that, in case of obtaining no more than L-bit leakage information of a key, the adversary gains enough key entropy, we use a statistically indistinguishable theorem to specify the bounded leakage function. The *statistical distance* between two random variables X and Y over a finite domain χ is defined as $\mathsf{SD}(X, Y) \triangleq \frac{1}{2} \sum_{v \in \chi} |Pr[X = v] - Pr[Y = v]|$. We say that two variables are ϵ-close if their statistical distance is at most ϵ. We denote the computational indistinguishability of two distributions X and Y by $X \approx_c Y$.

The following theorems show that, given some sufficiently small leakage on a random matrix, it is hard to distinguish the spanned random vectors from uniformly random vectors [8,17].

Theorem 1. *(Subspace Hiding with Leakage) [1] Let p be a prime, and let $n \geq d \geq u$, s be integers, $\boldsymbol{S} \in \mathbb{Z}_p^{d \times s}$ be an arbitrary matrix and* $\mathsf{Leak}\colon \{0,1\}^* \to \{0,1\}^L$ *be an arbitrary function with L-bit output. For randomly sampled $\boldsymbol{A} \leftarrow \mathbb{Z}_p^{n \times d}$, $\boldsymbol{V} \leftarrow \mathbb{Z}_p^{n \times u}$, we have $(\mathsf{Leak}(\boldsymbol{A}), \boldsymbol{AS}, \boldsymbol{V}, \boldsymbol{AV}) \approx_c (\mathsf{Leak}(\boldsymbol{A}), \boldsymbol{AS}, \boldsymbol{V}, \boldsymbol{U})$, as long as $L \leq (d - s - u) \log p + \omega(\log \tau)$ and $n = \mathsf{poly}(\tau)$.*

Theorem 2. *[8] Let p be a prime, $m, l, d \in \mathbb{N}$, $2d \leq l \leq m$. Let $\boldsymbol{V} \xleftarrow{\$} \mathbb{Z}_p^{m \times l}$, $\boldsymbol{A} \xleftarrow{\$} \mathbb{Z}_p^{m \times d}$, and $\boldsymbol{T} \xleftarrow{\$} Rank_d(\mathbb{Z}_p^{l \times d})$, where $Rank_d(\mathbb{Z}_p^{l \times d})$ denotes the set of $l \times d$*

matrices of rank d. For any map Leak : $\mathbb{Z}_p^{m \times d} \to \pi$, *there exists* $SD((\text{Leak}(\boldsymbol{VT}), \boldsymbol{V}),$ $(\text{Leak}(\boldsymbol{A}), \ \boldsymbol{V})) \leq \mu(p)$, *as long as* $\|\pi\| \leq 4(1 - \frac{1}{p}) \cdot p^{l-2d+1} \cdot \mu(p)^2$.

In particular, if the leakage Leak($\mathbf{VT}$) reveals bounded information $\mathbf{V}$, then (Leak($\mathbf{VT}$), $\mathbf{V}$) and (Leak($\mathbf{A}$), $\mathbf{V}$) are statistically close. In the latter pair, $\mathbf{A}$ is a random vector and the leakage function reveals nothing about the subspace $\mathbf{V}$. We give the following Corollary to describe the statistical indistinguishability of two-dimensional orthogonal vectors with arbitrary function outputs.

Corollary 1. *Let p be a prime and $m \geq 3$ be an integer. Let $\Delta, \boldsymbol{v} \xleftarrow{\$} \mathbb{Z}_p^m$ and $\boldsymbol{v}'$ be uniformly chosen from the set of vector in $\mathbb{Z}_p^m$ that are orthogonal to Δ under the dot product modulo p. For any function* Leak : $\mathbb{Z}_p^m \to \pi$, *there exists $SD((\text{Leak}(\boldsymbol{v}), \Delta), (\text{Leak}(\boldsymbol{v}'), \Delta)) \leq \mu(p)$, as long as $\|\pi\| \leq 4p^{m-3}(p-1) \cdot \mu(p)^2$.*

Definition 1. *(Access Structure) Let $P_1, \cdots, P_n$ be a set of parties. A collection $\mathbb{A} \subseteq 2^{P_1, \cdots, P_n}$ is monotonic if $\forall B \in \mathbb{A}$ and $B \subseteq C$, then $C \in \mathbb{A}$. An access structure (AS) is a collection $\mathbb{A}$ of non-empty subsets of $\{P_1, \cdots, P_n\}$, i.e., $\mathbb{A} \subseteq 2^{P_1, \cdots, P_n} \backslash \{\phi\}$. The set in $\mathbb{A}$ is called authorized set, and the set not in $\mathbb{A}$ is called unauthorized set.*

Remark 1. In attribute-based encryption, the attributes will play the role of parties and we will consider only monotonic access structure. Actually, it is also possible to (inefficiently) realize general access structures using our techniques by having the "not" of an attribute (non-monotonic attribute) as a separate attribute altogether.

Definition 2. *(Linear Secret-Sharing Scheme(LSSS)) A secret sharing scheme over a set of parties $\mathcal{P}$ is called linear if*

1. *The share of each party forms a vector over $\mathbb{Z}_p$;*
2. *There exists a $l \times n$ matrix A. For all $j = 1, \cdots, l$, the j-th row of A is labeled by a party $\rho(j)$. When we consider the column vector $v = (s, r_2, \cdots, r_n)$, where $s \in \mathbb{Z}_p$ is the secret to be shared and $r_2, \cdots, r_n$ are randomly picked, then Av is the vector of l shares of the secret s.*
3. *There is an efficient secret reconstruction algorithm. Let S be the authorized set and $I \subseteq \{1, \cdots, l\}$ as $I = \{j | \rho(j) \in S\}$, then the vector $(1, 0, \cdots, 0)$ is in the span of rows of A indexed by I, and there exists constants $\{\omega_j \in \mathbb{Z}_p\}_{j \in I}$ such that, for any valid shares $\{\lambda_j\}$ of a secret s, we have $\sum_{j \in I} \omega_j \lambda_j = s$. For all unauthorized sets, no such constants $\{\omega_j\}$ exists.*

It is shown that these constants ω_j can be found in time polynomial in the size of the share-generating matrix A.

3 Model of ABE of Key Resilient-Leakage and Attribute Direct-Revocation

3.1 Algorithm Definition

A directly revocable attribute-based encryption $\mathcal{E}$ resilient to leakage is comprised of five probabilistic polynomial time algorithms ADR-lrABE $\triangleq$ (Initialize, Extract,

Encrypt, Decrypt, Update). We now present the ciphertext-policy attribute-based encryption scheme that is resilient to leakage from many keys capable of decrypting the challenge ciphertext. Note that we additionally devise an update algorithm to perform key refresh and then defeat the continual leakage attacks.

In this paper, we denote the term $\mathcal{U}$ as the universal attribute set, and denote $\mathcal{R}$ as the attribute revocation set. We also use $\mathcal{I}$ to denote the identity set of the user. We denote the term Γ as the access structure described by an LSSS, i.e., $\Gamma = (A, \rho)$, and we use $\overline{\Gamma}$ to denote the complementary set of Γ, i.e., $\overline{\Gamma} = \mathcal{U} - \Gamma$.

Definition 3. *(ADR-lrABE Algorithm) An attribute directly revocable attribute-based encryption scheme resilient to key-leakage (ADR-lrABE) is defined as:*

1. **Initialize**$(1^\tau, L, \mathcal{U}, \mathcal{I})$ *The system initialization algorithm takes as input the security parameter τ, a leakage bound L, a universal attribute set $\mathcal{U} = \{1, 2, \cdots, m\}$ and a user set $\mathcal{I} = \{1, 2, \cdots, n\}$, and outputs system public key PP and master secret key MK.*

2. **Extract**$(MK, I, \mathcal{S})$ *The key generation algorithm takes as input the master key MK, and a user identity $I \in \mathcal{I}$ and the associated attribute set $\mathcal{S} \subseteq \mathcal{U}$ as inputs, and outputs a secret key $SK_{I,\mathcal{S}}$. Note that a key implicitly contains the attribute set $\mathcal{S}$ and the user identity I.*

3. **Encrypt**$(\mathfrak{m}, \Gamma = (A, \rho), \mathcal{R} = \{R_i\}_{i \in \overline{\Gamma}})$ *The encryption algorithm takes as input a message $\mathfrak{m}$, an access structure $\Gamma = (A, \rho)$ and a revocation user list $\{R_i\}$ for each attribute $i \in \mathcal{U}$, and outputs a ciphertext CT_Γ. Note that a ciphertext contains an access structure Γ and the corresponding revocation attribute set $\{R_i\}_{i \in \overline{\Gamma}}$.*

4. **Decrypt**$(SK_{I,\mathcal{S}}, CT_\Gamma)$ *Let $\mathcal{S}' = \{i | i \in \mathcal{S} \cap \overline{\Gamma}, i \notin \mathcal{R}\}$. The decryption algorithm takes as input a ciphertext CT_Γ and a secret key $SK_\mathcal{S}$, and outputs a message $\mathfrak{m}$ if $\mathcal{S}'$ satisfies Γ.*

5. **Update**$(SK_\mathcal{S}, I, \mathcal{S})$ *The key update algorithm takes as input a key $SK_\mathcal{S}$ and outputs a refreshed key $SK'_\mathcal{S}$.*

Remark 2. 1. The system public key is be used in all other algorithms, and all algorithms take implicitly PP as input.

2. We note that an update key has the same decryption functionality as the previous one.

3. In our model, we require that the scheme must be secure in the presence of a key leaked under some bound L.

The robustness of algorithm ADR-lrABE will hold in the following conditions: Let L be a leakage bound, $\mathcal{U}$ and $\mathcal{I}$ be a universal attribute set and a user set respectively, and $\mathcal{M}$ be the message space. Let Leak_i be any polynomial-time computable function. For all correctly created PP and MK from the system initialization algorithm, and $SK_{I,\mathcal{S}} \leftarrow \mathsf{Extract}(MK, I, \mathcal{S})$, $CT_\Gamma \leftarrow \mathsf{Encrypt}(\mathfrak{m}, \Gamma = (A, \rho), \{R_i\}_{i \in \overline{\Gamma}})$, then $\mathsf{Decrypt}(CT_\Gamma, SK_\mathcal{S}) = \mathfrak{m}$ with probability 1 if the user attribute set (excluding the revocation attributes) $\mathcal{S}'$ satisfies the access structure Γ, where $\mathcal{S}' = \{i | i \in \mathcal{S} \cap \overline{\Gamma}, I \notin \{R_i\}\}$. That is,

$$\Pr\begin{bmatrix}(\mathsf{PP},\mathsf{MK}) \leftarrow \mathsf{Initialize}(1^\tau, L, \mathcal{U}, \mathcal{I}) \\ \mathsf{m} \in \mathcal{M},\ \mathcal{S} \subseteq \mathcal{U},\ I \in \mathcal{I} \\ \forall i \in \mathcal{S},\ \Gamma(\mathcal{S}) = 1 \\ \mathsf{Leak}_i : \{0,1\}^* \to \{0,1\}^o \text{ where } o \leq L \\ \mathsf{SK}_{I,\mathcal{S}} \leftarrow \mathsf{Extract}(\mathsf{MK}, I, \mathcal{S}) \\ \mathsf{SK}'_{I,\mathcal{S}} \leftarrow \mathsf{Update}(\mathsf{SK}_{I,\mathcal{S}}, I, \mathcal{S}) \\ \sum_i |\mathsf{Leak}_i(\mathsf{SK}_{I,\mathcal{S}}, I, \mathcal{S})| \leq L, \\ \sum_i |\mathsf{Leak}_i(\mathsf{SK}'_{I,\mathcal{S}}, I, \mathcal{S})| \leq L \\ \mathsf{CT}_\Gamma \leftarrow \mathsf{Encrypt}(\mathsf{m}, \Gamma = (A, \rho), \{R_i\}_{i \in \overline{\Gamma}}) \\ \mathsf{m} \neq \mathsf{Decrypt}(\mathsf{CT}_\Gamma, \mathsf{SK}_{I,\mathcal{S}}) \neq \mathsf{Decrypt}(\mathsf{CT}_\Gamma, \mathsf{SK}'_{I,\mathcal{S}})\end{bmatrix} \leq \mu(\tau)$$

As the system public key PP is fully published, we only consider the secret key as the input of the leakage function Leak.

In the rest of this paper, we use a boolean function $\mathsf{Match}(\Gamma, \mathcal{S}, I, \mathcal{R})$ to denote the output of the match of attribute set $\mathcal{S}$ of user I to satisfy an access structure Γ. i.e.,

$$\Gamma(\mathcal{S}) = \begin{cases} 1 & \text{set } \mathcal{S} \text{ satisfies access structure } \Gamma \\ 0 & \text{otherwise} \end{cases}$$

and

$$\mathsf{Match}(\Gamma, \mathcal{S}, I, \mathcal{R}) = \begin{cases} 1 & \Gamma(\mathcal{S}')=1 \text{ for } \mathcal{S}' = \{i | i \in \mathcal{S} \cap \overline{\Gamma}, i \notin \{R_i\}\} \\ 0 & \text{otherwise} \end{cases}$$

We have the computational indistinguishability relation between key/ciphertext spaces and plaintext space, that is,

$$\mathsf{Decrypt}(\mathsf{Encrypt}(\mathsf{m}, \Gamma, \mathcal{R}), \mathsf{Update}(\mathsf{Extract}(\mathsf{MK}, I, \mathcal{S}))) = \mathsf{m} \approx_c \mathsf{Match}(\Gamma, \mathcal{S}, I, \mathcal{R}) = 1$$

3.2   Security Definition

Semantic security of an encryption scheme requires that an adversary, with two messages and a ciphertext encrypting one of them, must not be able to guess which of the two messages is encrypted. But if we let the adversary learn arbitrary functions of several secret keys, then it could ask for a function that decrypts the challenge ciphertext and provides the output. We provide the security of ADR-IrABE to be key-leakage resilient and fine-grained attribute revocable in the sense that the semantic security still holds when any adversary can specify any efficiently computable function and learns the bounded outputs of keys from the function.

As a key may be leaked by leakage functions Leak_i repeatedly, in our security experiment, we devise the oracles for an adversary queries as: (i) key creation oracle $\mathcal{O}_C$, (ii) key leak oracle $\mathcal{O}_L$, (iii) key update oracle $\mathcal{O}_U$ and, (iv) key reveal oracle $\mathcal{O}_R$. In order to model the leakage is bounded, we allow the adversary to get access to the leakage oracle $\mathcal{O}_L$ on the secret key with only the constraint that the amount outputs of the leakage can not get more than L bits per key. For a key leak or reveal oracle, we first create the key from Extract algorithm and store it in a queue $\mathcal{L}$. A leakage oracle $\mathcal{O}_L$ is parameterized by secret key $SK_{I,\mathcal{S}}$ and leakage bound L.

When an adversary requests a leakage query, we search the key in the queue $\mathcal{L}$ and outputs the leakage from function $\text{Leak}_i(SK)$ if the amount output of SK is less than L. For a key reveal query, we at first obtain the key in $\mathcal{L}$, and return the key directly (this simulates the traditional key extraction query in ABE). At the same time, we will record the revealed key into another queue $\mathcal{T}$ since the key can be updated and we should record all revealed keys.

We define the security experiment $\text{Exp}_{\mathcal{E},\mathcal{A}}$ in the presence of the key leakage. The $\text{Exp}_{\mathcal{E},\mathcal{A}}$ that interacts between a challenger $\mathcal{C}$ and an adversary $\mathcal{A}$ is formally described as follows:

1. *Prepare.* The challenger $\mathcal{C}$ runs Initialize algorithm to create system parameter PP and master key MK, and sends PP to adversary $\mathcal{A}$. Moreover, the challenger $\mathcal{C}$ creates two initially empty queues $\mathcal{L} = \langle \propto, \mathcal{S}, I, SK_{I,\mathcal{S}}, \text{Inum} \rangle$ and $\mathcal{T} = \langle \propto, \mathcal{S}, I \rangle$, in which we use $\propto$ as a handle to associate the record and use Inum to store the amount bits of key leakage.

2. *Query-I.* By adaptive manner, adversary $\mathcal{A}$ issues a number of queries to the oracles as follows:

   Create key oracle $(\mathcal{O}_C(\propto, \mathcal{S}, I))$: $\mathcal{C}$ first searches the record in $\mathcal{L}$. If there is no record found, $\mathcal{C}$ makes a call to Extract algorithm to obtain a secret key $SK_{I,\mathcal{S}}$ and adds $(\propto +1, \mathcal{S}, I, SK_{I,\mathcal{S}}, 0)$ into $\mathcal{L}$.

   Key leakage oracle $(\mathcal{O}_L(\propto, \text{Leak}))$: $\mathcal{A}$ provides a leakage function Leak to request a key leakage query. $\mathcal{C}$ first searches $\mathcal{L}$ to obtain the key $SK_{I,\mathcal{S}}$, answers the query with $\text{Leak}(SK_{I,\mathcal{S}})$ if $\text{Inum} + \text{Leak}(SK_{I,\mathcal{S}}) \leq L$, and updates Inum with $\text{Inum} + \text{Leak}(SK_{I,\mathcal{S}})$; $\mathcal{C}$ responds with ϕ otherwise.

   Key update oracle $(\mathcal{O}_U(\propto, SK_{I,\mathcal{S}}))$: $\mathcal{C}$ first search the key in $\mathcal{L}$. If there is no record found, $\mathcal{C}$ makes a call to $\mathcal{O}_C$ to create a new key and store it in $\mathcal{L}$. Otherwise $\mathcal{C}$ calls Update to refresh the key and sets $\text{Inum} = 0$. Finally, $\mathcal{C}$ answers the query with the key associated with handle $\propto$.

   Key reveal oracle $(\mathcal{O}_R(\propto))$: $\mathcal{C}$ searches $\mathcal{L}$ to find the record, adds the tuple $(\propto, \mathcal{S}, I)$ into $\mathcal{T}$ and answers the query with $SK_{I,\mathcal{S}}$.

3. *Challenge.* $\mathcal{A}$ provides the challenge: an access structure Γ^*, a revocation list $\mathcal{R}^*$ and two messages $\mathfrak{m}_0^*$ and $\mathfrak{m}_1^*$, with the restriction that (i) $|\mathfrak{m}_0^*| = |\mathfrak{m}_1^*|$, (ii) for all tuples $(\mathcal{S}, I) \in \mathcal{T}$, $\text{Match}(\Gamma^*, I, \mathcal{S}, \mathcal{R}^*) = 0$. $\mathcal{C}$ flips a random coin $\psi \in \{0, 1\}$, and encrypts $\mathfrak{m}_\psi$ under access structure Γ^*, receiver identity I and attribute set $\mathcal{S}$, and revocation list $\mathcal{R}^*$.

4. *Query-II.* This stage is the same as Query-I, with the restriction that the query to the oracles $\mathcal{O}_C$, $\mathcal{O}_U$ and $\mathcal{O}_R$ must satisfy $(\mathcal{S}, I) \in \mathcal{T}$, $\text{Match}(\Gamma^*, \mathcal{S}, I, \mathcal{R}^*) = 0$.

5. *Output.* $\mathcal{A}$ outputs a bit $\hat{\psi}$.

$\mathcal{A}$'s advantage in $\text{Exp}_{\mathcal{E},\mathcal{A}}$ is defined as $\text{Adv}_{\mathcal{E},\mathcal{A}}(\tau, L, \mathcal{U}, \mathcal{I}) \triangleq 2Pr[\hat{\psi} = \psi] - 1$.

Definition 4. *(Key-leakage resilient semantic security of ADR-lrABE) An attribute-based encryption scheme ADR-lrABE is (τ, L)-key leakage resilient and attribute revocably secure if all probabilistic polynomial-time adversaries have at most a negligible advantage $\mathsf{Adv}_{\mathcal{E},\mathcal{A}}(\tau, L, \mathcal{U}, \mathcal{I})$ in the experiment $\mathsf{Exp}_{\mathcal{E},\mathcal{A}}$.*

Definition 5. *(Continual key-leakage resilience of ADR-lrABE) If a leakage-resilient encryption scheme is equipped with an update algorithm that takes in a secret key as input and outputs a re-randomized key from the same distribution, then the scheme is called continual-leakage resilient in different key periods.*

4 Our Construction

Our ADR-lrABE scheme uses a composite order bilinear group of order $N = p_1 p_2 p_3$, where p_1, p_2, p_3 are distinct primes. The main system resides in $\mathbb{G}_{p_1}$ while $\mathbb{G}_{p_2}$ subgroup acts for the semi-functional space. $\mathbb{G}_{p_3}$ subgroup provides the additional randomness on keys to isolate keys in our hybrid games. Also, we extend the composite-order group to multiple dimensional to tolerate the possible leakage. We can convert our scheme to the construction in prime-order group by using the translation technique in [11,14].

Secret Key Structure. Let $\mathcal{S}$ be a set of attributes of user I that satisfies an access structure Γ. A secret key of $\mathcal{S} = \{S_1, S_2, \cdots, S_k\}$ has the form

$$\mathsf{SK}_{I,\mathcal{S}} = \langle K_{i,1}, K_{j,2}, K_{j,3} \rangle_{i \in [\theta], j \in \mathcal{S}}$$

$$= \langle (g^{\rho_i})_{i \in [\theta]}, \ (g^{\alpha^I h_j + \beta + t_j r_j - \langle \rho, \sigma \rangle})_{j \in \mathcal{S}}, \ (g^{r_j})_{j \in \mathcal{S}} \rangle \times X_3^{\theta + 2k}$$

where θ is a leakage resilience parameter and $\rho, \sigma \in \mathbb{Z}_N^\theta$. We note that $(g^{t_j})_{j \in \mathcal{U}}$, $(g^{\alpha^j})_{j \in [1, \cdots, n, n+2, \cdots, 2n]}$, $(g^\sigma)_{i \in [\theta]}$ are system public parameters and $(\alpha, \beta, h_j, t_j)_{j \in \mathcal{U}}$ are system master keys.

We note that the components of $\mathsf{SK}_{I,\mathcal{S}}$ are the elements in $\mathbb{G}_{p_1 p_3}$. Actually, since we hide the generators $\mathbb{G}_{p_2}$ and N cannot factor, then from the view of adversary the elements of secret key $\mathsf{SK}_{I,\mathcal{S}}$ is computationally indistinguishable from the elements in $\mathbb{G}$.

In our scheme, θ ($\theta \geq 2$) is a positive constant that determines the leakage-resilient strength. The larger θ leads to a better leakage rate being tolerated, and the smaller θ yields a smaller size of key and ciphertext. We can adjust the system parameter to obtain a better leverage of security and efficiency.

Ciphertext Structure. The encryption algorithm takes as input an LSSS access structure (A, ρ), in which the function ρ associates rows of matrix A to attributes. In our construction, we limit ρ to be an injective function, that is, an attribute is associated with at most one row of A. Let $\Gamma = (A_{l \times k}, \rho)$ be an access structure that formally describes as an LSSS, and $\mathcal{R} = \{R_{\rho(x)}\}_{x \in \{1, 2, \cdots, l\}}$ be an attribute revocation list. For each row x in matrix A, we let $\boldsymbol{A}_x$ denote the x-th row vector of A. A ciphertext CT_Γ has the following form:

$$\mathrm{CT}_\Gamma = \langle C_0, (B_{x,i})_{i \in [\theta]}, \{C_{x,0}, C_{x,1}, C_{x,2}, C_{x,3}, C_{x,4}\}_{x \in [l]}\rangle$$

$$= \langle \mathrm{m} \cdot (g_T)^s, T_{\rho(x)}^{\sigma_i s}, \ g^{\lambda_x}, \ T_{\rho(x)}^{\lambda_x}, g^{\eta_x}(H_{\rho(x)} \prod_{j \in S_{\rho(x)}} g_{n+1-j})^{\lambda_x}, g^{s_x}, \ g^{\eta_x}(\prod_{j \in R_{\rho(x)}} g_{n+1-j})^{s_x}\rangle$$

where $v = (s, v_2, \cdots, v_k)$ is picked from $\mathbb{Z}_N^k$ randomly, and $\lambda_x = A_x \cdot v$ and $S_{\rho(x)} = \mathcal{U} - R_{\rho(x)}$. Note that we use components $C_{x,3}$ and $C_{x,4}$ to associate with the list of attribute revocation. Here T_j and H_j are published, and we use T_j to associate with authorized attribute and H_j to associate with revocation attribute.

In our construction, we assume that there are m attributes in $\mathcal{U}$ and n users in the system. The concrete construction is described as follows.

Initialize$(1^\tau, L, \mathcal{U}, \mathcal{I})$. On input a system security parameter $1^\tau \in \mathbb{N}$, an allowable leakage bound L, a universal attribute set $\mathcal{U}$ and a user list $\mathcal{I}$, this algorithm creates system public key PP and master key MK as follows: Taking as input a system security parameter 1^τ to generate a description of bilinear group $\mathcal{P} = (N = p_1 p_2 p_3, \mathbb{G}, \mathbb{G}_t, \hat{e})$, where p_1, p_2 and p_3 are distinct primes of size τ_1, τ_2, τ_3-bit, and for $1 \le i \le 3$, $2^{\tau_i - 1} \le p_i \le 2^{\tau_i}$ and $\tau_i = \mathsf{poly}(\tau)$; Set $\theta = 1 + 2\xi + L/\log p_2$ where ξ is a constant and $\varepsilon = p_2^{-\xi}$ is a negligible probability in guessing the secret key when obtaining the leakage;[1] And then at random pick $g \in \mathbb{G}_{p_1}, X_3 \in \mathbb{G}_{p_3}$. Let $\mathcal{U} = \{1, 2 \cdots, m\}$ and $\mathcal{I} = \{1, 2, \cdots, n\}$. For $j \in \mathcal{U}$, at random choose $t_j, h_j \in \mathbb{Z}_N$ and set $T_j = g^{t_j}, H_j = g^{h_j}$; At random select $\alpha, \beta \in \mathbb{Z}_N$, and for $k \in \{1, 2, \cdots, n, n+2, \cdots, 2n\}$ set $g_k = g^{\alpha^k}$; For $i \in [\theta]$, choose $\rho_i, \sigma_i \in \mathbb{Z}_N$ randomly, keep the master key MK $:= (\alpha, \beta, (\rho_i)_{i \in [\theta]}, (t_j, h_j)_{j \in \mathcal{U}}, X_3)$, and set the system public key PP $:= (\mathcal{P}, g, (g^{\sigma_i})_{i \in [\theta]}, (T_j, H_j)_{j \in \mathcal{U}}, (g_k)_{k \in [2n] \setminus \{n+1\}}, g_T = \hat{e}(g_1, g_n)^\beta)$.

Extract$(\mathrm{MK}, I, \mathcal{S})$. Let $\mathcal{S} \subseteq \mathcal{U}$, $k = |\mathcal{S}|$ and $I \in \mathcal{I}$. The key generation algorithm creates a secret key $\mathrm{SK}_{I,\mathcal{S}}$ for user I of attribute set $\mathcal{S}$ as follows: Choose $X \in \mathbb{G}_{p_3}^{\theta+2k}$ randomly. Note that a random element in $\mathbb{G}_{p_3}$ can be obtained by raising X_3 to a random exponent from $\mathbb{Z}_N$; For $j \in \mathcal{S}$, at random select $r_j \in \mathbb{Z}_N$. For $i \in [\theta], j \in \mathcal{S}$, select $\vartheta_{i,j} \in \mathbb{Z}_N$ s.t. $g^{\langle \rho, \sigma \rangle} = g^{\langle \vartheta_j, \sigma \rangle}$, and then output the secret key $\mathrm{SK}_{I,\mathcal{S}}$, where

$$\mathrm{SK}_{I,\mathcal{S}} = \langle K_{i,1}, K_{j,2}, K_{j,3}\rangle_{i \in [\theta], j \in \mathcal{S}}$$

$$= \langle (g^{\sigma_i})_{i \in [\theta]}, \ (g^{\alpha^I h_j + \beta + t_j r_j - \langle \vartheta_j, \sigma \rangle})_{j \in \mathcal{S}}, \ (g^{r_j})_{j \in \mathcal{S}}\rangle \times X_3^{\theta+2k} \quad (1)$$

Encrypt$(\mathrm{m}, \Gamma, \mathcal{R})$. Let $\Gamma = (A_{l \times k}, \rho)$ be the associated access structure and $\mathcal{R} = \{R_{\rho(x)}\}_{i \in [l]}$ be the attribute revocation list. The encryption algorithm proceeds as follows: At first select a random vector $v = \{s, v_2, \cdots, v_k\}$, and set $C_0 = \mathrm{m} \cdot (g_T)^s = \mathrm{m} \cdot \hat{e}(g_1, g_n)^{\beta s}$, randomly; Let A_x denote the x-th row of matrix A. For each row x in matrix A, set $\lambda_x = A_x \cdot v$ and $S_{\rho(x)} = \mathcal{U} - R_{\rho(x)}$; For each row x in A, pick $\eta_x, s_x \in \mathbb{Z}_N$ randomly; Output the ciphertext CT_Γ along with $R_{\rho(x)}$, where

---

[1] In elliptic curve cryptography (ECC), the order p_2 is at least 160-bit, and thus ε is negligible if $\xi \ge 1$.

$$\mathrm{CT}_\Gamma = \langle C_0, \{(B_{x,i})_{i\in[\theta]}, C_{x,0}, C_{x,1}, C_{x,2}, C_{x,3}, C_{x,4}\}_{x\in[l]}\rangle$$

$$= \langle \mathfrak{m}\cdot(g_T)^s, (T_{\rho(x)})^{\sigma_i s}{}_{i\in[\theta]}, g^{\lambda_x}, (T_{\rho(x)})^{\lambda_x}, g^{\eta_x}(H_{\rho(x)}\prod_{j\in S_{\rho(x)}} g_{n+1-j})^{\lambda_x},$$

$$g^{s_x}, g^{\eta_x}(\prod_{j\in R_{\rho(x)}} g_{n+1-j})^{s_x}\rangle \tag{2}$$

Remark 3. Obviously, the key does not contain the attribute revocation list, but only the ciphertext does. Thus, only the sender (encrypter) decides the receivers that own the attribute set out of the revocation list.

Remark 4. Attribute direct revocation does not need to re-distribute the user key in the system, and the system is very flexible in practice.

Decrypt($\mathrm{CT}_\Gamma, \mathrm{SK}_{I,S}$). Let $\mathcal{R} = \{x|\rho(x)\in S, x\notin R_{\rho(x)}\}$ and $\mathcal{S}' = \{\rho(x)\}_{x\in R}$. If Match($\Gamma, \mathcal{S}, \mathcal{I}, \mathcal{R}$) = 1 then $\Gamma(\mathcal{S}') = 1$, and the decryption algorithm computes

$$D_{x,1} = \frac{\hat{e}(C_{x,0}, K_{\rho(x),2}\cdot\prod_{j\in S_{\rho(x)}, j\neq I} g_{n+1-j+I})}{\hat{e}(C_{x,1}, K_{\rho(x),3})}, \quad D_{x,2} = \frac{\hat{e}(C_{x,4}/C_{x,2}, g_I)\hat{e}_\omega(B_x, K_1)}{\hat{e}(C_{x,3}, \prod_{j\in R_{\rho(x)}} g_{n+1-j+I})}$$

Compute constants ω_x such that $\sum_{\rho(x)\in S}\omega_x A_x = (1, 0, \cdots, 0)$, and then return $\mathfrak{m} \leftarrow C_0\prod_{x\in R}(D_{x,1}D_{x,2})^{\omega_x}$.

Update($\mathrm{SK}_{I,S}, I, S$). On input a secret key $\mathrm{SK}_{I,S}$, the key update algorithm re-randomizes and produces a same distributed secret key $\mathrm{SK}'_{I,S}$ as follows: Parse $\mathrm{SK}_{I,S}$ as $\langle K_1, K_2, K_3\rangle$; At random select $\delta\in\mathbb{Z}_N^\theta$. For $j\in S$, choose $\varsigma_j\in\mathbb{Z}_N^\theta$ and $z_j\in\mathbb{Z}_N$ s.t. $\sum_{j\in S}\varsigma_{i,j} = \delta_i$ for $i = 1, \cdots, \theta$; Select $Z_1, Z_2, Z_3\in\mathbb{G}_{p_3}^\theta\times\mathbb{G}_{p_3}^k\times\mathbb{G}_{p_3}^k$ randomly, where $k = |S|$; Output the key $\mathrm{SK}'_{I,S}$

$$\mathrm{SK}'_{I,S} = \left(\begin{pmatrix} K_1 \\ K_2 \\ K_3 \end{pmatrix}\times\begin{pmatrix} g^\delta \\ T_j^{z_j}g^{-\langle\varsigma_j,\sigma\rangle} \\ g^{z_j} \end{pmatrix}\times\begin{pmatrix} Z_1 \\ Z_2 \\ Z_3 \end{pmatrix}\right)$$

$$= \langle(g^{\rho_i+\delta_i})_{i\in[\theta]}, (g^{\alpha^I h_j+\beta+t_j(r_j+z_j)-\langle\vartheta_j+\varsigma_j,\sigma\rangle})_{j\in S}, (g^{r_j+z_j})_{j\in S}\rangle\times X_3^{\theta+2k} \tag{3}$$

It is easy to see that an updated key has the same distribution to the previous key, since the fresh exponents are added by uniform randomness δ_i, ς_j and z_j, and the $\mathbb{G}_{p_3}$ part has the similar update. As all randomness in $\mathrm{SK}_{I,S}$ will be removed by the pairing operations in decryption procedure, the update key and the old key have the same decryption ability.

5 Performance

We first analyze and discuss the *leakage bound L* and *leakage probability* ε. To obtain a leakage tolerance in subspace hiding theorem, in Corollary 1, by setting

$\theta = m - 1$ and $d = 1$, and we have $L = \log_2 \|\pi\| = 2 + (\theta - 1 - 2\xi) \log_2 p_2$-bit, where θ is a positive constant defined in Section 4. We can obtain $\varepsilon(\cdot) = p_2^{-\xi}$ is negligible if $\xi \geq 1$ and $p_2 = \mathsf{poly}(\tau)$. The leakage bound L is mainly decided by the order of subgroup $\mathbb{G}_{p_2}$. The sizes of system public key, secret key and ciphertext are $(\theta + m + 2n)\|\mathbb{G}\| + \|\mathbb{G}_2\|$, $(\theta + 2k)\|\mathbb{G}\|$ and $(\theta + 4)l\|\mathbb{G}\| + \|\mathbb{G}\|$, respectively, which are described in Tab.2.

Table 1. Size of public key, secret key and ciphertext

	size	remark
# of PP	$(\theta + m + 2n)\|\mathbb{G}\| + \|\mathbb{G}_2\|$	m: number of elements in universal attribute set
		n: number of elements in user identity set
# of SK	$(\theta + 2k)\|\mathbb{G}\|$	k: number of elements in attribute set $\mathcal{S}$
# of CT	$(\theta + 4)l\|\mathbb{G}\| + \|\mathbb{G}_2\|$	l: row of LSSS matrix A

θ: leakage parameter, $\|\mathbb{G}\|$: bits of an element of group $\mathbb{G}$, $\|\mathbb{G}_2\|$: bits of an element of group $\mathbb{G}_2$.

We give the performance of *leakage rate* γ that describes the allowable leakage of a key divided by the size of total key SK, more concretely, $\gamma = \frac{L}{\|\mathsf{SK}\|}$. As discussed in Section 4, we suppose that p_1, p_2 and p_3 are distinct primes of τ_1, τ_2 and τ_3 bits respectively, which are associated with the system security parameter τ. By ascertaining $\tau_1 = w_1\tau$, $\tau_2 = \tau$ and $\tau_3 = w_3\tau$ where w_1 and w_3 are positive, we can obtain the leakage rate of a secret key $\mathsf{SK}_{\mathcal{S}}$ is $\frac{\theta - 1 - 2\xi}{(1 + w_1 + w_3)(\theta + 2k)} \approx \frac{1}{(1 + w_1 + w_3)(1 + \frac{2k}{\theta})}$. Obviously, the larger w_1 and w_3 provide stronger security in subgroups $\mathbb{G}_{p_1}$ and $\mathbb{G}_{p_3}$, but will emerge lower leakage rate since the security of these subgroups is determined by the parameter τ_1 or τ_3. We can obtain the leverage of security and efficiency by choosing suitable factors w_1 and w_3. Actually, we can set $w_1 = w_3 = w$ to allow $\|p_1\| = \|p_3\|$ since our construction is only in $\mathbb{G}_{p_1 p_3}$.

Table 2. Performance of leakage resilience

performance	value
leakage bound L	$\lfloor (\theta - 1 - 2\xi) \log p_2 \rfloor$
leakage rate γ	$\frac{1}{1+2w} \cdot \frac{1 - \frac{1+2\xi}{\theta}}{1 + \frac{2k}{\theta}} \approx \frac{1}{1+2w} \cdot \frac{1}{1 + \frac{2k}{\theta}}$
leakage probability ε	$p_2^{-\xi}$

ξ: a constant that decides the leakage probability, k: size of attribute set $\mathcal{S}$
p_2: order of subgroup $\mathbb{G}_{p_2}$, θ: leakage parameter

We now give the practical evaluation of our scheme in 112-bit standard security recommended by NIST, which can be securely used in practice in the next twenty years [19][2]. Our scheme is constructed in pairing-based cryptographic

---

[2] From NIST recommendation, 112-bit standard is secure till year 2030.

system, in which $\mathbb{G}$ is an elliptic curve group. NIST shows that, elliptic curve cryptography in pairing-based cryptography appears to be secure with shorter keys than those needed by other asymmetric key algorithms, and elliptic curve cryptography keys should be twice the length of equivalent strength symmetric key algorithms [19]. For example, a 224-bit ECC key would have roughly the same strength as a 112-bit symmetric key in AES. Meanwhile, we guarantee that the factorization of N is hard, then we require $N = 2048$-bit under 112-bit security level. Thus an element of $\mathbb{G}$ is 2048-bit and an element of $\mathbb{G}_2$ is 4096-bit. In order to obtain better performance of leakage resilience, we set $\|p_1\| = \|p_3\| = 224$-bit and $\|p_2\| = 2048 - 2*224 = 1600$-bit. Thus, we can calculate $w = \frac{224}{2048} = 0.11$, and then the allowable maximum leakage rate is $\frac{\theta-1-2\xi}{1.22*(\theta+\frac{2k}{\theta})} \approx \frac{1}{1.22*(1+\frac{2k}{\theta})}$. For an enough large leakage parameter θ, the extreme value of leakage rate is $1/1.22 = 82\%$. The simulations of leakage bound and the adversary's possible attack probability are shown in Fig.1 and Fig.2.

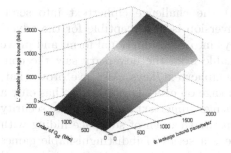

Fig. 1. Leakage bound L (bits)   **Fig. 2.** Leakage probability

6   Security

Intuitively, our scheme is equipped with an update algorithm that takes input a secret key and outputs a re-randomized key from the same distribution, and then we can obtain continual leakage tolerance in different key periods. We can specify the leakage parameter L as the entropy loss that a secret key can tolerate, and update the key when the entropy loss of that secret key will draw near the threshold.

The semantic security is obtained via a hybrid argument over a series of games, which employs DSE mechanism in [18,16,17]. At first we let Game_0 denote the real game as defined in Section 4 and its security model is defined in Section 3. Then we describe the remainder of games as the semi-functional versions in ciphertext and keys, respectively. We prove that all these games are computationally indistinguishable. At the last game, we show that an adversary has no advantage in outputting a successful guess ψ defined in security experiment $\text{Exp}_{\mathcal{E},\mathcal{A}}$ in Section 3.2. We have the following theorem.

Theorem 3. *Under the subgroup decisional assumptions hold in composite order bilinear groups, the ADR-lrABE scheme defined in Section 4 achieves semantic security and key-leakage resilience in the presence of attribute direct revocation.*

Proof. We only give the proof idea due to page limitation. We fist give the construction of the semi-functional ciphertext and two types of semi-functional keys by attaching the $\mathbb{G}_{p_2}$ parts in the corresponding ciphertext/key in Eq.(1) and Eq.(2) respectively. The semi-functional ciphertext has the form $\hat{CT}_\Gamma = (\hat{C}_0, \{(\hat{B}_{x_i})_{i \in [\theta]}, \hat{C}_{x,1}, \hat{C}_{x,2}, \hat{C}_{x,3}, \hat{C}_{x,4}\}_{x \in [l]})$, where $\hat{C}_0 = C_0$, $\hat{B}_{x,i} = B_{x_i}W_{x,i}$, $\hat{C}_{x,1} = C_{x,1}Y_{x,1}$, $\hat{C}_{x,2} = C_{x,2}Y_{x,2}$, $\hat{C}_{x,3} = C_{x,3}$, $\hat{C}_{x,4} = C_{x,4}$ in which $W_{x,i}, Y_{x,1}$ and $Y_{x,2}$ are at random picked from $\mathbb{G}_{p_2}$ for $i \in [\theta]$ and $x \in [l]$.

The semi-functional key has two forms: Type-1 form and Type-2 form. The first form of semi-functional key is $\hat{SK}_{I,\mathcal{S}} = (\hat{K}_{i,1}, \hat{K}_{j,2}, \hat{K}_{j,3})_{i \in [\theta], j \in \mathcal{S}}$, where $\hat{K}_{i,1} = K_{i,1}X_{i,1}$, $\hat{K}_{i,2} = K_{i,2}X_{i,2}$ and $\hat{K}_{i,3} = K_{i,3}X_{i,3}$ in which $X_{i,1}, X_{i,2}$ and $X_{i,3}$ are picked from $\mathbb{G}_2$ randomly. In the second semi-functional key, only the second component $\hat{K}_{i,2}$ has $\mathbb{G}_{p_2}$ part, that is $\overline{SK}_{I,\mathcal{S}} = (\hat{K}_{i,1} = K_{i,1}, \hat{K}_{i,2} = K_{i,2}X_{i,2}, \hat{K}_{i,2} = K_{i,3})_{i \in [\theta], j \in \mathcal{S}}$.

By the DSE mechanism, we convert the challenge ciphertext into semi-functional form and prove that this conversion is imperceptible for the adversary. By turn, we convert the queried keys into semi-functional form, and prove that these conversions are indistinguishable even the adversary saw the converted normal/semi-functional challenge ciphertext/keys. Also, we prove that, even the adversary has at most L bits leakage on every key, s/he also has only a negligible advantage to decrypt the challenge ciphertext and break the security experiment in $\mathsf{Exp}_{\mathcal{E},\mathcal{A}}$, which is based on the theorem of subspace hiding with leakage in Theorem 2. Finally, we achieve a series of indistinguishable games between normal key and normal challenge ciphertext in real construction and truly semi-functional key and ciphertext in last game. We use a series of games to prove the leakage-resilient security. More concretely, we prove that these games are computationally indistinguishable, and thus conclude the theorem.

7   Concluding Remarks

We presented the model of attribute-based encryption that supports both key leakage resilience and attribute direct revocation, and then gave the concrete construction and performance evaluation. We proved the security in the standard model under the static subgroup decision assumptions, analyzed the leakage-resilient performance, and showed that the scheme is semantically secure in the presence of about $(82 + o(1))$ fraction of the bits of decryption key being leaked. Our scheme can be used in secure data transmission and access control in large scale open networks with potential noise attacks or side-channel attacks such as public cloud computing, Internet of Things, smart grids, etc.

Acknowledgement. The author would like to thank the anonymous reviewers for their valuable comments from ACISP 2014. In particular, the author would like to express his thanks to Dr. Xinyi Huang for his suggestion and improvement in this work.

References

1. Agrawal, S., Dodis, Y., Vaikuntanathan, V., Wichs, D.: On continual leakage of discrete log representations. In: Sako, K., Sarkar, P. (eds.) ASIACRYPT 2013, Part II. LNCS, vol. 8270, pp. 401–420. Springer, Heidelberg (2013)
2. Akavia, A., Goldwasser, S., Vaikuntanathan, V.: Simultaneous hardcore bits and cryptography against memory attacks. In: Reingold, O. (ed.) TCC 2009. LNCS, vol. 5444, pp. 474–495. Springer, Heidelberg (2009)
3. Attrapadung, N., Herranz, J., Laguillaumie, F., Libert, B., et al.: Attribute-based encryption schemes with constant-size ciphertexts. Theoretical Computer Sciences 422, 15–38 (2012)
4. Attrapadung, N., Imai, H.: Conjunctive broadcast and attribute-based encryption. In: Shacham, H., Waters, B. (eds.) Pairing 2009. LNCS, vol. 5671, pp. 248–265. Springer, Heidelberg (2009)
5. Attrapadung, N., Imai, H.: Attribute-based encryption supporting direct/indirect revocation modes. In: Parker, M.G. (ed.) Cryptography and Coding 2009. LNCS, vol. 5921, pp. 278–300. Springer, Heidelberg (2009)
6. Boldyreva, A., Goyal, V., Kumar, V.: Identity-based encryption with efficient revocation. In: ACM-CCS 2008, pp. 417–426 (2008)
7. Brakerski, Z., Goldwasser, S.: Circular and leakage resilient public-key encryption under subgroup indistinguishability. In: Rabin, T. (ed.) CRYPTO 2010. LNCS, vol. 6223, pp. 1–20. Springer, Heidelberg (2010)
8. Brakerski, Z., Kalai, Y.T., Katz, J., Vaikuntanathan, V.: Overcoming the hole in the bucket: Publickey cryptography resilient to continual memory leakage. In: FOCS 2010, pp. 501–510 (2010)
9. Chow, S., Dodis, Y., Rouselakis, Y., Waters, B.: Practical leakage-resilient identity-based encryption from simple assumptions. In: ACM-CCS 2010, pp. 152–161 (2010)
10. Dodis, Y., Haralambiev, K., López-Alt, A., Wichs, D.: Efficient public-key cryptography in the presence of key leakage. In: Abe, M. (ed.) ASIACRYPT 2010. LNCS, vol. 6477, pp. 613–631. Springer, Heidelberg (2010)
11. Freeman, D.M.: Converting pairing-based cryptosystems from composite-order groups to prime-order groups. In: Gilbert, H. (ed.) EUROCRYPT 2010. LNCS, vol. 6110, pp. 44–61. Springer, Heidelberg (2010)
12. Goyal, V., Pandey, O., Sahai, A., Waters, B.: Attribute-based encryption for fine-grained access control of encrypted data. ACM-CCS 2006, pp. 89–98 (2006)
13. Han, J., Susilo, W., Mu, Y., Yan, J.: Attribute-based oblivious access control. Computer Journal 55(10), 1202–1215 (2012)
14. Lewko, A.: Tools for simulating features of composite order bilinear groups in the prime order setting. In: Pointcheval, D., Johansson, T. (eds.) EUROCRYPT 2012. LNCS, vol. 7237, pp. 318–335. Springer, Heidelberg (2012)
15. Lewko, A., Waters, B.: New proof methods for attribute-based encryption: achieving full security through selective techniques. In: Safavi-Naini, R., Canetti, R. (eds.) CRYPTO 2012. LNCS, vol. 7417, pp. 180–198. Springer, Heidelberg (2012)
16. Lewko, A., Okamoto, T., Sahai, A., Takashima, K., Waters, B.: Fully secure functional encryption: attribute-based encryption and (hierarchical) inner product encryption. In: Gilbert, H. (ed.) EUROCRYPT 2010. LNCS, vol. 6110, pp. 62–91. Springer, Heidelberg (2010)
17. Lewko, A., Rouselakis, Y., Waters, B.: Achieving leakage resilience through dual system encryption. In: Ishai, Y. (ed.) TCC 2011. LNCS, vol. 6597, pp. 70–88. Springer, Heidelberg (2011)

18. Lewko, A., Waters, B.: New techniques for dual system encryption and fully secure hibe with short ciphertexts. In: Micciancio, D. (ed.) TCC 2010. LNCS, vol. 5978, pp. 455–479. Springer, Heidelberg (2010)
19. Polk, W.T., Dodson, D.F., Burr, W.E., Ferraiolo, H., Cooper, D.: Cryptographic algorithms and key sizes for personal identity verification. NIST Special Publication 800-78-3 (2010),
    csrc.nist.gov/publications/nistpubs/800-78-3/sp800-78-3.pdf
20. Naor, M., Segev, G.: Public-key cryptosystems resilient to key leakage. In: Halevi, S. (ed.) CRYPTO 2009. LNCS, vol. 5677, pp. 18–35. Springer, Heidelberg (2009)
21. Sahai, A., Waters, B.: Fuzzy identity based encryption. In: Cramer, R. (ed.) EUROCRYPT 2005. LNCS, vol. 3494, pp. 457–473. Springer, Heidelberg (2005)
22. Wang, G., Liu, Q., Wu, J., Guo, M.: Hierarchical attribute-based encryption with scalable user revocation for data sharing in cloud servers. Computer and Security 30, 320–331 (2011)
23. Wang, P., Feng, D., Zhang, L.: Towards attribute revocation in key-policy attribute based encryption. In: Lin, D., Tsudik, G., Wang, X. (eds.) CANS 2011. LNCS, vol. 7092, pp. 272–291. Springer, Heidelberg (2011)
24. Waters, B.: Ciphertext-policy attribute-based encryption: an expressive, efficient, and provably secure realization. In: Catalano, D., Fazio, N., Gennaro, R., Nicolosi, A. (eds.) PKC 2011. LNCS, vol. 6571, pp. 53–70. Springer, Heidelberg (2011)
25. Yu, S., Wang, C., Ren, K., Lou, W.: Attribute based data sharing with attribute revocation. In: ASIACCS 2010, pp. 261–270. ACM (2010)
26. Zhang, M., Shi, W., Wang, C., Chen, Z., Mu, Y.: Leakage-resilient attribute-based encryption with fast decryption: models, analysis and constructions. In: Deng, R.H., Feng, T. (eds.) ISPEC 2013. LNCS, vol. 7863, pp. 75–90. Springer, Heidelberg (2013)
27. Zhang, M., Yang, B., Takagi, T.: Bounded leakage-resilient functional encryption with hidden vector predicate. The Computer Journal 56(4), 464–477 (2013)

Expressive Bandwidth-Efficient Attribute Based Signature and Signcryption in Standard Model

Y. Sreenivasa Rao and Ratna Dutta

Indian Institute of Technology Kharagpur
Kharagpur-721302, India
{ysrao,ratna}@maths.iitkgp.ernet.in

Abstract. This paper proposes an efficient key-policy attribute based signature (ABS) scheme with *constant-size* signature for expressive linear secret-sharing scheme (LSSS)-realizable monotone access structures with only 3 pairings for the verification algorithm, which is an affirmative answer for one of the open problems left in Pairing 2012 by Gagné *et al.* Our ABS provides signer privacy, and the existential unforgeability is achieved in selective security model. We also propose a new attribute based signcryption (ABSC) scheme for LSSS-realizable access structures utilizing only 6 pairings and making the ciphertext size *constant.* Our scheme is significantly more efficient than existing ABSC schemes. While the secret key size increases by a factor of number of attributes used in the system, the number of pairing evaluations is reduced to constant. Our protocol achieves (a) *ciphertext indistinguishability* under adaptive chosen ciphertext attacks assuming the hardness of decisional Bilinear Diffie-Hellman Exponent problem, (b) *existential unforgeability* under adaptive chosen message attack assuming the hardness of computational Diffie-Hellman Exponent problem and (c) *strong unforgeability* against insider adversary. The security proofs are in selective security model without using any random oracle. In addition, our ABSC achieves *public verifiability of the ciphertext,* enabling any party to verify the integrity and validity of the ciphertext.

Keywords: attribute based signature, signcryption, public ciphertext verifiability, signer privacy, LSSS-realizable access structure.

1 Introduction

Signcryption (SC) is an important cryptographic primitive for applications where both confidentiality and authenticity are at prime concern. As encryption offers confidentiality and signature provides authenticity, one can perform encryption and signing sequentially to achieve this. However, the complexity of the resulting framework is sum of the complexities of the individual primitives. Signcryption, first introduced by Zheng [9], is a logical mixture of encryption and signature in a single primitive, cost of which is significantly smaller than the cumulative cost of encryption and signature.

W. Susilo and Y. Mu (Eds.): ACISP 2014, LNCS 8544, pp. 209–225, 2014.
© Springer International Publishing Switzerland 2014

Attribute Based Signcryption (ABSC) which combines the functionalities of Attribute Based Encryption (ABE) [1–8] and Attribute Based Signature (ABS) [10–13] are appropriate to ensure fine-grained data access control in large-scale distributed environments like online social networks, cloud technology, etc. For instance, in cloud technology, users can outsource their data to the clouds in order to share their data efficiently with other users of their choice and also access their data from any place through the Internet when required. In this scenario, storing the information securely in the cloud may not be enough and the users should also be able to prove their genuineness at the cloud servers, so that illegal data storage can be avoided by the cloud. Designing efficient ABSC scheme is not a trivial task and has received considerable attention to the recent research community due to increasing demand of protecting sensitive data as well as achieving authenticity of the data for fine-grained access control in large distributed network.

Attribute Based Signature (ABS) introduced by Maji et al. [10] facilitates several applications such as attribute based messaging, attribute based authentication, trust-negotiation and leaking secrets. In ABS, messages are signed according to some predicate of signer's attributes and the verifier is assured that a signer has endorsed the message with a set of attributes satisfying the signing predicate. Especially, the signature exhibits no other attribute information about the original signer. Later, a number of ABS schemes [11–14, 23, 24] are proposed.

Previous Work. The first ABSC was introduced by Gagné et al. [15] with formal security models of *message confidentiality* and *ciphertext unforgeability* for signcryption in attribute based setting. Following this, a number of ABSC are proposed [16–19, 22]. To provide different rights for signature and decryption, signing attributes are separated from encryption/decryption attributes in [15]. The ABSC scheme of [18] is dynamic in the sense that it allows updation of signing access structures without re-issuing secret keys of users. Another interesting feature exhibited by [18], in contrast to [15–17, 19, 22], is the *public ciphertext verifiability* which allows any intermediate party (e.g., firewalls) to check the ciphertext's validity before sending to actual recipient. This reduces unnecessary burden on the receiver for unsigncrypting invalid ciphertexts. While [15, 18] achieve chosen ciphertext attack (CCA) security against message confidentiality in standard model, [17] is chosen plaintext attack (CPA) secure and [22] is CCA secure in random oracle model. The scheme of [16] has no formal security proof for ciphertext unforgeability in existing security models and can be shown to violate even the CPA security. The ABSC and its extension to support traceability in [19] which are claimed to be CCA secure can be shown incorrect (see Appendix B). The communication and computation overhead in the existing ABSC schemes [15–19, 22] proliferates linearly with the number of required attributes and none of these utilizes linear secret-sharing scheme (LSSS)-realizable access structures. This motivates us to address the problem of constructing ABSC with constant complexity (constant-size ciphertext and constant computation cost) for more expressive access structure and featuring public verifiability along with security in standard model.

1.1   Our Contributions

ABS with constant-size signature. To design an ABSC with the mentioned objectives, we first construct a key-policy ABS scheme with constant-size signature for monotone LSSS-realizable access structure employing threshold public key encryption framework of [20], where signature verification requires only 3 pairings. The existential unforgeability of this new ABS is reduced to computational Diffie-Hellman Exponent (cDHE) problem in standard model. Our ABS construction preserves signer privacy which is one of the essential design goals of the signature schemes in attribute based setting. The existing ABS schemes [11–13, 23, 24] with constant-size signature admit only limited access structures like threshold or AND-gate policies. Our ABS is the *first* LSSS-realizable ABS construction with constant-size signature in key-policy setting, which is an affirmative answer for one of the open problems left in [13].

ABSC with constant-size ciphertext. We then propose an ABSC scheme that is a logical combination of the KP-ABE [8] and our proposed ABS. The main technical difficulty of designing signcryption is how to unify encryption and signature primitives, so that the resulting signcryption is rich in functionality. We overcome this by adapting the technique of ID based signcryption [21] and employing some new technical ideas. Following are the silent features of our ABSC scheme:

- The proposed ABSC is proven to be CCA secure under the hardness of decisional Bilinear Diffie-Hellman Exponent (dBDHE) problem [8] and achieves existential unforgeability (EUF) under the hardness of cDHE problem [12], in standard model against *selective* adversary. Our security definitions are more general than the existing ones.
- The properties of strong unforgeability (sEUF) and public ciphertext verifiability are achieved without using any strongly unforgeable one-time signature scheme unlike [18] (this is the only existing scheme satisfying these two properties, see Table 2) to establish a connection between encryption and signature. The proposed ABSC also provides insider security with respect to both confidentiality and unforgeability as in [15].
- The ciphertext size in the proposed framework reduces to 6 group elements, thereby more suitable for bandwidth limited applications (see Table 1).
- Moreover, the amount of computation required to generate ciphertexts and to recover plaintexts is independent of the number of attributes involved in the respective process unlike existing schemes (see Table 1). Precisely, the signcryption process creates a ciphertext by performing 10 exponentiations. On the other hand, the unsigncryption requires only 2 exponentiations and 6 pairing evaluations to recover any message. We achieve this at the expense of large secret key size that is quadratic in the number of attributes. However, storage is much cheaper nowadays even for a large amount (e.g., smart phones [7]), while the main concerns lie with low bandwidth and computation overhead.
- The proposed ABSC exploits more expressive monotone LSSS-realizable access structures, whereas the existing key-policy ABSC schemes [15, 16, 19, 22] support only threshold access structures. We present the functionality comparison in Table 2.

Table 1. Comparison of communication and computation costs of ABSC schemes

Scheme	Secret Key (SK) Size		Ciphertext Size	Signcryption Cost		Unsigncryption Cost	
	Signing SK	Decryption SK		Exp.	Pair.	Exp.	Pair.
[15]	$2L_s$	$3L_e$	$\mathcal{O}(\phi_s + w_e)$	$\mathcal{O}(\phi_s + w_e)$	-	$\mathcal{O}(\phi_e)$	$\mathcal{O}(\phi_s + \phi_e)$
[16]	$2L_s$	$2L_e$	$\mathcal{O}(\phi_s + w_e)$	$\mathcal{O}(\phi_s + w_e)$	-	$\mathcal{O}(\phi_e)$	$\mathcal{O}(\phi_e)$
[17]	$2L_s + 1$	$2L_e + 1$	$\mathcal{O}(\phi_s + w_e)$	$\mathcal{O}(\phi_s + w_e)$	1	$\mathcal{O}(\phi_s + \phi_e)$	$\mathcal{O}(\phi_s + \phi_e)$
[18]	$2L_s$	$2L_e + 2vk + 1$	$\mathcal{O}(L_s + u_e)$	$\mathcal{O}(L_s + u_e)$	-	-	$\mathcal{O}(L_s + u_e)$
[22]	$L_s + d - 1$	$L_e + d - 1$	$\mathcal{O}(\phi_s + w_e)$	$\mathcal{O}(\phi_s + w_e)$	-	$\mathcal{O}(\phi_e + w_e)$	$\mathcal{O}(\phi_e)$
[19]	$(L_s + d)^2$	$2L_e$	$\mathcal{O}(id + w_e)$	$\mathcal{O}(id + w_e)$	-	$\mathcal{O}(\phi_e)$	$\mathcal{O}(id + \phi_e)$
[8] + [12]	$(2b_s + 2)(b_s + L_s)$	$u_e L_e$	7	$\mathcal{O}(b_s)$	-	$\mathcal{O}(b_s)$	9
Our ABSC	$u_s L_s$	$u_e L_e$	6	10	-	2	6

Note that by size, we mean the number of involved group elements. We exclude the message size from the ciphertext size in all the schemes listed in the table. L_s = number of signature attributes annotated to a user's signing secret key, b_s = maximum size of the admitted signing access structure, L_e = number of decryption attributes annotated to a user's decryption secret key, ϕ_s = number of signature attributes involved in the signcryption, ϕ_e = minimum number of decryption attributes required to recover a message, w_e = number of encryption attributes used to encrypt a message, u_s = number of signature attributes in the signature attribute space $\mathcal{U}_s$, u_e = number of decryption attributes in the decryption attribute space $\mathcal{U}_e$, vk = bit length of verification key, d = threshold value of the system, id = length of user's identity.

Table 2. Functionality comparison of ABSC schemes

Scheme	KP/CP	Access Structure (AS)		Security		Hardness Assumption		PV	SM
		Signature AS	Decryption AS	MC	CU	MC	CU		
[15]	KP	Threshold policy	Threshold policy	IND-CCA	EUF-CMA	dHmBDH	cmDH	No	Yes
[16]	KP	Threshold policy	Threshold policy	insecure	-	-	-	No	-
[17]	CP	Monotone tree	Monotone tree	IND-CPA	EUF-CMA	Generic group	DHI	No	No
[18]	CP	Monotone tree	AND-gate policy	IND-CCA	sEUF-CMA	dBDH	cDH	Yes	Yes
[22]	KP	Threshold policy	Threshold policy	IND-CCA	EUF-CMA	dBDH	cDH	No	No
[19]	KP	Threshold policy	Threshold policy	IND-CPA	EUF-CMA	dBDH	cDHE	No	No
[8] + [12]	KP	Threshold policy	LSSS-realizable	IND-CCA	EUF-CMA	dBDHE	cDHE	No	Yes
Our	KP	LSSS-realizable	LSSS-realizable	IND-CCA	sEUF-CMA	dBDHE	cDHE	Yes	Yes

Note that all the schemes listed in the table are selectively secure. MC = message confidentiality, CU = ciphertext unforgeability, d(Hm)BDH = decisional (hashed modified) bilinear Diffie-Hellman, c(m)DH = computational (modified) Diffie-Hellman, DHI = computational Diffie-Hellman inversion, IND-CP(C)A = indistinguishability of ciphertexts under chosen plaintext (ciphertext) attack, (s)EUF-CMA = (strongly) existential unforgeability under chosen message attack, KP/CP = key-policy/ciphertext-policy, PV = Public Verifiability, SM = Standard Model.

The unsigncryption process in [CCA secure KP-ABE of [8]] + [our ABS] requires 9 paring operations, while that for our ABSC is only 6. All other complexities are almost identical for both the approaches. This in turn implies that cost[our ABSC] < cost[CCA secure KP-ABE of [8]] + cost[our ABS]. In addition, the new ABSC outperforms all the existing ABSC schemes in terms of communication and computation cost while realizing more expressive access policies, namely LSSS-realizable access structures. One can obtain constant-size ciphertext ABSC by merging KP-ABE of [7] and one of the existing constant-size signature ABS schemes [11–13, 23, 24]. However, the computation cost (in terms of exponentiations) during signcryption and unsigncryption grows linearly with the number of encryption attributes used to signcrypt a message, and the signing access structure is limited to either threshold or AND-gate policy.

2   Preliminaries

We use the following notations in the rest of the paper.

$x \in_R X$	: operation of picking an element x uniformly at random from a set X
$[n]$	: set $\{1, 2, \ldots, n\}$ of positive integers

In this section, we recall necessary background from [6, 8, 15].

Definition 1 (Access Structure). *Let $\mathcal{U}$ be the universe of attributes and $\mathcal{P}(\mathcal{U})$ be the collection of all subsets of $\mathcal{U}$. Every non-empty subset $\mathbb{A}$ of $\mathcal{P}(\mathcal{U}) \backslash \{\emptyset\}$ is called an access structure. The sets in $\mathbb{A}$ are called authorized sets and the sets not in $\mathbb{A}$ are called unauthorized sets with respect to $\mathbb{A}$. An access structure $\mathbb{A}$ is said to be monotone access structure (MAS) if every superset of an authorized set is again authorized in $\mathbb{A}$, i.e., for any $C \in \mathcal{P}(\mathcal{U})$, with $C \supseteq B$ where $B \in \mathbb{A}$ implies $C \in \mathbb{A}$. An attribute set L satisfies $\mathbb{A}$ (in other words, $\mathbb{A}$ accepts L) if and only if L is an authorized set in $\mathbb{A}$, i.e., $L \in \mathbb{A}$.*

Definition 2 (Linear Secret-Sharing Scheme (LSSS)). *Let $\mathcal{U}$ be the universe of attributes. A secret-sharing scheme $\Pi_{\mathbb{A}}$ for the access structure $\mathbb{A}$ over $\mathcal{U}$ is called linear (in $\mathbb{Z}_p$) if $\Pi_{\mathbb{A}}$ consists of the following two polynomial time algorithms, where $\mathbb{M}$ is a matrix of size $\ell \times k$, called the share-generating matrix for $\Pi_{\mathbb{A}}$ and $\rho : [\ell] \to I_{\mathcal{U}}$ is a row labeling function that maps each row of the matrix $\mathbb{M}$ to an attribute in $\mathbb{A}$, $I_{\mathcal{U}}$ being the index set of $\mathcal{U}$.*

- Distribute($\mathbb{M}, \rho, \alpha$). *This algorithm takes as input the share-generating matrix $\mathbb{M}$, row labeling function ρ and a secret $\alpha \in \mathbb{Z}_p$ which is to be shared. It selects $z_2, z_3, \ldots, z_k \in_R \mathbb{Z}_p$ and sets $v = (\alpha, z_2, z_3, \ldots, z_k) \in \mathbb{Z}_p^k$. It outputs a set $\{M_i \cdot v : i \in [\ell]\}$ of ℓ shares, where $M_i \in \mathbb{Z}_p^k$ is the i-th row of the matrix $\mathbb{M}$. The share $\lambda_{\rho(i)} = M_i \cdot v$ belongs to an attribute $\rho(i)$.*
- Reconstruct($\mathbb{M}, \rho, W$). *This algorithm will accept as input $\mathbb{M}, \rho$ and a set of attributes $W \in \mathbb{A}$. Let $I = \{i \in [\ell] : \rho(i) \in I_W\}$, where I_W is the index set of the attribute set W. It returns a set $\{\omega_i : i \in I\}$ of secret reconstruction constants such that $\sum_{i \in I} \omega_i \lambda_{\rho(i)} = \alpha$, if $\{\lambda_{\rho(i)} : i \in I\}$ is a valid set of shares of the secret α according to $\Pi_{\mathbb{A}}$.*

The target vector which is used to characterize access structures is $(1, 0, \ldots, 0)$, i.e., a set $W \in \mathbb{A}$ iff $(1, 0, \ldots, 0)$ is in the linear span of the rows of $\mathbb{M}$ that are indexed by W.

Lemma 1. *[6] Let $(\mathbb{M}, \rho)$ be a LSSS access structure realizing an access structure $\mathbb{A}$ over the universe U of attributes, where $\mathbb{M}$ is share-generating matrix of size $\ell \times k$. For any $W \subset U$ such that $W \notin \mathbb{A}$, there exists a polynomial time algorithm that outputs a vector $w = (-1, w_2, \ldots, w_k) \in \mathbb{Z}_p^k$ such that $M_i \cdot w = 0$, for each row i of $\mathbb{M}$ for which $\rho(i) \in I_W$, here I_W is index set of attribute set W.*

Bilinear Map. We use multiplicative cyclic groups $\mathbb{G}, \mathbb{G}_T$ of prime order p with an efficiently computable mapping $e : \mathbb{G} \times \mathbb{G} \to \mathbb{G}_T$ such that $e(u^a, v^b) = e(u, v)^{ab}, \forall u, v \in \mathbb{G}, a, b \in \mathbb{Z}_p$ and $e(u, v) \neq 1_{\mathbb{G}_T}$ whenever $u, v \neq 1_{\mathbb{G}}$.

2.1   Attribute Based Signcryption (ABSC)

In this section, we define attribute based signcryption as a set of five algorithms following [15] wherein $\mathcal{U}_e$ and $\mathcal{U}_s$ respectively are disjoint universes of encryption/decryption attributes and signature attributes. A Central Authority (CA) manages all the (encryption and signature) attributes and their public-secret key pairs by executing **Setup** algorithm. When a decryptor requests a decryption secret key, the CA creates a decryption access structure $\mathbb{A}_d$ over $\mathcal{U}_e$ according to her role in the system and then computes the decryption secret key $\mathsf{SK}_{\mathbb{A}_d}$ by running **dExtract** algorithm, and finally sends to the decryptor. Similarly, the CA computes the signing secret key $\mathsf{SK}_{\mathbb{A}_s}$ by executing **sExtract** algorithm with the input a signing access structure $\mathbb{A}_s$ over $\mathcal{U}_s$ and sends to the signcryptor. While the decryption access structure enables what type of ciphertexts the user can decrypt, the signing access structure is used to signcrypt a message.

When a signcryptor wants to signcrypt a message M, it selects a set W_e of encryption attributes that decides a group of legitimate recipients and an authorized signing attribute set W_s of its signing access structure $\mathbb{A}_s$ (i.e., $W_s \in \mathbb{A}_s$), and then executes **Signcrypt** algorithm with the input $M, \mathsf{SK}_{\mathbb{A}_s}, W_s, W_e$. Here, W_e is used to encrypt a message and W_s is used to sign a message. On receiving the ciphertext $\mathsf{CT}_{(W_s, W_e)}$ of some message M, the decryptor/recipient performs **Unsigncrypt** algorithm with the input $\mathsf{CT}_{(W_s, W_e)}, \mathsf{SK}_{\mathbb{A}_d}$. The unsigncryption will correctly returned M only if $W_e \in \mathbb{A}_d$ and the ciphertext $\mathsf{CT}_{(W_s, W_e)}$ contains a valid signature with signing attributes W_s used in the ciphertext.

We denote this ABSC system as follows.

$$\Sigma_{\mathsf{ABSC}} = \begin{bmatrix} (\mathsf{PK}, \mathsf{MK}) & = \mathbf{Setup}(\kappa, \mathcal{U}_e, \mathcal{U}_s) \\ \mathsf{SK}_{\mathbb{A}_s} & = \mathbf{sExtract}(\mathsf{PK}, \mathsf{MK}, \mathbb{A}_s) \\ \mathsf{SK}_{\mathbb{A}_d} & = \mathbf{dExtract}(\mathsf{PK}, \mathsf{MK}, \mathbb{A}_d) \\ \mathsf{CT}_{(W_s, W_e)} & = \mathbf{Signcrypt}(\mathsf{PK}, M, \mathsf{SK}_{\mathbb{A}_s}, W_s, W_e) \\ M \text{ or } \bot & = \mathbf{Unsigncrypt}(\mathsf{PK}, \mathsf{CT}_{(W_s, W_e)}, \mathsf{SK}_{\mathbb{A}_d}) \end{bmatrix}$$

2.2   Security Definitions for ABSC

Following [15], the security definitions of *message confidentiality* and *ciphertext unforgeability* for ABSC are given below.

Message Confidentiality. This security notion is defined on indistinguishability of ciphertexts under adaptive chosen ciphertext attack in the selective attribute set model (IND-ABSC-sCCA) through the following game between a challenger $\mathfrak{C}$ and an adversary $\mathcal{A}$.

Init. The adversary $\mathcal{A}$ outputs the target set W_e^* of encryption attributes that will be used to create the challenge ciphertext during Challenge Phase.

Setup. The challenger $\mathfrak{C}$ executes **Setup**$(\kappa, \mathcal{U}_e, \mathcal{U}_s)$, gives the public key PK to $\mathcal{A}$ and keeps the master secret key MK to itself.

Query Phase 1. The adversary $\mathcal{A}$ is given access to the following oracles which are simulated by $\mathfrak{C}$.

- *sExtract oracle* $\mathcal{O}_{sE}(\mathbb{A}_s)$: on input any signing access structure $\mathbb{A}_s$ over signature attributes, $\mathfrak{C}$ runs **sExtract**$(PK, MK, \mathbb{A}_s)$ and returns $SK_{\mathbb{A}_s}$ to $\mathcal{A}$.
- *dExtract oracle* $\mathcal{O}_{dE}(\mathbb{A}_d)$: on input a decryption access structure $\mathbb{A}_d$ over encryption attributes such that $W_e^* \notin \mathbb{A}_d$, $\mathfrak{C}$ executes **dExtract**$(PK, MK, \mathbb{A}_d)$ and sends $SK_{\mathbb{A}_d}$ to the adversary $\mathcal{A}$.
- *Signcrypt oracle* $\mathcal{O}_{SC}(M, W_s, W_e)$: on input a message M, a signing attribute set W_s and an encryption attribute set W_e, the challenger $\mathfrak{C}$ samples a signing access structure $\mathbb{A}_s$ such that $W_s \in \mathbb{A}_s$ and returns the ciphertext $CT_{(W_s, W_e)} =$ **Signcrypt**$(PK, M, SK_{\mathbb{A}_s}, W_s, W_e)$ to $\mathcal{A}$, where $SK_{\mathbb{A}_s} = $ **sExtract**$(PK, MK, \mathbb{A}_s)$.
- *Unsigncrypt oracle* $\mathcal{O}_{US}(CT_{(W_s, W_e)}, \mathbb{A}_d)$: on input $CT_{(W_s, W_e)}$ and a decryption access structure $\mathbb{A}_d$ used to decrypt, $\mathfrak{C}$ obtains $SK_{\mathbb{A}_d} = $ **dExtract**$(PK, MK, \mathbb{A}_d)$ and gives the output of **Unsigncrypt**$(PK, CT_{(W_s, W_e)}, SK_{\mathbb{A}_d})$ to the adversary.

Challenge. The adversary $\mathcal{A}$ outputs two equal length messages M_0^*, M_1^* and a signing attribute set W_s^*. The challenger $\mathfrak{C}$ selects a signing access structure $\mathbb{A}_s^*$ such that $W_s^* \in \mathbb{A}_s^*$ and returns the challenge ciphertext $CT_{(W_s^*, W_e^*)}^*$ to the adversary $\mathcal{A}$ that is output of **Signcrypt**$(PK, M_b^*, SK_{\mathbb{A}_s^*}, W_s^*, W_e^*)$, where $SK_{\mathbb{A}_s^*} = $ **sExtract**$(PK, MK, \mathbb{A}_s^*)$ and $b \in_R \{0, 1\}$.

Query Phase 2. The adversary $\mathcal{A}$ can continue adaptively to make queries as in Query Phase 1 except the queries: $\mathcal{O}_{US}(CT_{(W_s^*, W_e^*)}^*, \mathbb{A}_d^*)$, for any $\mathbb{A}_d^*$ with $W_e^* \in \mathbb{A}_d^*$.

Guess. The adversary $\mathcal{A}$ outputs a guess bit $b' \in \{0, 1\}$ and wins the game if $b' = b$.

The advantage of $\mathcal{A}$ in the above game is defined to be $Adv_{\mathcal{A}}^{\mathsf{IND-ABSC-sCCA}} = |\Pr[b' = b] - \frac{1}{2}|$, where the probability is taken over all random coin tosses.

Remark 1. The adversary $\mathcal{A}$ is allowed to issue the queries $\mathcal{O}_{sE}(\mathbb{A}_s)$, for any signing access structure $\mathbb{A}_s$ with $W_s^* \in \mathbb{A}_s$, during Query Phase 2. This provides *insider* security, which means that $\mathcal{A}$ cannot get any additional advantage in the foregoing game even though the signing secret key corresponding to the challenge signing attribute set W_s^* is revealed.

Definition 3. *An ABSC scheme is said to be* $(\mathcal{T}, q_{sE}, q_{dE}, q_{SC}, q_{US}, \epsilon)$*-IND-ABSC-sCCA secure if the advantage* $Adv_{\mathcal{A}}^{\mathsf{IND-ABSC-sCCA}} \leq \epsilon$, *for any PPT adversary* $\mathcal{A}$ *running in time at most* $\mathcal{T}$ *that makes at most* q_{sE} *sExtract queries,* q_{dE} *dExtract queries,* q_{SC} *Signcrypt queries and* q_{US} *Unsigncrypt queries in the above game.*

Ciphertext Unforgeability. This notion of security is defined on existential unforgeability under adaptive chosen message attack in the selective attribute set model (EUF-ABSC-sCMA) through the following game between a challenger $\mathfrak{C}$ and an adversary $\mathcal{A}$.

Init. The adversary $\mathcal{A}$ outputs a set of signature attributes W_s^* to $\mathfrak{C}$ that will be used to forge a signature.

Setup. The challenger $\mathfrak{C}$ runs **Setup**$(\kappa, \mathcal{U}_e, \mathcal{U}_s)$ and sends the public key PK to the adversary $\mathcal{A}$.

Query Phase. The adversary $\mathcal{A}$ is given access to the following oracles.

- $sExtract$ $oracle$ $\mathcal{O}'_{sE}(\mathbb{A}_s)$: on input a signing access structure $\mathbb{A}_s$ over signature attributes such that $W_s^* \notin \mathbb{A}_s$, the challenger $\mathfrak{C}$ runs $\mathbf{sExtract}(\mathsf{PK}, \mathsf{MK}, \mathbb{A}_s)$ and returns $\mathsf{SK}_{\mathbb{A}_s}$ to the adversary $\mathcal{A}$.
- $dExtract$ $oracle$ $\mathcal{O}'_{dE}(\mathbb{A}_d)$: on input any decryption access structure $\mathbb{A}_d$ over encryption attributes, the challenger $\mathfrak{C}$ executes $\mathbf{dExtract}(\mathsf{PK}, \mathsf{MK}, \mathbb{A}_d)$ and sends $\mathsf{SK}_{\mathbb{A}_d}$ to the adversary $\mathcal{A}$.
- $Signcrypt$ $oracle$ $\mathcal{O}'_{SC}(M, W_s, W_e)$: on input a message M, a signing attribute set W_s and an encryption attribute set W_e, the challenger $\mathfrak{C}$ samples a signing access structure $\mathbb{A}_s$ such that $W_s \in \mathbb{A}_s$ and returns the ciphertext $\mathsf{CT}_{(W_s, W_e)} = \mathbf{Signcrypt}(\mathsf{PK}, M, \mathsf{SK}_{\mathbb{A}_s}, W_s, W_e)$ to $\mathcal{A}$, where $\mathsf{SK}_{\mathbb{A}_s} = \mathbf{sExtract}(\mathsf{PK}, \mathsf{MK}, \mathbb{A}_s)$.
- $Unsigncrypt$ $oracle$ $\mathcal{O}'_{US}(\mathsf{CT}_{(W_s, W_e)}, \mathbb{A}_d)$: on input $\mathsf{CT}_{(W_s, W_e)}$ and a decryption access structure $\mathbb{A}_d$ used to decrypt, $\mathfrak{C}$ obtains $\mathsf{SK}_{\mathbb{A}_d} = \mathbf{dExtract}(\mathsf{PK}, \mathsf{MK}, \mathbb{A}_d)$ and forwards the output of $\mathbf{Unsigncrypt}(\mathsf{PK}, \mathsf{CT}_{(W_s, W_e)}, \mathsf{SK}_{\mathbb{A}_d})$ to the adversary $\mathcal{A}$.

Forgery Phase. The adversary $\mathcal{A}$ outputs a forgery $\mathsf{CT}^*_{(W_s^*, W_e^*)}$ for some message M^* with a decryption access structure $\mathbb{A}_d^*$.

$\mathcal{A}$ wins if the ciphertext $\mathsf{CT}^*_{(W_s^*, W_e^*)}$ is valid and is not obtained from $Signcrypt$ oracle, i.e., $\mathbf{Unsigncrypt}(\mathsf{PK}, \mathsf{CT}^*_{(W_s^*, W_e^*)}, \mathbf{dExtract}(\mathsf{PK}, \mathsf{MK}, \mathbb{A}_d^*)) = M^* \neq \perp$ and $\mathcal{A}$ did not issue $\mathcal{O}'_{SC}(M^*, W_s^*, W_e^*)$.

The advantage of $\mathcal{A}$ in the above game is defined as $Adv_{\mathcal{A}}^{\mathsf{EUF-ABSC-sCMA}} = \Pr[\mathcal{A} \text{ wins}]$.

Remark 2. In this security model, $\mathcal{A}$ can query $dExtract$ oracle for the receiver's decryption access structure to whom the forgery is created in the foregoing game which captures the *insider* security model for signature unforgeability.

Definition 4. *An ABSC scheme is said to be* $(\mathcal{T}, q_{sE}, q_{dE}, q_{SC}, q_{US}, \epsilon)$-*EUF-ABSC-sCMA secure if the advantage* $Adv_{\mathcal{A}}^{\mathsf{EUF-ABSC-sCMA}} \leq \epsilon$, *for any PPT adversary* $\mathcal{A}$ *running in time at most* $\mathcal{T}$ *that makes at most* q_{sE} *sExtract queries,* q_{dE} *dExtract queries,* q_{SC} *Signcrypt queries and* q_{US} *Unsigncrypt queries in the above game.*

Strong Unforgeability. An ABSC system is said to be strongly unforgeable if it is existentially unforgeable with the condition that given signcryptions on some message M, the adversary cannot create a new signcryption on the same message M. In the foregoing existential unforgeability model, if the adversary is allowed to produce a forgery on a message M that has already queried to the Signcrypt oracle with the restriction that the forged signcryption for M cannot be the output of Signcrypt oracle for the same message M with the same signing and encryption attribute sets as the forgery, it is called as strongly existential unforgeability under adaptive chosen message attack in the selective attribute set model (sEUF-ABSC-sCMA).

Definition 5. *An ABSC scheme is said to be* $(\mathcal{T}, q_{sE}, q_{dE}, q_{SC}, q_{US}, \epsilon)$-*sEUF-ABSC-sCMA secure if* $Adv_{\mathcal{A}}^{\mathsf{sEUF-ABSC-sCMA}} \leq \epsilon$, *for any PPT adversary* $\mathcal{A}$ *running in time at most* $\mathcal{T}$ *that makes at most* q_{sE} *sExtract queries,* q_{dE} *dExtract queries,* q_{SC} *Signcrypt queries and* q_{US} *Unsigncrypt queries in the above game.*

3 Our Expressive ABS Scheme with Constant-Size Signature

In this section, we present our ABS with constant-size signature that supports any monotone LSSS-realizable access structure in key-policy setting as a tuple $\Sigma_{\mathsf{ABS}} = (\mathbf{Setup}, \mathbf{Extract}, \mathbf{Sign}, \mathbf{Verify})$ of the following four algorithms.

Setup$(\kappa, \mathcal{U}_s)$:

Here, $\mathcal{U}_s = \{\mathsf{att}'_x\}$ is the universe of signing attributes used in the system. Let $\{0,1\}^*$ be the message space and let $\mathcal{H} : \{0,1\}^* \to \{0,1\}^\ell$ be a collision resistant hash function, where ℓ is large enough that the hash function is collision resistant. The CA generates multiplicative cyclic groups $\mathbb{G}, \mathbb{G}_T$ of prime order p whose size is determined by the security parameter κ. Let $e : \mathbb{G} \times \mathbb{G} \to \mathbb{G}_T$ be an efficiently computable bilinear mapping. It samples $\alpha \in_R \mathbb{Z}_p, g \in_R \mathbb{G}$ and sets $Y = e(g,g)^\alpha$. It then selects $T_0, u_0, u_1, \ldots, u_\ell \in_R \mathbb{G}$. For each attribute $\mathsf{att}'_x \in \mathcal{U}_s$, it chooses $T_x \in_R \mathbb{G}$. The system's master secret is $\mathsf{MK} = \alpha$ and the public key is $\mathsf{PK} = \langle p, g, e, Y, T_0, \{T_x : \mathsf{att}'_x \in \mathcal{U}_s\}, u_0, u_1, \ldots, u_\ell, \mathcal{H}\rangle$.

Extract$(\mathsf{PK}, \mathsf{MK}, (\mathbb{S}, \rho))$:

The CA generates the secret key for signing LSSS access structure $(\mathbb{S}, \rho)$ as follows. Each row i of the signing share-generating matrix $\mathbb{S}$ of size $\ell_s \times k_s$ is associated with an attribute $\mathsf{att}'_{\rho(i)}$. Execute $\mathsf{Distribute}(\mathbb{S}, \rho, \alpha)$ and obtain a set $\{\lambda_{\rho(i)} = \boldsymbol{S}_i \cdot \boldsymbol{v} : i \in [\ell_s]\}$ of ℓ_s shares one for each row of the matrix, where $\boldsymbol{S}_i$ is the i-th row of $\mathbb{S}$ and $\boldsymbol{v} \in_R \mathbb{Z}_p^{k_s}$ such that $\boldsymbol{v} \cdot \boldsymbol{1} = \alpha$, $\boldsymbol{1} = (1,0,\ldots,0)$ being a vector of length k_s. For each row $i \in [\ell_s]$, choose $r_i \in_R \mathbb{Z}_p$ and compute $D_i = g^{\lambda_{\rho(i)}}(T_0 T_{\rho(i)})^{r_i}, D'_i = g^{r_i}, D''_i = \{D''_{i,x} : D''_{i,x} = T_x^{r_i}, \forall\, \mathsf{att}'_x \in \mathcal{U}_s \setminus \{\mathsf{att}'_{\rho(i)}\}\}$. The signing secret key of $(\mathbb{S}, \rho)$ is $\mathsf{SK}_{(\mathbb{S},\rho)} = \langle (\mathbb{S}, \rho), \{D_i, D'_i, D''_i : i \in [\ell_s]\}\rangle$.

Sign$(\mathsf{PK}, M, \mathsf{SK}_{(\mathbb{S},\rho)}, W_s)$:

The signer with signing secret key $\mathsf{SK}_{(\mathbb{S},\rho)}$ calculates the signature of a message $M \in \{0,1\}^*$ as follows.

- Choose an *authorized* signature attribute set W_s of the signing LSSS access structure $(\mathbb{S}, \rho)$ and obtain $\{\omega_i : i \in I_s\} = \mathsf{Reconstruct}(\mathbb{S}, \rho, W_s)$, here $I_s = \{i \in [\ell_s] : \mathsf{att}'_{\rho(i)} \in W_s\}$.
- Select $\theta, \xi \in_R \mathbb{Z}_p$.
- Compute $\sigma_1 = g^\theta, \sigma_2 = g^\xi \prod_{i \in I_s} (D'_i)^{\omega_i}, (m_1, m_2, \ldots, m_\ell) = \mathcal{H}(M \| \sigma_2 \| W_s)$,
  $$\sigma_3 = \prod_{i \in I_s} \left(D_i \cdot \prod_{\mathsf{att}'_x \in W_s, x \neq \rho(i)} D''_{i,x}\right)^{\omega_i} \cdot \left(T_0 \prod_{\mathsf{att}'_x \in W_s} T_x\right)^\xi \cdot \left(u_0 \prod_{j \in [\ell]} u_j^{m_j}\right)^\theta.$$
- The signature of a message M for the attribute set W_s is $\Gamma = \langle \sigma_1, \sigma_2, \sigma_3\rangle$.

Note: This algorithm requires only 4 exponentiations if the access structure is a boolean formula, since the exponents $\{\omega_i\}$ are 1 for boolean formulas [25].

Verify$(\mathsf{PK}, M, \Gamma, W_s)$:

To check if $\Gamma = \langle \sigma_1, \sigma_2, \sigma_3\rangle$ is a signature of a message M for an attribute set W_s, the verifier proceeds as follows.

- Compute $(m_1, m_2, \ldots, m_\ell) = \mathcal{H}(M \| \sigma_2 \| W_s)$.
- Verify the equation $e(\sigma_3, g) \stackrel{?}{=} Y \cdot e(T_0 \prod_{\mathsf{att}'_x \in W_s} T_x, \sigma_2) \cdot e(u_0 \prod_{j \in [\ell]} u_j^{m_j}, \sigma_1)$. If it is valid, output 1; otherwise, output 0.

The correctness of **Verify** algorithm follows from Correctness of Eq. (1) detailed in Section 4.

Security. The existential unforgeability of the above ABS scheme against adaptive chosen message attack in the selective attribute set model (without random oracles) follows from the proof of Theorem 3 (given in Section 5), assuming the hardness of computational n-DHE problem [12]. (Due to page restriction, we omit the proof.)

Signer Privacy. An ABS scheme is private if the distribution of the signature is independent of the secret key that is used to generate the signature. That is, no one can deduce any information about the access structure $\mathbb{A}_s = (\mathbb{S}, \rho)$ held by the signer from a signature $\Gamma = \langle \sigma_1, \sigma_2, \sigma_3 \rangle$ of a message M for the attribute set W_s, other than the fact that W_s satisfies $\mathbb{A}_s$.

Following [13], we formalize the signer privacy to key-policy ABS as follows.

Definition 6. *A key-policy ABS is private if for any message M, all $(\mathsf{PK}, \mathsf{MK})$ generated by* Setup *algorithm, all signing access structures $\mathbb{A}_s$ and $\mathbb{A}'_s$, all signing secret keys $\mathsf{SK}_{\mathbb{A}_s} = \mathrm{Extract}(\mathsf{PK}, \mathsf{MK}, \mathbb{A}_s)$ and $\mathsf{SK}_{\mathbb{A}'_s} = \mathrm{Extract}(\mathsf{PK}, \mathsf{MK}, \mathbb{A}'_s)$, all attribute sets W_s such that W_s satisfies both $\mathbb{A}_s$ and $\mathbb{A}'_s$, the distributions of $\mathrm{Sign}(\mathsf{PK}, M, \mathsf{SK}_{\mathbb{A}_s}, W_s)$ and $\mathrm{Sign}(\mathsf{PK}, M, \mathsf{SK}_{\mathbb{A}'_s}, W_s)$ are equal.*

Theorem 1. *Our ABS scheme is private.*

The proof will be given in Appendix A.

4   Proposed ABSC Construction with Constant-Size Ciphertext

Let $\mathcal{U}_e = \{\mathrm{att}_y\}$ and $\mathcal{U}_s = \{\mathrm{att}'_x\}$ be the universes of encryption and signature attributes, respectively. In our construction, both signing and decryption access structures are LSSS-realizable. We denote a *signing* LSSS access structure by $(\mathbb{S}, \rho)$ and a *decryption* LSSS access structure by $(\mathbb{D}, \phi)$. We describe now our attribute based signcryption as a set of the following five algorithms.

Setup$(\kappa, \mathcal{U}_e, \mathcal{U}_s)$:
To initialize the system the CA performs the following steps. Generate multiplicative cyclic groups $\mathbb{G}$ and $\mathbb{G}_T$ of prime order p whose size is determined by the security parameter κ. Let g be a generator of the group $\mathbb{G}$ and $e : \mathbb{G} \times \mathbb{G} \to \mathbb{G}_T$ be an efficiently computable bilinear mapping. Choose $\alpha \in_R \mathbb{Z}_p, K_0, T_0, \delta_1, \delta_2 \in_R \mathbb{G}$ and set $Y = e(g, g)^\alpha$. For each attribute $\mathrm{att}'_x \in \mathcal{U}_s$ (resp., $\mathrm{att}_y \in \mathcal{U}_e$), select $T_x \in_R \mathbb{G}$ (resp., $K_y \in_R \mathbb{G}$). Let $\{0,1\}^{\ell_m}$ be the message space, i.e., ℓ_m is the length of each message sent. Sample four one-way, collision resistant cryptographic hash functions $\mathcal{H}_1 : \mathbb{G}_T \times \mathbb{G} \times \{0,1\}^{\ell_\tau} \to \{0,1\}^{\ell_m}, \mathcal{H}_2 : \{0,1\}^* \to \{0,1\}^\ell,$ $\mathcal{H}_3 : \mathbb{G} \to \mathbb{Z}_p$ and $\mathcal{H}_4 : \{0,1\}^* \to \mathbb{Z}_p$ from appropriate families of such functions, where ℓ is large enough (a typical value of ℓ could be 256) so that the hash functions are collision resistant and $\ell_\tau \approx 40$. Pick $u_0, u_1, \ldots, u_\ell \in_R \mathbb{G}$. The master secret key is $\mathsf{MK} = \alpha$ and the public key is $\mathsf{PK} = \langle p, g, e, Y, T_0, K_0, \{T_x : \mathrm{att}'_x \in \mathcal{U}_s\}, \{K_y : \mathrm{att}_y \in \mathcal{U}_e\}, \delta_1, \delta_2, u_0, u_1, \ldots, u_\ell, \mathcal{H}_1, \mathcal{H}_2, \mathcal{H}_3, \mathcal{H}_4 \rangle$.

sExtract$(\mathsf{PK}, \mathsf{MK}, (\mathbb{S}, \rho))$:

The CA carries out the following steps and returns the signing secret key to a legitimate signcryptor. Each row i of the signing share-generating matrix $\mathbb{S}$ of size $\ell_s \times k_s$ is associated with an attribute $\mathsf{att'}_{\rho(i)}$. Execute $\mathsf{Distribute}(\mathbb{S}, \rho, \alpha)$ and obtain a set $\{\lambda_{\rho(i)} = \boldsymbol{S_i} \cdot \boldsymbol{v_s} : i \in [\ell_s]\}$ of ℓ_s shares, where $\boldsymbol{S_i}$ is the i-th row of $\mathbb{S}$, $\boldsymbol{v_s} \in_R \mathbb{Z}_p^{k_s}$ such that $\boldsymbol{v_s} \cdot \boldsymbol{1} = \alpha$, $\boldsymbol{1} = (1, 0, \dots, 0)$ being a vector of length k_s. For each row $i \in [\ell_s]$, choose $r_i \in_R \mathbb{Z}_p$ and compute $D_{s,i} = g^{\lambda_{\rho(i)}} (T_0 T_{\rho(i)})^{r_i}, D'_{s,i} = g^{r_i}, D''_{s,i} = \{D''_{s,i,x} : D''_{s,i,x} = T_x^{r_i}, \forall \, \mathsf{att'}_x \in \mathcal{U}_s \setminus \{\mathsf{att'}_{\rho(i)}\}\}$. Return the signing secret key as $\mathsf{SK}_{(\mathbb{S}, \rho)} = \langle (\mathbb{S}, \rho), \{D_{s,i}, D'_{s,i}, D''_{s,i} : i \in [\ell_s]\}\rangle$.

dExtract$(\mathsf{PK}, \mathsf{MK}, (\mathbb{D}, \phi))$:

In order to issue the decryption secret key to a legitimate decryptor, the CA executes as follows. Each row i of the decryption share-generating matrix $\mathbb{D}$ of size $\ell_e \times k_e$ is associated with an attribute $\mathsf{att}_{\phi(i)}$. Execute $\mathsf{Distribute}(\mathbb{D}, \phi, \alpha)$ and obtain a set $\{\lambda_{\phi(i)} = \boldsymbol{D_i} \cdot \boldsymbol{v_e} : i \in [\ell_e]\}$ of ℓ_e shares, where $\boldsymbol{D_i}$ is the i-th row of $\mathbb{D}$, $\boldsymbol{v_e} \in_R \mathbb{Z}_p^{k_e}$ such that $\boldsymbol{v_e} \cdot \boldsymbol{1} = \alpha$, $\boldsymbol{1} = (1, 0, \dots, 0)$ being a vector of length k_e. For each row $i \in [\ell_e]$, choose $\tau_i \in_R \mathbb{Z}_p$ and compute $D_{e,i} = g^{\lambda_{\phi(i)}} (K_0 K_{\phi(i)})^{\tau_i}, D'_{e,i} = g^{\tau_i}, D''_{e,i} = \{D''_{e,i,y} : D''_{e,i,y} = K_y^{\tau_i}, \forall \, \mathsf{att}_y \in \mathcal{U}_e \setminus \{\mathsf{att}_{\phi(i)}\}\}$. Return the secret decryption key as $\mathsf{SK}_{(\mathbb{D}, \phi)} = \langle (\mathbb{D}, \phi), \{D_{e,i}, D'_{e,i}, D''_{e,i} : i \in [\ell_e]\}\rangle$.

Signcrypt$(\mathsf{PK}, M, \mathsf{SK}_{(\mathbb{S}, \rho)}, W_s, W_e)$:

To signcrypt a message $M \in \{0, 1\}^{\ell_m}$, the signcryptor selects an authorized signature attribute set W_s of the signing LSSS access structure $(\mathbb{S}, \rho)$ held by the signcryptor and chooses a set of encryption attributes W_e which describe the target recipients. Since W_s satisfies $\mathbb{S}$, the signcryptor first runs $\mathsf{Reconstruct}(\mathbb{S}, \rho, W_s)$ and obtains a set $\{\omega_i : i \in I_s\}$ of reconstruction constants, where $I_s = \{i \in [\ell_s] : \mathsf{att'}_{\rho(i)} \in W_s\}$ such that $\sum_{i \in I_s} \omega_i \lambda_{\rho(i)} = \alpha$ (this implicitly holds and we use this fact in correctness below). Note that the secret shares $\{\lambda_{\rho(i)}\}_{i \in I_s}$ are not explicitly known to the signcryptor and hence so is α. However, as $(\mathbb{S}, \rho)$ accepts W_s, the secret α can correctly be embedded in the exponent as $g^{\sum_{i \in I_s} \omega_i \lambda_{\rho(i)}} = g^\alpha$ in the ciphertext component σ_3 given below by using the secret key components $\{D_{s,i}\}_{i \in I_s}$ (see correctness described below for details). Parse $\mathsf{PK}, \mathsf{SK}_{(\mathbb{S}, \rho)}$ as above. The signcryptor then

- chooses $\theta, \vartheta \in_R \mathbb{Z}_p$ and computes $C_1 = g^\theta, C_2 = (K_0 \prod_{\mathsf{att}_y \in W_e} K_y)^\theta, \sigma_1 = g^{\theta \vartheta}$,
- encrypts the message as $C_3 = \mathcal{H}_1(Y^\theta, \sigma_1, \tau) \oplus M$, where $\tau \in_R \{0, 1\}^{\ell_\tau}$,
- picks $\xi \in_R \mathbb{Z}_p$ and sets $\sigma_2 = g^\xi \prod_{i \in I_s}(D'_{s,i})^{\omega_i}$,
- calculates $\mu = \mathcal{H}_3(C_1)$ and sets $C_4 = (\delta_1^\mu \delta_2)^\theta$,
- computes $(m_1, m_2, \dots, m_\ell) = \mathcal{H}_2(\sigma_2 || \tau || W_s || W_e)$, $\beta = \mathcal{H}_4(\sigma_1 || C_2 || C_3 || C_4 || W_s || W_e)$ and

$$\sigma_3 = \prod_{i \in I_s} \left(D_{s,i} \cdot \prod_{\mathsf{att'}_x \in W_s, x \neq \rho(i)} D''_{s,i,x}\right)^{\omega_i} \cdot \left(T_0 \prod_{\mathsf{att'}_x \in W_s} T_x\right)^\xi \cdot \left(u_0 \prod_{j \in [\ell]} u_j^{m_j}\right)^\theta \cdot C_4^{\beta \vartheta},$$

where $m_i \in \{0, 1\}$ for all $i \in [\ell]$,
- sets $\sigma_4 = \tau$.

The signcryption of M is $\mathsf{CT}_{(W_s, W_e)} = \langle W_s, W_e, C_1, C_2, C_3, C_4, \sigma_1, \sigma_2, \sigma_3, \sigma_4 \rangle$.

Unsigncrypt$(\mathsf{PK}, \mathsf{CT}_{(W_s, W_e)}, \mathsf{SK}_{(\mathbb{D}, \phi)})$:

The secret decryption key $\mathsf{SK}_{(\mathbb{D}, \phi)}$ and the ciphertext $\mathsf{CT}_{(W_s, W_e)}$ are parsed as above. The decryptor

- computes $\mu = \mathcal{H}_3(C_1)$, $(m_1, m_2, \ldots, m_\ell) = \mathcal{H}_2(\sigma_2 \| \sigma_4 \| W_s \| W_e)$, $\beta = \mathcal{H}_4(\sigma_1 \| C_2 \| C_3 \| C_4 \| W_s \| W_e)$ and checks the validity of the ciphertext $\mathsf{CT}_{(W_s, W_e)}$ using the following equation as

$$e(\sigma_3, g) \overset{?}{=} Y \cdot e\left(T_0 \prod_{\text{att}'_x \in W_s} T_x, \sigma_2\right) \cdot e\left(u_0 \prod_{j \in [\ell]} u_j^{m_j}, C_1\right) \cdot e((\delta_1^\mu \delta_2)^\beta, \sigma_1), \quad (1)$$

if it is invalid, outputs $\bot$; otherwise, proceeds as follows

- obtains secret reconstruction constants $\{\nu_i : i \in I_e\} = \mathsf{Reconstruct}(\mathbb{D}, \phi, W_e)$, where $I_e = \{i \in [\ell_e] : \text{att}_{\phi(i)} \in W_e\}$
- computes $E_1 = \prod_{i \in I_e} \left(D_{e,i} \cdot \prod_{\text{att}_y \in W_e, y \neq \phi(i)} D''_{e,i,y}\right)^{\nu_i}$, $E_2 = \prod_{i \in I_e} (D'_{e,i})^{\nu_i}$ and recovers Y^θ by computing

$$Y^\theta = e(C_1, E_1)/e(C_2, E_2) \quad (2)$$

- obtains the message $M = C_3 \oplus \mathcal{H}_1(Y^\theta, \sigma_1, \sigma_4)$.

Note. As mentioned earlier, the exponents $\{\omega_i\}$ and $\{\nu_i\}$ are 1 for boolean formulas. Hence, Signcrypt and Unsigncrypt algorithms require only 10 and 2 exponentiations, respectively. For LSSS matrices over $\mathbb{Z}_p$, i.e., general LSSS monotone access structures, Signcrypt performs $\mathcal{O}(\phi_s)$ exponentiations, and Unsigncrypt computes $\mathcal{O}(\phi_e)$ exponentiations and 6 pairings, where $\phi_s = |I_s|$ and $\phi_e = |I_e|$. Thus, we achieve low computation cost when compare with previous schemes (see Table 1) even in case we use general LSSS access policies instead of boolean formulas. In this case also, the size of ciphertext is constant.

Remark 3. We note here that the verification process stated in Eq. (1) is formulated based on the public key parameters and the ciphertext components, thereby any user who has access to the ciphertext can verify the integrity and validity of the sender and the ciphertext. This provides the property of *Public Ciphertext Verifiability* to our scheme.

The correctness of the unsigncryption process follows from the following arguments.

Correctness of Eq. (1). Since W_s satisfies $\mathbb{S}$, we have $\sum_{i \in I_s} \omega_i \lambda_{\rho(i)} = \alpha$. Then,

$$\prod_{i \in I_s} \left(D_{s,i} \cdot \prod_{\text{att}'_x \in W_s, x \neq \rho(i)} D''_{s,i,x}\right)^{\omega_i} = \prod_{i \in I_s} \left(g^{\lambda_{\rho(i)}}(T_0 T_{\rho(i)})^{r_i} \cdot \prod_{\text{att}'_x \in W_s, x \neq \rho(i)} T_x^{r_i}\right)^{\omega_i}$$

$$= g^{\sum_{i \in I_s} \omega_i \lambda_{\rho(i)}} \prod_{i \in I_s} \left(T_0^{r_i} \prod_{\text{att}'_x \in W_s} T_x^{r_i}\right)^{\omega_i}$$

$$= g^\alpha \left(T_0 \prod_{\text{att}'_x \in W_s} T_x\right)^{\sum_{i \in I_s} r_i \omega_i},$$

$$\sigma_3 = g^\alpha \Big(T_0 \prod_{\text{att}'_x \in W_s} T_x\Big)^{\sum_{i \in I_s} r_i \omega_i} \cdot \Big(T_0 \prod_{\text{att}'_x \in W_s} T_x\Big)^\xi \cdot \Big(u_0 \prod_{j \in [\ell]} u_j^{m_j}\Big)^\theta \cdot (\delta_1^\mu \delta_2)^{\theta \beta \vartheta}.$$

Now, $\sigma_2 = g^\xi \prod_{i \in I_s} (D'_{s,i})^{\omega_i} = g^\xi g^{\sum_{i \in I_s} r_i \omega_i} = g^{\xi + \sum_{i \in I_s} r_i \omega_i}$. Hence,

$e(\sigma_3, g)$

$$= e\Big(g^\alpha (T_0 \prod_{\text{att}'_x \in W_s} T_x)^{\sum_{i \in I_s} r_i \omega_i} \cdot (T_0 \prod_{\text{att}'_x \in W_s} T_x)^\xi \cdot (u_0 \prod_{j \in [\ell]} u_j^{m_j})^\theta \cdot (\delta_1^\mu \delta_2)^{\theta \beta \vartheta}, g\Big)$$

$$= e(g^\alpha, g) \cdot e\Big(T_0 \prod_{\text{att}'_x \in W_s} T_x, \ g^{\xi + \sum_{i \in I_s} r_i \omega_i}\Big) \cdot e\Big(u_0 \prod_{j \in [\ell]} u_j^{m_j}, g^\theta\Big) \cdot e((\delta_1^\mu \delta_2)^\beta, g^{\theta \vartheta})$$

$$= Y \cdot e\Big(T_0 \prod_{\text{att}'_x \in W_s} T_x, \sigma_2\Big) \cdot e\Big(u_0 \prod_{j \in [\ell]} u_j^{m_j}, C_1\Big) \cdot e((\delta_1^\mu \delta_2)^\beta, \sigma_1).$$

Correctness of Eq. (2). We have $\sum_{i \in I_e} \nu_i \lambda_{\phi(i)} = \alpha$ since W_e satisfies $(\mathbb{D}, \phi)$. Then,

$$E_1 = \prod_{i \in I_e} \Big(g^{\lambda_{\phi(i)}} (K_0 K_{\phi(i)})^{\tau_i} \cdot \prod_{\text{att}_y \in W_e, y \neq \phi(i)} K_y^{\tau_i}\Big)^{\nu_i}$$

$$= g^{\sum_{i \in I_e} \nu_i \lambda_{\phi(i)}} \prod_{i \in I_e} \Big(K_0^{\tau_i} \prod_{\text{att}_y \in W_e} K_y^{\tau_i}\Big)^{\nu_i} = g^\alpha \Big(K_0 \prod_{\text{att}_y \in W_e} K_y\Big)^{\sum_{i \in I_e} \tau_i \nu_i},$$

$$E_2 = \prod_{i \in I_e} (D'_{e,i})^{\nu_i} = \prod_{i \in I_e} g^{\tau_i \nu_i} = g^{\sum_{i \in I_e} \tau_i \nu_i}.$$

Therefore, $\dfrac{e(C_1, E_1)}{e(C_2, E_2)} = \dfrac{e(g^\theta, g^\alpha (K_0 \prod_{\text{att}_y \in W_e} K_y)^{\sum_{i \in I_e} \tau_i \nu_i})}{e((K_0 \prod_{\text{att}_y \in W_e} K_y)^\theta, g^{\sum_{i \in I_e} \tau_i \nu_i})} = e(g^\theta, g^\alpha) = Y^\theta.$

5   Security Analysis

Theorem 2 (Indistinguishability). *Assume the encryption attribute universe $\mathcal{U}_e$ has n attributes and collision-resistant hash functions exist. Then our attribute based signcryption scheme is $(\mathcal{T}, q_{sE}, q_{dE}, q_{SC}, q_{US}, \epsilon)$-IND-ABSC-sCCA secure, assuming the decisional n-BDHE problem in $(\mathbb{G}, \mathbb{G}_T)$ is $(\mathcal{T}', \epsilon')$-hard, where $\mathcal{T}' = \mathcal{T} + \mathcal{O}(|\mathcal{U}_s|^2 \cdot (q_{sE} + q_{SC}) + n^2 \cdot (q_{dE} + q_{US})) \cdot \mathcal{T}_{exp} + \mathcal{O}(q_{US}) \cdot \mathcal{T}_{pair}$ and $\epsilon' = \epsilon - (q_{US}/p)$. Here, $\mathcal{T}_{exp}$ and $\mathcal{T}_{pair}$ denote the running time of one exponentiation and one pairing computation, respectively.*

Theorem 3 (Unforgeability). *Assume the signing attribute universe $\mathcal{U}_s$ has n attributes and collision-resistant hash functions exist. Then our attribute based signcryption scheme is $(\mathcal{T}, q_{sE}, q_{dE}, q_{SC}, q_{US}, \epsilon)$-sEUF-ABSC-sCMA secure, assuming that the computational n-DHE problem in $\mathbb{G}$ is $(\mathcal{T}', \epsilon')$-hard, where $\mathcal{T}' = \mathcal{T} + \mathcal{O}(n^2 \cdot (q_{sE} + q_{SC}) + |\mathcal{U}_e|^2 \cdot (q_{dE} + q_{US})) \cdot \mathcal{T}_{exp} + \mathcal{O}(q_{SC} + q_{US}) \cdot \mathcal{T}_{pair}$ and $\epsilon' = \epsilon/(\kappa(\ell_m + 1))$. Here, $\mathcal{T}_{exp}$ and $\mathcal{T}_{pair}$ denote the running time of one exponentiation and one pairing computation, respectively.*

Due to page restriction, the proofs are omitted. These are available in the full version of the paper at the eprint server maintained by IACR.

6   Some Extended Constructions

Traceable ABSC construction. We further extend our ABSC to support traceability exploiting the technique used in [19]. The resulting traceable ABSC preserves the same functionality as that of our ABSC and greatly improves upon the existing one [19].

Non-monotone access structure (non-MAS) realization. We can extend our ABSC to support *negative* attributes by treating the negation of an attribute as a separate attribute. This doubles the total number of attributes used in the system [25]. However, the resulting non-MAS ABSC attains the same efficiency as that of our monotone access structure ABSC.

Large attribute universe extension. It is also possible to extend our techniques to construct large universe ABSC scheme, where the public parameters of attributes are computed even after system setup by using a collision resistant hash function. In this case, the size of ciphertext will be linear in the number of encryption attributes and independent of the size of signing attribute set. Hence, we can achieve short ciphertext-size (although not constant) when compare with previous schemes. However, the number of pairing computations is still constant.

7   Conclusion

We present the first LSSS-realizable ABS scheme with constant-size signature and 3 pairing computations for signature verification. We show that our ABS provides signer privacy. We further present the first constant-size ciphertext ABSC for expressive LSSS-realizable access structures with constant computation cost. Both ciphertext confidentiality and strong unfogeability against selective adversary have been proven under decisional BDHE and computational DHE assumptions, respectively, in standard model. Additionally, it provides public ciphertext verifiability property which allows any third party to check the integrity and validity of the ciphertext. The secret key size in our schemes increases by a factor of number of attributes used in the system.

Acknowledgement. The authors would like to thank the anonymous reviewers of this paper for their valuable comments and suggestions.

References

1. Sahai, A., Waters, B.: Fuzzy Identity-Based Encryption. In: Cramer, R. (ed.) EUROCRYPT 2005. LNCS, vol. 3494, pp. 457–473. Springer, Heidelberg (2005)
2. Goyal, V., Pandey, O., Sahai, A., Waters, B.: Attribute Based Encryption for Fine-Grained Access Control of Encrypted Data. In: ACM Conference on Computer and Communications Security, pp. 89–98 (2006)
3. Bethencourt, J., Sahai, A., Waters, B.: Ciphertext-Policy Attribute-Based Encryption. In: IEEE Symposium on Security and Privacy, pp. 321–334 (2007)

4. Ostrovksy, R., Sahai, A., Waters, B.: Attribute Based Encryption with Non-Monotonic Access Structures. In: ACM Conference on Computer and Communications Security, pp. 195–203 (2007)
5. Lewko, A., Okamoto, T., Sahai, A., Takashima, K., Waters, B.: Fully Secure Functional Encryption: Attribute-Based Encryption and (Hierarchical) Inner Product Encryption. In: Gilbert, H. (ed.) EUROCRYPT 2010. LNCS, vol. 6110, pp. 62–91. Springer, Heidelberg (2010)
6. Waters, B.: Ciphertext-Policy Attribute-Based Encryption: An Expressive, Efficient, and Provably Secure Realization. In: Catalano, D., Fazio, N., Gennaro, R., Nicolosi, A. (eds.) PKC 2011. LNCS, vol. 6571, pp. 53–70. Springer, Heidelberg (2011)
7. Attrapadung, N., Herranz, J., Laguillaumie, F., Libert, B., de Panafieu, E., Ràfols, C.: Attribute-Based Encryption Schemes with Constant-Size Ciphertexts. Theor. Comput. Sci. 422, 15–38 (2012)
8. Rao, Y.S., Dutta, R.: Computationally Efficient Expressive Key-Policy Attribute Based Encryption Schemes with Constant-Size Ciphertext. In: Qing, S., Zhou, J., Liu, D. (eds.) ICICS 2013. LNCS, vol. 8233, pp. 346–362. Springer, Heidelberg (2013)
9. Zheng, Y.: Digital Signcryption or How to Achieve Cost(Signature & Encryption) << Cost(Signature) + Cost(Encryption). In: Kaliski Jr., B.S. (ed.) CRYPTO 1997. LNCS, vol. 1294, pp. 165–179. Springer, Heidelberg (1997)
10. Maji, H.K., Prabhakaran, M., Rosulek, M.: Attribute-Based signatures. In: Kiayias, A. (ed.) CT-RSA 2011. LNCS, vol. 6558, pp. 376–392. Springer, Heidelberg (2011)
11. Ge, A., Ma, C., Zhang, Z.: Attribute-Based Signature Scheme with Constant Size Signature in the Standard Model. IET Information Security 6(2), 1–8 (2012)
12. Herranz, J., Laguillaumie, F., Libert, B., Ràfols, C.: Short Attribute-Based Signature for Threshold Predicates. In: Dunkelman, O. (ed.) CT-RSA 2012. LNCS, vol. 7178, pp. 51–67. Springer, Heidelberg (2012)
13. Gagné, M., Narayan, S., Safavi-Naini, R.: Short Pairing-Efficient Threshold-Attribute-Based signature. In: Abdalla, M., Lange, T. (eds.) Pairing 2012. LNCS, vol. 7708, pp. 295–313. Springer, Heidelberg (2013)
14. Li, J., Au, M.H., Susilo, W., Xie, D., Ren, K.: Attribute-based signature and its application. In: ASIACCS 2010, pp. 60–69. ACM, New York (2010)
15. Gagné, M., Narayan, S., Safavi-Naini, R.: Threshold Attribute-Based Signcryption. In: Garay, J.A., De Prisco, R. (eds.) SCN 2010. LNCS, vol. 6280, pp. 154–171. Springer, Heidelberg (2010)
16. Hu, C., Zhang, N., Li, H., Cheng, X., Liao, X.: Body Area Network Security: A Fuzzy Attribute-based Signcryption Scheme. IEEE Journal on Selected Areas in Communications 31(9), 37–46 (2013)
17. Wang, C., Huang, J.: Attribute-based Signcryption with Ciphertext-policy and Claim-predicate Mechanism. In: CIS 2011, pp. 905–909 (2011)
18. Emura, K., Miyaji, A., Rahman, M.S.: Dynamic Attribute-Based Signcryption without Random Oracles. Int. J. Applied Cryptography 2(3), 199–211
19. Wei, J., Hu, X., Liu, W.: Traceable attribute-based signcryption. Security Comm. Networks (2013), doi:10.1002/sec.940
20. Qin, B., Wu, Q., Zhang, L., Domingo-Ferrer, J.: Threshold Public-Key Encryption with Adaptive Security and Short Ciphertexts. In: Soriano, M., Qing, S., López, J. (eds.) ICICS 2010. LNCS, vol. 6476, pp. 62–76. Springer, Heidelberg (2010)
21. Selvi, S.S.D., Vivek, S.S., Vinayagamurthy, D., Rangan, C.P.: ID Based Signcryption Scheme in Standard Model. In: Takagi, T., Wang, G., Qin, Z., Jiang, S., Yu, Y. (eds.) ProvSec 2012. LNCS, vol. 7496, pp. 35–52. Springer, Heidelberg (2012)

22. Guo, Z., Li, M., Fan, X.: Attribute-based ring signcryption scheme. Security Comm. Networks 6, 790–796 (2013), doi:10.1002/sec.614
23. Zeng, F., Xu, C., Li, Q., Zhang, X.: Attribute-based Signature Scheme with Constant Size Signature. Journal of Computational Information Systems 8(7), 2875–2882 (2012)
24. Chen, C., Chen, J., Lim, H.W., Zhang, Z., Feng, D., Ling, S., Wang, H.: Fully secure attribute-based systems with short ciphertexts/signatures and threshold access structures. In: Dawson, E. (ed.) CT-RSA 2013. LNCS, vol. 7779, pp. 50–67. Springer, Heidelberg (2013)
25. Lewko, A., Waters, B.: Decentralizing attribute-based encryption. Cryptology ePrint Archive, Report 2010/351 (2010), http://eprint.iacr.org/

A   Proof of Theorem 1

Proof. A signature of a message M using an attribute set W_s is of the form $\Gamma = \langle \sigma_1, \sigma_2, \sigma_3 \rangle$, where $\sigma_1 = g^\theta$, $\quad \sigma_2 = g^\xi \prod_{i \in I_s} (D_i')^{\omega_i}$,

$\sigma_3 = \prod_{i \in I_s} \left(D_i \cdot \prod_{\mathrm{att'}_x \in W_s, x \neq \rho(i)} D_{i,x}'' \right)^{\omega_i} \cdot \left(T_0 \prod_{\mathrm{att'}_x \in W_s} T_x \right)^\xi \cdot \left(u_0 \prod_{j \in [\ell]} u_j^{m_j} \right)^\theta$.

Here, $\theta, \xi \in_R \mathbb{Z}_p$ and $(m_1, m_2, \dots, m_\ell) = \mathcal{H}(M \| \sigma_2 \| W_s)$. By simplification (as in Correctness of Eq. (1) in Section 4), we have

$$\sigma_3 = g^\alpha \cdot \left(T_0 \prod_{\mathrm{att'}_x \in W_s} T_x \right)^{\xi + \sum_{i \in I_s} r_i \omega_i} \cdot \left(u_0 \prod_{j \in [\ell]} u_j^{m_j} \right)^\theta, \quad \sigma_2 = g^{\xi + \sum_{i \in I_s} r_i \omega_i}, \quad \sigma_1 = g^\theta.$$

Let $\gamma = \xi + \sum_{i \in I_s} r_i \omega_i$. Then, γ is random since ξ is random and

$$\sigma_3 = g^\alpha \cdot \left(T_0 \prod_{\mathrm{att'}_x \in W_s} T_x \right)^\gamma \cdot \left(u_0 \prod_{j \in [\ell]} u_j^{m_j} \right)^\theta, \quad \sigma_2 = g^\gamma, \quad \sigma_1 = g^\theta,$$

where $(m_1, m_2, \dots, m_\ell) = \mathcal{H}(M \| \sigma_2 \| W_s)$ and γ, θ are random exponents. Thus, the distribution of the signature is clearly the same regardless of the secret key that is used to compute it.   □

B   Cryptanalysis of ABSC Schemes [16, 19]

Hu et al. [16] proved that their scheme is IND-CCA secure—given a ciphertext for the message M_b *randomly* chosen from M_0 and M_1, no polynomial-time adversary (with an access to unsigncrypt oracle) can determine from which message M_0 or M_1 the ciphertext is computed, i.e., $M_b = M_0$ or $M_b = M_1$, with a non-negligible advantage. But, the ABSC in [16] is not even IND-CPA secure, i.e., any adversary is able to decide wether $M_b = M_0$ or $M_b = M_1$ with certainty, without accessing the unsigncrypt oracle. This follows from the argument that the adversary first guesses $M_b = M_0$ and then performs the signature verification test in unsigncryption process using public parameters and challenge ciphertext components. If the test passes, $M_b = M_0$; otherwise, $M_b = M_1$. This violates the IND-CPA security of the ABSC proposed in [16].

Wei et al. [19] proposed an ABSC with identity, called ID-ABSC, and then extends this construction to support traceability, i.e., the authority can recover the identity of the signcryptor when necessary. Wei et al. [19] claimed that ID-ABSC is proven to have the security of IND-CCA in the random oracle model. However, this conclusion does not hold from the following argument. The adversary obtains the challenge ciphertext of M_b after submitting M_0, M_1 to the challenger that is of the form $\mathsf{CT}^* = [u, W_e, \Gamma_{k,W_s}(\cdot), \Omega', X, \{E_i\}_{i \in W_e}, C, \sigma_1, \sigma_2, \sigma_3, \sigma_4]$. Then the adversary computes $\sigma_1' = \sigma_1 \cdot R^\vartheta$ and $\sigma_3' = \sigma_3 \cdot g_1^\vartheta$, where R is publicly computable parameter[1], ϑ is a random exponent and g_1 is a public parameter, and sets $\mathsf{CT}' = [u, W_e, \Gamma_{k,W_s}(\cdot), \Omega', X, \{E_i\}_{i \in W_e}, C, \sigma_1', \sigma_2, \sigma_3', \sigma_4]$. The adversary queries the unsigncrypt oracle with CT' as input. This query is allowed since $\mathsf{CT}' \neq \mathsf{CT}^*$. Note that the adversary cannot query the unsigncrypt oracle with the challenge ciphertext as input. Since the adversary randomizes only the signature terms σ_1 and σ_3, the unsigncrypt oracle can correctly recover the message M_b. Hence the signature verification test will pass always without detecting the changes made by the adversary because of the fact that the randomized terms are canceled out automatically. Finally, the unsigncrypt oracle returns M_b. If $M_b = M_0$, the adversary knows that M_0 is the plaintext of the challenge ciphertext CT^*. Otherwise, if $M_b = M_1$, he knows that M_1 is the plaintext of CT^*. This violates the IND-CCA security of ID-ABSC. In the manner described above, the traceable ABSC proposed in [19] also cannot achieve IND-CCA security as it is a simple extension of ID-ABSC.

---

[1] Note that $R = T_0 \prod_{j \in W_s \cup \Omega'} T_{2,j}$. Where $T_0, T_{2,j}$ are public parameters for all j and W_s, Ω' are in CT^*.

Incrementally Executable Signcryptions

Dan Yamamoto, Hisayoshi Sato, and Yasuko Fukuzawa

Hitachi, Ltd., Yokohama Research Laboratory, 292 Yoshida-cho,
Totsuka-ku, Yokohama, Kanagawa 244-0817, Japan
{dan.yamamoto.vx,hisayoshi.sato.th,yasuko.fukuzawa.pd}@hitachi.com

Abstract. We present the concept of incrementally executable signcryptions, which is a generalization of traditional on-line/off-line signcryption and facilitates optimizing the sender's off-line computation. With an incrementally executable signcryption scheme, the sender can activate signcryption process *incrementally* by its given sequential input: the sender's key pair, a recipient's public key, and a plaintext message to be sent to the recipient. Furthermore, we present an efficient generic construction of incrementally executable signcryption scheme. In our construction, the signing process can be done *before* being given the recipient's public key as well as the message to be sent. This feature enables us to accelerate the subsequent processes. Moreover, our construction achieves the strongest security notions without relying on random oracles. In addition, it requires a weak assumption for the underlying signature scheme, i.e., the underlying signature scheme is sufficient to be unforgeable under generic chosen message attack. Furthermore, it supports the *parallel unsigncryption* feature, which allows receivers to perform two potentially expensive computations, i.e., the verification of off-line signature and the key-decapsulation, in parallel.

Keywords: signcryption, on-line/off-line, insider security, multi-user setting, generic construction.

1 Introduction

The concept of signcryption was introduced by Zheng [30] as a public-key cryptographic primitive offering confidentiality and authenticity simultaneously. A signcryption scheme performs the functions of both digital signature and public-key encryption at the same time, which enables end-to-end secure message transmissions required in many applications such as e-mailing and e-commerce.

A large number of signcryption schemes have been proposed in the literature (see, e.g., [30,2,3,23,12,18,11,4,26,22,31,8]). These schemes provide different security levels depending on the used security model. Chiba et al. [8] proposed two generic constructions of signcryption, which are the first to achieve the strongest confidentiality and authenticity properties, i.e., indistinguishability against insider chosen ciphertext attacks in the dynamic multi-user model (dM-IND-iCCA) and strong unforgeability against insider chosen message attacks in the dynamic multi-user model (dM-sUF-iCMA), without relying on random oracles.

W. Susilo and Y. Mu (Eds.): ACISP 2014, LNCS 8544, pp. 226–241, 2014.

Although signcryption schemes are useful building blocks for end-to-end secure message transmissions, they are not suitable for computationally-restricted devices (e.g., RFID tags, mobile phones, and sensors) due to their signing and public-key encryption parts that usually require expensive operations such as exponentiation or pairing computation.

To overcome this difficulty, the notion of on-line/off-line signcryption were introduced by An et al. [2]. As in the case of on-line/off-line signatures [13,24,16,7], a on-line/off-line signcryption process (i.e., simultaneous signing and public-key encryption) is split into two phases. The first phase is performed *off-line*, i.e., before the message to be signcrypted is given, and the second phase is performed *on-line*, i.e., after the message to be signcrypted is given. The major computational overhead is shifted to the off-line phase, whereas the on-line phase requires only a low computational overhead.

In [2], An et al. also presented the first generic construction of on-line/off-line signcryption, which is an on-line/off-line variant of "commit-then-encrypt-and-sign" composition (hereinafter referred to as OCtEaS). We point out that OCtEaS has two drawbacks in terms of efficiency and security. First, the off-line signing in the OCtEaS construction requires a recipient's public key as an additional input parameter, which is essential for their scheme to achieve the unforgeability in the multi-user setting. This causes practical issues because a sender cannot start expensive off-line signing until she determines who is her target recipient, even if her device has enough idle time. Second, the OCtEaS construction only achieves the weaker security notions than the above strong notions of dM-IND-iCCA and dM-sUF-iCMA. More concretely, it only achieves the indistinguishability against *publicly detectable replayable CCA* [6] and *standard* (i.e., not strong) unforgeability notion.

1.1 Our Contribution

The above efficiency drawback of OCtEaS arises because the traditional two-phase definition of off-line and on-line cannot capture the state transition of the sender precisely. In other words, the syntax of the traditional off-line signcrypt algorithm $\mathsf{sc}_{\mathsf{off}}(sk_S, pk_S, pk_R)$ is ambiguous as to whether its internal computations (e.g., expensive off-line signing) can be executed *prior to* knowing the recipient's public key pk_R or not. To overcome this ambiguity, we split the traditional off-line phase in two, which results in the following three sequential phases: ▷ *Phase 1 (Setup):* The identity of the sender is determined. Specifically, the sender generates (or securely obtains from a trusted authority) her own key pair (sk_S, pk_S). ▷ *Phase 2 (Handshake):* The sender recognizes the target recipient to whom she might send some messages. Specifically, the sender obtains the receiver's public key pk_R. ▷ *Phase 3 (On-Line):* The sender finally decides a message m to be sent to the target recipient determined in the previous phase.

The essential point for efficiency is that the sender could have significant idle time in the above *setup* phase as well as the handshake phase. For instance, imagine a situation where the sender, say Alice, uses her mobile device to securely communicate with her friends. After generating her key pair sk_S, pk_S, the device can execute sc_1 as many times as possible and stores the results in its secure storage. After a few seconds, minutes, hours, or days of the executions of sc_1, Alice decides to contact to one of her friends, say Bob. She chooses the address of Bob from an address book on the device, then sc_2 can be performed as many times as possible by consuming the stored results of sc_1. Finally, after a few second or minute, she types some message for Bob and submit it, which enables the device to run sc_3 algorithm. Note that we can utilize these meaningful intervals between these three algorithm invocations to perform as much pre-computation as possible.

Incrementally Executable Signcryptions. Based on the above observation, we present the concept of *incrementally executable signcryptions*, which consists of three algorithms corresponding to the above three phases: $sc_1(sk_S, pk_S)$, $sc_2(pk_R)$, and $sc_3(m)$, With an incrementally executable signcryption scheme, the sender can activate signcryption process *incrementally* by its given sequential input: the sender's key pair (sk_S, pk_S), a recipient's public key pk_R, and a plaintext message m to be sent to the recipient.

We notice that the incrementally executable signcryption helps the scheme designer to pay more attention to the efficiency of the off-line computation. The design principle of efficient signcryptions can be much simpler: Let as many expensive computations move to the earlier phases as possible. This principle is especially useful for applications like the mobile communication example we mentioned earlier as well as MANETs (Mobile Ad-hoc Networks), in which the sender has significant idle time to execute pre-computation not only in the handshake phase (i.e., after knowing the neighbor node) but also in the setup phase (i.e., prior to knowing the neighborhood). Pre-computations in the setup phase save the computational resource in the handshake phase.

According to the concept of incrementally executable signcryptions, the limitation of OCtEaS construction we mentioned earlier can be explained as the disadvantage that the underlying signing procedure can be executed in the handshake phase (i.e., in $sc_2(pk_R)$) but not in the earlier setup phase (i.e., in $sc_1(sk_S, pk_S)$).

Generic Construction with Strong Security and Parallel Un-Signcryption. Furthermore, we present an efficient generic construction of incrementally executable signcryption scheme: GIESC. In our construction, the signing process can be done in $sc_1(sk_S, pk_S)$ computation. This feature enables us to accelerate the subsequent processes after the target recipient and message are decided. Moreover, GIESC achieves the strong security notions of dM-IND-iCCA and dM-sUF-iCMA without relying on random oracles. In addition, GIESC requires a weak assumption for the underlying signature scheme, i.e., the underlying signature scheme is sufficient to have *standard* (i.e., not strong) unforgeability under *generic* chosen message attack (UF-GMA). Furthermore, it supports the *parallel un-signcryption* feature, which allows receivers to perform two potentially expensive computations, i.e., the verification of off-line signature and the key-decapsulation, in parallel. This feature results in efficiency improvements on parallel machines.

1.2   Related Work

Although several on-line/off-line signcryption schemes have also been proposed in the literature (see, e.g., [29,27]), none of them achieves the strong security notions of dM-IND-iCCA and dM-sUF-iCMA without relying on random oracles. Several *hybrid* signcryption schemes have been proposed (see, e.g., [11,10,5]), where the research goal is rather establishing a hybrid paradigm for signcryption schemes than providing on-line/off-line feature. Several *identity-based* on-line/off-line signcryption schemes have been proposed (see, e.g., [25,19]). In particular, the construction in [19] has a desirable property that enables the sender to perform all expensive computation before given the receiver's identity. However, this feature takes advantage of the ID-based setting, as ID-based on-line/off-line *encryption* schemes [14,20,9] do. We cannot find a trivial application of this technique to the non-ID-based (i.e., PKI) setting and leave it as an open problem.

2   Preliminaries

We denote by $x \leftarrow_\$ \mathcal{X}$ the operation of selecting a random element x from a set $\mathcal{X}$ and by $x \leftarrow y$ the assignment of value y to x. We denote by $[pred]$ Boolean value of a predicate *pred*. For instance, $[1 = 1]$ equals to 1 (true) and $[1 = 1 \text{ and } 1 = 0]$ equals to 0 (false). We denote by $\langle x_1 \parallel \ldots \parallel x_n \rangle$ a concatenate string encoding of $x_1, \ldots, x_n$ from which the latter are uniquely recoverable. We write A.x to indicate explicitly that the algorithm x belongs to the scheme A. Unless otherwise indicated, algorithms are randomized, i.e., it takes a source of randomness to make random choices during execution. We write $z \leftarrow \mathcal{A}(x, y, \ldots; \texttt{oracle}_1, \texttt{oracle}_2, \ldots)$ to indicate the operation of a Turing machine $\mathcal{A}$ with inputs $x, y, \ldots$ and access to oracles $\texttt{oracle}_1, \texttt{oracle}_2, \ldots$, and letting z be the output. In all the experiments (games), every number, set, and bit string is implicitly initialized by 0, ϕ, and empty string, respectively.

2.1   Tag-Based Key Encapsulation Mechanism

A tag-based key encapsulation mechanism (TBKEM) is a KEM-analogue of tag-based encryption (TBE) [21,17] [1]. Its encapsulation and decapsulation algorithms take an arbitrary string (tag) as an additional input.

A TBKEM TK consists of the following algorithms:

init() $\to \lambda$: The initialization algorithm. It outputs public parameters λ, which includes a description of a key space TK.$\mathcal{K}$. We will generally assume that all algorithms take λ as an implicit input, even if it is not explicitly stated.

gen(λ) $\to (sk, pk)$: The key generation algorithm. It generates a private/public key pair (sk, pk) for decapsulation and encapsulation.

---

[1] Note that the notion of TBKEM is different from the notion of tag-KEMs formalized by Abe et al. [1]

$\mathsf{enc}(\lambda, pk, \tau) \to (K, C)$: The encapsulation algorithm. It takes as input the public key pk, and a tag $\tau \in \{0,1\}^*$, and outputs a pair (K, C), where $K \in \mathsf{TK}.\mathcal{K}$ is a generated key and C is an encapsulation of K.

$\mathsf{dec}(\lambda, sk, \tau, C) \to K$: The (deterministic) decapsulation algorithm. It takes as input the secret key sk, a tag $\tau \in \{0,1\}^*$, and an encapsulation C, and outputs either a key $K \in \mathsf{TK}.\mathcal{K}$ or an error symbol $\bot$.

For correctness, we require that for all $\lambda \leftarrow \mathsf{init}()$, all $(sk, pk) \leftarrow \mathsf{gen}(\lambda)$, all tag $\tau \in \{0,1\}^*$, and all $(K, C) \leftarrow \mathsf{enc}(\lambda, pk, \tau)$, it must hold that $\mathsf{dec}(\lambda, sk, \tau, C) = K$.

We recall the security notion of indistinguishability against adaptive tag [2] and adaptive chosen ciphertext attacks (IND-tag-CCA). The IND-tag-CCA-*advantage of $\mathcal{A}$ against* TK is defined as

$$\mathsf{Adv}_{\mathsf{TK}}^{\mathsf{IND\text{-}tag\text{-}CCA}}(\mathcal{A}) = \left| 2\Pr\left[\mathsf{Exp}_{\mathsf{TK}}^{\mathsf{IND\text{-}tag\text{-}CCA}}(\mathcal{A}) = 1 \right] - 1 \right|,$$

where the experiment $\mathsf{Exp}_{\mathsf{TK}}^{\mathsf{IND\text{-}tag\text{-}CCA}}$ is described in Algorithm 1. The adversary $\mathcal{A}$ is given accesses to the oracles encap and decap. The challenge encapsulation oracle encap can be queried only once. The decapsulation oracle decap can be called multiple times. After interactions with encap and decap, adversary $\mathcal{A}$ outputs a bit b^*. We say that TK is $(t, q_{\mathsf{decap}}, \epsilon)$-IND-tag-CCA-*secure* if for any adversary $\mathcal{A}$ that runs in time t and makes at most q_{decap} queries to the oracle decap, the IND-tag-CCA-advantage of $\mathcal{A}$ against TK has an upper bound ϵ, i.e., $\mathsf{Adv}_{\mathsf{TK}}^{\mathsf{IND\text{-}tag\text{-}CCA}}(\mathcal{A}) \leq \epsilon$.

Game $\mathsf{Exp}_{\mathsf{TK}}^{\mathsf{IND\text{-}tag\text{-}CCA}}(\mathcal{A})$:
  $b \leftarrow_\$ \{0,1\}$; $\lambda \leftarrow \mathsf{TK.init}()$; $(sk^*, pk^*) \leftarrow \mathsf{TK.gen}(\lambda)$
  $b^* \leftarrow \mathcal{A}(\lambda, pk^*; \mathsf{encap}_{b,pk^*}, \mathsf{decap}_{sk^*})$; $v^* \leftarrow [b^* = b]$; return v^*

Oracle $\mathsf{encap}_{b,pk^*}(\tau^*)$:
  $(K_1^*, C^*) \leftarrow \mathsf{TK.enc}(\lambda, pk^*, \tau^*)$; $K_0^* \leftarrow_\$ \mathsf{TK}.\mathcal{K}$; return (K_b^*, C^*)

Oracle $\mathsf{decap}_{sk^*}(\tau, C)$:
  if $(\tau, C) = (\tau^*, C^*)$: return $\bot$ else: return $K \leftarrow \mathsf{TK.dec}(\lambda, sk^*, \tau, C)$

Algorithm 1. Experiment for defining IND-tag-CCA security of TBKEM

2.2 Data Encapsulation Mechanism

A data encapsulation mechanism DEM consists of the following algorithms:

$\mathsf{enc}(K, m) \to C$: The encryption algorithm. It takes as input the secret key $K \in \mathsf{DEM}.\mathcal{K}$, and a message m from the associated message space, and outputs a ciphertext C.

---

[2] We need the adaptive-tag flavor of tag-based security, which is stronger than the selective-tag security property used by Kiltz [17].

$dec(K, C) \to m$: The (deterministic) decryption algorithm. It takes as input the secret key $K \in DEM.\mathcal{K}$, and a ciphertext C, and outputs either a message m or an error symbol $\perp$.

For correctness, we require that for all $K \in DEM.\mathcal{K}$ and for all m in the associated message space, it must hold that $dec(K, enc(K, m)) = m$.

A DEM is said to be *one-to-one* if for any K, C, and C', $dec(K, C) = dec(K, C') \neq \perp$ implies $C = C'$. In other words, for any given K and m, there is at most one ciphertext C such that $dec(K, C) = m$. As described in [8], this property is quite natural for a large number of DEMs.

We recall the security notion of indistinguishability against one-time adaptive chosen ciphertext attacks (IND-OTCCA). The IND-OTCCA-*advantage of $\mathcal{A}$ against* DEM is defined as

$$\mathsf{Adv}_{\mathsf{DEM}}^{\mathsf{IND\text{-}OTCCA}}(\mathcal{A}) = \left| 2 \Pr\left[\mathsf{Exp}_{\mathsf{DEM}}^{\mathsf{IND\text{-}OTCCA}}(\mathcal{A}) = 1 \right] - 1 \right|,$$

where the experiment $\mathsf{Exp}_{\mathsf{DEM}}^{\mathsf{IND\text{-}OTCCA}}$ is described in Algorithm 2. The challenge encryption oracle enc can be queried only once. The decryption oracle dec can be called multiple times. After interactions with these oracles, adversary $\mathcal{A}$ outputs a bit b^*. We say that DEM is $(t, q_{\mathsf{dec}}, \epsilon)$-IND-OTCCA-*secure* if for any adversary $\mathcal{A}$ that runs in time t and makes at most q_{dec} queries to the oracle dec, the IND-OTCCA-advantage of $\mathcal{A}$ against DEM has an upper bound ϵ, i.e., $\mathsf{Adv}_{\mathsf{DEM}}^{\mathsf{IND\text{-}OTCCA}}(\mathcal{A}) \leq \epsilon$.

Game $\mathsf{Exp}_{\mathsf{DEM}}^{\mathsf{IND\text{-}OTCCA}}(\mathcal{A})$:
$b \leftarrow_\$ \{0, 1\}$; $K^* \leftarrow_\$ DEM.\mathcal{K}$; $b^* \leftarrow \mathcal{A}(; enc_{b, K^*}, dec_{K^*})$; return $[b^* = b]$
Oracle $enc_{b, K^*}(m_0^*, m_1^*)$: // called only once; $|m_0^*| = |m_1^*|$ $\quad C^* \leftarrow DEM.enc(K^*, m_b^*)$; return C^*
Oracle $dec_{K^*}(C)$: $\quad$ if $C = C^*$: return $\perp$ else: return $m \leftarrow DEM.dec(K^*, C)$

Algorithm 2. Experiment for defining IND-OTCCA security of DEM.

2.3 Digital Signature

A digital signature scheme DS consists of the following algorithms:

$init() \to \lambda$: The initialization algorithm. It outputs public parameters λ. We will generally assume that all algorithms take λ as an implicit input, even if it is not explicitly stated.

$gen(\lambda) \to (sk, pk)$: The key generation algorithm. It generates a private/public key pair (sk, pk).

$sign(\lambda, sk, m) \to \sigma$: The signing algorithm. It takes as input the signer's secret key sk, and a message m from the associated message space, and outputs a signature σ.

$\mathsf{ver}(\lambda, pk, m, \sigma) \to v$: The (deterministic) verification algorithm. It takes as input the signer's public key pk, a message m, and an alleged signature σ, and outputs $v \in \{0, 1\}$.

For correctness, we require that for all $\lambda \leftarrow \mathsf{init}()$, all $(sk, pk) \leftarrow \mathsf{gen}(\lambda)$, and all m in the associated message space, it must hold that $\mathsf{ver}(\lambda, pk, m, \mathsf{sign}(\lambda, sk, m)) = 1$.

We recall the security notion of strong and standard unforgeability against chosen message attacks (sUF-CMA and UF-CMA) as well as generic chosen message attacks (sUF-GMA and UF-GMA). For each $X \in \{\mathsf{sUF}, \mathsf{UF}\}$, the X-CMA-*advantage* and X-GMA-*advantage* of $\mathcal{A}$ against DS is defined as

$$\mathsf{Adv}_{\mathsf{DS}}^{\mathsf{X\text{-}CMA}}(\mathcal{A}) = \Pr\left[\mathsf{Exp}_{\mathsf{DS}}^{\mathsf{X\text{-}CMA}}(\mathcal{A}) = 1\right], \quad \mathsf{Adv}_{\mathsf{DS},n}^{\mathsf{X\text{-}GMA}}(\mathcal{A}) = \Pr\left[\mathsf{Exp}_{\mathsf{DS},n}^{\mathsf{X\text{-}GMA}}(\mathcal{A}) = 1\right],$$

where the experiments $\mathsf{Exp}_{\mathsf{DS}}^{\mathsf{X\text{-}CMA}}$ and $\mathsf{Exp}_{\mathsf{DS},n}^{\mathsf{X\text{-}GMA}}$ are described in Algorithm 3. The adversary $\mathcal{A}$ is given access to the signing oracle sign or gsign. Both oracles can be called multiple times. After interactions with sign or gsign, adversary $\mathcal{A}$ outputs an alleged forgery (m^*, σ^*). The message m^* should not be queried to the signing oracle. In addition, in the strong unforgeability game, i.e., sUF-CMA and sUF-GMA, the forged signature σ^* should not be returned from the signing oracle as a response of m^*. For each $X \in \{\mathsf{sUF}, \mathsf{UF}\}$, we say that DS is $(t, q_{\mathsf{sign}}, \epsilon)$-X-CMA-*secure* if for any adversary $\mathcal{A}$ that runs in time t and makes at most q_{sign} queries to the oracle sign, the X-CMA-advantage of $\mathcal{A}$ against DS has an upper bound ϵ, i.e., $\mathsf{Adv}_{\mathsf{DS}}^{\mathsf{X\text{-}CMA}}(\mathcal{A}) \le \epsilon$. Similarly, for each $X \in \{\mathsf{sUF}, \mathsf{UF}\}$, we say that DS is (t, n, ϵ)-X-GMA-*secure* if for any adversary $\mathcal{A}$ that runs in time t and makes only one query to the oracle gsign, the X-GMA-advantage of $\mathcal{A}$ against DS has an upper bound ϵ, i.e., $\mathsf{Adv}_{\mathsf{DS},n}^{\mathsf{X\text{-}GMA}}(\mathcal{A}) \le \epsilon$. The query to gsign consists of n messages.

Both a $(t, 1, \epsilon)$-X-CMA-secure digital signature scheme and a $(t, 1, \epsilon)$-X-GMA-secure digital signature scheme are called *one-time*. Roughly speaking, an one-time digital signature scheme OTS can be used to securely sign a single message per a signing/verification key pair.

3   Incrementally Executable Signcryptions

We define incrementally executable signcryptions by generalizing a syntactical definition of standard signcryption schemes.

Definition 1 (Incrementally Executable Signcryptions). *An incrementally executable signcryption scheme* IESC *consists of the following algorithms:*

$\mathsf{init}() \to \lambda$: *The initialization algorithm. It outputs public parameters* λ. *We will generally assume that all algorithms take* λ *as an implicit input, even if it is not explicitly stated.*

$\mathsf{gen}_S(\lambda) \to (sk_S, pk_S)$: *The sender key generation algorithm. It generates a private/public key pair* (sk_S, pk_S) *for a sender.*

Game $\mathsf{Exp}_{\mathsf{DS}}^{\mathsf{X\text{-}CMA}}(\mathcal{A})$:
  $\lambda \leftarrow \mathsf{DS.init}()$; $(sk^*, pk^*) \leftarrow \mathsf{DS.gen}(\lambda)$; $(m^*, \sigma^*) \leftarrow \mathcal{A}(\lambda, pk^*; \mathsf{sign}_{sk^*})$
  $v^* \leftarrow \mathsf{DS.ver}(\lambda, pk^*, m^*, \sigma^*) \wedge [(m^*, \boxed{\sigma^*}) \notin \mathcal{Q}]$; return v^*

Oracle $\mathsf{sign}_{sk^*}(m)$:
  $\sigma \leftarrow \mathsf{DS.sign}(\lambda, sk^*, m)$; $\mathcal{Q} \leftarrow \mathcal{Q} \cup \{(m, \sigma)\}$; return σ

Game $\mathsf{Exp}_{\mathsf{DS},n}^{\mathsf{X\text{-}GMA}}(\mathcal{A})$:
  $\lambda \leftarrow \mathsf{DS.init}()$; $(m^*, \sigma^*) \leftarrow \mathcal{A}(\lambda; \mathsf{gsign})$
  $v^* \leftarrow \mathsf{DS.ver}(\lambda, pk^*, m^*, \sigma^*) \wedge [(m^*, \boxed{\sigma^*}) \notin \mathcal{Q}]$; return v^*

Oracle $\mathsf{gsign}(m_1, \ldots, m_n)$:
  $(sk^*, pk^*) \leftarrow \mathsf{DS.gen}(\lambda)$
  for $j \in \{1, \ldots, n\}$: $\sigma_j \leftarrow \mathsf{DS.sign}(\lambda, sk^*, m_j)$; $\mathcal{Q} \leftarrow \mathcal{Q} \cup \{(m_j, \sigma_j)\}$
  return $(pk^*, \sigma_1, \ldots, \sigma_n)$

Algorithm 3. Experiment for defining the unforgeability notions of digital signatures. Boxed parts are evaluated only in sUF games.

$\mathsf{gen_R}(\lambda) \to (sk_R, pk_R)$: *The receiver key generation algorithm. It generates a private/public key pair* (sk_R, pk_R) *for a receiver.*

$\mathsf{sc_1}(\lambda, sk_S, pk_S) \to st_1$: *The signcryption algorithm partially executed with the sender's key pair. It takes as input the public parameters* λ *and the sender S's key pair* (sk_S, pk_S) *to output an internal state* st_1, *which must be secretly stored and eventually used only once in the next algorithm* $\mathsf{sc_2}$.

$\mathsf{sc_2}(st_1, pk_R) \to st_2$: *The signcryption algorithm partially executed with the recipient's public key. It takes as input the precomputed results* st_1 *and the receiver R's public (encryption) key* pk_R, *and outputs an internal state* st_2, *which must be secretly stored and eventually used only once in the next algorithm* $\mathsf{sc_3}$.

$\mathsf{sc_3}(st_2, m) \to \Sigma$: *The on-line signcryption algorithm. It takes as input the precomputed results* st_2 *and a message m from the associated message space, and outputs a ciphertext* Σ.

$\mathsf{unsc}(\lambda, pk_S, sk_R, pk_R, \Sigma) \to m$: *The (deterministic) un-signcryption algorithm. It takes as input the sender S's public (verification) key* pk_S, *the receiver R's key pair* (sk_R, pk_R), *and a ciphertext* Σ, *and outputs either a message m or an error symbol* $\perp$.

For correctness, we require that for all $\lambda \leftarrow \mathsf{init}()$, *all* $(pk_S, sk_S) \leftarrow \mathsf{gen_S}(\lambda)$, *all* $(pk_R, sk_R) \leftarrow \mathsf{gen_R}(\lambda)$, *and all m in the associated message space, it must hold that* $\mathsf{unsc}(\lambda, pk_S, sk_R, pk_R, \mathsf{sc_3}(\mathsf{sc_2}(\mathsf{sc_1}(\lambda, sk_S, pk_S), pk_R), m)) = m$.

We adapt the strongest security notion of indistinguishability against insider chosen ciphertext attacks in the dynamic multi-user model (dM-IND-iCCA) [22] to our notion.

Definition 2 (Confidentiality). *Let* IESC *be an incrementally executable signcryption scheme and let* $\mathcal{A}$ *be an adversary. The* dM-IND-iCCA-*advantage of* $\mathcal{A}$ *against* IESC *is defined as*

$$\mathsf{Adv}_{\mathsf{IESC}}^{\mathsf{dM\text{-}IND\text{-}iCCA}}(\mathcal{A}) = \left|2\Pr\left[\mathsf{Exp}_{\mathsf{IESC}}^{\mathsf{dM\text{-}IND\text{-}iCCA}}(\mathcal{A}) = 1\right] - 1\right|,$$

where the experiment $\mathsf{Exp}_{\mathsf{IESC}}^{\mathsf{dM\text{-}IND\text{-}iCCA}}$ *is described in Algorithm 4. The adversary* $\mathcal{A}$ *is given access to the oracles* sc *and* unsc. *The challenge signcryption oracle* sc *can be queried only once, with a sender key pair* (sk_S^*, pk_S^*) *and a message pair* m_0^*, m_1^* *that are of the same length. We require that* (sk_S^*, pk_S^*) *is a valid key pair. The un-signcryption oracle* unsc *can be called multiple times, with a sender key* pk_S *and a ciphertext* Σ. *After interactions with* sc *and* unsc, *adversary* $\mathcal{A}$ *outputs a bit* b^*. *We say that* IESC *is* $(t, q_{\mathsf{unsc}}, \epsilon)$-dM-IND-iCCA-*secure if for any adversary* $\mathcal{A}$ *that runs in time* t *and makes at most* q_{unsc} *queries to the oracle* unsc, *the* dM-IND-iCCA-*advantage of* $\mathcal{A}$ *against* IESC *has an upper bound* ϵ, *i.e.,* $\mathsf{Adv}_{\mathsf{IESC}}^{\mathsf{dM\text{-}IND\text{-}iCCA}}(\mathcal{A}) \le \epsilon$.

Game $\mathsf{Exp}_{\mathsf{IESC}}^{\mathsf{dM\text{-}IND\text{-}iCCA}}(\mathcal{A})$:

    $b \leftarrow_\$ \{0,1\}$; $\lambda \leftarrow \mathsf{IESC.init}()$; $(sk_R^*, pk_R^*) \leftarrow \mathsf{IESC.gen}_R(\lambda)$

    $b^* \leftarrow \mathcal{A}(\lambda, pk_R^*;\ \mathsf{sc}_{b, pk_R^*}, \mathsf{unsc}_{sk_R^*, pk_R^*})$; return $[b^* = b]$

Oracle $\mathsf{sc}_{b, pk_R^*}(sk_S^*, pk_S^*, m_0^*, m_1^*)$:

    $st_1^* \leftarrow \mathsf{IESC.sc}_1(\lambda, sk_S^*, pk_S^*)$; $st_2^* \leftarrow \mathsf{IESC.sc}_2(st_1^*, pk_R^*)$; return $\Sigma^* \leftarrow \mathsf{IESC.sc}_3(st_2^*, m_b^*)$

Oracle $\mathsf{unsc}_{sk_R^*, pk_R^*}(pk_S, \Sigma)$:

    if $(pk_S, \Sigma) = (pk_S^*, \Sigma^*)$: return $\bot$ else: return $m \leftarrow \mathsf{IESC.unsc}(\lambda, pk_S, sk_R^*, pk_R^*, \Sigma)$

Algorithm 4. Experiment for defining dM-IND-iCCA security.

For unforgeability, we also adapt the strongest security definition of strong unforgeability against insider chosen message attacks in the dynamic multi-user model (dM-sUF-iCMA) [22] to our notion.

Definition 3 (Unforgeability). *Let* IESC *be an incrementally executable signcryption scheme and let* $\mathcal{A}$ *be an adversary. The* dM-sUF-iCMA-*advantage of* $\mathcal{A}$ *against* IESC *is defined as*

$$\mathsf{Adv}_{\mathsf{IESC}}^{\mathsf{dM\text{-}sUF\text{-}iCMA}}(\mathcal{A}) = \Pr\left[\mathsf{Exp}_{\mathsf{IESC}}^{\mathsf{dM\text{-}sUF\text{-}iCMA}}(\mathcal{A}) = 1\right],$$

where the experiment $\mathsf{Exp}_{\mathsf{IESC}}^{\mathsf{dM\text{-}sUF\text{-}iCMA}}$ *is described in Algorithm 5. Adversary* $\mathcal{A}$ *is given access to the signcryption oracle* sc, *which can be called multiple times with a receiver public key* pk_R *and a message* m. *After interactions with oracle* sc, *adversary* $\mathcal{A}$ *outputs a receiver key pair* (sk_R^*, pk_R^*) *and a forgery* Σ^*. *We require that* (sk_R^*, pk_R^*) *is a valid key pair. We say that* IESC *is* $(t, q_{\mathsf{sc}}, \epsilon)$-dM-sUF-iCMA-*secure if for any adversary* $\mathcal{A}$ *that runs in time* t *and makes at most* q_{sc} *queries to the oracle* sc, *the* dM-sUF-iCMA-*advantage of* $\mathcal{A}$ *against* IESC *has an upper bound* ϵ, *i.e.,* $\mathsf{Adv}_{\mathsf{IESC}}^{\mathsf{dM\text{-}sUF\text{-}iCMA}}(\mathcal{A}) \le \epsilon$.

Game $\mathsf{Exp}_{\mathsf{IESC}}^{\mathsf{dM\text{-}sUF\text{-}iCMA}}(\mathcal{A})$:

$\quad \lambda \leftarrow \mathsf{IESC.init}()$; $\ (sk_S^*, pk_S^*) \leftarrow \mathsf{IESC.gen}_S(\lambda)$; $\ (sk_R^*, pk_R^*, \Sigma^*) \leftarrow \mathcal{A}(\lambda, pk_S^*; \ \mathsf{sc}_{sk_S^*, pk_S^*})$

$\quad m^* \leftarrow \mathsf{IESC.unsc}(\lambda, pk_S^*, sk_R^*, pk_R^*, \Sigma^*)$; $\ \mathsf{return} \ [m^* \neq \bot] \wedge [(pk_R^*, m^*, \Sigma^*) \notin \mathcal{Q}]$

Oracle $\mathsf{sc}_{sk_S^*, pk_S^*}(pk_R, m)$:

$\quad st_1 \leftarrow \mathsf{IESC.sc}_1(\lambda, sk_S^*, pk_S^*)$; $\ st_2 \leftarrow \mathsf{IESC.sc}_2(st_1, pk_R)$; $\ \Sigma \leftarrow \mathsf{IESC.sc}_3(st_2, m)$

$\quad \mathcal{Q} \leftarrow \mathcal{Q} \cup \{(pk_R, m, \Sigma)\}$; $\ \mathsf{return} \ \Sigma$

Algorithm 5. Experiment for defining dM-sUF-iCMA security.

4 Generic Construction with Strong Security and Parallel Un-Signcryption

In this section, we show a generic construction of incrementally executable signcryption scheme that achieves the confidentiality and unforgeability notions without relying on random oracles. Our construction is based on the TBKEM-based composition methods from [8] (hereinafter referred to as $\mathsf{CMSM}_{\mathsf{tk}}$) and the signature transformation technique proposed by Huang et al. [16,15].

Let TK be a tag-based key encapsulation mechanism and DEM a data encapsulation mechanism, where their key spaces are identical, i.e., $\mathsf{TK}.\mathcal{K} = \mathsf{DEM}.\mathcal{K}$. Let DS be a digital signature scheme and OTS an one-time digital signature scheme. Then, our generic construction GIESC is defined as described in Algorithm 6, respectively. The correctness properties of the schemes are easy to verify.

$\mathsf{init}()$:

$\quad \lambda_S \leftarrow \mathsf{DS.init}()$; $\ \lambda_K \leftarrow \mathsf{TK.init}()$; $\ \lambda_O \leftarrow \mathsf{OTS.init}()$; $\ \mathsf{return} \ \lambda \leftarrow (\lambda_S, \lambda_K, \lambda_O)$

$\mathsf{gen}_S(\lambda)$:

$\quad \mathsf{return} \ (sk_S, pk_S) \leftarrow \mathsf{DS.gen}(\lambda_S)$

$\mathsf{gen}_R(\lambda)$:

$\quad \mathsf{return} \ (sk_R, pk_R) \leftarrow \mathsf{TK.gen}(\lambda_K)$

$\mathsf{sc}_1(\lambda, sk_S, pk_S)$:

$\quad (osk, opk) \leftarrow \mathsf{OTS.gen}(\lambda_O)$; $\ \sigma_1 \leftarrow \mathsf{DS.sign}(sk_S, opk)$

$\quad \mathsf{return} \ st_1 \leftarrow (\lambda, osk, opk, pk_S, \sigma_1)$

$\mathsf{sc}_2(st_1, pk_R)$:

$\quad (\lambda, osk, opk, pk_S, \sigma_1) \leftarrow st_1$; $\ (K, C_1) \leftarrow \mathsf{TK.enc}(pk_R, \langle opk \, \| \, \sigma_1 \, \| \, pk_S \rangle)$

$\quad \mathsf{return} \ st_2 \leftarrow (\lambda, osk, opk, \sigma_1, pk_R, K, C_1)$

$\mathsf{sc}_3(st_2, m)$:

$\quad (\lambda, osk, opk, \sigma_1, pk_R, K, C_1) \leftarrow st_2$; $\ \sigma_2 \leftarrow \mathsf{OTS.sign}(osk, \langle \sigma_1 \, \| \, pk_R \, \| \, C_1 \, \| \, m \rangle)$

$\quad C_2 \leftarrow \mathsf{DEM.enc}(K, \langle \sigma_2 \, \| \, m \rangle)$; $\ \mathsf{return} \ \Sigma \leftarrow (opk, \sigma_1, C_1, C_2)$

$\mathsf{unsc}(pk_S, sk_R, pk_R, \Sigma)$:

$\quad (opk, \sigma_1, C_1, C_2) \leftarrow \Sigma$

$\quad K \leftarrow \mathsf{TK.dec}(sk_R, \langle opk \, \| \, \sigma_1 \, \| \, pk_S \rangle, C_1)$; $\ v_1 \leftarrow \mathsf{DS.ver}(pk_S, opk, \sigma_1)$

$\quad \langle \sigma_2 \, \| \, m \rangle \leftarrow \mathsf{DEM.dec}(K, C_2)$; $\ v_2 \leftarrow \mathsf{OTS.ver}(opk, \langle \sigma_1 \, \| \, pk_R \, \| \, C_1 \, \| \, m \rangle, \sigma_2)$

$\quad \mathsf{if} \ \neg v_1 \vee \neg v_2 \vee [K = \bot]: \ \mathsf{return} \ \bot \ \mathsf{else}: \ \mathsf{return} \ m$

Algorithm 6. GIESC: Generic construction of incrementally executable signcryption. Note that in unsc algorithm, DS.ver and TK.dec can be performed in parallel.

We integrate the signature transformation paradigm from Huang et al. [16,15], which weaken the underlying assumption, i.e., the underlying signature scheme is sufficient to be *not necessarily strong* unforgeable under *generic* chosen message attack. Furthermore, GIESC supports the *parallel un-signcryption* feature, which allows receivers to perform two potentially expensive computations, i.e., the verification of off-line signature and the key-decapsulation, in a parallel fashion. For realizing this, we avoid encrypting opk and σ_1 so that the receiver need not wait for the decryption process to verify the validity of opk and σ_1. In order to preserve dM-IND-iCCA security, these two visible component opk and σ_1 are given into TK.enc as additional tags.

The following theorems guarantee the security of our construction.

Theorem 1 (Confidentiality of GIESC). *If* TK *is* $(t', q_{\text{decap}}, \epsilon_{\text{TK}})$-IND-tag-CCA-*secure and* DEM *is* $(t', q_{\text{dec}}, \epsilon_{\text{DEM}})$-IND-OTCCA-*secure, then* GIESC *is* $(t, q_{\text{unsc}}, \epsilon_{\text{IESC}})$-dM-IND-iCCA-*secure, where* $t = t' - O(q_{\text{unsc}})$, $q_{\text{unsc}} \leq \min\{q_{\text{decap}}, q_{\text{dec}}\}$, *and* $\epsilon_{\text{IESC}} \geq 2\epsilon_{\text{TK}} + \epsilon_{\text{DEM}}$.

Proof. Assume we have a t-time adversary $\mathcal{A}$ that makes at most q_{unsc} queries to unsc oracle in order to break the confidentiality of our GIESC. Then, we construct two adversaries $\mathcal{B}_{\mathcal{A}}$ and $\mathcal{C}_{\mathcal{A}}$ that exploit $\mathcal{A}$ as a black-box. For any $\mathcal{A}$ we will show the following equation holds:

$$\text{Adv}_{\text{GIESC}}^{\text{dM-IND-iCCA}}(\mathcal{A}) \leq 2\text{Adv}_{\text{TK}}^{\text{IND-tag-CCA}}(\mathcal{B}_{\mathcal{A}}) + \text{Adv}_{\text{DEM}}^{\text{IND-OTCCA}}(\mathcal{C}_{\mathcal{A}}). \quad (1)$$

Combined Eq. (1) with the assumptions that TK is $(t', q_{\text{decap}}, \epsilon_{\text{TK}})$-IND-tag-CCA-secure and DEM is $(t', q_{\text{dec}}, \epsilon_{\text{DEM}})$-IND-OTCCA-secure, we have $\text{Adv}_{\text{GIESC}}^{\text{dM-IND-iCCA}}(\mathcal{A})$ $\leq 2\epsilon_{\text{TK}} + \epsilon_{\text{DEM}}$, which implies that GIESC is $(t, q_{\text{unsc}}, \epsilon_{\text{IESC}})$-dM-IND-iCCA-secure for any $\epsilon_{\text{IESC}} \geq 2\epsilon_{\text{TK}} + \epsilon_{\text{DEM}}$, as desired.

In order to prove Eq. (1), we define four games G_0, G_1, $G_{0 \to 1}$, and G_2 as well as two adversaries $\mathcal{B}_{\mathcal{A}}$ and $\mathcal{C}_{\mathcal{A}}$ in Algorithm 7.

We briefly explain the game chain. ▷ Game G_0 is equivalent to the original attack game played by $\mathcal{A}$ against GIESC. Hence, we have $\text{Adv}_{\text{GIESC}}^{\text{dM-IND-iCCA}}(\mathcal{A}) = \Pr[G_0(\mathcal{A}) \Rightarrow 1]$ ▷ Game G_1 behaves just like game G_0, except that we use a random key K_0^* to compute the fourth component C_2^* of the challenge ciphertext. Moreover, The unsc oracle uses this K_0^* to decrypt a ciphertext C_2 when $(\langle opk \| \sigma_1 \| pk_S \rangle, C_1) = (\langle opk^* \| \sigma_1^* \| pk_S^* \rangle, C_1^*)$ holds. ▷ Game $G_{0 \to 1}$ interpolates between G_0 and G_1. This game behaves like game G_1, except that we use additional random bit $b' \leftarrow_\$ \{0, 1\}$ and call two oracles encap and decap instead of TK.enc and TK.dec, respectively. Note that the specifications of encap and decap are defined in the IND-tag-CCA game described in Algorithm 1.

Lemma 1 $(G_0 \to \{G_{0 \to 1}, G_1\})$. *From $\mathcal{A}$'s viewpoint, game $G_{0 \to 1}$ is equivalent to G_0 when $b' = 1$, and is equivalent to G_1 otherwise. More specifically, we have* $\Pr_{G_0}[b^* = b] = \Pr_{G_{0 \to 1}}[b^* = b \mid b' = 1]$ *and* $\Pr_{G_1}[b^* = b] = \Pr_{G_{0 \to 1}}[b^* = b \mid b' = 0]$.

Using this lemma, we have

$$\Pr[G_0(\mathcal{A}) \Rightarrow 1] = (\Pr_{G_0}[b^* = b] - \Pr_{G_1}[b^* = b]) + \Pr_{G_1}[b^* = b]$$
$$= (\Pr_{G_{0 \to 1}}[b^* = b \mid b' = 1] - \Pr_{G_{0 \to 1}}[b^* = b \mid b' = 0]) + \Pr_{G_1}[b^* = b]$$
$$= (2\Pr_{G_{0 \to 1}}[[b^* = b] = b'] - 1) + \Pr_{G_1}[b^* = b]$$
$$= (2\Pr[G_{0 \to 1}(\mathcal{A}) \Rightarrow 1] - 1) + \Pr[G_1(\mathcal{A}) \Rightarrow 1]. \tag{2}$$

From the description of game $G_{0 \to 1}$, we construct an adversary $\mathcal{B}_\mathcal{A}$ as described in Algorithm 7. Adversary $\mathcal{B}_\mathcal{A}$ exploits $\mathcal{A}$ to break the confidentiality of TK, i.e., it plays $\mathsf{Exp}_{\mathsf{TK}}^{\mathsf{IND\text{-}tag\text{-}CCA}}(\mathcal{B}_\mathcal{A})$. The adversary $\mathcal{B}_\mathcal{A}$ provides $\mathcal{A}$ with two simulated oracles sc_{b,pk_R^*} and $\mathsf{unsc}_{sk_R^*,pk_R^*}$. When $\mathcal{A}$ queries these oracles, $\mathcal{B}_\mathcal{A}$ replies to the query using its given oracle encap and decap, in the same manner as $G_{0 \to 1}$. The goal of $\mathcal{B}_\mathcal{A}$ is guessing a random bit b' embedded in $\mathsf{encap}_{b',pk_R^*}$. We can see that its running time satisfies $t' = t + O(q_{\mathsf{unsc}})$ since it takes in time t to run $\mathcal{A}$ as a black-box and takes in time $O(q_{\mathsf{unsc}})$ to simulate unsc oracle for at most at most q_{unsc} times. Note that oracle encap is queried only once and oracle decap is queried at most q_{unsc} times.

Lemma 2 ($G_{0 \to 1} \to \mathcal{B}_\mathcal{A}$). *Game $G_{0 \to 1}(\mathcal{A})$ is equivalent to* $\mathsf{Exp}_{\mathsf{TK}}^{\mathsf{IND\text{-}tag\text{-}CCA}}(\mathcal{B}_\mathcal{A})$ *from $\mathcal{A}$'s viewpoint. Specifically, we have*

$$\Pr[G_{0 \to 1}(\mathcal{A}) \Rightarrow 1] = \Pr\left[\mathsf{Exp}_{\mathsf{TK}}^{\mathsf{IND\text{-}tag\text{-}CCA}}(\mathcal{B}_\mathcal{A}) \Rightarrow 1\right].$$

Now we transform game G_1 into game G_2, which uses two oracles enc and dec instead of $\mathsf{DEM.encrypt}$ and $\mathsf{DEM.decrypt}$, respectively. Note that enc and dec are defined in the IND-CCA game described in Algorithm 2.

Lemma 3 ($G_1 \to G_2$). *Game G_2 is equivalent to G_1 from $\mathcal{A}$'s viewpoint. More specifically, we have* $\Pr[G_1(\mathcal{A}) \Rightarrow 1] = \Pr[G_2(\mathcal{A}) \Rightarrow 1]$.

From the description of game G_2, we construct an adversary $\mathcal{C}_\mathcal{A}$ as described in Algorithm 7. Adversary $\mathcal{C}_\mathcal{A}$ exploits $\mathcal{A}$ to break the confidentiality of DEM, i.e., it plays $\mathsf{Exp}_{\mathsf{DEM}}^{\mathsf{IND\text{-}OTCCA}}(\mathcal{C}_\mathcal{A})$. The adversary $\mathcal{C}_\mathcal{A}$ provides $\mathcal{A}$ with two simulated oracles sc_{b,pk_R^*} and $\mathsf{unsc}_{sk_R^*,pk_R^*}$. When $\mathcal{A}$ queries these oracles, $\mathcal{C}_\mathcal{A}$ replies to the query using its given oracle enc and dec, in the same manner as G_2. The goal of $\mathcal{C}_\mathcal{A}$ is guessing a random bit b embedded in enc_{b,K^*}. We can see that its running time satisfies $t' = t + O(q_{\mathsf{unsc}})$ since it takes in time t to run $\mathcal{A}$ as a black-box and takes in time $O(q_{\mathsf{unsc}})$ to simulate unsc oracle for at most q_{unsc} times. Note that oracle enc is queried only once and oracle dec is queried at most q_{unsc} times.

Lemma 4 ($G_2 \to \mathcal{C}_\mathcal{A}$). *Game $G_2(\mathcal{A})$ is equivalent to* $\mathsf{Exp}_{\mathsf{DEM}}^{\mathsf{IND\text{-}CCA}}(\mathcal{C}_\mathcal{A})$ *from $\mathcal{A}$'s viewpoint. More specifically, we have* $\Pr[G_2(\mathcal{A}) \Rightarrow 1] = \mathsf{Adv}_{\mathsf{DEM}}^{\mathsf{IND\text{-}OTCCA}}(\mathcal{C}_\mathcal{A})$.

From Eq. (2) and each lemmas, we can obtain Eq. (1). $\qquad\square$

Theorem 2 (Unforgeability of GIESC). *If DEM is one-to-one, DS is $(t', q_{\mathsf{sign}}, \epsilon_{\mathsf{DS}})$-UF-GMA-secure, and OTS is $(t', 1, \epsilon_{\mathsf{OTS}})$-sUF-CMA-secure, then GIESC is $(t, q_{\mathsf{sc}}, \epsilon_{\mathsf{IESC}})$-dM-sUF-iCMA-secure, where $t = t' - O(q_{\mathsf{sc}})$, $q_{\mathsf{sc}} \leq q_{\mathsf{sign}}$, and $\epsilon_{\mathsf{IESC}} \geq \epsilon_{\mathsf{DS}} + q_{\mathsf{sc}}\epsilon_{\mathsf{OTS}}$.*

Game $G_0, G_1, G_{0\to1}, G_2$:
$\quad b \leftarrow_\$ \{0,1\}; \boxed{b' \leftarrow_\$ \{0,1\}}^{(G_{0\to1})}; \boxed{K^* \leftarrow_\$ \text{DEM}.\mathcal{K}}^{(G_2)}$
$\quad \lambda_S \leftarrow \text{DS.init}(); \ \lambda_R \leftarrow \text{TK.init}(); \ \lambda_C \leftarrow \text{OTS.init}(); \ \lambda \leftarrow (\lambda_S, \lambda_R, \lambda_C)$
$\quad (sk_R^*, pk_R^*) \leftarrow \text{TK.gen}(\lambda_R); \ b^* \leftarrow \mathcal{A}(\lambda, pk_R^*; \text{sc}_{b,pk_R^*}, \text{unsc}_{sk_R^*, pk_R^*})$
$\quad \boxed{v^* \leftarrow [b^* = b]}^{(G_0, G_1, G_2)}; \ \boxed{v^* \leftarrow [[b^* = b] = b']}^{(G_{0\to1})}; \ \text{return } v^*$

Oracle $\text{sc}_{b,pk_R^*}(sk_S^*, pk_S^*, m_0^*, m_1^*)$:
$\quad (osk^*, opk^*) \leftarrow \text{OTS.gen}(\lambda_C); \ \sigma_1^* \leftarrow \text{DS.sign}(sk_S^*, opk^*)$
$\quad \boxed{(K_1^*, C_1^*) \leftarrow \text{TK.enc}(pk_R^*, \langle opk^* \parallel \sigma_1^* \parallel pk_S^* \rangle)}^{(G_0, G_1, G_2)}; \ \boxed{K^* \leftarrow K_1^*}^{(G_0)}$
$\quad \boxed{K_0^* \leftarrow_\$ \text{TK}.\mathcal{K}; \ K^* \leftarrow K_0^*}^{(G_1)}; \ \boxed{(K^*, C_1^*) \leftarrow \text{encap}_{b', pk_R^*}(\langle opk^* \parallel \sigma_1^* \parallel pk_S^* \rangle)}^{(G_{0\to1})}$
$\quad \boxed{\sigma_2^* \leftarrow \text{OTS.sign}(osk^*, \langle \sigma_1^* \parallel pk_R^* \parallel C_1^* \parallel m_b^* \rangle)}^{(G_0, G_{0\to1}, G_1)}$
$\quad \boxed{\sigma_{2,0}^* \leftarrow \text{OTS.sign}(osk^*, \langle \sigma_1^* \parallel pk_R^* \parallel C_1^* \parallel m_0^* \rangle)}^{(G_2)}$
$\quad \boxed{\sigma_{2,1}^* \leftarrow \text{OTS.sign}(osk^*, \langle \sigma_1^* \parallel pk_R^* \parallel C_1^* \parallel m_1^* \rangle)}^{(G_2)}$
$\quad \boxed{C_2^* \leftarrow \text{DEM.enc}(K^*, \langle \sigma_2^* \parallel m_b^* \rangle)}^{(G_0, G_{0\to1}, G_1)}$
$\quad \boxed{C_2^* \leftarrow \text{enc}_{b,K^*}(\langle \sigma_{2,0}^* \parallel m_0^* \rangle, \langle \sigma_{2,1}^* \parallel m_1^* \rangle)}^{(G_2)}; \ \text{return } \Sigma^* \leftarrow (opk^*, \sigma_1^*, C_1^*, C_2^*)$

Oracle $\text{unsc}_{sk_R^*, pk_R^*}(pk_S, \Sigma)$:
$\quad \text{if } (pk_S, \Sigma) = (pk_S^*, \Sigma^*): \text{ return } \perp$
$\quad (opk, \sigma_1, C_1, C_2) \leftarrow \Sigma; \ v_1 \leftarrow \text{DS.ver}(pk_S, opk, \sigma_1)$
$\quad \boxed{K \leftarrow \text{TK.dec}(sk_R^*, \langle opk \parallel \sigma_1 \parallel pk_S \rangle, C_1); \ \langle \sigma_2 \parallel m \rangle \leftarrow \text{DEM.dec}(K, C_2)}^{(G_0, G_1, G_2)}$
$\quad \text{if } (\langle opk \parallel \sigma_1 \parallel pk_S \rangle, C_1) = (\langle opk^* \parallel \sigma_1^* \parallel pk_S^* \rangle, C_1^*):$
$\quad\quad \boxed{K \leftarrow K^*; \ \langle \sigma_2 \parallel m \rangle \leftarrow \text{DEM.dec}(K, C_2)}^{(G_{0\to1}, G_1)}$
$\quad\quad \boxed{\text{if } C_2 = C_2^*: \text{ return } \perp \text{ else}: \langle \sigma_2 \parallel m \rangle \leftarrow \text{dec}_{K^*}(C_2)}^{(G_2)}$
$\quad \text{else}:$
$\quad\quad \boxed{K \leftarrow \text{decap}_{sk_R^*}(\langle opk \parallel \sigma_1 \parallel pk_S \rangle, C_1); \ \langle \sigma_2 \parallel m \rangle \leftarrow \text{DEM.decrypt}(K, C_2)}^{(G_{0\to1})}$
$\quad v_2 \leftarrow \text{OTS.ver}(opk, \langle \sigma_1 \parallel pk_R \parallel C_1 \parallel m \rangle, \sigma_2)$
$\quad \text{if } \neg v_1 \vee \neg v_2 \vee [K = \perp]: \text{ return } \perp \text{ else: return } m$

Adversary $\mathcal{B}_\mathcal{A}(\lambda_R, pk_R^*; \text{encap}_{b', pk_R^*}, \text{decap}_{sk_R^*})$:
$\quad b \leftarrow_\$ \{0,1\}; \ \lambda_S \leftarrow \text{DS.init}(); \ \lambda_O \leftarrow \text{OTS.init}(); \ \lambda \leftarrow (\lambda_S, \lambda_K, \lambda_O)$
$\quad b^* \leftarrow \mathcal{A}(\lambda, pk_R^*; \text{sc}_{b,pk_R^*}, \text{unsc}_{sk_R^*, pk_R^*}); \ \text{return } [b^* = b]$
$\quad \text{// sc and unsc are the same as } G_{0\to1}$

Adversary $\mathcal{C}_\mathcal{A}(\text{DEM}.\mathcal{K}; \text{enc}_{b,K^*}, \text{dec}_{K^*})$:
$\quad \lambda_S \leftarrow \text{DS.init}(); \ \lambda_K \leftarrow \text{TK.init}(); \ \lambda_O \leftarrow \text{OTS.init}(); \ \lambda \leftarrow (\lambda_S, \lambda_K, \lambda_O)$
$\quad (sk_R^*, pk_R^*) \leftarrow \text{TK.gen}(\lambda_K); \ b^* \leftarrow \mathcal{A}(\lambda, pk_R^*; \text{sc}_{b,pk_R^*}, \text{unsc}_{sk_R^*, pk_R^*}); \ \text{return } b^*$
$\quad \text{// sc and unsc are the same as } G_2$

Algorithm 7. Experiments for proving dM-IND-iCCA security of GIESC. Boxed parts are evaluated only in the game indicated as its superscript.

Due to space limitations, the proofs of Theorem 2 and the lemmas are given in the full version [28].

4.1 Comparison

We present in Table 1 a comparison of our GIESC construction with previous signcryption constructions in various viewpoints. We consider only generic constructions not relying on random oracles.

From the second to the fourth row, we describe the building blocks computed in sc_1, sc_2, and sc_3. The computation with the dagger mark (†) is potentially expensive process. Note that the expensive signing process DS.sign (underlined parts in Table 1) can be performed even in sc_1 (i.e., *before* being given the recipient's public key) with our construction, whereas it can be only in sc_2 (i.e., *after* being given the recipient's public key) with OCtEaS as well as in sc_3 (i.e., after being given the message to be sent) with $CMSM_{tk}$. The fifth row shows whether the scheme achieves the strong security notions of dM-IND-iCCA and dM-sUF-iCMA. The sixth row shows whether the scheme supports the parallel un-signcryption feature. The seventh row shows the security assumption for the underlying signature scheme DS to prove the strong security of each construction. The eighth row shows the difference between the ciphertext size and the plaintext size, where $|C|$ denotes the size of the encapsulation generated by TBKEM.enc or KEM.enc; $|\sigma_1|$ denotes the size of the signature generated by DS.sign; $|c|$ and $|r|$ denote the size of commitment and randomness generated by trapdoor commitment schemes; $|opk|$ denotes the size of the public key generated by OTS.gen; and $|\sigma_2|$ denotes the size of the signature generated by OTS.sign.

Table 1. Comparison of previous and our proposed signcryption schemes

	$CMSM_{tk}$[8]	OCtEaS [2]	Ours: GIESC
Setup Computation (sc_1) (with sk_S and pk_S only)	-	-	DS.sign†
Handshake Computation (sc_2) (with sk_S, pk_S, and pk_R)	TBKEM.enc†	DS.sign† KEM.enc†	TBKEM.enc†
On-line Computation (sc_3)	DS.sign† DEM.enc	TCMT.switch DEM.enc	OTS.sign DEM.enc
Strong Security	yes	no	yes
Parallel Un-Signcryption	no	yes	yes
Security Assumption for DS	sUF-CMA	sUF-CMA	UF-GMA (**weakest**)
Ciphertext Overhead	$|C| + |\sigma_1|$	$|C| + |\sigma_1|$	$|C| + |\sigma_1| + |opk| + |\sigma_2|$

5   Conclusion

This paper presents the concept of incrementally executable signcryptions, which is a generalization of traditional on-line/off-line signcryption and facilitates optimizing the sender's off-line computation. With an incrementally executable signcryption scheme, the sender can activate signcryption process incrementally by its given sequential input: the sender's key pair, a recipient's public key, and a plaintext message to be sent to the recipient. We defined the syntax of incrementally executable signcryptions and proposed formal security models for confidentiality and unforgeability.

Furthermore, we presented an generic construction of incrementally executable signcryption scheme. In our construction, the signing process can be done before being given the recipient's public key as well as the message to be sent. This feature enables us to accelerate the subsequent processes. Moreover, we showed that our construction achieves the strongest security notions without relying on random oracles. We also showed that it requires a weak assumption for the underlying signature scheme and our construction supports the parallel un-signcryption feature, which allows receivers to perform two potentially expensive computations, i.e., the verification of off-line signature and the key-decapsulation, in parallel.

References

1. Abe, M., Gennaro, R., Kurosawa, K., Shoup, V.: Tag-kem/dem: A new framework for hybrid encryption and a new analysis of kurosawa-desmedt kem. In: Cramer, R. (ed.) EUROCRYPT 2005. LNCS, vol. 3494, pp. 128–146. Springer, Heidelberg (2005)
2. An, J.H., Dodis, Y., Rabin, T.: On the security of joint signature and encryption. In: Knudsen, L.R. (ed.) EUROCRYPT 2002. LNCS, vol. 2332, pp. 83–107. Springer, Heidelberg (2002)
3. Baek, J., Steinfeld, R., Zheng, Y.: Formal proofs for the security of signcryption. In: Naccache, D., Paillier, P. (eds.) PKC 2002. LNCS, vol. 2274, pp. 80–98. Springer, Heidelberg (2002)
4. Baek, J., Steinfeld, R., Zheng, Y.: Formal proofs for the security of signcryption. Journal of Cryptology 20(2), 203–235 (2007)
5. Bjørstad, T.E., Dent, A.W.: Building better signcryption schemes with tag-kems. In: Yung, M., Dodis, Y., Kiayias, A., Malkin, T. (eds.) PKC 2006. LNCS, vol. 3958, pp. 491–507. Springer, Heidelberg (2006)
6. Canetti, R., Krawczyk, H., Nielsen, J.B.: Relaxing chosen-ciphertext security. In: Boneh, D. (ed.) CRYPTO 2003. LNCS, vol. 2729, pp. 565–582. Springer, Heidelberg (2003)
7. Catalano, D., Di Raimondo, M., Fiore, D., Gennaro, R.: Off-line/on-line signatures: theoretical aspects and experimental results. In: Cramer, R. (ed.) PKC 2008. LNCS, vol. 4939, pp. 101–120. Springer, Heidelberg (2008)
8. Chiba, D., Matsuda, T., Schuldt, J.C.N., Matsuura, K.: Efficient generic constructions of signcryption with insider security in the multi-user setting. In: Lopez, J., Tsudik, G. (eds.) ACNS 2011. LNCS, vol. 6715, pp. 220–237. Springer, Heidelberg (2011)
9. Chow, S.S., Liu, J.K., Zhou, J.: Identity-based online/offline key encapsulation and encryption. In: Proceedings of the 6th ACM Symposium on Information, Computer and Communications Security, ASIACCS 2011, pp. 52–60. ACM (2011)
10. Dent, A.W.: Hybrid signcryption schemes with insider security. In: Boyd, C., González Nieto, J.M. (eds.) ACISP 2005. LNCS, vol. 3574, pp. 253–266. Springer, Heidelberg (2005)
11. Dent, A.W.: Hybrid signcryption schemes with outsider security. In: Zhou, J., López, J., Deng, R.H., Bao, F. (eds.) ISC 2005. LNCS, vol. 3650, pp. 203–217. Springer, Heidelberg (2005)
12. Dodis, Y., Freedman, M.J., Jarecki, S., Walfish, S.: Optimal signcryption from any trapdoor permutation. Cryptology ePrint Archive, Report 2004/020 (2004), http://eprint.iacr.org/

13. Even, S., Goldreich, O., Micali, S.: On-line/off-line digital signatures. In: Brassard, G. (ed.) CRYPTO 1989. LNCS, vol. 435, pp. 263–275. Springer, Heidelberg (1990)
14. Guo, F., Mu, Y., Chen, Z.: Identity-based online/offline encryption. In: Tsudik, G. (ed.) FC 2008. LNCS, vol. 5143, pp. 247–261. Springer, Heidelberg (2008)
15. Huang, Q., Wong, D.S., Li, J., Zhao, Y.M.: Generic transformation from weakly to strongly unforgeable signatures. Journal of Computer Science and Technology 23(2), 240–252 (2008)
16. Huang, Q., Wong, D.S., Zhao, Y.: Generic transformation to strongly unforgeable signatures. In: Katz, J., Yung, M. (eds.) ACNS 2007. LNCS, vol. 4521, pp. 1–17. Springer, Heidelberg (2007)
17. Kiltz, E.: Chosen-ciphertext security from tag-based encryption. In: Halevi, S., Rabin, T. (eds.) TCC 2006. LNCS, vol. 3876, pp. 581–600. Springer, Heidelberg (2006)
18. Libert, B., Quisquater, J.-J.: Efficient signcryption with key privacy from gap diffie-hellman groups. In: Bao, F., Deng, R., Zhou, J. (eds.) PKC 2004. LNCS, vol. 2947, pp. 187–200. Springer, Heidelberg (2004)
19. Liu, J.K., Baek, J., Zhou, J.: Online/offline identity-based signcryption revisited. In: Lai, X., Yung, M., Lin, D. (eds.) Inscrypt 2010. LNCS, vol. 6584, pp. 36–51. Springer, Heidelberg (2011)
20. Liu, J.K., Zhou, J.: An efficient identity-based online/offline encryption scheme. In: Abdalla, M., Pointcheval, D., Fouque, P.-A., Vergnaud, D. (eds.) ACNS 2009. LNCS, vol. 5536, pp. 156–167. Springer, Heidelberg (2009)
21. MacKenzie, P.D., Reiter, M.K., Yang, K.: Alternatives to non-malleability: Definitions, constructions, and applications. In: Naor, M. (ed.) TCC 2004. LNCS, vol. 2951, pp. 171–190. Springer, Heidelberg (2004)
22. Matsuda, T., Matsuura, K., Schuldt, J.C.N.: Efficient constructions of signcryption schemes and signcryption composability. In: Roy, B., Sendrier, N. (eds.) INDOCRYPT 2009. LNCS, vol. 5922, pp. 321–342. Springer, Heidelberg (2009)
23. Pieprzyk, J., Pointcheval, D.: Parallel authentication and public-key encryption. In: Safavi-Naini, R., Seberry, J. (eds.) ACISP 2003. LNCS, vol. 2727, pp. 383–401. Springer, Heidelberg (2003)
24. Shamir, A., Tauman, Y.: Improved online/offline signature schemes. In: Kilian, J. (ed.) CRYPTO 2001. LNCS, vol. 2139, pp. 355–367. Springer, Heidelberg (2001)
25. Sun, D., Mu, Y., Susilo, W.: A generic construction of identity-based online/offline signcryption. In: International Symposium on Parallel and Distributed Processing with Applications, ISPA 2008, pp. 707–712. IEEE (2008)
26. Tan, C.H.: Signcryption scheme in multi-user setting without random oracles. In: Matsuura, K., Fujisaki, E. (eds.) IWSEC 2008. LNCS, vol. 5312, pp. 64–82. Springer, Heidelberg (2008)
27. Xu, Z., Dai, G., Yang, D.: An efficient online/offline signcryption scheme for MANET. In: 21st International Conference on Advanced Information Networking and Applications Workshops, AINAW 2007, vol. 2, pp. 171–176. IEEE (2007)
28. Yamamoto, D., Sato, H., Fukuzawa, Y.: Incrementally executable signcryptions, http://eprint.iacr.org/ (submitted)
29. Zhang, F., Mu, Y., Susilo, W.: Reducing security overhead for mobile networks. In: Advanced Information Networking and Applications, AINA 2005, vol. 1, pp. 398–403. IEEE (2005)
30. Zheng, Y.: Digital signcryption or how to achieve cost (signature & encryption) ≪ cost (signature) + cost (encryption). In: Kaliski Jr., B.S. (ed.) CRYPTO 1997. LNCS, vol. 1294, pp. 165–179. Springer, Heidelberg (1997)
31. Zheng, Y., Yung, M., Dent, A.W.: Practical signcryption. Springer (2010)

Hierarchical Identity-Based Broadcast Encryption

Weiran Liu[1], Jianwei Liu[1], Qianhong Wu[2,1], and Bo Qin[3]

[1] School of Electronic and Information Engineering, Beihang University,
XueYuan Road No.37, Haidian District, Beijing, China
liuweiran900217@gmail.com, liujianwei@buaa.edu.cn, qhwu@xidian.edu.cn
[2] The Academy of Satellite Application, Beijing, 100086, China
[3] School of Information, Renmin University of China,
ZhongGuanCun Street No. 59, Haidian District, Beijing, China
bo.qin@ruc.edu.cn

Abstract. We elaborate Hierarchical Identity-Based Encryption (HIBE) with a new primitive referred to as Hierarchical Identity-Based Broadcast Encryption (HIBBE). Similar to HIBE, HIBBE organizes users in a tree-like structure and users can delegate their decryption capability to their subordinates, which mirrors hierarchical social organizations in the real world. Unlike HIBE merely allowing a single decryption path, HIBBE enables encryption to any subset of the users and only the intended users (and their supervisors) can decrypt. We define ciphertext indistinguishability against adaptively chosen-identity-vector-set and chosen-ciphertext attack (IND-CIVS-CCA2) which captures the most powerful attacks on HIBBE in the real world. We construct an efficient HIBBE scheme against chosen-identity-vector-set and chosen-plaintext attack (IND-CIVS-CPA). The construction is built from composite order bilinear pairings and has constant size ciphertext. Analyses show that our HIBBE is efficient in terms of communication and computation that is suitable into practical usage.

Keywords: Hierarchical Identity-Based Broadcast Encryption, Hierarchical Identity-Based Encryption, Broadcast Encryption.

1 Introduction

Identity-Based Encryption (IBE), introduced by Shamir [22], allows one to securely communicate with others if he/she knows their public identities. In IBE, users' recognizable identities such as their social security number, IP or email address, are used as their public keys. A Private Key Generator (PKG) is employed to generate secret keys associated with the users' public identities. One can encrypt to any user by specifying the user's identity and only the intended user can decrypt.

Hierarchical IBE (HIBE) extends IBE to host a large number of users with a delegation mechanism. HIBE [14] organizes users in a tree-like structure which is consistent with the structure of many social organizations. PKG's burden is

W. Susilo and Y. Mu (Eds.): ACISP 2014, LNCS 8544, pp. 242–257, 2014.
© Springer International Publishing Switzerland 2014

shared by upper-level users who can delegate secret keys to their subordinates. In the encryption process, the sender associates the ciphertext with an identity vector, instead of the single identity in an IBE system. Then only the users whose identities appearing in the specified identity vector can decrypt. For instance, to securely communicate with a professor in a university, one just needs to encrypt with a specified identity vector "university: XXX | school: XXX | laboratory: XXX | professor: XXX", which is very convenient in practice.

In applications similar to the above, one may have to simultaneously communicate with multiple users in hierarchical organizations. For example, a company may cooperate with a number of professors from different laboratories in a university for developing a new software system. Trivially, the company can separately encrypt to these professors by specifying their respective decryption paths. However, this trivial solution incurs heavy encryption burden and long ciphertexts. Another application comes from the IP-based multicast networks, in which all nodes in the networks are organized in hierarchy. The nodes are identified by their IP addresses and subnet masks. Since sensitive contents in such networks can be easily intercepted by sniffer-like hack software, secure cryptographic systems are needed. Applying existing HIBE systems in multicast network would be a possible solution. However, it becomes inefficient when the number of nodes from different IP paths increases. We are interested in more practical solutions to such applications.

1.1   Our Contributions

Motivated by the above scenarios, we propose a new cryptographic primitive referred to as Hierarchical Identity-Based Broadcast Encryption (HIBBE). Users in a tree-like structure can delegate their decryption capabilities to their subordinates, so that the burden of the PKG can be shared when the system hosts a large number of users. One can encrypt to any subset of the users and only the intended ones and their supervisors can decrypt.

We define ciphertext indistinguishability against adaptively chosen-identity-vector-set and chosen-ciphertext attack (IND-CIVS-CCA2). In this notion, the attacker is simultaneously allowed to adaptively query for the secret keys of users recognized by identity vectors of its choice and to issue decryption queries for receiver identity vector sets at will. Even such an attacker cannot distinguish the encrypted messages, provided that the attacker does not query for the secret keys of the target users or their supervisors. Clearly, this definition captures the most powerful attacks on HIBBE in the real world.

We construct an HIBBE scheme with chosen-identity-vector-set and chosen-plaintext security (IND-CIVS-CPA) in the standard model. This construction is built from composite order bilinear pairings and has constant size ciphertext. The encryption and decryption procedures are considerably efficient. Thorough theoretical analyses show the feasibility and efficiency of our HIBBE in terms of communication and computation. All of these features show the proposed HIBBE is suitable for practical applications.

1.2 Related Work

Identity-Based Encryption. Since the concept of Identity-Based Encryption (IBE) was introduced by Shamir [22], it took long time for researchers to construct a practical and fully functional scheme. In 2001, Boneh and Franklin [3] precisely defined the security model of IBE systems and proposed the first practical IBE construction by using bilinear pairings. In the Boneh-Franklin security model, the adversary can adaptively request secret keys for the identities of its choice and can choose the challenge identity it wants to attack at any point during the key-requesting process, provided that the challenging identity is not queried. The security of their systems [3] requires cryptographic hash functions to be modeled as random oracles. Canetti *et al.* [7,8] formalized a slightly weaker security notion, called Selective-ID security, in which the adversary must disclose the challenge identity before the public parameters are generated. They illustrated a Selective-ID secure IBE scheme without using random oracles. Since then, more practical IBE schemes have been proposed that are shown to be secure without random oracles in the selective-ID security model [1] or in the full security model [23].

Broadcast Encryption. In Broadcast Encryption (BE) systems [12], a dealer is employed to generate decryption keys for the users. A sender can encrypt to a subset of the users and only the privileged ones can decrypt. Since the concept of BE was introduced in 1994 [12], many BE schemes have been proposed to gain more preferable properties. We mention just a few properties: "Stateless Receivers" (after getting the decryption keys, users do not need to update it) [9,17], "Fully Collusion Resistant" (even if all users outside the receiver set collude, they can obtain no information about the encrypted message) [5], "Dynamic" (the dealer can dynamically recruit new members while the other members will not be affected) [11], and "Anonymity" (a receiver does not need to know who are the other receivers when decrypting the encrypted messages) [18].

Identity-Based Broadcast Encryption. Identity-Based Broadcast Encryption (IBBE) incorporates the idea of BE into IBE and recognizes the users in a BE scheme with their identities, instead of indexes assigned by the system. When one needs to send confidential messages to multiple users, with IBE the sender has to encrypt to the receivers separately, which is inefficient in practice. The sender in IBBE can efficiently encrypt the message one time to multiple users and simply broadcasts the resulting ciphertext. Fully functional IBBE was formalized and realized by Delerablée with constant size ciphertext and secret key [10], although it is only selective-ID secure in the random oracle model. The up-to-date IBBE schemes [15,21] are shown to be secure in the full security model.

Hierarchical Identity-Based Encryption. Horwitz and Lynn [16] first proposed the concept of HIBE and presented a two-level HIBE system in the same article. The first fully functional HIBE construction was proposed by Gentry and Silverberg [14]. The security relies on the Bilinear Diffie-Hellman assumption in the random oracle model. Subsequently, Boneh and Boyen [1] introduced HIBE schemes in the selective-ID model without using random oracles. Boneh, Boyen and Goh [2] presented a selective-ID secure HIBE with constant size ciphertext.

Gentry and Halevi [13] constructed a fully secure HIBE that supports polynomial depth of hierarchy. In 2009, Waters [24] proposed a new approach, called Dual System, for proving full security in IBE and HIBE. This approach has become a powerful security proof tool [19,20].

Generalized Identity-Based Encryption. Boneh and Hamburg [6] proposed a general framework for constructing IBE systems, referred to as Generalized Identity-Based Encryption (GIBE), to incorporate different properties in IBE via a product rule. Their framework is rather general and can cover different primitives, e.g., HIBE, inclusive IBE, co-inclusive IBE, in an identity-based like settings. HIBBE can also be derived from GIBE. However, the HIBBE derived from their GIBE only has selective security.

1.3 Paper Organization

The rest of the paper is organized as follows. In Section 2, we review composite order bilinear groups and the assumptions used in our constructions. Section 3 formalizes HIBBE and its security definitions. We propose a IND-CIVS-CPA secure HIBBE system in Section 4. Finally, we conclude the paper in Section 5.

2 Preliminaries

2.1 Composite Order Bilinear Groups

Composite order bilinear groups were first introduced in [4]. Let $\mathcal{G}$ be an algorithm which takes a security parameter λ as input and outputs the description of a bilinear group, $(N, \mathbb{G}, \mathbb{G}_T, e)$, where $N = p_1 p_2 p_3$ is a composite integer with three distinct large prime factors p_1, p_2 and p_3, $\mathbb{G}$ and $\mathbb{G}_T$ are cyclic groups of order N, and a bilinear map $e : \mathbb{G} \times \mathbb{G} \to \mathbb{G}_T$ satisfying the following properties:

1. *Bilinearity*: for all $g, h \in \mathbb{G}$ and $a, b \in \mathbb{Z}_N$, $e(g^a, h^b) = e(g, h)^{ab}$;
2. *Non-degeneracy*: there exists at least an element $g \in \mathbb{G}$ such that $e(g, g)$ has order N in $\mathbb{G}_T$;
3. *Computability*: There exists an efficient algorithm (in polynomial time with respect to λ) to compute the bilinear pairing $e(u, v)$ for all $u, v \in \mathbb{G}$.

Aside from these properties, the three subgroups of order p_1, p_2 and p_3 in $\mathbb{G}$ (we respectively denote them by $\mathbb{G}_{p_1}$, $\mathbb{G}_{p_2}$ and $\mathbb{G}_{p_3}$) satisfy the orthogonality property: $\forall h_i \in \mathbb{G}_{p_i}, h_j \in \mathbb{G}_{p_j}$, if $i \neq j$, then $e(h_i, h_j) = 1$. This property is essential in our construction and the security proof.

2.2 Assumptions in Composite Order Bilinear Groups

We will use three static assumptions to prove the security of our HIBBE systems. These three assumptions, which were first introduced by Lewko and Waters [19], hold if it is hard to find a nontrivial factor of the group order. Let $\mathcal{G}$ be a group generator algorithm that outputs a composite order bilinear group

($N = p_1 p_2 p_3, \mathbb{G}, \mathbb{G}_T, e$). For ease of description, we let $\mathbb{G}_{p_i p_j}$ denote the subgroup of order $p_i p_j$ in $\mathbb{G}$.

Let $g \xleftarrow{R} \mathbb{G}_{p_1}$ be a random generator of $\mathbb{G}_{p_1}$ and $X_3 \xleftarrow{R} \mathbb{G}_{p_3}$ be a random element in $\mathbb{G}_{p_3}$. The **Assumption 1** is to determine whether T is a random element in $\mathbb{G}_{p_1 p_2}$, or a random element in $\mathbb{G}_{p_1}$ by given $D_1 \leftarrow (g, X_3)$ as input. We define the advantage of an algorithm $\mathcal{A}$ that outputs $b \in \{0, 1\}$ in solving the first assumption in $\mathbb{G}$ to be

$$Adv1_{\mathcal{A}}(\lambda) = \left| \Pr \left[\mathcal{A} \left(D_1, T \xleftarrow{R} \mathbb{G}_{p_1 p_2} \right) = 1 \right] - \Pr \left[\mathcal{A} \left(D_1, T \xleftarrow{R} \mathbb{G}_{p_1} \right) = 1 \right] \right|$$

Definition 1. *Assumption 1 states that $Adv1_{\mathcal{A}}(\lambda)$ is negligible for all polynomial time algorithms $\mathcal{A}$.*

Let $g \xleftarrow{R} \mathbb{G}_{p_1}$ be a random generator of $\mathbb{G}_{p_1}$, choose random elements $X_1 \xleftarrow{R} \mathbb{G}_{p_1}$, $X_2, Y_2 \xleftarrow{R} \mathbb{G}_{p_2}$ and $X_3, Y_3 \xleftarrow{R} \mathbb{G}_{p_3}$, the **Assumption 2** is, given $D_2 = (g, X_1 X_2, X_3, Y_2 Y_3)$ as input, to determine whether T is a random element in $\mathbb{G}$ or a random element in $\mathbb{G}_{p_1 p_3}$. We define the advantage of an algorithm $\mathcal{A}$ that outputs $b \in \{0, 1\}$ in solving the second assumption in $\mathbb{G}$ to be

$$Adv2_{\mathcal{A}}(\lambda) = \left| \Pr \left[\mathcal{A} \left(D_2, T \xleftarrow{R} \mathbb{G} \right) = 1 \right] - \Pr \left[\mathcal{A} \left(D_2, T \xleftarrow{R} \mathbb{G}_{p_1 p_3} \right) = 1 \right] \right|$$

Definition 2. *Assumption 2 states that $Adv2_{\mathcal{A}}(\lambda)$ is negligible for all polynomial time algorithms $\mathcal{A}$.*

Similarly, let $g \xleftarrow{R} \mathbb{G}_{p_1}$ be a random generator of $\mathbb{G}_{p_1}$, $X_2, Y_2, Z_2 \xleftarrow{R} \mathbb{G}_{p_2}$ be random elements in $\mathbb{G}_{p_2}$, $X_3 \xleftarrow{R} \mathbb{G}_{p_3}$ be a random element in $\mathbb{G}_{p_3}$, $\alpha, s \xleftarrow{R} \mathbb{Z}_N$ be random exponents chosen in $\mathbb{Z}_N$. The **Assumption 3** states that, given $D_3 = (g, g^{\alpha} X_2, X_3, g^s Y_2, Z_2)$ as input, to determine whether T is $e(g, g)^{\alpha s}$, or a random element in $\mathbb{G}_T$. We define the advantage of an algorithm $\mathcal{A}$ that outputs $b \in \{0, 1\}$ in solving the third assumption in $\mathbb{G}$ to be

$$Adv3_{\mathcal{A}}(\lambda) = \left| \Pr \left[\mathcal{A} \left(D_3, T \leftarrow e(g, g)^{\alpha s} \right) = 1 \right] - \left[\mathcal{A} \left(D_3, T \xleftarrow{R} \mathbb{G}_T \right) \right] = 1 \right|$$

Definition 3. *Assumption 3 states that $Adv3_{\mathcal{A}}(\lambda)$ is negligible for all polynomial time algorithms $\mathcal{A}$.*

3   Syntax

3.1   Terminologies and Notations

We introduce several notations to simplify the description of HIBBE systems. Table 1 summarizes these notations and their corresponding meanings that will be used in the paper.

We use $[a, b]$ to denote integers in $\{a, a+1, \cdots, b\}$. For a set S, its cardinality is denoted by $|S|$. For an identity vector $\mathbf{ID} = (ID_1, ID_2, \cdots, ID_d)$, we define

Table 1. Notations

Notation	Description	Notation	Description
λ	Security Parameter	PK	Public Key
MSK	Master Key	CT	Ciphertext
ID	Identity	**ID**	Identity Vector
$\mathbb{I}_{\textbf{ID}}$	Identity Vector Position	$SK_{\textbf{ID}}$	Secret Key for Identity Vector
$\|\textbf{ID}\|$	Depth of **ID**	$S_{\textbf{ID}}$	Identity Set Associating with **ID**
V	Identity Vector Set	$\mathbb{I}_{\textbf{V}}$	Identity Vector Set Position
$\|\textbf{V}\|$	Depth of **V**	$S_{\textbf{V}}$	Identity Set Associating with **V**

$\|\textbf{ID}\| = d$ as the depth of **ID** and $S_{\textbf{ID}} = \{ID_1, \cdots, ID_d\}$ as the identity set associating with **ID**. The identity vector position of **ID** is defined by $\mathbb{I}_{\textbf{ID}} = \{i : ID_i \in S_{\textbf{ID}}\}$. Similarly, we define the maximal depth of an identity vector set as $\|\textbf{V}\| = \max\{\|\textbf{ID}\| : \textbf{ID} \in \textbf{V}\}$. The associating identity set $S_{\textbf{V}}$ of **V** and the identity vector set position $\mathbb{I}_{\textbf{V}}$ of **V** can be defined accordingly.

We slightly abuse the term prefix and define the prefix of an identity vector $\textbf{ID} = (ID_1, \cdots, ID_d)$ as an identity vector set denoted by $Pref(\textbf{ID}) = \{(ID_1, \cdots, ID_{d'}) : d' \leq d\}$. Clearly, $|Pref(\textbf{ID})| = \|\textbf{ID}\| = d$. We similarly define the prefix of an identity vector set **V** as $Pref(\textbf{V}) = \bigcup_{\textbf{ID} \in \textbf{V}} Pref(\textbf{ID})$.

In practice, a user may have more than one identity or parent node. In this case, we will treat them as different users with the same identity. Hence, without loss of generality, we assume that each user has a unique identity vector and can have at most one parent node.

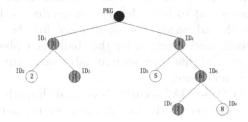

Fig. 1. A Typical Example of an HIBBE System

For example, assume that the users are organized as in Figure 1. For the user with identity vector $\textbf{ID} = (ID_1, ID_3)$, we have that $\|\textbf{ID}\| = 2$, $S_{\textbf{ID}} = \{ID_1, ID_3\}$, and $\mathbb{I}_{\textbf{ID}} = \{1, 3\}$. The prefix of **ID** is $Pref(\textbf{ID}) = \{(ID_1), (ID_1, ID_3)\}$. Similarly, for the broadcast identity vector set $\textbf{V} = \{(ID_1, ID_3), (ID_4, ID_6, ID_7)\}$, we have that $\|\textbf{V}\| = \max\{2, 3\} = 3$, $S_{\textbf{V}} = \{ID_1, ID_3, ID_4, ID_6, ID_7\}$, and $\mathbb{I}_{\textbf{V}} = \{1, 3, 4, 6, 7\}$. The prefix of **V** is

$$Pref(\textbf{V}) = \{(ID_1), (ID_1, ID_3), (ID_4), (ID_4, ID_6), (ID_4, ID_6, ID_7)\}$$

3.2   Hierarchical Identity-Based Broadcast Encryption (HIBBE)

A (D, n)-HIBBE system consists of five polynomial time algorithms: **Setup**, **KeyGen**, **Delegate**, **Encrypt** and **Decrypt** defined as follows:

- **Setup**(D, n, λ). The algorithm **Setup** takes as inputs the maximal depth D of the hierarchy, the maximal size n of users, and the security parameter λ. It outputs a masker key MSK and a public key PK.
- **Encrypt**(PK, M, **V**). The algorithm **Encrypt** takes as inputs the public key PK, a message $M \in \mathcal{M}$, and a receiver identity vector set **V**. The algorithm outputs the ciphertext CT for M.
- **KeyGen**(MSK, **ID**). The algorithm **KeyGen** takes as inputs the master key MSK and an identity vector **ID**. It outputs a secret key $SK_{\mathbf{ID}}$ for the user with identity vector **ID**.
- **Delegate**($SK_{\mathbf{ID}'}$, ID). The algorithm **Delegate** takes as inputs a secret key for a user with identity vector **ID**$'$ of depth d and an identity ID. It returns a secret key $SK_{\mathbf{ID}}$ for the user with identity **ID** $= (\mathbf{ID}', ID)$.
- **Decrypt**(**V**, CT, $SK_{\mathbf{ID}}$). The algorithm **Decrypt** takes as inputs a receiver identity vector set **V**, a ciphertext CT for a message M, and a secret key $SK_{\mathbf{ID}}$ for a user with identity vector **ID**. If **ID** $\in Pref(\mathbf{V})$, it returns M.

An HIBBE system must satisfy the standard consistency constraint, namely for all $D \le n \in \mathbb{N}$, all $(PP, MSK) \leftarrow$ **Setup**(D, n, λ), all $SK_{\mathbf{ID}} \leftarrow$ **KeyGen**$(MSK,$ **ID**$)$ or $SK_{\mathbf{ID}} \leftarrow$ **Delegate**$(SK_{\mathbf{ID}'}, ID)$ with $\|\mathbf{ID}\| \le D$, all $M \in \mathcal{M}$, and all $CT \leftarrow$ **Encrypt**$(PP, M,$ **V**$)$ with $\|\mathbf{V}\| \le D$ and $|S_{\mathbf{V}}| \le n$, if **ID** $\in Pref(\mathbf{V})$, then **Decrypt**(**V**, CT, $SK_{\mathbf{ID}}$) $= M$.

We next define the indistinguishability against chosen-identity-vector-set and chosen-ciphertext attacks (IND-CIVS-CCA2) in HIBBE. In this security model, the adversary is allowed to obtain the secret keys associated with any identity vectors **ID** of its choice and to issue decryption queries for its chosen ciphertexts, provided that the adversary does not query for the secret keys of its chosen receivers or their supervisors, or for the challenge ciphertext of one of its chosen message. We require that even such an adversary cannot distinguish the encrypted messages of its choice.

Formally, the IND-CIVS-CCA2 security is defined through a game played by an adversary and a challenger. Both of them are given the parameters D, n and λ as inputs.

- **Setup.** The challenger runs **Setup** algorithm to obtain the public key PK and gives it to the adversary $\mathcal{A}$.
- **Phase 1.** The adversary $\mathcal{A}$ adaptively issues two kinds of queries:
  - Secret key query for an identity vector **ID**. The challenger generates a secret key for **ID** and gives it to the adversary.
  - Decryption query for the ciphertext CT with a receiver identity vector set **V**. The challenger responds by running algorithm **KeyGen** to generate a secret key $SK_{\mathbf{ID}}$ for identity vector **ID** satisfying **ID** $\in Pref(\mathbf{V})$. It then runs algorithm **Decrypt** to decrypt the ciphertext CT and returns the resulting message to the adversary.

- **Challenge.** When adversary $\mathcal{A}$ decides that Phase 1 is over, it outputs two equal-length messages M_0 and M_1 on which it wishes to be challenged. Also, adversary $\mathcal{A}$ outputs a challenge identity vector set $\mathbf{V}^*$ in which contains all the users that it wishes to attack. The identity vector set $\mathbf{V}^*$ should satisfy that for all the secret key queries for $\mathbf{ID}$ issued in Phase 1, $\mathbf{ID} \notin Pref(\mathbf{V}^*)$. The challenger flips a random coin $b \in \{0,1\}$ and encrypts M_b under the challenge identity vector set $\mathbf{V}^*$. The challenger returns the resulting challenge ciphertext CT^* to $\mathcal{A}$.
- **Phase 2.** The adversary $\mathcal{A}$ further adaptively issues two kinds of queries:
  - Secret key query for identity vectors $\mathbf{ID}$ such that $\mathbf{ID} \notin Pref(\mathbf{V}^*)$.
  - Decryption query for the ciphertext CT such that $CT \neq CT^*$.
  The challenger responds the same as in Phase 1.
- **Guess.** Finally, the adversary $\mathcal{A}$ outputs a guess $b' \in \{0,1\}$ and wins in the game if $b = b'$.

The advantage of such an adversary $\mathcal{A}$ in attacking the (D,n)-HIBBE system with security parameter λ is defined as $Adv_{\mathcal{A},D,n}^{IND-CIVS-CCA2}(\lambda) = \left|\Pr[b' = b] - \frac{1}{2}\right|$.

Definition 4. *A (D,n)-HIBBE system is (τ, q, q_d, ϵ)-secure if for any τ-time IND-CIVS-CCA2 adversary $\mathcal{A}$ that makes at most q secret key queries and q_d decryption queries, we have that $Adv_{\mathcal{A},D,n}^{IND-CIVS-CCA2}(\lambda) < \epsilon$*

As usual, we define chosen-identity-vector-set and chosen-plaintext (IND-CIVS-CPA) security for an HIBBE system as in the preceding game, with the constraint that the adversary is not allowed to issue any decryption query. The adversary is still able to adaptively issue secret key queries.

Definition 5. *A (D,n)-HIBBE system is (τ, q, ϵ)-secure if for any τ-time IND-CIVS-CPA adversary $\mathcal{A}$ that makes at most q secret key queries, we have that $Adv_{\mathcal{A},D,n}^{IND-CIVS-CPA}(\lambda) < \epsilon$.*

It is challenging to achieve full (identity/identity-vector) security in BE and (H)IBE, some weaker security notions have been proposed to bridge security proofs or cater for special applications which require only moderate security level. One useful security notion, called selective security, was firstly proposed by Canetti, Halevi, and Katz [7,8] in IBE systems. In this notion, the adversary should commits ahead of time to the challenge identity it will attack. Similar security notions can also be found in HIBE systems [1] and IBBE systems [10]. A counterpart security notion can be naturally defined in HIBBE systems, by requiring the adversary in HIBBE to submit a challenge identity vector set before seeing the public parameters.

Another useful security notion, named semi-static security, can also be extended in HIBBE systems. This security notion was firstly defined by Gentry and Waters [15] in BE systems. In this notion, the adversary must first commit to a set $\overline{S}$ before **Setup** phase. The adversary cannot query for secret key of any user in $\overline{S}$, but it can attack any target set $S^* \subseteq \overline{S}$. This security notion is weaker than full security but stronger than selective security, since the adversary can partly decide which set is allowed to query adaptively. In HIBBE systems, a similar security notion can be defined by requiring the adversary to submit an identity vector set $\overline{\mathbf{V}}$ before **Setup** phase and later allowing the adversary to challenge any identity vector set $\mathbf{V}^* \subseteq Pref(\overline{\mathbf{V}})$.

4 IND-CIVS-CPA Secure HIBBE with Constant Size Ciphertext

In this section, we propose an IND-CIVS-CPA secure HIBBE with constant size ciphertext over composite order bilinear groups of order $N = p_1p_2p_3$. Our starting point is the Lewko-Waters fully secure HIBE scheme [19] which was inspired by Boneh-Boyen-Goh selective secure HIBE scheme [2]. To support broadcast, every user in our system, instead of every depth of hierarchy in [2,19], is associated with a random element for blinding its own identity vector in their secret keys. Since users' identities have been randomized by different elements, users cannot reveal any information for other users' secret key from their own ones.

We realize the functionalities in $\mathbb{G}_{p_1}$, while randomizing secret keys in $\mathbb{G}_{p_3}$. The $\mathbb{G}_{p_2}$ space, called semi-functional space, is only used in security proofs.

4.1 Our Construction

We first assume that the identity vectors $\mathbf{ID} = (ID_1, \cdots, ID_k)$ at depth k are vector elements in $(\mathbb{Z}_N)^k$. We later extend the construction to identity vectors over $(\{0,1\}^*)^k$ by first hashing each component $ID_j \in S_{\mathbf{ID}}$ using a collision resistant hash function $H : \{0,1\}^* \to \mathbb{Z}_N$. Similarly to HIBE systems, we also assume that users' positions in HIBBE are publicly known with the processing of **KeyGen, Delegate, Encrypt** and **Decrypt**. Our (D, n)-HIBBE scheme works as follows.

Setup(D, n, λ). Run $(N, \mathbb{G}, \mathbb{G}_T, e) \leftarrow \mathcal{G}(1^\lambda)$ to generate a composite integer $N = p_1p_2p_3$, two groups $\mathbb{G}$, $\mathbb{G}_T$ of order N, and a bilinear map $e : \mathbb{G} \times \mathbb{G} \to \mathbb{G}_T$. Then, select a random generator $g \xleftarrow{R} \mathbb{G}_{p_1}$, two random elements $h \xleftarrow{R} \mathbb{G}_{p_1}$, $X_3 \xleftarrow{R} \mathbb{G}_{p_3}$, and a random exponent $\alpha \xleftarrow{R} \mathbb{Z}_N$. Next, pick random elements $u_i \xleftarrow{R} \mathbb{G}_{p_1}$ for all $i \in [1, n]$. The public key PK includes the description of $(N, \mathbb{G}, \mathbb{G}_T, e)$, as well as

$$(g, h, u_1, \cdots, u_n, X_3, e(g, g)^\alpha)$$

The master key is $MSK \leftarrow g^\alpha$.

KeyGen$(MSK, \mathbf{ID})$. For an identity vector $\mathbf{ID}$ of depth $d \leq D$, the key generation algorithm picks a random exponent $r \xleftarrow{R} \mathbb{Z}_N$ and two random elements $A_0, A_1 \xleftarrow{R} \mathbb{G}_{p_3}$. It then chooses random elements $U_j \xleftarrow{R} \mathbb{G}_{p_3}$ for all $j \in [1, n]\backslash I_{\mathbf{ID}}$ and outputs

$$SK_{\mathbf{ID}} \leftarrow \left(g^\alpha \left(h \cdot \prod_{i \in I_{\mathbf{ID}}} u_i^{ID_i} \right)^r A_0, g^r A_1, \{u_j^r U_j\}_{j \in [1,n]\backslash I_{\mathbf{ID}}} \right)$$

Delegate$(SK_{\mathbf{ID}'}, ID)$. Given a secret key

$$SK_{\mathbf{ID}'} = \left(g^\alpha \left(h \cdot \prod_{i \in I_{\mathbf{ID}'}} u_i^{ID_i} \right)^{r'} A_0', g^{r'} A_1', \left\{ u_j^{r'} U_j' \right\}_{j \in [1,n] \backslash I_{\mathbf{ID}'}} \right)$$

$$= \left(a_0, a_1, \{b_j\}_{j \in [1,n] \backslash I_{\mathbf{ID}'}} \right)$$

the delegation algorithm generates a secret key for $\mathbf{ID} = (\mathbf{ID}', ID)$ as follows. It first picks a random exponent $t \xleftarrow{R} \mathbb{Z}_N$, and also chooses two random elements $R_0, R_1 \xleftarrow{R} \mathbb{G}_{p_3}$. Next, for all $j \in [1,n] \backslash I_{\mathbf{ID}}$, it chooses random elements $T_j \xleftarrow{R} \mathbb{G}_{p_3}$. The algorithm outputs

$$SK_{\mathbf{ID}} = \left(a_0 \left(b_i^{ID} \right)_{i \in I_{\mathbf{ID}} \backslash I_{\mathbf{ID}'}} \left(h \prod_{i \in I_{\mathbf{ID}}} u_i^{ID_i} \right)^t R_0, a_1 g^t R_1, \left\{ b_j u_j^t T_j \right\}_{j \in [1,n] \backslash I_{\mathbf{ID}}} \right)$$

Note that by implicitly setting $r = r' + t \in \mathbb{Z}_N$, $A_0 = A_0' U_i' R_0 \in \mathbb{G}_{p_3}$ with $i \in I_{\mathbf{ID}} \backslash I_{\mathbf{ID}'}$, $A_1 = A_1' R_1 \in \mathbb{G}_{p_3}$, and $U_j = U_j' T_j \in \mathbb{G}_{p_3}$ for all $j \in [1,n] \backslash I_{\mathbf{ID}}$, this delegated secret key can be written in the form

$$SK_{\mathbf{ID}} \leftarrow \left(g^\alpha \left(h \cdot \prod_{i \in I_{\mathbf{ID}}} u_i^{ID_i} \right)^r A_0, g^r A_1, \left\{ u_j^r U_j \right\}_{j \in [1,n] \backslash I_{\mathbf{ID}}} \right)$$

which is well-formed as if it were generated by the **KeyGen** algorithm. Hence it is a properly distributed secret key for $\mathbf{ID} = (\mathbf{ID}', ID)$.

Encrypt$(PP, M, \mathbf{V})$. For the receiver identity vector set $\mathbf{V}$ the encryption algorithm picks a random exponent $\beta \xleftarrow{R} \mathbb{Z}_N$ and outputs the ciphertext

$$CT = (C_0, C_1, C_2) = \left(g^\beta, \left(h \cdot \prod_{i \in I_{\mathbf{V}}} u_i^{ID_i} \right)^\beta, e(g,g)^{\alpha\beta} \cdot M \right)$$

Decrypt$(\mathbf{V}, CT, SK_{\mathbf{ID}})$. Given the ciphertext $CT = (C_0, C_1, C_2)$, any user with identity vector $\mathbf{ID} \in Pref(\mathbf{V})$ can use its secret key $SK_{\mathbf{ID}} = \left(a_0, a_1, \{b_j\}_{j \in [1,n] \backslash I_{\mathbf{ID}}} \right)$ to compute

$$K = a_0 \cdot \prod_{j \in I_{\mathbf{V}} \backslash I_{\mathbf{ID}}} b_j^{ID_j}$$

Then it outputs the message by calculating $M = C_2 \cdot e(C_1, a_1)/e(K, C_0)$.

Consistency. If the ciphertext $CT = (C_0, C_1, C_2)$ is well-formed, then we have

$$K = a_0 \cdot \prod_{j \in I_{\mathbf{V}} \backslash I_{\mathbf{ID}}} b_j^{ID_j} = g^\alpha \left(h \cdot \prod_{i \in I_{\mathbf{V}}} u_i^{ID_i} \right)^r \cdot \left(A_0 \prod_{j \in I_{\mathbf{V}} \backslash I_{\mathbf{ID}}} U_j \right)$$

Note that all random elements in $\mathbb{G}_{p_3}$ can be cancelled in the pairing operations due to the orthogonality property. Therefore, for the blinding factor in C_2, the following equalities hold:

$$\frac{e(C_1, a_1)}{e(K, C_0)} = \frac{e\left(\left(h \cdot \prod_{i \in \mathbb{I}_\mathbf{V}} u_i^{ID_i}\right)^\beta, g^r A_1\right)}{e\left(g^\alpha\left(h \cdot \prod_{i \in \mathbb{I}_\mathbf{V}} u_i^{ID_i}\right)^r \cdot \left(A_0 \prod_{j \in \mathbb{I}_\mathbf{V} \backslash \mathbb{I}_{\mathbf{ID}}} U_j\right), g^\beta\right)}$$

$$= \frac{e\left(\left(h \cdot \prod_{i \in \mathbb{I}_\mathbf{V}} u_i^{ID_i}\right)^\beta, g^r\right)}{e\left(g^\alpha, g^\beta\right) \cdot e\left(h \cdot \left(\prod_{i \in \mathbb{I}_\mathbf{V}} u_i^{ID_i}\right)^r, g^\beta\right)} = \frac{1}{e\left(g, g\right)^{\alpha\beta}}$$

It follows that $C_2 \cdot e(C_1, a_1)/e(K, C_0) = M \cdot e(g, g)^{\alpha\beta}/e(g, g)^{\alpha\beta} = M$.

4.2   A Toy Example of the Proposed HIBBE Scheme

To achieve intuition in our basic construction, we provide a toy example of the proposal. Assume that the users are organized as in the right side of Figure 2 (same as in Figure 1). The secret keys for all users can be illustrated in the left matrix, in which r_i denotes the random exponent chosen for randomizing the secret key of the identity vector $\mathbf{ID}_i$. For ease of illustration, all random elements in $\mathbb{G}_{p_3}$ used for blinding secret keys are omitted in this matrix.

When an encryptor wants to broadcast a message M to an identity vector set $\mathbf{V} = \{\mathbf{ID}_3, \mathbf{ID}_7\} = \{(ID_1, ID_3), (ID_4, ID_6, ID_7)\}$, it combines $u_1^{ID_1}$, $u_3^{ID_3}$, $u_4^{ID_4}$, $u_6^{ID_6}$, $u_7^{ID_7}$ and randomizes them by the randomly choosing exponent $\beta \xleftarrow{R} \mathbb{Z}_N$. The ciphertext is formed as

$$CT = (C_1, C_2, C_3) = \left(g^\beta, \left(h \cdot u_1^{ID_1} u_3^{ID_3} u_4^{ID_4} u_6^{ID_6} u_7^{ID_7}\right)^\beta, e(g, g)^{\alpha\beta} \cdot M\right)$$

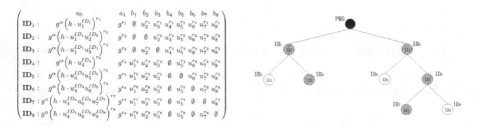

Fig. 2. The Illustration of our HIBBE construction

When decrypting, any user with identity vector $\mathbf{ID} \in Pref(\mathbf{V})$ can compute

$$K = g^\alpha \left(h \cdot u_1^{ID_1} u_3^{ID_3} u_4^{ID_4} u_6^{ID_6} u_7^{ID_7} \right)^{r_i}$$

Hence, the users defined by the receiver vectors can successfully recover the message using the decryption algorithm by eliminating $\left(h u_1^{ID_1} u_3^{ID_3} u_4^{ID_4} u_6^{ID_6} u_7^{ID_7} \right)^\beta$ from the ciphertext. However, users who are not in the receiver identity vector set cannot decrypt since their $u_i^{ID_i}$ do not appear in the ciphertext but are combined in the a_0 component of their own secret keys. If they try to correctly decrypt the ciphertext, they need to eliminate $\left(u_i^{ID_i} \right)^{r_i}$ from their secret keys, which is impossible without knowing the randomizing number r_i.

4.3   Security Analysis

To prove the chosen-identity-vector-set and chosen-plaintext security of our scheme, we apply the Dual System Encryption technique introduced by Waters [24] for obtaining adaptively secure IBE and HIBE schemes. This technique has been shown a powerful tool for security proofs [19,20]. In a Dual System Encryption system, the ciphertexts and keys can take one of two indistinguishable forms: normal and semi-functional. Normal keys can decrypt normal or semi-functional ciphertexts, and semi-functional ciphertexts can be decrypted by normal or semi-functional keys. However, decryption will fail when ones use a semi-functional key to decrypt a semi-functional ciphertext. Since these two kinds of keys and ciphertexts are indistinguishable, the simulator can replace all normal ciphertexts and keys with semi-functional ones in the security game. When all ciphertexts and keys are semi-functional, the adversary can obtain no information about the challenge ciphertext as none of the given keys are useful to decrypt the challenge ciphertext.

We first need to define the semi-functional key and the semi-functional ciphertext. They will only be used in the security proof. Let $g_2 \xleftarrow{R} \mathbb{G}_{p_2}$ be a random generator of $\mathbb{G}_{p_2}$, the semi-functional ciphertext and the semi-functional key are defined as follows:

Semi-Functional Ciphertext. Run **Encrypt** algorithm to construct a normal ciphertext $CT = (C_0', C_1', C_2')$. Then, choose random exponents $x, y_c \xleftarrow{R} \mathbb{Z}_N$ and set $C_0 = C_0', C_1 = C_1' g_2^{x y_c}, C_2 = C_2' g_2^x$.

Semi-Functional Key. For an identity vector $\mathbf{ID}$, run **KeyGen** algorithm to generate its normal secret key $SK = (a_0', a_1', \{b_j'\}_{j \in [1,n] \backslash I_{ID}})$. Then, choose random exponents $\gamma, y_k \in \mathbb{G}_N$, $z_j \in \mathbb{G}_N$ for all $j \in [1, n] \backslash I_{ID}$ and set $a_0 = a_0' g_2^\gamma, a_1 = a_1' g_2^{\gamma y_k}, \{b_j = b_j' g_2^{\gamma z_j}\}_{j \in [1,n] \backslash I_{ID}}$.

It can be seen that the **Decrypt** algorithm will correctly output the message M when decrypting a semi-functional ciphertext using a normal key or a semi-functional key since the added elements in $\mathbb{G}_{p_2}$ can be cancelled due to the orthogonality property. However, the blinding factor will be multiplied by the additional term $e(g_2, g_2)^{x\gamma(y_k - y_c)}$ when trying to decrypt the semi-functional ciphertext using a semi-functional key, unless $y_k = y_c$ with probability $\frac{1}{N}$. In this case, we call the key is *nominally semi-functional*.

We prove the security by using a sequence of games:

- **Game$_{Real}$**. This game is the real HIBBE security game.
- **Game$_{Restricted}$**. This game is identical with **Game$_{Real}$**, except that in Phase 2, the attacker cannot ask for any identity vector $\mathbf{ID} = (ID_1, \cdots, ID_d)$ satisfying that $\exists \mathbf{ID}^* = (ID_1^*, \cdots, ID_{d'}^*) \in Pref(\mathbf{V}^*)$ with $d' \leq d$, s.t. $\forall i \in [1, d'], ID_i = ID_i^* \bmod p_2$, where $\mathbf{V}^*$ is the challenge identity vector set.
- **Game$_k$**. Suppose that the adversary can make q secret key queries in Phase 1 and Phase 2. This game is identical with the **Game$_{Restricted}$**, except that the challenge ciphertext is semi-functional and the first k keys are semi-functional, while the rest of the keys are normal. We note that in **Game$_0$**, only the challenge ciphertext is semi-functional; in **Game$_q$**, the ciphertext and all keys are semi-functional.
- **Game$_{Final}$**. This game is the same as **Game$_q$**, except that the challenge ciphertext is a semi-functional encryption for a random message in $\mathbb{G}_T$, not one of the messages given by the adversary.

The security of our scheme is guaranteed by the following Theorem. In a high level, the proof of our HIBBE system follows the proof framework of the Lewko-Waters HIBE system [19], with an extra effort to generate ciphertexts for supporting broadcast. The above games are indistinguishable and in the final game the encrypted message is information-theoretically hidden from the attacker. The details of the proof can be seen in the full version of this paper.

Theorem 1. *Let $\mathbb{G}$ be a group (of composite order N) equipped with an efficient bilinear map. Our HIBBE scheme is IND-CIVS-CPA secure if all the three assumptions defined in Definition 1, Definition 2 and Definition 3 hold in $\mathbb{G}$.*

4.4   Efficiency Analysis

The public/secret key size in our HIBBE construction is linear with the maximal number of active users n. For any subset of receivers, the ciphertext only has three groups elements, which is preferable in broadcast encryption systems. The **Encrypt** algorithm requires one pairing operation (which can be pre-computed). The **Decrypt** algorithm only requires two pairing operations. Table 2 shows the efficiency of the proposed HIBBE scheme in details. In Table 2, we denote τ_e as one exponent operation time in $\mathbb{G}$, τ_m as one multiplication operation time in $\mathbb{G}$, and τ_p as one pairing operation time in $\mathbb{G}$. From Table 2, it can be seen that our HIBBE system is efficient in practical usage.

4.5   HIBBE with Shorter Secret Keys

In our HIBBE scheme, while the ciphertext contains only three group elements, the secret key for user at depth d contains $n - d + 2$ elements. In some scenarios,

Table 2. Efficiency Analysis for Our (D,n)-HIBBE

	(D,n)-HIBBE
Active Users	n
Public Key Size	$n+4$
Secret Key Size	$\leq n+1$
Ciphertext Size	3
Encryption Time	$(2+|S_{\mathbf{V}}|)\cdot(\tau_e+\tau_m)$
Decryption Time	$\leq (1+|S_{\mathbf{V}}|)\cdot(\tau_e+\tau_m)+2\tau_p$

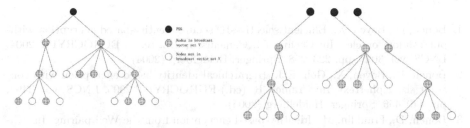

Fig. 3. Original HIBBE   **Fig. 4.** Shorter Secret keys HIBBE

e.g., the storage capacity of the receivers are limited, one may expect an efficient tradeoff between key size and ciphertext size. Note that users in an HIBBE system are organized as a tree T with n nodes (PKG as the sink is not countered). We divide T into $\mathcal{T}$ subtrees with n_i nodes, where $i \in [1, \mathcal{T}]$. To achieve better balance, as shown in Figure 4, all the subtrees may be obtained in a way satisfying: (1) The number of nodes for each subtree is approximately equal. That is, for the ith subtree with $i \in [1, \mathcal{T}]$, we have $n_i \approx n/\mathcal{T}$; (2) All subtrees only share necessarily minimum number of higher-level nodes.

We then implement independent HIBBE instances in each subtree. When broadcasting, one encrypts the messages with each instance where the broadcast subsets are the intersection of the original broadcast set and the subtrees. Each receiver can decrypt the ciphertext component corresponding to its subtree. By using this subtree method, the key size is $O(\frac{n}{\mathcal{T}})$ and the ciphertext size is $O(\mathcal{T})$. By setting $\mathcal{T} = \sqrt{n}$, both the key size and the ciphertext size are $O(\sqrt{n})$.

5   Conclusion

We formalized a new cryptographic primitive, referred to as Hierarchical Identity-Based Broadcast Encryption (HIBBE) to cater for applications in which one needs to encrypt to multiple receivers in a hierarchically organized organization. We formalized IND-CIVS-CCA2 security to capture the realistic attacks against HIBBE to be deployed in the real world. We presented an IND-CIVS-CPA secure HIBBE scheme in the standard model. Theoretical analyses illustrate high efficiency of our HIBBE in terms of communication and computation. All these features show that our HIBBE is secure and practical.

Acknowledgment. This paper is partially supported by the Natural Science Foundation through projects 61272501, 61173154, 61370190 and 61003214, by the National Key Basic Research Program (973 program) through project 2012CB315905, by the Beijing Natural Science Foundation through project 4132056, and by the Fundamental Research Funds for the Central Universities, and the Research Funds(No.14XNLF02) of Renmin University of China and the Open Research Fund of Beijing Key Laboratory of Trusted Computing.

References

1. Boneh, D., Boyen, X.: Efficient selective-ID secure identity-based encryption without random oracles. In: Cachin, C., Camenisch, J.L. (eds.) EUROCRYPT 2004. LNCS, vol. 3027, pp. 223–238. Springer, Heidelberg (2004)
2. Boneh, D., Boyen, X., Goh, E.J.: Hierarchical identity based encryption with constant size ciphertext. In: Cramer, R. (ed.) EUROCRYPT 2005. LNCS, vol. 3494, pp. 440–456. Springer, Heidelberg (2005)
3. Boneh, D., Franklin, M.: Identity-based encryption from the Weil pairing. In: Kilian, J. (ed.) CRYPTO 2001. LNCS, vol. 2139, pp. 213–229. Springer, Heidelberg (2001)
4. Boneh, D., Goh, E.-J., Nissim, K.: Evaluating 2-dnf formulas on ciphertexts. In: Kilian, J. (ed.) TCC 2005. LNCS, vol. 3378, pp. 325–341. Springer, Heidelberg (2005)
5. Boneh, D., Gentry, C., Waters, B.: Collusion resistant broadcast encryption with short ciphertexts and private keys. In: Shoup, V. (ed.) CRYPTO 2005. LNCS, vol. 3621, pp. 258–275. Springer, Heidelberg (2005)
6. Boneh, D., Hamburg, M.: Generalized identity based and broadcast encryption schemes. In: Pieprzyk, J. (ed.) ASIACRYPT 2008. LNCS, vol. 5350, pp. 455–470. Springer, Heidelberg (2008)
7. Canetti, R., Halevi, S., Katz, J.: A forward-secure public-key encryption scheme. In: Biham, E. (ed.) EUROCRYPT 2003. LNCS, vol. 2656, pp. 255–271. Springer, Heidelberg (2003)
8. Canetti, R., Halevi, S., Katz, J.: Chosen-ciphertext security from identity-based encryption. In: Cachin, C., Camenisch, J.L. (eds.) EUROCRYPT 2004. LNCS, vol. 3027, pp. 207–222. Springer, Heidelberg (2004)
9. Dodis, Y., Fazio, N.: Public key broadcast encryption for stateless receivers. In: Feigenbaum, J. (ed.) DRM 2002. LNCS, vol. 2696, pp. 61–80. Springer, Heidelberg (2003)
10. Delerablée, C.: Identity-based broadcast encryption with constant size ciphertexts and private keys. In: Kurosawa, K. (ed.) ASIACRYPT 2007. LNCS, vol. 4833, pp. 200–215. Springer, Heidelberg (2007)
11. Delerablée, C., Paillier, P., Pointcheval, D.: Fully collusion secure dynamic broadcast encryption with constant-size ciphertexts or decryption keys. In: Takagi, T., Okamoto, T., Okamoto, E., Okamoto, T. (eds.) Pairing 2007. LNCS, vol. 4575, pp. 39–59. Springer, Heidelberg (2007)
12. Fiat, A., Naor, M.: Broadcast encryption. In: Stinson, D.R. (ed.) Advances in Cryptology - CRYPTO 1993. LNCS, vol. 773, pp. 480–491. Springer, Heidelberg (1994)

13. Gentry, C., Halevi, S.: Hierarchical identity based encryption with polynomially many levels. In: Reingold, O. (ed.) TCC 2009. LNCS, vol. 5444, pp. 437–456. Springer, Heidelberg (2009)
14. Gentry, C., Silverberg, A.: Hierarchical ID-based cryptography. In: Zheng, Y. (ed.) ASIACRYPT 2002. LNCS, vol. 2501, pp. 548–566. Springer, Heidelberg (2002)
15. Gentry, C., Waters, B.: Adaptive security in broadcast encryption systems (with short ciphertexts). In: Joux, A. (ed.) EUROCRYPT 2009. LNCS, vol. 5479, pp. 171–188. Springer, Heidelberg (2009)
16. Horwitz, J., Lynn, B.: Toward hierarchical identity-based encryption. In: Knudsen, L.R. (ed.) EUROCRYPT 2002. LNCS, vol. 2332, pp. 466–481. Springer, Heidelberg (2002)
17. Halevy, D., Shamir, A.: The LSD broadcast encryption scheme. In: Yung, M. (ed.) CRYPTO 2002. LNCS, vol. 2442, pp. 47–60. Springer, Heidelberg (2002)
18. Libert, B., Paterson, K.G., Quaglia, E.A.: Anonymous broadcast encryption: Adaptive security and efficient constructions in the standard model. In: Fischlin, M., Buchmann, J., Manulis, M. (eds.) PKC 2012. LNCS, vol. 7293, pp. 206–224. Springer, Heidelberg (2012)
19. Lewko, A., Waters, B.: New techniques for dual system encryption and fully secure HIBE with short ciphertexts. In: Micciancio, D. (ed.) TCC 2010. LNCS, vol. 5978, pp. 455–479. Springer, Heidelberg (2010)
20. Lewko, A., Waters, B.: New proof methods for attribute-based encryption: Achieving full security through selective techniques. In: Safavi-Naini, R., Canetti, R. (eds.) CRYPTO 2012. LNCS, vol. 7417, pp. 180–198. Springer, Heidelberg (2012)
21. Ren, Y., Gu, D.: Fully CCA2 secure identity based broadcast encryption without random oracles. Information Processing Letters 109, 527–533 (2009)
22. Shamir, A.: Identity-based cryptosystems and signature schemes. In: Blakely, G.R., Chaum, D. (eds.) CRYPTO 1984. LNCS, vol. 196, pp. 47–53. Springer, Heidelberg (1985)
23. Waters, B.: Efficient identity-based encryption without random oracles. In: Cramer, R. (ed.) EUROCRYPT 2005. LNCS, vol. 3494, pp. 114–127. Springer, Heidelberg (2005)
24. Waters, B.: Dual system encryption: Realizing fully secure IBE and HIBE under simple assumptions. In: Halevi, S. (ed.) CRYPTO 2009. LNCS, vol. 5677, pp. 619–636. Springer, Heidelberg (2009)

Continuous After-the-Fact Leakage-Resilient Key Exchange

Janaka Alawatugoda[1], Colin Boyd[3], and Douglas Stebila[1,2]

[1] School of Electrical Engineering and Computer Science,
[2] Mathematical Sciences School,
Queensland University of Technology, Brisbane, Australia
{janaka.alawatugoda,stebila}@qut.edu.au
[3] Department of Telematics, Norwegian University of Science and Technology,
Trondheim, Norway
colin.boyd@item.ntnu.no

Abstract. Security models for two-party authenticated key exchange (AKE) protocols have developed over time to provide security even when the adversary learns certain secret keys. In this work, we advance the modelling of AKE protocols by considering more granular, *continuous leakage* of long-term secrets of protocol participants: the adversary can adaptively request arbitrary leakage of long-term secrets even after the test session is activated, with limits on the amount of leakage per query but no bounds on the total leakage. We present a security model supporting continuous leakage even when the adversary learns certain ephemeral secrets or session keys, and give a generic construction of a two-pass leakage-resilient key exchange protocol that is secure in the model; our protocol achieves continuous, after-the-fact leakage resilience with not much more cost than a previous protocol with only bounded, non-after-the-fact leakage.

Keywords: leakage resilience, key exchange, continuous leakage, after-the-fact leakage, security models.

1   Introduction

In order to capture leakage (side-channel) attacks, the notion of leakage resilience has been developed. Examples of information considered by leakage or side-channel attacks includes timing information [6,10,19], electromagnetic radiation [16], and power consumption information [23]. Leakage may reveal information about the secret parameters which have been used for computations in cryptosystems. To abstractly model leakage attacks, cryptographers have proposed the notion of *leakage-resilient* cryptography [1,4,9,13,14,18,17,22], where the information that leaks is not fixed, but instead chosen adversarially. As authenticated key exchange is one of the most important cryptographic primitives in practice, it is important to construct key exchange protocols in a leakage-resilient manner.

W. Susilo and Y. Mu (Eds.): ACISP 2014, LNCS 8544, pp. 258–273, 2014.

Earlier key exchange security models, such as the Bellare–Rogaway [5], Canetti–Krawczyk [11], and extended Canetti–Krawczyk (eCK) [21] models, aim to capture security against an adversary who can fully compromise some, but not all secret keys. For example, in the eCK model, a session key should be secure even if the adversary has compromised either the long-term or ephemeral key at the client, and either the long-term or ephemeral key at the server, but not all of the values at one party. This is not a very granular form of leakage, and thus is not fully suitable for modelling side-channel attacks.

This motivates the development of leakage-resilient key exchange security models and protocols. Moriyama and Okamoto [25] and Alawatugoda, Stebila and Boyd [3] proposed key exchange security models to analyze security of leakage-resilient key exchange protocols, using a variant of the eCK model. There are two central limitations in the Moriyama–Okamoto model. First, the total amount of leakage allowed in the Moriyama–Okamoto model is bounded. Second, the adversary cannot obtain any leakage information after the "test" session is activated. The former restriction is troublesome because, in practice, ongoing executions of a protocol may reveal a small amount of leakage each time, and we would like to provide security against this "continuous" leakage. The latter restriction is problematic because we would like to provide security of one session, even if some leakage happens in subsequent sessions. Alawatugoda et al. [3] overcome the limitations of the Moriyama-Okamoto model by proposing a generic key exchange security model (ASB model), which can be instantiated using either continuous leakage model or bounded leakage, both instantiations allowing leakage after the "test" session is activated. Moreover, they proposed a generic construction of a protocol which can be proven secure in their generic model. However, concrete construction of their generic protocol with available cryptographic primitives can only be proven in the ASB bounded leakage model, because currently there exist no continuous leakage-resilient public-key cryptosystems. In this paper, we aim to propose a generic protocol which provides leakage resilience against continuous leakage, even after the "test" session is activated. In order to prove the security of our protocol, we use a slightly weakened variant of the ASB continuous leakage security model.

We now review few different approaches to modelling leakage. These leakage models generally allow the adversary to adaptively choose the leakage function that is evaluated against the long-term secret. The early leakage models generally did not allow leakage after a challenge had been issued, thus prevents the adversary from using subsequent calls to the leakage function to trivially solve the challenge. More recently, *after-the-fact leakage* schemes have been proposed to remove that restriction. We will review these schemes, then describe our contributions.

1.1   Leakage Models

In this section we review few leakage models, which have been widely used to define leakage-resilient security of cryptographic schemes.

Inspired by "cold boot" attacks, Akavia et al. [1] constructed a general framework to model memory attacks for public-key cryptosystems. With the knowledge of the public-key, the adversary can choose an efficiently computable arbitrary leakage function, f, and send it to the leakage oracle. The leakage oracle gives $f(sk)$ to the adversary where sk is the secret key. The only restriction here is that the sum of output length of all the leakage functions that an adversary can obtain is bounded by some parameter λ which is smaller than the size of sk. This model is widely known as *bounded* leakage model.

In the work of Micali et al. [24], a general framework was introduced to model the leakage that occurs during computation with secret parameters. This framework relies on the assumption that *only computation leaks information* and that leakage only occurs from the secret memory portions which are actively involved in a computation. The adversary is allowed to obtain leakage from many computations. Therefore, the overall leakage amount is *unbounded* and in particular it can be larger than the size of the secret key.

Brakerski et al. [9] proposed a leakage model in which it is not assumed that the information is only leaked from the secret memory portions involved in computations. Instead it is assumed that leakage happens from the entire secret memory, but the amount of leakage is bounded per occurrence. In this model, number of leakage occurrences are allowed continuously. Therefore, the overall leakage amount is arbitrarily large. This model is widely known as *continuous* leakage model.

The above leakage models generally address the leakage which happens *before* the *challenge* is given to the adversary. In security experiments for public-key cryptosystems, the challenge is to distinguish the real plaintext corresponding to a particular ciphertext from a random plaintext, whereas in key exchange security models, the challenge is to identify the real session key of a chosen session from a random session key.

After-the-fact Leakage. Leakage which happens after the *challenge* is given to the adversary can be considered as after-the-fact leakage. In leakage models for public-key cryptosystems, after-the-fact leakage is the leakage which happens after the challenge ciphertext is given whereas in leakage security models for key exchange protocols, after-the-fact leakage is the leakage which happens after the test session is activated.

For leakage-resilient public-key encryption there are three properties which may be important differentiators for the different models. One is whether the model allows access to decryption of chosen ciphertexts before (CCA1) or after (CCA2) the challenge is known. The second is whether the leakage allowed to the adversary is *continuous* or *bounded*. The third is whether the leakage is allowed only before the challenge ciphertext is known or also after the fact.

In earlier models, such as that of Naor et al. [26], it was expected that although the adversary is given access to the decryption oracle (CCA2), the adversary cannot be allowed to obtain leakage after the challenge ciphertext is given. This is because the adversary can encode the decryption algorithm and challenge ciphertext with the leakage function and by revealing a few bits of the decrypted value of the challenge ciphertext trivially win the challenge. Subsequently, Halevi et al. [15] introduced chosen plaintext after-the-fact leakage-resilient security on public-key cryptosystems. In their security experiment, the adversary is not allowed to access the decryption oracle. Further, the total leakage amount is also bounded.

Dziembowski et al. [12] defined an adaptively chosen ciphertext attack (CCA2) security experiment in which the adversary is allowed to obtain leakage information even after the challenge ciphertext is given. Their security experiment defines adaptively chosen ciphertext after-the-fact leakage (CCLA2) which can be considered as the strongest security notion of public-key cryptosystems; it allows the adversary adaptive access to the decryption oracle and leakage information even after the challenge ciphertext is given. Furthermore, they allow continuous leakage so the total leakage amount is unbounded. This is achieved by keeping the secret key in a split state, an idea earlier introduced by Kiltz et al. [18], using the reasonable assumption that leakage occurs only when computation takes place, leakage is only bounded per invocation of the secret key while the state is updated after each invocation.

Recall that in key exchange security models, the challenge to the adversary is to distinguish the real session key of a chosen session from a random session key. In the Moriyama–Okamoto [25] key exchange security model, the adversary is not allowed to obtain leakage after the test session is activated, whereas in the ASB model, the adversary is allowed to obtain leakage even after the test session is activated. In the literature there are no key exchange protocols available that are secure against continuous leakage after the test session is activated. Alawatugoda et al. [3] proposed a generic construction of a key exchange protocol which provides security against leakage after the test session is activated, but when instantiated with available cryptographic primitives it does not provide continuous leakage resilience.

1.2 Our Contribution

Alawatugoda et al. [3] mentioned that constructing a continuous after-the-fact leakage-resilient key exchange protocol in the ASB continuous leakage model is an open problem. In this paper, we aim to construct a continuous after-the-fact leakage-resilient key exchange protocol using existing leakage-resilient cryptographic primitives. In order to prove the security of our protocol, we use a *weaker* variant of the generic ASB model's continuous leakage instantiation. The meaning of "weaker" is defined by means of the freshness condition. While weakening a model is generally undesirable, introducing the restrictions allow us to actually achieve the security definition, whereas no instantiation of the ASB continuous leakage-resilient key exchange protocol is known. Thus, we begin by presenting the **continuous after-the-fact leakage model** (CAFL model).

We summarize the adversarial powers of CAFL model in comparison with the adversarial powers of CK model [11], eCK model [21], Moriyama–Okamoto model (MO) [25] and the generic Alawatugoda–Stebila–Boyd model (ASB) [3] in Table 1. There are four Corrupt-EphemeralKeyReveal query combinations which do not trivially expose the session key. In the column "Combinations" of

Table 1. Security models with combinations of allowed reveal and leakage queries

Security model	SessionKey	EphemeralKey	Corrupt	Combinations	Leakage resilience
eCK [21]	Yes	Yes	Yes	4/4	None
MO [25]	Yes	Yes	Yes	4/4	Bounded, not after-the-fact
ASB [3]	Yes	Yes	Yes	4/4	Bounded/Continuous, after-the-fact
CAFL (this paper)	Yes	Yes	Yes	2/4	Continuous, after-the-fact

Table 2. Security and efficiency comparison of key exchange protocols

Protocol	Initiator cost	Responder cost	Security model	Proof model
NAXOS [21]	4 **Exp**	4 **Exp**	eCK	Random oracle
MO [25]	8 **Exp**	8 **Exp**	MO	Standard
ASB [3]	12 **Exp**	12 **Exp**	ASB (Bounded)	Standard
π instantiation	10 **Exp**	10 **Exp**	CAFL	Standard

Table 1, we mention how many of them are allowed in the corresponding security model. We discuss more about query combinations in detail in Section 3.3.

We then construct a generic protocol π which can be proven secure in this model; the protocol is a "key agreement"-style protocol, and it relies on a public-key cryptosystem that is secure against adaptively chosen ciphertext attacks with after-the-fact leakage-resilience (abbreviated as CCLA2). In Table 2, we compare an instantiation of the proposed generic protocol π, with the NAXOS protocol [21], the Moriyama-Okamoto (MO) protocol [25] and the generic ASB protocol instantiation, by means of computation cost, security model and the proof model. The protocol π is instantiated using the CCLA2-secure public-key cryptosystem of Dziembowski et al. [12].

Table 2 shows that the instantiation of protocol π provides significant leakage resilience properties for practically achievable computation costs, and thus π is a viable framework for construction of CAFL-secure protocols. The generic protocol π can be instantiated with any CCLA2-secure public-key cryptosystem. Our proof shows that protocol π can achieve the same leakage tolerance as the underlying public-key cryptosystem tolerates. Moreover, protocol π can be instantiated with smaller computational cost by using *cost effective* CCLA2-secure public-key encryption schemes.

2   Background

In this section we review the formal definitions of the tools we will use to construct our protocol.

2.1   CCLA2-Secure Public-Key Cryptosystems

Dziembowski et al. [12] constructed an adaptively chosen ciphertext after-the-fact leakage-resilient public-key cryptosystem which is secure against continuous leakage.

Definition 1 (Security Against Adaptively Chosen Ciphertext After-the-fact Leakage Attacks (CCLA2)). *Let $k \in \mathbb{N}$ be the security parameter. A public-key cryptosystem* PKE $=$ (KG, Enc, Dec) *is λ-CCLA2 secure if for any probabilistic polynomial time adversary $\mathcal{D}$, the advantage of winning the following distinguishing game is negligible.*

1. $(sk, pk) \leftarrow \mathrm{KG}(1^k)$.

2. $(m_0, m_1, state) \leftarrow \mathcal{D}^{\mathrm{Leak}(\cdot),\mathrm{Dec}(sk,\cdot)}(pk)$
   such that $|m_0| = |m_1|$.

3. $b \leftarrow \{0, 1\}$.

4. $C \leftarrow \mathrm{Enc}(pk, m_b)$.

5. $b' \leftarrow \mathcal{D}^{\mathrm{Leak}(\cdot),\mathrm{Dec}_{\neq C}(sk,\cdot)}(C, state)$.

6. *Output b'. $\mathcal{D}$ wins if $b' = b$.*

Decryption Oracle

$\mathrm{Dec}(sk, c) \rightarrow (sk', m)$ *where m is the corresponding plaintext of the ciphertext c. Update the secret state sk to sk'.*

Leakage Oracle

For any adversary chosen efficiently computable leakage function f, $\mathrm{Leak}(f) \rightarrow f(sk)$ *whenever $|f(sk)| \leq \lambda$. The* **Leakage Oracle** *is called whenever the* **Decryption Oracle** *is called.*

In the Dziembowski et al. [12] public-key cryptosystem, the secret key $sk = (x_1, x_2) \in \mathbb{Z}_p^2$ is split into two parts ℓ_{sk}, r_{sk} such that $\ell_{sk} \leftarrow \mathbb{Z}^n$ at random and $r_{sk} \leftarrow \mathbb{Z}^{n \times 2}$ holding $\ell_{sk} \cdot r_{sk} = sk$, where n is the statistical security parameter. They proved their public-key cryptosystem is CCLA2 secure for $\lambda = 0.15 \cdot n \cdot \log p - 1$. So if we consider $n = 80$ and $\log p$ to be 1024, we can allow $\lambda = 12276$ bits of leakage. Considering only the most expensive computations, the computation cost of Enc and Dec is 5**Exp** where **Exp** is the computational cost of an exponentiation.

2.2 Key Derivation Functions

We review the definitions of key derivation functions proposed by Krawczyk [20]. Secure and efficient key derivation functions are available in the literature, for example based on HMAC [20].

Definition 2 (Key Derivation Function). *A key derivation function* KDF *is an efficient algorithm that accepts as input four arguments: a value σ sampled from a source of keying material Σ, a length value k and two additional arguments, a salt value r defined over a set of possible salt values and a context variable c, both of which are optional i.e., can be set to a null. The* KDF *output is a string of k bits.*

Definition 3 (Source of Key Material). *A source of keying material Σ is a two-valued (σ, κ) probability distribution generated by an efficient probabilistic algorithm, where σ is the secret source key material to be input to the* KDF *and κ is some public knowledge about σ or its distribution.*

Definition 4 (Security of key derivation function with respect to a source of key material). *A key derivation function* KDF *is said to be secure with respect to a source of key material Σ if no feasible attacker $\mathcal{B}$ can win the following distinguishing game with probability significantly better than 1/2:*

1. $(\sigma, \kappa) \leftarrow \Sigma$. *(Both the probability distribution as well as the generating algorithm have been referred by Σ)*
2. *A salt value r is chosen at random from the set of possible salt values defined by* KDF. *(r may be set to a constant or a null value if so defined by* KDF*)*
3. *The attacker $\mathcal{B}$ is provided with κ and r.*
4. *$\mathcal{B}$ chooses arbitrary value k and c.*
5. *A bit $b \leftarrow \{0,1\}$ is chosen at random. If $b = 0$, attacker $\mathcal{B}$ is provided with the output of* KDF(σ, r, k, c) *else $\mathcal{B}$ is given a random string of k bits.*
6. *$\mathcal{B}$ outputs a bit $b' \leftarrow \{0,1\}$. $\mathcal{B}$ wins if $b' = b$.*

2.3   Decision Diffie-Hellman Problem

The decision Diffie-Hellman (DDH) problem is a computational hardness assumption based on discrete logarithms in a cyclic group [7]. Consider a cyclic group $\mathbb{G}$ of order q, with a generator g. For $a, b, c \in \mathbb{Z}_p$, the DDH problem is to distinguish the triple (g^a, g^b, g^{ab}) from the triple (g^a, g^b, g^c).

3   Continuous After-the-Fact Leakage Model

A *key agreement* protocol is an interactive protocol executed between two parties to establish a shared secret key. In this section we introduce the continuous after-the-fact leakage model, (CAFL model), for key exchange. In the CAFL model, the adversary is allowed to adaptively obtain partial leakage on the long-term secret keys even after the test session is activated, as well as reveal session keys, long-term keys, and ephemeral keys.

3.1   Protocol Execution

Parties and Long-term Keys. Let $\mathcal{U} = \{U_1, \ldots, U_{N_P}\}$ be a set of N_P parties. Each party U_i where $i \in [1, N_P]$ has a pair of long-term public and secret keys, (pk_{U_i}, sk_{U_i}).

Sessions. Each party may run multiple instances of the protocol concurrently or sequentially; we use the term *principal* to refer a party involved in a protocol instance, and the term *session* to identify a protocol instance at a principal. The notation $\Pi_{U,V}^s$ represents the sth session at the owner principal U, with intended partner principal V. The principal which sends the first protocol message of a session is the *initiator* of the session, and the principal which responds to the first protocol message is the *responder* of the session. A session $\Pi_{U,V}^s$ enters an *accepted* state when it computes a session key. Note that a session may terminate without ever entering into the accepted state. The information of whether a session has terminated with or without acceptance is public.

Adversary Interaction. The adversary (a probabilistic algorithm) controls all interaction and communication between parties. In particular, the adversary initiates sessions at parties and delivers protocol messages; it can create, change, delete, or reorder messages. The adversary can also compromise certain short-term and long-term secrets. Notably, whenever the party performs an operation using its long-term key, the adversary obtains some leakage information about the long-term key.

The following query allows the adversary $\mathcal{A}$ to run the protocol, modelling normal communication.

- Send$(U, V, s, m, \mathbf{f})$ query: The oracle $\Pi_{U,V}^s$, computes the next protocol message according to the protocol specification on receipt of m, and sends it to the adversary $\mathcal{A}$, along with the leakage $\mathbf{f}(sk_U)$ as described in Section 3.2. $\mathcal{A}$ can also use this query to activate a new protocol instance as an initiator with blank m and $\mathbf{f}$.

The following queries allow the adversary $\mathcal{A}$ to compromise certain session specific ephemeral secrets and long-term secrets from the protocol principals.

- SessionKeyReveal(U, V, s) query: $\mathcal{A}$ is given the session key of the oracle $\Pi_{U,V}^s$, if the oracle $\Pi_{U,V}^s$ is in the accepted state.
- EphemeralKeyReveal(U, V, s) query: $\mathcal{A}$ is given the ephemeral keys of the oracle $\Pi_{U,V}^s$.
- Corrupt(U) query: $\mathcal{A}$ is given the long-term secrets of the principal U. This query does not reveal any session keys or ephemeral keys to $\mathcal{A}$.

3.2   Modelling Leakage

In this key exchange security model we consider *continuous leakage of the long-term secret keys* of protocol principals, because long-term secret keys are not one-time secrets, but they last for multiple protocol sessions. Leakage of long-term secret key from one session affects to the security of another session which uses the same long-term secret key. Considering side-channel attacks which can be mounted against key exchange protocols, the most realistic way to obtain the leakage information of long-term secret keys is from the protocol computations which use long-term secret keys. Hence, following the premise "only computation leaks information" [24], we have modeled the leakage to occur where computation takes place using secret keys. By issuing a Send query, the adversary will get a protocol message which is computed according to the normal protocol computations. Therefore, the instance of a Send query would be the appropriate instance to address the leakage occurs due to a computation which uses a long-term secret key. Thus, sending an adversary-chosen leakage function, $\mathbf{f}$, with the Send query would reflect the premise "only computation leaks information".

Further, we assume that the amount of leakage of a secret key is bounded by a leakage parameter λ, per computation. The adversary is allowed to obtain leakage from many computations continuously. Hence, the overall leakage amount is unbounded.

Remark 1 (Corrupt query vs Leakage queries). By issuing a Corrupt query, the adversary gets the party's entire long-term secret key. Separately, by issuing leakage queries (using leakage function **f** embedded with the Send query) the adversary gets λ-bounded amount of leakage information about the long-term secret key. It may seem paradoxical to consider Corrupt and Leakage queries at the same time. But there are good reasons to consider both.

- A *non-leakage* version of CAFL model (Send query without **f**) addresses KCI attacks, because the adversary is allowed to corrupt the owner of the test session before the activation of the test session. In the CAFL model, we allow the adversary to obtain leakage from the partner of the test session, in addition to allowing the adversary to corrupt the owner of the test session.
- A *non-leakage* version of CAFL model (Send query without **f**) addresses partial weak forward secrecy, because the adversary is allowed to corrupt either of the protocol principals, but not both, after the test session is activated. In the CAFL model, we allow the adversary to obtain leakage from the uncorrupted principal, in addition to allowing the adversary to corrupt one of the protocol principals.

Hence, the CAFL model allows the adversary to obtain more information than a *non-leakage* version of CAFL model.

3.3   Defining Security

In this section we give formal definitions for partner sessions, freshness of a session and security in the CAFL model.

Definition 5 (Partner sessions in CAFL model). *Two oracles $\Pi_{U,V}^s$ and $\Pi_{U',V'}^{s'}$ are said to be partners if:*

1. *$\Pi_{U,V}^s$ and $\Pi_{U',V'}^{s'}$ have computed session keys and*
2. *Sent messages from $\Pi_{U,V}^s$ = Received messages to $\Pi_{U',V'}^{s'}$ and*
3. *Sent messages from $\Pi_{U',V'}^{s'}$ = Received messages to $\Pi_{U,V}^s$ and*
4. *$U' = V$ and $V' = U$ and*
5. *If U is the initiator then V is the responder, or vise versa.*

A protocol is said to be *correct* if two partner oracles compute identical session keys in the presence of a passive adversary. Once the oracle $\Pi_{U,V}^s$ has accepted a session key, asking the following query the adversary $\mathcal{A}$ attempt to distinguish it from a random session key. The Test query is used to formalize the notion of the semantic security of a key exchange protocol.

- Test(U, V, s) query: When $\mathcal{A}$ asks the Test query, the oracle $\Pi_{U,V}^s$ first chooses a random bit $b \leftarrow \{0, 1\}$ and if $b = 1$ then the actual session key is returned to $\mathcal{A}$, otherwise a random string chosen from the same session key space is returned to $\mathcal{A}$. This query is only allowed to be asked once across all sessions.

We now define what it means for a session to be λ-CAFL-*fresh* in the CAFL model.

Definition 6 (λ-CAFL-freshness). *Let λ be the leakage bound per occurrence. An oracle $\Pi_{U,V}^s$ is said to be λ-CAFL-fresh if and only if:*

1. *The oracle $\Pi_{U,V}^s$ or its partner, $\Pi_{V,U}^{s'}$ (if it exists) has not been asked a* SessionKeyReveal.
2. *If the partner $\Pi_{V,U}^{s'}$ exists, none of the following combinations have been asked:*
   (a) Corrupt(U) *and* Corrupt(V).
   (b) Corrupt(U) *and* EphemeralKeyReveal(U, V, s).
   (c) Corrupt(V) *and* EphemeralKeyReveal(V, U, s').
   (d) EphemeralKeyReveal(U, V, s) *and* EphemeralKeyReveal(V, U, s').
3. *If the partner $\Pi_{V,U}^{s'}$ does not exist, none of the following combinations have been asked:*
   (a) Corrupt(V).
   (b) Corrupt(U) *and* EphemeralKeyReveal(U, V, s).
4. *For each* Send($\cdot, U, \cdot, \cdot, \mathbf{f}$) *query, the output of $\mathbf{f}$ is at most λ bits.*
5. *For each* Send($\cdot, V, \cdot, \cdot, \mathbf{f}$) *query, the output of $\mathbf{f}$ is at most λ bits.*

When the adversary asks EphemeralKeyReveal and Corrupt queries, there are two Corrupt–EphemeralKeyReveal query combinations which trivially expose the session key of an oracle.

1. Corrupt(U) and EphemeralKeyReveal(U, V, s).
2. Corrupt(V) and EphemeralKeyReveal(V, U, s').

As in the other models we have compared with [21,25,3] we do not allow above combinations in the freshness condition, as they trivially expose the session key of oracles $\Pi_{U,V}^s$ and $\Pi_{V,U}^{s'}$. Differently, there are four Corrupt–EphemeralKeyReveal query combinations which do not trivially expose the session key an oracle.

1. Corrupt(U) and Corrupt(V).
2. Corrupt(U) and EphemeralKeyReveal(V, U, s).
3. Corrupt(V) and EphemeralKeyReveal(U, V, s').
4. EphemeralKeyReveal(V, U, s) and EphemeralKeyReveal(U, V, s').

All the models we consider [21,25,3] allow above combinations in the freshness condition, whereas our CAFL model does not allow the query combinations 1 and 4 in the freshness condition. In that sense the CAFL model is weaker than the ASB continuous leakage model.

Security of a key exchange protocol in the CAFL model is defined using the following security game, which is played by a probabilistic polynomial time adversary $\mathcal{A}$ against the protocol challenger.

– **Stage 1:** $\mathcal{A}$ may ask any of Send, SessionKeyReveal, EphemeralKeyReveal and Corrupt queries to any oracle at will.
– **Stage 2:** $\mathcal{A}$ chooses a λ-CAFL-fresh oracle and asks a Test query.

- **Stage 3:** $\mathcal{A}$ continues asking Send, SessionKeyReveal, EphemeralKeyReveal and Corrupt queries. $\mathcal{A}$ may not ask a query that violates the λ-CAFL-freshness of the test session.
- **Stage 4:** Eventually, $\mathcal{A}$ outputs the bit $b' \leftarrow \{0, 1\}$ which is its guess of the value b on the test session. $\mathcal{A}$ wins if $b' = b$.

$Succ(\mathcal{A})$ is the event that $\mathcal{A}$ wins the above security game. The definition of security follows.

Definition 7 (λ-**CAFL-security**). *A protocol π is said to be λ-CAFL-secure if there is no probabilistic polynomial time algorithm $\mathcal{A}$ that can win the above game with non-negligible advantage. The advantage of an adversary $\mathcal{A}$ is defined as $Adv_{\pi}^{\mathrm{CAFL}}(\mathcal{A}) = |2\Pr(Succ_{\mathcal{A}}) - 1|$.*

3.4 Practical Interpretation of Security of CAFL Model

We review the relationship between the CAFL model and real world attack scenarios.

- **Active adversarial capabilities:** Send queries address the powers of an active adversary who can control the message flow over the network.
- **Side-channel attacks:** Leakage functions are embedded with the Send query. Thus, a wide variety of side-channel attacks based on **continuous leakage of long-term secrets** are addressed, assuming that the leakage happens when computations take place in principals.
- **Cold-boot attacks:** Corrupt queries address situations which reveal the long-term secret keys of protocol principals like in cold-boot attacks.
- **Malware attacks:** EphemeralKeyReveal queries cover the malware attacks which steal stored ephemeral keys, given that the long-term keys may be securely stored separately from the ephemeral keys in places such as smart cards or hardware security modules. Separately, Corrupt queries address malware attacks which steal the long-term secret keys of protocol principals.
- **Weak random number generators:** After knowing a previous set of randomly generated ephemeral values the adversary may be able to identify the statistical pattern of the random number generator and hence correctly guess the next value with a high probability. EphemeralKeyReveal query addresses situations where the adversary can get the ephemeral secrets.
- **Known key attacks:** SessionKeyReveal query covers the attacks which can be mounted by knowing past session keys.
- **Key compromise impersonation attacks:** λ-CAFL-freshness allows the adversary to corrupt the owner of the test session before the activation of the test session. Hence, the CAFL model security protects against the key compromise impersonation attacks.
- **Partial weak forward secrecy:** λ-CAFL-freshness allows the adversary to corrupt either of the protocol principals, but not both, after the test session is activated. Hence, the CAFL model addresses partial weak forward secrecy.

Table 3. Protocol π. Underline denotes operations to which leakage functions apply

A (Initiator)		B (Responder)
	Initial Setup	
$sk_A, pk_A \leftarrow \mathrm{KG}(1^k)$		$sk_B, pk_B \leftarrow \mathrm{KG}(1^k)$
	Protocol Execution	
$r_A \leftarrow \{0,1\}^k$		$r_B \leftarrow \{0,1\}^k$
$C_A \leftarrow \mathrm{Enc}(pk_B, r_A)$	$\xrightarrow{A, C_A}$	$(sk'_B, r_A) \leftarrow \underline{\mathrm{Dec}}(sk_B, C_A)$
		$sk_B \leftarrow sk'_B$
$(sk'_A, r_B) \leftarrow \underline{\mathrm{Dec}}(sk_A, C_B)$	$\xleftarrow{B, C_B}$	$C_B \leftarrow \mathrm{Enc}(pk_A, r_B)$
$sk_A \leftarrow sk'_A$		
$K_{AB} \leftarrow \mathrm{KDF}(A, B, r_A, r_B)$		$K_{AB} \leftarrow \mathrm{KDF}(A, B, r_A, r_B)$
	K_{AB} is the session key	

Although our model is a weaker variant of the ASB continuous leakage model, it addresses all the attack scenarios which are addressed by the ASB model, except *weak forward secrecy*. Instead, our model addresses *partial weak forward secrecy*. Hence, our model is very similar to the generic ASB model and interprets most of real world attack scenarios.

4 Protocol π

In Table 3 we show the generic construction of protocol π. Enc and Dec are the encryption and decryption algorithms of the underlying adaptively chosen ciphertext after-the-fact leakage (CCLA2) secure public-key cryptosystem, PKE. KDF is a secure key derivation function which generates the session key of length k. The protocol π is a key agreement protocol, in which each of the principals randomly chooses its ephemeral secret key, encrypts it with the public-key of the intended partner principal using the encryption algorithm Enc, and sends the encrypted message to the intended partner principal. After exchanging the ephemeral secrets both principals compute the session key with ephemeral secrets and identities of the two principals, using the key derivation function KDF. We underlined the computations which could leak information about secret keys.

Theorem 1. *The protocol π is λ-CAFL-secure, whenever the underlying public-key cryptosystem PKE is CCLA2 secure and the key derivation function KDF is secure with respect to a uniformly random key material.*

In order to formally prove the CAFL-security of the protocol π we use the game hopping technique [27]; define a sequence of games and relate the adversary's advantage of distinguishing each game from the previous game to the advantage of breaking one of the underlying cryptographic primitive. The proof structure is similar to Boyd et al. [8]. Following the proof sketch of Theorem 1 is presented while the complete security proof is available in the full version of this paper [2].

Proof sketch. Assume that the adversary $\mathcal{A}$ can win the challenge against the protocol π challenger with non negligible advantage $Adv_\pi^{\mathrm{CAFL}}(\mathcal{A})$. The proof is split into two cases.

Case 1: The owner of the test session is corrupted In this case we consider the situation that $\mathcal{A}$ corrupts the owner of the test session but not the partner.

Game 1: This game is the original game. When the Test query is asked, the Game 1 challenger chooses a random bit $b \leftarrow \{0,1\}$. If $b = 1$, the real session key is given to $\mathcal{A}$, otherwise a random value chosen from the same session key space is given.

Game 2: Same as Game 1 with the following exception: before $\mathcal{A}$ begins, two distinct random principals $U^*, V^* \leftarrow \{U_1, \ldots, U_{N_P}\}$ are chosen and two random numbers $s^*, t^* \leftarrow \{1, \ldots, N_s\}$ are chosen, where N_P is the number of protocol principals and N_S is the number of sessions on a principal. The oracle $\Pi_{U^*,V^*}^{s^*}$ is chosen as the *target session* and the oracle $\Pi_{V^*,U^*}^{t^*}$ is chosen as the *partner* to the target session. If the test session is *not* the oracle $\Pi_{U^*,V^*}^{s^*}$ or the partner to the oracle is not $\Pi_{V^*,U^*}^{t^*}$, the Game 2 challenger aborts the game.

Game 3: Same as Game 2 with the following exception: the Game 3 challenger chooses a random value $r' \leftarrow \{0,1\}^k$.

- If the test session is on the initiator, the challenger computes $K_{U^*V^*} \leftarrow \text{KDF}(U^*, V^*, r', r_{V^*})$.
- If the test session is on the responder, the challenger computes $K_{U^*V^*} \leftarrow \text{KDF}(V^*, U^*, r_{V^*}, r')$.

Game 4: Same as Game 3 with the following exception: the Game 4 challenger randomly chooses $K \leftarrow \{0,1\}^k$ and sends it to the adversary $\mathcal{A}$ as the answer to the Test query.

Differences between Games

In this section the adversary's advantage of distinguishing each game from the previous game is investigated. $Succ_{\text{Game }x}(\mathcal{A})$ denotes the event that the adversary $\mathcal{A}$ wins Game x, $Adv_{\text{Game }x}(\mathcal{A})$ denotes the advantage of the adversary $\mathcal{A}$ of winning Game x.

Game 1 is the original game. Hence,

$$Adv_{\text{Game 1}}(\mathcal{A}) = Adv_\pi^{\text{CAFL}}(\mathcal{A}). \tag{1}$$

Game 1 and Game 2. The probability of Game 2 to be halted due to incorrect choice of the test session is $1 - \frac{1}{N_P^2 N_s^2}$. Unless the incorrect choice happens, Game 2 is identical to Game 1. Hence,

$$Adv_{\text{Game 2}}(\mathcal{A}) = \frac{1}{N_P^2 N_s^2} Adv_{\text{Game 1}}(\mathcal{A}). \tag{2}$$

Game 2 and Game 3. We introduce an algorithm $\mathcal{D}$ which is constructed using the adversary $\mathcal{A}$. If $\mathcal{A}$ can distinguish the difference between Game 2 and Game 3, then $\mathcal{D}$ can be used against the CCLA2 challenger of underlying public-key cryptosystem, PKE. The algorithm $\mathcal{D}$ uses the public-key of the CCLA2 challenger as the public-key of the protocol principal V^* and generates public/secret key pairs for all other protocol principals. $\mathcal{D}$ runs a copy of $\mathcal{A}$ and interacts with $\mathcal{A}$, such that it is interacting with either Game 2 or Game 3. $\mathcal{D}$ picks two random strings, $r_0', r_1' \leftarrow \{0,1\}^k$ and passes them to the CCLA2 challenger. From the CCLA2 challenger, $\mathcal{D}$ receives a challenge ciphertext C such that $C \leftarrow \text{Enc}(pk_{V^*}, r')$ where $r' = r_0'$ or $r' = r_1'$. The procedure of answering queries is explained in detail in full version of this paper [2].

If r_1' is the decryption of C coming *from* the owner of the test session, U^*, the simulation constructed by $\mathcal{D}$ is identical to Game 2 whereas if r_0' is the decryption of C, the simulation constructed by $\mathcal{D}$ is identical to Game 3. If $\mathcal{A}$ can distinguish the difference between Game 2 and Game 3, then $\mathcal{D}$ can distinguish whether $C \leftarrow \text{Enc}(pk_{V^*}, r_0')$ or $C \leftarrow \text{Enc}(pk_{V^*}, r_1')$.

The algorithm $\mathcal{D}$ plays the CCLA2 game against the public-key cryptosystem PKE according to the Definition 1 since $\mathcal{D}$ does not ask the decryption of the challenge ciphertext C. Hence,

$$|Adv_{\text{Game } 2}(\mathcal{A}) - Adv_{\text{Game } 3}(\mathcal{A})| \leq Adv^{\text{PKE}}(\mathcal{D}). \tag{3}$$

Game 3 and Game 4. We introduce an algorithm $\mathcal{B}$ which is constructed using the adversary $\mathcal{A}$. If $\mathcal{A}$ can distinguish the difference between Game 3 and Game 4, then $\mathcal{B}$ can be used to distinguish whether the value K is computed using KDF or randomly chosen. $\mathcal{B}$ receives K from the KDF challenger, such that K is computed using the KDF or randomly chosen from the session key space. If K is computed using the KDF, the simulation constructed by $\mathcal{B}$ is identical to Game 3 whereas if K is randomly chosen, the simulation constructed by $\mathcal{B}$ is identical to Game 4. If $\mathcal{A}$ can distinguish the difference between Game 3 and Game 4, then $\mathcal{B}$ can distinguish whether the value K is computed using KDF or randomly chosen. Hence,

$$|Adv_{\text{Game } 3}(\mathcal{A}) - Adv_{\text{Game } 4}(\mathcal{A})| \leq Adv^{\text{KDF}}(\mathcal{B}). \tag{4}$$

Semantic security of the session key in Game 4. Since the session key K of $\Pi_{U^*, V^*}^{s^*}$ is chosen randomly and independently from all other values, $\mathcal{A}$ does not have any advantage in Game 4. Hence,

$$Adv_{\text{Game } 4}(\mathcal{A}) = 0. \tag{5}$$

Using equations (1)–(5) we find,

$$Adv_{\pi}^{\text{CAFL}}(\mathcal{A}) \leq N_P^2 N_s^2 \big(Adv^{\text{PKE}}(\mathcal{D}) + Adv^{\text{KDF}}(\mathcal{B}) \big). \tag{6}$$

Case 2: The owner of the test session is not corrupted In this case we consider the situation that $\mathcal{A}$ corrupts the partner of the test session but not the owner. The proof structure and games are similar to the previous case. The only difference in this case is that the algorithm $\mathcal{D}$ uses the public-key of the CCLA2 challenger as the public-key of the protocol principal U^*. In this case we find,

$$Adv_\pi^{\text{CAFL}}(\mathcal{A}) \leq N_P^2 N_s^2 \big(Adv^{\text{PKE}}(\mathcal{D}) + Adv^{\text{KDF}}(\mathcal{B})\big). \tag{7}$$

Combining Case 1 and Case 2. In both cases we can see the adversary $\mathcal{A}$'s advantage of winning against the protocol π challenger is

$$Adv_\pi^{\text{CAFL}}(\mathcal{A}) \leq N_P^2 N_s^2 \big(Adv^{\text{PKE}}(\mathcal{D}) + Adv^{\text{KDF}}(\mathcal{B})\big).$$

5 Future Work

The challenge is to achieve a secure protocol in the ASB continuous leakage model. The ASB continuous leakage model is a continuous leakage variant of the eCK model. There are two main techniques for constructing (non-leakage-resilient) eCK-secure protocols: use of the so-called "NAXOS trick", in which the long-term and ephemeral secret keys are hashed together to derive the ephemeral Diffie–Hellman exponent, and MQV-style protocols, which algebraically combine ephemeral and static Diffie–Hellman computations. Since the NAXOS trick involves a calculation based on the secret key, adapting such a protocol requires the use of a continuous leakage-resilient NAXOS trick. By using pair-generation-indistinguishable continuous-after-the-fact-leakage-resilient public-key cryptosystems, it would be possible to obtain a continuous leakage-resilient NAXOS trick as shown in Alawatugoda et al. [3]. A leakage-resilient protocol based on MQV-style computations is also an interesting open question.

References

1. Akavia, A., Goldwasser, S., Vaikuntanathan, V.: Simultaneous hardcore bits and cryptography against memory attacks. In: Reingold, O. (ed.) TCC 2009. LNCS, vol. 5444, pp. 474–495. Springer, Heidelberg (2009)
2. Alawatugoda, J., Boyd, C., Stebila, D.: Continuous after-the-fact leakage-resilient key exchange (full version). IACR Cryptology ePrint Archive, Report 2014/264 (2014)
3. Alawatugoda, J., Stebila, D., Boyd, C.: Modelling after-the-fact leakage for key exchange (full version). IACR Cryptology ePrint Archive, Report 2014/131 (2014)
4. Alwen, J., Dodis, Y., Wichs, D.: Leakage-resilient public-key cryptography in the bounded-retrieval model. In: Halevi, S. (ed.) CRYPTO 2009. LNCS, vol. 5677, pp. 36–54. Springer, Heidelberg (2009)
5. Bellare, M., Rogaway, P.: Entity authentication and key distribution. In: Stinson, D.R. (ed.) CRYPTO 1993. LNCS, vol. 773, pp. 232–249. Springer, Heidelberg (1994)
6. Bernstein, D.J.: Cache-timing attacks on AES. Technical report (2005), http://cr.yp.to/antiforgery/cachetiming-20050414.pdf

7. Boneh, D.: The decision Diffie-Hellman problem. In: Buhler, J.P. (ed.) ANTS 1998. LNCS, vol. 1423, pp. 48–63. Springer, Heidelberg (1998)
8. Boyd, C., Cliff, Y., Nieto, J.M.G., Paterson, K.G.: One-round key exchange in the standard model. International Journal of Advanced Computer Technology, 181–199 (2009)
9. Brakerski, Z., Kalai, Y.T., Katz, J., Vaikuntanathan, V.: Overcoming the hole in the bucket: Public-key cryptography resilient to continual memory leakage. IACR Cryptology ePrint Archive, Report 2010/278 (2010)
10. Brumley, D., Boneh, D.: Remote timing attacks are practical. In: USENIX Security Symposium, pp. 1–14 (2003)
11. Canetti, R., Krawczyk, H.: Analysis of key-exchange protocols and their use for building secure channels. In: Pfitzmann, B. (ed.) EUROCRYPT 2001. LNCS, vol. 2045, pp. 453–474. Springer, Heidelberg (2001)
12. Dziembowski, S., Faust, S.: Leakage-resilient cryptography from the inner-product extractor. In: Lee, D.H., Wang, X. (eds.) ASIACRYPT 2011. LNCS, vol. 7073, pp. 702–721. Springer, Heidelberg (2011)
13. Dziembowski, S., Pietrzak, K.: Leakage-resilient cryptography. In: IEEE Symposium on Foundations of Computer Science, pp. 293–302 (2008)
14. Faust, S., Kiltz, E., Pietrzak, K., Rothblum, G.N.: Leakage-resilient signatures. IACR Cryptology ePrint Archive, Report 2009/282 (2009)
15. Halevi, S., Lin, H.: After-the-fact leakage in public-key encryption. In: Ishai, Y. (ed.) TCC 2011. LNCS, vol. 6597, pp. 107–124. Springer, Heidelberg (2011)
16. Hutter, M., Mangard, S., Feldhofer, M.: Power and EM attacks on passive 13.56MHz RFID devices. In: Paillier, P., Verbauwhede, I. (eds.) CHES 2007. LNCS, vol. 4727, pp. 320–333. Springer, Heidelberg (2007)
17. Katz, J., Vaikuntanathan, V.: Signature schemes with bounded leakage resilience. In: Matsui, M. (ed.) ASIACRYPT 2009. LNCS, vol. 5912, pp. 703–720. Springer, Heidelberg (2009)
18. Kiltz, E., Pietrzak, K.: Leakage resilient elgamal encryption. In: Abe, M. (ed.) ASIACRYPT 2010. LNCS, vol. 6477, pp. 595–612. Springer, Heidelberg (2010)
19. Kocher, P.C.: Timing attacks on implementations of Diffie-Hellman, RSA, DSS, and other systems. In: Koblitz, N. (ed.) CRYPTO 1996. LNCS, vol. 1109, pp. 104–113. Springer, Heidelberg (1996)
20. Krawczyk, H.: On extract-then-expand key derivation functions and an HMAC-based KDF (2008), http://webee.technion.ac.il/~hugo/kdf/kdf.pdf
21. LaMacchia, B.A., Lauter, K., Mityagin, A.: Stronger security of authenticated key exchange. In: Susilo, W., Liu, J.K., Mu, Y. (eds.) ProvSec 2007. LNCS, vol. 4784, pp. 1–16. Springer, Heidelberg (2007)
22. Malkin, T., Teranishi, I., Vahlis, Y., Yung, M.: Signatures resilient to continual leakage on memory and computation. In: Ishai, Y. (ed.) TCC 2011. LNCS, vol. 6597, pp. 89–106. Springer, Heidelberg (2011)
23. Messerges, T., Dabbish, E., Sloan, R.: Examining smart-card security under the threat of power analysis attacks. IEEE Transactions on Computers, 541–552 (2002)
24. Micali, S., Reyzin, L.: Physically observable cryptography (extended abstract). In: Naor, M. (ed.) TCC 2004. LNCS, vol. 2951, pp. 278–296. Springer, Heidelberg (2004)
25. Moriyama, D., Okamoto, T.: Leakage resilient eCK-secure key exchange protocol without random oracles. In: ASIACCS, pp. 441–447 (2011)
26. Naor, M., Segev, G.: Public-key cryptosystems resilient to key leakage. In: Halevi, S. (ed.) CRYPTO 2009. LNCS, vol. 5677, pp. 18–35. Springer, Heidelberg (2009)
27. Shoup, V.: Sequences of games: a tool for taming complexity in security proofs. IACR Cryptology ePrint Archive, Report 2004/332 (2004)

Sakai-Ohgishi-Kasahara Identity-Based Non-Interactive Key Exchange Scheme, Revisited

Yu Chen[1], Qiong Huang[2], and Zongyang Zhang[3,4,*]

[1] State Key Laboratory of Information Security (SKLOIS),
Institute of Information Engineering, Chinese Academy of Sciences, China
chenyu@iie.ac.cn
[2] College of Informatics, South China Agricultural University, China
csqhuang@gmail.com
[3] National Institute of Advanced Industrial Science and Technology, Japan
[4] Shanghai Jiao Tong University, China
zongyang.zhang@aist.go.jp

Abstract. Identity-based non-interactive key exchange (IB-NIKE) is a powerful but a bit overlooked primitive in identity-based cryptography. While identity-based encryption and signature have been extensively investigated over the past three decades, IB-NIKE has remained largely unstudied. Currently, there are only few IB-NIKE schemes in the literature. Among them, Sakai-Ohgishi-Kasahara (SOK) scheme is the first efficient and secure IB-NIKE scheme, which has great influence on follow-up works. However, the SOK scheme required its identity mapping function to be modeled as a random oracle to prove security. Moreover, the existing security proof heavily relies on the ability of programming the random oracle. It is unknown whether such reliance is inherent.

In this work, we intensively revisit the SOK IB-NIKE scheme, and present a series of possible and impossible results in the random oracle model and the standard model. In the random oracle model, we first improve previous security analysis for the SOK IB-NIKE scheme by giving a tighter reduction. We then use meta-reduction technique to show that the SOK scheme is unlikely proven to be secure based on the computational bilinear Diffie-Hellman (CBDH) assumption without programming the random oracle. In the standard model, we show how to instantiate the random oracle in the SOK scheme with a concrete hash function from admissible hash functions (AHFs) and indistinguishability obfuscation. The resulting scheme is fully adaptive-secure based on the decisional bilinear Diffie-Hellman inversion (DBDHI) assumption. To the best of our knowledge, this is first fully adaptive-secure IB-NIKE scheme in the standard model that does not explicitly require multilinear maps. Previous schemes in the standard model either have merely selective security or use multilinear maps as a key ingredient. Of particular interest, we generalize the definition of AHFs, and propose a generic construction which enables AHFs with previously unachieved parameters.

---

* Corresponding author.

W. Susilo and Y. Mu (Eds.): ACISP 2014, LNCS 8544, pp. 274–289, 2014.

1   Introduction

Identity-based non-interactive key exchange (IB-NIKE) is a natural extension of NIKE [11] in the identity-based setting, which enables any two parties registered in the same key generator center (KGC) to agree on a unique shared key without any interaction. IB-NIKE has important applications in managing keys and enabling secure communications in mobile ad hoc and sensor networks. The advantages of IB-NIKE, in terms of reducing communication costs and latency in a realistic adversarial environment, are demonstrated in [8].

In 2000, Sakai, Ohgishi and Kasahara [22] proposed the first efficient and secure IB-NIKE scheme in the random oracle model, namely the SOK scheme (with security models and formal proofs in follow up works [12, 20]). Despite the appearing of IB-NIKE in this celebrated work on identity-based cryptography, it had received less attention as a fundamental primitive in its own right over the past decade. In the last year, we have seen remarkable progress on this topic. Freire et al. [15] constructed (poly, 2)-programmable hash functions (PHFs) from multilinear maps. By substituting the random oracle in the original SOK scheme with (poly, 2)-PHFs, they obtained the first IB-NIKE scheme in the standard model. Boneh and Waters [6] demonstrated that constrained pseudo-random functions that support left/right predicate imply IB-NIKE. Particularly, they constructed such specific constrained PRFs based on the decisional bilinear Diffie-Hellman (DBDH) assumption, and the resulting IB-NIKE scheme (the BW scheme) can be viewed as a variant of the SOK scheme, which is also only proven secure in the random oracle model. Boneh and Zhandry [7] proposed a construction of multiparty IB-NIKE from PRG, constrained PRFs, and indistinguishability obfuscation. However, their construction only has selective security. Hnece, how to achieve fully adaptive security is left as an open problem.

1.1   Motivations

For a security reduction $\mathcal{R}$ that converts any adversary $\mathcal{A}$ with advantage $\mathsf{Adv}_{\mathcal{A}}$ against some hard problem in running time $\mathsf{Time}_{\mathcal{A}}$ to an algorithm $\mathcal{B}$ with advantage $\mathsf{Adv}_{\mathcal{B}}$ against the target cryptographic scheme in running time $\mathsf{Time}_{\mathcal{B}}$, we say it is tight if $\mathsf{Adv}_{\mathcal{B}}/\mathsf{Adv}_{\mathcal{A}}$ (advantage loose factor) is close to 1 and $\mathsf{Time}_{\mathcal{B}} - \mathsf{Time}_{\mathcal{A}}$ (time loose factor) is close to 0, and loose otherwise. It has been well known that besides theoretical interest, a tighter reduction is of utmost practical importance. To obtain the same security level, cryptographic schemes with tighter reduction generally admits more efficient implementations [1]. The exisiting proof [20] for the SOK scheme programs the random oracle H (acting as the identity mapping function in the construction) with "all-but-one" technique to implement partitioning strategy.[1] As a consequence, the advantage loose

---

[1] In the case of IB-NIKE, the partitioning strategy is to partition the set of all identities into "extractable" and "unextractable" ones. The reduction hopes that all identities for which an adversary requests for a secret key are extractable, while the target identities are unextractable.

factor is around $1/2^{180}$, which is far from tight. It is interesting to know if we can provide an alternative proof with tighter reduction.

Both the original security reduction [20] and our new security reduction (as we will show in Section 3.1) for the SOK scheme exploit full programmability of the random oracle model (ROM) to implement partitioning strategy. Such property allows the reduction to program the random oracle (RO) arbitrarily as long as the output distributes uniformly and independently over the range. This full-fledged model is usually refereed as fully programming ROM (FPROM). Full programmability is a strong property in that it does not quite match with the features of cryptographic hash functions. Therefore, two weaker random oracle models are proposed by constraining the ability of the reduction to program the RO. The randomly programming ROM (RPROM) [14] allows the reduction to program the RO with random instead of arbitrary values, while the non-programming ROM (NPROM) forbids the reduction to program the RO. Since the NPROM is the weakest one among the above three random oracle models and is closest to the standard model, it is curious to know if the SOK scheme could be proven secure in the NPROM.

As previously mentioned, Freire et al. [15] successfully instantiated the SOK scheme in the standard model by substituting the random oracle H with (poly, 2)-programmable hash functions (PHFs). However, the construction of (poly, 2)-PHFs requires multilinear maps [16]. So far, we do not have candidates for multilinear maps between groups with cryptographically hard problems. Instead, we only have concrete candidate for an "approximation" of multilinear maps, named graded encoding systems [16]. Hence, we are motivated to find an alternative approach of substituting the random oracle in the SOK scheme, with the hope that the replacements are not explicitly involved with multilinear maps. Recently, Hohenberger, Sahai and Waters [19] gave a way to instantiate the random oracle with concrete hash functions from indistinguishability obfuscation[2] in the "full domain hash" signatures. It is natural to ask if their approach can extend to other applications, and in particular, the SOK scheme.

1.2   Our Results

In the remainder of this paper, we give negative or affirmative answers to the above questions. We summarize our main results as below.

Being aware of the usage of "all-but-one" programming technique is the reason that makes the original reduction loose, we are motivated to find an alternative programming technique that admits tighter reduction. Observing the structural similarities between the SOK IB-NIKE scheme and the Boneh-Franklin [4] IBE scheme and the Boneh-Lynn-Shacham (BLS) [5] short signature, we are inspired to program the random oracle H in the SOK scheme with the flipping coin technique developed in [10], which were successfully employed in the reductions for

---

[2] Although currently the only known construction of indistinguishability obfuscation ($i\mathcal{O}$) is from multilinear maps [18], it is still possible that $i\mathcal{O}$ can be constructed from other primitives.

the latter two well-known schemes. Roughly speaking, the flipping coin technique usually conducts as follows: to program $H(x)$ (x is an identity in the IBC setting or a message in the signature setting), the reduction flips a random coin once, then programs $H(x)$ according to the coin value in two different manners. One allows the reduction to embed a trapdoor in order to extract a secret key or produce a signature, while the other allows the reduction to embed some fixed component of the challenge instance. However, this approach does not work well in the case of the SOK scheme. This is because the reduction has to embed two group elements g_2 and g_3 from the CBDH instance to $H(id_a^*)$ and $H(id_b^*)$ respectively, where id_a^* and id_b^* are two target identities adaptively chosen by the adversary. We overcome this difficulty by flipping random coins twice. Looking ahead, to program $H(x)$, the reduction first flips a random biased coin to determine the partitioning, namely either embedding a trapdoor or embedding a component from the CBDH instance. If the first round coin value indicates the latter choice, then $\mathcal{R}$ further flips an independent and unbiased coin to determine which component is going to be embedded. As a result, we obtain a new reduction with a loose factor around $1/2^{120}$, which significantly improves the original result. The same technique can also be used to improve Boneh-Waters constrained PRFs supporting left/right predicate [6], by minimizing the number of RO and tightening the reduction.

Following the work of Fischlin and Fleischhacker [13], we use meta-reduction technique to show that the SOK scheme is unlikely proven secure to be based on the CBDH assumption in NPROM, assuming the hardness of an intractable problem called one-more CBDH problem. We obtain this result by showing that if there is a black-box reduction $\mathcal{R}$ basing the fully adaptive security of the SOK IB-NIKE scheme on the CBDH assumption in NPROM, then there exists a meta-reduction $\mathcal{M}$ breaking the one-more CBDH assumption. Our black-box separation result holds with respect to single-instance reduction which invokes only one instance of the adversary and can rewind it arbitrarily to the point after sending over the master public key. Though single-instance reduction is a slightly restricted type of reductions, it is still general enough to cover the original reduction [20] and our new reduction shown in Section 3.1. Moreover, our result holds even for selective semi-static one-way security.

Realizing the technical heart of Hohenberger-Sahai-Waters approach [19] is to replace the programmable RO with a specific hash function H satisfying suitable programmability, we successfully extend their approach in the case of IB-NIKE, going beyond the "full domain hash" signatures. More precisely, we first create a replacement hash function H for RO from puncturable PRFs. The resulting IB-NIKE scheme is selective-secure in the standard model. To attain fully adaptive security, we hope to create a specific hash function H with (poly, 2)-programmability from admissible hash functions (AHFs). This potentially requires the AHF to be (poly, 2)-admissible, which is not met by current AHF constructions. We circumvent this technical difficulty by giving a generic construction of (poly, c)-AHF (c could be any constant integer) from any (poly, 1)-AHF, which utilizes Cartesian product as the key mathematical tool. We note that beyond the usage in the above construction, (poly, c)-AHF may find more important applications as a purely statistical cryptographic primitive.

2 Preliminaries and Definitions

Notations. For a distribution or random variable X, we write $x \xleftarrow{\text{R}} X$ to denote the operation of sampling a random x according to X. For a set X, we use $x \xleftarrow{\text{R}} X$ to denote the operation of sampling x uniformly at random from X, use U_X to denote the uniform distribution over set X, and use $|X|$ to denote its size. We write κ to denote the security parameter, and all algorithms (including the adversary) are implicitly given κ as input. We write $\mathsf{poly}(\kappa)$ to denote an arbitrary polynomial function in κ. We write $\mathsf{negl}(\kappa)$ to denote an arbitrary negligible function in κ, one that vanishes faster than the inverse of any polynomial. A probability is said to be overwhelming if it is $1 - \mathsf{negl}(\kappa)$, and said to be noticeable if it is $1/\mathsf{poly}(\kappa)$. A probabilistic polynomial-time (PPT) algorithm is a randomized algorithm that runs in time $\mathsf{poly}(\kappa)$.

2.1 Cartesian Product and Power of Vectors

The Cartesian product of a m-dimension vector $X = (x_1, \ldots, x_m)$ and a n-dimension vector $Y = (y_1, \ldots, y_n)$ over some finite set S is defined as:

$$X \times Y = \{z_{ij} := z_{(i-1)n+j} = (x_i, y_j)\}_{1 \le i \le m, 1 \le j \le n},$$

where $\times$ denotes the Cartesian product operation. $X \times Y$ can be viewed as a mn-dimension vector over S^2 or a $2mn$-dimension vector over S. The Cartesian k-power of a m-dimension vector $X = (x_1, \ldots, x_n)$ over S is defined as:

$$X^k = \underbrace{X \times \cdots \times X}_{k},$$

where X^k can be viewed as a m^k-dimension vector over S^k or a km^k-dimension vector over S.

2.2 Bilinear Maps and Related Hardness Assumptions

A bilinear group system consists of two cyclic groups $\mathbb{G}$ and $\mathbb{G}_T$ of prime order p, with a bilinear map $e : \mathbb{G} \times \mathbb{G} \to \mathbb{G}_T$ which satisfies the following properties:

- bilinear: $\forall g \in \mathbb{G}$ and $\forall a, b \in \mathbb{Z}_p$, we have $e(g^a, g^b) = e(g, g)^{ab}$.
- non-degenerate: $\forall g \in \mathbb{G}^*$, we have $e(g, g) \ne 1_{\mathbb{G}_T}$.

In the following, we write $\mathsf{BLGroupGen}$ to denote bilinear group system generator which on input security parameter κ, output $(p, \mathbb{G}, \mathbb{G}_T, e)$.

Assumption 2.1. *The computational bilinear Diffie-Hellman (CBDH) assumption in bilinear group system* $(p, \mathbb{G}, \mathbb{G}_T, e) \leftarrow \mathsf{BLGroupGen}(\kappa)$ *is that for any PPT adversary* $\mathcal{A}$*, it holds that:*

$$\Pr[\mathcal{A}(g, g^x, g^y, g^z) = e(g, g)^{xyz}] \leq \mathsf{negl}(\kappa),$$

where the probability is taken over the choice of $g \stackrel{R}{\leftarrow} \mathbb{G}$*,* $x, y, z \stackrel{R}{\leftarrow} \mathbb{Z}_p$*. Hereafter, we write* $\vec{v}$ *to denote a CBDH instance* $(g, g^x, g^y, g^y) \in \mathbb{G}^4$*. The decisional bilinear Diffie-Hellman (DBDH) assumption is that the two distributions* (g, g^x, g^y, g^z, T_0) *and* (g, g^x, g^y, g^z, T_1) *are computationally indistinguishable, where* $T_0 \stackrel{R}{\leftarrow} \mathbb{G}_T$ *and* $T_1 = e(g, g)^{xyz}$*.*

Assumption 2.2. *The n-one-more CBDH (n-omCBDH) assumption in bilinear group system* $(p, \mathbb{G}, \mathbb{G}_T, e) \leftarrow \mathsf{BLGroupGen}(\kappa)$ *is that for any PPT adversary* $\mathcal{A}$*, it holds that:*

$$\Pr[\mathcal{A}^{\mathsf{DL}_g(\cdot)}(g, \{g^{x_i}, g^{y_i}, g^{z_i}\}_{i=1}^{n+1}) = (\{e(g, g)^{x_i y_i z_i}\}_{i=1}^{n+1})] \leq \mathsf{negl}(\kappa),$$

where the probability is taken over the choices of $g \stackrel{R}{\leftarrow} \mathbb{G}$*, and* $x_i, y_i, z_i \stackrel{R}{\leftarrow} \mathbb{Z}_p$ *for* $i \in [n+1]$*. To solve* $n+1$ *CBDH instances,* $\mathcal{A}$ *is allowed to query* $\mathsf{DL}_g(\cdot)$ *at most* n *times, where* $\mathsf{DL}_g(\cdot)$ *is a discrete logarithm oracle which outputs* $t \in \mathbb{Z}_p$ *on input* $h = g^t$*. The hardness of the omCBDH problem is demonstrated by a recent result [23].*

Assumption 2.3. *The n-decisional bilinear Diffie-Hellman inversion (n-DBDHII) assumption in bilinear group system* $(p, \mathbb{G}, \mathbb{G}_T, e) \leftarrow \mathsf{BLGroupGen}(\kappa)$ *is that for any PPT adversary* $\mathcal{A}$*, it holds that:*

$$|\Pr[\mathcal{A}(g, g^x, \ldots, g^{x^n}, T_\beta) = 1] - 1/2| \leq \mathsf{negl}(\kappa),$$

where $T_0 \stackrel{R}{\leftarrow} \mathbb{G}_T, T_1 = e(g, g)^{1/x} \in \mathbb{G}_T$*, and the probability is taken over the choices of* $g \stackrel{R}{\leftarrow} \mathbb{G}$*,* $x \stackrel{R}{\leftarrow} \mathbb{Z}_p$*, and* $\beta \stackrel{R}{\leftarrow} \{0, 1\}$*.*

As observed in [2], the n-DBDHI assumption is equivalent to the n-DBDHI* assumption, which is identical to the standard one except that T_1 *is set as* $e(g, g)^{x^{2n+1}}$ *instead of* $e(g, g)^{1/x}$*. We will, for notational convenience, base our proofs on the n-DBDHI* assumption in this work.*

2.3 Indistinguishability Obfuscation

We recall the definition of indistinguishability obfuscator from [17] as below.

Definition 1 (Indistinguishability Obfuscator $(i\mathcal{O})$**).** *A uniform PPT machine* $i\mathcal{O}$ *is called an indistinguishability obfuscator for a circuit class* $\{\mathcal{C}_\kappa\}$ *if the following properties satisfied:*

- **Functionality Preserving:** *For all security parameters* $\kappa \in \mathbb{N}$*, for all* $C \in \mathcal{C}_\kappa$*, for all inputs* x*, we have that:*

$$\Pr[C'(x) = C(x) : C' \leftarrow i\mathcal{O}(\kappa, C)] = 1$$

- **Indistinguishability Obfuscation:** *For any pairs of PPT adversaries* $(\mathcal{S}, \mathcal{D})$, *there exists a negligible function* α *such that if* $\Pr[\forall x, C_0(x) = C_1(x) : (C_0, C_1, state) \leftarrow \mathcal{S}(\kappa)] \geq 1 - \alpha(\kappa)$, *then we have:*

$$|\Pr[\mathcal{D}(state, i\mathcal{O}(\kappa, C_0)) = 1] - \Pr[\mathcal{D}(state, i\mathcal{O}(\kappa, C_1)) = 1]| \leq \alpha(\kappa)$$

2.4 Puncturable PRFs

We then recall the notion of *puncturable* PRFs [19, 21], in which the key owner is able to generate a constrained key for all but polynomial number of elements in the domain.

Definition 2. *A family of puncturable PRFs* $\mathsf{F}_k : X \to Y$, *where X and Y may be parameterized by κ, is efficiently evaluable itself with secret key k. In addition, it consists of three polynomial-time algorithms* KeyGen, $\mathsf{Puncture}$, *and* Eval *satisfying the following properties:*

- **Evaluable under puncturing:** *For any $S \subseteq \{0, 1\}^n$ (containing polynomial number of punctured points), and any $x \in X$ but $x \notin S$, we have:*

$$\Pr[\mathsf{Eval}(k_S, x) = \mathsf{F}_k(x) : k_S \leftarrow \mathsf{Puncture}(k, S)] = 1$$

- **Pseudorandom at punctured points:** *For any PPT adversary* $\mathcal{A} = (\mathcal{A}_1, \mathcal{A}_2)$ *such that* $\mathcal{A}_1(\kappa)$ *outputs a set* $S \subseteq X$ *and state* τ, *we have:*

$$|\Pr[\mathcal{A}_2(\tau, k_S, S, \mathsf{F}_k(S)) = 1] - \Pr[\mathcal{A}_2(\tau, k_S, S, U_{Y^{|S|}}) = 1]| \leq \mathsf{negl}(\kappa)$$

where $S = \{x_1, \ldots, x_t\}$ *is the enumeration of the elements of S in lexicographic order,* $k_S \leftarrow \mathsf{Puncture}(k, S)$, $\mathsf{F}_k(S)$ *denotes the concatenation of* $\mathsf{F}_k(x_1), \ldots, \mathsf{F}_k(x_t)$. *The probability is defined over the choice of* $k \leftarrow \mathsf{KeyGen}(\kappa)$.

For ease of notation, sometimes we write $\mathsf{F}_{k_S}(x)$ *to represent* $\mathsf{Eval}(k_S, x)$, *and write* $k(S)$ *to represent the punctured key* $k_S \leftarrow \mathsf{Puncture}(k, S)$.

2.5 Non-Interactive Identity-Based Key Exchange

An non-interactive identity-based key exchange (IB-NIKE) scheme consists of the following polynomial-time algorithms:

- $\mathsf{Setup}(\kappa)$: on input security parameter κ, output master public key mpk and master secret key msk. Let I be the identity space and SHK be the shared key space.
- $\mathsf{Extract}(msk, id)$: on input msk and identity $id \in I$, output a secret key sk_{id} for id.
- $\mathsf{Share}(sk_{id_a}, id_b)$: on input secret key sk_{id_a} for identity id_a and another identity id_b, output a shared key shk for (id_a, id_b).

Correctness: For any $\kappa \in \mathbb{N}$, any $(mpk, msk) \leftarrow \mathsf{Setup}(\kappa)$, any pair of identities (id_a, id_b), any $sk_{id_a} \leftarrow \mathsf{Extract}(msk, id_a)$, $sk_{id_b} \leftarrow \mathsf{Extract}(msk, id_b)$, we have:

$$\mathsf{Share}(sk_{id_a}, id_b) = \mathsf{Share}(sk_{id_b}, id_a)$$

Security: Let $\mathcal{A}$ be an adversary against IB-NIKE and define its advantage as:

$$\mathrm{Adv}_{\mathcal{A}}(\kappa) = \Pr\left[\beta = \beta' : \begin{array}{l} (mpk, msk) \leftarrow \mathsf{Setup}(\kappa); \\ (id_a^*, id_b^*) \leftarrow \mathcal{A}^{\mathcal{O}_{\mathrm{extract}}(\cdot), \mathcal{O}_{\mathrm{reveal}}(\cdot, \cdot)}(mpk); \\ shk_0^* \xleftarrow{\mathrm{R}} SHK, shk_1^* \leftarrow \mathsf{Share}(id_a^*, id_b^*); \\ \beta \xleftarrow{\mathrm{R}} \{0, 1\}; \\ \beta' \leftarrow \mathcal{A}^{\mathcal{O}_{\mathrm{extract}}(\cdot), \mathcal{O}_{\mathrm{reveal}}(\cdot, \cdot)}(shk_\beta^*); \end{array}\right] - \frac{1}{2},$$

where $\mathcal{O}_{\mathrm{extract}}(id) = \mathsf{Extract}(msk, id)$, $\mathcal{O}_{\mathrm{reveal}}(id_a, id_b) = \mathsf{Share}(sk_{id_a}, id_b)$, and $\mathcal{A}$ is not allowed to query $\mathcal{O}_{\mathrm{extract}}(\cdot)$ for the target identities id_a^* and id_b^* and query $\mathcal{O}_{\mathrm{reveal}}(\cdot, \cdot)$ for (id_a^*, id_b^*) and (id_b^*, id_a^*). We say IB-NIKE is fully adaptive-secure if no PPT adversary has non-negligible advantage in the above security experiment. The fully adaptive security is the strongest security notion for IB-NIKE so far. The selective security can be defined similarly as above by requiring the adversary to commit the target identities (id_a^*, id_b^*) before it seeing mpk, while the semi-static security can be defined similarly above by discarding $\mathcal{O}_{\mathrm{reveal}}(\cdot, \cdot)$.

3 Revisit Sakai-Ohgishi-Kasahara IB-NIKE

We begin this section by recalling the SOK IB-NIKE scheme [22], which is given by the following three algorithms:

- $\mathsf{Setup}(\kappa)$: run $\mathsf{BLGroupGen}(\kappa)$ to generate $(p, \mathbb{G}, \mathbb{G}_T, e)$, pick $x \xleftarrow{\mathrm{R}} \mathbb{Z}_p$, set $h = g^x$; output $mpk = (h, \mathsf{H}, \mathsf{G})$ and $msk = x$, where $\mathsf{H} : I \to \mathbb{G}$ is the identity mapping function and $\mathsf{G} : \mathbb{G}_T \to \{0, 1\}^n$ is the key mapping function.
- $\mathsf{Extract}(msk, id)$: on input $msk = x$ and $id \in I$, output $sk_{id} \leftarrow \mathsf{H}(id)^x$.
- $\mathsf{Share}(sk_{id_a}, id_b)$: on input sk_{id_a} and id_b, output $shk \leftarrow \mathsf{G}(e(sk_{id_a}, \mathsf{H}(id_b)))$.

3.1 An Improved Proof for the SOK IB-NIKE

The original reduction [20] for the SOK IB-NIKE lose a factor of $1/Q_1^2 Q_2$. In this subsection, we show that the fully adaptive security for the SOK scheme can be reduced to the CBDH problem with a tighter security reduction.

Theorem 1. *The SOK IB-NIKE scheme is fully adaptive-secure in the random oracle model assuming the CBDH assumption holds in bilinear group system generated by $\mathsf{BLGroupGen}(\kappa)$. Suppose H and G are random oracles, for any adversary $\mathcal{A}$ breaking the SOK IB-NIKE scheme with advantage $\mathrm{Adv}_{\mathcal{A}}(\kappa)$ that makes at most Q_e extraction queries and Q_r reveal queries and Q_2 random oracle queries to G, there is an algorithm $\mathcal{B}$ that solves the CBDH problem with advantage $4\mathrm{Adv}_{\mathcal{A}}(\kappa)/e^2(Q_e + Q_r)^2 Q_2$, where e is the natural logarithm.*

Due to space limitation, we defer the proof of Theorem 1 in the full version.

3.2 SOK IB-NIKE Is Not Provably Secure under NPROM

We now show that the SOK IB-NIKE can not be proven secure without programming the random oracle with respect to a slightly restricted type of reductions, which is called *single-instance* reduction in [13]. In the case of identity-based schemes (including IBE, IBS as well as IB-NIKE), the restrictions lie at such a type of reductions can only invoke a single instance of the adversary and, can not rewind the adversary to a point before it hands over *mpk* for the first time. We have the following theorem whose proof appears in the full version.

Theorem 2 (Non-Programming Irreducibility for SOK IB-NIKE). *Assume the 1-omCBDH assumption holds in bilinear group system generated by* BLGroupGen(κ), *then there exists no non-programming single-instance fully-black-box reduction that reduces the fully adaptive security of SOK IB-NIKE to the CBDH problem. More precisely, assume there exists such a reduction $\mathcal{R}$ that converts any adversary $\mathcal{A}$ against the SOK IB-NIKE into an algorithm against the CBDH problem. Assume further that the reduction $\mathcal{R}$ has success probability* $\mathrm{Succ}_{\mathcal{R}^{\mathcal{A}}}^{\mathrm{CBDH}}$ *for given $\mathcal{A}$ and runtime* $\mathrm{Time}_{\mathcal{R}}(\kappa)$. *Then, there exists a family $\mathbb{A}$ of successful (but possibly inefficient) adversaries $\mathcal{A}_{\mathcal{R},a}$ against fully adaptive security of SOK IB-NIKE and a meta-reduction $\mathcal{M}$ that breaks the 1-omCBDH assumption with success probability* $\mathrm{Succ}_{\mathcal{M}}^{\text{1-omCBDH}}(\kappa) \geq (\mathrm{Succ}_{\mathcal{R}^{\mathcal{A}_{\mathcal{R},a}}}^{\mathrm{CBDH}}(\kappa))^2$ *for a random $\mathcal{A}_{\mathcal{R},a} \in \mathbb{A}$ and runtime* $\mathrm{Time}_{\mathcal{M}}(\kappa) = 2 \cdot \mathrm{Time}_{\mathcal{R}}(\kappa) + \mathrm{poly}(\kappa)$.

4   IB-NIKE from Indistinguishability Obfuscation

4.1   Warmup: Selectively Secure IB-NIKE from $i\mathcal{O}$

As a warmup, we show how to create a replacement for the RO H($\cdot$) in the SOK scheme from puncturable PRFs and $i\mathcal{O}$. The resulting scheme is selective-secure in the standard model.

Selectively Secure Construction from $i\mathcal{O}$

- Setup(κ): run BLGroupGen(κ) to generate $(p, \mathbb{G}, \mathbb{G}_T, e)$, pick $x \xleftarrow{\text{R}} \mathbb{Z}_p$ and $g \xleftarrow{\text{R}} \mathbb{G}^*$; pick a secret key k for puncturable PRF F : $I \to \mathbb{Z}_p$; then create an obfuscation of the program H shown in Fig. 1. The size of the program is padded to be the maximum of itself and the program H* shown in Fig. 2. We refer to the obfuscated program as the function H : $I \to \mathbb{G}$, which acts as the random oracle type hash function in the SOK scheme. The *msk* is x, whereas *mpk* is the hash function H($\cdot$).
- Algorithm Extract and Share are identical to that in the SOK scheme.

Theorem 3. *The above IB-NIKE scheme is selective-secure if the obfuscation scheme is indistinguishably secure, F is a secure punctured PRF, and the DBDH assumption holds.*

Due to space limitation, we defer the proof of Theorem 3 in the full version.

Selective Hash H

Constants: Punctured PRF key k, $g \in \mathbb{G}^*$.
Input: Identity id.

1. Output $g^{F_k(id)}$.

Fig. 1. Selective Hash H

Selective Hash H*

Constants: Punctured PRF key $k(S)$ for $S = \{id_a^*, id_b^*\}$, $id_a^*, id_b^* \in I$, $z_1^*, z_2^* \in \mathbb{G}$,
$g \in \mathbb{G}^*$.
Input: Identity id.

1. If $id = id_a^*$ output z_1^* and exit.
2. If $id = id_b^*$ output z_2^* and exit.
3. Else output $g^{F_{k(S)}(id)}$.

Fig. 2. Selective Hash H*

4.2 Main Result: Adaptively Secure IB-NIKE from $i\mathcal{O}$

We now show how to create a replacement for the RO $H(\cdot)$ in the SOK IB-NIKE
scheme from (poly, 2)-AHF and $i\mathcal{O}$ to attain adaptive security in the standard
model. We first recap the definition of AHF and present a generic construction
of (poly, 2)-AHF.

Admissible Hash Functions. Our definition below is generalization of "admissible hash function"(AHF) [3,9,15].

Definition 3 (AHF). *Let ℓ, l, and θ be efficiently computable univariate polynomials of κ. For an efficiently computable function $\mathsf{AHF} : \{0,1\}^\ell \to \{0,1\}^l$, define the predicate $P_u : \{0,1\}^\ell \to \{0,1\}$ for any $u \in \{0,1,\bot\}^l$ as $P_u(x) = 0 \iff \forall i : \mathsf{AHF}(x)_i \neq u_i$, where $\mathsf{AHF}(x)_i$ denotes the i-th component of $\mathsf{AHF}(x)$. We say that AHF is (m,n)-admissible if there exists a PPT algorithm $\mathsf{AdmSample}$ and a polynomial $\theta(\kappa)$, such that for all $x_1, \ldots, x_m, z_1, \ldots, z_n \in \{0,1\}^\ell$, where $x_i \neq z_j$ for all $1 \leq i \leq m$ and $1 \leq j \leq n$, we have that:*

$$\Pr[P_u(x_1) = \cdots = P_u(x_m) = 1 \wedge P_u(z_1) = \cdots = P_u(z_n) = 0] \geq 1/\theta(\kappa) \quad (1)$$

where the probability is over the choice of $u \leftarrow \mathsf{AdmSample}(\kappa)$. Particularly, we say that AHF is (poly, n)-admissible if AHF is (q,n)-admissible for any polynomial $q = q(\kappa)$ and constant $n > 0$. Note that in the standard definition of AHF, the second parameter n is fixed to 1. To show the existence of (q,n)-AHF for $n \geq 1$, we present the following theorem.

Theorem 4. *Let $q = q(\kappa)$ be a polynomial, n be a constant, and* AHF *(with* AdmSample*) be a $(q, 1)$-AHF from $\{0, 1\}^\ell$ into $\{0, 1\}^l$. Then* AHF′ *with:*

- AHF′$(x) = \underbrace{\text{AHF}(x) \times \cdots \times \text{AHF}(x)}_{n}$.

- $P'_u : \{0, 1\}^\ell \to \{0, 1\}$ *for any $u \in \{0, 1, \perp\}^{nl^n}$ is defined as $P'_u(x) = 0 \iff \forall i : \text{AHF}'(x)_i \neq u_i$, where $\text{AHF}'(x)_i$ denotes the i-th component of* AHF′(x).

- AdmSample′(κ): *run* AdmSample(κ) *independently n times to generate u_1, ..., $u_n \in \{0, 1\}^l$, output $u = \underbrace{u_1 \times \cdots \times u_n}_{n}$.*

is a (q, n)-AHF from $\{0, 1\}^\ell$ into $\{0, 1\}^{nl^n}$. Here $\times$ denotes the Cartesian product defined in Section 2.1. AHF′(x) *can be viewed as a nl^n-dimension vector over $\{0, 1\}$, and u can be viewed as a nl^n-dimension vector over $\{0, 1, \perp\}$.*

Proof. We first note that the definition of P'_u for AHF′ is compatible with that of P_u for AHF. According the construction of AHF′ and AdmSample′(κ), we have $P'_u(x) = P_{u_1}(x) \wedge \cdots \wedge P_{u_n}(x)$. Now fix $q+n$ distinct elements $x_1, \ldots, x_q, z_1, \ldots, z_n \in \{0, 1\}^\ell$. For each $i \in [n]$, define event A_i as: $P_{u_i}(x_j) = 1$ for all $1 \leq j \leq q$ and $P_{u_i}(z_i) = 0$ (the predicate values on the rest $n - 1$ elements could be either 0 or 1). Define event A as: $P'_u(x_j) = 1$ for all $1 \leq j \leq q$ and $P'_u(z_i) = 0$ for all $1 \leq i \leq n$. According to the definition of P'_u, we have: $A \supseteq A_1 \wedge \cdots \wedge A_n$. Since AHF is a $(q, 1)$-AHF, thus each event A_i happens independently with probability at least $1/\theta(\kappa)$ (over the choice of $u_i \leftarrow$ AdmSample(κ)). Therefore, we have: $\Pr[A] \geq \prod_{i=1}^{n} \Pr[A_i] \geq 1/(\theta(\kappa))^n$, which indicates AHF′ is a (q, n)-AHF. This proves the theorem.

Adaptively Secure Construction from $i\mathcal{O}$

- Setup(κ): run BLGroupGen(κ) to generate $(p, \mathbb{G}, \mathbb{G}_T, e)$, pick $x \xleftarrow{\text{R}} \mathbb{Z}_p$ and $g \xleftarrow{\text{R}} \mathbb{G}^*$; pick a secret key k for puncturable PRF $F : I \to \mathbb{Z}_p$; pick uniformly at random $(c_{1,0}, c_{1,1}), \ldots, (c_{n,0}, c_{n,1})$ each from $\mathbb{Z}_p$; then create an obfuscation of the program H shown in Fig. 3, where the size of the program is padded to be the maximum of itself and the program of H* shown in Fig. 4. The msk is x, whereas mpk is the hash function $\mathsf{H}(\cdot)$.
- Algorithms Extract and Share are identical to that in the SOK IB-NIKE.

Theorem 5. *The above IB-NIKE scheme is adaptively secure if the obfuscation scheme is indistinguishable secure and the n-DBDHI assumption holds in bilinear group system.*

Proof. We proceed via a sequence of hybrid games, where the first game corresponds to the standard adaptive security game. We first prove that any two successive games are computationally indistinguishable. We then show that any PPT adversary in the final game that succeeds with non-negligible probability can be used to break the n-DBDHI assumption.

Adaptive Hash H

Constants: $g \in \mathbb{G}^*$, exponents $c_{i,\alpha} \in \mathbb{Z}_p$ for $i \in [n]$ and $\alpha \in \{0,1\}$.
Input: Identity id.

1. Compute $w \leftarrow \mathsf{AHF}(id)$.
2. Output $g^{\prod_{i=1}^n c_{i,w_i}}$.

Fig. 3. Adaptive Hash H

Adaptive Hash H*

Constants: $g \in \mathbb{G}^*$, $g^x, \ldots, g^{x^n} \in \mathbb{G}$ for some $x \in \mathbb{Z}_p$, exponents $y_{i,\alpha} \in \mathbb{Z}_p$ for $i \in [n]$ and $\alpha \in \{0,1\}$, $u \in \{0,1,\perp\}^n$.
Input: Identity id.

1. Compute $w \leftarrow \mathsf{AHF}(id)$.
2. Compute the set size $|\mu(w)|$, where $\mu(w)$ is the set i such that $w_i \neq u_i$.
3. Output $(g^{x^{|\mu(w)|}})^{\prod_{i=1}^n y_{i,w_i}}$.

Fig. 4. Adaptive Hash H*

Game 0: This game is identical to standard adaptive security game played between adversary $\mathcal{A}$ and challenger $\mathcal{CH}$:

- Setup: $\mathcal{CH}$ runs $\mathsf{BLGroupGen}(\kappa)$ to generate $(p, \mathbb{G}, \mathbb{G}_T, e)$, picks $x \xleftarrow{\mathrm{R}} \mathbb{Z}_p$ and $g \xleftarrow{\mathrm{R}} \mathbb{G}^*$, then chooses exponents $c_{i,\alpha}$ uniformly at random $\mathbb{Z}_p$ for $i \in [n]$ and $\alpha \in \{0,1\}$, creates the hash function $\mathsf{H}(\cdot)$ as an obfuscation of the program of H shown in Fig. 3, and pads its size to be the maximum of itself and the program of H* shown in Fig. 4. $\mathcal{CH}$ sets $msk = x$ and $mpk = \mathsf{H}$.
- Phase 1: $\mathcal{A}$ can issue the following two types of queries:
  - extraction query $\langle id \rangle$: $\mathcal{CH}$ responds with $sk_{id} = \mathsf{H}(id)^x$.
  - reveal query $\langle id_a, id_b \rangle$: $\mathcal{CH}$ first extracts secret key sk_{id_a} for id_a, then responds with $shk \leftarrow \mathsf{Share}(sk_{id_a}, id_b)$.
- Challenge: $\mathcal{A}$ submits id_a^* and id_b^* as the target identities with the restriction that either id_a^* or id_b^* has not been queried for secret key. $\mathcal{CH}$ picks $shk_0^* \xleftarrow{\mathrm{R}} SHK$ and computes $shk_1^* \leftarrow \mathsf{Share}(sk_{id_a^*}, id_b^*)$, then picks $\beta \xleftarrow{\mathrm{R}} \{0,1\}$ and sends shk_β^* to $\mathcal{A}$ as the challenge.
- Phase 2: $\mathcal{A}$ can continue to issue the extraction queries and the reveal queries, $\mathcal{CH}$ proceeds the same way as in Phase 1 except that the extraction queries to id_a^* or id_b^* and reveal query for (id_a^*, id_b^*) are not allowed.
- Guess: $\mathcal{A}$ outputs its guess β' and wins if $\beta = \beta'$.

Game 1: same as Game 0 except that $\mathcal{CH}$ generates the exponents $c_{i,\alpha}$ as follows: first samples $u \in (\{0,1,\perp\})^n$ via $\mathsf{AdmSample}(\kappa, Q)$, where Q is the upper bound on the number of queries made by $\mathcal{A}$ (including extraction queries and reveal queries), then for $i \in [n]$ and $\alpha \in \{0,1\}$ chooses $y_{i,\alpha} \xleftarrow{\text{R}} \mathbb{Z}_p$, and sets:

$$c_{i,\alpha} = \begin{cases} y_{i,\alpha} & \text{if } \alpha = u_i \\ x \cdot y_{i,\alpha} & \text{if } \alpha \neq u_i \end{cases}$$

Game 2: same as Game 1 except that $\mathcal{CH}$ creates the hash function $\mathsf{H}(\cdot)$ as an obfuscation of program H^* shown in Fig. 4.

Lemma 1. *Game 0 and Game 1 are statistically indistinguishable.*

Proof. This lemma immediately follows from the facts: (1) in Game 1 the sampling of u only determines the generation of $c_{i,\alpha}$ and it is independent of the rest game; (2) the value of $c_{i,\alpha}$ distributes uniformly at random from $\mathbb{Z}_p$ in both Game 0 and Game 1.

Lemma 2. *Game 1 and Game 2 are computationally indistinguishable if the underlying obfuscation scheme is indistinguishability secure.*

Proof. We prove this lemma by giving a reduction to the indistinguishability security of the obfuscator. More precisely, suppose there is an PPT adversary $\mathcal{A}$ can distinguish Game 1 and Game 2, then we can build algorithms $(\mathcal{S}, \mathcal{D})$ against the indistinguishability of the obfuscator by interacting with $\mathcal{A}$ as follows.

Sample: $\mathcal{S}$ runs $\mathsf{BLGroupGen}(\kappa)$ to generate $(p, \mathbb{G}, \mathbb{G}_T, e)$, picks $x \xleftarrow{\text{R}} \mathbb{Z}_p$ and $g \xleftarrow{\text{R}} \mathbb{G}$, prepares g^{x^i} for $i \in [n]$, runs $\mathsf{AdmSample}(\kappa, Q)$ to obtain a string $u \in (\{0, 1, \perp\})^n$, and for $i \in [n]$ and $\alpha \in \{0,1\}$ chooses $y_{i,\alpha} \xleftarrow{\text{R}} \mathbb{Z}_p$, then sets:

$$c_{i,\alpha} = \begin{cases} y_{i,\alpha} & \text{if } \alpha = u_i \\ x \cdot y_{i,\alpha} & \text{if } \alpha \neq u_i \end{cases}$$

It sets $\tau = (c_{i,\alpha}, y_{i,\alpha}, u)$ and builds C_0 as the program of H, and C_1 as the program of H^*. Before describing $\mathcal{D}$, we observe that by construction, the circuits C_0 and C_1 always behave identically on every input. To show program equivalence, note that for all $w \in \{0,1\}^n$, we have that:

$$g^{\prod_i^n c_{i,\alpha_i}} = g^{x^{|\mu(w)|} \cdot \prod_i^n y_{i,w_i}} = (g^{x^{|\mu(w)|}})^{\prod_i^n y_{i,w_i}}$$

With suitable padding, both C_0 and C_1 have the same size. Thus, $\mathcal{S}$ satisfies the conditions needed for invoking the indistinguishability property of the obfuscator. Now, we can describe the algorithm $\mathcal{D}$, which takes as input τ as given above, and the obfuscation of either C_0 or C_1.

Distinguish: $\mathcal{D}$ sets $msk = x$ and builds mpk from C_β, then invokes $\mathcal{A}$ in the adaptive security game for IB-NIKE. When $\mathcal{A}$ issues extraction queries and reveal queries, $\mathcal{D}$ responds with msk. If $\mathcal{A}$ wins, $\mathcal{D}$ outputs 1.

By construction, if $\mathcal{D}$ receives an obfuscation of C_0, then the probability that $\mathcal{D}$ outputs 1 is exactly the probability that $\mathcal{A}$ wins in Game 1. On the other hand, if $\mathcal{D}$ receives an obfuscation of C_1, then the probability that $\mathcal{D}$ outputs 1 is the probability that $\mathcal{A}$ wins in Game 2. The indistinguishability of the obfuscator implies Game 1 and Game 2 are computationally indistinguishable. The lemma immediately follows.

Lemma 3. $\mathcal{A}$'s advantage in Game 2 is negligible in κ.

Proof. We prove this lemma by showing that any adversary $\mathcal{A}$ has non-negligible advantage in Game 2 implies an algorithm $\mathcal{B}$ that has non-negligible advantage against the n-DBDHI problem. Given a n-DBDHI instance $(g, g^x, \ldots, g^{x^n}, T_\beta)$, $\mathcal{B}$ interacts with $\mathcal{A}$ as follows:

- Setup: $\mathcal{B}$ first runs $\mathsf{AdmSample}(\kappa, Q)$ to obtain $u \in \{0, 1, \bot\}^n$, where Q is the sum of Q_e (the maximum number of extraction queries) and Q_r (the maximum number of the reveal queries). For $i \in [n]$ and $\alpha \in \{0, 1\}$, $\mathcal{B}$ chooses random $y_{i,\alpha} \in \mathbb{Z}_p$, then creates the hash function $\mathsf{H}(\cdot)$ as an obfuscation of the program H^* using the input DBDHI instance as well as $y_{i,\alpha}$ and u.
- Phase 1: $\mathcal{A}$ can issue the following two types of queries:
  - extraction queries $\langle id \rangle$: If $P_u(id) = 0$, then $\mathcal{B}$ aborts and outputs a random guess for β. Else, $\mathcal{B}$ extracts the secret key from the input n-DBDHI instance and the $y_{i,\alpha}$ values. $\mathcal{B}$ could to do so since $P_u(id) = 1$ implies there exists at least one i such that $w_i = u_i$. In this case $\mathsf{H}(id)$ will contain a power of x that is strictly less than n.
  - reveal queries $\langle id_a, id_b \rangle$: If $P_u(id_a) = 0 \wedge P_u(id_b) = 0$, then $\mathcal{B}$ aborts and outputs a random guess for β. Otherwise, either $P_u(id_a) = 1$ or $P_u(id_b) = 1$. Therefore, $\mathcal{B}$ can at least extract a secret key for one identity and then computes the shared key.
- Challenge: $\mathcal{A}$ outputs the target identities (id_a^*, id_b^*). If $P_u(id_a^*) = 1 \vee P_u(id_b^*) = 1$, then $\mathcal{B}$ aborts and outputs a random guess for β. Else, we have $P_u(id_a^*) = 0 \wedge P_u(id_b^*) = 0$, which means $\mathsf{AHF}(id_a^*)_i \neq u_i$ and $\mathsf{AHF}(id_b^*) \neq u_i$ for all $i \in [n]$. In this situation, both the hash values of id_a^* and id_b^* will be g^{a^n} raised to some known product of some $y_{i,\alpha}$ values. Denote the products by y_a^* and y_b^*, respectively. $\mathcal{B}$ thus sends $shk_\beta^* = (T_\beta)^{y_a^* y_b^*}$ to $\mathcal{A}$ as the challenge. It is easy to verify that if $T_\beta \xleftarrow{\text{R}} \mathbb{G}_T$ then shk_β^* also distributes uniformly over $\mathbb{G}_T$, else if $T_\beta = e(g, g)^{x^{2n+1}}$ then $shk_\beta^* = e(\mathsf{H}(id_a^*), \mathsf{H}(id_b^*))^a$.
- Phase 2: same as in Phase 1 except that the extraction queries $\langle id_a^* \rangle$, $\langle id_b^* \rangle$ and the reveal query $\langle id_a^*, id_b^* \rangle$ are not allowed.
- Guess: When $\mathcal{A}$ outputs its guess β', $\mathcal{B}$ forwards β' to its own challenger.

Since the choice of $u \leftarrow \mathsf{AdmSample}(\kappa, Q)$ determines whether or not $\mathcal{B}$ aborts and it is independent of the rest of the interaction. We conclude that conditioned on $\mathcal{B}$ does not abort, $\mathcal{A}$'s view in the above game is identical to that in Game 2. Let F be the event that $\mathcal{B}$ does not abort, we have $\mathsf{Adv}_\mathcal{B}(\kappa) = \Pr[F] \cdot \mathsf{Adv}_\mathcal{A}(\kappa)$. In what follows, we estimate the low bound of $\Pr[F]$. Let $\{id_i\}_{1 \leq i \leq Q_e}$ be Q_e distinct extraction queries, $\{(id_{j,1}, id_{j,2})\}_{1 \leq j \leq Q_r}$ be Q_r distinct reveal queries. During the game, $\mathcal{B}$ will abort if one of the following events does not happen.

$$F_1 : \bigwedge_{i=1}^{Q_e} (P(id_i) = 1)$$
$$F_2 : \bigwedge_{j=1}^{Q_r} (P(id_{j,1}) = 1 \vee P(id_{j,2}) = 1)$$
$$F_3 : P_u(id_1^*) = 0 \wedge P_u(id_2^*) = 0$$

We have $F = F_1 \wedge F_2 \wedge F_3$. Note that in each extraction query, there exists at least one identity different from both id_1^* and id_2^*. Suppose $Q_e + Q_r \leq Q$, then according to the fact that AHF is a $(Q, 2)$-AHF, we have $\Pr[F] \geq \theta(\kappa)$. The lemma immediately follows.

Combining the above three lemma, our main theorem immediately follows.

Acknowledgement. We greatly thank Dennis Hofheinz for helpful clarifications on admissible hash functions. In particular, we thank Dennis for suggesting the construction of (poly, c)-AHFs in Section 4.2. The first author is supported the National Natural Science Foundation of China under Grant No. 61303257, the Strategic Priority Research Program of CAS (Chinese Academy of Sciences) under Grant No. XDA06010701, and the National 973 Program of China under Grant No. 2011CB302400. The second author is supported by the National Natural Science Foundation of China under Grant No. 61103232, the Guangdong Natural Science Foundation under Grant No. S2013010011859, and the Research Fund for the Doctoral Program of Higher Education of China under Grant No. 20114404120027. The third author is an International Research Fellow of JSPS and supported by the National Natural Science Foundation of China under Grant No. 61303201.

References

1. Bellare, M., Ristenpart, T.: Simulation without the artificial abort: Simplified proof and improved concrete security for waters' ibe scheme. In: Joux, A. (ed.) EUROCRYPT 2009. LNCS, vol. 5479, pp. 407–424. Springer, Heidelberg (2009)
2. Boneh, D., Boyen, X.: Efficient selective-ID secure identity-based encryption without random oracles. In: Cachin, C., Camenisch, J.L. (eds.) EUROCRYPT 2004. LNCS, vol. 3027, pp. 223–238. Springer, Heidelberg (2004)
3. Boneh, D., Boyen, X.: Secure identity based encryption without random oracles. In: Franklin, M. (ed.) CRYPTO 2004. LNCS, vol. 3152, pp. 443–459. Springer, Heidelberg (2004)
4. Boneh, D., Franklin, M.: Identity-based encryption from the weil pairing. In: Kilian, J. (ed.) CRYPTO 2001. LNCS, vol. 2139, pp. 213–229. Springer, Heidelberg (2001)
5. Boneh, D., Lynn, B., Shacham, H.: Short signatures from the weil pairing. In: Boyd, C. (ed.) ASIACRYPT 2001. LNCS, vol. 2248, pp. 514–532. Springer, Heidelberg (2001)
6. Boneh, D., Waters, B.: Constrained pseudorandom functions and their applications. In: Sako, K., Sarkar, P. (eds.) ASIACRYPT 2013, Part II. LNCS, vol. 8270, pp. 280–300. Springer, Heidelberg (2013)
7. Boneh, D., Zhandry, M.: Multiparty key exchange, efficient traitor tracing, and more from indistinguishability obfuscation (2013),
http://eprint.iacr.org/2013/642

8. Capar, C., Goeckel, D., Paterson, K.G., Quaglia, E.A., Towsley, D., Zafer, M.: Signal-flow-based analysis of wireless security protocols. Information and Computation 226, 37–56 (2013)
9. Cash, D., Hofheinz, D., Kiltz, E., Peikert, C.: Bonsai trees, or how to delegate a lattice basis. In: Gilbert, H. (ed.) EUROCRYPT 2010. LNCS, vol. 6110, pp. 523–552. Springer, Heidelberg (2010)
10. Coron, J.S.: On the exact security of full domain hash. In: Bellare, M. (ed.) CRYPTO 2000. LNCS, vol. 1880, pp. 229–235. Springer, Heidelberg (2000)
11. Diffie, W., Hellman, M.E.: New directions in cryptograpgy. IEEE Transactions on Infomation Theory 22(6), 644–654 (1976)
12. Dupont, R., Enge, A.: Provably secure non-interactive key distribution based on pairings. Discrete Applied Mathematics 154(2), 270–276 (2006)
13. Fischlin, M., Fleischhacker, N.: Limitations of the meta-reduction technique: The case of schnorr signatures. In: Johansson, T., Nguyen, P.Q. (eds.) EUROCRYPT 2013. LNCS, vol. 7881, pp. 444–460. Springer, Heidelberg (2013)
14. Fischlin, M., Lehmann, A., Ristenpart, T., Shrimpton, T., Stam, M., Tessaro, S.: Random oracles with(out) programmability. In: Abe, M. (ed.) ASIACRYPT 2010. LNCS, vol. 6477, pp. 303–320. Springer, Heidelberg (2010)
15. Freire, E.S.V., Hofheinz, D., Paterson, K.G., Striecks, C.: Programmable hash functions in the multilinear setting. In: Canetti, R., Garay, J.A. (eds.) CRYPTO 2013, Part I. LNCS, vol. 8042, pp. 513–530. Springer, Heidelberg (2013)
16. Garg, S., Gentry, C., Halevi, S.: Candidate multilinear maps from ideal lattices. In: Johansson, T., Nguyen, P.Q. (eds.) EUROCRYPT 2013. LNCS, vol. 7881, pp. 1–17. Springer, Heidelberg (2013)
17. Garg, S., Gentry, C., Halevi, S., Raykova, M., Sahai, A., Waters, B.: Candidate indistinguishability obfuscation and functional encryption for all circuits (2013), http://eprint.iacr.org/2013/451
18. Garg, S., Gentry, C., Halevi, S., Sahai, A., Waters, B.: Attribute-based encryption for circuits from multilinear maps. In: Canetti, R., Garay, J.A. (eds.) CRYPTO 2013, Part II. LNCS, vol. 8043, pp. 479–499. Springer, Heidelberg (2013)
19. Hohenberger, S., Sahai, A., Waters, B.: Replacing a random oracle: Full domain hash from indistinguishability obfuscation (2013), http://eprint.iacr.org/2013/509
20. Paterson, K.G., Srinivasan, S.: On the relations between non-interactive key distribution, identity-based encryption and trapdoor discrete log groups. Des. Codes Cryptography 52(2), 219–241 (2009)
21. Sahai, A., Waters, B.: How to use indistinguishability obfuscation: Deniable encryption, and more (2013), http://eprint.iacr.org/2013/454
22. Sakai, R., Ohgishi, K., Kasahara, M.: Cryptosystems based on pairing. In: The 2000 Symposium on Cryptography and Information Security, Japan, vol. 45, pp. 26–28 (2000)
23. Zhang, J., Zhang, Z., Chen, Y., Guo, Y., Zhang, Z.: Generalized "one-more" problems and black-box separations. In: CRYPTO 2014 (submitted, 2014)

On the Impossibility of Proving Security of Strong-RSA Signatures via the RSA Assumption

Masayuki Fukumitsu[1], Shingo Hasegawa[2], Shuji Isobe[2], and Hiroki Shizuya[2]

[1] Faculty of Information Media, Hokkaido Information University,
Nishi-Nopporo 59-2 Ebetsu, Hokkaido, 069-8585 Japan
`fukumitsu@do-johodai.ac.jp`
[2] Graduate School of Information Sciences, Tohoku University,
41 Kawauchi, Aoba-ku, Sendai, 980–8576 Japan
`{hasegawa,iso,shizuya}@cite.tohoku.ac.jp`

Abstract. We pose a question whether or not the standard RSA assumption is sufficient to prove the security of the strong RSA-based (SRSA-based, for short) signatures. In this paper, we show a negative circumstantial evidence for the question. Namely, several SRSA-based signatures cannot be proven to be sEUF-CMA, or even EUF-KOA, under the RSA assumption as far as a modulus-preserving algebraic reduction is concerned. Our result is obtained as an important application of the adaptive pseudo-free group introduced by Catalano, Fiore and Warinschi that can be regarded as an abstract framework of signatures. We in fact show that the adaptive pseudo-freeness of the RSA group $\mathbb{Z}_N^\times$ cannot be proven from the RSA assumption via such reductions.

Keywords: Strong-RSA Signature Schemes, Pseudo-Free Groups, Adaptive Pseudo-Free Groups, RSA Assumption, Algebraic Reduction.

1 Introduction

Gennaro, Halevi and Rabin [18] and Cramer and Shoup [12] independently proposed digital signature schemes whose security is proven under the strong RSA (SRSA, for short) assumption [5,16]. Their SRSA-based signatures are known as one of secure and efficient signature schemes without random oracles [6]. Several enhanced variants of their schemes were introduced by Fischlin [13], Camenisch and Lysyanskaya [9], Zhu [37,38] and Hofheinz and Kiltz [22]. Joye [25] studied some potential security flaws of CS-like signatures for the purpose of showing the vulnerability of some specific SRSA-based signatures.

For security proofs, it is important that a reduction is tight in a sense that the loss factor of the reduction is asymptotically small enough. Naccache, Pointcheval and Stern [27], Chevallier-Mames and Joye [11] and Schäge [32] introduced SRSA-based signatures that are proven to be secure by tight reductions, respectively. Schäge [33] gave tight security proofs for the SRSA-based signatures proposed by Cramer-Shoup, Fischlin, Camenisch-Lysyanskaya and Zhu.

W. Susilo and Y. Mu (Eds.): ACISP 2014, LNCS 8544, pp. 290–305, 2014.
© Springer International Publishing Switzerland 2014

Another important issue on signatures is to prove their security under a weaker cryptographic assumption. In this paper, we consider a question whether or not SRSA-based signatures are secure under the RSA assumption rather than the SRSA assumption. The difficulty of breaking RSA is that the exponent e of $z^e \equiv y \pmod{N}$ is forced by a given RSA instance (N, e, y), whereas in the case of SRSA, an adversary is allowed to conveniently choose such an exponent e so that $z^e \equiv y \pmod{N}$ for a given SRSA instance (N, y). It is not known that this question has been formally solved so far.

In this paper, we give a negative circumstantial evidence for this question. We show that several SRSA-based signatures cannot be proven to be strongly existentially unforgeable against the chosen message attack (sEUF-CMA, for short) from the RSA assumption via some reasonably restricted reductions. This result is obtained as an important application of the framework concerning the adaptive pseudo-free group [10].

The notion of adaptive pseudo-free group is put forward by Catalano, Fiore and Warinschi [10]. Intuitively, a computational group family $\{\mathbb{G}_N\}$ is adaptive pseudo-free if any PPT adversary $\mathcal{A}$ cannot find a new witness for distinguishing the group $\mathbb{G}_N$ from a free group, even though $\mathcal{A}$ is allowed to adaptively receive such witnesses. In [10], they showed that the RSA group $\mathbb{Z}_N^\times$ can be proven to be adaptive pseudo-free from the SRSA assumption. They also proposed a generic construction of secure signatures from adaptive pseudo-free groups. Applying their construction to the adaptive pseudo-freeness of $\mathbb{Z}_N^\times$, several SRSA-based signatures given in [9,12,13,18,22,37] can be obtained.

We restrict ourselves in this paper to "CFW-type signatures", namely SRSA-based signatures yielded from their generic construction. Note that there are some SRSA-based signatures that seem not to be CFW-type, for example [11,27,32], and such signatures are excluded from our discussion. Our impossibility result on CFW-type signatures is obtained by the following theorem.

Theorem 1 (Informal). *It cannot be proven that $\mathbb{Z}_N^\times$ is adaptive pseudo-free from the RSA assumption via modulus-preserving algebraic reductions.*

More precisely, if there exists a modulus-preserving algebraic reduction algorithm $\mathcal{R}$ that breaks RSA with black-box access to an adversary $\mathcal{A}$ violating the adaptive pseudo-freeness of $\mathbb{Z}_N^\times$, then the RSA assumption does not hold.

Moreover, we also show that if CFW-type signatures are sEUF-CMA, then $\mathbb{Z}_N^\times$ is adaptive pseudo-free. Combining this fact and Theorem 1, we show that CFW-type signatures cannot be proven to be sEUF-CMA from the RSA assumption via modulus-preserving algebraic reductions, as long as the RSA assumption holds.

Theorem 1 is proven by using the *meta-reduction* technique. This technique has been employed in e.g. [1,2,7,8,17,20,28,30,34] to give impossibility results on the security proofs of cryptographic schemes and relationships among cryptographic assumptions. In Theorem 1, we only consider a modulus-preserving algebraic reduction $\mathcal{R}$. The *modulus-preserving* means that an RSA modulus N submitted from $\mathcal{R}$ to the adversary $\mathcal{A}$ is the same as that of an RSA instance (N, e, y) input to $\mathcal{R}$. On the other hand, $\mathcal{R}$ is informally *algebraic with respect to a group* $\mathbb{G}$ [28] if $\mathcal{R}$ performs only group operations for elements in $\mathbb{G}$ and its execution can be easily traced. Theorem 1 intuitively means that the adaptive pseudo-freeness of $\mathbb{Z}_N^\times$ cannot be proven from the RSA assumption, as long as the concerning reduction $\mathcal{R}$ is modulus-preserving and algebraic. We should note that our setting that $\mathcal{R}$ is required to be modulus-preserving and algebraic is not exceedingly restricted: in fact, most reductions concerning the pseudo-free groups [10,24,26] and ordinary security proofs (e.g. [9,12]) are modulus-preserving and algebraic. The algebraic condition has been employed in order to give impossibility results for constructing security proofs of several cryptographic schemes [1,2,17,20,34], and to investigate relationships among cryptographic assumptions [8,36]. Note also that Theorem 1 does not exclude the possibility that there exists a non-modulus-preserving and/or non-algebraic reduction $\mathcal{R}$ that proves the adaptive pseudo-freeness of $\mathbb{Z}_N^\times$ from the RSA assumption.

Especially, Theorem 1 can be shown even when an adversary $\mathcal{A}$ is restricted to being *static*, namely $\mathcal{A}$ is not allowed to receive any witness. In the case of signatures, such an adversary corresponds to a key only attacker rather than a chosen message attacker. Therefore, our result actually means that CFW-type signatures cannot be proven to be existentially unforgeable against even the key only attack via modulus-preserving algebraic reductions, as long as the RSA assumption holds.

Since $\mathbb{Z}_N^\times$ is adaptive pseudo-free under the SRSA assumption [10], and the reduction algorithm in [10] can be described as a modulus-preserving algebraic one, Theorem 1 is regarded as a negative circumstantial evidence that the SRSA assumption is not equivalent to the RSA assumption. For the relationship between the RSA assumption and the SRSA assumption, Aggarwal, Maurer and Shparlinski [3] gave an opposite evidence. Namely they showed that the RSA modulus N can be factored if SRSA is broken in some specific restricted model. We should note that the Aggarwal-Maurer-Shparlinski's result does not contradict our result. This is because in our result, the operations of the reduction algorithm are restricted, whereas in [3], they restricted the oracle operations.

2   Preliminaries

A prime P is *safe* if $P = 2P' + 1$ for some prime P'. Let $\mathbb{N}_{\mathsf{RSA}}^{\mathsf{safe}}$ be the set of all RSA composites $N = PQ$ such that P and Q are distinct safe primes, and let $\mathbb{N}_{\mathsf{RSA}(k)}^{\mathsf{safe}}$ be the set of all $N = PQ \in \mathbb{N}_{\mathsf{RSA}}^{\mathsf{safe}}$ such that P and Q are distinct primes of binary length $k/2$. It is widely believed that there are infinitely many safe primes, e.g. [4]. For any $N \in \mathbb{N}$, we use $\mathbb{Z}_N$ and $\mathbb{Z}_N^\times$ to denote the residue ring $\mathbb{Z}/N\mathbb{Z}$ and its group of units, respectively. QR_N designates the group of quadratic residues mod N.

For any integers $a \leq b$, let $[a, b] = \{n \in \mathbb{Z} \mid a \leq n \leq b\}$ and let $(a, b) = \{n \in \mathbb{Z} \mid a < n < b\}$. We denote by $x \in_{\mathrm{R}} S$ that the element x is randomly chosen from the set S according to some specific probabilistic distribution. In particular, we write $x \in_{\mathrm{U}} S$ when a uniform distribution on S is designated.

A function $\nu(k)$ is *negligible* if for any polynomial p, there exists a constant k_0 such that $\nu(k) < 1/p(k)$ for any $k \geq k_0$. We denote by $\mathrm{negl}(k)$ any negligible function in k. Let X be a probability distribution over a finite set S. For any $a \in S$, $X(a)$ indicates the probability that a is chosen according to X. We write $\mathsf{Supp}(X)$ to denote the *support* of X. Namely, $\mathsf{Supp}(X)$ is the set of all elements $a \in S$ such that $X(a) > 0$. Let $\{X_N\}_{N \in \mathbb{N}}$ and $\{U_N\}_{N \in \mathbb{N}}$ be ensembles of probability distributions, where for each $N \in \mathbb{N}$, X_N is defined over a finite set S_N, and U_N is the uniform distribution over S_N. $\{X_N\}$ is said to be *almost uniform* if the statistical distance $1/2 \cdot \sum_{a \in S_N} |X_N(a) - U_N(a)|$ between X_N and U_N is negligible in the binary length of N.

2.1 Adaptive Pseudo-Free Groups

We describe the notion of adaptive pseudo-free groups introduced by Catalano, Fiore and Warinschi [10]. It is a generalization of Rivest's pseudo-freeness [31]. We now prepare the definition of computational groups and free (abelian) groups.

Computational Groups [26,31]. Let $\{\mathbb{G}_N\}_{N \in \mathcal{N}}$ be a family of finite abelian groups indexed by an index set $\mathcal{N} = \bigcup_{k \geq 0} \mathcal{N}(k)$. We assume that each group index $N \in \mathcal{N}(k)$ and each element of $\mathbb{G}_N$ (with $N \in \mathcal{N}(k)$) are expressed as a word of polynomial length in k, respectively. Then, $\{\mathbb{G}_N\}_{N \in \mathcal{N}}$ is said to be a *family of computational groups* if its group operations such as the group law and the sampling can be efficiently executed. Note that the sampling is not necessarily uniform probability distribution. For the more formal definition, refer to [26,31].

Free Abelian Groups. We denote by $\mathcal{F}(A)$ the free abelian group generated by a set $A = \{a_1, a_2, \ldots, a_m\}$ of distinct m symbols. (For the detail, refer to [10,21,26,31].) Any element of $\mathcal{F}(A)$ is uniquely expressed by a word of the form $\prod_{i=1}^{m} a_i^{s_i}$ with some exponents $s_1, s_2, \ldots, s_m \in \mathbb{Z}$. We focus only on univariate equations as in [10]. An *equation in x with symbols in A* is a pair $\lambda = (w_1, w_2)$, where w_1 is a word of the form x^E with some exponent $E \in \mathbb{N}$, and w_2 is an element $\prod_{i=1}^{m} a_i^{s_i} \in \mathcal{F}(A)$. Then we express the equation $\lambda = (w_1, w_2)$ as $x^E = \prod_{i=1}^{m} a_i^{s_i}$ or the tuple (E, s) of exponents, where $s = (s_1, s_2, \ldots, s_m)$. Equations that have solutions in $\mathcal{F}(A)$ are *trivial over $\mathcal{F}(A)$*, others are *nontrivial over $\mathcal{F}(A)$*.

Let $\mathbb{G}$ be any finite abelian group, and let $\alpha : A \to \mathbb{G}$ be an *assignment map* that interprets each symbol $a \in A$ to a group element $\alpha(a) \in \mathbb{G}$. We write λ_α for the equation $\lambda : x^E = \prod_{i=1}^{m} a_i^{s_i}$ interpreted over $\mathbb{G}$ via α, namely λ_α is the equation $x^E = \prod_{i=1}^{m} \alpha(a_i)^{s_i}$ over $\mathbb{G}$. $\psi \in \mathbb{G}$ is a *solution* for λ_α if $\psi^E = \prod_{i=1}^{m} \alpha(a_i)^{s_i}$ holds over $\mathbb{G}$.

A pair (λ^*, ψ^*) is called a *witness* pair for distinguishing $\mathbb{G}$ from $\mathcal{F}(A)$, if λ^* is a nontrivial equation over $\mathcal{F}(A)$ and ψ^* is a solution over $\mathbb{G}$ of the interpreted equation λ_α^*. Existence of such a pair (λ^*, ψ^*) witnesses that $\mathbb{G}$ is not a free group, because λ_α^* should have no solution if $\mathbb{G}$ is indeed a free group.

Adaptive Pseudo-Freeness. Intuitively, a computational group family $\{\mathbb{G}_N\}$ is adaptive pseudo-free if any probabilistic polynomial-time (PPT, for short) adversary cannot find a new witness pair (λ^*, ψ^*), even though the adversary is allowed to adaptively receive such witnesses.

The formal definition is described by the following adaptive pseudo-free (APF, for short) game [10]. It is played by a challenger $\mathcal{C}$ and an adversary $\mathcal{A}$. Let k be a security parameter, and let A be a set of $m = m(k)$ symbols. We suppose that for each k and m, a class $\mathcal{E}_{k,m}$ of pairs (λ, r) of an equation λ and an auxiliary string r is designated, and we provide a family $\rho_{k,m} = \{\rho_{k,m}(M)\}$ of probabilistic distributions $\rho_{k,m}(M)$ over $\mathcal{E}_{k,m}$. We say that $\rho = \{\rho_{k,m}\}_{k,m}$ is a *computational parametric distribution* if for any k, m and M, $\rho_{k,m}(M)$ is efficiently samplable, and the description of $\rho_{k,m}(M)$ can be efficiently obtained. Given k and A, the APF game proceeds as follows:

Setup. The challenger $\mathcal{C}$ chooses a random group index $N \in_{\mathrm{U}} \mathcal{N}(k)$. Then, $\mathcal{C}$ specifies an assignment map $\alpha : A \to \mathbb{G}_N$ by independently choosing an element $\alpha(a) \in_{\mathrm{R}} \mathbb{G}_N$ at random according to the designated sampling algorithm for each $a \in A$. The adversary $\mathcal{A}$ is given the *game tuple* $(N, \alpha, \rho_{k,m})$.

Equations queries. On t-th query, $\mathcal{A}$ chooses a parameter M_t for determining a distribution $\rho_{k,m}(M_t)$, and hands it to $\mathcal{C}$. Then, $\mathcal{C}$ chooses a pair $(\lambda^{(t)}, r_t) \in \mathcal{E}_{k,m}$ of an equation $\lambda^{(t)} = (E_t, s_t)$ and an auxiliary string r_t according to the distribution $\rho_{k,m}(M_t)$, and then returns the pair $(\lambda^{(t)}, r_t)$ and a solution $\psi_t \in \mathbb{G}_N$ of the interpreted equation $\lambda_\alpha^{(t)} : x^{E_t} = \prod_{i=1}^m \alpha(a_i)^{s_{t,i}}$ to $\mathcal{A}$.

Challenge. Eventually, $\mathcal{A}$ outputs a tuple $((\lambda^*, r^*), \psi^*)$. Then $\mathcal{C}$ outputs 1 if (1) λ^* is *nontrivial with respect to* $\Lambda = \{(\lambda^{(t)}, \psi_t)\}_t$, (2) $(\lambda^*, r^*) \in \mathcal{E}_{k,m}$, and (3) ψ^* is a solution of λ_α^*, or 0 otherwise.

For the condition (1), the equation λ^* is intuitively said to be *nontrivial with respect to* Λ if the equation λ^* cannot be efficiently derived from the queried equations $\lambda \in \Lambda$ by using the group laws and the following fact: for any coprime integer e to the order $\mathrm{ord}(\mathbb{G}_N)$ of the group $\mathbb{G}_N$, if $w_1^e = w_2^e$ over $\mathbb{G}_N$ then $w_1 = w_2$. In [10], the nontriviality of the adaptive case is formally defined. An adversary $\mathcal{A}$ is said to *win the APF game of the family* $\mathcal{G}$ *with respect to the parametric distribution* $\rho = \{\rho_{k,m}\}_{k,m}$ if the challenger $\mathcal{C}$ outputs 1 in the game between $\mathcal{C}$ and $\mathcal{A}$.

Definition 1 (Adaptive Pseudo-Free Groups w.r.t. ρ [10]). *Let k be a security parameter, let m be a polynomial in k, and let $\rho = \{\rho_{k,m}\}_{k,m}$ be a computational parametric distribution. A family $\mathcal{G} = \{\mathbb{G}_N\}_{N \in \mathcal{N}}$ of computational groups is* adaptive pseudo-free with respect to ρ, *if there exists no PPT adversary $\mathcal{A}$ such that for any set A of m symbols, $\mathcal{A}$ wins the APF game of the family $\mathcal{G}$ with respect to ρ in nonnegligible probability in k, where the probability is taken over the random choices of the index $N \in_{\mathrm{U}} \mathcal{N}(k)$, $\alpha(a) \in_{\mathrm{R}} \mathbb{G}_N$ for each $a \in A$ and each pair $(\lambda^{(t)}, r_t) \in_{\mathrm{R}} \mathcal{E}_{k,m}$, and the internal coin flips of $\mathcal{A}$.*

We say that an adversary $\mathcal{A}$ is *static* if $\mathcal{A}$ is not allowed to query in Equations queries phase. A family $\mathcal{G}$ is *adaptive pseudo-free with respect to a computational parametric distribution* ρ *against static adversaries* if $\mathcal{G}$ is adaptive pseudo-free with respect to ρ even when an adversary is static. Note that the nontriviality is exactly equivalent to that over $\mathcal{F}(A)$ when an APF adversary is static [10,14]. In such a case, the nontriviality can be verified by the following lemma.

Lemma 1 ([31]). *An equation $x^E = \prod_{i=1}^m a_i^{s_i}$ is trivial over $\mathcal{F}(A)$ if and only if $E \mid s_i$ for any $1 \le i \le m$.*

KGen: on input $(1^k, m)$, KGen chooses a game tuple $(N, \alpha, \rho_{k,m})$ as in Setup phase of the APF game, and then outputs a public key $pk := (N, \alpha, \rho_{k,m})$ and a secret key $sk := \mathrm{ord}(\mathbb{G}_N)$.

Sign: on input (pk, sk, M), Sign issues a signature in the following way. Sign chooses a pair (λ, r) of an equation λ and a string r as in Equations queries phase of the APF game, and then finds a solution ψ of the interpreted equation λ_α by using the secret key $sk = \mathrm{ord}(\mathbb{G}_N)$. It returns a signature $\sigma = (\lambda, r, \psi)$.

Verify: on input (pk, M, σ), Verify outputs 1 if $(\lambda, r) \in \mathsf{Supp}(\rho_{k,m}(M))$ and ψ is actually a solution of the interpreted equation λ_α, or 0 otherwise.

Fig. 1. Construction of $\mathsf{PFSig}_{\mathcal{G},\rho}$

2.2   Digital Signature Schemes

A *signature scheme* $\mathcal{S}$ consists of the following three polynomial-time algorithm (KGen, Sign, Verify). KGen is a PPT algorithm that on input 1^k, generates a public key pk and a secret key sk. Sign is a PPT algorithm that on input (sk, pk, M), issues a signature σ on the message M. Verify is a deterministic algorithm that on input (pk, M, σ), outputs 1 if σ is a signature on the message M under the public key pk, or 0 otherwise. For the security, we consider *strongly existentially unforgeable security against the chosen message attack (sEUF-CMA security, for short)*, and *existentially unforgeable security against the key only attack (EUF-KOA security, for short)*. For the formal definition, please refer to [19].

Catalano, Fiore and Warinschi [10] proposed a generic construction of a secure signatures based on an adaptive pseudo-free group. Let $\mathcal{G} = \{\mathbb{G}_N\}_{N \in \mathcal{N}}$ be a computational group family and let $\rho = \{\rho_{k,m}\}$ be a computational parametric distribution such that for any k, m and M, the membership of the support $\mathsf{Supp}(\rho_{k,m}(M))$ of the distribution $\rho_{k,m}(M)$ can be efficiently verified. In Fig. 1, we depict their signature $\mathsf{PFSig}_{\mathcal{G},\rho}$. In [10, Theorem 1], they showed that $\mathsf{PFSig}_{\mathcal{G},\rho}$ is sEUF-CMA provided that $\mathcal{G}$ is adaptive pseudo-free with respect to ρ.

In order to give a negative circumstantial evidence on the security proof of some SRSA-based signatures, we now show the converse of Theorem 1 of [10]. More specifically, we show that if there exists a winning APF adversary $\mathcal{A}$ for the group $\mathcal{G}$ with respect to the parametric distribution ρ, then one can construct a forger violating the sEUF-CMA security of $\mathsf{PFSig}_{\mathcal{G},\rho}$. Our strategy is to prove that a witness $((\lambda^*, r^*), \psi^*)$ output from $\mathcal{A}$ can be regarded as a forgery for $\mathsf{PFSig}_{\mathcal{G},\rho}$. However, $\mathcal{A}$ would not output a message M^* so that $(\lambda^*, r^*) \in \mathsf{Supp}(\rho_{k,m}(M^*))$, whereas the forger is required to output such a message. We therefore consider the following modification of the APF game: in Challenge phase, an adversary $\mathcal{A}$ outputs a parameter M^* together with $((\lambda^*, r^*), \psi^*)$ such that $(\lambda^*, r^*) \in \mathsf{Supp}(\rho_{k,m}(M^*))$. It should be noted that this modification does not affect the adaptive pseudo-freeness. Namely, if $\mathcal{G}$ is APF with respect to ρ, then it is so under this modified sense.

Lemma 2. *Let $\mathcal{G} = \{\mathbb{G}_N\}_{N \in \mathcal{N}}$ be any computational group family, and let $\rho = \{\rho_{k,m}\}$ be any computational parametric distribution such that for any parameter*

M, the membership of $\mathsf{Supp}(\rho_{k,m}(M))$ can be efficiently verified. If $\mathsf{PFSig}_{\mathcal{G},\rho}$ is sEUF-CMA, then $\mathcal{G}$ is adaptive pseudo-free with respect to ρ.

It should be noted in Lemma 2 that $\mathcal{G}$ is adaptive pseudo-free with respect to ρ against static adversaries provided that $\mathsf{PFSig}_{\mathcal{G},\rho}$ is EUF-KOA. This is because an adversary makes no query.

2.3 Algebraic Algorithms

The concept of the algebraic algorithm was introduced by Paillier and Vergnaud [28]. Intuitively, an algorithm $\mathcal{R}$ is *algebraic with respect to a computational group* $\mathbb{G}$ if $\mathcal{R}$ performs only the group operation for the elements in $\mathbb{G}$ and the execution of $\mathcal{R}$ can be easily traced. In particular, on any input elements $y_1, \ldots, y_n \in \mathbb{G}$, any element $g \in \mathbb{G}$ produced in the execution of $\mathcal{R}$ belongs to the subgroup $\langle y_1, \ldots, y_n \rangle$ generated by the input elements, and moreover the expression $g = \prod_{i=1}^n y_i^{c_i}$ should be easily retrieved.

We follow the formal definition given in [34]. An algorithm $\mathcal{R}$ is *algebraic* for a computational group family $\{\mathbb{G}_N\}_{N \in \mathcal{N}}$, if the following algorithm Extract is provided. Extract receives any tuple $(N, y_1, \ldots, y_n, \mathsf{aux}, g, \omega)$ as input, where $N \in \mathcal{N}$ is a group index, $y_1, \ldots, y_n \in \mathbb{G}_N$ are elements that are given to $\mathcal{R}$ as input, aux is any word given to $\mathcal{R}$ as an auxiliary input, $g \in \mathbb{G}_N$ is a *target* group element and ω denotes a random coin used in $\mathcal{R}$. Then Extract finds a tuple $(c_1, \ldots, c_n)$ of exponents such that $g = \prod_{i=1}^n y_i^{c_i}$, provided that g is actually produced in the execution of $\mathcal{R}$ on the input tuple $(N, y_1, \ldots, y_n, \mathsf{aux})$ with the random coin ω. If there is no correct exponents $(c_1, \ldots, c_n)$, then Extract may output any word. Extract is required to run in polynomial-time in the running time of $\mathcal{R}$. In particular, if $\mathcal{R}$ runs in polynomial-time in the security parameter k, then Extract should run in polynomial-time in k.

We consider an algebraic algorithm $\mathcal{R}$ that has an access to an oracle $\mathcal{A}$. In the case where a target element $g \in \mathbb{G}$ is produced after $\mathcal{R}$ has received an answer for a u-th input to $\mathcal{A}$, Extract correctly retrieves exponents $(c_1, \ldots, c_n)$ for the given target g if besides the input tuple $(N, y_1, \ldots, y_n, \mathsf{aux})$, Extract is also given all the u correct answers from the first input through the u-th input. Note that if the target element g is produced before $\mathcal{R}$ invokes $\mathcal{A}$ on the first input, it is not required to provide any additional inputs to Extract as in [8].

2.4 RSA Assumption

A key generator $\mathsf{KGen}_{\mathsf{RSA}}$ outputs a pair $(N, e) \in \mathbb{N}^{\mathsf{safe}}_{\mathsf{RSA}(\ell)} \times \mathbb{Z}^\times_{\varphi(N)}$ on each input 1^k, where ℓ is a polynomial in a security parameter k and φ is Euler's function.

Definition 2 (RSA assumption). *The* RSA assumption holds *if there exists no PPT adversary $\mathcal{R}$ such that*

$$\Pr\left[z^e \equiv y \pmod N : (N, e) \leftarrow \mathsf{KGen}_{\mathsf{RSA}}(1^k), y \in_{\mathsf{U}} \mathrm{QR}_N, z \leftarrow \mathcal{R}(N, e, y)\right]$$

is nonnegligible in k, where the probability is taken over the coin flips of $\mathsf{KGen}_{\mathsf{RSA}}$ and $\mathcal{R}$, and the uniform random choice y from QR_N.

We follow the setting of [23] that an RSA composite N is restricted to a product of two safe primes. We also assume that y is restricted to a quadratic residue mod N. Note that this is not an essential restriction, because breaking RSA for $y \in \mathrm{QR}_N$ leads to breaking RSA for an arbitrary $y \in \mathbb{Z}_N^\times$ [26]. In our main theorem, we employ the following lemma.

Lemma 3 ([35]). *Let $N \in \mathbb{N}$ with binary length k. Let e and E^* be any integers of length at most polynomial in k, and let $z^*, y \in \mathbb{Z}_N^\times$ such that $(z^*)^e \equiv y^{E^*}$ (mod N). If $\gcd(e, E^*) = 1$, then the element $z \in \mathbb{Z}_N^\times$ such that $z^e \equiv y$ (mod N) can be computed in polynomial-time in k on the input (N, e, E^*, z^*, y).*

3 Impossibility Result on the Adaptive Pseudo-Freeness of $\mathbb{Z}_N^\times$ under the RSA Assumption

Catalano, Fiore and Warinschi [10] presented a class $\mathfrak{D}^{\mathsf{CFW}}$ of computational parametric distributions so that the RSA group family $\{\mathbb{Z}_N^\times\}$ can be proven to be adaptive pseudo-free with respect to $\rho \in \mathfrak{D}^{\mathsf{CFW}}$ from the SRSA assumption, where $\{\mathbb{Z}_N^\times\}$ stands for the RSA group family $\{\mathbb{Z}_N^\times\}_{N \in \mathcal{N}}$ with $\mathcal{N} = \mathbb{N}_{\mathsf{RSA}}^{\mathsf{safe}}$.

The main purpose of this paper is to give a negative circumstantial evidence on the security proof of *CFW-type signatures* under the RSA assumption, namely signatures obtained by applying the generic construction $\mathsf{PFSig}_{\mathbb{Z}_N^\times, \rho}$ to the RSA group family $\{\mathbb{Z}_N^\times\}$ with $\rho \in \mathfrak{D}^{\mathsf{CFW}}$. For the purpose, we show in this section that if the RSA group family $\{\mathbb{Z}_N^\times\}$ is proven to be adaptive pseudo-free with respect to any parametric distribution $\rho \in \mathfrak{D}^{\mathsf{CFW}}$ (against static adversaries) from the RSA assumption via some restricted reductions, then the RSA assumption does not hold. As a consequence of this impossibility result and Lemma 2, we will show that if CFW-type signatures are proven to be EUF-KOA from the RSA assumption via some restricted reductions, then the RSA assumption does not hold. Recall that in Lemma 2, we require the modification on the adaptive pseudo-freeness as described in Section 2.2. Hereafter, we focus on the modified version of the adaptive pseudo-freeness. Note that the impossibility result on the ordinary adaptive pseudo-freeness can also be proven in a similar manner.

We now describe the class $\mathfrak{D}^{\mathsf{CFW}}$. The set $\mathcal{E}_{k,m}^{\mathsf{CFW}}$ is defined in the following manner. We fix any nonconstant polynomials $\ell_{\mathsf{msg}} = \ell_{\mathsf{msg}}(k)$, $\ell_{\mathsf{exp}} = \ell_{\mathsf{exp}}(k)$ and $\ell_{\mathsf{seed}} = \ell_{\mathsf{seed}}(k)$ such that $\ell_{\mathsf{exp}} \le \ell/2 - 2$, and any (single-valued) division-intractable hash function $H : \{0,1\}^{\ell_{\mathsf{seed}}} \to [0, 2^{\ell_{\mathsf{exp}}} - 1]$. For each k and m, let $\mathcal{E}_{k,m}^{\mathsf{CFW}}$ be the set of all pairs (λ, r) of an equation $\lambda = (E, (s_1, \ldots, s_m))$ and a string $r \in \{0,1\}^{\ell_{\mathsf{seed}}}$ such that $E = H(r) \in [0, 2^{\ell_{\mathsf{exp}}} - 1]$, $s_1 = 1$ and $s_2, \ldots, s_m \in \mathbb{Z}$. Then, $\mathfrak{D}^{\mathsf{CFW}}$ is a class of computational parametric distributions $\rho = \{\rho_{k,m}\}_{k,m}$ such that for each k and m, $\rho_{k,m}(M) \in \rho_{k,m}$ is a probabilistic distribution over the set $\mathcal{E}_{k,m}^{\mathsf{CFW}}$ so that a string r is uniformly distributed over $\{0,1\}^{\ell_{\mathsf{seed}}}$. For a single-valued division-intractable hash function, the following lemma holds.

Lemma 4. *If $H : \{0,1\}^{\ell_{\mathsf{seed}}} \to [0, 2^{\ell_{\mathsf{exp}}} - 1]$ is a division-intractable hash function, then for any integer $E \in [0, 2^{\ell_{\mathsf{exp}}} - 1]$, $\Pr_{r \in_{\mathsf{U}} \{0,1\}^{\ell_{\mathsf{seed}}}} [H(r) = E] = \mathrm{negl}(k)$.*

It should be noted that we have described a lager class than the class actually proposed in [10] in a sense that elements $s_2, \ldots, s_m$ are not restricted to belonging to $\mathbb{Z}_E$.

The Situation. We describe the situation that *the RSA assumption implies the adaptive pseudo-freeness of the RSA group family* $\{\mathbb{Z}_N^\times\}$ *with respect to a computational parametric distribution* $\rho = \{\rho_{k,m}\}_{k,m}$ *against static adversaries*, and then we write $\mathsf{RSA} \leq \mathsf{APFG}_{\mathbb{Z}_N^\times, \rho}$ to denote such a situation. We formalize this statement by the following contrapositive setting as in [8,28]: there exist a PPT algorithm $\mathcal{R}$ and a polynomial m such that $\mathcal{R}$ breaks RSA in nonnegligible probability with a black-box access to a static adversary $\mathcal{A}$ that wins the APF game for the family $\{\mathbb{Z}_N^\times\}$ with respect to $\rho = \{\rho_{k,m}\}_{k,m}$ in nonnegligible probability. Through the black-box access, $\mathcal{R}$ would play the APF game with the adversary $\mathcal{A}$ in which $\mathcal{R}$ is placed at the challenger's position. For ease of explanation for the proof, we now consider the case where $\mathcal{R}$ invokes $\mathcal{A}$ only once. Note that one can extend our main theorem to cover the case where $\mathcal{R}$ invokes $\mathcal{A}$ polynomially many times in a natural way. The detail will be given in the full version of this paper.

Here, $\mathsf{KGen}_{\mathsf{RSA}}$ is forced to generate a *good* pair (N, e) with probability at least $1/\tau_{\mathsf{Good}}$ for some polynomial $\tau_{\mathsf{Good}}(k)$ for any sufficiently large k. The good pair (N, e) means that e is a prime in $\mathbb{Z}_{\varphi(N)}^\times$ and $e \geq 2^{\ell_{\exp}}$. Note that this assumption on $\mathsf{KGen}_{\mathsf{RSA}}$ is not exceedingly strong. For instance, if e is (almost) uniformly distributed over $\mathbb{Z}_{\varphi(N)}^\times$ with respect to each specific modulus N, then our assumption holds. This fact can be proven as in [15, Lemma 5]. Throughout this paper, we assume that a group index $N \in \mathcal{N}(k)$ chosen by an APF challenger is distributed according to N chosen by such a generator $\mathsf{KGen}_{\mathsf{RSA}}(1^k)$ for each security parameter k. Moreover, following the setting in [10,14,26], we adopt any sampling algorithm of the family $\{\mathbb{Z}_N^\times\}$ which chooses an element g almost uniformly at random over QR_N. For example, such a sampling can be done [26, Lemma 2] by choosing an exponent $d \in_{\mathsf{U}} \{0, 1, \ldots, B-1\}$ with sufficiently large B and then setting $g := (y^*)^d$, where y^* is any fixed generator of QR_N. Note that QR_N is cyclic when $N \in \mathsf{N}_{\mathsf{RSA}}^{\mathsf{safe}}$ [26].

Let (N, e, y^*) be any RSA instance given to $\mathcal{R}$. Following Setup phase of the APF game, $\mathcal{R}$ sets a game tuple $(N, \alpha, \rho_{k,m})$, and then invokes $\mathcal{A}$ on $(N, \alpha, \rho_{k,m})$. In this paper, we assume as in [10,14,26] that $\mathcal{R}$ is *modulus-preserving* in a sense that the index N is always the same as the modulus N of the given RSA instance. Since $\mathcal{R}$ now plays the role of the challenger for the APF game of $\{\mathbb{Z}_N^\times\}$, the assignment α is specified by selecting $\alpha(a)$ almost uniformly at random from QR_N for each $a \in A$. Eventually, the game completes with $\mathcal{A}$'s output: a "winning" witness $(M^*, (\lambda^*, r^*), \psi^*)$ of the APF game, or "losing" symbol $\bot$. After the game, $\mathcal{R}$ would find a correct solution z^* for the given RSA instance (N, e, y^*) with nonnegligible probability ϵ_0.

In this paper, we force the reduction $\mathcal{R}$ to be *algebraic with respect to* QR_N. Consequently, any element $g \in \mathrm{QR}_N$ produced in the execution of $\mathcal{R}(N, e, y^*)$ before $\mathcal{R}$ invokes $\mathcal{A}$ is generated by the given RSA ciphertext $y^* \in \mathrm{QR}_N$ and the expression $g = (y^*)^d$ is retrieved by the polynomial-time extractor Extract.

On each RSA instance (N, e, y), $\mathcal{M}$ proceeds as follows.

(M-1) $\mathcal{M}$ sets an integer $E^* := H(r^*)$ by choosing a string $r^* \in_U \{0, 1\}^{\ell_{\text{seed}}}$.

(M-2) $\mathcal{M}$ aborts if $E^* \leq 1$, or proceeds to the following step otherwise.

(M-3) $\mathcal{M}$ chooses a random coin ω of $\mathcal{R}$, sets $y^* := y^{E^*}$, and then executes $\mathcal{R}$ on the RSA instance (N, e, y^*) with ω.

(M-4) When $\mathcal{R}$ invokes an APF adversary on a game tuple $(N, \alpha, \rho_{k,m})$ of the group index N, an assignment $\alpha : A \to \mathrm{QR}_N$ and the distribution family $\rho_{k,m}$, $\mathcal{M}$ operates as follows:

    (a) $\mathcal{M}$ executes $\mathsf{Sim}_\mathcal{A}$ on $(N, \alpha, \rho_{k,m})$ with using the auxiliary tuple (e, y, r^*, ω);

    (b) $\mathcal{M}$ receives a witness $(M^*, (\lambda^*, r^*), \psi^*)$ from $\mathsf{Sim}_\mathcal{A}$; and

    (c) $\mathcal{M}$ hands the tuple $(M^*, (\lambda^*, r^*), \psi^*)$ to $\mathcal{R}$ as an adversary's response.

(M-5) $\mathcal{M}$ receives a solution z^* for the RSA instance (N, e, y^*) from $\mathcal{R}$.

(M-6) $\mathcal{M}$ finds a solution z for the target RSA instance (N, e, y) by applying Lemma 3 to the tuple (N, e, E^*, z^*, y), and halts with output z.

Fig. 2. Configuration of $\mathcal{M}$

We now ready to state our main theorem.

Theorem 1. *Assume that* $\mathsf{KGen}_{\mathsf{RSA}}$ *outputs a good public key* (N, e) *with probability* $1/\tau_{\mathsf{Good}}$ *for sufficiently large* k, *where* τ_{Good} *is a polynomial in* k. *Let* $\rho \in \mathfrak{D}^{\mathsf{CFW}}$. *If* $\mathsf{RSA} \leq \mathsf{APFG}_{\mathbb{Z}_N^\times, \rho}$, *then the RSA assumption does not hold.*

Proof. (*Sketch*) Assume that $\mathsf{RSA} \leq \mathsf{APFG}_{\mathbb{Z}_N^\times, \rho}$. Then, there exist a PPT algorithm $\mathcal{R}$ and a polynomial m such that $\mathcal{R}$ is algebraic with respect to QR_N, and $\mathcal{R}$ breaks RSA in nonnegligible probability with a black-box access to any static adversary $\mathcal{A}$ that wins the APF game of the family $\{\mathbb{Z}_N^\times\}$ with respect to $\rho = \{\rho_{k,m}\}_{k,m}$ in nonnegligible probability. This means that for any security parameter k, $\mathcal{R}$ breaks RSA with at least nonnegligible probability ϵ_0 for a given RSA instance (N, e, y^*), where $(N, e) \leftarrow \mathsf{KGen}_{\mathsf{RSA}}(1^k)$ and $y^* \in_U \mathrm{QR}_N$.

Construction of Meta-Reduction $\mathcal{M}$. We shall construct a PPT algorithm $\mathcal{M}$ that breaks RSA with no oracle access. As a subroutine of $\mathcal{M}$, we shall provide for the reduction $\mathcal{R}$ a simulator $\mathsf{Sim}_\mathcal{A}$ that plays a role of a winning APF adversary. In other words, from the $\mathcal{R}$'s viewpoint, $\mathsf{Sim}_\mathcal{A}$ looks like an adversary that really wins the APF game with nonnegligible probability. If $\mathsf{Sim}_\mathcal{A}$ behaves as the adversary, then $\mathcal{R}$ breaks RSA via playing the game with $\mathsf{Sim}_\mathcal{A}$. Thus, our meta-reduction $\mathcal{M}$ is constructed by involving $\mathcal{R}$ and $\mathsf{Sim}_\mathcal{A}$. If such an $\mathsf{Sim}_\mathcal{A}$ is provided, then $\mathcal{M}$ is constructed as depicted in Fig 2.

By using the following claims, we estimate the probability $\Pr[\mathsf{Succ}_\mathcal{M}]$ that $\mathcal{M}$ outputs a correct solution z for the target RSA instance (N, e, y) in (M-6), where $(N, e) \leftarrow \mathsf{KGen}_{\mathsf{RSA}}(1^k)$ and $y \in_U \mathrm{QR}_N$.

Claim 1. $\mathcal{M}$ *aborts in (M-2) with negligible probability in* k.

This is a direct implication of Lemma 4.

Claim 2. *Assume that $\mathcal{M}$ does not abort in (M-2). For the target RSA instance (N, e, y) and the natural number E^* chosen in (M-1), $y^* = y^{E^*}$ is distributed uniformly at random over QR_N.*

Proof. Let P and Q be distinct safe primes such that $N = PQ$, $P = 2P' + 1$ and $Q = 2Q' + 1$ for some primes P' and Q'. We now assume that $E^* \in \mathbb{Z}_{P'Q'}^{\times}$. Then, we consider for the given RSA modulus N, a map $\mathcal{B}_{N,E^*}$ that maps each element $y \in \mathrm{QR}_N$ to $y^{E^*} \bmod N \in \mathrm{QR}_N$. It follows from $E^* \in \mathbb{Z}_{P'Q'}^{\times}$ and QR_N of the order $P'Q'$ that $\mathcal{B}_{N,E^*}$ is bijective. Since the RSA ciphertext y given to $\mathcal{M}$ is chosen uniformly at random from QR_N, $y^* = y^{E^*}$ is uniformly distributed over QR_N.

We now show that $E^* = H(r^*) \in \left[0, 2^{\ell_{\exp}} - 1\right]$ set in (M-1) is in $\mathbb{Z}_{P'Q'}^{\times}$. Under the assumption that $\mathcal{M}$ does not abort in (M-2), we have $E^* > 1$. On the other hand, it follows from $N = PQ \in \mathrm{N}_{\mathsf{RSA}(\ell)}^{\mathsf{safe}}$, namely $P, Q \in \left(2^{\ell/2-1}, 2^{\ell/2}\right)$, that $P' > 2^{\ell/2-2} - 1$. The inequality $\ell_{\exp} \leq \ell/2 - 2$ implies that $1 < E^* \leq 2^{\ell_{\exp}} - 1 \leq 2^{\ell/2-2} - 1 < P'$. In a similar manner, we also have $1 < E^* < Q'$. Since P' and Q' are prime, $E^* \in \mathbb{Z}_{P'Q'}^{\times}$ holds. □

Claim 3. *Assume that the RSA public key (N, e) is good, and $\mathcal{M}$ does not abort in (M-2). If $\mathcal{R}$ outputs a correct solution z^* for the RSA instance (N, e, y^*) in (M-5), $\mathcal{M}$ correctly finds a solution z for the RSA instance (N, e, y) in (M-6).*

Proof. Assume that the given RSA public key (N, e) is good. Namely, e is a prime and $e \geq 2^{\ell_{\exp}}$. On the other hand, the assumption that $\mathcal{M}$ does not abort implies that $E^* > 1$. It therefore follows from $E^* = H(r^*) < 2^{\ell_{\exp}}$ that $1 < E^* < 2^{\ell_{\exp}} \leq e$. Since e is prime, we have $\gcd(e, E^*) = 1$. Thus, if $\mathcal{R}$ outputs a correct solution z^* for the RSA instance (N, e, y^*), $\mathcal{M}$ correctly finds a solution z for the target RSA instance (N, e, y) by Lemma 3. □

Note that it is shown in [26] that one can easily verify whether or not $y^* = y^{E^*}$ is a generator of QR_N, and the solution z^* of the RSA instance (N, e, y^*) can be efficiently found if y^* is not a generator. When y^* is not a generator, $\mathcal{M}$ can therefore proceed to (M-6) without employing $\mathcal{R}$ and $\mathsf{Sim}_{\mathcal{A}}$. Hereafter, we assume that y^* is a generator.

It follows from **Claim 1** and **Claim 2** that $(N, e) \leftarrow \mathsf{KGen}_{\mathsf{RSA}}(1^k)$ and $y^* \in_{\mathrm{U}} \mathrm{QR}_N$ for the RSA instance (N, e, y^*) submitted by $\mathcal{M}$ in (M-3). We note that $\mathsf{Sim}_{\mathcal{A}}$ will be constructed so that from the $\mathcal{R}$'s viewpoint, its outcome $(M^*, (\lambda^*, r^*), \psi^*)$ in the step (c) of (M-4) is indeed a winning witness tuple on the game tuple $(N, \alpha, \rho_{k,m})$. These imply that $\mathcal{R}$ outputs a correct solution z^* with nonnegligible probability $\epsilon_0 - \mathrm{negl}(k)$ in (M-5). Therefore, by **Claim 3**, $\mathcal{M}$ outputs a correct solution z for the target RSA instance (N, e, y) with probability at least $\epsilon_0 - \mathrm{negl}(k)$ provided that the RSA public key (N, e) is good. Since we now assume that for the polynomial τ_{Good}, $\mathsf{KGen}_{\mathsf{RSA}}$ outputs a good public key (N, e) with probability $1/\tau_{\mathsf{Good}}$ for sufficiently large k, it holds that

On each game tuple $(N, \alpha, \rho_{k,m})$ with the auxiliary tuple (e, y, r^*, ω), as in the step (a) of (M-4), $\mathsf{Sim}_\mathcal{A}$ proceeds as follows.

(A-1) $\mathsf{Sim}_\mathcal{A}$ sets $E^* := H(r^*)$ and $y^* := y^{E^*}$, and then for each index $i \in [1, m]$, $\mathsf{Sim}_\mathcal{A}$ retrieves an exponent d_i of the element $\alpha(a_i) \in \mathrm{QR}_N$ such that $\alpha(a_i) = (y^*)^{d_i}$ by executing $\mathsf{Extract}(N, e, y^*, \alpha(a_i), \omega)$.

(A-2) $\mathsf{Sim}_\mathcal{A}$ chooses a random parameter M^*, chooses exponents $s_2^*, \ldots, s_m^*$ according to the distribution $\rho_{k,m}(M^*)$, and then sets $\boldsymbol{s}^* := (1, s_2^*, \ldots, s_m^*)$.

(A-3) $\mathsf{Sim}_\mathcal{A}$ sets $\lambda^* := (E^*, \boldsymbol{s}^*)$ and sets $\psi^* := y^{\sum_{i=1}^m d_i s_i^*}$.

(A-4) $\mathsf{Sim}_\mathcal{A}$ outputs the tuple $(M^*, (\lambda^*, r^*), \psi^*)$, and then halts.

Fig. 3. Configuration of $\mathsf{Sim}_\mathcal{A}$

$$\Pr[\mathsf{Succ}_\mathcal{M}] \geq \Pr[\mathsf{Succ}_\mathcal{M} \wedge (N, e) \text{ is good}]$$
$$= \Pr[(N, e) \text{ is good}] \Pr[\mathsf{Succ}_\mathcal{M} \mid (N, e) \text{ is good}]$$
$$\geq \frac{1}{\tau_{\mathsf{Good}}} \epsilon_0 - \mathrm{negl}(k).$$

Thus, $\mathcal{M}$ can break RSA with nonnegligible probability.

Construction of $\mathsf{Sim}_\mathcal{A}$. In order to construct the algorithm $\mathcal{M}$, it suffices to construct the subroutine $\mathsf{Sim}_\mathcal{A}$ of $\mathcal{M}$. Since $\mathcal{R}$ is algebraic with respect to QR_N, there exists a polynomial-time algorithm $\mathsf{Extract}$ that on a tuple (N, e, y^*, g, ω), where g is a target element in QR_N that is produced in the execution of $\mathcal{R}$ on the input (N, e, y^*) given from $\mathcal{M}$ with the random coin ω, returns an exponent d such that $g = (y^*)^d$. The algorithm $\mathsf{Sim}_\mathcal{A}$ is depicted in Fig 3. Note that we use the extractor $\mathsf{Extract}$ only to find the exponent d_i of $\alpha(a_i) = (y^*)^{d_i}$ in (A-1). For example if $\mathcal{R}$ has been constructed the assignment map α in a way that $\alpha(a_i) = (y^*)^{d_i}$ by choosing $d_i \in_U \{0, 1, \ldots, B - 1\}$ for some sufficiently large B with the generator y^*, then it suffices to hand the exponent d_i to $\mathsf{Sim}_\mathcal{A}$.

We now show that $\mathsf{Sim}_\mathcal{A}$ is a PPT simulator that wins the APF game with probability 1 on each game tuple $(N, \alpha, \rho_{k,m})$. Because $\mathsf{Extract}$ is a polynomial-time algorithm, $\mathsf{Sim}_\mathcal{A}$ runs in polynomial-time. For the tuple $(M^*, (\lambda^*, r^*), \psi^*)$, the following claims hold.

Claim 4. *The equation* λ^* *is nontrivial, and* $(\lambda^*, r^*) \in \mathsf{Supp}(\rho_{k,m}(M^*))$.

Proof. We now show that the equation $\lambda^* = (E^*, \boldsymbol{s}^*)$ is nontrivial, where $\boldsymbol{s}^* = (s_1, s_2, \ldots, s_m)$. Since $\mathsf{Sim}_\mathcal{A}$ is static, the nontriviality is exactly equivalent to that over $\mathcal{F}(A)$ as mentioned in Section 2.1. Hence, the nontriviality is determined by Lemma 1. Recall that the exponent E^* given to $\mathsf{Sim}_\mathcal{A}$ is strictly greater than 1 and the integer s_1^* chosen in (A-2) is 1, This implies that $E^* \nmid s_1^*$. It follows from Lemma 1 that the equation λ^* is nontrivial.

In (M-1) of Fig. 2, the string r^* and the exponent E^* are chosen so that $r^* \in_U \{0, 1\}^{\ell_{\mathsf{seed}}}$ and $E^* = H(r) \in [0, 2^{\ell_{\mathsf{exp}}} - 1]$. In (A-2), $s_1^*, s_2^*, \ldots, s_m^*$ are chosen according to $\rho_{k,m}(M^*)$. It therefore holds that $(\lambda^*, r^*) \in \mathsf{Supp}(\rho_{k,m}(M^*))$. $\square$

Claim 5. ψ^* *is a correct solution of the interpreted equation* λ_α^*.

Proof. It follows from $y^* = y^{E^*}$, $\alpha(a_i) = (y^*)^{d_i}$ for each $i \in [1, m]$ and $\psi^* = y^{\sum_{i=1}^m d_i s_i^*}$ that for the equation $\lambda^* = (E^*, (s_1^*, s_2^*, \ldots, s_m^*))$, in $\mathbb{Z}_N^\times$,

$$(\psi^*)^{E^*} = \left(y^{\sum_{i=1}^m d_i s_i^*} \right)^{E^*} = \prod_{i=1}^m \left(y^{E^* d_i} \right)^{s_i^*} = \prod_{i=1}^m \alpha(a_i)^{s_i^*}.$$

ψ^* is therefore a correct solution of the interpreted equation λ^*.   □

Thus, $\mathsf{Sim}_\mathcal{A}$ always wins the APF game of $\{\mathbb{Z}_N^\times\}$ with respect to the parametric distribution ρ when $\mathcal{R}$ plays the role of a challenger.   □

Recall that the SRSA assumption implies the adaptive pseudo-freeness of $\{\mathbb{Z}_N^\times\}$ with respect to $\rho \in \mathfrak{D}^{\mathsf{CFW}}$ [10], and the reduction algorithm in [10] can be described as a modulus-preserving algebraic one. Putting together with this fact and Theorem 1, the following corollary is obtained as a negative circumstantial evidence that the RSA assumption is not equivalent to the SRSA assumption.

Corollary 1. *Assume that* $\mathsf{KGen}_{\mathsf{RSA}}$ *outputs a good public key* (N, e) *with probability* $1/\tau_{\mathsf{Good}}$ *for sufficiently large* k, *where* τ_{Good} *is a polynomial in* k. *If the RSA assumption implies the SRSA assumption as far as a modulus-preserving algebraic reduction is concerned, then the RSA assumption does not hold.*

4   Impossibility Result on the Security Proofs of SRSA-Based Signatures

We now give an impossibility result on the security proof of *CFW-type signatures* under the RSA assumption. As such signatures, we cite several SRSA-based signatures such as the Camenisch-Lysyanskaya (CL, for short) signature [9], the Cramer-Shoup (CS, for short) signature [12], the Fischlin signature [13], the Gennaro-Halevi-Rabin (GHR, for short) signature [18], the Hofheinz-Kiltz (HK, for short) signature [22], and the Zhu signature [37,38]. In order to prove the impossibility, we give the following lemma. This can be shown by applying Theorem 1 and Lemma 2 to the RSA group family $\{\mathbb{Z}_N^\times\}$ with any parametric distribution $\rho \in \mathfrak{D}^{\mathsf{CFW}}$.

Lemma 5. *Let* $\rho = \{\rho_{k,m}\}$ *be a parametric distribution such that* $\rho \in \mathfrak{D}^{\mathsf{CFW}}$ *and for any* k, m *and* M, *the membership of* $\mathsf{Supp}(\rho_{k,m}(M))$ *can be efficiently verified. Assume that* $\mathsf{KGen}_{\mathsf{RSA}}$ *outputs a good public key* (N, e) *with probability* $1/\tau_{\mathsf{Good}}$ *for sufficiently large* k, *where* τ_{Good} *is a polynomial in* k. *If* $\mathsf{PFSig}_{\mathbb{Z}_N^\times, \rho}$ *is proven to be sEUF-CMA (EUF-KOA, resp.) from the RSA assumption via modulus-preserving algebraic reductions, then the RSA assumption does not hold.*

By employing Lemma 5, we give the impossibility result on the SRSA-based signatures. Catalano, Fiore and Warinschi [10] constructed a parametric distribution $\rho^{\mathsf{CL}} = \left\{ \rho_{k,m}^{\mathsf{CL}} \right\}_{k,m}$ (ρ^{CS}, ρ^{Fis}, ρ^{GHR}, ρ^{HK} and ρ^{Zhu}, resp.) so that $\mathsf{PFSig}_{\mathbb{Z}_N^\times, \rho^{\mathsf{CL}}}$

Let $\ell_{msg} + 2 \le \ell_{exp}$, and let ℓ_{parm} be a polynomial in k. For each k and m, $\rho^{CL}_{k,m}(M)$ outputs a tuple $((E, s), r)$ by the following rules:

(1) choose $r \in_U \{0,1\}^{\ell_{seed}}$, and then set $E := H_{PRIMES}(r)$, where $H_{PRIMES} : \{0,1\}^{\ell_{seed}} \to (2^{\ell_{exp}-1}, 2^{\ell_{exp}})$ denotes a division-intractable prime-valued hash function; and
(2) for the vector $s = (s_1, s_2, \ldots, s_m)$, set $s_1 := 1$, $s_2 \in_U [0, 2^{\ell+\ell_{msg}+\ell_{parm}} - 1]$, $s_3 := M$ and $s_i := 0$ for each $i \in [4, m]$.

Fig. 4. The parametric distribution ρ^{CL} for Camenisch-Lysyanskaya Signature [10]

coincides with the CL (CS, Fischlin, GHR, HK and Zhu, resp.) scheme. The parametric distribution ρ^{CL} is depicted in Fig. 4. The parametric distributions for the other signatures can be obtained in a similar manner. For the detail, refer to [10]. It follows that $\rho^{CL}, \rho^{Fis}, \rho^{HK}, \rho^{Zhu} \in \mathfrak{D}^{CFW}$. In fact, a pair (λ, r) chosen according to each of these parametric distributions satisfies that r is uniformly distributed over $\{0,1\}^{\ell_{seed}}$, E is computed by using a division-intractable hash function, $s_1 = 1$ and $s_2, \ldots, s_m \in \mathbb{Z}$. Therefore, one can apply Lemma 5 to $\mathsf{PFSig}_{\mathbb{Z}_N^\times, \rho^{CL}}$ (the CL signature), $\mathsf{PFSig}_{\mathbb{Z}_N^\times, \rho^{Fis}}$ (the Fischlin signature), $\mathsf{PFSig}_{\mathbb{Z}_N^\times, \rho^{HK}}$ (the HK signature) and $\mathsf{PFSig}_{\mathbb{Z}_N^\times, \rho^{Zhu}}$ (the Zhu signature), respectively. Note that Lemma 5 can be also applied to $\mathsf{PFSig}_{\mathbb{Z}_N^\times, \rho^{CS}}$ (the CS signature) and $\mathsf{PFSig}_{\mathbb{Z}_N^\times, \rho^{GHR}}$ (the GHR signature) by slight modifications on $\mathsf{Sim}_{\mathcal{A}}$, respectively. We will elaborate on such modifications in the full version of this paper. Thus, the following corollary can be shown.

Corollary 2. *Assume that $\ell_{seed} = \ell_{msg}$ and $\ell_{exp} \le \ell/2 - 2$. Assume also that KGen_{RSA} outputs a good public key (N, e) with probability $1/\tau_{Good}$ for sufficiently large k. The CL scheme, the CS scheme, the Fischlin scheme, the GHR scheme, the HK scheme and the Zhu scheme cannot be proven to be EUF-KOA under the RSA assumption via modulus-preserving algebraic reductions, as long as the RSA assumption holds.*

References

1. Abe, M., Groth, J., Ohkubo, M.: Separating Short Structure-Preserving Signatures from Non-Interactive Assumptions. In: Lee, D.H., Wang, X. (eds.) ASIACRYPT 2011. LNCS, vol. 7073, pp. 628–646. Springer, Heidelberg (2011)
2. Abe, M., Haralambiev, K., Ohkubo, M.: Group to Group Commitments Do Not Shrink. In: Pointcheval, D., Johansson, T. (eds.) EUROCRYPT 2012. LNCS, vol. 7237, pp. 301–317. Springer, Heidelberg (2012)
3. Aggarwal, D., Maurer, U., Shparlinski, I.: The Equivalence of Strong RSA and Factoring in the Generic Ring Model of Computation. In: Augot, D., Canteaut, A. (eds.) WCC 2011, pp. 17–26 (2011)
4. Agrawal, M., Kayal, N., Saxena, N.: PRIMES Is in P. Annals of Mathematics 160(2), 781–793 (2004)
5. Barić, N., Pfitzmann, B.: Collision-Free Accumulators and Fail-Stop Signature Schemes Without Trees. In: Fumy, W. (ed.) EUROCRYPT 1997. LNCS, vol. 1233, pp. 480–494. Springer, Heidelberg (1997)

6. Bellare, M., Rogaway, P.: Random Oracles Are Practical: A Paradigm for Designing Efficient Protocols. In: ACM CCS 1993, Fairfax, Virginia, USA, pp. 62–73. ACM Press, New York (1993)

7. Boneh, D., Venkatesan, R.: Breaking RSA May Not Be Equivalent to Factoring. In: Nyberg, K. (ed.) EUROCRYPT 1998. LNCS, vol. 1403, pp. 59–71. Springer, Heidelberg (1998)

8. Bresson, E., Monnerat, J., Vergnaud, D.: Separation Results on the "One-More" Computational Problems. In: Malkin, T. (ed.) CT-RSA 2008. LNCS, vol. 4964, pp. 71–87. Springer, Heidelberg (2008)

9. Camenisch, J., Lysyanskaya, A.: A Signature Scheme with Efficient Protocols. In: Cimato, S., Galdi, C., Persiano, G. (eds.) SCN 2002. LNCS, vol. 2576, pp. 268–289. Springer, Heidelberg (2003)

10. Catalano, D., Fiore, D., Warinschi, B.: Adaptive Pseudo-Free Groups and Applications. In: Paterson, K.G. (ed.) EUROCRYPT 2011. LNCS, vol. 6632, pp. 207–223. Springer, Heidelberg (2011)

11. Chevallier-Mames, B., Joye, M.: A Practical and Tightly Secure Signature Scheme Without Hash Function. In: Abe, M. (ed.) CT-RSA 2007. LNCS, vol. 4377, pp. 339–356. Springer, Heidelberg (2006)

12. Cramer, R., Shoup, V.: Signature Schemes Based on the Strong RSA Assumption. In: ACM CCS 1999, Kent Ridge Digital Labs, Singapore, pp. 46–51. ACM Press, New York (1999)

13. Fischlin, M.: The Cramer-Shoup Strong-RSA Signature Scheme Revisited. In: Desmedt, Y.G. (ed.) PKC 2003. LNCS, vol. 2567, pp. 116–129. Springer, Heidelberg (2002)

14. Fukumitsu, M., Hasegawa, S., Isobe, S., Koizumi, E., Shizuya, H.: Toward Separating the Strong Adaptive Pseudo-Freeness from the Strong RSA Assumption. In: Boyd, C., Simpson, L. (eds.) ACISP 2013. LNCS, vol. 7959, pp. 72–87. Springer, Heidelberg (2013)

15. Fukumitsu, M., Hasegawa, S., Isobe, S., Shizuya, H.: The RSA Group Is Adaptive Pseudo-Free under the RSA Assumption. IEICE Trans. Fundamentals, Special Section on Cryptography and Information Security E97-A(1), 200–214 (2014)

16. Fujisaki, E., Okamoto, T.: Statistical Zero Knowledge Protocols to Prove Modular Polynomial Relations. In: Kaliski Jr., B.S. (ed.) CRYPTO 1997. LNCS, vol. 1294, pp. 16–30. Springer, Heidelberg (1997)

17. Garg, S., Bhaskar, R., Lokam, S.V.: Improved Bounds on Security Reductions for Discrete Log Based Signatures. In: Wagner, D. (ed.) CRYPTO 2008. LNCS, vol. 5157, pp. 93–107. Springer, Heidelberg (2008)

18. Gennaro, R., Halevi, S., Rabin, T.: Secure Hash-and-Sign Signatures Without the Random Oracle. In: Stern, J. (ed.) EUROCRYPT 1999. LNCS, vol. 1592, pp. 123–139. Springer, Heidelberg (1999)

19. Goldwasser, S., Micali, S., Rivest, R.L.: A Digital Signature Scheme Secure against Adaptive Chosen-Message Attacks. SIAM Journal of Computing 17(2), 281–308 (1988)

20. Hanaoka, G., Matsuda, T., Schuldt, J.C.N.: On the Impossibility of Constructing Efficient Key Encapsulation and Programmable Hash Functions in Prime Order Groups. In: Safavi-Naini, R., Canetti, R. (eds.) CRYPTO 2012. LNCS, vol. 7417, pp. 812–831. Springer, Heidelberg (2012)

21. Hasegawa, S., Isobe, S., Shizuya, H., Tashiro, K.: On the Pseudo-Freeness and the CDH Assumption. International Journal of Information Security 8(5), 347–355 (2009)

22. Hofheinz, D., Kiltz, E.: Programmable Hash Functions and Their Applications. J. Cryptology 25(3), 484–527 (2012)
23. Hohenberger, S., Waters, B.: Short and Stateless Signatures from the RSA Assumption. In: Halevi, S. (ed.) CRYPTO 2009. LNCS, vol. 5677, pp. 654–670. Springer, Heidelberg (2009)
24. Jhanwar, M.P., Barua, R.: Sampling from Signed Quadratic Residues: RSA Group Is Pseudofree. In: Roy, B., Sendrier, N. (eds.) INDOCRYPT 2009. LNCS, vol. 5922, pp. 233–247. Springer, Heidelberg (2009)
25. Joye, M.: How (Not) to Design Strong-RSA Signatures. Designs, Codes and Cryptography 59(1-3), 169–182 (2011)
26. Micciancio, D.: The RSA Group is Pseudo-Free. J. Cryptology 23(2), 169–186 (2010)
27. Naccache, D., Pointcheval, D., Stern, J.: Twin Signatures: An Alternative to the Hash-and-Sign Paradigm. In: ACM CCS 2001, Philadelphia, PA, USA, pp. 20–27. ACM Press, New York (1993)
28. Paillier, P., Vergnaud, D.: Discrete-Log-Based Signatures May Not Be Equivalent to Discrete Log. In: Roy, B. (ed.) ASIACRYPT 2005. LNCS, vol. 3788, pp. 1–20. Springer, Heidelberg (2005)
29. Paillier, P., Villar, J.L.: Trading One-Wayness Against Chosen-Ciphertext Security in Factoring-Based Encryption. In: Lai, X., Chen, K. (eds.) ASIACRYPT 2006. LNCS, vol. 4284, pp. 252–266. Springer, Heidelberg (2006)
30. Paillier, P.: Impossibility Proofs for RSA Signatures in the Standard Model. In: Abe, M. (ed.) CT-RSA 2007. LNCS, vol. 4377, pp. 31–48. Springer, Heidelberg (2006)
31. Rivest, R.L.: On the Notion of Pseudo-Free Groups. In: Naor, M. (ed.) TCC 2004. LNCS, vol. 2951, pp. 505–521. Springer, Heidelberg (2004)
32. Schäge, S.: Twin Signature Schemes, Revisited. In: Pieprzyk, J., Zhang, F. (eds.) ProvSec 2009. LNCS, vol. 5848, pp. 104–117. Springer, Heidelberg (2009)
33. Schäge, S.: Tight Proofs for Signature Schemes without Random Oracles. In: Paterson, K.G. (ed.) EUROCRYPT 2011. LNCS, vol. 6632, pp. 189–206. Springer, Heidelberg (2011)
34. Seurin, Y.: On the Exact Security of Schnorr-Type Signatures in the Random Oracle Model. In: Pointcheval, D., Johansson, T. (eds.) EUROCRYPT 2012. LNCS, vol. 7237, pp. 554–571. Springer, Heidelberg (2012)
35. Shamir, A.: On the Generation of Cryptographically Strong Pseudorandom Sequences. ACM Trans. on Computer Systems 1(1), 38–44 (1983)
36. Villar, J.L.: Optimal Reductions of Some Decisional Problems to the Rank Problem. In: Wang, X., Sako, K. (eds.) ASIACRYPT 2012. LNCS, vol. 7658, pp. 80–97. Springer, Heidelberg (2012)
37. Zhu, H.: New Digital Signature Scheme Attaining Immunity to Adaptive Chosen-Message Attack. Chinese Journal of Electronics 10(4), 484–486 (2001)
38. Zhu, H.: A Formal Proof of Zhu's Signature Scheme. Cryptology ePrint Archive, Report 2003/155 (2003), http://eprint.iacr.org/

ELmE: A Misuse Resistant Parallel Authenticated Encryption

Nilanjan Datta and Mridul Nandi

Indian Statistical Institute, Kolkata, India
nilanjan_isi_jrf@yahoo.com, mridul.nandi@gmail.com

Abstract. The authenticated encryptions which resist misuse of initial value (or nonce) at some desired level of privacy are two-pass or Mac-then-Encrypt constructions (inherently inefficient but provide full privacy) and online constructions, e.g., McOE, sponge-type authenticated encryptions (such as duplex) and COPA. Only the last one is almost parallelizable with some bottleneck in processing associated data. In this paper, *we design a new online secure authenticated encryption, called* ELmE *or Encrypt-Linear mix-Encrypt, which is completely (two-stage)* **parallel** *(even in associated data) and* **pipeline implementable**. It also provides full privacy when associated data (which includes initial value) is not repeated. The basic idea of our construction is based on EME, an Encrypt-Mix-Encrypt type SPRP constructions (secure against chosen plaintext and ciphertext). But unlike EME, we have used an on-line computable efficient **linear mixing** instead of a non-linear mixing. Our construction optionally supports **intermediate tags** which can be verified faster with less buffer size. Intermediate tag provides security against block-wise adversaries which is meaningful in low-end device implementation.

Keywords: Authenticated Encryption, Privacy, Misuse Resistant, EME.

1 Introduction

The common application of cryptography is to implement a secure channel between two or more users and then exchanging information over that channel. These users can initially set up their one-time shared key. Otherwise, a typical implementation first calls a key-exchange protocol for establishing a shared key or a session key (used only for the current session). Once the users have a shared key, either through the initial key set-up or key-exchange, they use this key to authenticate and encrypt the transmitted information using efficient symmetric-key algorithms such as a *message authentication code* Mac($\cdot$) and (symmetric-key) *encryption* Enc($\cdot$). The encryption provides **privacy** or **confidentiality** (hiding the sensitive data M, we call it *plaintext* or *message*) resulting a ciphertext C, whereas a message authentication code provides **data-integrity** (authenticating the transmitted message M or the ciphertext C) resulting a tag T. An authenticated encryption or AE is an integrated scheme which provides both privacy

W. Susilo and Y. Mu (Eds.): ACISP 2014, LNCS 8544, pp. 306–321, 2014.
© Springer International Publishing Switzerland 2014

of plaintext and authenticity or data integrity of message or ciphertext. An authenticated encryption scheme F_K takes associated data D (which may include initial value or nonce) and message M and produces tagged-ciphertext (C, T). Its inverse F_K^{-1} returns $\perp$ for all those (D, C, T) for which no such M exists, otherwise it returns M. Note that the associated data D must be sent along with tagged-ciphertext to decrypt correctly.

1.1 Examples of Authenticated Encryptions

So far, cryptography community put a lot of effort of designing different authenticated encryptions. CAESAR [1], a competition for Authenticated Encryption is going on, which will identify a portfolio of authenticated ciphers that offer advantages over AES-GCM and are suitable for widespread adoption. We have submitted ELmD v1.0 [1], a variant of ELmE (main difference is in the masking) in the competition and believe that it would be a strong candidate for this competition. We quickly mention some of the popularly known competitive constructions putting into different categories based on construction types.

ENCRYPT-AND-MAC AND ENCRYPT-THEN-MAC. It relies on non-repeating IV (or nonce), e.g. CCM [16], EAX [4], GCM [35], CHM [17], Sarkar's generic construction [34] and dedicated Stream Ciphers like Grain [15], Zuc [2] etc. All these constructions combine counter type encryption and a Mac.

MAC-THEN-ENCRYPT. It is a two-pass IV misuse resistant category e.g., SIV [33], BTM [19], HBS [18]. These compute a tag first and then based on this tag, counter type encryption is used to encrypt.

ONLINE FEED BACK ENCRYPTION. It uses feedback type encryption, e.g. IACBC [21], XCBC [8], CCFB [24], McOE [11], sponge-type constructions (Duplex [6]). These constructions have a bottleneck that they are not fully parallelizable. Our construction ELmE and COPA [3] also fall in this category which use basic structure of completely parallel EME, Encrypt-Mix-Encrypt constructions [14] with linear mixing in the middle layer, and hence parallelizable.

ENCRYPT-THEN-CHECKSUM. It uses IV-based block-wise encryption (non-repeating IV is required) and then finally checksum is used to compute tag. For example, different versions of OCB [5,30,22] and IAPM [21].

1.2 Encrypt Mix Encrypt

Encrypt Mix Encrypt or EME [14] is a block-cipher mode of operation, that turns a block cipher into a tweakable enciphering scheme. The mode is parallelizable, and as serial-efficient as the non-parallelizable mode CMC [13]. EME algorithm entails two layers of ECB encryption and a non-linear mixing in between. In the non-linear mixing, the blockcipher is again used. EME is proved to provide SPRP [23] security in the standard, provable security model assuming that the underlying block cipher is SPRP secure. Moreover, the designers of EME showed a CCA-distinguisher if non-linear mixing is replaced by a binary linear mixing.

1.3   Our Contribution

In this paper, we have observed that replacing non-linear mixing by an efficient online linear mixing actually helps to have faster and parallel implementation of the construction and gives online prp [23] security. (We know that, an online function is a function whose i^{th} block output is determined by the first i blocks of input) the Based on this observation, we have designed an online authenticated cipher ELmE based on Encrypt Mix Encrypt structure where the non-linear mixing is replaced by efficient online linear mix. ELmE has the following advantages over other popular authenticated schemes :

Nonce Misuse Resistant. Most of the IV based authenticated encryption schemes [31] like all the versions of OCB [5], GCM [35] needed to ensure that nonce must be distinct for every invocation of the tagged-encryption. Failure to do so, leads easy attacks on the privacy of the scheme. In practice, it is challenging to ensure that the nonce is never reused. For example, in lightweight applications, it is quite challenging to generate distinct nonce as it either needs to store a non-tamperable state or require some hardware source of randomness. Apart from that, there are various issues like flawed implementations or bad management by the user, for example where users with same key uses the same nonce. Our construction ELmE does not have the distinct nonce requirement, instead it generates an IV from the associated data. In section 4, we prove that, ELmE provides **online privacy** under IV repetition and **full privacy** when distinct IVs are used.

Fully Pipeline Implementable. Most of the popular online constructions like McOE [11] (uses MHCBC [25], later generalized and called TC3 [32]) has a hardware bottleneck of not being fully pipelined (see the bottom layer of McOE in Figure 1. It has CBC like structure, which is sequential and hence can not be pipelined). Our construction ELmE has a Encrypt-Linear mix-Decrypt type structure, making it fully parallel and pipeline implementable.

Efficient. Deterministic AE Schemes (for example : SIV, BTM, HBS) doesn't use any nonce. Instead it uses a derived IV using the message and the

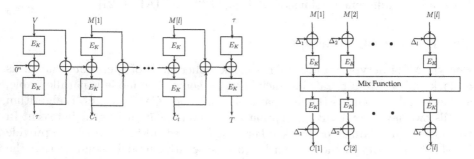

Fig. 1. (1) McOE-D construction : cannot be pipelined. (2) Encrypt-Mix-Encrypt : completely parallel and pipeline implementable.

associated data, which ensures that it is distinct for each different associated data-message tuples but such constructions are two passed, and hence not efficient. Having Encrypt- Linear mix-Encrypt type layered design, makes our construction single pass and efficient.

Minimized Area in Combined Implementation. The construction of ELmE ensures that encryption and decryption behave almost in a similar fashion (see figure 3 and remark 2 in section 3). This helps us to implement both encryption and decryption in hardware with a smaller area. Nowadays in all application environment, both encryption and decryption of blockciphers to be implemented and hence we can share the architectures to have a compact combined hardware implementation of it.

Secure against Block-wise Adaptive Adversaries. Due to limited memory in some environment such as low end devices the decryption oracle has to release a part of the plaintext before it authenticates. That raises some attacks on popular constructions [20]. We consider similar advantages such as privacy and authenticity, however the adversaries (called blockwise adaptive adversary) would have access of partial decryption oracles for authenticity security. To resist such attacks, intermediate tags can be used. In section 5, we have shown that ELmE can be extended to incorporates intermediate tags, hence it provides security against Block-wise adaptive adversaries.

2   Preliminaries

Definitions and Notation. By convention, $\mathbb{B} = \{0,1\}^n$ where n is the block size of the underlying blockcipher. An ℓ-tuple $x \in \mathbb{B}^\ell$ is denoted by $(x[1], x[2], \ldots, x[\ell])$. We call $\ell := \|x\|$ block-length of x. For $0 \le a \le b < \ell$ we denote $x[a..b] := (x[a], x[a+1], \ldots, x[b])$, $x[..b] = x[1..b]$. A plaintext P is represented as a tuple (D, M) where M is the message and D is the associated data and the corresponding ciphertext is represented as (C, T) where C is the ciphertext and T is the generated tag.

2.1   Full and Online Privacy

We give a particularly strong definition of privacy, one asserting indistinguishability from random strings. Consider an adversary A who has access of one of two types of oracles: a "real" encryption oracle or an "ideal" authenticated encryption oracle. A real authenticated encryption oracle, F_K, takes as input (D, M) and returns $(C, T) = F_K(D, M)$. Whereas an ideal authenticated encryption oracle $\$$ returns a random string R with $\|R\| = \|M\| + 1$ for every fresh pair (D, M). Given an adversary A (w.l.o.g. throughout the paper we assume a **deterministic adversary**) and an authenticated encryption scheme F, we define the (full) **privacy-advantage** of A by the distinguishing advantage of A distinguishing F from $\$$. More formally,

$$\mathbf{Adv}_F^{\mathrm{priv}}(A) := \mathbf{Adv}_F^{\$}(A) = \Pr_K[A^{F_K} = 1] - \Pr_{\$}[A^{\$} = 1].$$

We include initial value IV as a part of associated data D and so for nonce-respecting adversary A (never repeats a nonce or initial value and hence the view obtained by the adversary is nonce-respecting) the response of ideal oracle for every query is random as all queries are fresh. Similarly, we define online privacy for which the the ideal online authenticated encryption oracle $\$_{ol}$ responses random string keeping the online property. The online privacy advantage of an adversary A against F is defined as $\mathbf{Adv}_F^{\mathrm{opriv}}(A) := \mathbf{Adv}_F^{\$_{ol}}(A)$.

VIEW AND A-REALIZABLE. We define view of a deterministic adversary A interacting with an oracle $\mathcal{O}$ by a tuple $\tau(A^{\mathcal{O}}) := (Q_1, R_1, \ldots, Q_q, R_q)$ where Q_i is the ith query and R_i is the response by $\mathcal{O}$. It is also called $\mathcal{O}$-view. A tuple $\tau = (Q_1, R_1, \ldots, Q_q, R_q)$ is called A-realizable if it makes query Q_i after obtaining all previous responses $R_1, \ldots, R_{i-1}$. As A is assumed to be deterministic, given $R_1, \ldots, R_q$, there is an unique q-tuple $Q_1, \ldots, Q_q$ for which the combined tuple is A-realizable. Now we describe the popular coefficient H-technique [27] which can be used to bound distinguish advantage. Suppose f and g are two oracles and V denotes all possible A-realizable views while A interacts with f or g (they have same input and output space).

Lemma 1 (Coefficient H Technique). If $\forall v \in V_{good} \subseteq V$ (as defined above), $\Pr[\tau(A^g(\cdot)) = v] \geq (1 - \epsilon)\Pr[\tau(A^f(\cdot)) = v]$, then the distinguishing advantage $\mathbf{Adv}_g^f(A)$ of A is at most $\epsilon + \Pr[\tau(A^f(\cdot)) \notin V_{good}]$.

We skip the proof as it can be found in many papers, e.g. [27,36].

2.2 Authenticity

We say that an adversary A **forges** an authenticated encryption F if A outputs (D, C, T) where $F_K(D, C, T) \neq \bot$ (i.e. it accepts and returns a plaintext), and A made no earlier query (D, M) for which the F-response is (C, T). It can make s attempts to forge after making q queries. We define that A forges if it makes at least one forges in all s attempts and the **authenticity-advantage** of A by

$$\mathbf{Adv}_F^{\mathrm{auth}}(A) = \Pr_K[A^{F_K} \text{ forges}].$$

Suppose for any valid tuple of associate data and tagged ciphertext (D, C, T), the tag T can be computed from (D, C). We write $T = T_K(D, C)$. So (D, C, T) is a valid tagged ciphertext if and only if $T_K(D, C) = T$. Almost all known authenticated encryptions F (including those following encrypt-then-mac paradigm) have this property for a suitably defined ciphertext C and tag function T. We know that PRF implies Mac. We use similar concept to bound authenticity. More formally, for any forgery B, there is a distinguisher A such that

$$\mathbf{Adv}_F^{\mathrm{auth}}(B) \leq \mathbf{Adv}_{(F,T)}^{\mathcal{O},\$}(A) + \frac{s}{2^n} \qquad (1)$$

where $\mathcal{O}$ and $\$$ are independent oracles and $\$$ is a random function. This can be easily seen by defining A as follows:

- A first makes the q many F-queries (D_i, M_i) which are made by B and obtains responses (C_i, T_i), $1 \le i \le q$.
- Then it makes s many T-queries (D_j, C_j), $q < j \le q + s$ where (D_j, C_j, T_j)'s are returned by B.
- A returns 1 (interpreting that interacting with real) if and only if $T(D_j, C_j) = T'_j$ for some j.

The distinguishing advantage of A is clearly at least $\Pr[B \text{ forges}] - \frac{s}{2^n}$ and hence our claim follows.

TRIVIAL QUERIES. As $F(D, M) = (C, T)$ implies that $T(D, C) = T$, we call such T-query (D, C) trivial (after obtaining response (C, T) response of the F-query (D, M)). The repetition of queries are also called trivial. Without loss of generality we assume that all adversaries A is **deterministic and does not make any trivial query**. These assumptions are useful to simplify the analysis.

3 ELmE: An Online Authenticated Encryption Algorithm

In this section, we demonstrate our new construction ELmE. It is an online authenticated encryption which takes an associated data $D \in \mathbb{B}^d$ and a messages $M \in \mathbb{B}^e$ and returns a tagged-ciphertext $C \in \mathbb{B}^{e+1}$ for all integers $d \ge 1$, $e \ge 1$. We assume associated data to be non-empty. The case when the associated data is empty, is taken care in the remark 1. To process incomplete blocks, one can either apply an injective padding rule (e.g., first pad 1 and then a sequence of zeros to make the padded message or associate data size multiple of n) or some standard methods (e.g., ciphertext stealing [9], the method used in Hash Counter Hash type constructions [10], XLS [29] etc.). It uses Encrypt-Mix-Encrypt type construction with a specified simple linear mixing (see in Algorithm 1) and a keyed block cipher $E_k : \mathbb{B} \to \mathbb{B}$ for the ECB layers. The ECB layers are masked by separate keys L_1 (for associated data), L_2 (for the message) and L_3 (for the ciphertext) chosen uniformly from $\mathbb{B}$. However, L_1, L_2, L_3 can be simply computed from E_k as $E_K(0) = L_1$, $E_K(1) = L_2$, $E_k(2) = L_3$ and can be preprocessed. The complete construction is described below in Algorithm 1 and illustrated in Fig. 2 below.

Remark 1 (Case when Associated data is empty). Here we consider the case when the associated data is non empty, using the initial value of the sequence $W[0] = 0$, one can have a trivial attack against the privacy of the construction : Query any message M_1 with $M_1[1] = 0$. It produces the ciphertext with $C_1[1] = L_2 + L_3$. Now querying any message M_2 with $M_2[1] = C_1[1]$ will produce $C_2[1] = 0$ with probability 1.

Note that, Algorithm 1 is defined for non-empty associated data. One can ensure associated data to be non-empty by including a non-empty public message number, in the first block of the associated data. Still, if we want to incorporate empty associated data in our algorithm, we make a small modification and initialize the value $W[0]$ to 1, to resist against any attack. The rest computations, to generate the tagged ciphertext, are identical to the above algorithm.

> **Input:** $(D, M) \in \mathbb{B}^d \times \mathbb{B}^e$
> **Output:** $Z = (C, T) \in \mathbb{B}^e \times \mathbb{B}$
>
> **Algorithm ELmE**(D, M) **(Key:** (L_1, L_2, L_3, K)**)**
> parse D and M into n-length blocks.
> 1 $D = D[1] \| \cdots \| D[d]$
> 2 $M = M[1] \| M[2] \| \cdots \| M[e]$
> 3 $W[0] = 0$
> 4 $M[e+1] = D[1] + \cdots + D[d] + M[1] + \cdots + M[e]$ **(checksum)**
> process D
> 5   **For all** $j = 1$ **to** d
> 6 $DD[j] = D[j] + \alpha^{j-1}.L_1$ **(Masking the associate data blocks)**
> 7 $Z[j] = E_K(DD[j])$ **(Layer-I Encryption)**
> 8 $(Y'[j], W[j]) \leftarrow \rho(Z[j], W[j-1])$ **(Linear Mixing)**
> process M
> 9   **For all** $j = 1$ **to** e
> 10 $MM[j] = M[j] + \alpha^{j-1}.L_2$ **(Masking the message blocks)**
> 11 $X[j] = E_K(MM[j])$ **(Layer-I Encryption)**
> 12 $(Y[j], W[d+j]) \leftarrow \rho(X[j], W[d+j-1])$ **(Linear Mixing)**
> 13 $CC[j] = E_K^{-1}(Y[j])$ **(Layer-II Encryption)**
> 14 $C[j] = CC[j] + \alpha^{j-1}.L_3$ **(Masking the ciphertext blocks)**
> **Tag generation**
> 15 $MM[e+1] = M[e+1] + \alpha^e.L_2$
> 16 $X[e+1] = E_K(MM[e+1])$
> 17 $(Y[e+1], W[d+e+1]) \leftarrow \rho(X[d+e+1], W[d+e])$
> 18 $TT = E_K^{-1}(Y[e+1] + 0^{n-1}1)$
> 19 $T = TT + \alpha^e.L_3$
> 20   **Return** $(C = C[1] \| C[2] \| \cdots \| C[e], T)$
>
> **Subroutine** $\rho(x, w)$ **Onlinear Linear Mixing Function**
> 21 $y = x + (\alpha + 1) \cdot w$
> 22 $w = x + \alpha \cdot w$
> 23   **Return** (y, w)

Algorithm 1. ELmE Authenticated Encryption Algorithm. Here α is a primitive element of the binary field $(GF(2^n), +, .)$.

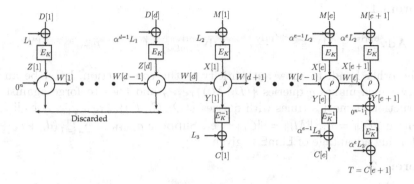

Fig. 2. Construction of ELmE Authenticated Encryption

Remark 2 (Similarity in Encryption and Decryption). Observe that, the second ECB layer is based on blockcipher decryption instead of encryption. Due to this, both encryption and decryption behave almost in a similar fashion (only with few changes in masking layers due to different keys and in linear mixing which should be inverse of the forward mixing). This helps us to implement both encryption and decryption in hardware with a smaller area.

Note that, from the definition of ρ, we see that the following online linear mixing has been performed :

When d is non-empty :

$$Y[i] = \alpha^{d+i-2}(\alpha+1)Z[1] + \cdots + \alpha^{i-1}(\alpha+1)Z[d]$$
$$+\alpha^{i-2}(\alpha+1)X[1] + \alpha^{i-3}(\alpha+1)X[2] + \cdots + (\alpha+1)X[i-1] + X[i]$$

When d is empty :

$$Y[i] = \alpha^{i-2}(\alpha+1)X[1] + \alpha^{i-3}(\alpha+1)X[2] + \cdots + (\alpha+1)X[i-1] + X[i] + \alpha^{i-1}(\alpha+1)$$

4   Privacy and Authenticity of ELmE

To prove the online Privacy of ELmE, let A be an adversary which makes at most q queries $\{(D_i, M_i)\}_{1 \le i \le q}$ in order to distinguish it from an online function, with same domain and range size chosen uniformly at random. Assume $\|D_i\| = d_i$, $\|M_i\| = e_i$. Let $\sigma_{priv} = \sum_{i=1}^{q}(d_i + e_i + 1)$ (the total number of blocks processed). Let $\$_{perm}$ denotes the random n-bit permutation and $\eta_{priv} := \max_B \mathbf{Adv}_{E,E^{-1}}^{\$_{perm},\$_{perm}^{-1}}(B)$ denotes the maximum advantage over all adversaries B making at most σ_{priv} queries and running in time T_0 which is about time of the adversary A plus some overhead which can be determined from the hybrid technique. The advantage of A is given by,

Theorem 1

$$\mathbf{Adv}^{opriv}_{ELmE_{\Pi},\mathbf{L}}(A) \leq \frac{5\sigma^2_{priv}}{2^n}, \quad \mathbf{Adv}^{opriv}_{ELmE_{E_K},\mathbf{L}}(A) \leq \eta_{priv} + \frac{5\sigma^2_{priv}}{2^n}.$$

On the other hand, to show authenticity of the construction, let A be an adversary which makes q queries $\{(D_i, M_i)\}_{1 \leq i \leq q}$ and tries to forge against the construction at most s times with queries $\{(D_i, C_i, T_i)\}_{q+1 \leq i \leq q+s}$. For all i, let us denote $\|D_i\| = d_i$, $\|M_i\| = \|C_i\| = e_i$. Suppose $\sigma_{\mathbf{auth}} = \sum_{i=1}^{q+s}(d_i + e_i + 1)$. The forging advantage of ELmE is given by:

Theorem 2

$$\mathbf{Adv}^{forge}_{ELmE_{\Pi},\mathbf{L}}(A) \leq \frac{9\sigma^2_{auth}}{2^n} + \frac{s}{2^n}, \quad \mathbf{Adv}^{forge}_{ELmE_{E_K},\mathbf{L}}(A) \leq \eta_{auth} + \frac{9\sigma^2_{auth}}{2^n} + \frac{s}{2^n}.$$

where η_{auth} is exactly same to η_{priv} except that it can make atmost σ_{auth} queries.

4.1 Proof of Theorem 1

First part of the theorem follows using the coefficient H technique (see Lemma 1) and following Propositions 1 and 2. Second part follows from the standard hybrid argument.

Let us fix q message and associate data pairs $P_1 = (D_1, M_1), \ldots, P_q = (D_q, M_q)$ with $\|D_i\| = d_i$, $\|M_i\| = e_i$, $\ell_i = d_i + e_i$ and $\sigma = \sum_i \ell_i$. We denote $(P_1, \ldots, P_q)$ by τ_{in}. We assume that all P_i's are distinct.

Definition 1 (Good views). *A tagged ciphertext tuple $\tau_{out} = (C_1, \ldots, C_q)$ (also the complete view $\tau = (\tau_{in}, \tau_{out})$) is called **good** online view (belongs to τ_{good}) w.r.t. τ_{in} if (τ_{in}, τ_{out}) is an online view (i.e., it must be realized by an online cipher, see section 2) and the following conditions hold:*

1. $C_i[j] = C_{i'}[j]$ implies that $D_i = D_{i'}$, $M_i[..j] = M_{i'}[..j]$ and
2. $\forall\ (i, l_i + 1) \neq (i', j')$, $T_i \neq C_{i'}[j']$.

The first condition says that we can have collision of ciphertext blocks in a position only if they are ciphertexts of two messages with same prefixes up to that block. The second conditions says that all tag blocks are fresh as if these are independently generated. It is easy to check that, in case of ideal online cipher, generating a bad view (i.e. not a good view) has negligible probability:

Proposition 1 (Obtaining a Good view has high probability)

$$\Pr[\tau(A^{\$_{ol}}) \notin \tau_{good}] \leq \frac{\sigma^2_{priv}}{2^n}.$$

We Now Fix a Good View $\tau = (\tau_{in}, \tau_{out})$ **as Mentioned above.** The tagged ciphertext of P_i is given by C_i which has $e_i + 1$ blocks where the last block $T_i := C_i[e_i + 1]$ denotes the tag. In the following result, we compute the interpolation probability, i.e. $\Pr[\tau(A^F) = \tau]$.

Proposition 2 (High interpolation probability of ELmE). $\forall \tau \in V_{good}$,

$$Pr[\tau(A^{ELmE_{\Pi,L}}) = \tau] \geq (1 - \frac{4\sigma_{priv}^2}{2^n}) \times Pr[\tau(A^{\$^{ol}}) = \tau].$$

Note that $Pr[\tau(A^{\$^{ol}}) = \tau] = 2^{-nP}$ where P denotes the number of non-empty prefixes of (D_i, M_i), $1 \leq i \leq q$ as for every different prefixes, $\$^{ol}$ assigns an independent and uniform ciphertext blocks. Proof of the above proposition can be found in the full version [7].

Remark 3. If associated datas are distinct for all the q messages, then $P = \sigma_{priv}$ and hence, we'll have full privacy i.e. the construction becomes indistinguishable from a random cipher with same domain and range.

4.2 Proof of Theorem 2

First part of theorem 2 follows using the coefficient H technique (see Lemma 1) and following Propositions 3 and 4 and then using equation 1. Second part follows from the standard hybrid argument.

Let $\mathbf{L} = (L_1, L_2, L_3)$ be the triple of masking keys and Π be the uniform random permutation. For notational simplicity, we write $ELmE_{\Pi,L}$ by F. Note that for a valid tuple of associate data and tagged ciphertext (D, C, T), the tag T can be computed from C and the key. We write $T = T_{\Pi,L}(D, C) := T(D, C)$. So (D, C, T) is a valid tagged ciphertext if and only if $T(D, C) = T$. As we have observed in Eq. 1, we only need to show indistinguishability for which we apply the coefficient H technique again. For this, we need to identify set of good views for which we have high interpolation probability.

GOOD FORGE VIEW. A (F, T)-forge view of a distinguisher A is the pair $\tau = (\tau_F, \tau_T)$ where $\tau_F = (D_i, M_i, C_i, T_i)_{1 \leq i \leq q}$ is an q-tuple of F-online view and $\tau_F = (D_j, C_j, T_j)_{q < j \leq q+s}$ is an s-tuple non-trivial T-view. τ is called **good forge view** (belongs to τ_{good}) if τ_F is good (as defined in Definition 1) and for all $q < j \leq q + s$, T_j's are fresh - distinct and different from all other T_i's and $C_i[j]$'s. We recall the notation $|M_i| = e_i$, $|D_i| = d_i$ and $\ell_i = d_i + e_i$. Let $\sigma_{auth} = \sum_{i=1}^{q+s}(\ell_i + 1)$. Since F is online function we consider pair of independent oracles $(\$_{ol}, \$)$ where $\$_{ol}$ denotes the random online function and $\$$ is simply a random function.

Proposition 3 (Obtaining a good forge view has high probability)

$$Pr[\tau(A^{\$_{ol},\$}) \in \tau_{good}] \leq \frac{(q + \sum_{i=1}^q e_i)^2}{2^{n+1}} + \frac{s(q + s + \sum_{i=1}^{q+s} e_i)}{2^n} \leq \frac{2\sigma_{auth}^2}{2^n}.$$

The first summand takes care the collisions in $C_i[j]$'s (i.e., the bad view for τ_F as in Proposition 1) and the second summand takes care the collision between T_i's ($q < i \leq q + s$) and all other $C_i[j]$'s.

Now we fix a good view $\tau = (\tau_F, \tau_T)$ as defined above (following same notations). It is easy to see that obtaining τ interacting with $(\$_{ol}, \$)$ has probability

$2^{-ns} \times 2^{-n\sigma_{pf}} = 2^{-n(s+\sigma_{pf})}$ where σ_{pf} denotes the number of non-empty prefixes of (C_i, T_i), $1 \leq i \leq q$ (at those blocks random online function returns randomly). Now, one can show the following result :

Proposition 4 (Good forge view has high interpolation probability). *For any good (F, T)-view τ and $\epsilon' = \frac{7\sigma_{auth}^2}{2^n}$, we have*

$$Pr[F(D_i, M_i) = (C_i, T_i), 1 \leq i \leq q, \ T(D_j, C_j) = T_j, q < j \leq q+s] \geq (1-\epsilon')2^{-n(\sigma_{pf}+s)}.$$

Proof of this proposition can be found in the full version [7].

5   ELmE Incorporating Intermediate Tags

Intermediate tags can be used in authenticated encryption to provide quick rejection of invalid decryption queries. This also helps in low-end implementation where the message has to be released depending on buffer size. If we have an intermediate tag in appropriate positions so that we can reject before we release some message blocks. Our construction can be easily extended to produce intermediate tags also, as described in the figure below. Suppose, we want ELmE with intermediate tags generated after each k blocks. In this case, for a message $M \in \mathbb{B}^e$, ELmE generates a ciphertext $C \in \mathbb{B}^e$ and $T \in \mathbb{B}^h$ where $h = \lceil \frac{e}{k} \rceil$. Processing of D remains same. For Processing of M, the calculation of $C[j]$ is changed to $CC[j] + \alpha^{j-1+\lfloor \frac{j-1}{k} \rfloor}.L_3$. $\forall \ j < e$ s.t. $k|j$, the intermediate tags are generated by $T[\frac{j}{k}] = E_K^{-1}(W[d+j]) + \alpha^{j-1+\lceil \frac{j-1}{k} \rceil}.L_3$. Final tag $T[h]$ is generated similar to the generation of T in the case of ELmE without intermediate tags (Here $\alpha^{e+h-1}L_3$ is used as the mask). Tag T is given by $T[1] \ || \ T[2] \ || \cdots || \ T[h]$. For verification during decryption, each $T[i]$ is verified and as soon as, a $T[i]$ doesn't matched with it's calculated value, the ciphertext gets rejected. Here, we have used intermediate tags after processing of each $k < n$ blocks of message. Let $\mathbf{F}$ be our construction incorporating intermediate tags after each $k < n$ blocks. In the following subsection, we show the privacy and authenticity of $\mathbf{F}$.

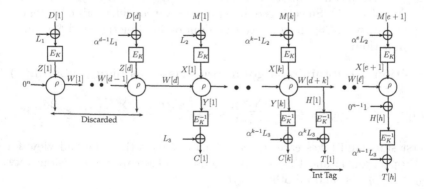

Fig. 3. ELmE with intermediate tags

Remark 4. Sponge duplex [6], is another authenticated encryption that incorporates intermediate tags but the dependency is such that, during decryption, the plaintext depends on the values of the intermediate tags. In our construction, during decryption, the plaintext does not depend on the intermediate tags and hence the extra computations required for the intermediate tags, can be skipped, if intermediate verifications are not required.

5.1 Online Privacy and Authenticity of F

Let A be an adversary which makes q queries (D_i, M_i) and obtains responses (C_i, T_i), $1 \leq i \leq q$. We denote $\|D_i\| = d_i$, $\|M_i\| = \|C_i\| = e_i$ and $\|T_i\| = h_i$. Let $\sigma_{\mathsf{priv}} = \sum_{i=1}^{q}(d_i + e_i + h_i)$ (the total number of ciphertext blocks with the tag blocks). The online Privacy of $\mathbf{F}$ is given by:

Theorem 3

$$\mathbf{Adv}^{\mathrm{opriv}}_{\mathbf{F}_{\Pi,\mathbf{L}}}(A) \leq \frac{5\sigma^2_{\mathsf{priv}}}{2^n}, \quad \mathbf{Adv}^{\mathrm{opriv}}_{\mathbf{F}_{E_K,\mathbf{L}}}(A) \leq \eta_{\mathsf{priv}} + \frac{5\sigma^2_{\mathsf{priv}}}{2^n}.$$

On the other hand, let A be an adversary which makes q queries $\{(D_i, M_i)\}_{1 \leq i \leq q}$ and tries to forge against the construction at most s times with queries $\{(D_i, C_i, T_i)\}_{q+1 \leq i \leq q+s}$. For all i, let us denote $\|D_i\| = d_i$, $\|M_i\| = \|C_i\| = e_i$ and $\|T_i\| = h_i$. Suppose $\sigma_{\mathsf{auth}} = \sum_{i=1}^{q+s}(d_i + e_i + h_i)$ (the total number of ciphertext blocks with the tag blocks). The forging advantage of F is given by:

Theorem 4

$$\mathbf{Adv}^{\mathrm{forge}}_{\mathbf{F}_{\Pi,\mathbf{L}}}(A) \leq \frac{10\sigma^2_{\mathsf{auth}}}{2^n} + \frac{s}{2^n}, \quad \mathbf{Adv}^{\mathrm{forge}}_{\mathbf{F}_{E_K,\mathbf{L}}}(A) \leq \eta_{\mathsf{auth}} + \frac{10\sigma^2_{\mathsf{auth}}}{2^n} + \frac{s}{2^n}.$$

The proofs of Theorem 3 and 4 are skipped due to page limit and can be found in the full version of the paper [7].

5.2 Including Intermediate Tags : Comparison with COPA

Intermediate tags are used to provide block-wise security. Suppose we consider a construction with intermediate tag size of k blocks. At each k blocks, we check the intermediate tag, hold the k block message and finally release the k blocks of the message if the tag is verified. For that, we need to store all the intermediate computations and the already computed messages in order to perform the verification. As we are using low end device, we need to minimize the buffer size.

Now, generating intermediate tags for COPA is not as straight forward as ELmE as similar approach won't provide any security because identical last two blocks will produce same intermediate tag.

Moreover, we claim that even if intermediate tags are produced for COPA as if the final tag, then it also has the disadvantage of requiring additional buffer storage. Now we compare the 20 round pipeline implementations which is keeping

Table 1. Comparative study on the performance of block-cipher based Authenticated Encryptions. Here #BC AD, #BC M and #BC T denotes no. of block-cipher call per associated data, message and tag block respectively.

Construction	#BC AD	#BC M	#BC T	speed up	Misuse Resistance	Bottleneck
OCB	1	1	1	p	No	Nonce Processing
McOE-D	1	2	2	2	Yes	Lower level Processing
CoPA	1	2	2	p	Yes	Associated data Processing
ELmE	1	2	1	p	Yes	None

computing the messages even after intermediate tag to keep the pipeline full. For each k block of intermediate tags, the pipelined implementation of 20 round AES for COPA requires to store k block messages and in addition 20 blocks of intermediate values for the subsequent ciphertext blocks. On the other hand ELmE requires k blocks messages and 10 blocks of intermediate computation for next 10 next subsequent ciphertext. We save 10 blocks in buffer mainly due to faster verification (ELmE verifies after one layer, whereas COPA verifies after two layers). It has great advantage for low-end devices (keeping in mind that, block-wise adversaries are considered only when buffer size is limited implying low-end device). Keeping the above benefits into consideration, we opt for the linear mix ρ function rather than using a simple xor operation, as used in COPA.

6   Conclusion and Future Works

In the following paragraph, we mainly provide theoretical comparisons of OCB3, McOE-D, COPA and our construction ELmE. All the constructions have same key size and similar number of random mask (which can be preprocessed) for masking layers. The number of blockcipher calls for processing every message, associate data and tag blocks are given in the Table 1. The speed up for OCB, COPA and ELmE is p with parallel implementations by p processors as their construction support parallel execution. Due to the sequential nature of the lower level of McOE-D, the speed up factor can be at most 2.

Now, we briefly discuss bottlenecks issues of the other constructions, that our construction overcome.

OCB versions are IV based constructions and require distinct nonce in each invocation, hence not misuse resistant. Moreover OCB3 (which has minimum bottleneck among all versions) has a bottleneck in the nonce processing. As the encryption of the IV is needed in the masking of the messages, hence the encryption of the messages can start only after the encryption of IV, hence has the bottleneck of having additional clock cycles required for one block encryption.

As already mentioned in section 1, McOE-D uses TC3 type encryption and it's lower level has a CBC type structure which can not be executed in parallel implying the construction can not be pipelined. Hence it has a hardware bottleneck.

COPA has the bottleneck during the processing of associated data, as the last blockcipher input depends on the previous blockcipher outputs. Hence, the last block cipher invocation must be done after the completion of all the block-cipher invocations, making it sequential for one block-cipher invocation. So, complete parallelization can not be achieved.

On the other hand, our construction ELmE is completely parallel with no such bottleneck as described above. Moreover the construction treats the additional data and message exactly in a similar way (except with different masking keys). The encryption and decryption also behave similarly and hence ensures less chip area in combined hardware implementation. Moreover, to resist against blockwise adversaries, ELmE can incorporate intermediate tags very efficiently, which the other constructions do not take care of and could be hard to generate.

Note that, the above comparison is given from theoretical point of view. Experimental measurements to support these claim is a possible future scope. We've planned to implement a portable reference software implementation of our cipher as well as include a reference hardware design in verilog.

Acknowledgement. This work is supported by the Centre of Excellence in Cryptology (CoEC), Indian Statistical Institute, Kolkata.

References

1. (no editor), CAESAR: Competition for Authenticated Encryption: Security, Applicability, and Robustness, http://competitions.cr.yp.to/caesar.html, Citations in this document: §1.1, §1.1
2. (no editor), Specification of the 3GPP Confidentiality and Integrity Algorithms 128-EEA3 and 128-EIA3. Document 2: ZUC Specification. ETSI/SAGE Specification, Version: 1.5 (2011), Citations in this document: §1.1
3. Andreeva, E., Bogdanov, A., Luykx, A., Mennink, B., Tischhauser, E., Yasuda, K.: Parallelizable and authenticated online ciphers. In: Sako, K., Sarkar, P. (eds.) ASIACRYPT 2013, Part I. LNCS, vol. 8269, pp. 424–443. Springer, Heidelberg (2013), Citations in this document: §1.1
4. Bellare, M., Rogaway, P., Wagner, D.: The EAX Mode of Operation. In: Roy, B., Meier, W. (eds.) FSE 2004. LNCS, vol. 3017, pp. 389–407. Springer, Heidelberg (2004), Citations in this document: §1.1
5. Bellare, M., Blake, J., Rogaway, P.: OCB: A Block-Cipher Mode of Operation for Efficient Authenticated Encryption 6, 365–403 (2005), Citations in this document: §1.3
6. Bertoni, G., Daemen, J., Peeters, M., Van Assche, G.: Duplexing the Sponge: Single Pass Authenticated Encryption and Other Applications. In: Miri, A., Vaudenay, S. (eds.) SAC 2011. LNCS, vol. 7118, pp. 320–337. Springer, Heidelberg (2012), Citations in this document: §1.1, §4

7. Datta, N., Nandi, M.: Misuse Resistant Parallel Authenticated Encryptions, IACR Cryptology ePrint Archive (2013), http://eprint.iacr.org/2013/767.pdf, Citations in this document: §4.1, §4.2, §5.1

8. Gligor, V.D., Donescu, P.: Fast Encryption and Authentication: XCBC Encryption and XECB Authentication Modes. In: Matsui, M. (ed.) FSE 2001. LNCS, vol. 2355, pp. 92–108. Springer, Heidelberg (2002), Citations in this document: §1.1

9. Dworkin, M.: Recommendation for block cipher modes of operation: three variants of ciphertext stealing for CBC mode. Addendum to NIST Special Publication 80038A (2010), Citations in this document: §3

10. Wang, P., Feng, D., Wu, W.: HCTR: A Variable-Input-Length Enciphering Mode. In: Feng, D., Lin, D., Yung, M. (eds.) CISC 2005. LNCS, vol. 3822, pp. 175–188. Springer, Heidelberg (2005), Citations in this document: §3

11. Fleischmann, E., Forler, C., Lucks, S.: McOE: A Family of Almost Foolproof On-Line Authenticated Encryption Schemes. In: Canteaut, A. (ed.) FSE 2012. LNCS, vol. 7549, pp. 196–215. Springer, Heidelberg (2012), Citations in this document: §1.1, §1.3

12. Fouque, P.-A., Joux, A., Martinet, G., Valette, F.: Authenticated On-Line Encryption. In: Matsui, M., Zuccherato, R.J. (eds.) SAC 2003. LNCS, vol. 3006, pp. 145–159. Springer, Heidelberg (2004)

13. Halevi, S., Rogaway, P.: A Tweakable Enciphering Mode. In: Boneh, D. (ed.) CRYPTO 2003. LNCS, vol. 2729, pp. 482–499. Springer, Heidelberg (2003), Citations in this document: §1.2

14. Halevi, S., Rogaway, P.: A parallelizable enciphering mode. In: Okamoto, T. (ed.) CT-RSA 2004. LNCS, vol. 2964, pp. 292–304. Springer, Heidelberg (2004), Citations in this document: §1.1, §1.2

15. Hell, M., Johansson, T., Maximov, A., Meier, W.: A Stream Cipher Proposal: Grain-128, eSTREAM, ECRYPT Stream Cipher Project, Report 2006/071 (2005), http://www.ecrypt.eu.org/stream, Citations in this document: §1.1

16. Housley, R., Whiting, D., Ferguson, N.: Counter with CBC-MAC, CCM, RFC 3610 (Informational) (2003), Citations in this document: §1.1

17. Iwata, T.: New blockcipher modes of operation with beyond the birthday bound security. In: Robshaw, M. (ed.) FSE 2006. LNCS, vol. 4047, pp. 310–327. Springer, Heidelberg (2006), Citations in this document: §1.1

18. Iwata, T., Yasuda, K.: HBS: A Single-Key mode of Operation for Deterministic Authenticated Encryption. In: Dunkelman, O. (ed.) FSE 2009. LNCS, vol. 5665, pp. 394–415. Springer, Heidelberg (2009), Citations in this document: §1.1

19. Iwata, T., Yasuda, K.: A Single-Key, Inverse-Cipher-Free Mode for Deterministic Authenticated Encryption. In: Jacobson Jr., M.J., Rijmen, V., Safavi-Naini, R. (eds.) SAC 2009. LNCS, vol. 5867, pp. 313–330. Springer, Heidelberg (2009), Citations in this document: §1.1

20. Joux, A., Martinet, G., Valette, F.: Blockwise-Adaptive Attackers: Revisiting the (In)Security of Some Provably Secure Encryption Models: CBC, GEM, IACBC. In: Yung, M. (ed.) CRYPTO 2002. LNCS, vol. 2442, pp. 17–30. Springer, Heidelberg (2002), Citations in this document: §1.3

21. Jutla, C.S.: Encryption Modes with Almost Free Message Integrity. In: Pfitzmann, B. (ed.) EUROCRYPT 2001. LNCS, vol. 2045, pp. 529–544. Springer, Heidelberg (2001), Citations in this document: §1.1, §1.1

22. Krovetz, T., Rogaway, P.: The Software Performance of Authenticated-Encryption Modes. In: Joux, A. (ed.) FSE 2011. LNCS, vol. 6733, pp. 306–327. Springer, Heidelberg (2011)

23. Luby, M., Rackoff, C.: How to construct pseudorandom permutations from pseudorandom functions. SIAM Journal of Computing, 373–386 (1988), Citations in this document: §1.2, §1.3
24. Lucks, S.: Two Pass Authenticated Encryption Faster than Generic Composition. In: Gilbert, H., Handschuh, H. (eds.) FSE 2005. LNCS, vol. 3557, pp. 284–298. Springer, Heidelberg (2005), Citations in this document: §1.1
25. Nandi, M.: Two new efficient CCA-secure online ciphers: MHCBC and MCBC. In: Chowdhury, D.R., Rijmen, V., Das, A. (eds.) INDOCRYPT 2008. LNCS, vol. 5365, pp. 350–362. Springer, Heidelberg (2008), Citations in this document: §1.3
26. Nandi, M.: A Generic Method to Extend Message Space of a Strong Pseudorandom Permutation. Computacin y Sistemas 12 (2009)
27. Patarin, J.: The "Coefficients H" technique. In: Avanzi, R.M., Keliher, L., Sica, F. (eds.) SAC 2008. LNCS, vol. 5381, pp. 328–345. Springer, Heidelberg (2009), Citations in this document: §2.1
28. Preneel, B., Wu, H.: AEGIS: A Fast Authenticated Encryption Algorithm, Cryptology ePrint Archive: Report 2013/695
29. Ristenpart, T., Rogaway, P.: How to Enrich the Message Space of a Cipher. In: Biryukov, A. (ed.) FSE 2007. LNCS, vol. 4593, pp. 101–118. Springer, Heidelberg (2007), Citations in this document: §3
30. Rogaway, P.: Efficient Instantiations of Tweakable Blockciphers and Refinements to Modes OCB and PMAC. In: Lee, P.J. (ed.) ASIACRYPT 2004. LNCS, vol. 3329, pp. 16–31. Springer, Heidelberg (2004)
31. Rogaway, P.: Nonce-based symmetric encryption. In: Roy, B., Meier, W. (eds.) FSE 2004. LNCS, vol. 3017, pp. 348–359. Springer, Heidelberg (2004), Citations in this document: §1.3
32. Rogaway, P., Zhang, H.: Online Ciphers from Tweakable Blockciphers. In: CT-RSA, pp. 237–249 (2011), Citations in this document: §1.3
33. Rogaway, P., Shrimpton, T.: A Provable-Security Treatment of the Key-Wrap Problem. In: Vaudenay, S. (ed.) EUROCRYPT 2006. LNCS, vol. 4004, pp. 373–390. Springer, Heidelberg (2006), Citations in this document: §1.1
34. Sarkar, P.: On Authenticated Encryption Using Stream Ciphers Supporting an Initialisation Vector. IACR Cryptology ePrint Archive, 299–299 (2011), http://eprint.iacr.org/2011/299.pdf; capsulating Security Payload (ESP), Citations in this document: §1.1
35. Viega, J., McGraw, D.: The use of Galois/Counter Mode (GCM) in IPsec En, RFC 4106 (2005), Citations in this document: §1.1, §1.3
36. Vaudenay, S.: Decorrelation: A Theory for Block Cipher Security. Journal of Cryptology, 249–286 (2003)

Lattice Decoding Attacks on Binary LWE

Shi Bai and Steven D. Galbraith

Department of Mathematics,
University of Auckland,
New Zealand
S.Bai@auckland.ac.nz,
S.Galbraith@math.auckland.ac.nz

Abstract. We consider the binary-LWE problem, which is the learning with errors problem when the entries of the secret vector are chosen from $\{0,1\}$ or $\{-1,0,1\}$. Our main result is an improved lattice decoding algorithm for binary-LWE, by translating to the inhomogeneous short integer solution (ISIS) problem, and then re-scaling the lattice. We also discuss modulus switching as an approach to the problem. Our conclusion is that binary-LWE is easier than general LWE. We give experimental results, and theoretical estimates for parameters that achieve certain security levels.

Keywords: lattice attacks, learning with errors, closest vector problem.

1 Introduction

The learning with errors problem is: Given an $m \times n$ matrix $\mathbf{A}$ and a vector $\mathbf{b} \equiv \mathbf{As} + \mathbf{e} \pmod{q}$, where $\mathbf{e} \in \mathbb{Z}_q^m$ is a "short" error vector, to compute $\mathbf{s} \in \mathbb{Z}_q^n$. This is a computational problem of major current importance in cryptography. Recently, Brakerski, Langlois, Peikert, Regev and Stehlé [7] and Micciancio and Peikert [19] have considered variants of this problem where the secret vectors are chosen uniformly from the set $\{0,1\}^n$ (or $\{-1,0,1\}^n$), rather than from $\mathbb{Z}_q^n$. These variants of the problem are called binary-LWE.

It is natural to expect that the binary-LWE problem is easier than the standard LWE problem, but it is an open question to determine how much easier. Both papers [7, 19] give reductions that imply that binary-LWE is hard, but those results require increasing the parameter n to approximately $n \log_2(q) = O(n \log_2(n))$ (it is usually the case that q is a low-degree polynomial in n). An interesting problem is to determine whether these results are optimal. As an example, taking $n = 256$ for standard LWE would lead to a parameter of at least $n \log_2(n) = 2048$ for binary LWE, which seems excessive.

Our goal is to develop and analyse improved algorithms for the binary-LWE problem. We first translate the problem to a related problem called the inhomogeneous short integer solution problem (ISIS). Our main tool is to *rescale* the lattice so that the standard lattice methods to solve the closest vector problem are more effective. We also consider other approaches to the problem, such as

W. Susilo and Y. Mu (Eds.): ACISP 2014, LNCS 8544, pp. 322–337, 2014.

modulus switching. We show that modulus switching is not a helpful tool in this setting, which may be counter-intuitive. We also give theoretical and experimental analysis of the algorithm.

Experimental results with the new algorithm do confirm that the parameter n needs to be increased when using binary-LWE. Returning to the example of $n = 256$, our results suggest that a parameter around 440 may be sufficient to achieve the same security level as standard LWE with parameter 256.

Our approaches are all based on lattice decoding attacks. There is another class of algorithms for LWE that are more combinatorial, originating with Blum, Kalai and Wasserman [5, 1]. However, these algorithms require an extremely large number of samples from the LWE distribution, which may not be realistic in certain applications.

The paper is organised as follows. Sections 2 and 3 give precise definitions for the LWE and binary-LWE problems. Section 4 recalls the current state-of-the-art for lattice attacks on LWE. Section 5 describes modulus switching and evaluates its performance. Section 6 contains our algorithm and its analysis, specifically the description of the rescaling in Section 6.1 and the discussion of why modulus switching is unhelpful in Section 6.3. Some experimental results, that confirm our improvement over previous methods, are given in Section 7.

2   LWE

Let $\sigma \in \mathbb{R}_{>0}$. Define $\rho_\sigma(x) = \exp(-x^2/(2\sigma^2))$ and $\rho_\sigma(\mathbb{Z}) = 1 + 2\sum_{x=1}^{\infty} \rho_\sigma(x)$. The discrete Gaussian distribution D_σ on $\mathbb{Z}$ with standard deviation σ is the distribution that associates to $x \in \mathbb{Z}$ the probability $\rho_\sigma(x)/\rho_\sigma(\mathbb{Z})$.

We fix parámeters (n, m, q, σ). Typical choices of parameters are $(n, m, q, \sigma) = (256, 640, 4093, 32)$. Let $\mathbf{A}$ be a uniformly chosen $m \times n$ matrix with entries in $\mathbb{Z}_q$. Let $\mathbf{s}$ and $\mathbf{e}$ be integer vectors of lengths n and m respectively whose entries are sampled independently from the discrete Gaussian distribution with parameter σ (this is the case of LWE with secrets chosen from the error distribution, which is no loss of generality [3]). We call $\mathbf{s}$ the "secret vector" and $\mathbf{e}$ the "error vector". The LWE distribution is the distribution on $(\mathbb{Z}_q^{m \times n}, \mathbb{Z}_q^m)$ induced by pairs $(\mathbf{A}, \mathbf{b} \equiv \mathbf{As} + \mathbf{e} \pmod q)$ sampled as above. The search-LWE problem is: Given $(\mathbf{A}, \mathbf{b})$ chosen from the LWE distribution, to compute the pair $(\mathbf{s}, \mathbf{e})$. We refer to [20–22] for further details of LWE.

The $(m, n, q, \mathcal{B})$-SIS problem is: Given an $n \times m$ integer matrix $\mathbf{A}'$ (where typically m is much bigger than n) and an integer q to find a vector $\mathbf{y} \in \mathbb{Z}^m$, if it exists, such that $\mathbf{A}'\mathbf{y} \equiv 0 \pmod q$ and $\mathbf{y} \in \mathcal{B}$. Here $\mathcal{B}$ is a set of vectors that are "short" in some sense (e.g., $\mathcal{B} = \{-1, 0, 1\}^m$). One can also define an inhomogeneous version of the SIS problem (ISIS): Given $\mathbf{A}'$ and $\mathbf{v}$ find $\mathbf{y} \in \mathcal{B}$, if it exists, such that $\mathbf{A}'\mathbf{y} \equiv \mathbf{v} \pmod q$.

The LWE problem can be rephrased as inhomogenous-SIS: Given $(\mathbf{A}, \mathbf{b} \equiv \mathbf{As} + \mathbf{e} \pmod q)$ one can form the ISIS instance

$$(\mathbf{A}|\mathbf{I}_m) \begin{pmatrix} \mathbf{s} \\ \mathbf{e} \end{pmatrix} \equiv \mathbf{b} \pmod q$$

where $\mathbf{I}_m$ is the $m \times m$ identity matrix. An alternative transformation of LWE to ISIS is mentioned in Remark 1 of Section 4.3. Conversely, ISIS can be translated to LWE, for details see Lemmas 9 and 10 of Micciancio and Mol [18].

2.1 Size of the Error Vector

Let D_σ be the discrete Gaussian distribution on $\mathbb{Z}$ with standard deviation σ. Let $\mathbf{e}$ be sampled from D_σ^m, which means that $\mathbf{e} = (e_1, \ldots, e_m)$ is formed by taking m independent samples from D_σ. We need to know the distribution of $\|\mathbf{e}\|$. If the entries e_i were chosen from a true Gaussian with standard deviation σ then $\|\mathbf{e}\|^2$ comes from the chi-squared distribution, and so has mean $m\sigma^2$. Since our case is rather close, we assume that $\|\mathbf{e}\|^2$ is also close to a chi-squared distribution, and we further assume that the expected value of $\|\mathbf{e}\|$ is close to $\sqrt{m}\sigma$. Lyubashevsky (Lemma 4.4(3) of the full version of [16]) shows that

$$\Pr\left(\|\mathbf{e}\| \leq k\sigma\sqrt{m}\right) \geq 1 - \left(ke^{\frac{1-k^2}{2}}\right)^m$$

for $k > 0$. This supports our assumption that $\|\mathbf{e}\| \approx \sqrt{m}\sigma$. To achieve overwhelming probability, we may use $k \approx 2$. In practice, this bound is quite useful for $k \gtrsim 1$. In practice, we can easily estimate the expected value of $\|\mathbf{e}\|$ for any fixed parameters by sampling.

3   Binary LWE and Related Work

We now restrict the LWE problem so that the secret vector $\mathbf{s}$ is chosen to lie in a much smaller set. Fix (n, m, q, σ). To be compatible with Regev's results (e.g., see Theorem 1.1 of [22]), we usually take $\sigma \approx 2\sqrt{n}$. Let $\mathbf{A}$ be a uniformly chosen $m \times n$ matrix with entries in $\mathbb{Z}_q$. Let $\mathbf{s} \in \mathbb{Z}^n$ have entries chosen independently and uniformly from $\{0, 1\}$. Let $\mathbf{e} \in \mathbb{Z}^m$ have entries sampled independently from the discrete Gaussian distribution on $\mathbb{Z}$ with standard deviation σ. The binary-LWE distribution is the distribution on $(\mathbb{Z}_q^{m \times n}, \mathbb{Z}_q^m)$ induced by pairs $(\mathbf{A}, \mathbf{b} = \mathbf{A}\mathbf{s} + \mathbf{e} \pmod{q})$ sampled as above. The search-binary-LWE problem is: Given $(\mathbf{A}, \mathbf{b})$ chosen from the binary-LWE distribution, to compute the pair $(\mathbf{s}, \mathbf{e})$. One can also consider a decisional problem, but in this paper we focus on the search problem.

The binary-LWE problem (where secret vectors $\mathbf{s}$ are from $\{0, 1\}^n$) has been considered in work by Brakerski, Langlois, Peikert, Regev and Stehlé [7]. The main focus of their paper is to prove hardness results for LWE in the classical setting (i.e., without using quantum algorithms as in Regev's original result). Micciancio and Peikert [19] have considered the binary-LWE problem where $\mathbf{s} \in \{-1, 0, 1\}^n$. Their main result is a hardness result for the case where not only the secrets are small but even the errors are small. Of course, due to the Arora-Ge attack [4] this is only possible if one makes the (realistic) assumption that one has access to a very restricted number of samples from the LWE distribution.

Both papers [7, 19] give reductions that imply that binary-LWE is hard, assuming certain other lattice problems are hard. Essentially, the papers relate (n, q)-binary-LWE to $(n/t, q)$-LWE (where $t = O(\log(n)) = O(\log(q))$). In other words, we can be confident that binary-LWE is hard as long as we increase the parameter n by a factor of $\log(n)$. For example, taking $n = 256$ as a reasonably hard case for standard LWE, we can be confident that binary-LWE is hard for $n = 256 \log_2(256) = 2048$. Our feeling is that these reductions are too conservative, and that binary-LWE is harder than these results would suggest.

The main goal of our paper is to study the LWE problem where the secret vector is binary, but the errors are still discrete Gaussians. We focus on the case $\mathbf{s} \in \{-1, 0, 1\}^n$, but our methods are immediately applicable to the case $\mathbf{s} \in \{-B, \ldots, -1, 0, 1, \ldots, B\}$ for any $B < \sigma$.

4   Standard Lattice Attack on LWE

We recall the standard lattice decoding attack on LWE, and its analysis. Let $L = \Lambda_q(\mathbf{A}^T) = \{\mathbf{v} \in \mathbb{Z}^m : \mathbf{v} \equiv \mathbf{A}\mathbf{s} \pmod{q}, \mathbf{s} \in \mathbb{Z}^n\}$. This is a lattice of rank m. Typically the rank of $\mathbf{A}$ will be n, and so L has volume q^{m-n}. Suppose one can solve the closest vector problem (CVP) instance $(L, \mathbf{b})$. Then one finds a vector $\mathbf{v} \in L$ such that $\|\mathbf{b} - \mathbf{v}\|$ is small. Writing $\mathbf{e} = \mathbf{b} - \mathbf{v}$ and $\mathbf{v} \equiv \mathbf{A}\mathbf{s} \pmod{q}$ for some $\mathbf{s} \in \mathbb{Z}^n$ (it is easy to solve for $\mathbf{s}$ using linear algebra when $m \geq n$), then

$$\mathbf{b} \equiv \mathbf{A}\mathbf{s} + \mathbf{e} \pmod{q}.$$

Hence, if we can solve CVP then we have a chance to solve LWE.

The CVP instance can be solved using the embedding technique [12] (reducing CVP to SVP in a lattice of dimension one larger) or an enumeration algorithm (there are several such algorithms, but Liu and Nguyen [14] argue that all variants can be considered as cases of pruned enumeration algorithms). For the complexity analysis here we use the embedding technique, so we recall this now. Some discussions of enumeration algorithms will be given in Section 7.3.

Let $L \subseteq \mathbb{Z}^m$ be a lattice of rank m with (column) basis matrix $\mathbf{B}$, and suppose $\mathbf{b} \in \mathbb{Z}^m$ is a target vector. We wish to find $\mathbf{v} = \mathbf{B}\mathbf{u} \in L$ such that $\mathbf{e} = \mathbf{v} - \mathbf{b} = \mathbf{B}\mathbf{u} - \mathbf{b}$ is a short vector. The idea is to consider the basis matrix, where $M \in \mathbb{N}$ is chosen appropriately (e.g., $M \approx \sqrt{m}\sigma$),

$$\mathbf{B}' = \begin{pmatrix} \mathbf{B} & \mathbf{b} \\ 0 & M \end{pmatrix}. \tag{1}$$

This is the basis for a lattice L' of rank $d = m + 1$ and volume $M \cdot \text{vol}(L)$. Note that

$$\mathbf{B}' \begin{pmatrix} \mathbf{u} \\ -1 \end{pmatrix} = \begin{pmatrix} \mathbf{B}\mathbf{u} - \mathbf{b} \\ -M \end{pmatrix} = \begin{pmatrix} \mathbf{e} \\ -M \end{pmatrix}.$$

Hence, the (column) lattice generated by $\mathbf{B}'$ contains a short vector giving a potential solution to our problem. One therefore applies an SVP algorithm (e.g., LLL or BKZ lattice basis reduction).

Lyubashevsky and Micciancio (Theorem 1 of [15]) argue that the best choice for M above is $\|\mathbf{e}\|$, which is approximately $\sqrt{m}\sigma$ in our case. However, in our experiments $M = 1$ worked fine (and leads to a more powerful attack [2] in practice).

4.1   Unique-SVP

Gama and Nguyen [10] have given a heuristic approach to estimate the capability of lattice basis reduction algorithms. Consider a lattice basis reduction algorithm that takes as input a basis for a lattice L of dimension d, and outputs a list of vectors $\mathbf{b}_1, \ldots, \mathbf{b}_d$. Gama and Nguyen define the root Hermite factor of such an algorithm to be $\delta \in \mathbb{R}$ such that

$$\|\mathbf{b}_1\| \leq \delta^d \mathrm{vol}(L)^{1/d}$$

for all d and almost all lattices L.

The standard LLL algorithm corresponds to $\delta = 1.021$. The paper [10] argues that $\delta = 1.01$ is about the limit of practical algorithms (i.e., variants of BKZ using extreme pruning and large block size). Chen and Nguyen [9] extended this analysis to algorithms with greater running time. Their heuristic argument is that a Hermite factor corresponding to $\delta = 1.006$ might be reachable with an algorithm performing around 2^{110} operations.

In Section 3.3 of [10], Gama and Nguyen turn their attention to the unique-SVP problem. One seeks a short vector in a lattice L when one knows that there is a large gap $\gamma = \lambda_2(L)/\lambda_1(L)$, where $\lambda_i(L)$ denotes the i-th successive minima of the lattice. The unique-SVP problem arises when solving CVP using the embedding technique. The standard theoretical result is that if one is using a lattice reduction algorithm with Hermite factor δ, then the algorithm outputs the shortest vector if the lattice gap satisfies $\gamma > \delta^{2m}$. However, Gama and Nguyen observe that practical algorithms will succeed as long as $\gamma > c\delta^m$ for some small constant c (their paper gives $c = 0.26$ and $c = 0.45$ for different families of lattices). Moreover, Luzzi, Stehlé and Ling [17] gave some theoretical justification that the unique-SVP problem is easier to solve when the gap is large.

4.2   Application to LWE

Consider running the embedding technique on an LWE instance, using the lattice L' given by the matrix $\mathbf{B}'$ from equation (1). We have a good chance of getting the right answer if the error vector $\mathbf{e}$ is very short compared with the second shortest vector in the lattice L', which we assume to be the shortest vector in the original lattice L.

The Gaussian heuristic suggests that the shortest vector in a lattice L of rank d has Euclidean norm about $\frac{1}{\sqrt{\pi}}\Gamma(1 + \frac{d}{2})^{1/d}\mathrm{vol}(L)^{1/d}$ which is approximately $\sqrt{\frac{d}{2\pi e}}\mathrm{vol}(L)^{1/d}$. In lattice L (of rank m), this is $\sqrt{\frac{m}{2\pi e}}q^{(m-n)/m}$. Note also that our lattices contain known vectors of Euclidean length equal to q. Hence, our estimate of the Euclidean length of known short vectors is

$$\lambda_2(L') \approx \lambda_1(L) \approx \min\left\{q, \sqrt{\frac{m}{2\pi e}}\, q^{\frac{m-n}{m}}\right\}.$$

In contrast, the vector $\mathbf{e}$ has Euclidean length around $\sqrt{m}\sigma$ on average (see Section 2.1), and so the vector $(\frac{\mathbf{e}}{M})$ has length approximately $\sqrt{2m}\sigma$ when $M = \sqrt{m}\sigma$. In our experiments we take $M = 1$ and so assume that $\lambda_1(L') \approx \sqrt{m}\sigma$. Hence the gap is

$$\gamma(m) = \frac{\lambda_2(L')}{\lambda_1(L')} \approx \frac{\min\{q, \frac{1}{\sqrt{\pi}}\Gamma(1+\frac{m}{2})^{1/m}q^{\frac{m-n}{m}}\}}{\sqrt{m}\sigma} \approx \frac{\min\{q, \sqrt{\frac{m}{2\pi e}}q^{\frac{m-n}{m}}\}}{\sqrt{m}\sigma}. \quad (2)$$

For a successful attack we want this gap to be large, so we will need

$$\sigma \ll q^{\frac{m-n}{m}} < \frac{q}{\sqrt{m}}.$$

To determine whether an LWE instance can be solved using the embedding technique and a lattice reduction algorithm with a given (root) Hermite factor δ, one can choose a suitable subdimension m and verify that the corresponding gap satisfies the condition $\gamma = \gamma(m) > c\delta^m$ for a suitable value c. Since the constant c is unknown, we can maximize $\min\{q, q^{(m-n)/m}\}/\delta^m$ for fixed n, q, δ to get the "optimal" sub-dimension (which maximizes the success probability of the algorithm) to be

$$m = \sqrt{\frac{n\log(q)}{\log(\delta)}}, \quad (3)$$

where δ is the Hermite factor of the lattice basis reduction algorithm used.

Furthermore, we may assume c is upper bounded by 1 according to the experimental results of Gama and Nguyen [10]. For fixed $n, q, \sigma = 2\sqrt{n}$, we can easily compute values (m, δ) satisfying the constraint $\gamma^{1/m} \geq \delta$ and such that δ is maximal. These values have lattice dimension m as in equation (3). By doing this we obtained Table 1 (for $n \geq 160$ the length of the second shortest vector is taken to be q and this leads to very large dimensions; enlarging q to around 13000 in the case $n = 300$ leads to $m = 1258$ and $\delta \approx 1.002$). The last row consists of the estimated time

$$\log(T_{BKZ}) = \frac{1.8}{\log_2(\delta)} - 110 \quad (4)$$

for running the BKZ lattice basis reduction algorithm, based on Lindner and Peikert's work [13].

The running times and values for δ in Table 1 are worse than those reported in some other papers on LWE. This is because we consider rather large values $\sigma = 2\sqrt{n}$ for the error distribution, instead of very small values like $\sigma = 3$. Since LWE can always be reduced to the case where the secrets are chosen from the error distribution, the question of the hardness of binary-LWE is most interesting when the error distribution itself is not very small.

Table 1. Theoretical prediction of (optimal) root Hermite factor δ and running time T of the standard embedding technique algorithm using BKZ for LWE instances with $q = 4093$, $\sigma = 2\sqrt{n}$ for the given values for n. The lattice dimension $d = m + 1$ is calculated using equation (3) and the running time T is estimated using equation (4).

n	30	40	50	60	70	100	150	200	250	300
d	110	151	194	239	284	425	673	1144	1919	3962
$\delta \approx$	1.0208	1.0147	1.0111	1.0088	1.0072	1.0046	1.0028	1.0013	1.0006	1.0002
$\log(T) \approx$	0	0	3	33	63	161	343	872	2100	7739

4.3 How to Solve ISIS

Recall the inhomogeneous-SIS (ISIS) problem: Given $(\mathbf{A}', \mathbf{v})$ to find a short vector $\mathbf{y} \in \mathbb{Z}^m$ such that $\mathbf{v} \equiv \mathbf{A}'\mathbf{y} \pmod{q}$. It is standard that ISIS is also attacked by reducing to CVP: One considers the lattice $L' = \Lambda_q^{\perp}(\mathbf{A}') = \{\mathbf{y} \in \mathbb{Z}^m : \mathbf{A}'\mathbf{y} \equiv 0 \pmod{q}\}$, finds any vector (not necessarily short) $\mathbf{w} \in \mathbb{Z}^m$ such that $\mathbf{A}'\mathbf{w} \equiv \mathbf{v} \pmod{q}$, then solves CVP for $(L', \mathbf{w})$ to find some $\mathbf{y}$ close to $\mathbf{w}$ and so returns $\mathbf{w} - \mathbf{y}$ as the ISIS solution.

We sketch the details of solving LWE (in the case of short secrets) by reducing to ISIS and then solving by CVP (more details are given in Section 6). Given $(\mathbf{A}, \mathbf{b})$ we define $\mathbf{A}' = (\mathbf{A}|\mathbf{I}_m)$ to get an ISIS instance $(\mathbf{A}', \mathbf{b})$. Choose any vector $\mathbf{w} \in \mathbb{Z}^{n+m}$ such that $\mathbf{A}'\mathbf{w} \equiv \mathbf{b} \pmod{q}$. Then the lattice $L' = \Lambda_q^{\perp}(\mathbf{A}') = \{\mathbf{y} \in \mathbb{Z}^{n+m} : \mathbf{A}'\mathbf{y} \equiv 0 \pmod{q}\}$ is seen to have rank $m' = n + m$ and (assuming the rank of $\mathbf{A}'$ is n) determinant $q^m = q^{m'-n}$ (the determinant condition can be seen by considering the index of the subgroup $q\mathbb{Z}^{n+m}$ in the additive group L'). The condition for success in the algorithm is $\sigma \ll q^{m/(n+m)}$. Writing $m' = n + m$ this is $q^{(m'-n)/m'}$, which is the same as the LWE condition above.

Remark 1. We can also reduce LWE to ISIS using the approach of Micciancio and Mol [18]. In particular, one can construct a matrix $\mathbf{A}^{\perp} \in \mathbb{Z}_q^{(m-n)\times m}$ such that $\mathbf{A}^{\perp}\mathbf{A} \equiv 0 \pmod{q}$. The LWE problem $(\mathbf{A}, \mathbf{b})$ is therefore transformed into the ISIS instance $(\mathbf{A}^{\perp}, \mathbf{A}^{\perp}\mathbf{b} \equiv \mathbf{A}^{\perp}\mathbf{e} \pmod{q})$. It follows that a solution to the ISIS problem gives a value for $\mathbf{e}$ and hence solves the LWE problem. It is easy to see that this approach is equivalent to the previous one in the case where the secret vector $\mathbf{s}$ is chosen from the error distribution. However, since this reduction eliminates the vector $\mathbf{s}$, we are no longer able to take advantage of the "smallness" of $\mathbf{s}$ compared with $\mathbf{e}$, as we will do in the following sections. So we do not consider this approach further.

5 Modulus Switching

Modulus switching was first proposed by Brakerski and Vaikuntanathan [6], in the context of homomorphic encryption. Write the LWE instance $(\mathbf{A}, \mathbf{b} \equiv \mathbf{As} + \mathbf{e} \pmod{q})$ as

$$\mathbf{b} = \mathbf{As} + \mathbf{e} + q\mathbf{u}$$

for some $\mathbf{u} \in \mathbb{Z}^m$. Now suppose q' is another integer and define $\mathbf{A}' = [\frac{q'}{q}\mathbf{A}]$ and $\mathbf{b}' = [\frac{q'}{q}\mathbf{b}]$, where the operation $[\ ]$ applied to a vector or matrix means rounding each entry to the nearest integer. Write $\mathbf{A}' = \frac{q'}{q}\mathbf{A} + \mathbf{W}$ and $\mathbf{b}' = \frac{q'}{q}\mathbf{b} + \mathbf{w}$ where $\mathbf{W}$ is an $m \times n$ matrix with entries in $[-1/2, 1/2]$ and $\mathbf{w}$ is a length m vector with entries in $[-1/2, 1/2]$. One can now verify that

$$\begin{aligned}
\mathbf{b}' - \mathbf{A}'\mathbf{s} &= \tfrac{q'}{q}\mathbf{b} + \mathbf{w} - (\tfrac{q'}{q}\mathbf{A} + \mathbf{W})\mathbf{s} \\
&= \tfrac{q'}{q}(\mathbf{As} + \mathbf{e} + q\mathbf{u} - \mathbf{As}) + \mathbf{w} - \mathbf{Ws} \\
&= \tfrac{q'}{q}\mathbf{e} + \mathbf{w} - \mathbf{Ws} + q'\mathbf{u}.
\end{aligned}$$

One sees that $(\mathbf{A}', \mathbf{b}')$ is an LWE instance modulo q', with the same secret vector, and that the "error vector" has length

$$\left\| \tfrac{q'}{q}\mathbf{e} + \mathbf{w} - \mathbf{Ws} \right\| \leq \tfrac{q'}{q}\|\mathbf{e}\| + \|\mathbf{w}\| + \|\mathbf{Ws}\|.$$

Note that the final term $\|\mathbf{Ws}\|$ has the potential to be small only when $\mathbf{s}$ has small entries, as is the case for binary LWE. The term $\|\mathbf{w}\|$ is bounded by $\frac{1}{2}\sqrt{m}$. The term $\|\mathbf{Ws}\|$ is easily bounded, but it is more useful to determine its expected value. Each entry of the vector $\mathbf{Ws}$ is a sum of n (or around $n/2$ in the case where $\mathbf{s} \in \{0,1\}^n$) rational numbers in the interval $[-1/2, 1/2]$. Assuming the entries of $\mathbf{W}$ are uniformly distributed then the central limit theorem suggests that each entry of $\mathbf{Ws}$ has absolute value roughly $\frac{1}{4}\sqrt{n/2}$. Hence, it seems plausible to think that $\|\mathbf{Ws}\|$ can be as small as $\frac{1}{4}\sqrt{nm}$.

Modulus switching was originally proposed to control the growth of the noise under homomorphic operations. The standard scenario is that if $\|\mathbf{e}\|$ becomes too large then, by taking q' much smaller than q, one can reduce the noise by the factor $\frac{q'}{q}$ while only adding a relatively small additional noise. However, the idea is also interesting for cryptanalysis: One can perform a modulus switching to make the error terms smaller and hence the scheme more easily attacked. We will consider such an attack in the case of binary LWE in the next section.

We now give a back-of-the-envelope calculation that shows modulus switching can be a useful way to improve lattice attacks on LWE. Note that modulus switching reduces the error vector by a factor of $\frac{q'}{q}$, as long as the other terms (dominated by $\frac{1}{4}\sqrt{nm}$) introduced into the noise are smaller than $\frac{q'}{q}\sigma\sqrt{m}$. However, note that the volume of the lattice is also reduced, since it goes from $q^{(m-n)/m}$ to $q'^{(m-n)/m}$. Let us write ϵ for the reduction factor $\frac{q'}{q}$. All other parameters remaining the same, the lattice gap $\gamma = \lambda_2/\lambda_1 \approx q^{(m-n)/m}/(\sigma\sqrt{2\pi e})$ changes to

$$\gamma' \approx (\epsilon q)^{(m-n)/m}/(\epsilon\sigma\sqrt{2\pi e}) = (\epsilon^{1-n/m}/\epsilon)\gamma = \epsilon^{-n/m}\gamma. \tag{5}$$

Now, $0 < \epsilon < 1$ and so this is a positive improvement to the lattice gap (and hence the Hermite factor).

For LWE we usually have errors chosen from a discrete Gaussian with standard deviation at most $2\sqrt{n}$, and so $\|\mathbf{e}\|$ is typically $O(\sqrt{mn})$. As discussed above, the additional noise introduced by performing modulus reduction (from the $\mathbf{W}\mathbf{s}$ term) will typically be around $\frac{1}{4}\sqrt{nm}$. Hence, it seems the best we can hope for is $q'/q \approx \frac{1}{8}$ giving an error vector of norm reduced by a factor of approximately $\frac{1}{4}$ (from $2\sqrt{mn}$ to $\sqrt{mn}/2$). This does give a modest improvement to the performance of lattice decoding algorithms for LWE.

6   New Attacks on Binary-LWE

We now present our original work. We want to exploit the fact that $\mathbf{s}$ is small. The standard lattice attack on LWE (reducing to CVP) cannot use this information. However, going via ISIS seems more appropriate.

6.1   Reducing Binary-LWE to ISIS and then Rescaling

Let $(\mathbf{A}, \mathbf{b})$ be the (n, m, q, σ)-LWE instance. We may discard rows to reduce the value for m. We write $m' = n + m$. Write $\mathbf{A}' = (\mathbf{A}|\mathbf{I}_m)$, being an $m \times m'$ matrix, and consider the ISIS instance

$$\mathbf{b} \equiv \mathbf{A}'(\tfrac{\mathbf{s}}{\mathbf{e}}) \pmod{q}$$

where the target short vector is $(\tfrac{\mathbf{s}}{\mathbf{e}})$.

The next step is to reduce this ISIS instance to CVP in a lattice. So define the vector $\mathbf{w} = (0, \mathbf{b}^T)^T$. Clearly $\mathbf{A}'\mathbf{w} \equiv \mathbf{b} \pmod{q}$. We now construct a basis matrix $\mathbf{B}$ for the lattice $L' = \{\mathbf{v} \in \mathbb{Z}^{m'} : \mathbf{A}'\mathbf{v} \equiv 0 \pmod{q}\}$. This can be done as follows: The columns of the $(n + m) \times (m + 2n)$ matrix

$$\mathbf{M} = \begin{pmatrix} \mathbf{I}_n & \\ & q\mathbf{I}_{n+m} \\ -\mathbf{A} & \end{pmatrix}$$

span the space of all vectors $\mathbf{v}$ such that $\mathbf{A}'\mathbf{v} \equiv 0 \pmod{q}$. Computing the column Hermite normal form of $\mathbf{M}$ gives an $m' \times m'$ matrix $\mathbf{B}$ whose columns generate the lattice L'.

One can confirm that $\det(\mathbf{B}) = q^m = q^{m'-n}$. As before, we seek a vector $\mathbf{v} \in \mathbb{Z}^{m'}$ such that $\mathbf{B}\mathbf{v} \equiv 0 \pmod{q}$ and $\mathbf{v} \approx \mathbf{w}$. We hope that $\mathbf{w} - \mathbf{v} = (\tfrac{\mathbf{s}}{\mathbf{e}})$ and so $\mathbf{v} = (\tfrac{\mathbf{s}}{*})$, where $*$ is actually going to be $\mathbf{b} - \mathbf{e}$. Our main observation is that $\|\mathbf{s}\| \ll \|\mathbf{e}\|$ and so the CVP algorithm is trying to find an unbalanced solution. It makes sense to try to rebalance things.

Our proposal is to multiply the first n rows of $\mathbf{B}$ by σ (or some other appropriate scaling factor). This increases the volume of the lattice, without significantly increasing the norm of the error vector in the CVP instance. As a result, the Hermite factor of the problem is increased and hence the range of the lattice attack for a given security level is increased.

A further trick, when $\mathbf{s} \in \{0,1\}^n$, is to rebalance $\mathbf{s}$ so that it is symmetric around zero. In this case we rescale by multiplying the first n rows of $\mathbf{B}$ by 2σ and then subtract $(\sigma, \ldots, \sigma, 0, \ldots, 0)^T$ from $\mathbf{w}$. Now the difference $\mathbf{w} - \mathbf{v}$ is of the form

$$(\pm\sigma, \ldots, \pm\sigma, \mathbf{e}_1, \ldots, \mathbf{e}_m)^T$$

which is more balanced.

6.2 Gap in the Unique-SVP

The determinant has been increased by a factor of σ^n (or $(2\sigma)^n$ in the $\{0,1\}$ case). So the gap in the re-scaled lattice is expected to be larger compared to the original lattice. In the embedded lattice formed by the standard attack, $\lambda_1(L') \approx \sqrt{m} \cdot \sigma$ and $\lambda_2(L') \approx q^{(m-n)/m}\sqrt{\frac{m}{2\pi e}}$ where m is the subdimension being used. In the embedded lattice formed by the new attack, $\lambda_1(L') \approx \sqrt{m+n} \cdot \sigma$ and $\lambda_2(L') \approx (q^m \sigma^n)^{1/(m+n)}\sqrt{\frac{m+n}{2\pi e}}$ where m is the number of LWE samples being used. Hence the new lattice gap is $\gamma = \lambda_2(L')/\lambda_1(L')$ and so we will need to use lattice reduction algorithms with Hermite factor $\delta \leq \gamma^{1/(m+n)}$.

Lemma 1. *Let q, n, σ and δ be fixed. Let $m' \approx m + n$ be the dimension of the embedded lattice in the new attack. For a given Hermite factor δ, the optimal value for m' is approximately*

$$\sqrt{\frac{n(\log q - \log \sigma)}{\log \delta}}. \tag{6}$$

Proof. The goal is to choose m' (and hence m) to minimize the function $f(m') = q^{(m'-n)/m'}\sigma^{n/m'}\delta^{-m'}$. It suffices to find a minimum for the function $F(x) = \log(f(x)) = ((x - n)/x)\log(q) + (n/x)\log(\sigma) - x\log(\delta)$. Differentiating gives $n(\log(q) - \log(\sigma)) = x^2\log(\delta)$ and the result follows.

Table 2. Theoretical prediction of (optimal) root Hermite factor δ and running time T of embedding technique for rescaled binary-LWE instances $\mathbf{s} \in \{-1, 0, 1\}^n$ with $q = 4093$, $\sigma = 2\sqrt{n}$ for the given values for n. The lattice dimension d' ($\approx m'$) is calculated using equation (6) and the running time T is estimated using equation (4).

n	30	40	50	60	70	100	150	200	250	300
d'	78	105	132	160	187	271	414	558	799	1144
δ	1.0296	1.0212	1.0164	1.0132	1.0111	1.0073	1.0045	1.0032	1.0019	1.0011
$\log(T)$	0	0	0	0	3	63	169	280	545	1031

Given n, q and σ, we use Lemma 1 to obtain Table 2 of optimal subdimensions m' and values for δ. Comparing this table with Table 1 one sees that the lattice dimensions m' and the Hermite factors δ are all much improved.

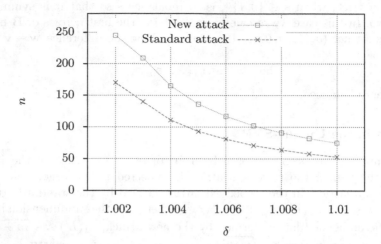

Fig. 1. Theoretical prediction of the largest binary-LWE parameter n that can be solved using an algorithm with the given root Hermite factor

By fixing a lattice reduction algorithm that has the ability to produce some fixed Hermite factor δ, we can compare the maximum n that this algorithm can attack, based on the standard attack or our new attack. Figure 1 indicates that, for instance, the binary LWE with secret in $\{-1, 0, 1\}$ and $n \approx 100$ provides approximately the same security as the regular LWE with $n \approx 70$.

6.3 Using Modulus Switching

It is natural to consider applying modulus switching before performing the improved lattice attack. We now explain that this is not a good idea in general.

As discussed in Section 5, the best we can try to do is to have $q'/q \approx 1/8$ and the error vector is reduced in size from elements of standard deviation σ to elements of standard deviation approximately $\sigma/4$.

Consider the desired Hermite factor $\delta = \gamma^{1/m'}$ to attack a lattice with gap

$$\gamma = (\sigma^{n/m'} q^{(m'-n)/m'} / (\sigma\sqrt{2\pi e}))^{1/m'}$$

as in our improved lattice attack using rescaling. Applying this attack to the lattice after modulus switching gives Hermite factor

$$\left((\tfrac{1}{4}\sigma)^{n/m'} (\tfrac{1}{8}q)^{(m'-n)/m'} / (\tfrac{1}{4}\sigma\sqrt{2\pi e}) \right)^{1/m'} = \delta \left(\frac{1}{2^{(m'-n)/m'}} \right)^{1/m'} \quad (7)$$

which is strictly smaller than δ. Hence, the instance after modulus switching is harder than the instance before modulus switching. Intuitively, the problem is this: Modulus switching reduces the size of q and also the size of the error.

But it reduces q by a larger factor than it reduces the size of the error (due to the additional error arising from the modulus switching process). When we do the rescaling, we are also rescaling by a smaller factor relative to q. Hence, the crucial lattice gap property is weakened by modulus switching.

7   Experiments

Our theoretical analysis (Figure 1) indicates that our new algorithm is superior to previous methods when solving CVP using the embedding technique. In this section we give experimental evidence that confirms these theoretical predictions. However, the state-of-the-art for solving CVP is not to use the embedding technique, but to use enumeration methods with suitable pruning strategies. Hence, in this section we also report some predictions based on experiments of using enumeration algorithms to solve binary-LWE using the standard method and our new method. For full details on enumeration algorithms in lattices see [9–11].

The binary LWE problem considered in this section has secret vectors $\mathbf{s} \in \{-1, 0, 1\}^n$ (i.e., it follows Micciancio and Peikert's definition [19]). Thus our results are more conservative compared to the case where $\mathbf{s} \in \{0, 1\}^n$. In the experiments, we fix parameters $q = 4093$ and vary $n \in [30, 80]$. We use $\sigma = 2\sqrt{n}$.

7.1   Embedding

We first consider the embedding technique with $M = 1$ to solve the CVP problems (we used FPLLL [8] on a 2.4G desktop). In Tables 1 and 2, we have determined the optimal (root) Hermite factor and subdimension that maximize the success probability using the embedding technique. However, when (the Hermite factor of) a lattice reduction algorithm is fixed (call it δ), the optimal subdimension m is the one that minimizes the running time while satisfying the lattice gap argument: $\gamma(m) > c\delta^m$ for some constant c (where $\gamma(m)$ is defined in equation (2)).

For a successful attack we want the lattice gap $\gamma(m)$ to be larger than δ^m which is to assume c is upper bounded by 1. As long as this condition is satisfied, we can reduce m in order to minimize the running time.

In the meantime, we want to maintain a certain success probability. In the LWE problem, the norm of the error vector is unknown to the attacker, so we guess that its value is equal to the average norm of 10^4 randomly sampled vectors from the error distribution. We choose a bound for the norm of the error vector so that the expected success probability is $\geq 1/2$. In this way, we can decide an optimal m. Also in our experiments, we restrict to $m \geq n$. On the other hand, if $\gamma(m) < \delta^m$ for all m, we set $m \approx \sqrt{n \log q / \log \delta}$ which maximizes $\gamma(m)/\delta^m$ for given δ. Of course, the reduction algorithm is likely to fail in such cases.

In Table 3, we use BKZ-60 with pruned enumeration [10]. To decide the optimal subdimension as described above, we assume the Hermite factor $\delta \gtrapprox 1.011$. This is verified experimentally in Table 3 and in [10]. Note that using a smaller dimension than the "optimum" may be slightly faster. In the standard

Table 3. Results of the embedding technique using BKZ for binary-LWE using the standard approach and the new lattice rescaling (with and without modulus switching). The columns m_i are the number of LWE samples used for the experiments (the value in parenthesis is the theoretical value for m_i from equation (3) or equation (6) as appropriate). The lattice dimensions are $d_1 = m_1 + 1$, $d_2 = m_2 + n + 1$ and $d_3 = m_3 + n + 1$. The lattice gap γ_i is estimated as in equation (2) and the corresponding Hermite factor is $\delta_i = \gamma_i^{1/d_i}$. Column Succ is the success probability observed from 10 trials (where $-$ denotes no success at all).

	Standard embedding attack				New attack				New attack with modulus switching			
n	m_1	γ_1^{1/d_1}	Succ	Time	m_2	γ_2^{1/d_2}	Succ	Time	m_3	γ_3^{1/d_3}	Succ	Time
30	68 (151)	1.013	1.0	0.83s	30 (97)	1.027	1.0	0.32s	53 (90)	1.023	1.0	3.76s
40	105 (174)	1.012	1.0	6.70s	40 (105)	1.019	1.0	1.30s	67 (96)	1.018	1.0	6.29s
50	195 (195)	1.011	0.5	61.71s	50 (111)	1.015	1.0	3.61s	84 (101)	1.014	1.0	10.58s
60	214 (214)	1.009	$-$	90.20s	115 (115)	1.013	1.0	27.83s	104 (104)	1.011	0.4	17.17s
70	231 (231)	1.007	$-$	127.82s	117 (117)	1.011	0.5	42.41s	105 (105)	1.010	$-$	29.11s
80	247 (247)	1.005	$-$	189.25s	119 (119)	1.009	$-$	56.54s	106 (106)	1.009	$-$	43.88s

attack, the optimal subdimension is m_1 and the lattice dimension is $d_1 = m_1 + 1$. In the new attack, the re-scaled lattice has dimension $d_2 = m_2 + n + 1$. We record the average running time for ten instances. The values for $\gamma_i = \lambda_2/\lambda_1$ are computed by assuming λ_1 is the length of the error vector and that λ_2 is given by the Gaussian heuristic. The success probability reflects the fact that we are using BKZ for the embedding technique, and so for larger n the shortest vector in the reduced basis is not the desired target vector. To get a higher success probability one uses enumeration, as discussed in Section 7.3.

7.2 Modulus Switching

We also experimented with modulus switching for the new algorithm. We confirm our theoretical analysis that the performance is worse. As mentioned in Section 5, the best choice for modulus switching is to use q' such that $q'/q \approx 1/8$. The third block in Table 3 records the running time and success probability of the new attack based on modulus switching. Note that we use $q' = 512$. The table shows that the success probability is worse than the new attack without modulus switching.

7.3 Enumeration

When solving CVP for practical parameters the state of the art method [13, 14] is to use BKZ pre-processing of the lattice basis followed by pruned enumeration. This is organised so that the time spent on pre-processing and enumeration is roughly equal. We consider these algorithms here. Note that one can expect a similar speedup from our lattice rescaling for the binary-LWE problem, since the volume of the lattice is increased, which creates an easier CVP instance.

We give predictions of the running time for larger parameters using Chen, Liu and Nguyen's methods [9, 14]: we first preprocess the CVP basis by BKZ-β for some large β and then enumerate on the reduced basis.

Write $\delta(\beta)$ for the Hermite factor achieved by BKZ with blocks of size β. Given a target $\delta(\beta)$ and dimension m, Chen and Nguyen [9] described an algorithm to estimate the BKZ time. It is observed that a small number of calls to the enumeration routine (for each block reduction in the BKZ-β) is often sufficient to achieve the targeted δ. It boils down to estimating the enumeration time (either for the local basis within BKZ or the full enumeration later), which depends on the number of nodes visited in the enumeration. We use the approach of [9, 14] to estimate the enumeration time, which assumes the Gaussian heuristic and the Geometric Series Assumption (GSA) [23]. Following this approach, and under those assumptions, we estimate the running time for solving binary-LWE with $n = 128, q = 4093$ in Table 4.

Table 4. Predictions of the running time for solving binary-LWE with $(n, q, \sigma) = (128, 4093, 22.6)$ using BKZ lattice reduction followed by pruned enumeration. Columns d_i are the lattice dimensions. The BKZ reduction (preprocessing) achieves the targeted Hermite factor δ_i. Column T_{Red} is an estimate of the BKZ reduction time (in seconds). Column $\#E$ denotes the estimated number of nodes in the enumeration. Column T denotes the estimated total running-time in seconds.

Standard attack					New attack				
δ_1	d_1	$\log(T_{Red})$	$\log(\#E)$	$\log(T)$	δ_2	d_2	$\log(T_{Red})$	$\log(\#E)$	$\log(T)$
1.008	366	42.94	197.96	175	1.009	273	29.35	57.22	34
1.007	391	59.13	152.99	130	1.0085	280	34.27	48.07	35
1.0065	405	76.82	129.54	107	1.008	289	42.61	39.19	43
1.006	422	93.04	105.71	94	1.007	309	58.74	23.09	59

8   Conclusion

We have given theoretical and experimental results that confirm the benefit of our lattice rescaling approach to the binary-LWE problem. These results are most interesting when the standard deviation of the error distribution is large.

Figure 2 plots (the comparison of) the running time of our attack (using the embedding technique) for binary LWE and standard LWE. This graph should only be interpreted as a very rough approximation to the truth, but it allows us to compare the relative security. The papers [7, 19] have shown that to match the hardness of standard LWE for parameter n one can use binary-LWE with parameter $n \log(n)$. Figure 2 suggests that this is overkill and that even $n \log(\log(n))$ may be more than sufficient. However, it seems to be not sufficient to take parameter cn where c is a constant.

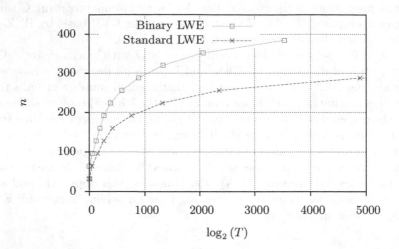

Fig. 2. Plot of predicted running time with respect to LWE parameter n for embedding attack on standard LWE and binary LWE

Acknowledgements. The authors are grateful to Chris Peikert for suggesting the lattice re-scaling idea. The authors would also like to thank Robert Fitzpatrick, Mingjie Liu, Phong Q. Nguyen and the Program Chairs for helpful comments and discussions.

The authors wish to acknowledge NeSI (New Zealand eScience Infrastructure) and the Centre for eResearch at the University of Auckland for providing CPU hours and support.

References

1. Albrecht, M.R., Cid, C., Faugère, J.-C., Fitzpatrick, R., Perret, L.: On the Complexity of the BKW Algorithm on LWE. In: Designs, Codes and Cryptography (Published online July 19, 2013) (to appear)
2. Albrecht, M.R., Fitzpatrick, R., Göpfert, F.: On the Efficacy of Solving LWE by Reduction to Unique-SVP. In: Proceedings of 2013 International Conference on Information Security and Cryptology (2013) (to appear)
3. Applebaum, B., Cash, D., Peikert, C., Sahai, A.: Fast Cryptographic Primitives and Circular-Secure Encryption Based on Hard Learning Problems. In: Halevi, S. (ed.) CRYPTO 2009. LNCS, vol. 5677, pp. 595–618. Springer, Heidelberg (2009)
4. Arora, S., Ge, R.: New Algorithms for Learning in Presence of Errors. In: Aceto, L., Henzinger, M., Sgall, J. (eds.) ICALP 2011, Part I. LNCS, vol. 6755, pp. 403–415. Springer, Heidelberg (2011)
5. Blum, A., Kalai, A., Wasserman, H.: Noise-tolerant learning, the parity problem, and the statistical query model. Journal of ACM 50(4), 506–519 (2003)
6. Brakerski, Z., Vaikuntanathan, V.: Efficient Fully Homomorphic Encryption from (Standard) LWE. In: Ostrovsky, R. (ed.) IEEE FOCS 2011, pp. 97–106 (2011)

7. Brakerski, Z., Langlois, A., Peikert, C., Regev, O., Stehlé, D.: Classical hardness of learning with errors. In: Boneh, D., Roughgarden, T., Feigenbaum, J. (eds.) ACM STOC 2013, pp. 575–584 (2013)
8. Cadé, D., Pujol, X., Stehlé, D.: FPLLL (2013), http://perso.ens-lyon.fr/damien.stehle/fplll
9. Chen, Y., Nguyen, P.Q.: BKZ 2.0: Better Lattice Security Estimates. In: Lee, D.H., Wang, X. (eds.) ASIACRYPT 2011. LNCS, vol. 7073, pp. 1–20. Springer, Heidelberg (2011)
10. Gama, N., Nguyen, P.Q.: Predicting Lattice Reduction. In: Smart, N.P. (ed.) EUROCRYPT 2008. LNCS, vol. 4965, pp. 31–51. Springer, Heidelberg (2008)
11. Gama, N., Nguyen, P.Q., Regev, O.: Lattice enumeration using extreme pruning. In: Gilbert, H. (ed.) EUROCRYPT 2010. LNCS, vol. 6110, pp. 257–278. Springer, Heidelberg (2010)
12. Kannan, R.: Minkowski's convex body theorem and integer programming. Mathematics of Operations Research 12(3), 415–440 (1987)
13. Lindner, R., Peikert, C.: Better key sizes (and attacks) for LWE-based encryption. In: Kiayias, A. (ed.) CT-RSA 2011. LNCS, vol. 6558, pp. 319–339. Springer, Heidelberg (2011)
14. Liu, M., Nguyen, P.Q.: Solving BDD by Enumeration: An Update. In: Dawson, E. (ed.) CT-RSA 2013. LNCS, vol. 7779, pp. 293–309. Springer, Heidelberg (2013)
15. Lyubashevsky, V., Micciancio, D.: On Bounded Distance Decoding, Unique Shortest Vectors, and the Minimum Distance Problem. In: Halevi, S. (ed.) CRYPTO 2009. LNCS, vol. 5677, pp. 577–594. Springer, Heidelberg (2009)
16. Lyubashevsky, V.: Lattice signatures without trapdoors. In: Pointcheval, D., Johansson, T. (eds.) EUROCRYPT 2012. LNCS, vol. 7237, pp. 738–755. Springer, Heidelberg (2012)
17. Luzzi, L., Stehlé, D., Ling, C.: Decoding by Embedding: Correct Decoding Radius and DMT Optimality. IEEE Transactions on Information Theory 59(5), 2960–2973 (2013)
18. Micciancio, D., Mol, P.: Pseudorandom Knapsacks and the Sample Complexity of LWE Search-to-Decision Reductions. In: Rogaway, P. (ed.) CRYPTO 2011. LNCS, vol. 6841, pp. 465–484. Springer, Heidelberg (2011)
19. Micciancio, D., Peikert, C.: Hardness of SIS and LWE with Small Parameters. In: Canetti, R., Garay, J.A. (eds.) CRYPTO 2013, Part I. LNCS, vol. 8042, pp. 21–39. Springer, Heidelberg (2013)
20. Micciancio, D., Regev, O.: Lattice-based cryptography. In: Bernstein, D.J., Buchmann, J., Dahmen, E. (eds.) Post Quantum Cryptography, pp. 147–191. Springer (2009)
21. Regev, O.: On lattices, learning with errors, random linear codes, and cryptography. In: Gabow, H.N., Fagin, R. (eds.) STOC 2005, pp. 84–93. ACM (2005)
22. Regev, O.: On lattices, learning with errors, random linear codes, and cryptography. Journal of the ACM 56(6), article 34 (2009)
23. Schnorr, C.P.: Lattice reduction by random sampling and birthday methods. In: Alt, H., Habib, M. (eds.) STACS 2003. LNCS, vol. 2607, pp. 145–156. Springer, Heidelberg (2003)

Privacy-Preserving Wildcards Pattern Matching Using Symmetric Somewhat Homomorphic Encryption

Masaya Yasuda[1], Takeshi Shimoyama[1], Jun Kogure[1],
Kazuhiro Yokoyama[2], and Takeshi Koshiba[3]

[1] FUJITSU Laboratories Ltd.,
1-1, Kamikodanaka 4-chome, Nakahara-ku, Kawasaki, 211-8588, Japan
{yasuda.masaya,shimo-shimo,kogure}@jp.fujitsu.com
[2] Department of Mathematics, Rikkyo University,
Nishi-Ikebukuro, Tokyo 171-8501, Japan
kazuhiro@rikkyo.ac.jp
[3] Division of Mathematics, Electronics and Informatics,
Graduate School of Science and Engineering, Saitama University,
255 Shimo-Okubo, Sakura, Saitama, 338-8570, Japan
koshiba@mail.saitama-u.ac.jp

Abstract. The basic pattern matching problem is to find the locations where a pattern occurs in a text. We give several computations enabling a client to obtain matching results from a database so that the database can not learn any information about client's queried pattern. For such computations, we apply the symmetric-key variant scheme of somewhat homomorphic encryption proposed by Brakerski and Vaikuntanathan (CRYPTO 2011), which can support a limited number of both polynomial additions and multiplications on encrypted data. We also utilize the packing method introduced by Yasuda et al. (CCSW 2013) for efficiency. While they deal with only basic problems for binary vectors, we address more complex problems such as the approximate and wildcards pattern matching for non-binary vectors. To demonstrate the efficiency of our method, we implemented the encryption scheme for secure wildcards pattern matching of DNA sequences. Our implementation shows that a client can privately search real-world genomes of length 16,500 in under one second on a general-purpose PC.

1 Introduction

Pattern matching is an essential tool in computer science and it can be applied to various applications such as text processing, image recognition, database search, computational biology, and network security. Given an alphabet Σ and a text $\mathcal{T} \in \Sigma^k$ of length k. Assume that Σ is represented as a set of positive integers (e.g., the DNA alphabet $\Sigma = \{A, C, G, T\}$ can be represented as the set $\{1, 2, 3, 4\}$). The *exact pattern matching* is the most basic, and its problem is to find all the occurrence of a given pattern $\mathcal{P}$ of length $\ell \leq k$ in $\mathcal{T}$. In addition to

W. Susilo and Y. Mu (Eds.): ACISP 2014, LNCS 8544, pp. 338–353, 2014.

the exact version problem, the following problems are required in wider retrieval applications (see [9, Section 3.1] for details):

(a) The *approximate pattern matching* problem is to find the locations where the Hamming distance between $\mathcal{P}$ and substrings of $\mathcal{T}$ of length ℓ is less than a pre-defined threshold τ. Sometimes, this problem is called the *substring* or the *threshold pattern matching*.

(b) Let "$\star$" $\notin \Sigma$ denote a special character, called the wildcard character, that matches any "single-character" of Σ (the wildcard character is usually represented as 0). Then the problem of *pattern matching with wildcards* is to find all the occurrence of a pattern $\mathcal{P} \in (\Sigma \cup \{\star\})^{\ell}$ in a text $\mathcal{T} \in (\Sigma \cup \{\star\})^{k}$. For example, the pattern "$TA\star$" matches any texts including "TAA", "TAC", "TAG", and "TAT" when we use the DNA alphabet.

Recently, pattern matching with preserving a pattern $\mathcal{P}$ and/or a text $\mathcal{T}$ has been received much attention in various areas such as privacy-preserving matching of DNA sequences [2,17,29], secure Hamming distance based biometric authentication [5,26], and anomaly detection in RFID [18].

1.1 Application Scenario Using Homomorphic Encryption

As an application scenario, we consider the following private search problem; A server (Bob) has a text $\mathcal{T}$ and a client (Alice) has a pattern $\mathcal{P}$. Then Alice wants to find the locations where her pattern $\mathcal{P}$ (approximately) occurs in Bob's text $\mathcal{T}$, but she does not want to reveal her queried pattern to Bob. On the other hand, Bob can not bring his text outside (i.e., we assume that Alice can not search his text locally), but he has powerful computational resources to search. In this scenario, Alice wants to know only the matching results, and also wants to securely outsource expensive matching computations to Bob. Then we apply the privacy homomorphism approach [28], in which we make use of homomorphic encryption supporting meaningful operations on encrypted data without decryption. Since current homomorphic encryption (e.g., fully homomorphic encryption) can support any targeted operation or circuit on encrypted data, we can "theoretically" construct the following protocol:

1. Alice generates keys of homomorphic encryption. Then she encrypts the pattern $\mathcal{P}$, and sends the encrypted pattern to Bob for private search (note that only Alice knows the secret key).
2. Bob performs pattern matching computations between $\mathcal{T}$ and $\mathcal{P}$ on encrypted data, and sends encrypted computation results back to Alice.
3. Using her own secret key, Alice decrypts data sent from Bob to obtain her desired matching results.

As long as the secret key is privately managed by Alice herself, Bob can not learn any information about both her queried pattern and desired matching results.

Typical Applications. In the real world, an application example of the above protocol is privately searching of DNA sequences in a genome database such as GenBank (see http://www.ncbi.nlm.nih.gov/genbank/), which is a typical database containing publicly available DNA sequences. In addition, the description in [16] tells that the Human Mitochondrial Genome Database (shortly, *mtDB*) has provided a comprehensive database of complete human mitochondrial genome collected from GenBank since early 2000. The mtDB gives an online repository for mitochondrial DNA sequences and it will provide both medical and human population genetic researchers with access to a common resource for future studies. In studying with such databases, it is obliviously important to prevent leakage of queried DNA sequences because it may indicate pre-exposure of certain health risks. At present, any researcher can bring DNA sequences in the mtDB locally for studying, but in this paper we assume the restrictive case where the DNA sequences can not be brought outside (e.g., for privacy regulation), and then we try to apply our homomorphic encryption technology to search in the mtDB (see §4.3 below). We believe that the above protocol would be useful for many researchers to securely and privately search in such DNA databases under strong regulation on privacy of DNA sequences.

1.2   Our Contributions

In evaluating a certain function by homomorphic encryption, performance and the size of encrypted data are main issues for practical usage. As in [31], we apply the somewhat homomorphic encryption (SHE) scheme proposed by Brakerski and Vaikuntanathan [7] to evaluate several matching computations homomorphically. Their scheme can be used as a building block for the construction of a fully homomorphic encryption (FHE) scheme, and it can support only a limited number of both additions and multiplications but it is much more practical than FHE[1]. The authors in [31] also introduced a new method in the scheme to pack a vector of certain length into a single ciphertext, and gave efficient matching computations over packed ciphertexts. In the following, we summarize our contributions;

- The authors in [31] used the public-key scheme of [7, Section 3.2], whereas we apply the *symmetric-key scheme* of [7, Section 3.1], which is more suitable for our scenario of §1.1 and gives more practical performance (see Remark 1 in §4.2). In addition, while the authors in [31] dealt with only basic pattern matching problems for binary vectors, we utilize their packing method for efficient computations of *various* matching problems (e.g., the wildcards matching) for *non-binary* vectors (see §3). Our method can be applied in the public-key scheme, and hence this work gives an extension of [31].
- Our main contribution is rather to give informative implementation results for secure wildcards pattern matching of DNA sequences (see §4.2 and Table

---

[1] We clarify the difference between FHE and SHE; FHE can support any operation or circuit, while SHE should be designed to evaluate a targeted operation or circuit so as to avoid the decryption failure (e.g., see §4.1 below for choosing SHE parameters).

2). These results show how practically our method can applied to a real-world genome database such as the mtDB (see §4.3).

Notation. The symbols $\mathbb{Z}$, $\mathbb{Q}$, and $\mathbb{R}$ denote the ring of integers, the field of rational numbers, and the field of real numbers, respectively. For a prime number p, the finite field with p elements is denoted by $\mathbb{F}_p$. For two integers z and d, let $[z]_d$ denote the reduction of z modulo d included in the interval $[-d/2, d/2)$ (the reduction of z modulo d included in the interval $[0, d)$ is denoted by $z \bmod d$ as usual). For a vector $\boldsymbol{A} = (a_0, a_1, \ldots, a_{n-1}) \in \mathbb{R}^n$, let $||\boldsymbol{A}||_\infty$ denote the ∞-norm defined by $\max_i |a_i|$. Let $\langle \boldsymbol{A}, \boldsymbol{B} \rangle$ denote the inner product between two vectors $\boldsymbol{A}$ and $\boldsymbol{B}$. We let $\lg(q)$ denote the logarithm value of an integer q with base 2.

2 Symmetric Encryption Scheme

In this section, we review the construction and the correctness of the symmetric SHE scheme proposed by Brakerski and Vaikuntanathan [7].

2.1 Construction of the Scheme

The following four parameters are required for the construction;

- n: an integer of 2-power, which defines the base ring $R = \mathbb{Z}[x]/(f(x))$ with the cyclotomic polynomial $f(x) = x^n + 1$ of degree n. The parameter n is often called the *lattice dimension*.
- q: a prime number with $q \equiv 1 \bmod 2n$, which defines the base ring $R_q = R/qR = \mathbb{F}_q[x]/(f(x))$ of a ciphertext space.
- t: an integer with $t < q$ to determine a plaintext space $R_t = (\mathbb{Z}/t\mathbb{Z})[x]/(f(x))$.
- σ: the parameter to define a discrete Gaussian error distribution $\chi = D_{\mathbb{Z}^n, \sigma}$ with the standard deviation σ.

An element in the ring R_q (resp. the ring R_t) can be represented as a polynomial of degree $(n-1)$ with coefficients in $\{0, 1, \ldots, q-1\}$ (resp. $\{0, 1, \ldots, t-1\}$). The security of the scheme constructed below relies on the following polynomial learning with errors (LWE) assumption $\mathsf{PLWE}_{n,q,\chi}$ [7, Section 2] (note that it does not depend on the parameter t), which is a simplified version of the ring-LWE assumption of [21] (see also [22, Section 2.4]);

Definition 1 (Polynomial LWE). *Given (n, q, σ) with $\chi = D_{\mathbb{Z}^n, \sigma}$, the polynomial LWE assumption $\mathsf{PLWE}_{n,q,\chi}$ (in the Hermite normal form) is that it is infeasible to distinguish the following two distributions (with a polynomial number of samples);*

- *One samples (a_i, b_i) uniformly from $(R_q)^2$.*
- *One first draws $s \leftarrow \chi = D_{\mathbb{Z}^n, \sigma}$ uniformly and then samples $(a_i, b_i) \in (R_q)^2$ by sampling $a_i \leftarrow R_q$ uniformly, $e_i \leftarrow \chi$ and setting $b_i = a_i s + e_i$.*

- **Key Generation.** Choose an element $R \ni s \leftarrow \chi$ as the secret key sk.
- **Encryption.** For a plaintext $m \in R_t$ and sk $= s$, the encryption first samples $a \leftarrow R_q$ and $e \leftarrow \chi$, and then compute the "fresh" ciphertext given by

$$\mathsf{Enc}(m, \mathsf{sk}) = (c_0, c_1) = (as + te + m, -a) \in (R_q)^2,$$

where $m \in R_t$ is regarded as an element of R_q in the natural way due to the condition $t < q$ (cf. the public-key scheme of [7, Section 3.2]).
- **Homomorphic Operations.** Here we only consider homomorphic operations between a fresh ciphertext ct $= (c_0, c_1) \in (R_q)^2$ and a plaintext $m' \in R_t$ (in general, homomorphic operations are defined between any two ciphertexts). The homomorphic addition "$\dotplus$" and multiplication "$*$" are respectively given by

$$\begin{cases} \mathsf{ct} \dotplus m' = (c_0 + m', c_1) \\ \mathsf{ct} * m' = (c_0 \cdot m', c_1 \cdot m') \end{cases}$$

where m' is regarded as an element of R_q as in the above encryption procedure. Similarly, the homomorphic subtraction is computed by $(c_0 - m', c_1)$. Note that the above homomorphic operations do not increase the length of the original ciphertext (cf. as mentioned in [7, Section 3], the homomorphic multiplication between two fresh ciphertexts gives a ciphertext with three elements in R_q).
- **Decryption.** For a fresh or homomorphically operated ciphertext ct $= (c_0, c_1) \in (R_q)^2$, the decryption with the secret key sk $= s$ is computed by

$$\mathsf{Dec}(\mathsf{ct}, \mathsf{sk}) = [\tilde{m}]_q \bmod t \in R_t,$$

where $\tilde{m} = c_0 + c_1 s \in R_q$. For the secret key vector $\boldsymbol{s} = (1, s)$ of length 2, we can rewrite $\mathsf{Dec}(\mathsf{ct}, \mathsf{sk}) = [\langle \mathsf{ct}, \boldsymbol{s} \rangle]_q \bmod t$.

2.2 Correctness of the Scheme

By *correctness*, we mean that the decryption can recover the operated result over plaintexts after certain homomorphic operations over ciphertexts. It follows from the description in [7, Section 1.1] that we have

$$\begin{cases} \mathsf{Dec}(\mathsf{ct} \dotplus m') = m + m' \\ \mathsf{Dec}(\mathsf{ct} * m') = m \cdot m' \end{cases} \tag{1}$$

for a ciphertext ct corresponding $m \in R_t$ and a plaintext $m' \in R_t$. In this paper, we use the correctness (1) for our application scenario of §1.1. We note that the encryption scheme constructed in §2.1 merely gives an SHE scheme (not an FHE scheme), and its correctness holds under the following condition:

Lemma 1 (Condition for successful decryption). *For a ciphertext* ct, *the decryption* $\mathsf{Dec}(\mathsf{ct}, \mathsf{sk})$ *recovers the correct result if* $\langle \mathsf{ct}, \boldsymbol{s} \rangle \in R_q$ *does not wrap around mod* q, *namely, if the condition* $||\langle \mathsf{ct}, \boldsymbol{s} \rangle||_\infty < \frac{q}{2}$ *is satisfied, where let* $||a||_\infty = \max |a_i|$ *for an element* $a = \sum_{i=0}^{n-1} a_i x^i \in R_q$.

3   Secure Pattern Matching Computations

In this section, we introduce a method to homomorphically evaluate various pattern matching computations (e.g., exact, approximate, and wildcards pattern matching introduced in §1) in the symmetric SHE scheme of §2. For simplicity, we here assume that $\Sigma \subset \mathbb{N}$ and the wildcard character $\star \notin \Sigma$ is represented as 0, and let $\Sigma_0 = \Sigma \cup \{0\}$ denote the alphabet with the wildcard character.

3.1   Review of Packing Method

A certain special message encoding can considerably reduce performance and the ciphertext size in performing several meaningful computations on encrypted data. In this paper, we make use of the packing method proposed in [31]. Its packing method transforms a vector of length less than n into a certain polynomial of the plaintext space R_t, and then packs it into a single ciphertext. This idea is fundamentally based on the encoding techniques introduced in [19], which gives efficient sums and products over large integers such as 128-bit integers. The main extension of [31] is to give two types of polynomials, and it enables to efficiently compute "multiple inner products" between two vectors. We begin with the definition of two types of polynomials in the packing method of [31];

Definition 2. *Let n be the lattice dimension parameter. For a vector $\boldsymbol{A} = (a_0, a_1, \ldots, a_{m-1}) \in \mathbb{Z}^m$ of length $m \leq n$, we define two types of polynomials in the ring $R = \mathbb{Z}[x]/(x^n + 1)$ as follows:*

(I) $\mathsf{pm}_1(\boldsymbol{A}) = \displaystyle\sum_{i=0}^{m-1} a_i x^i \in R,$

(II) $\mathsf{pm}_2(\boldsymbol{A}) = -\displaystyle\sum_{i=0}^{m-1} a_i x^{n-i} = a_0 - \displaystyle\sum_{i=1}^{m-1} a_i x^{n-i} \in R.$

The following property gives us a fundamental idea to obtain efficient multiple inner products; Let $\boldsymbol{A} = (a_0, a_1, \ldots, a_{k-1})$ and $\boldsymbol{B} = (b_0, b_1, \ldots, b_{\ell-1})$ with $\ell \leq k \leq n$. Since $x^n = -1$ in the ring R, the polynomial multiplication between $\mathsf{pm}_1(\boldsymbol{A})$ and $\mathsf{pm}_2(\boldsymbol{B})$ is equal to

$$\left(\sum_{i=0}^{k-1} a_i x^i\right) \times \left(-\sum_{j=0}^{\ell-1} b_j x^{n-j}\right) = -\sum_{j=0}^{\ell-1} \sum_{h=-j}^{k-j-1} a_{h+j} \cdot b_j x^{n+h} \quad \text{(take } h = i - j)$$

$$= \sum_{h=0}^{k-\ell} \langle \boldsymbol{A}^{(h)}, \boldsymbol{B} \rangle x^h + \text{terms of deg.} \geq k-\ell+1, \quad (2)$$

where $\boldsymbol{A}^{(h)}$ denotes the h-th subvector $(a_h, a_{h+1}, \ldots, a_{h+\ell-1})$ of length ℓ for $0 \leq h \leq k-\ell$. The expression (2) tells us that only one time polynomial multiplication between $\mathsf{pm}_1(\boldsymbol{A})$ and $\mathsf{pm}_2(\boldsymbol{B})$ gives multiple inner products $\langle \boldsymbol{A}^{(h)}, \boldsymbol{B} \rangle$ for $0 \leq h \leq k - \ell$ simultaneously.

For our application scenario of §1.1, we only need to consider the encryption of the queried pattern $\mathcal{P}$ of length ℓ which Alice holds. For simplicity, we assume $\ell \leq n$, and encrypt the pattern $\mathcal{P}$ with the secret key sk as

$$\mathsf{ct}_2(\mathcal{P}) := \mathsf{Enc}\left(\mathsf{pm}_2(\mathcal{P}), \mathsf{sk}\right) \in (R_q)^2, \tag{3}$$

where we consider the polynomial $\mathsf{pm}_2(\mathcal{P}) \in R$ as an element of the plaintext space R_t for sufficiently large t (in this paper, we only use the second type for the encryption of $\mathcal{P}$, but we can use the first type similarly). The property (2) and the correctness (1) of the symmetric SHE scheme give the following result on secure multiple inner products (cf. [31, Proposition 1]):

Proposition 1. *We assume $\ell \leq k \leq n$ and let $\mathcal{T} = (t_0, t_1, \ldots, t_{k-1}) \in \Sigma_0^k$ be a text of length k. For a pattern $\mathcal{P} = (p_0, p_1, \ldots, p_{\ell-1}) \in \Sigma_0^\ell$ of length ℓ, let $\mathsf{ct}_2(\mathcal{P})$ be its ciphertext given by (3). Then, under the condition of Lemma 1, the decryption of the homomorphic multiplication*

$$\mathsf{pm}_1(\mathcal{T}) * \mathsf{ct}_2(\mathcal{P}) \in (R_q)^2$$

gives a polynomial of R_t with the x^i-th coefficient equal to $\langle \mathcal{T}^{(i)}, \mathcal{P} \rangle = \sum_{j=0}^{\ell-1} t_{i+j} \cdot p_j$ for $0 \leq i \leq k - \ell$ modulo t. In other words, for sufficiently large t, the homomorphic multiplication of $\mathsf{pm}_1(\mathcal{T})$ and $\mathsf{ct}_2(\mathcal{P})$ simultaneously computes multiple inner products $\langle \mathcal{T}^{(i)}, \mathcal{P} \rangle$ for each $0 \leq i \leq k - \ell$ on encrypted data.

3.2   Exact and Approximate Pattern Matching

Set $\mathcal{T} = (t_0, t_1, \ldots, t_{k-1}) \in \Sigma^k$, $\mathcal{P} = (p_0, p_1, \ldots, p_{\ell-1}) \in \Sigma^\ell$ with $\ell \leq k$ (we here do not consider the wildcard character). For the exact and approximate pattern matching problems (see the first paragraph in §1 for the problems), we consider the squared Euclidean distance between $\mathcal{T}^{(i)}$ and $\mathcal{P}$ given by

$$\sum_{j=0}^{\ell-1} (p_j - t_{i+j})^2 = \sum_{j=0}^{\ell-1} \left(p_j^2 - 2p_j \cdot t_{i+j} + t_{i+j}^2\right) \tag{4}$$

for each $0 \leq i \leq k - \ell$. A simple observation shows that for fixed i, the pattern $\mathcal{P}$ occurs at the i-th position in $\mathcal{T}$ if and only if the distance (4) is equal to zero. Therefore the computation (4) tells us an answer of the exact pattern matching problem. Moreover, for binary vectors $\mathcal{T}$ and $\mathcal{P}$, the computation (4) is just the Hamming distance, and hence it also gives the approximate pattern matching computation. On the other hand, for non-binary vectors $\mathcal{T}$ and $\mathcal{P}$, we need to transform $\mathcal{T}$ and $\mathcal{P}$ to unary encoded vectors, that is, each entry $t_i, p_j \in \Sigma$ can be encoded as $t_i', p_j' \in \{0, 1\}^{|\Sigma|}$ with all 0s except for a single 1 in the place representing t_i, p_j lexicographically. Note that if $t_i \neq p_j$, then the computation (4) between two vectors $t_i', p_j' \in \{0, 1\}^{|\Sigma|}$ gives the Hamming distance 2 instead of 1. Therefore the computation (4) between unary encoded vectors $\mathcal{T}' = (t'_0, \ldots, t'_{k-1})$ and $\mathcal{P}' = (p'_0, \ldots, p'_{\ell-1})$ gives $2d_H(\mathcal{T}^{(i)}, \mathcal{P})$, where let d_H denote the Hamming distance between two strings.

To homomorphically evaluate multiple distance values (4) for $0 \leq i \leq k - \ell$ in the symmetric SHE scheme, we define the following notation; For a positive integer m, let $\boldsymbol{v}_m$ denote the vector $(1, 1, \ldots, 1)$ of length m. Furthermore, for a vector $\boldsymbol{A} = (a_0, a_1, \ldots, a_k)$, its component-wise m-power vector $(a_0^m, a_1^m, \ldots, a_k^m)$ is denoted by $\boldsymbol{A}^m$. Then we obtain the following result on secure exact and approximate pattern matching computations:

Theorem 1. *Under the condition of Lemma 1, the linear combination of homomorphic operations*

$$\mathsf{pm}_1(\mathcal{T}^2) * \mathsf{pm}_2(\boldsymbol{v}_\ell) \dotplus \mathsf{pm}_1(\boldsymbol{v}_k) * \mathsf{ct}_2(\mathcal{P}^2) \dotplus (-2\mathsf{pm}_1(\mathcal{T})) * \mathsf{ct}_2(\mathcal{P}) \qquad (5)$$

simultaneously computes multiple values (4) for $0 \leq i \leq k - \ell$ on encrypted data. Concretely, the homomorphic operation (5) gives a polynomial of R_t with the x^i-coefficient equal to the value (4) for each $0 \leq i \leq k - \ell$ on encrypted data.

Proof. The property (2) shows that each x^i-coefficient of $\mathsf{pm}_1(\mathcal{T}^2) * \mathsf{pm}_2(\boldsymbol{v}_\ell)$ is equal to the sum

$$(t_i^2, t_{i+1}^2, \ldots, t_{i+\ell-1}^2) \cdot (1, 1, \ldots, 1)^T = \sum_{j=0}^{\ell-1} t_{i+j}^2 \text{ for } 0 \leq i \leq k - \ell,$$

where $\boldsymbol{A}^T$ denotes the transpose of a vector $\boldsymbol{A}$. In addition, Proposition 1 tells that the homomorphic multiplication $\mathsf{pm}_1(\boldsymbol{v}_k) * \mathsf{ct}_2(\mathcal{P}^2)$ (resp. $(-2\mathsf{pm}_1(\mathcal{T})) * \mathsf{ct}_2(\mathcal{P})$) computes a polynomial with the x^i-coefficient equal to the sum

$$\sum_{j=0}^{\ell-1} p_j^2 \quad \left(\text{resp. } -2\sum_{j=0}^{\ell-1} p_j \cdot t_{i+j} \right)$$

for each $0 \leq i \leq k - \ell$ on encrypted data. Finally, by the correctness (1), the homomorphic operation (5) computes a polynomial of R_t with the x^i-coefficient equal to the value (4) for each $0 \leq i \leq k - \ell$ on encrypted data, which completes the proof. $\square$

3.3   Wildcards Pattern Matching

Set $\mathcal{T} = (t_0, t_1, \ldots, t_{k-1}) \in \Sigma_0^k$, $\mathcal{P} = (p_0, p_1, \ldots, p_{\ell-1}) \in \Sigma_0^\ell$ with $\ell \leq k$ (unlike in §3.2, we consider the alphabet Σ_0 with the wild character). According to [30], for each $0 \leq i \leq k - \ell$, we need to consider the sum

$$\sum_{j=0}^{\ell-1} p_j \cdot t_{i+j} (p_j - t_{i+j})^2 = \sum_{j=0}^{\ell-1} (p_j^3 \cdot t_{i+j} - 2p_j^2 \cdot t_{i+j}^2 + p_j \cdot t_{i+j}^3) \qquad (6)$$

for wildcards pattern matching (see the problem (b) in §1). Note that if p_j or t_{i+j} is a wildcard, the j-th term in the sum equals to 0. Similarly, if $p_j = t_{i+j}$,

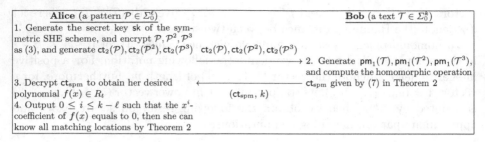

Fig. 1. Our protocol of secure wildcards pattern matching, which preserves the privacy of a queried pattern and matching results from Bob (assume $\ell \leq k \leq n$ for the packing method described in §3.1)

the j-th term is also equal to 0. Thus the entire sum equals to 0 if and only if the pattern $\mathcal{P}$ matches the i-th substring $\mathcal{T}^{(i)}$. Hence, for wildcards pattern matching, it is enough to compute the sum (6) for all $0 \leq i \leq k - \ell$. Here we give the following result on evaluation of multiple values (6) for $0 \leq i \leq k - \ell$ in the symmetric SHE scheme;

Theorem 2. *Under the condition of Lemma 1, the linear combination of homomorphic operations*

$$\mathsf{pm}_1(\mathcal{T}) * \mathsf{ct}_2(\mathcal{P}^3) \dotplus \mathsf{pm}_1(\mathcal{T}^3) * \mathsf{ct}_2(\mathcal{P}) \dotplus (-2\mathsf{pm}_1(\mathcal{T}^2)) * \mathsf{ct}_2(\mathcal{P}^2) \qquad (7)$$

simultaneously computes multiple values (6) *for* $0 \leq i \leq k - \ell$ *on encrypted data. As in Theorem 1, the computation* (7) *gives a polynomial of* R_t *such that the* x^i*-coefficient is equal to the value* (6) *for each* $0 \leq i \leq k - \ell$ *on encrypted data.*

Proof. The proof is almost the same as that of Theorem 1. In particular, we remark that three homomorphic multiplications $\mathsf{pm}_1(\mathcal{T}) * \mathsf{ct}_2(\mathcal{P}^3)$, $\mathsf{pm}_1(\mathcal{T}^3) * \mathsf{ct}_2(\mathcal{P})$, and $-2\mathsf{pm}_1(\mathcal{T}^2) * \mathsf{ct}_2(\mathcal{P}^2)$ respectively correspond to three sums

$$\sum_{j=0}^{\ell-1} p_j^3 \cdot t_{i+j}, \ \sum_{j=0}^{\ell-1} p_j \cdot t_{i+j}^3, \ \text{and} \ -2\sum_{j=0}^{\ell-1} p_j^2 \cdot t_{i+j}^2$$

on the plaintext space by Proposition 1. $\qquad \square$

By (5) and (7), we can perform a variety of secure pattern matching computations by combinations of only a few homomorphic additions and multiplications. In particular, for secure wildcards pattern matching, we give the detailed protocol flow in Figure 1 (as noted in §1.1, as long as the secret key sk is managed by Alice herself, Bob cannot learn any information about both her queried pattern and matching results). The protocol is secure under the assumption that Bob is *semi-honest* (also known as *honest-but-curious*), i.e., he always follows the protocol but tries to learn information from the protocol. Furthermore, note that the security of the protocol holds under the polynomial LWE assumption $\mathsf{PLWE}_{n,q,\chi}$, on which the security of the symmetric SHE scheme relies.

As in [31], our protocol gives a decryptor (i.e., Alice in this paper) more information than desired matching positions, but there is no problem in our application because Alice wants to search in a database only with preserving the confidentiality of her queried pattern. However, more useful applications would be required to compute the minimum Hamming distance between a pattern and string texts, and in such applications, this work only gives a building block for secure pattern matching. For such complex applications, other techniques such as zero-knowledge protocols and oblivious transfer would be necessary (e.g., see the survey paper [9]).

4   Experimental Evaluation

In this section, we give informative implementation results to demonstrate the efficiency of our method. Specifically, we implemented the protocol shown in Figure 1 for the application scenario of §1.1 on the private search problem with wildcards. For simplicity, we assume $\Sigma = \{1, 2, 3, 4\}$, which can be typically used as a representation of the DNA alphabet (i.e., $\Sigma_0 = \{0, 1, 2, 3, 4\}$).

4.1   Chosen Parameters of Symmetric SHE Scheme

In the protocol of Figure 1, we need to evaluate the computation (7). Our method to choose suitable parameters is based on the methodology in [19], which is also based on [20]. For simplicity, we assume $n \geq k \geq \ell \geq 1$, which condition enables to handle each vector of a text $\mathcal{T} \in \Sigma_0^k$ and a pattern $\mathcal{P} \in \Sigma_0^\ell$ as only one block (if $n < k$, the packing method of §3.1 enforces to divide $\mathcal{T}$ into $\lceil n/k \rceil$ blocks of length less than n, and it causes difficulty of handling boundary of blocks).

Correctness Side. For the correctness of the ciphertext $\mathsf{ct}_{\mathrm{spm}}$ given by the equation (7), it requires the condition of Lemma 1. The homomorphic property of the symmetric SHE scheme shows that the element $\langle \mathsf{ct}_{\mathrm{spm}}, s \rangle$ is equal to

$$\mathsf{pm}_1(\mathcal{T}) \cdot \langle \mathsf{ct}_2(\mathcal{P}^3), s \rangle + \mathsf{pm}_1(\mathcal{T}^3) \cdot \langle \mathsf{ct}_2(\mathcal{P}), s \rangle - 2\mathsf{pm}_1(\mathcal{T}^2) \cdot \langle \mathsf{ct}_2(\mathcal{P}^2), s \rangle$$

in the ring R_q (see also the proof of [19, Lemma 3.3]). Note that we clearly have $||\mathsf{pm}_1(\mathcal{T}^m)||_\infty \leq 4^m$ for $m \geq 1$ by the assumption of $\Sigma_0 = \{0, 1, 2, 3, 4\}$ and $\mathcal{T} \in \Sigma_0^k$. Set U to be an upper bound of the ∞-norm size $||\langle \mathsf{ct}, s \rangle||_\infty$ for any fresh ciphertext $\mathsf{ct} \in (R_q)^2$. Then we have an inequality

$$||\langle \mathsf{ct}_{\mathrm{spm}}, s \rangle||_\infty \leq 4nU + 4^3 nU + 2 \cdot 4^2 nU \leq 2^7 nU \qquad (8)$$

by $||\langle \mathsf{ct}_2(\mathcal{P}^m), s \rangle||_\infty \leq U$ for $m = 1, 2, 3$ and the fact [19, Lemma 3.2] that we have $||a + b||_\infty \leq ||a||_\infty + ||b||_\infty$ and $||a \cdot b||_\infty \leq n \cdot ||a||_\infty \cdot ||b||_\infty$ for any two elements $a, b \in R_q$. For a fresh ciphertext ct, the size $||\langle \mathsf{ct}, s \rangle||_\infty$ is approximately equal to $t \cdot ||e||_\infty$ with $e \leftarrow \chi = D_{\mathbb{Z}^n, \sigma}$ from the encryption procedure in §2.1. Here we assume $||e||_\infty \leq 8\sigma$ for any noises $e \leftarrow \chi$ since the value $\mathrm{erfc}(8) \approx 2^{-96}$ of complementary error function is sufficiently small (cf. $\mathrm{erfc}(2) \approx 2^{-8}$

and erfc(4) $\approx 2^{-26}$). Then we set $U = 8t\sigma$ for the successful correctness with overwhelming probability $1 - 2^{-96}$. Then, by the inequality (8) and Lemma 1, we estimate that the correctness of the ciphertext ct_{spm} holds if

$$2^7 n \cdot 8t\sigma = 2^{10} nt\sigma < \frac{q}{2} \iff 2^{11} nt\sigma < q, \tag{9}$$

which condition gives a lower bound of the prime q.

Security Side. As noted in §2.1, the security of the symmetric SHE scheme relies on the polynomial LWE assumption $\mathsf{PLWE}_{n,q,\chi}$. In this work, we follow the methodology of Lindner and Peikert [20] for the security analysis of the more general LWE problem. According to their work, there are two efficient attacks against the LWE problem, namely, the distinguishing attack proposed in [23], and the decoding attack proposed in [20]. Although the analysis in [20] shows that the decoding attack is always stronger than the distinguishing one, the two attacks have a similar performance for practical advantages such as $\varepsilon = 2^{-32}$ and 2^{-64}. Therefore, as in [19], we consider the security against only the distinguishing attack. The security of the distinguishing attack can be measured by so called *the root Hermite factor*, which was firstly introduced in [11] (as the root Hermite factor is smaller, the security is higher). For given parameters (n, q, t, σ) of the symmetric SHE scheme, the analysis of [20] gives us the relation

$$c \cdot q/\sigma = 2^{2\sqrt{n \cdot \lg(q) \cdot \lg(\delta)}} \tag{10}$$

between n, q and δ, where c is the constant determined by the attack advantage ε, and we here assume $c = 3.758$ corresponding to $\varepsilon = 2^{-64}$ for higher security than [19], in which $\varepsilon = 2^{-32}$ is considered ($c = 2.657$ in this case).

Chosen Parameters and Their Security Level. Set $\sigma = 8$ to make the scheme secure against combinatorial style attacks as noted in [13, Appendix D]. Since the sum of the equation (6) is included in the range $[0, 2^8 \ell]$, we set $t = 2^8 n \geq 2^8 \ell$ in order to avoid the carry operation. We also consider five lattice dimensions $n = 2048 \sim 32768$ in order to correspond various applications. For each lattice dimension, the prime parameter q is determined by the condition (9), and then the root Hermite factor δ can be calculated by the relation (10). In Table 1, we show our chosen five parameters (i)-(v).

According to the state-of-the-art security analysis of Chen and Nguyen [8] for lattice-based cryptography, a root Hermite factor smaller than $\delta = 1.0050$ is estimated to have much more than 80-bit security (note that lattice dimensions less than $n = 2048$ have the root Hermite factor larger than 1.0050, and hence such dimensions do not give the enough security). Therefore all parameters in Table 1 are estimated to have 80-bit security level with an enough margin against the distinguishing attack with advantage $\varepsilon = 2^{-64}$, and also against the more powerful decoding attack (as the lattice dimension n is larger, the security level becomes higher). Different from [8], the authors in [20] simply estimate the running time from NTL implementation experiments of the BKZ algorithm,

Table 1. Chosen parameters (n, q, t, σ) of the symmetric SHE scheme for the protocol of Figure 1 (see Appendix A for the root Hermite factor δ and the "roughly" estimated running time $\lg(t_{\mathsf{Adv}})$ of the distinguishing attack)

	n	q	t	σ	δ	$\lg(t_{\mathsf{Adv}})$
(i)	2048	45-bit	$2^8 n$	8	1.00363	234
(ii)	4096	47-bit	$2^8 n$	8	1.00190	547
(iii)	8192	49-bit	$2^8 n$	8	1.00099	1150
(iv)	16384	51-bit	$2^8 n$	8	1.00052	2290
(v)	32768	53-bit	$2^8 n$	8	1.00027	4530

which is one of the most practical attacks against lattice problems. In [20], they also derive a relation of the expected running time t_{Adv} of the distinguishing attack with the root Hermite factor δ given by

$$\lg(t_{\mathsf{Adv}}) = \frac{1.8}{\lg(\delta)} - 110. \tag{11}$$

For chosen parameters (i)-(v) in Table 1, the expected running time t_{Adv} by the above relation is also given in the same table. We remark that their security analysis seems no longer state-of-the-art due to the old NTL implementation, and hence the expected running time in Table 1 is just at the reference level. However, their analysis tells us a rough standard of the security level of each parameter. According to the values $\lg(t_{\mathsf{Adv}})$ in Table 1, all our chosen parameters are estimated to have much more than 80-bit security level as noted in the first paragraph. In particular, three parameters (iii)-(v) are estimated to have more than 1000-bit security level.

4.2 Implementation Details

For five parameters (i)-(v) in Table 1, we implemented the symmetric SHE scheme for our protocol of secure wildcards pattern matching shown in Figure 1. Our experiments ran on an Intel Xeon X3480 at 3.07 GHz with 16 GB memory, and we used our software library using inline assembly language x86_64 in C programs for all computations in the base ring $R_q = \mathbb{F}_q[x]/(x^n + 1)$ of the ciphertext space. Our C code was complied using gcc 4.6.0 on Linux. In particular, we used the Montgomery reduction algorithm and the FFT (Fast Fourier Transform) method for efficient multiplication in the ring R_q (in our implementation, the FFT method gives the faster performance than the Karatsuba multiplication algorithm). In Table 2, we summarize the performance and the bandwidth of the protocol of Figure 1 for DNA sequences. As described in Figure 1, for a fixed lattice dimension n, our protocol can pack a queried pattern vector $\mathcal{P}$ of length less than n into three ciphertexts $\mathsf{ct}_2(\mathcal{P}), \mathsf{ct}_2(\mathcal{P}^2), \mathsf{ct}_2(\mathcal{P}^3)$, and the homomorphic operation (7) in Theorem 2 enables to perform secure wildcards pattern matching for DNA sequences of length less than n. In the following, we give details of the performances and the sizes only for the parameter (i) with

$n = 2048$ in Table 1 (due to our optimized implementation, our performance is faster than [19, Table 2], in which the computer algebra system *Magma* is used);

- The size of the key sk $= s \in R_q$ of the scheme is $n \cdot \lg(q) \approx 11.5$ KB. A fresh ciphertext has two elements in the ring R_q, and hence its size is $2n \cdot \lg(q) \approx 23$ KB. Therefore the size of three packed ciphertexts $\mathsf{ct}_2(\mathcal{P}), \mathsf{ct}_2(\mathcal{P}^2), \mathsf{ct}_2(\mathcal{P}^3)$ is about $3 \times 23 = 69$ KB. Furthermore, the ciphertext $\mathsf{ct}_{\mathrm{spm}}$ given by the homomorphic operation (7) has only two ring elements in R_q as well as a fresh ciphertext, and its size is about 23 KB.
- The packed encryption for three vectors $\mathcal{P}, \mathcal{P}^2, \mathcal{P}^3$ of length less than $n = 2048$ took about $3 \times 3.498 \approx 10.49$ milliseconds (ms) to generate three packed ciphertexts $\mathsf{ct}_2(\mathcal{P}), \mathsf{ct}_2(\mathcal{P}^2), \mathsf{ct}_2(\mathcal{P}^3)$, the secure wildcards pattern matching computation (7) took about 18.33 ms, and finally the decryption took about 5.99 ms. Hence the total time is about 34.92 ms for secure wildcards pattern matching for DNA sequences of length less than $n = 2048$.

Remark 1. Our platform and implementation level are almost the same as in [31]. In particular, as well as in [31], our software library with assembly-level optimizations give the fast performance of the 64-bit $\times$ 64-bit $\rightarrow$ 128-bit multiplication, which needs only about 4 clocks on our platform. When we implement the same operations in standard C programs without assembly-level optimizations, it needs about $4 \times 4 = 16$ clocks and hence our performance results in Table 2 would be $4 \sim 5$ times slower.

Although we implemented the *symmetric* scheme in this paper, the performance of our protocol for each lattice dimension n in Table 2 is slower than [31, Table 3], in which the *public-key* scheme is used. The main reason is that our secure computation (7) is more complex than the matching computation in [31, Theorem 1] in order to perform the wildcards matching, and our parameters are chosen to handle DNA sequences (cf. only the exact and approximate matching computations for binary vectors can be performed in [31]). Specifically, when we evaluate the secure computation (7) homomorphically in the public-key scheme as in [31], larger q must be chosen for the correctness. For example, we estimate that it needs to set $q > 64$-bit ($q \approx 70$-bit is sufficient) for the case $n = 32768$ (cf. it needs $q < 64$-bit for the parameter (v) in Table 1). Therefore, in this case, we need to compute the 128-bit $\times$ 128-bit $\rightarrow$ 256-bit multiplication for efficient multiplication in the base ring R_q of the ciphertext space, and hence the performance of the secure computation (7) in the public-key scheme is estimated to be at least $2 \sim 3$ times slower (in fact, it would be $5 \sim 10$ times slower) than our performance shown in Table 2 (v).

4.3   Use Case: Application to the mtDB

As introduced in §1.1, the mtDB [16] is a database in which anyone can search for comprehensive information on human mitochondrial genome. According to [16], a full mitochondrial DNA sequence in the mtDB has at most 16,500 characters in length, and any user can input up to 10 DNA characters including the wildcards

Table 2. Performance and bandwidth of the protocol of Figure 1 (the secure matching computation (7) in Theorem 2 enables to perform secure wildcards pattern matching for DNA sequences of length less than n)

Parameters in Table 1	Performance (ms)				Bandwidth (KB)	
	Packed enc. for $\mathcal{P}, \mathcal{P}^2, \mathcal{P}^3$	Secure match comp. (7)	Decryption	Total time of the protocol	Alice to Bob	Bob to Alice
(i)	10.49	18.33	5.99	34.92	69	23
(ii)	22.72	39.88	13.07	75.90	144	48
(iii)	50.90	90.10	29.59	171.03	300	100
(iv)	118.31	212.06	69.79	404.05	627	209
(v)	257.76	467.51	152.99	880.04	1302	434

character as a queried pattern (see http://www.mtdb.igp.uu.se/ for the web page of searching in the mtDB). In applying our protocol of Figure 1 to the mtDB, the parameter (i) in Table 1 with $n = 2048$ enforces us to divide a DNA sequence of length 16,500 into at least $8 \approx 16500/2048$ blocks of length 2048. On the other hand, the parameter (v) with $n = 32768$ is sufficient to handle a DNA sequence in the mtDB as "only one block", and hence it can release difficulty of handing boundary of blocks for privacy-preserving matching computations in the mtDB. Moreover, according to Table 2, the parameter (v) enables to perform secure wildcards pattern matching in about 880.04 ms, which would be sufficiently practical in real life. In 2013, Beck and Kerschbaum [4] proposed a privacy-preserving string matching protocol using encrypted Bloom filters by the additively homomorphic encryption scheme proposed by Naccache and Stern [25]. As well as in this paper, they reported in [4, Section VI] that in applying their protocol to the mtDB, it took about 286 seconds on a Linux laptop with an Intel Core2 Duo T9600 at 2.8 GHz, which is much slower than ours (though platforms and implementation levels are quite different). This gives an evidence in support of the claim that our protocol has the considerably fast performance for privacy-preserving pattern matching of DNA sequences in the setting of §1.1. In addition, our protocol has the much lower bandwidth than their protocol. Specifically, while their protocol for DNA sequences of length 12,800 requires 18636 KB bandwidth for transmission from Alice to Bob, and 123 KB from Bob to Alice (see [4, Table 1] for the bandwidth of their protocol), our protocol requires only 1,302 KB from Alice to Bob, and 434 KB from Bob to Alice in using the parameter (v) (see the bandwidth of our protocol shown in Table 2).

5 Conclusions

We utilized the packing method of [31] in the symmetric-key variant of SHE scheme of [7] to obtain practical secure computations of various pattern matching problems. In this paper, we implemented several parameters of the encryption scheme with $n = 2048 \sim 32768$ in order to correspond various applications. Our implementation showed that our protocol of secure wildcards pattern matching computation for DNA sequences has both faster performance and lower communication cost than the state-of-the-art work. In particular, we showed that the lattice dimension $n = 32768$ can be practically applied to a private search in the mtDB [16] including DNA sequences of length up to 16,500.

References

1. Atallah, M.J., Frikken, K.B.: Securely outsourcing linear algebra computations. In: ACM Symposium on Information, Computer and Communication Security, ASIACCS 2010, pp. 48–59. ACM Press, New York (2010)
2. Baldi, P., Baronio, R., De Crisofaro, E., Gasti, P., Tsudik, G.: Countering gattaca: efficient and secure testing of fully-sequenced human genomes. In: ACM Conference on Computer and Communications Security, CCS 2011, pp. 691–702. ACM (2011)
3. Baron, J., El Defrawy, K., Minkovich, K., Ostrovsky, R., Tressler, E.: 5PM: secure pattern matching. In: Visconti, I., De Prisco, R. (eds.) SCN 2012. LNCS, vol. 7485, pp. 222–240. Springer, Heidelberg (2012),
   http://eprint.iacr.org/2012/698.pdf
4. Beck, M., Kerschbaum, F.: Approximate two-party privacy-preserving string matching with linear complexity. In: IEEE International Congress on Big Data, pp. 31–37. IEEE (2013)
5. Blanton, M., Gasti, P.: Secure and efficient protocols for iris and fingerprint identification. In: Atluri, V., Diaz, C. (eds.) ESORICS 2011. LNCS, vol. 6879, pp. 190–209. Springer, Heidelberg (2011)
6. Boneh, D., Gentry, C., Halevi, S., Wang, F., Wu, D.J.: Private database queries using somewhat homomorphic encryption. In: Jacobson, M., Locasto, M., Mohassel, P., Safavi-Naini, R. (eds.) ACNS 2013. LNCS, vol. 7954, pp. 102–118. Springer, Heidelberg (2013)
7. Brakerski, Z., Vaikuntanathan, V.: Fully homomorphic encryption from ring-LWE and security for key dependent messages. In: Rogaway, P. (ed.) CRYPTO 2011. LNCS, vol. 6841, pp. 505–524. Springer, Heidelberg (2011)
8. Chen, Y., Nguyen, P.Q.: BKZ 2.0: better lattice security estimates. In: Lee, D.H., Wang, X. (eds.) ASIACRYPT 2011. LNCS, vol. 7073, pp. 1–20. Springer, Heidelberg (2011)
9. El Defrawy, K., Faber, S.: Blindfolded searching of data via secure pattern matching. IEEE Computer Magazine's Special Issue (2013) (to appear)
10. Frikken, K.B.: Practical private DNA string searching and matching through efficient oblivious automata evaluation. In: Gudes, E., Vaidya, J. (eds.) Data and Applications Security XXIII. LNCS, vol. 5645, pp. 81–94. Springer, Heidelberg (2009)
11. Gama, N., Nguyen, P.Q.: Predicting lattice reduction. In: Smart, N.P. (ed.) EUROCRYPT 2008. LNCS, vol. 4965, pp. 31–51. Springer, Heidelberg (2008)
12. Gennaro, R., Hazay, C., Sorensen, J.S.: Text search protocols with simulation based security. In: Nguyen, P.Q., Pointcheval, D. (eds.) PKC 2010. LNCS, vol. 6056, pp. 332–350. Springer, Heidelberg (2010)
13. Gentry, C., Halevi, S., Smart, N.P.: Homomorphic evaluation of the AES circuit. In: Safavi-Naini, R., Canetti, R. (eds.) CRYPTO 2012. LNCS, vol. 7417, pp. 850–867. Springer, Heidelberg (2012)
14. Hazay, C., Lindell, Y.: Efficient protocols for set intersection and pattern matching with security against malicious and convert adversaries. In: Canetti, R. (ed.) TCC 2008. LNCS, vol. 4948, pp. 155–175. Springer, Heidelberg (2008)

15. Hazay, C., Toft, T.: Computationally secure pattern matching in the presence of malicious adversaries. In: Abe, M. (ed.) ASIACRYPT 2010. LNCS, vol. 6477, pp. 195–212. Springer, Heidelberg (2010)

16. Ingman, M., Gyllensten, U.: mtDB: Human Mitochondrial Genome Database, a resource for population genetics and medical sciences. Nucleic Acids Research 34, 749–751 (2006)

17. Katz, J., Malka, L.: Secure text processing with applications to private DNA matching. In: ACM Conference on Computer and Communication Security, CCS 2010, pp. 485–492. ACM (2010)

18. Kerschbaum, F., Oertel, N.: Privacy-preserving pattern matching for anomaly detection in RFID anti-counterfeiting. In: Ors Yalcin, S.B. (ed.) RFIDSec 2010. LNCS, vol. 6370, pp. 124–137. Springer, Heidelberg (2010)

19. Lauter, K., Naehrig, M., Vaikuntanathan, V.: Can homomorphic encryption be practical? In: ACM Workshop on Cloud Computing Security Workshop, CCSW 2011, pp. 113–124. ACM (2011)

20. Lindner, R., Peikert, C.: Better key sizes (and attacks) for LWE-based encryption. In: Kiayias, A. (ed.) CT-RSA 2011. LNCS, vol. 6558, pp. 319–339. Springer, Heidelberg (2011)

21. Lyubashevsky, V., Peikert, C., Regev, O.: On ideal lattices and learning with errors over rings. In: Gilbert, H. (ed.) EUROCRYPT 2010. LNCS, vol. 6110, pp. 1–23. Springer, Heidelberg (2010)

22. Lyubashevsky, V., Peikert, C., Regev, O.: A toolkit for ring-LWE cryptography. In: Johansson, T., Nguyen, P.Q. (eds.) EUROCRYPT 2013. LNCS, vol. 7881, pp. 35–54. Springer, Heidelberg (2013)

23. Micciancio, D., Regev, O.: Worst-case to average-case reduction based on gaussian measures. SIAM J. Computing 37(1), 267–302 (2007)

24. Mohassel, P., Niksefat, S., Sadeghian, S., Sadeghiyan, B.: An efficient protocol for oblivious DFA evaluation and applications. In: Dunkelman, O. (ed.) CT-RSA 2012. LNCS, vol. 7178, pp. 398–415. Springer, Heidelberg (2012)

25. Naccache, D., Stern, J.: A new cryptosystem based on higher residues. In: ACM Conference on Computer and Communication Security, CCS 1998, pp. 59–66 (1998)

26. Osadchy, M., Pinkas, B., Jarrous, A., Moskovich, B.: SCiFI - a system for secure face recognition. In: IEEE Security and Privacy, pp. 239–254. IEEE (2010)

27. Paillier, P.: Public-key cryptosystems based on composite degree residuosity classes. In: Stern, J. (ed.) EUROCRYPT 1999. LNCS, vol. 1592, pp. 223–238. Springer, Heidelberg (1999)

28. Rivest, R.L., Adleman, L., Dertouzos, M.L.: On data banks and privacy homomorphism. Foundations of Secure Computation, 169–177 (1978)

29. Troncoso-Pastoriza, J.R., Katzenbeisser, S., Celik, M.: Privacy preserving error resilient DNA searching through oblivious automata. In: ACM Conference on Computer and Communications Security, CCS 2007, pp. 519–528. ACM (2007)

30. Vergnaud, D.: Efficient and secure generalized pattern matching via fast fourier transform. In: Nitaj, A., Pointcheval, D. (eds.) AFRICACRYPT 2011. LNCS, vol. 6737, pp. 41–58. Springer, Heidelberg (2011)

31. Yasuda, M., Shimoyama, T., Kogure, J., Yokoyama, K., Koshiba, T.: Secure pattern matching using somewhat homomorphic encryption. In: ACM Workshop on Cloud Computing Security Workshop, CCSW 2013, pp. 65–76. ACM (2013)

Once Root Always a Threat: Analyzing the Security Threats of Android Permission System*

Zhongwen Zhang[1,2,3], Yuewu Wang[1,2], Jiwu Jing[1,2],
Qiongxiao Wang[1,2], and Lingguang Lei[1,2]

[1] Data Assurance and Communication Security Research Center, Beijing, China
[2] State Key Laboratory of Information Security,
Institute of Information Engineering, CAS, Beijing, China
[3] University of Chinese Academy of Sciences, Beijing, China
{zwzhang,ywwang,jing,qxwang,lglei}@lois.cn

Abstract. Android permission system enforces access control to those privacy-related resources in Android phones. Unfortunately, the permission system could be bypassed when the phone is rooted. On a rooted phone, processes can run with root privilege and can arbitrarily access any resources without permission. Many people are willing to root their Android phones to uninstall pre-installed applications, flash third party ROMs, backup their phones and so on. People use rootkit tools to root their phones. The mainstream rootkit tools in China are provided by some well-known security vendors. Besides root, these vendors also provide the *one-click-unroot* function to unroot a phone. The unroot process gives users a feeling that their phones will roll back to the original safe state. In this paper, we present the security threats analysis of permission system on phones rooted once and unrooted later. On these phones, two categories of attacks: tampering data files attack and tampering code files attack are carried out. Also, the attacks' detection rate, damage degree, influence range, and survivability in the real word are analyzed. Analysis result shows even under Antivirus' monitoring, these attacks towards permission system can still be carried out and survive after the phone is unrooted. Therefore, the permission system faces a long-term compromise. The potential defense solutions are also discussed.

Keywords: Android, Permission System, Rooted Time Window.

1 Introduction

Android permission system is one of the most important security mechanism for protecting critical system resources on Android phones. Android phones contain numerous privacy-related system resources, such as various sensors, sensitive data, and important communication modules. Abusing these resources will

---

* The work is supported by a grant from the National Basic Research Program of China (973 Program, No. 2013CB338001).

W. Susilo and Y. Mu (Eds.): ACISP 2014, LNCS 8544, pp. 354–369, 2014.

result in serious leakage of users' private data and even financial loss. To prevent the privacy-related resources from being abused, permission system ensures only the applications (apps) granted certain permissions can access corresponding resources. Otherwise, the access request will be rejected. In Android system, permissions that an app possesses represent the app's capability to access resources.

Besides permissions, root privilege is another resource access capability. Nowadays, it is common for users to root Android phones. According to [23], 23% Android phones are rooted at least one time in China mainland by the first half of 2012. After a phone is rooted, users can fully control it. For example, they can remove the disliked pre-installed apps, custom personalized system, backup their phones, and flash third party ROMs.

Getting root privilege is a big challenge to permission system. With root privilege, the highest privilege in user mode, malware can access sensitive database files (e.g. SMS and Contact databases files) and hardware interfaces (e.g. Camera, Microphone) without getting corresponding permissions beforehand. In this kind of resource accessing, permission system does not play any role. That is to say, the permission system can be bypassed. We call this kind of attacks as bypass attacks. Moreover, YaJin Zhou et al.'s work [33] reveals 36.7% malware leveraged root-level exploits to fully compromise the Android security. As the threats brought by root become more and more serious, users are motivated to unroot their Android phones. Besides, the mainstream rootkits in China mainland provide the *one-click-unroot* function, which makes unroot process easy to be carried out. For example, the unroot process of *Baidu, Tencent*, and *360* takes less than 1 minute. For convenience of description, we call the time between root and unroot as a rooted time window.

Will unroot prevent Android system from suffering security threat? Unrooting a phone will make malware lose root privilege. For the bypass attacks, without root privilege, malware cannot access system resources any more. Also, that the permissions system is bypassed not means it is compromised. When malware lose root privilege, they subject to the permission system's access control again. Therefore, unroot can defend the bypass attack towards permission system. However, we wonder if there are other attacks happened in rooted time window and cannot be defended by unroot. To answer this question, we analyzed the implementation of permission system.

Permission system is composed of data files and code files. Data files include a metadata file named *packages.xml* and installation files (*apk* files). Both of them contain app's permissions, and they are protected by nothing but the UNIX file system access control mechanism. By tampering the *packages.xml* file or the *apk* files with root privilege, we carry out 3 kinds of attacks to escalate permissions. By doing this, even after a phone is unrooted, the escalated permissions still open a backdoor for malware to abuse system resources. What is more, we also explore the feasibility of removing access control of permission system by tampering its code files. The feasibility of this attack is verified on Galaxy Nexus, which is a phone supporting Android Open Source Project. This way could fully compromise the permission system and open a backdoor for all apps.

To evaluate the practical effectiveness of these attacks, we run our demo malware under Antivirus' (AV) monitoring at the rooted time window. The result shows these attacks have a 100% rate to evade detection of AVs in China and 80% abroad. To permission escalation attacks, more than one half of escalated permissions can hide from permission list provided by AVs. Besides this, damage degree, influence range, and survivability after unroot are also analyzed.

The main contributions of this paper are listed as follows:

- To the best of our knowledge, we primarily analyzed the implementation of permission system and illustrated 4 attack models from the perspective of tampering data files or tampering code files of permission system.
- We evaluated the attacks in the aspects of evasion rate, damage degree, influence range, and survivability. The analysis result indicates that even under AVs' monitoring, attacks can be carried out at rooted time window and survive after the phone is unrooted.

The remaining part of this paper is organized as follows. Section 2 describes the problem statement; Section 3 shows tampering data files attacks; Section 4 describes tampering code files attacks; Section 5 evaluates the attacks; Section 6 discusses potential defenses solutions, Section 7 discusses the related work, and Section 8 shows our conclusion.

2 Problem Statement

Android gives each app a distinct Linux user ID (UID) at installation time. Normally, the UID given to each app is bigger than 10000. Once the UID is given, it cannot be changed on the same phone. Each app is regarded as an unique Linux user and runs in its own process space. The *systemserver* is the most important process in Android system. Many significant system services, such as *PackageManager* service, *ActivityManager* service, are running as a thread of the *systemserver* process. Many system resources, such as GPS, Bluetooth, are managed by the *systemserver* process. The *systemserver* also has an independent process space, whose UID is set as 1000. When the phone is rooted, an app could change its UID to 0, which is the UID of root. The UID of the *systemserver* is not affected, which is still 1000.

Users can use rootkit tools to root their phones. The mainstream rootkit tools in China are provided by *Baidu, Tencent, LBE*, and *360* etc. These tools provide not only the *one-click-root* function but also the *one-click-unroot* function. When a user wants to root his phone, he only needs to push the *one-click-root* button. After several minutes, the rooting process is finished and his phone is rooted. During the rooting process, the rootkit tool first exploits Linux vulnerabilities [10] to temporarily get root privilege. The Linux vulnerabilities could be: *ASHMEM, Exploid, Gingerbeak, Levitator, Mempodroid, RageAgainstTheCage, Wunderbar, ZergRush*, and *Zimperlich*. Next, the tool places a customized *"su"* binary file into */system/bin* or */system/xbin* directory. At last, the tool sets the *s* attribute to the *"su"* binary file. With *s* attribute, the *"su"* binary file could run with root privilege. If the user pushes the *one-click-unroot* button, the added *"su"* file will be deleted, which means the phone is unrooted. The unrooting process takes less than 1 minute.

Several reasons attract people to root their phones. After the phone is rooted, they can uninstall the disliked system apps, which cannot be uninstalled before. Besides this, the user also could flash a third party ROM to his phone, backup his phone, customize Android system and so on. The website [20] lists 10 reasons attracting users to root their phones, let alone those mobile forums. According to [23], 23% Android phones had been rooted at least once in China mainland by the first half of 2012.

Taking advantage of the rooted phone vulnerability, many attacks can be carried out. After a phone is rooted, attackers could do anything using a malware, which is in the form of an app. For example, with root privilege, the malware could directly call *libgps.so* to access GPS location without using the *system-server* process. Moreover, YaJin Zhou et al.'s work [33] reveals 36.7% malware leveraged root-level exploits to fully compromise the Android security. The malware *DroidKungFu* [22] is a typical example. As the security threats on a rooted phone become more and more serious, users want to unroot their phones as soon as possible.

We assume that the attacker's malware can get root privilege on a rooted phone. Since users want to unroot their phones as soon as possible, the malware will quickly lose root privilege. We suppose the attacker's goal is stealing users' private data such as GPS location, photos, and SMS. These data are frequently updated. Hence, the attacker wants to steal the private data all the time regardless the phone is unrooted or not. For example, the attacker would keep an eye on users' GPS location all the time. Moreover, some private data may be created after the phone is unrooted, such as a newly applied credit card account. The attacker may want to steal these new data as well. Therefore, the malware should keep working even the phone is unrooted. The attacker knows after a phone is unrooted, his malware will lose root privilege. So, the malware should not rely on root privilege all the time.

An effective way to make the malware keep working after the phone is unrooted is opening a backdoor during the rooted time window. In this way, two kinds of attacks can be carried out. The first kind is tampering data files to escalate required permissions. For example, tampering the *packages.xml* file to escalate the *"android.permission.ACCESS_FINE_LOCATION"* permission to get GPS location. This way enables malware to pass the access control checks of permission system all the time. The other one is tampering the code files of permission system to remove the access control. This way makes private data freely accessible to all apps. Therefore, even if the phone is unrooted, the above attacks open a backdoor for malware.

3   Tampering Data Files Attack

3.1   Inserting Permissions into the *packages.xml* File

The heart of permission system is a system service named *PackageManager* service (PMS). After an app is installed, PMS writes its permissions into the *packages.xml* file. At the next system boot time, PMS directly grants the permissions preserved in the *packages.xml* file to each app. Therefore, adding permissions into the *packages.xml* file is one way to escalate apps' permission.

The *packages.xml* file is only protected by the user-based UNIX file system access control mechanism. Normally, the file belongs to the *systemserver*, and other users (processes) cannot access it. However, as long as a malware gets root privilege, it becomes a superuser. Superuser can read and write any files in file system. Furthermore, Android supports the Java APIs of executing external command. Through the Java APIs, malware could execute the *"su"* command to gain root privilege on a rooted phone. The attack flow is shown as Figure 1.

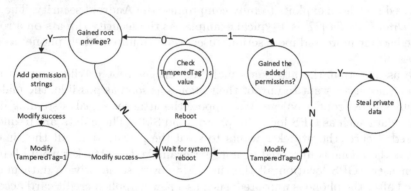

Fig. 1. The attack flow of escalating permissions by modifying the *packages.xml* file

The attack flow can be divided into two parts: tampering the *packages.xml* file to add permission and starting attack based on the added permission. To control the attack flow, we introduce a flag *TamperedTag*, whose value 1 or 0 indicates that the *packages.xml* file has or has not been tampered.

The demo app first checks the *TamperedTag*'s value. If its value is 0, which means that the *packages.xml* file has not been tampered, the demo app will take a further step to check whether the phone has been rooted. One way of doing this is executing the *"su"* command, and then see the execution result. If the command is successfully executed, the demo app can get root privilege and do the following steps of the attack. Otherwise, the demo app will do nothing but wait for the system reboot (see Figure 1). With root privilege, the demo app adds, for example, the *android.permission.READ_SMS* permission into the *packages.xml* file for itself. Once added, the value of *TamperedTag* should be changed to 1.

If the *TamperedTag*'s value is 1, which means that the *packages.xml* file has successfully been modified, the demo app checks if it has indeed got the READ_SMS permission. If yes, the demo app could read and steal SMS. Otherwise, the demo app changes the *TamperedTag*'s value to 0 to restart the attack. This step increases the robustness of the attack.

The demo app has less than 430 lines of code and can successfully run on any rooted Android phones. Furthermore, the demo app can be extended to escalate any permission in the real world.

3.2 Bypassing Signature Verification to Share UID with High Privileged Apps

By default, each app has a distinct UID and runs as an independent Linux user. For these independently running apps, Android has no restriction on their certificates. Android also allows different apps to share the same UID. For the apps running with the same UID, Android enforces that they must be signed by the same certificate.

Apps with the same UID can run with the same permission set and access each other's data and, if desired, run in the same process. Some system apps share the same high privileged UID. For example, *SystemUI* and *SettingsProvider* share the UID: *android.uid.system*. This UID has a bunch of privacy-related permissions such as READ_CONTACTS, CALL_PHONE; and many hardware-related permissions such as INTERNET, BLUETOOTH.

Normally, malware cannot share the same UID with other apps because their signatures are mismatched. However, if an app satisfies the following optimization terms, PMS will not verify the app's signature.

1) The package setting info of the app, denoted as a <*package*> node, exists in the *packages.xml* file;
2) The path of the app is consistent with that preserved in the <*package*> node;
3) The last modification time of the app is the same as the timestamp preserved in the <*package*> node;
4) The <*sig*> sub-node of the <*package*> node exists;
5) The certificate value exists in the <*sig*> sub-node.

By satisfying the above terms, malware can escape the signature verification step enforced by the permission system. As a result, the malware can break the certificate restriction of sharing UID, and shares UID with any privileged app. A demo attack flow can be described as follows.

We use a cover app and shadow app model to illustrate how to start an attack. The cover app does not contain malicious code of stealing private data, but contains the code of loading the shadow app into Android system. The shadow app contains malicious code to steal private data as well as necessary permissions to access the private data. To start an attack, the attacker should develop a cover app first. The cover app is not over privileged that can escape detection tools based on permission analysis like Kirin [13], Stowaway [14], and

Pscout [2]. Then, following the cover app, the attacker develops a shadow app. For concealment considerations, they should have the similar appearance. The shadow app can be loaded into Android system as the cover app's payload or by remote downloading. These ways of loading malicious code are widely used [33].

In this attack, the attacker should set the value of the shadow app's *android:sharedUserId* attribute to the UID that it wants to share. The UID could be an app's package name or a shared user's name defined by Android system such as *android.uid.system*. The *android:sharedUserId* attribute is defined in the shadow app's *AndroidManifest.xml* file (manifest file). Every Android app has a manifest file to declare the desired permissions, assign the desired UIDs, and list its components, etc. To meet the optimization requirement, the cover app can modify either the attribute of the shadow app's *apk* file or the content of the *packages.xml* file to make the value of *path* and *ft* matched. The *ft* is the timestamp of the last modified time of the *apk* file.

Then, the cover app traverses the *packages.xml* file to get the shared UID's certificate info (preserved in <*sig*> sub-node), and uses that info to replace the cover app's <*sig*> sub-node. At last, the cover app uses the shadow app's *apk* file to replace the cover app's *apk* file (stays in the */data/app directory*). After reboot, the shadow app can turn into a shared user running with a higher privileged permission set and can access other shared users' data.

This kind of attack not only extends malware's permissions but also extends the influence from one app to multiple apps. The feasibility of the attack is verified on Nexus S, Nexus 4g, Galaxy Nexus, and Sony LT29i.

3.3   Escalating Permission by Silent Update

The permissions escalated using the way described in Section 3.1 and 3.2 are fully depend on the *packages.xml* file. When the file is deleted, the escalated permissions will be gone. In this section, we will discuss another way of permission escalating that is not depend on the *packages.xml* file.

All the installed apps including system and non-system apps will be reinstalled at system boot time. During the re-installation, the permissions will be re-parsed from each app's manifest file. After the re-installation is done, PMS will update each app's permissions based on the following policy. For system apps, PMS updates each system app's permissions to those declared in its manifest file. While for non-system apps, PMS will not update any permission, except the permissions updated by Android platform, which is rarely happened. Therefore, the actual permissions of a system app is a union of the permissions declared in the manifest file and the permissions stored in the *packages.xml* file, while the actual permissions of a non-system app are only the permissions stored in the *packages.xml* file.

Attacks towards Non-system Apps. Normally, non-system apps cannot be given more permissions than those stored in the *packages.xml* file. However, when the <*package*> node of an app is removed from the file, PMS will grant all permissions declared in the app's manifest file to this app. Malware can use this way to escalate permissions, which could be called as silent update.

The attack flow is described as follows. With root privilege, the cover app remounts the *data* directory to be writable. Then, it moves the shadow app into */data/app* directory to replace the cover app's *apk* file. Next, the cover app should delete its *<package>* node or delete the entire *packages.xml* file. At the next system boot time, PMS will recover the cover app's permissions from its manifest file, which is contained in the *apk* file. As the cover app's *apk* file is replaced with the shadow app's, the permissions are actually recovered from the shadow app's manifest file. And, the permission info will be written into the *packages.xml* file. Finally, the cover app is updated to a malicious one silently. A typical example in the real world is the *BaseBridge* [28], which exploits root privilege to silently install apps without user intervention [33].

The attacker can use the same way to replace any installed apps with malicious ones as long as he can remove the target app's *<package>* node. After the node is removed, the target app is actually regarded as uninstalled, and the malicious one will be installed as a new app. Android adopts self-signed mechanism, and the signature of the shadow app is verified by self-signed certificate, so there is no need for the shadow app to be signed with the same certificate as the target app.

We validated the feasibility of the attack on Nexus S, Nexus 4g, Galaxy Nexus, and Sony LT29i.

Attacks towards System Apps. Android regards apps in the */system/app* directory as system apps. Also, Android pre-installs several system apps to provide the basic phone functions. For example, the pre-installed *Phone.apk* is used to place phone call, the *Mms.apk* is used to send multimedia message, and the *Contact.apk* is used to manage contacts. Compared to non-system apps, system apps play a more important role in Android system. However, there is no special requirement for the system apps' certificate. The system apps also apply to the self-signed certificate mechanism. Therefore, malware can also replace system apps with malicious ones.

The attack flow is similar to that of the non-system apps', while this one is much easier. The only thing that the cover app needs to do is replacing the target system app with a shadow app. There is no need to remove the target app's *<package>* node. That is because, when the shadow app is put into the */system/app* directory, it will be regarded as a system app. According to the update policy, system apps could gain full permissions declared in the manifest file directly. The shadow app can be developed by re-packing or re-coding since Android is open-source.

Besides replacing original system apps, malware can also disguise as a system app and gain full permissions declared in the manifest file. Simply, the cover app places the shadow app into */system/app* directory and deletes the original *apk* file from the */data/app* directory.

We verified the feasibility and effectiveness of this attack on Nexus S, Nexus 4g, Galaxy Nexus, but not Sony LT29i. That is because, this phone has blocked modification to the *system* partition. The */system/app* directory belongs to this partition. When the *system* partition is modified, the phone will reboot automatically, which makes all modifications fail to go into effect.

Compared to the above two attacks described in Section 3.1 and 3.2, the permissions escalated by silence update do not depend on the *packages.xml* file. No matter what happened to the *packages.xml* file, the permission escalated in this way will not disappear.

4   Tampering Code Files Attack

All system code are stored as files in the file system. With root privilege, attackers can also tamper the code file of permission system to fully compromise it.

Permission system carries out the access control by checking whether an app has certain permission strings. The check function is provided by Android APIs such as *checkPermission, checkCallingPermission*, and *checkCallingUriPermission*. The difference between them is they taking different parameters. Taking *checkPermission* as an example, it takes a permission name and a package name of an app as the parameters. When the method is called, it first checks whether the app (identified by the package name) is a shared user. If yes, the method checks the shared user's *grantedPermissions* field. Otherwise, it checks the app's *grantedPermissions* field. The *grantedPermissions* field exists in a data structure (*PackageSetting*), which stores all info of an app needed to run. If the field contains the required permission string, the *checkPermission* API will return *PERMISSION_GRANTED*, or else it will return *PERMISSION_DENIED*.

An available way to compromise permission system is tampering the return value of those APIs. A typical compromise example is tampering the *checkpermission* API to return *PERMISSION_GRANTED* always.

The source code of permission system are compiled into a file named *services.jar*, which is located in the */system/framework* directory. Provide that the malware is designed as adaptive, it needs to analyze the construction of the *jar* file and identify the exact point to tamper. However, we doubt the feasibility of automatic analysis without manual intervention. Therefore, we assume that the attacker would temper the code files in the way of replacing the original *services.jar* with a malicious one prepared ahead.

Two ways can be used to create a malicious *services.jar* file. The first one is decompiling and recompiling the target phone's *services.jar* or *services.odex* file using tools such as *baksmali, smali*, and *dex2jar*. The *services.odex* file is an optimized version of the *services.jar* file. Some vendors shipped their phones with *odex* version of code files in order to increase the phones' performance. The other one is exploiting Android Open Source Project (AOSP). Several phones, such as the Nexus series phones published by Google, support AOSP. By fetching the source code of these phones, the attacker can customize his own permission system, let alone modify the return value of an Android API.

Even the attacker successfully gets a customized *services.jar* file, he cannot directly use it to replace the original one. Some issues should be overcome. The first one is optimization. In the real world, most vendors such as Samsung, Sony,

HTC optimize the *jar* file to the *odex* file in their factory image. The optimization is hardware-related. Even the source code is identical, the *odex* file generated on a phone cannot run on a different versions of phone. Only the same *odex* file running on the same version of phone is allowed. The other issue that the attacker should overcome is signature. During the system boot time, the Dalvik Virtual Machine (DVM) will load all Java classes into memory to create the runtime for Android system. In this process, the DVM verifies the *dex* or *odex* files' signature and the dependencies with other *dex* or *odex* files.

There are two ways can be used to overcome the signature issue. The first way is tampering the code file of the DVM to remove the piece of code doing the verification work. The DVM is compiled into a file called *libdvm.so*. Android has no signature restriction to *so* files. Therefore, replacing a *so* file does not face the signature issue. However, decompiling a *so* file to modify the code is difficult. An optional way to remove the verification code is getting the source code of the target phone. This way only fits attacking phones supporting AOSP.

The second way is extracting signature from the original *odex* file and using it to replace the malicious one's signature. After analyzing the *odex* file's construction, we find that the signature has a 20-bytes length and has a 52-bytes offset from the file header. To obtain the signature value, we use the *dd* command: *dd if=services.odex of=myservices.odex bs=1 count=20 skip=52 seek=52* The whole command means that reads 20 bytes (signature) from the original *service.odex* file, and writes the 20 bytes (signature) to the *myservices.odex* file. Both reading and writing should skip 52 bytes from the header.

Based on the second way to overcome the signature issue, a demo attack is carried out on a Galaxy Nexus phone running 4.1.2 code version. This phone supports AOSP and runs *odex* version of code files. Using this phone, we successfully replace the original *odex* file provided by Google's factory image with the one we generated from Android source code.

5 Attack Evaluation

5.1 Evasion Rate Evaluation

We implement all attacks on one demo malware. To understand the attacks' efficacy in the real world, we evaluate the demo malware's evading detection rate and permission hidden rate under Antivirus' (AVs) monitoring. We select the top 5 AVs in China and abroad, respectively. In China, we download the top 5 popular AVs on Google Play, which are *360, LBE, Tencent, Kingsoft,* and *Anguanjia*. At abroad, according to [29], we select the top 5 **free** AVs, which are *Lookout, McAfee, Kaspersky, ESET,* and *Trend*.

As AVs do a scanning when apps are installed, we test whether the malware can evade detection at installation time. We first install 10 AVs on our test phones, then install the demo malware and waiting for the 10 AVs' scanning result. The result shows that 9 of 10 AVs assert it is clean, only 1 AV detects it out but mistakenly classify the threat as *"Exploit.Android.RageAgainstTheCage.a"*, which we have not exploited. Then, we run the demo malware under the 10

AVs' monitoring to see if the malware could evade detection at runtime. The result is, none of the AVs detect the malware out when it is running. Therefore, these attacks can evade 100% AV's detection in China and 80% AV's detection at abroad at installation time and evade 100% AV's detection at runtime. Since rooting a phone mainly happens in China mainland, evading AVs in this area is the main goal of our attacks, which has been achieved.

Towards attacks of tampering data files to escalate permissions, we test whether the escalated permission can hide from the permission list provided by the 10 AVs. Permissions escalated by silence update are not necessary to test, as they exist in both the manifest file and the *packages.xml* file. What worth testing are those escalated by the attacks of tampering the *packages.xml* file, which are described in section 3.1 and 3.2. We only checked permissions listed by AVs in China except *360*, as *360* and the AVs abroad do not offer the function of listing permissions when this paper is written. The demo malware used to launch the two attacks do not apply any permission in its manifest file. For testing the attacks described in Section 3.1 (denoted as InsertPerm attack), the demo malware inserts 5 different permissions into the *packages.xml* file. While for the attacks described in Section 3.2 (denoted as ShareUID attack), the demo malware shares UID with an app possesses 24 permissions. The test result is shown in table 1. It should be mentioned that *Kingsoft* relies on Android system to list permissions.

Table 1. Permission detection rate

AVs	LBE	Tencent	Kingsoft (Android system)	Anguanjia	Android system	Avg. Dtc. Rate
InsertPerm	3/5	0/5	0/5	3/5	0/5	24%
ShareUID	4/24	0/24	24/24	6/24	24/24	48.3%

The result shows that the 4 AVs have an average detection rate of 24% and 48.3% towards the two attacks, respectively. Most escalated permissions are not detected out. The InsertPerm attack completely cheated 3 in 5 AVs, while the ShareUID attack completely cheated 1 due to the effectiveness of Android system in listing shared user's permissions.

5.2 Damage Degree Analysis

The two kinds of attacks have a different damage degree.

Tampering data files attack only makes the malware itself pass permission checking process, while other apps' permissions are still constrained by the permission system. Therefore, this type of attack only opens a backdoor for the malware itself, and the extent of damage is limited in the malware.

Tampering code files is an extreme damage to the permission system. Section 4 shows a demo attack that removes the resource access control of permission system, which makes apps freely access private data such as *SMS, Contact.* While the hardware resources cannot be freely accessed, as the access control towards these resources are based on UNIX groups rather than permission strings. However, in the real world, attackers can modify any part of the permission system. To address the hardware access issue, they can modify permission system to automatically set an app as a member of all UNIX groups. For example, the attacker could tamper permission system to set an app as a member of groups like *camera, radio, net_admin.* Then, all apps could take pictures, place phone calls, and access the Internet without applying permissions. By doing this, permission system will comprehensively loss its efficacy and all resources could be freely accessed. This type of attack opens a backdoor for all apps. Obviously, attacks of tampering code files are a disaster to Android security. However, this kind of attack has a quite limited range, which will be discussed in the next section.

5.3 Influence Range Analysis

Another dimension to analyze an attack is the influence range. The two kinds of attacks have a different damage degree as well as a different influence range.

Regarding the tampering data files attack, malware only require the read and write ability towards data files. The *package.xml* file and non-system *apk* files are placed in the *userdata* partition. This partition will be frequently written by Android system. For example, installing and uninstalling an app should write the *userdata* partition. Therefore, this partition is designed as modifiable. Attacks writing this partition can be carried out on all rooted devices. However, system *apk* files stay in */system/app* directory, which belongs to the *system* partition. This partition is used to store system code, which should never be modified; therefore it is designed as read only. Some vendors such as *Sony* restrict modifying this partition even with root privilege. On these phones, the attacks of tampering system apps cannot be carried out. The influence range of replacing or disguising as a system app depends on the phone's version.

Regarding the tampering code files attack, there are three limitations. First, as different vendors make different modifications to Android source code to customize their own system, the code of permission system may differ from each phone version. Therefore, one tampering way may only fit one phone version. Second, the code of permission system on most phones is optimized into *odex* files. The optimization is hardware-related, which makes the *odex* file hardware-related as well. Even the source code is the same, the *odex* file generated on a phone cannot run on another version of phone, which makes the attack not only limited by source code but also limited by phone version. Third, as described above, some vendors block the *system* partition from being written. Take a rooted Sony LT 29i phone as an example, when we try to write the *system* partition, the phone automatically reboots. Vendor's constrain is another limitation. Therefore, the influence of tampering code files attacks has a rather limited range. Based on our experience, those phones supporting AOSP are particularly vulnerable to this kind of attack.

5.4 Survivability Analysis

Both tampering data files to escalate permissions and tampering code files to compromise permission system cannot be blocked by unroot.

As we illustrated in section 2, unroot is deleting the "su" file. Without "su" file, the "su" command cannot be executed. As a result, the root privilege cannot be obtained. However, the attacks described in this paper do not depend on root privilege all the time. The truth is, once the attacks are carried out at the rooted time window, the root privilege is no longer needed any more. Blocking the usage of root privilege has no effect on the attacks. First, the escalated permissions open a backdoor for malware to abuse system resources. Second, tampering code files attack makes permission system compromised, which is irreversible. Even unroot cannot make permission system roll back to the normal state.

Therefore, although the phone is unrooted, these attacks can survive and make permission system suffer a long-term threat.

6 Potential Solution Discussion

6.1 SEAndroid

Google has officially merged SEAndroid [27] onto the 4.3 version of AOSP to mitigate security issues brought by root exploits. It constrains the read and write ability of some root-privileged processes such as *init* and can confine apps running with root privilege. By introducing SEAndroid, the *packages.xml* file and the *system, userdata* partitions cannot be freely read/written by super users any more. Therefore, malware even with root privilege cannot launch the attacks mentioned in this paper.

However, although SEAndroid [27] does a great job in mitigating root exploits, as the authors mentioned in their paper, it cannot mitigate all kernel root exploits. Further, Pau Oliva shows the other two weakness of SEAndroid and gives out 4 ways to bypass SEAndroid [31]. Since SEAndroid has been introduced into Android not long ago, there are some imperfections, and it still has a long way to go to be widespread.

6.2 Our Proposal

SEAndroid has done a lot of work from the perspective of protecting the existing Android system. Unlike SEAndroid, we provide some proposals from the perspective of improving the implementation of permission system to confront the permission escalation attacks mentioned in this paper.

Firstly, removing the *packages.xml* file from disk immediately after it has been successfully loaded and re-generate the file after all apps have been shut down. Since the *packages.xml* file is only loaded at system boot time and never be loaded till next boot. There is no need to keep the file on disk always. As the file cannot be accessed by malware, attacks exploiting the *packages.xml* file can be blocked. Secondly, for non-system apps, only installing the ones recorded in the *packages.xml* file at system boot time. If the file does not exist at this time, Android system should warn users there may be an attack and offer users some options such as letting users re-grant permissions to each app. Thirdly, for system apps, using certificate to identify their identification rather than directory. In this way, malware cannot disguise as system apps as they cannot pass identity authentication.

These proposals can work together with SEAndroid to provide a better security protection to Android. Even if SEAndroid is bypassed, these proposals can combat the permission escalation attacks mentioned in this paper.

7 Related Work

7.1 Defence against Privilege Escalation Attack

The tampering data files attack is a type of privilege escalation attack. Privilege escalation attacks have drawn much attention these years. These works [12][18][26] show that the privilege escalation attack is a serious threat to users' privacy.

A number of detection tools [5] [14] [2] [16] [13] have been proposed mainly aiming to detect whether an app has unprotected interface that can induce privilege escalation attacks. These static analysis tools are likely to be incomplete, because they cannot completely predict the confused deputy attack that will occur at runtime. Confused deputy attack is a kind of privilege escalation attack. Some enhanced frameworks [15] [9] [4] [17] [3] have been proposed to confront this kind of attack at runtime. But all these works cannot confront the privilege escalation attacks mentioned in this paper. It is because that, these attacks do not depend on other apps to start attacks. Malware in these attacks have all required permissions themselves.

Some framework security extension solutions [21] [34] [25] [6] enforce runtime permission control to restrict app's permission at runtime. However, these works do not consider the situation that malware get root privilege. Although these works can control an app's permission at runtime, all of them rely on policy database files and lack of protection to the file. When malware get root privilege, the policy file could be tampered or deleted. Once the policy file is tampered or deleted, the solution loses its effectiveness.

7.2 Protections towards System Code

Some solutions aim at protecting the integrity of system code, which could be used to confront the tampering code files attack mentioned in this paper.

One way to protect the integrity of system code is making sure that the phone is trustily booted. Some techniques, like Mobile Trusted Module (MTM) [30] and TrustZone [1], can be used to ensure that the system is booted in a trusted manner. Based on MTM, paper [8] and [19] implement two different secure-boot prototypes; patent [24] and [11] give out two different secure-boot architecture reference designs. In addition, paper [32] outlines an approach to merge MTM with TrustZone technology to build a trusted computing platform, on which the secure-boot process can be provided by TrustZone.

Another way of protecting system code is making sure that the system code is correctly executed at runtime. MoCFI [7] provides a general countermeasure against runtime attacks on smartphone platforms, which can be applied to Android platform and ensures that the Android software stack can be correctly executed.

8   Conclusion

To the best of our knowledge, this paper is the first work focusing on analyzing the security threat faced by permission system at rooted time window. At rooted time window, two kinds of attacks can be carried out. The first kind attack is tampering data files managed by permission system to gain stable resource access capabilities, which still hold even if system is unrooted. Tampering code files is another attack way that can be carried out on rooted time window and influences forever. This way is more destructive than the former one, but its influence range is limited by the phone's version. Even under AV's monitoring, these attacks can be carried out and make permission system suffer a long-term threat.

References

1. Alves, T., Felton, D.: Trustzone: Integrated hardware and software security. ARM White Paper 3(4) (2004)
2. Au, K.W.Y., Zhou, Y.F., Huang, Z., Lie, D.: Pscout: analyzing the android permission specification. In: ACM CCS (2012)
3. Bugiel, S., Davi, L., Dmitrienko, A., Fischer, T., Sadeghi, A.R.: XMandroid: a new android evolution to mitigate privilege escalation attacks. Technische Universität Darmstadt, Technical Report TR-2011-04 (2011)
4. Bugiel, S., Davi, L., Dmitrienko, A., Fischer, T., Sadeghi, A.R., Shastry, B.: Towards taming privilege-escalation attacks on android. In: 19th NDSS (2012)
5. Chin, E., Felt, A.P., Greenwood, K., Wagner, D.: Analyzing inter-application communication in android. In: 9th MobiSys (2011)
6. Conti, M., Nguyen, V.T.N., Crispo, B.: Crepe: Context-related policy enforcement for android. In: Burmester, M., Tsudik, G., Magliveras, S., Ilić, I. (eds.) ISC 2010. LNCS, vol. 6531, pp. 331–345. Springer, Heidelberg (2011)
7. Davi, L., Dmitrienko, A., Egele, M., Fischer, T., Holz, T., Hund, R., Nürnberger, S., Sadeghi, A.R.: Mocfi: A framework to mitigate control-flow attacks on smartphones. In: NDSS (2012)
8. Dietrich, K., Winter, J.: Secure boot revisited. In: ICYCS (2008)
9. Dietz, M., Shekhar, S., Pisetsky, Y., Shu, A., Wallach, D.S.: Quire: Lightweight provenance for smart phone operating systems. In: USENIX Security (2011)
10. Duo Security: X-ray for Android (2012), http://www.xray.io/
11. Ekberg, J.E.: Secure boot with trusted computing group platform registers, US Patent US20120297175 A1 (November 22, 2012)
12. Enck, W., Ongtang, M., McDaniel, P.: Mitigating android software misuse before it happens. Technical Report NAS-TR-0094-2008 (September 2008)

13. Enck, W., Ongtang, M., McDaniel, P.: On lightweight mobile phone application certification. In: 16th ACM CCS (2009)
14. Felt, A.P., Chin, E., Hanna, S., Song, D., Wagner, D.: Android permissions demystified. In: 18th ACM CCS (2011)
15. Felt, A.P., Wang, H.J., Moshchuk, A., Hanna, S., Chin, E.: Permission redelegation: Attacks and defenses. In: USENIX Security Symposium (2011)
16. Fuchs, A.P., Chaudhuri, A., Foster, J.S.: Scandroid: Automated security certification of android applications. Univ. of Maryland (2009) (manuscript)
17. Grace, M., Zhou, Y., Wang, Z., Jiang, X.: Systematic detection of capability leaks in stock android smartphones. In: Proceedings of the 19th NDSS (2012)
18. Hornyack, P., Han, S., Jung, J., Schechter, S., Wetherall, D.: These aren't the droids you're looking for: retrofitting android to protect data from imperious applications. In: 18th ACM CCS (2011)
19. Kai, T., Xin, X., Guo, C.: The secure boot of embedded system based on mobile trusted module. In: ISDEA (2012)
20. LifeHacker: Top 10 reasons to root your android phone, http://lifehacker.com/top-10-reasons-to-root-your-android-phone-1079161983
21. Nauman, M., Khan, S., Zhang, X.: Apex: extending android permission model and enforcement with user-defined runtime constraints. In: 5th ACM CCS (2010)
22. NC State University: Security alert: New sophisticated android malware droidkungfu found in alternative chinese app markets (2011), http://www.csc.ncsu.edu/faculty/jiang/DroidKungFu.html
23. NetQin: 2012 moblie phone security report (2012), http://cn.nq.com/neirong/2012shang.pdf
24. Nicolson, K.A.: Secure boot with optional components method, US Patent US20100318781 A1 (December 16, 2010)
25. Ongtang, M., McLaughlin, S., Enck, W., McDaniel, P.: Semantically rich application-centric security in android. In: SCN (2012)
26. Schlegel, R., Zhang, K., Zhou, X.Y., Intwala, M., Kapadia, A., Wang, X.: Soundcomber: A stealthy and context-aware sound trojan for smartphones. In: NDSS (2011)
27. Smalley, S., Craig, R.: Security Enhanced (SE) Android: Bringing Flexible MAC to Android. In: NDSS (2013)
28. Symantec: Android.basebridge (2011), http://www.symantec.com/security_response/writeup.jsp?docid=2011-060915-4938-99
29. Toptenreviews: 2014 Best Mobile Security Software Comparisons and Reviews (2014), http://mobile-security-software-review.toptenreviews.com/
30. Trusted Computing Group (TCG): Mobile Phone Work Group Mobile Trusted Module Specification (2010), http://www.trustedcomputinggroup.org/developers/mobile/specifications
31. viaForensics: Defeating SEAndroid C DEFCON 21 Presentation, http://viaforensics.com/mobile-security/implementing-seandroid//-defcon-21-presentation.html (March 8, 2013)
32. Winter, J.: Trusted computing building blocks for embedded linux-based arm trustzone platforms. In: 3rd ACM Workshop on Scalable Trusted Computing (2008)
33. Zhou, Y., Jiang, X.: Dissecting android malware: Characterization and evolution. In: Security and Privacy (SP), pp. 95–109. IEEE (2012)
34. Zhou, Y., Zhang, X., Jiang, X., Freeh, V.W.: Taming information-stealing smartphone applications (on android). In: McCune, J.M., Balacheff, B., Perrig, A., Sadeghi, A.-R., Sasse, A., Beres, Y. (eds.) Trust 2011. LNCS, vol. 6740, pp. 93–107. Springer, Heidelberg (2011)

A High-Throughput Unrolled ZUC Core for 100Gbps Data Transmission*

Qinglong Zhang[1,2,3], Zongbin Liu[1,2,**], Miao Li[1,2], Ji Xiang[1,2], and Jiwu Jing[1,2]

[1] Data Assurance and Communication Security Research Center, Beijing, China
[2] State Key Laboratory of Information Security,
Institute of Information Engineering, CAS, Beijing, China
[3] University of Chinese Academy of Sciences, Beijing, China
{qlzhang,zbliu,limiao12,jixiang,jing}@is.ac.cn

Abstract. In this paper, we propose a high-throughput encryption and decryption IP core based on ZUC, in order to satisfy the demand of confidentiality and data integrity in modern multi-gigabit communication system. Till now, a popular method for improvement of hardware implementation on ZUC is to apply pipeline technology to promote the design's performance. At the same time, there is another method to take advantage of the unrolling technology into hardware implementation. However, we find that the existing unrolled architecture on ZUC cannot improve the performance efficiently, even may reduce the performance. In this paper, we present our novel optimization techniques: computation rescheduling and single-feedback initialization for improving throughput. Combining these techniques, we propose two unrolled architectures: x2-ZUC and x3-ZUC, both of which significantly improve the performance both on FPGA and ASIC. The performance of our new unrolled architecture on FPGA in Virtex-5 is at least 63.5% higher than the previous design. Meanwhile, on ASIC of 65 nm technology the best performance of our architecture is up to 100 Gbps, which achieves the highest throughput for the hardware implementation of ZUC. The evaluation result suggests that our novel unrolled architecture with the high throughput is suitable for the high-speed and high-throughput data transmissions at a bandwidth of 100 Gbps.

Keywords: ZUC, unrolling technology, FPGA, high throughput, ASIC, 100 Gbps.

1 Introduction

ZUC [1–4] is an LFSR (Linear-Feedback Shift Register) based word oriented stream cipher, selected as one of the security algorithms for 3GPP LTE-Advanced

* The work is supported by a grant from the National High Technology Research and Development Program of China (863 Program, No.2013AA01A214) and the National Basic Research Program of China (973 Program, No. 2013CB338001).
** Corresponding author.

W. Susilo and Y. Mu (Eds.): ACISP 2014, LNCS 8544, pp. 370–385, 2014.

which is the leading candidate for 4G mobile services. With the development of 4G network, the demand of confidentiality and data integrity in high-speed and high-throughput data transmission is growing rapidly. Furthermore, since the IEEE 802.3ba Ethernet Standard was proposed in June 2010, data transmission at a bandwidth of 100 Gbps has been widely used. Therefore, it is significant to design a high-throughput encryption and decryption ZUC core with the purpose of providing efficient data protection for high-throughput data transmission.

FPGA (Field-Programmable Gate Array) and ASIC (Application-Specific Integrated Circuit) are two common hardware devices for cryptographic implementations. Up to now, there are several academic researches which proposed some hardware implementations of ZUC both on FPGA and ASIC aiming at throughput promotion. One popular method for improvement of the hardware implementation on ZUC is to apply pipeline in order to shorten the timing-critical path. The other method is to employ unrolling technology in a design which can output a keystream of 64 bits or 96 bits.

On FPGA, [5–8] focus on shortening the timing-critical path in the hardware implementation of ZUC to increase their design's throughput. Liu et al [6] propose a four-stage pipeline architecture on ZUC, but the design is just applied in the working stage. On ASIC, in order to design a full implementation on ZUC and promote throughput, Gupta et al [9] propose a three-stage pipeline architecture whose performance is 29.4 Gbps. Recently, Liu et al [10] propose a mixed two-stage pipeline architecture on ASIC to solve the problem of the lengthy timing-critical path in the initialization stage. The performance of the mixed two-stage pipeline design is 80 Gbps, but the frequency of the design is almost 2.5 GHz, which is too high to lead the design's instability since the stable frequency in 65 nm technology is about 1500 MHz and the max clock output of a normal PLL in 65 nm technology is 1500 MHz. Therefore if the frequency of a design is increased to 2.5 GHz, the designer should make many changes to avoid the signal interference in the architecture and need a special PLL whose output can be as high as 2.5 GHz. All these changes may bring down the performance of the design.

On FPGA, there are no results for the implementation of ZUC through unrolling technology. On ASIC, Gupta et al [9] propose Unrolled ZUC with the primary purpose of improving throughput. However, in [9], the result of ZUC is that the performance of ZUC is 29.4 Gbps and the performance of Unrolled ZUC is 27.2 Gbps. Thus Gupta et al [9] conclude that there is no throughput increase in Unrolled ZUC due to the long timing-critical path via self-feedback loop in the final pipeline stage.

Contribution. In this paper, we present our novel optimization techniques: computation rescheduling and single-feedback initialization for improving throughput. Combining these techniques, we propose our new unrolled architectures: x2-ZUC and x3-ZUC. Both of them can improve the throughput efficiently.

Computation rescheduling can efficiently shorten the long path to compute the self-feedback variables and can reduce the number of mod $2^{31} - 1$ adders.

Single-feedback initialization architecture can avoid the long timing-critical path via self-feedback loop in the previous design.

Furthermore, the performance of our new architecture in Virtex-5 is at least 63.5% higher than that of the previous full implementations on FPGA. The best performance of our architecture on ASIC of 65 nm technology is up to 100Gbps, 25% higher than that of the previous fastest implementation. Moreover, the frequency is 1045 MHz and it is stable in 65 nm technology. The new unrolled architecture will be competent for the demand of the high-speed and high-throughput data protection in the modern multi-gigabit communication system.

2 Preliminaries: ZUC Algorithm

The word-oriented stream cipher [1–4] is designed by the Data Assurance and Communication Security Research Center of the Chinese Academy of Science (DACAS). General structure of ZUC has three logical layers. The top layer is a linear feedback shift register (LFSR), having 16 blocks, each of length 31 bits, and the LFSR has an update function which is based on a series of modulo $(2^{31} - 1)$ multiplications and additions ($2^{31} - 1$ is a prime). The middle layer is bit-reorganization (BR), consisting of 4 32-bit registers X0, X1, X2 and X3 which are updated using 128-bit from LFSR. The bottom layer is a nonlinear filter with memory, which takes three 32-bit words from the LFSR as inputs and outputs a 32-bit word as well.

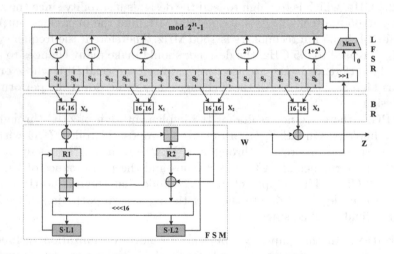

Fig. 1. The architecture of ZUC

2.1 The Linear Feedback Shift Register (LFSR)

The LFSR has two modes of operations: the initialization mode and the working mode. In the initialization mode, firstly, the LFSR receives a 128 bit key and a

128 bit IV to initialize the 16 blocks, then in the first 32 iterations, the update function of LFSR has a 31-bit input word u which is changed from the 32-bit output W of the nonlinear function F by removing the rightmost bit. The following is the computations of the LFSR in the initialization mode.

LFSRWithInitialisationMode (u)
{

1. $v = \{2^{15}S_{15} + 2^{17}S_{13} + 2^{21}S_{10} + 2^{20}S_4 + (1 + 2^8)S_0\} \pmod{2^{31} - 1}$
2. $S_{16} = v + u \pmod{2^{31} - 1}$
3. $If\ S_{16} = 0$ then set $S_{16} = 2^{31} - 1$
4. $(S_1, S_2, \ldots, S_{15}, S_{16}) \rightarrow (S_0, S_1, \ldots, S_{14}, S_{15})$

}

In the working mode, the LFSR does not receive any input, and it works as follows,

LFSRWithWorkMode()
{

1. $S_{16} = \{2^{15}S_{15} + 2^{17}S_{13} + 2^{21}S_{10} + 2^{20}S_4 + (1 + 2^8)S_0\} \pmod{2^{31} - 1}$
2. $If\ S_{16} = 0$ then set $S_{16} = 2^{31} - 1$
3. $(S_1, S_2, \ldots, S_{15}, S_{16}) \rightarrow (S_0, S_1, \ldots, S_{14}, S_{15})$

}

2.2   The Bit-Reorganization

The middle layer of the algorithm is the bit-reorganization. It extracts 128 bits from the state of the LFSR and forms 4 32-bits words, $X_0, X_1, X_2,$ and X_3. The first three words will be used by the nonlinear function F in the bottom layer, and the last word will be involved in producing the keystream.

Bitreorganization()
{

1. $X_0 = S_{15H} \parallel S_{14L}$
2. $X_1 = S_{11L} \parallel S_{9H}$
3. $X_2 = S_{7L} \parallel S_{5H}$
4. $X_3 = S_{2L} \parallel S_{0H}$

}

S_{15H} denotes the leftmost 16 bits of integer S_{15}. S_{14L} denotes the rightmost 16 bits of integer S_{14}. $S_{15H} \parallel S_{14L}$, denotes the concatenation of strings S_{15H} and S_{14L}. A detail specification can be found in [1].

2.3   The Nonlinear Filter F

The nonlinear filter F has two 32-bit memory cells R_1 and R_2. Let the inputs of F be X_0, X_1, X_2, which come from the outputs of the bit-reorganization. Then the filter F outputs a 32-bit word W. The detailed process of F is as follows:

$\mathbf{F}(X_0, X_1, X_2)$
{
1. $W = (X_0 \oplus R_1) \boxplus R_2$
2. $W_1 = R_1 \boxplus X_1$
3. $W_2 = R_2 \boxplus X_2$
4. $R_1 = S(L_1(W_{1L} \parallel W_{2H}))$
5. $R_2 = S(L_2(W_{2L} \parallel W_{1H}))$
}

$\parallel$ denotes the concatenation of strings. $\oplus$ denotes the bit-wise exclusive-OR operation of integers. $\boxplus$ denotes the modulo 2^{32} addition . In step 4 and 5, S is a 32×32 S-box which is composed of four 8×8 S-boxes, and L_1 and L_2 are linear transformations, which are defined as follows:

$$L_1(X) = X \oplus (X \lll 2) \oplus (X \lll 10) \oplus (X \lll 18) \oplus (X \lll 24) \qquad (1)$$

$$L_2(X) = X \oplus (X \lll 8) \oplus (X \lll 14) \oplus (X \lll 22) \oplus (X \lll 30) \qquad (2)$$

2.4   The Execution of ZUC

Key Loading. The key loading procedure will expand the initial key and the initial vector into 16 31-bit integers as the initial state of the LFSR. Let the 128-bit initial key k and the 128-bit initial vector iv be:

$$k = k_0 \parallel k_1 \parallel k_2 \parallel \cdots \parallel k_{15}$$

$$iv = iv_0 \parallel iv_1 \parallel iv_2 \parallel \cdots \parallel iv_{15}$$

Let D be a 240-bit long constant string composed of 16 substrings, each of which is 15 bits:

$$D = d_0 \parallel d_1 \parallel \cdots \parallel d_{15}$$

For $0 \le i \le 15$, let $s_i = k_i \parallel d_i \parallel iv_i$

The Initialization Stage. During the initialization stage, the algorithm calls the key procedure to load the 128-bit initial key k and the 128-bit initial vector iv into the LFSR, and sets the 32-bit memory cells R_1 and R_2 to be all 0. Then the cipher runs the following operations 32 times.

1. Bitreorganization();
2. W = F(X_0, X_1, X_2);
3. LFSRWithInitializationMode(W $\lll$ 1);

The Working Stage. After the initialization stage, the algorithm moves into the working stage. At the working stage, the algorithm executes the following operations once, and discards the output W of F:

1. Bitreorganization();
2. F(X_0, X_1, X_2);
3. LFSRWithWorkMode();

Then the algorithm goes into the stage of producing keystream, i.e., for each iteration, the following operations are executed once, and a 32-bit word Z is produced as an output:

1. Bitreorganization();
2. Z = F(X_0, X_1, X_2) $\oplus X_3$;
3. LFSRWithWorkMode();

3   Proposed x2-ZUC Architecture

3.1   The Selection of Modulo $2^{31} - 1$ Adder in x2-ZUC

In the implementation of ZUC algorithm, modulo $2^{31} - 1$ adder is the most time-consuming and resource-consuming component. In this section, we first give three basic adders, then give an efficient way to compute the sum of more than three numbers. The algorithm to compute $(a + b) \pmod{2^{31} - 1}$ is as follows:
Let $a, b \in GF(2^{31} - 1)$, the computation of $v = (a + b) \pmod{2^{31} - 1}$ can be done by computing $v = a + b$, then check the carry bit:

carry = 1, set $v = a + b + 1$.

carry = 0, set $v = a + b$.

Basic Adder 1
Basic adder 1 is the original adder prescribed in [6]. This is a direct hardware implementation of modulo $2^{31} - 1$ adder as the algorithm described as above. This architecture contains two 31-bit adders and a multiplexer, and its delay is mainly that of two 31-bit adders.

Basic Adder 2
Basic adder 2 is used by Gupta [11]. Compared to the basic adder 1, it slightly reduces the delay of modulo $2^{31} - 1$ adder by cutting down the multiplexer. However, its delay is also equal to that of two 31-bit adders.

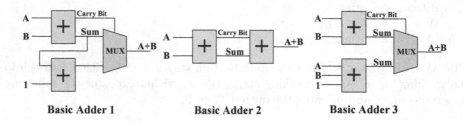

Fig. 2. The architecture of Modulo $2^{31} - 1$ Adder

Basic Adder 3

Basic adder 3 is proposed by Liu [6] in order to give a low-delay modulo $2^{31} - 1$ adder. As shown in Fig 2, the main idea is to calculate $a + b$ and $a + b + 1$ at the same time. So $a, b, 1$ are set to be three inputs of an adder, and a, b are set to be two inputs of another adder, then the result is selected by the carry-bit of $a + b$. The delay of this modulo $2^{31} - 1$ adder is just about that of one 31-bit adder.

3.2   An Efficient Way to Use the Modulo $2^{31} - 1$ Adder

In general, when there are more than three numbers to be added modulo $2^{31} - 1$, we will need two or more modulo $2^{31} - 1$ adders. If there are three numbers, we may need two modulo $2^{31} - 1$ adders, and if there are four numbers, we may need three modulo $2^{31} - 1$ adders. Liu in [10] proposed an efficient way to add more than three numbers just using one modulo $2^{31} - 1$ adder. When we add three numbers A, B, D together, we firstly use a CSA (carry save adder) to get two new numbers C, S and then add the two numbers by one modulo $2^{31} - 1$ adder. The procedure of the three numbers addition is as follows:

1. $C = (A \& B) | (A \& D) | (B \& D)$

2. $S = A \oplus B \oplus D$

3. $C * 2 \ (\mathrm{mod} \ 2^{31} - 1) = C \lll 1$

4. $C_C = C \lll 1$

5. $C_C + S = A + B + D$

In the same way, we can use two CSAs and one modulo $2^{31} - 1$ adder to add four numbers. The architecture is shown in Fig 3. Because the delay of a CSA is very short, so if we apply this CSA architecture to calculate modulo $2^{31} - 1$ addition, the delay of the modulo $2^{31} - 1$ addition will be shorter and the area will also be smaller. So in our paper, we use basic adder 3 and the CSA architecture in our design.

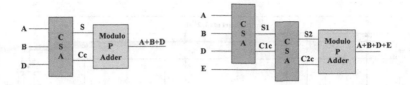

Fig. 3. The CSA architecture

3.3   Single-Feedback Initialization

Gupta et al [9] propose a structure of unrolled ZUC, and Gupta showed that the long timing-critical path via self-feedback loop of s_{16} and s_{17} remains in the final pipeline stage at the initialization mode. Because the result of s_{16} has to be fed back to compute s_{17}, Gupta wanted to compute s_{16} and s_{17} in the same clock cycle. The path is two 32-bit adders and two 'Basic adder 2' and some logic gates. The timing-critial path was so long that the frequency of the Gupta's unrolled ZUC was 425 MHz. In this section, we propose a new structure of unrolled ZUC (namely, x2-ZUC) whose critical path will not lie in the initialization mode. One optimization technique is single-feedback initialization. There are two kinds of ways to shift the registers in the LFSR of x2-ZUC. In the initialization stage of x2-ZUC, in order to shorten the long data path, the feedback variable in LFSR is just s_{16}. Then s_{17} will be computed in the next clock cycle. From Fig 4, there are one more 31-bit register s_{-1} in x2-ZUC. In the initialization stage, due to single-feedback initialization, x2-ZUC only needs to compute s_{16} in a clock cycle, and the way to shift the registers in LFSR is as follows.

$$(S_{16}, S_{15}, S_{14}, \ldots, S_2, S_1, S_{-1}) \rightarrow (S_{15}, S_{14}, S_{13}, \ldots, S_1, S_0, S_{-1})$$

The loop in the initialization stage of x2-ZUC has 32 steps as the same as general ZUC algorithm. Then in the working stage, x2-ZUC can compute the feedback variable s_{16}, s_{17} in the same clock cycle, because in the working stage, the data path will not have the 32-bit adders and the parallel computation of s_{16}, s_{17} will not result in the timing-critical path based on our computation rescheduling technique. The way to shift the registers at the working stage is as follows.

$$(S_{17}, S_{16}, S_{15}, \ldots, S_3, S_2, S_1) \rightarrow (S_{15}, S_{14}, S_{13}, \ldots, S_1, S_0, S_{-1})$$

3.4   Computation Rescheduling

In order to increase the throughput of our design and to achieve a high and stable operating frequency in our design, we propose the computation rescheduling techniques in x2-ZUC. Although in the initialization stage x2-ZUC just needs to compute s_{16}, in the working stage x2-ZUC needs to compute s_{16}, s_{17} in the same clock cycle. Computation rescheduling which is based on the CSA trees

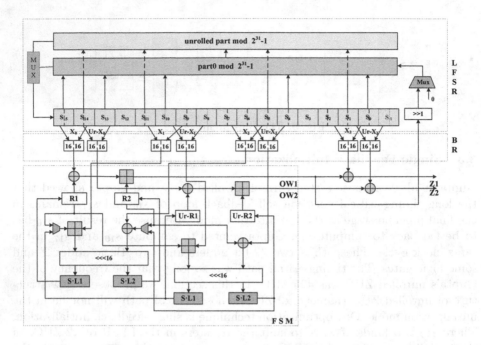

Fig. 4. The architecture of x2-ZUC

architecture can efficiently guarantee that the self-feedback loop will not be the timing-critical path in the design and also can save some resource. Because the path to compute the self-feedback variables s_{16}, s_{17} both cost some CSAs and one mod $2^{31} - 1$ adder. As is shown in Fig 4, part0 mod $2^{31} - 1$ is the update function in LFSR to compute s_{16}, and unrolled part mod $2^{31} - 1$ is the update function to compute s_{17}. Due to the dependency between the computation of s_{16} and s_{17}, part0 has some numbers to be fed back to unrolled part. As we know, in the working stage, the common procedure of computing s_{16}, s_{17} is as follows:

1. $S_{16} = \{2^{15}S_{15} + 2^{17}S_{13} + 2^{21}S_{10} + 2^{20}S_4 + (1 + 2^8)S_0\} \pmod{2^{31} - 1}$

2. *If* $S_{16} = 0$ *then set* $S_{16} = 2^{31} - 1$

3. $S_{17} = \{2^{15}S_{16} + 2^{17}S_{14} + 2^{21}S_{11} + 2^{20}S_5 + (1 + 2^8)S_1\} \pmod{2^{31} - 1}$

4. *If* $S_{17} = 0$ *then set* $S_{17} = 2^{31} - 1$

5. $(S_{17}, S_{16}, \ldots, S_3, S_2, S_1) \rightarrow (S_{15}, S_{14}, \ldots, S_1, S_0, S_{-1})$

Table 1 below shows the details of computation rescheduling, and the architecture of part0 and unrolled part are shown in Fig 5. From Fig 5, we can note that in the working stage, the data path to compute s_{16} consists of four CSAs and one modulo $2^{31} - 1$ adder and the data path to compute s_{17} consists of six CSAs and one modulo $2^{31} - 1$ adder.

Table 1. computation rescheduling in the update function of x2-ZUC

number	Computation
1	$S_{16} = 2^{15}S_{15} + 2^{17}S_{13} + 2^{21}S_{10} + 2^{20}S_4 + 2^8 S_0 + S_0$ $S_{17} = 2^{15}S_{16} + 2^{17}S_{14} + 2^{21}S_{11} + 2^{20}S_5 + 2^8 S_1 + S_1$ $\quad = 2^{15}(2^{15}S_{15} + 2^{17}S_{13} + 2^{21}S_{10} + 2^{20}S_4 + 2^8 S_0 + S_0)$ $\quad + 2^{17}S_{14} + 2^{21}S_{11} + 2^{20}S_5 + 2^8 S_1 + S_1$
2	$S_{18} = 2^{15}S_{17} + 2^{17}S_{15} + 2^{21}S_{12} + 2^{20}S_6 + 2^8 S_2 + S_2$ $S_{19} = 2^{15}S_{18} + 2^{17}S_{16} + 2^{21}S_{13} + 2^{20}S_7 + 2^8 S_3 + S_3$ $\quad = 2^{15}(2^{15}S_{17} + 2^{17}S_{15} + 2^{21}S_{12} + 2^{20}S_6 + 2^8 S_2 + S_2)$ $\quad + 2^{17}S_{16} + 2^{21}S_{13} + 2^{20}S_7 + 2^8 S_3 + S_3$
3	......

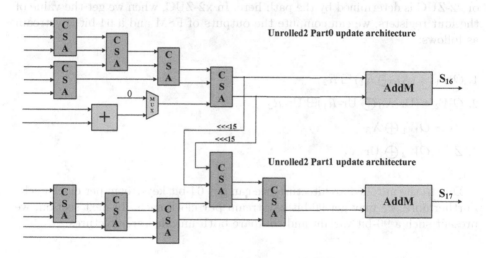

Fig. 5. The architecture of update functions in x2-ZUC

3.5 The Unrolled Architecture in FSM

The key stream of ZUC is computed from LFSR and the value of registers R_1 and R_2. As the ZUC algorithm described above, we know that registers R_1 and R_2 are updated every clock cycle and the values of the registers R_1 and R_2 in next clock cycle have dependency with that in current clock cycle. So if we want to get a keystream of 64-bit, we need to unroll the update of registers R_1 and R_2. In the architecture of x2-ZUC, there are four registers R_1, R_2, Ur-R_1 and Ur-R_2. The arithmetic operations between the four registers are as follows:

1. Ur-$W_1 = R_1 \boxplus$ Ur-X_1

2. Ur-$W_2 = R_2 \boxplus$ Ur-X_2

3. Ur-$R_1 = S(L_1($Ur-$W_{1L} \parallel$ Ur-$W_{2H}))$

4. Ur-$R_2 = S(L_2($Ur-$W_{2L} \parallel$ Ur-$W_{1H}))$

5. $W_1 =$Ur-$R_1 \boxplus X_1$

6. $W_2 =$Ur-$R_2 \boxplus X_2$

7. $R_1 = S(L_1(W_{1L} \parallel W_{2H}))$

8. $R_2 = S(L_1(W_{2L} \parallel W_{1H}))$

From the arithmetic operations, we can find that the timing-critical path in FSM is two 32-bit adders and two S-boxes(8 bit). Because of the fact that the timing-critical path here is longer than that in LFSR, so the operation frequency of x2-ZUC is determined by the path here. In x2-ZUC, when we get the value of the four registers, we can compute the outputs of FSM and a 64-bit keystream as follows:

1. $OW_1 = (X_0 \oplus R_1) \boxplus R_2$

2. $OW_2 =($Ur-$X_0 \oplus$ Ur-$R_1) \boxplus$ Ur-R_2

3. $Z_1 = OW_1 \oplus X_3$

4. $Z_2 = OW_2 \oplus$ Ur-X_3

Due to the unrolled architecture, we can get 64-bit keystream per clock cycle. Furthermore, we may get 96-bit keystream per clock cycle. In next section, we present such a 96-bit variant and compare both unrolled architectures.

3.6   x2-ZUC and x3-ZUC

When we apply the unrolled technology in our design, there comes a question that can we increase the degree of parallelism unlimitedly. So we propose a new unrolled implementation of ZUC (namely, x3-ZUC) which can output a keystream of 96-bit per clock cycle, then we will compare x2-ZUC with x3-ZUC. The architecture of x3-ZUC is shown in Fig 6. The initialization stage of x2-ZUC and x3-ZUC is the same, and both of them are based on single-feedback initialization. The main differences between them are the unrolled architectures in the update functions of LFSR and FSM. Because in the x3-ZUC we can get a keystream of 96-bit, there are three parts in the update function in LFSR. In x3-ZUC, there are also two kinds of ways to shift the registers in LFSR. The Fig 7 shows the computation rescheduling applied in the update functions of LFSR in x3-ZUC.

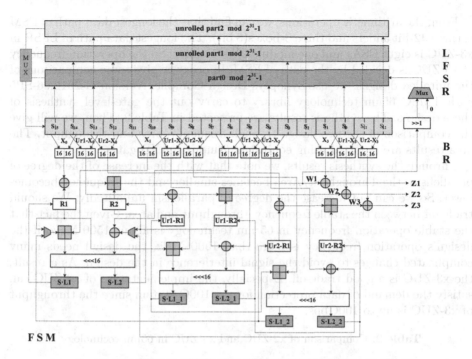

Fig. 6. The architecture of x3-ZUC

From Fig 6, the unrolled architecture of x3-ZUC is more complicated than that of x2-ZUC. In the FSM of x3-ZUC, there are six registers R_1, R_2, Ur1-R_1, Ur1-R_2, Ur2-R_1 and Ur2-R_2. The arithmetic operations between them are as follows:

1. Ur1-$W_1 = R_1 \boxplus$ Ur1-X_1

2. Ur1-$W_2 = R_2 \boxplus$ Ur1-X_2

3. Ur1-$R_1 = S(L_1($Ur1-$W_{1L} \parallel$ Ur1-$W_{2H}))$

4. Ur1-$R_2 = S(L_2($Ur1-$W_{2L} \parallel$ Ur1-$W_{1H}))$

5. Ur2-$W_1 =$Ur1-$R_1 \boxplus$ Ur2-X_1

6. Ur2-$W_2 =$Ur1-$R_2 \boxplus$ Ur2-X_2

7. Ur2-$R_1 = S(L_1($Ur2-$W_{1L} \parallel$ Ur2-$W_{2H}))$

8. Ur2-$R_2 = S(L_1($Ur2-$W_{2L} \parallel$ Ur2-$W_{1H}))$

9. $W_1 =$Ur2-$R_1 \boxplus X_1$

10. $W_2 =$Ur2-$R_2 \boxplus X_2$

11. $R_1 = S(L_1(W_{1L} \parallel W_{2H}))$

12. $R_2 = S(L_1(W_{2L} \parallel W_{1H}))$

From the arithmetic operations, we can find that the longest data path of FSM is three 32-bit adders and three S-boxes(8 bit). The longest data path of LFSR in x3-ZUC is eight CSAs and one modulo $2^{31} - 1$ adder. So the operation frequency of x3-ZUC is decided by the path of FSM. In order to give some comparisons of the unrolled designs, we use Synopsys Design Compiler Version G-2012.06-SP5 with TMSC 65nm technology library to carry out the gate-level synthesis of these designs. The synthesis results are presented in Table 2. Then, we will give the comparison of the two design through frequency, area and throughput. The area results are reported using equivalent 2-input NAND gates.

Through the synthesis results, we note that with the increase of the degree of parallelism, the Throughput/Area becomes smaller and the frequency becomes lower. So we can not increase the degree of parallelism unlimitedly. We should trade off between the stable frequency, throughput and area. Given the fact that the stable operation frequency in 65 nm technology is about 1500 MHz, if the design's operation frequency is more than 1500 MHz, the design needs many complicated changes to avoid the signal interference in the design. As a result, the x3-ZUC is a good trade-off. Especially, the implementation of x3-ZUC can satisfy the demand of data protection for the 100G system since the throughput of x3-ZUC is up to 100Gbps.

Table 2. Comparison of x2-ZUC and x3-ZUC in 65nm technology

Implementation	Technology	Max.Freq (MHz)	Area (KGates)	Throughput (Gbps)
x2-ZUC	TSMC 65nm	1495	22.69	95.68
x3-ZUC	TSMC 65nm	1045	33.16	100.32

4 Evaluation and Analysis

Through the above description, the timing-critical path in our unrolled design lies in FSM. The timing-critical path in x2-ZUC consists of two 32-bit adders, two s-boxes(8bit) and some logic gates. The timing-critical path in x3-ZUC is three 32-bit adders, three s-boxes(8bit) and some logic gates. In the initialization stage of our unrolled design, based on single-feedback initialization and two kinds of shift modes, we can avoid the long data path in the initialization mode. Meanwhile in our unrolled architecture, the data path of the update functions in LFSR becomes shorter by using computation rescheduling to compute the self-feedback variables. Firstly, in order to verify our unrolled design's correctness, we implement our architectures in Virtex-5 XC5VLX110T-3 and Virtex-6 XC6VLX75t-3 FPGA platform. The synthesis tool is ISE 13.2, and the synthesis result is given in Table 3. From Table 3, the performance of our new unrolled architecture is at least 8.99 Gbps, which is 63.5 % faster than the previous full implementations on FPGA.

Then, compared with the existing designs in ASIC, Liu et al [10] propose the mixed two-stage pipeline design, Gupta in [9] give an three-stage pipeline architecture and a kind of unrolled ZUC, and in the commercial area, both IP

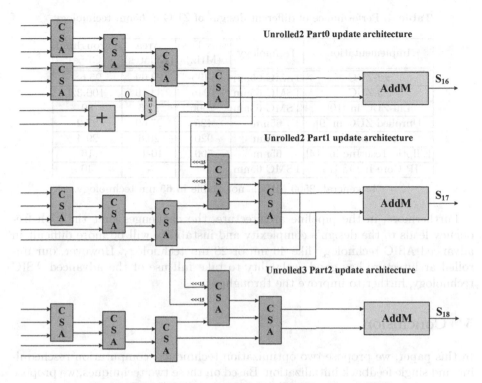

Fig. 7. The architecture of update functions in x3-ZUC

Table 3. Synthesis result of unrolled designs on FPGA

Implementation	Technology	Max.Freq (MHz)	Area (Slice)	Throughput (Gbps)
x2-ZUC	Virtex-5 XC5VLX110T-3	140.47	649	8.99
x2-ZUC	Virtex-6 XC6VLX75T-3	188.45	564	12.06
x3-ZUC	Virtex-5 XC5VLX110T-3	98.07	827	9.41
x3-ZUC	Virtex-6 XC6VLX75T-3	131.24	803	12.6
Kitsos et al [12]	Virtex 5	65	385	2.08
Wang et al [7]	Virtex-5 XC5VLX110T-3	108	356	3.46
Zhang et al [8]	Virtex-5 XC5VLX110T-3	172	395	5.50

Cores Inc [13] and Elliptic Tech Inc [14] proposed their ZUC IP cores in 65nm technology. In Table 4, we list the performance of these designs.

From Table 4, in the previous designs, the throughput of Liu-ZUC is 80 Gbps, but the frequency of Liu-ZUC is 2500 MHz, which is too high to result in the design's instability. The best performance of x3-ZUC achieves 100 Gbps, 25% higher than the previous fastest implementation, and the design frequency of x3-ZUC is 1045 MHz, which is stable in 65 nm technology. Also the throughput of x3-ZUC is 2.5 times higher than the previous unrolled architecture.

Table 4. Performance of different designs of ZUC in 65nm technology

Implementation	Technology	Max.Freq (MHz)	Area (KGates)	Throughput (Gbps)
x2-ZUC	TSMC 65nm	1495	22.69	95.68
x3-ZUC	TSMC 65nm	1045	33.16	100.32
Liu-ZUC in [10]	TSMC 65nm	2500*	12.5	80
Unrolled ZUC in [9]	65nm	425	27.69	27.2
ZUC in [9]	65nm	920	20.6	29.4
Elliptic Tech Inc in [14]	65nm	500	10-13	16
IP Core Inc in [13]	TSMC 65nm	-	-	40

*In general, 2500 MHz is not stable in 65 nm technology.

Furthermore, in the pipeline architecture, the challenges that the high frequency leads to the design's complexity and instability will be more difficult in advanced ASIC technology like 40 nm or 28 nm technology. However, our unrolled architecture has good scalability to take full use of the advanced ASIC technology, further to improve the throughput.

5   Conclusion

In this paper, we propose two optimization techniques: computation rescheduling and single feedback initialization. Based on these two techniques, we propose two unrolled architecture of ZUC: x2-ZUC and x3-ZUC. The two optimization techniques can solve the problem that the data path is too long in the initialization stage in the previous unrolled designs. Implementation results clearly indicate that our new unrolled architecture can improve throughput efficiently both on FPGA and ASIC. The best performance of x3-ZUC is up to 100Gbps. As far as we know, it is the fastest encryption and decryption ZUC IP core by now. With the challenge of the security of data transmission at a bandwidth of 100Gbps in the future, we hope this new architecture will be a standard for hardware implementation of ZUC.

References

1. Specification of the 3GPP Confidentiality and Integrity Algorithms 128-EEA3 & 128-EIA3. Document 2: ZUC Specification version: 1.6 (2011)
2. Specification of the 3GPP Confidentiality and Integrity Algorithms 128-EEA3 & 128-EIA3.Document 1: 128-EEA3 and 128-EIA3 Specificationversion: 1.6 (2011)
3. Specification of the 3GPP Confidentiality and Integrity Algorithms 128-EEA3 & 128-EIA3.Document 3: Implementors Test Dataversion: 1.6 (2011)
4. Specification of the 3GPP Confidentiality and Integrity Algorithms 128-EEA3 & 128-EIA3. Document 4: Design and Evaluation Report version: 1.6 (2011)
5. Kitsos, P., Sklavos, N., Skodras, A.: An FPGA Implementation of the ZUC Stream Cipher. In: 2011 14th Euromicro Conference on Digital System Design (DSD), pp. 814–817. IEEE (2011)

6. Liu, Z., Zhang, L., Jing, J., Pan, W.: Efficient Pipelined Stream Cipher ZUC Algorithm in FPGA. In: The First International Workshop on ZUC Algorithm, pp. 2–3 (December)
7. Wang, L., Jing, J., Liu, Z., Zhang, L., Pan, W.: Evaluating Optimized Implementations of Stream Cipher ZUC Algorithm on FPGA. In: Qing, S., Susilo, W., Wang, G., Liu, D. (eds.) ICICS 2011. LNCS, vol. 7043, pp. 202–215. Springer, Heidelberg (2011)
8. Zhang, L., Xia, L., Liu, Z., Jing, J., Ma, Y.: Evaluating the optimized implementations of snow3g and zuc on FPGA. In: 2012 IEEE 11th International Conference on Trust, Security and Privacy in Computing and Communications (TrustCom), pp. 436–442. IEEE (2012)
9. Gupta, S.S., Chattopadhyay, A., Khalid, A.: Designing integrated accelerator for stream ciphers with structural similarities. Cryptography and Communications 5(1), 19–47 (2013)
10. Liu, Z., Gao, N., Jing, J., Liu, P.: Hpaz: a high-throughput pipeline architecture of zuc in hardware (2013), http://eprint.iacr.org/
11. Sen Gupta, S., Chattopadhyay, A., Khalid, A.: HiPAcc-LTE: An Integrated High Performance Accelerator for 3GPP LTE Stream Ciphers. In: Bernstein, D.J., Chatterjee, S. (eds.) INDOCRYPT 2011. LNCS, vol. 7107, pp. 196–215. Springer, Heidelberg (2011)
12. Kitsos, P., Kostopoulos, G., Sklavos, N., Koufopavlou, O.: Hardware implementation of the RC4 stream cipher. In: 2003 IEEE International Symposium on Micro-NanoMechatronics and Human Science, vol. 3, pp. 1363–1366. IEEE (2005)
13. ZUC1 Ultra-Compact 3GPP Cipher Core, tech. rep., IP Cores Inc. (2012) http://ipcores.com/ZUC$_$cipher$_$IP$_$core.htm (retrieved on February 5, 2012)
14. ZUC1 KEY STREAM GENERATOR, tech. rep., Elliptic Tech Inc. (2012), http://elliptictech.com/zh/products-a-solutions/hardware/cryptographic-engines/clp-410 (retrieved on February 5, 2012)

Another Look at Privacy Threats in 3G Mobile Telephony

Mohammed Shafiul Alam Khan* and Chris J. Mitchell

Information Security Group, Royal Holloway, University of London
Egham, Surrey TW20 0EX, United Kingdom
shafiulalam@gmail.com, me@chrismitchell.net

Abstract. Arapinis et al. [1] have recently proposed modifications to the operation of 3G mobile phone security in order to address newly identified threats to user privacy. In this paper we critically examine these modifications. This analysis reveals that the proposed modifications are impractical in a variety of ways; not only are there security and implementation issues, but the necessary changes to the operation of the system are very significant and much greater than is envisaged. In fact, some of the privacy issues appear almost impossible to address without a complete redesign of the security system. The shortcomings of the proposed 'fixes' exist despite the fact that the modifications have been verified using a logic-based modeling tool, suggesting that such tools need to be used with great care.

1 Introduction

The 3GPP/ETSI 3G standards, which incorporate a range of security features [2,3], are the basis for a large part of the world's mobile telephony. As a result, any security or privacy flaws identified in these standards potentially have major implications.

We are primarily concerned with one particular feature of 3G security, namely the service known as *user identity confidentiality*. This service seeks to minimise the exposure of the mobile phone's long term identity (actually the long term identity of the USIM within the phone) on the *air interface*, i.e. the radio path between the phone and the network. The main security feature incorporated into the 3G system designed to provide this service is the use of frequently changing temporary identities, which act as pseudonyms.

A recently published paper by Arapinis et al. [1] describes two novel attacks on this service, which enable user device anonymity to be compromised. As well as describing the two attacks, modifications ('fixes') to the protocol are described which aim to prevent the attacks, and verifications of these fixes using ProVerif are also outlined.

---

* The first author would like to acknowledge the generous support of the Commonwealth Scholarship Commission.

W. Susilo and Y. Mu (Eds.): ACISP 2014, LNCS 8544, pp. 386–396, 2014.

This paper has the following main objectives. Firstly, the proposed fixes are re-examined, and are found to have significant shortcomings. Secondly, possible alternative approaches to some of the modifications are noted. Thirdly, it is argued that some of the weaknesses in user identity confidentiality are impossible to fix, meaning that making significant system changes to address some of them are unlikely to be worth the effort. Finally, conclusions are drawn about the effectiveness of tools such as ProVerif if not used with appropriate care, and in particular if used without a detailed understanding of the cryptographic primitives being used.

The remainder of the paper is structured as follows. In section 2 the key features of the 3G security architecture are briefly reviewed. The attacks of Arapinis et al. are then summarised in section 3, together with a description of their proposed fixes. Sections 4 and 5 provide an analysis of the 'fixes'. Finally, the findings of the paper are summarised and conclusions are drawn in section 6.

2   Relevant 3G Security Features

The purpose of this section is to introduce those 3G security features of relevance to this paper. Our description follows Niemi and Nyberg [3], and we use their notation.

2.1   The AKA Protocol

At the core of 3G air interface security is a mutual authentication and authenticated key establishment protocol known as AKA (Authentication and Key Agreement). This is regularly performed between the visited network and the mobile phone (the *user equipment (UE)*). It involves the network sending an *user authentication request* to the UE. The UE checks the validity of this request (thereby authenticating the network), and then sends a *user authentication response*. The network checks this response to authenticate the UE. As a result, if successful, the two parties have authenticated each other, and at the same time they establish two shared secret keys.

In order to participate in the protocol, the UE — in fact the User Subscriber Identity Module (USIM) installed inside the UE — must possess two values:

- a long term secret key K, known only to the USIM and to the USIM's 'home network', and
- a sequence number SQN maintained by both the USIM and the home network.

The key K never leaves the USIM, and the values of K and SQN are protected by the USIM's physical security features.

The 48-bit sequence number SQN is used to enable the UE to verify the 'freshness' of the user authentication request. More specifically, the request message contains two values: $RAND$ and $AUTN$, where $RAND$ is a 128-bit random number generated by the home network, and the 128-bit $AUTN$ consists of the concatenation of three values: $SQN \oplus AK$ (48 bits), AMF (16 bits), and MAC (64 bits). The value AMF is not relevant to our discussions here, and we do not discuss it further. The MAC is a Message Authentication Code (or *tag*) computed as a function of $RAND$, SQN, AMF, and the long term secret key K, using a MAC algorithm known as $f1$. The value AK, computed as a function of K and $RAND$, essentially functions as a means of encrypting SQN; this is necessary since, if sent in cleartext, the SQN value would potentially compromise user identity confidentiality, given that the value of SQN is USIM-specific.

On receipt of these two values, the USIM uses the received $RAND$, along with its stored value of K, to regenerate the value of AK, which it can then use to recover SQN. It next uses its stored key K, together with the received values of $RAND$ and SQN, in function $f1$ to regenerate the MAC value; if the newly computed value agrees with the value received in $AUTN$ then the first stage of authentication has succeeded. The USIM next checks that SQN is a 'new' value; if so it updates its stored SQN value and the network has been authenticated.

If authentication succeeds, then the USIM computes another message authentication code, called RES, from K and $RAND$ using another function $f2$, and sends it to the network as part of the user authentication response. If this RES agrees with the value expected by the network then the UE is deemed authenticated.

We note that if the authentication process fails for some reason, then the UE sends an error code (a *Failure Case Code*) as part of an *Authentication failure report*, sent instead of a user authentication response ([2], section 6.3.6). In particular, distinct error codes are sent to indicate an incorrect MAC and an incorrect SQN, i.e. depending whether the authentication process fails at the first or second stage.

Finally observe that the security properties of the AKA protocol itself have been proven to hold [4] — the problems we consider here arise from exchanges not actually part of the AKA protocol. This makes clear the necessity to consider the entirety of a system if robust results about security and privacy are to be achieved.

2.2 Session Keys

As part of a successful AKA procedure, the network and the USIM generate a pair of session keys, known as IK, the *integrity key*, and CK, the *ciphering key*. Both these keys are a function of K and $RAND$. The USIM exports these two keys to the UE. The IK is used for integrity protection of signalling messages sent across the radio path, and the CK is used for encryption of data sent across the air interface, using a stream ciphering technique.

2.3 User Identity Confidentiality

As mentioned previously, user identity confidentiality is provided by the use of temporary identities. Every USIM has a unique *International Mobile Subscriber Identity (IMSI)*. If this was routinely sent across the network then the UE, and hence its owner, could be traced. As a result, every UE also possesses a *Temporary Mobile Subscriber Identifier (TMSI)* which is sent instead.

The value of the TMSI, which is chosen by the network the UE is visiting, is changed regularly. A new TMSI is sent by the network to the UE in encrypted form, protected using the *CK*.

3   Privacy Threats and Fixes

3.1   The Attacks

Arapinis et al. [1] describe two apparently novel attacks that breach user identity confidentiality in 3G mobile telephony. These two threats operate as follows (for further details see [1]).

- *IMSI Paging Attack.* This attack exploits a specific type of signalling message known as a *Paging* message (or, more formally, a PAGING TYPE 1 message — see 8.1.2 of ETSI TS 125 331 [5]). Such messages are sent from the network to all mobile devices in a particular area, and can contain either an IMSI or a TMSI. If a UE detects such a message containing its IMSI or its current TMSI then it responds with a message containing its current TMSI. Most importantly, paging messages are not integrity protected (see 6.5.1 of ETSI TS 133 102 [2]), and hence a malicious third party can introduce spurious paging messages into the network. This can be used to both detect the presence of a UE with a specific IMSI, and also to learn the current TMSI for this device. This poses a threat to mobile identity privacy.
- *AKA Error Message Attack.* This attack exploits the error messages incorporated into the AKA protocol, as described in section 2.1 above. Suppose an attacker has intercepted a genuine ($RAND, AUTN$) pair sent to a particular UE. If these values are relayed to a specific UE, two possible outcomes will arise. If the recipient UE is the device to which the ($RAND, AUTN$) pair was originally sent then it will respond with an Authentication failure report containing an error code indicating a failed SQN, i.e. to indicate that the pair has been received previously. Otherwise, the UE will respond with a failure report containing an error code indicating an incorrect MAC value. That is, the error code can be used to distinguish between UEs, and this is clearly another means of breaching user identity confidentiality.

3.2   Observations

We start by observing that the first threat, whilst apparently novel, is closely related to another threat to user identity privacy. As described in section 6.2 of ETSI TS 133 102 [2], 'when the user registers for the first time in a serving network, or when the serving network cannot retrieve the IMSI from the TMSI by which the user identifies itself on the radio path', the serving network must obtain the IMSI from the UE — this is performed using a *User identity request/User identity response* message pair, where the latter message contains the IMSI. 'This represents a breach in the provision of user identity confidentiality'. This attack, called *user identity catching* (or *IMSI catching*), is further mentioned in A.1 of ETSI TS 121 133 [6], and is also noted by Arapinis et al. ([1], section 2.2).

Given that this attack exists, i.e. an active attacker can obtain the IMSI of any UE by impersonating the network, neither of the new attacks appear to significantly weaken the user privacy service any further. That is, neither of the new attacks appear to be any easier to launch than the IMSI catching attack — in particular, they both require active impersonation of the network.

Most interestingly, the second attack seems to be an issue that has not previously been discussed in the literature. It is just one example of a very broad class of threats arising from poorly designed error messages that reveal information of value to an attacker — see, for example, Vaudenay [7].

3.3   The Fixes

As well as describing the two privacy issues, Arapinis et al. [1] give three separate modifications to the operation of 3G mobile telephony designed to fix the two newly identified problems as well as the well known user identity catching attack. We next briefly describe these proposed modifications.

- *Fixing the IMSI Paging Attack.* This modification is not described in complete detail ([1], section 5.2), and as a result some suppositions need to be made. It involves cryptographically protecting the paging message using a secret key UK known only to the network and the UE. Like the CK and IK, this additional key is generated as a function of the $RAND$ and K during the AKA protocol.

   The paging message format is modified to incorporate two additional fields, namely a sequence number SQN and a random challenge $CHALL$. It is not clear whether SQN is in the same 'series' as the SQN sent in the $AUTN$ of whether this is a distinct sequence number used for this purpose only. This issue is discussed further in section 4 below.

   The entire paging message is then encrypted using UK. However, the method of encryption is not specified. This issue is also discussed further in section 4 below.

   Since this message is broadcast, it is received by all UEs currently attached to a base station. Each UE must use its current UK to decrypt the message. By some (unspecified) means the recipient UE decides whether the decrypted message is intended for it or not — Arapinis et al. simply state ([1], section 5.2) that each UE 'has to decrypt and check all the received IMSI paging to determine if it is the recipient' (sic). If it is the intended recipient, then the UE checks the SQN against its stored value to verify its freshness (as in AKA). If it is fresh then the USIM updates its stored SQN, and sends a paging response containing the TMSI and the received value of $CHALL$; otherwise, if the freshness check fails, the paging message is ignored.
- *Fixing the AKA Error Message Attack.* This fix involves leaving the 'normal' operation of AKA unchanged; the only modification is to require (asymmetric) encryption of authentication failure report messages, thereby hiding the

nature of the embedded error message. This encryption is performed using a public encryption key belonging to the visited network. Providing a reliable copy of this key to the UE requires the pre-establishment of a Public Key Infrastructure (PKI) involving all the 3G network operators, in which each network operator has an asymmetric encryption key pair *and* a signature key pair. Each operator must use its private signature key to create a certificate for every other network's public encryption key. Every USIM must be equipped with the public signature verification key of the issuing (home) network.

In order for the UE to obtain a trusted copy of the appropriate public encryption key, the visited network must send a copy of a certificate for its public encryption key, signed using the private signature key of the USIM's home network (this could be achieved by modifying an existing signalling message or by introducing a new such message). The USIM exports its trusted copy of the public verification key of its home network to the phone, and the phone can use this to verify the certificate, thereby obtaining the required trusted public encryption key. The phone can perform the encryption of the failure report message, obviating the need for the USIM to perform any computationally complex asymmetric encryption operations.

A further modification to the failure report message is proposed by Arapinis et al. [1], namely to include the USIM's current value of SQN. This change is designed to enable resynchronisation of this value by the network, but is not explained further.

– *Fixing User Identity Catching.* Finally, Arapinis et al. [1] also propose modifying the procedure by which a UE identifies itself when first joining a network. They propose that the UE asymmetrically encrypts the User identity response message containing the IMSI. As in the previous modification, this encryption is performed using the public encryption key of the visited network.

4 IMSI Paging Re-examined

There are a number of significant issues with the fix proposed to mitigate IMSI paging attacks. We enumerate some of the most serious.

1. Introducing a new type of session key, i.e. the UK, has major ramifications. To see why we first need to consider some issues surrounding the use of AKA. The long term K is not passed to a visited network. Instead, the home network of the USIM will generate, on request, sets of *authentication vectors*, i.e. 5-tuples $(RAND, XRES, CK, IK, AUTN)$, which are passed to the visited network. Each 5-tuple contains a random $RAND$ value and a distinct SQN value embedded in the $AUTN$. Note that several such 5-tuples will be passed to the visited network at the same time (to reduce the number of inter-network signalling messages), and the visited network must use them in the correct order, i.e. in ascending order of SQN values.

When it wishes to authenticate a UE, the visited network sends the ($RAND$, $AUTN$) pair from the 'next' authentication vector, and receives back RES, which it compares with the $XRES$ value from the authentication vector (the 'expected value of RES') to authenticate the UE. Introducing an additional key type means that the authentication vectors will need to become 6-tuples to include the UK value, which will involve changing the formats of messages sent between networks (this is, in itself, a significant change).

2. As noted in section 3.3 above, there are two possible ways in which the SQN might be generated and managed. It could be generated and verified using the same mechanism as employed for the AKA protocol, or a separate sequence number scheme could be involved. Unfortunately, there are major implementation difficulties with both options.

   (a) Using the same SQN values as are used in the AKA protocol is problematic. The visited network does not have a means of finding out these values, as they are not included in the authentication vectors sent to the visited network. Even if the current SQN value was sent as part of the authentication vector (which would affect the inter-network signalling infrastructure), two major problems remain. Firstly, if the visited network is permitted to generate new SQN values and have them accepted by the USIM, then this means that the visited network is able to modify the SQN value stored by the USIM. This could have the effect of invalidating any unused authentication vectors that the visited network retains for the UE. Secondly, giving the visited network the power to change the SQN value held by the USIM is a major change in the current trust model, and would give the visited network the power to deliberately or accidentally completely block the operation of the USIM by sending it a very large SQN value.

   (b) Using a different SQN value also raises major issues, as there is no obvious mechanism to keep multiple networks aware of the current value of the SQN for a particular UE. This would require the home network to maintain the current value, and for visited networks to exchange messages with the home network to maintain synchronisation between the value held by the USIM and the home network.

3. The 'encryption' of the paging message appears to be intended to provide two distinct security services: (a) guarantees to the recipient regarding the origin and integrity of the message, and (b) confidentiality of the contents so that passive interceptors cannot observe the link between an IMSI and a TMSI. It is well known that simple encryption cannot guarantee property (a), especially if that means use of a stream cipher (see, for example, section 9.6.5 of Menezes, van Oorschot and Vanstone [8]). However, stream cipher encryption is the only encryption primitive available in the current 3G security architecture. Clearly what is really required is the application of an authenticated encryption technique [9], which would provide the necessary security guarantees. However, this is never made explicit by Arapinis et al. [1]. Their success in proving the security of the modification using ProVerif

suggests that their input to ProVerif implicitly assumed the provision of properties (a) and (b), whereas their description of the necessary modifications to the system did not make these requirements explicit. This shows the danger of not carefully considering and making explicit all the properties of the cryptographic primitives being employed.

Of course, the visited network and UE share a pair of keys (CK and IK) designed explicitly for confidentiality and integrity protection of data and signalling messages. A much simpler solution, which achieves precisely the same objectives, would be to first encrypt the paging message using CK and then generate an accompanying MAC using IK. This would both achieve the security objectives and avoid the need to introduce an additional key type.

4. Finally, we note that, even if it could somehow be repaired, the fix imposes very significant burdens on the system. As stated by the authors (final sentence of 5.2 of [1]) the overheads of the proposed modification are non-trivial. This is because every UE that receives a paging message is required to decrypt it and somehow verify whether or not it is intended for them.

In conclusion, the number and seriousness of the issues identified with the fix, especially relating to the use of the SQN sequence number, suggest that it cannot work in practice. Moreover, finding an alternative fix without completely redesigning the 3G system appears highly problematic. As a result it would appear that accepting that user identity confidentiality is imperfect seems inevitable, a point we return to below.

5 Addressing the Error Message and Identity Catching Attacks

In evaluating the fix proposed to address the AKA error message attack, we start by considering the practicality of introducing a brand new PKI. Whilst the required PKI is relatively small scale, involving only the network operators, introducing such a PKI would nevertheless involve significant changes to the operation of the system. In particular, over and above requiring changes to all phones, all USIMs and all networks, every USIM would need to be equipped with a public key, every network would need to exchange public keys and certificates with every other network, certificates (potentially quite large) would need to be routinely sent across the air interface, and the USIM would need to routinely transfer a public key to its host phone (across a smart card interface with a very limited data transfer capability). That is, whilst the PKI itself might be relatively small-scale, the changes to the air interface protocol to allow its use would require fundamental changes to the system infrastructure. It is not even clear how a phased deployment could be undertaken, and changing the entire system (including all mobile phones) at a single point in time is clearly infeasible.

It is interesting to note that the difficulty of providing robust identity privacy without asymmetric cryptography has long been known — see, for example, Mitchell ([10], section 4.1). Indeed, this point is also made by Arapinis et al. ([1], section 5.5) who make similar remarks. This suggests that modifications analogous to the proposed fix have been considered in the past, and rejected for reasons of complexity and low pay off (a point we return to below).

Moreover, deploying the required PKI requires all networks to possess two key pairs, one for encryption/decryption and one for signature generation and verification. This is because, in general, the widely accepted principle of *key separation* (see, for example, 13.5.1 of Menezes, van Oorschot and Vanstone [8]) requires that different keys are used for different purposes. However, if sufficient care is taken, sometimes the same key pair can be securely used for both encryption and signature, although this is not without risks (see, for example, Degabriele et al. [11]).

We further note that if the private decryption key of any network is ever compromised, then security is compromised. The usual solution in a PKI is to deploy a revocation system, e.g. in the form of Certificate Revocation Lists (CRLs). However, deploying CRLs on the scale necessary would appear to be very challenging in a 3G system. Indeed, the difficulties of deploying CRLs across large networks are well-established, [12,13].

One alternative to the proposed solution would simply be to remove the error code from the error message, or, to minimise protocol modifications, to program mobile phones to always return the same error message regardless of how AKA actually fails. This is, in any case, clearly best practice for any security protocol, i.e. if an authentication procedure fails then the only information that should be provided is that the process has failed, and not how.

Finally we note that implementing the proposed fix to mitigate IMSI catching is problematic. Requiring a UE to encrypt the IMSI it sends to the network requires the phone to have a reliable copy of the network's public key. This will, in turn, require the network to send the UE a certificate — but which one? The UE will only be able to verify a certificate signed by the USIM's home network, but the visited network will not know what this is until it has seen the IMSI. That is, the UE will not be able to encrypt the IMSI for transmission to the network until the network knows the IMSI, and hence we have a classic 'chicken and egg' problem.

6   Summary and Conclusions

It would appear that the modifications proposed to address the identified privacy threats either do not work or impose a very major overhead on the network, over and above the huge cost in modifying all the network infrastructure. Very interestingly, the failures in the fixes arise despite a detailed analysis using formal techniques.

Of course, making significant changes to a protocol as widely deployed as the 3G air interface protocol is unlikely to be feasible, so the discussion here is perhaps rather moot. However, even where the fixes appear to work, in two cases significantly simpler approaches appear to have been ignored. That is, removing the error messages would mitigate the AKA error message attack (and would also conform to good practice), and it would appear that the introduction of a new key *UK* is unnecessary. If changes are to be made, then it is vital to try to minimise their impact on the operations of the system.

Most significantly in any discussion of whether it might be worth trying to implement 'fixed up' versions of the fixes, there exist 'passive' attacks on user identity confidentiality other than those discussed thus far. For example, a malicious party wishing to discover whether or not a particular phone is present in a cell could simply inaugurate a call to the phone or send it an SMS, simultaneously monitoring messages sent across the network. If such a procedure is repeated a few times, then it seems likely to be sufficient to reveal with high probability whether a particular phone is present, especially if the network is relatively 'quiet'. Such an attack only requires passive observation of the network, and hence would be simpler to launch than attacks requiring a false base station (which is the case for all the attacks we have discussed previously). Moreover, addressing such an attack would be almost impossible.

We can thus conclude that not only are the proposed fixes highly problematic, but providing a robust form of user identity confidentiality is essentially impossible in practice. That is, if robust identity confidentiality is not achievable, then it is very unlikely to be worth the huge cost of making changes of the type proposed. The 'pay off' in mitigating some threats but not others is small relative to the overall cost of implementing them.

Finally, the practical and security issues encountered in considering the detailed implementation of the proposed modifications suggests that the use of formal tools to try to guarantee security and privacy properties should be used with great care. In particular, any such analysis should always be accompanied by an analysis of the practical working environment for the security protocol.

References

1. Arapinis, M., Mancini, L., Ritter, E., Ryan, M., Golde, N., Redon, K., Borgaonkar, R.: New privacy issues in mobile telephony: Fix and verification. In: Yu, T., Danezis, G., Gligor, V.D. (eds.) ACM Conference on Computer and Communications Security, CCS 2012, Raleigh, NC, USA, October 16-18, pp. 205–216. ACM (2012)
2. European Telecommunications Standards Institute (ETSI): ETSI TS 133 102 V11.5.1 (2013-07): Digital cellular telecommunications system (Phase 2+); Universal Mobile Telecommunications System (UMTS); 3G Security; Security architecture (3GPP TS 33.102 version 11.5.1 Release 11) (2013)
3. Niemi, V., Nyberg, K.: UMTS Security. John Wiley and Sons, Chichester (2003)
4. Lee, M.F., Smart, N.P., Warinschi, B., Watson, G.J.: Anonymity guarantees of the UMTS/LTE authentication and connection protocol. Cryptology ePrint Archive: Report 2013/27 (2013)
5. European Telecommunications Standards Institute (ETSI): ETSI TS 125 331 V11.6.0 (2013-07): Universal Mobile Telecommunications System (UMTS); Radio Resource Control (RRC); Protocol specification (3GPP TS 25.331 version 11.6.0 Release 11) (2013)

6. European Telecommunications Standards Institute (ETSI): ETSI TS 121 133 V4.1.0 (2001-12): Universal Mobile Telecommunications System (UMTS); 3G Security; Security threats and requirements (3GPP TS 21.133 version 4.1.0 Release 4) (2001)

7. Vaudenay, S.: Security flaws induced by CBC padding - applications to SSL, IPSEC, WTLS... In: Knudsen, L.R. (ed.) EUROCRYPT 2002. LNCS, vol. 2332, pp. 534–545. Springer, Heidelberg (2002)

8. Menezes, A.J., van Oorschot, P.C., Vanstone, S.A.: Handbook of Applied Cryptography. CRC Press, Boca Raton (1997)

9. International Organization for Standardization Genève, Switzerland: ISO/IEC 19772:2009, Information technology — Security techniques — Authenticated encryption mechanisms (2009)

10. Mitchell, C.J.: The security of the GSM air interface protocol. Technical Report RHUL-MA-2001-3, Mathematics Department, Royal Holloway, University of London, Egham, Surrey TW20 0EX, UK (2001), http://www.ma.rhul.ac.uk/techreports

11. Degabriele, J.P., Lehmann, A., Paterson, K.G., Smart, N.P., Strefler, M.: On the joint security of encryption and signature in EMV. In: Dunkelman, O. (ed.) CT-RSA 2012. LNCS, vol. 7178, pp. 116–135. Springer, Heidelberg (2012)

12. Kocher, P.C.: On certificate revocation and validation. In: Hirschfeld, R. (ed.) FC 1998. LNCS, vol. 1465, pp. 172–177. Springer, Heidelberg (1998)

13. Myers, M.D.: Revocation: Options and challenges. In: Hirschfeld, R. (ed.) FC 1998. LNCS, vol. 1465, pp. 165–171. Springer, Heidelberg (1998)

ExBLACR: Extending BLACR System

Weijin Wang, Dengguo Feng, Yu Qin, Jianxiong Shao, Li Xi, and Xiaobo Chu

Trusted Computing and Information Assurance Laboratory,
Institute of Software, Chinese Academy of Sciences, Beijing, China
{wangweijin,feng,qin_yu,shaojianxiong,xili,chuxiaobo}@tca.iscas.ac.cn

Abstract. Reputation-based anonymous blacklisting systems allow users to anonymously authenticate their identities with a service provider (SP) directly, while enabling the service provider to score users' misbehaviour and deny access from users with insufficient reputation, without the assistance of a Trusted Third Party (TTP). Au, Kapadia and Susilo's reputation-based anonymous blacklisting system BLACR is an elegant solution except for the linear computational overhead in the size of the reputation list. Therefore, they proposed a more practical strategy for BLACR that allows active users to authenticate in the express lane. However, the strategy disables BLACR's ability to perform unblacklisting since removing entries from the blacklist invalidates the reputation proofs of express lane tokens. Another problem of BLACR is that the express lane tokens can be reused (replay attack). In this paper, we propose ExBLACR, which provides a solution to the above problems. Our construction directly builds from BLACR and we present an improvement of weighted-score adjusting protocol ($\mathfrak{G}_{WS-Adj}$) to support *unblacklisting* when BLACR employs the express lane authentication. We also make a minor change to the express lane tokens to resist replay attack.

Keywords: anonymous blacklisting, unblacklisting, revocation, BLACR, replay attack.

1 Introduction

Nowadays people are becoming increasingly concerned about their privacy matters during the use of web applications. For example, without the protection of privacy, users would not be willing to submit sensitive contents on Wikipedia, or express their real views on online forums due to being afraid of the consequences that might be faced from censorship. A trivial solution to protecting privacy on web applications is to use some kind of anonymous communications networks, such as Tor [12]. Nevertheless, anonymous communications networks cause another problem: misbehaved users will not be accountable for their bad actions. Given this situation, plenty of work has been done for permitting service providers (SPs) to blacklist misbehaved users while keeping their anonymity.

Anonymous Blacklisting Systems with TTP. These approaches allow a SP to blacklist a user in cooperation with a TTP, which can identify the user and link

W. Susilo and Y. Mu (Eds.): ACISP 2014, LNCS 8544, pp. 397–412, 2014.

the user's accesses. Two separate categories can be taken into account in the early literature. The first one is the pseudonym systems based on private credentials [11,21], blind signatures [13,1], and group signatures [10,24]. The other one is the Nymble-like systems [28,14,18,19]. Nonetheless, having a TTP capable of deanonymizing or linking a user's accesses is dangerous in that when the TTP is compromised, legitimate users' privacy will not be guaranteed. Recognizing this threat, the elimination of such TTP is desired.

Anonymous Blacklisting Systems without TTP. To eliminate the participation of TTPs, Tsang *et al.* proposed Blacklistable Anonymous Credentials (BLAC) [25,27]. In BLAC, a user proves in zero-knowledge that he holds a valid credential and the credential is not listed in the blacklist. At the same time, Brickll and Li proposed Enhanced Privacy ID (EPID) [7]. EPID is similar in spirit to BLAC, but is specially designed to enable a TPM device. However, the amount of computation that the SP requires for authentication in the BLAC and EPID is linear in the size L of the blacklist ($O(L)$). This drawback makes them impractical in practice due to the growing size of the blacklist. After that, Au *et al.* (some of them are the authors of BLAC) proposed BLACR [5], which stands for BLAC with reputation. In BLACR, the SP can score each entry with a positive or negative score on the reputation list (*meritlist/blacklist*) along with a category identifier. A user can be allowed to access the SP only if their reputation (or score) of each category is above a certain level. BLACR also implements the concept of 'express lane authentication' to improve performance. The original one can be called as 'normal lane authentication'. However, this improvement disables BLACR's ability to unblacklist forgiven misbehaviors since removing entries invalidates the reputation proofs of the express lane tokens. The 'normal lane authentication' does not have this problem because the user generates the reputation proof for the whole blacklist in the normal lane authentication, thus removing entries does not have an impact on the correctness of the reputation proof.

Tsang *et al.* also proposed a more practical TTP-Free scheme, PEREA [26], and Au *et al.* extended it in [3]. PEREA is an anonymous blacklisting scheme in which the time complexity of authentication at the SP is linearly independent of the size L of the blacklist. Instead, the amount of computation is linear in the size K of the *revocation window* ($K << L$). Nevertheless, a misbehaved user must be caught during his subsequent K ($5 \leq K \leq 15$) authentications, or he will escape from punishment. Vulnerability of the non-membership proof scheme in [17] has been presented by [23], which in turn breaks the security of PEREA. Another problem of PEREA is that the "naughtiness" extension can only capture the most recent K sessions. Yu *et al.* added a built-in positive reputation system and proposed $PE(AR)^2$ to fix these problems in [29]. However, a new vulnerability arises that a user may redeem again the score of a ticket that has been redeemed by another user if his initial set of tickets includes this ticket. Concurrently Au *et al.* did an excellent job to extend PEREA with memory called PERM [6] and solved these problems too, except the misbehavior must be scored within a revocation window (users are not willing to voluntarily upgrade negative reputation outside of this window). PERM takes a more efficient authentication at the user side than PEREA and $PE(AR)^2$.

Other practical schemes to eliminate TTPs include FAUST [20], which is based on Chaum's blind signature scheme [9]. FAUST alleviates the computation problem, but offers an even more limited form of reputation than PEREA. Recently, Henry and Goldberg [16] presented BLACRONYM to improve the performance of BLAC and its variants by incorporating novel batch zero-knowledge proof and verification techniques. However, these techniques can not deal with the "weighted" version of BLACR.

Problems with BLACR and Our Contribution. The major drawback of BLACR is that it has the same linear dependence of BLAC. BLACR improves the performance via express lane authentication, but *unblacklisting* will not working because *unblacklisting* invalidates the reputation proofs of the express lane tokens. For the purpose of supporting *unblacklisting* while enabling the express lane authentication, we propose ExBLACR that is directly built from BLACR. Two difficulties must be solved: (1) When some entries are removed from the a *meritlist/blacklist*, the "express lane tokens" must still be usable. (2) After removing the entries from a *meritlist/blacklist*, the weighted scores must be adjusted correctly. In our paper, ExBLACR fixes these difficulties by introducing an *demeritlist/unblacklist U* corresponding to a *meritlist/blacklist L*. Entries removed from L are added in the U and a new protocol is presented to adjust weighted scores. The time complexity of our scheme remains the same order of magnitude as BLACR except the constant factor is a little higher.

Another problem of BLACR is that the express lane tokens can be reused (replay attack). Consider the following attack scenario: in time period T_i, a user gets an express lane token tk_i. After j time periods, that is, in time period T_{i+j}, the user gets a new token tk_{i+j}. Assume that during the time $T_{i+j} - T_i$, the user achieves sufficient punishment while not have been revoked. At some point of time period T_{i+j+1}, the user wants to authenticate using tk_{i+j} in the express lane, but he/she finds that he/she cannot satisfy the policy. Thanks to the vulnerability of the express lane tokens, which do not consist of any labels to distinguish different time periods, the user can use the token tk_i at this point of the time period T_{i+j+1} to escape from the punishment during the time $T_{i+j} - T_i$. The solution to resist this attack is to append a timestamp for every signature of tokens.

2   Preliminaries

Zero Knowledge Proofs of Knowledge (ZKPoK). In a ZKPoK protocol, a prover convinces to a verifier that some statement is true while the verifier learns nothing except the validity of the statement. We use the standard notation

$SPK\{(x) : y = g^x\}(M)$ due to Camenisch and Stadler [8] to denote a proof knowledge of x where $y = g^x$, where M is a random challenge (message) to be signed.

Commitment Scheme. We use the commitment scheme proposed by Pedersen [22]. The commitment scheme is a triplet of algorithms $(\mathcal{S}, \mathcal{T}, \mathcal{R})$:

- $\mathcal{T}$: on input 1^k, outputs a common reference string $crs = (q, g, h)$, where q is prime order of a cyclic group $\mathbb{G}$ and g, h is the independent generators of $\mathbb{G}$.
- $\mathcal{S}$: on input crs and $x \in \mathbb{Z}_q$, choses a random value $r \in \mathbb{Z}_q$ and outputs a commitment $CMT(x) = g^x h^r$ in commit phase, then outputs (r, x) in reveal phase.
- $\mathcal{R}$: on input $crs, CMT(x)$ and (r, x), outputs accept if $CMT(x) = g^x h^r$.

BBS+ Signature. We employ the signature scheme proposed by Au *et al.* [2]. Let $(\mathbb{G}_1, \mathbb{G}_2)$ be a pair of groups of prime order q and $\hat{e}$ be a pairing defined over $(\mathbb{G}_1, \mathbb{G}_2)$. Let $g, g_0, g_1, ..., g_k, g_{k+1}$ be generators of $\mathbb{G}_1$ and h be a generator of $\mathbb{G}_2$ such that $g = \psi(h)$, where ψ is a computable isomorphism. The BBS+ signature scheme can be demonstrated as follow:

- KeyGen. Randomly chooses $\gamma \in \mathbb{Z}_q$ and computes $w = h^\gamma$, outputs the public key w.
- Sign. On input messages $(m_0, m_1, ..., m_k)$, chooses $e, y \in_R \mathbb{Z}_q$, computes $A = (g g_0^{m_0} g_1^{m_1} \cdots g_k^{m_k} g_{k+1}^y)^{\frac{1}{e+\gamma}}$ and outputs (A, e, y) as the signature on message $(m_0, m_1, ..., m_k)$.
- Verify. To verify the signature (A, e, y), checks if $\hat{e}(A, wh^e) = \hat{e}(g g_0^{m_0} g_1^{m_1} \cdots g_k^{m_k} g_{k+1}^y, h)$.

3 Review of BLACR

In this session, we review the construction of BLACR in brief. We recommend the readers to obtain more details of BLACR in [4,5], such as the definition of policy, the ∂-Approach and the details of some useful protocols.

3.1 Protocols Used in BLACR

Protocol $\mathfrak{G}_{Iss}(C_0, C_1, ..., C_k)$: allows a user to obtain a credential BBS+ signature $\sigma = (A, e, y)$ from the signer on values $(m_0, m_1, ..., m_k)$ committed in $(C_0, C_1, ..., C_k)$.

Protocol $\mathfrak{G}_{Sig}(C_0, C_1, ..., C_k)$: allows a prover to convince a verifier that he knows a credential signature $\sigma = (A, e, y)$ on messages $(m_0, m_1, ..., m_k)$ committed in $(C_0, C_1, ..., C_k)$.

Protocol $\mathfrak{G}_x(C_x, t, g)$: allows a prover to assure the verifier the value $log_g t$ is committed in $C_x = CMT(x)$.

Protocol $\mathfrak{G}_{WS-Adj}(C_x, C_s, C_n, C_c/\perp, \mathcal{L}, \mathcal{D})$: allows a user to convince any verifier that the value s committed in C_s is the weighted score of the user with secret value x committed in C_x with respect to the list $\mathcal{L}$, a set of adjusting factor $\mathcal{D}$, given a value $n = Cnt(\mathcal{L}, x)$ committed in C_n, where $Cnt(\mathcal{L}, x) = |\{\tau : (\tau, \cdot) \in \mathcal{L}\}|$ is the number of times this user has been put on $\mathcal{L}$ and τ stands for a ticket this user used in the authentication.

Protocol $\mathfrak{G}_{Pol}(Pol, C_1, C_2, ..., C_m)$: allows a prover to convince a verifier the set of reputation values committed in $(C_1, C_2, ..., C_m)$ would satisfy the authentication policy $Pol : \bigvee_{j=1}^{z}(\bigwedge_{i=1}^{m}(\neg)\mathcal{P}_{ji})$, where $\mathcal{P}_{ji}$ has the form (c_i, n_{ji}) which requires the authenticating user to have a reputation equal or higher than a threshold n_{ji} in category c_i.

3.2   Initialization

1. Let q $(|q| = \lambda)$ be a prime order of groups $\mathbb{G}, \mathbb{G}_1, \mathbb{G}_2$ and $\mathbb{G}_T$. Let $\hat{e} : \mathbb{G}_1 \times \mathbb{G}_2 = \mathbb{G}_T$ be a bilinear pairing and $\psi : \mathbb{G}_2 \to \mathbb{G}_1$ be an efficiently computable isomorphism. Let $g_0, g_1, g_2 \in \mathbb{G}_1$ and $h_0 \in \mathbb{G}_2$ be the generators of $\mathbb{G}_1$ and $\mathbb{G}_2$ respectively such that $g_0 = \psi(h_0)$. Let $H_0 : \{0,1\}^* \to \mathbb{G}$ be a collision-resistant hash function.

2. GM generates BBS+ signature key pair $(gsk, gpk) = (\gamma \in_R \mathbb{Z}_q, w = h_0^\gamma)$ for issuing credentials.

3. Let m be number of categories and sid be the unique identity of SP. Each SP publishes a set of generators $g_{sid}, g_{sid,0}, g_{sid,1}, ..., g_{sid,m}, g_{sid,m+1} \in \mathbb{G}_1$, $h_{sid} \in \mathbb{G}_2$ such that $g_{sid} = \psi(h_{sid})$ and generates a key pair $(gsk_{sid}, gpk_{sid}) = (\gamma_{sid} \in_R \mathbb{Z}_q, w_{sid} = h_{sid}^{\gamma_{sid}})$ for issuing the express lane tokens. SP initializes a meritlist $\mathcal{L}_i^+$ and blacklist $\mathcal{L}_i^-$ for each category c_i, as well as the set of adjusting factors $\mathcal{D}_i^+$ and $\mathcal{D}_i^-$ for each category c_i.

3.3   Registration

A user picks a secret key x and computes the commitment $C_x = CMT(x)$. Then the user get a credential signature (A, e, y) on x via executing protocol $\mathfrak{G}_{Iss}(C_x)$ with GM. The user stores the credential (A, e, x, y).

3.4   Authentication

In the authentication phase, the user must convince to a SP in zero-knowledge that he holds the following two properties.

Property 1. The user in possess of a secret value x holds a valid credential (A, e, x, y) and the ticket τ is formed by $(b, H_0(b||sid)^x)$, where $b \in_R \{0,1\}^\lambda$.

Property 2. The user computes m categories of reputation values correctly and the authentication policy Pol evaluates to 1 with respect to these reputation values.

Let tp be the current time period and $s_i^\diamond$ be the weighted score of the user with respect to $\mathcal{L}_i^\diamond$ in category c_i, where $\diamond \in \{+, -\}$. The authentication phase (both **Normal Lane Authentication** and **Express Lane Authentication**) can be summarised in high level as follow.

1. The SP sends to user the lists for each category, the adjusting factors, a random challenge M and the policy *Pol*.
2. The user computes the reputation $R_i = s_i^+ - s_i^-$ for each catogory and checks if it satisfies the policy *Pol*. If not, the user returns as failure.
3. If the user is not revoked, he/she generates a zero-knowledge proof Π to convince SP that **Property 1** and **Property 2** are satisfied. Then the user sends the Π to SP, together with other parameters, including the ticket τ.
4. On receiving the proof Π, SP checks this proof. If the proof Π is a valid proof, the SP outputs *success*. Then the user will obtain an express pass tk_{tp} with the assistance of SP for the express-lane authentication.

3.5   List Management

The *blacklisting* operation $Add(\mathcal{L}, (\tau, s))$ adds tuple (τ, s) to *meritlist/blacklist* $\mathcal{L}$. There is not *unblacklisting* operation due to the express lane authentication.

4   A Extended Scheme: ExBLACR

4.1   Category

The category method in ExBLACR is a bit different from BLACR. In BLACR, SP employs different scoring schemes in each category. But in ExBLACR, SP employs the same scoring scheme in each category and gives each category a base score. For examples, in BLACR, the SP can use different scoring schemes in the category of *comments* (e.g., vulgar language: -2, defamation: -5 and racism: -10). Instead, in ExBLACR, the SP can use three categories, each of which corresponds with a scoring scheme (category of *vulgar language comments*: -2, category of *defamation comments*: -5 and category of *racism comments*: -10).

4.2   Our Improvement to BLACR

Basic Ideal of *Unblacklisting*. To support *unblacklisting*, ExBLACR additionally introduces a *demeritlist* $\mathcal{U}_i^+$ and *unblacklist* $\mathcal{U}_i^-$ corresponding to a *meritlist* $\mathcal{L}_i^+$ and *blacklist* $\mathcal{L}_i^-$ respectively for each category c_i. An entry in the $\mathcal{L}_i^\diamond$ that has to be demeritlisted/unblacklisted will be added (copied) to $\mathcal{U}_i^\diamond$, where $\diamond \in \{+, -\}$. The weighted score s_i of a user in category c_i would be adjusted like this: subtracting the "most severity" score. For instance, let s_{c_i} be the base score of category c_i and $\mathcal{D}_i = \{\Delta_1 = 1, \Delta_2 = 2, ..., \Delta_k = k\}$ be the adjusting factors. Without loss of generality, we assume the entries in the blacklist only belong to this user in this example. Suppose a blacklist $\mathcal{L}_i^-$ of category c_i

is $\{(\tau_1, s_{c_i}), (\tau_2, s_{c_i}), (\tau_3, s_{c_i}), (\tau_4, s_{c_i}), (\tau_5, s_{c_i})\}$, then $n = |\mathcal{L}_i^-| = 5$ and $s_i = 1 \times s_{c_i} + 2 \times s_{c_i} + 3 \times s_{c_i} + 4 \times s_{c_i} + 5 \times s_{c_i}$. In principle, after a entry (τ_3, s_{c_i}) has been unblacklisted, the remaining entries would be $\{(\tau_1, s_{c_i}), (\tau_2, s_{c_i}), (\tau_4, s_{c_i}), (\tau_5, s_{c_i})\}$. And value s_i is equal to $1 \times s_{c_i} + 2 \times s_{c_i} + 3 \times s_{c_i} + 4 \times s_{c_i}$, in which the "most severity" score is gone. However, BLACR cannot directly remove the entries from $\mathcal{L}_i^-$ since it will invalidate the express lane authentication. Therefore, we take an equivalent way in ExBLACR. When the enty (τ_3, s_{c_i}) has to been unblacklisted, SP adds it into the *unblacklist* $\mathcal{U}_i^-$ while $\mathcal{L}_i^-$ remain unchanged. Then $\mathcal{U}_i^- = \{(\tau_3, s_{c_i})\}$ and $l = |\mathcal{U}_i^-| = 1$. The weighted score s_i can be computed as $\sum_{j=1}^{n} \Delta_j s_{c_i} - \sum_{j=n-l+1}^{n} \Delta_j s_{c_i} = 1 \times s_{c_i} + 2 \times s_{c_i} + 3 \times s_{c_i} + 4 \times s_{c_i}$, which is equal to the original one. The following protocol implements this functionality.

Protocol. $\mathfrak{G}'_{WS-Adj}(C_x, C_s, C_n, C_l, C_c, C_d, \mathcal{L}, \mathcal{U}, \mathcal{D})$: List $\mathcal{L}$ and $\mathcal{D}$ may be the sub-sequence of any longer list $\mathcal{L}_i = \mathcal{L}_{i-1} + \mathcal{L}$ and $\mathcal{U}_i = \mathcal{U}_{i-1} + \mathcal{U}$. Value s is the weighted score of a user with a secret value x with respect to the sub-sequence $\mathcal{L}$ and $\mathcal{U}$. We mark the values $n = Cnt(\mathcal{L}_{i-1}, x)$, $l = Cnt(\mathcal{U}_{i-1}, x)$, $c = Cnt(\mathcal{L}, x)$ and $d = Cnt(\mathcal{U}, x)$. The adjusting factors $\mathcal{D}$ can be parsed as $(i, \Delta_i, \sigma_i)_{i=1}^{D}$.

Protocal $\mathfrak{G}'_{WS-Adj}$ allows a user to convince any verifier that the value s committed in C_s is the weight score of the user with secret value x committed in C_x with respect to the list $\mathcal{L}$ and $\mathcal{U}$, the set of adjusting factors $\mathcal{D}$, and the value n, l, c and d committed in C_n, C_l, C_c and C_d respectively.

1. The prover picks additional inputs $x, r_x, s, r_s, n, r_n, l, r_l, c, r_c, d, r_d$ such that $C_x = g_1^x g_2^{r_x}, C_s = g_1^s g_2^{r_s}, C_n = g_1^n g_2^{r_n}, C_l = g_1^l g_2^{r_l}, C_c = g_1^c g_2^{r_c}, C_d = g_1^d g_2^{r_d}$. let

$$\mathcal{I}: \{i | (b_i, t_i, s_i) \in \mathcal{L}, \widehat{b}_i^x = t_i\}, \quad \mathcal{J}: \{j | (b_j, t_j, s_j) \in \mathcal{U}, \widehat{b}_j^x = t_j\},$$

where $\widehat{b}_i = H_0(b_i \| sid)$. For all $i \in \mathcal{I}$, let

$$k_i = |\{j : 1 \le j \le i \wedge t_j = \widehat{b}_j^x\}| + (n - l).$$

For all $j \in \mathcal{J}$, let

$$\ell_j = |\{i : 1 \le i \le j \wedge t_i = \widehat{b}_i^x\}| + (n + c) - (l + d).$$

2. The prover produces two auxiliary commitments: $aux_1(C_1^s, C_1^n, ..., C_L^s, C_L^n)$ for each score on the list $\mathcal{L}$ and $aux_2(C_1^{s'}, C_1^l, ..., C_L^{s'}, C_U^l)$ for each score on the list $\mathcal{U}$. Let $s_{\mathcal{L}}, s_{\mathcal{U}}$ be the base score of $\mathcal{L}, \mathcal{U}$ respectively (Therefore, $s_{\mathcal{L}} = s_{\mathcal{U}}$). He randomly generates $a_i, b_i \in_R \mathbb{Z}_p$ for $1 \le i \le L$ and $f_j, h_j \in_R \mathbb{Z}_p$ for $1 \le j \le U$, then computes:

$$(C_i^s, C_i^n) = \begin{cases} (g_1^{\Delta_{k_i} s_{\mathcal{L}}} g_2^{a_i}, g_1 g_2^{b_i}) & \text{for } i \in \mathcal{I} \\ (g_2^{a_i}, g_2^{b_i}) & \text{for } i \in [L] \backslash \mathcal{I} \end{cases}$$

$$(C_j^{s'}, C_j^l) = \begin{cases} (g_1^{\Delta_{\ell_j} s_{\mathcal{U}}} g_2^{f_j}, g_1 g_2^{h_j}) & \text{for } j \in \mathcal{J} \\ (g_2^{f_j}, g_2^{h_j}) & \text{for } j \in [U] \backslash \mathcal{J} \end{cases}$$

3. Let M be the random challenge. The prover generates a proof Π_1 to demonstrate the correctness of aux_1 (here $\beta_\imath = \sum_{j=1}^{\imath} b_j + r_n - r_l$).

$$\Pi_1 = SPK\left\{\begin{matrix}(x, r_x, \{\sigma_{k_\imath}, \Delta_{k_\imath}, k_\imath, \beta_\imath, a_\imath, b_\imath\}_{\imath=1}^{L}):\\\left(\left(\begin{matrix}C_x = g_1^x g_2^{r_x} \wedge\\ t_\imath \neq \widehat{b}_\imath^x \wedge\\ C_\imath^s = g_2^{a_\imath} \wedge\\ C_\imath^n = g_2^{b_\imath}\end{matrix}\right) \vee \left(\begin{matrix}C_x = g_1^x g_2^{r_x} \wedge\\ t_\imath = \widehat{b}_\imath^x \wedge\\ C_\imath^n = g_1 g_2^{b_\imath} \wedge\\ \frac{C_n}{C_l} \cdot \prod_{j=1}^{\imath} C_j^n = g_1^{k_\imath} g_2^{\beta_\imath} \wedge\\ 1 = \mathtt{Verify}(\sigma_{k_\imath}, k_\imath, \Delta_{k_\imath}) \wedge\\ C_\imath^s = g_1^{\Delta_{k_\imath} s_\imath} g_2^{a_\imath}\end{matrix}\right)\right)^L\\ _{\imath=1}\end{matrix}\right\}\quad(M)$$

4. The prover generates a proof Π_2 to demonstrate the correctness of aux_2 (here $\gamma_\jmath = \sum_{i=1}^{\jmath} h_i + r_n - r_l + r_c - r_d$).

$$\Pi_2 = SPK\left\{\begin{matrix}(x, r_x, \{\sigma_{\ell_\jmath}, \Delta_{l_\jmath}, l_\jmath, \gamma_\jmath, f_\jmath, h_\jmath\}_{\jmath=1}^{U}):\\\left(\left(\begin{matrix}C_x = g_1^x g_2^{r_x} \wedge\\ t_\jmath \neq \widehat{b}_\jmath^x \wedge\\ C_\jmath^{s'} = g_2^{f_\jmath} \wedge\\ C_\jmath^l = g_2^{h_\jmath}\end{matrix}\right) \vee \left(\begin{matrix}C_x = g_1^x g_2^{r_x} \wedge\\ t_\jmath = \widehat{b}_\jmath^x \wedge\\ C_\jmath^l = g_1 g_2^{h_\jmath} \wedge\\ \frac{C_n C_c}{C_l C_d} \cdot \prod_{i=1}^{\jmath} C_i^l = g_1^{\ell_\jmath} g_2^{\gamma_\jmath} \wedge\\ 1 = \mathtt{Verify}(\sigma_{\ell_\jmath}, \ell_\jmath, \Delta_{\ell_\jmath}) \wedge\\ C_\jmath^{s'} = g_1^{\Delta_{\ell_\jmath} s_\jmath} g_2^{f_\jmath}\end{matrix}\right)\right)^U\\ _{\jmath=1}\end{matrix}\right\}\quad(M)$$

5. The prover computes

$$C_s' = \prod_{i=1}^{L} C_i^s - \prod_{j=1}^{U} C_j^{s'}, \quad r_s' = \sum_{i=1}^{L} a_i - \sum_{j=1}^{U} f_j,$$

$$C_c' = \prod_{i=1}^{L} C_i^n, \quad r_c' = \sum_{i=1}^{L} b_i, \quad C_d' = \prod_{j=1}^{U} C_j^l, \quad r_d' = \sum_{j=1}^{U} h_j$$

and produces a proof Π_3 to demonstrate the correctness of C_s, C_c, C_d with respect to list $\mathcal{L}$ and $\mathcal{U}$.

$$\Pi_3 = SPK\left\{\begin{matrix}(s, r_s, r_s', c, r_c, r_c', d, r_d, r_d'):\\ C_s = g_1^s g_2^{r_s} \wedge C_s' = g_1^s g_2^{r_s'} \wedge\\ C_c = g_1^c g_2^{r_c} \wedge C_c' = g_1^c g_2^{r_c'} \wedge\\ C_d = g_1^d g_2^{r_d} \wedge C_d' = g_1^d g_2^{r_d'}\end{matrix}\right\}\quad(M)$$

6. The proof outputs $\mathfrak{P}_{\mathtt{WS-Adj}}$ as $(\Pi_1, \Pi_2, \Pi_3, aux_1, aux_2)$ and sends $(\mathfrak{P}_{\mathtt{WS-Adj}}, M)$ to the verifier.
7. The verifier outputs *accept* if Π_1, Π_2 and Π_3 are both valid proofs.

Token Revise. In BLACR, the express lane token can be expressed as $tk_{tp} = (\sigma_x, s_{1,tp}^+, n_{1,tp}^+, s_{1,tp}^-, n_{1,tp}^-, ..., s_{m,tp}^+, n_{m,tp}^+, s_{m,tp}^-, n_{m,tp}^-)$ in the time period

tp, where $\sigma_x \leftarrow \mathfrak{G}_{Iss}(C_x, C_{1,tp}^{s^+}, C_{1,tp}^{n^+}, C_{1,tp}^{s^-}, C_{1,tp}^{n^-}, ..., C_{m,tp}^{s^+}, C_{m,tp}^{n^+}, C_{m,tp}^{s^-}, C_{m,tp}^{n^-})$.
As we mentioned in the beginning, the signature σ_x can be verified successfully in any time periods using protocol $\mathfrak{G}_{Sig}$, which results in replay attack in some time period later. We revise the token as $tk_{tp} = (\sigma_x, tp + 1, s_{1,tp}^+, n_{1,tp}^+, s_{1,tp}^-, n_{1,tp}^-, ..., s_{m,tp}^+, n_{m,tp}^+, s_{m,tp}^-, n_{m,tp}^-)$, where $\sigma_x \leftarrow \mathfrak{G}_{Iss}(C_{tp+1}, C_x, C_{1,tp}^{s^+}, C_{1,tp}^{n^+}, C_{1,tp}^{s^-}, C_{1,tp}^{n^-}, ..., C_{m,tp}^{s^+}, C_{m,tp}^{n^+}, C_{m,tp}^{s^-}, C_{m,tp}^{n^-})$, in which $C_{tp+1} = CMT(tp + 1)$. Then the token tk_{tp} has to be used in the time period $tp + 1$ since in any other time periods the signature σ_x cannot be verified successfully.

4.3 Our Construction

The construction process is similar to BLACR [5], we detail the ExBLACR in the difference with BLACR. We focus on the lists' initialization and management, the normal lane authentication and express lane authentication. The readers can also achieve the processes of initialization and registration in section 3.

SP Initialization. Because we revised the express lane token via adding a timestamp tp, SP must additionally initial a generator $g_{tp,sid} \in \mathbb{G}_1$ for issuing a signature by protocol $\mathfrak{G}_{Iss}$.

List Initialization. Additionally, ExBLACR initials a *demeritlist* $\mathcal{U}_i^+$ and a *unblacklist* $\mathcal{U}_i^-$ for each category c_i more than a *meritlist* $\mathcal{L}_i^+$ and a *blacklist* $\mathcal{L}_i^-$.

Authentication. Similar to BLACR, the time is divided into time periods in ExBLACR. Let tp be the current time period and $\mathcal{L}_i^\diamond$, $\mathcal{U}_i^\diamond$ be the current lists of category c_i. The list $\mathcal{L}_i^\diamond$ can be parsed as $\mathcal{L}_{i,tp}^\diamond \cup \partial_{i,tp}^{\diamond,*}$, where $\mathcal{L}_{i,tp}^\diamond$ is the list up to the beginning of time period tp (or the end of time period $tp-1$), $\partial_{i,tp}^{\diamond,*}$ is the set of new entries between the beginning of time period tp and the time when the user is authenticating in the time period tp. $\mathcal{L}_{i,tp}^\diamond$ can be further parsed as $\mathcal{L}_{i,tp-1}^\diamond \cup \partial_{i,tp-1}^\diamond$, where $\partial_{i,tp-1}^\diamond$ is the set of entries during the time period $tp-1$. Similar to the list $\mathcal{L}_i^\diamond$, the list $\mathcal{U}_i^\diamond$ can be parsed as $\mathcal{U}_{i,tp}^\diamond \cup \eth_{i,tp}^{\diamond,*}$ and further $\mathcal{U}_{i,tp}^\diamond = \mathcal{U}_{i,tp-1}^\diamond \cup \eth_{i,tp-1}^\diamond$. A user who has authenticated in the time period $tp-1$ will get an express lane token tk_{tp-1} with respect to the list $\mathcal{L}_{i,tp-1}^\diamond$ and $\mathcal{U}_{i,tp-1}^\diamond$. When the user authenticates in the time period tp, he/she can use the tk_{tp-1} and execute protocol $\mathfrak{G}_{WS-Adj}'$ with respect to $\partial_{i,tp-1}^\diamond \cup \partial_{i,tp}^{\diamond,*}$ and $\eth_{i,tp-1}^\diamond \cup \eth_{i,tp}^{\diamond,*}$ in express lane authentication. Otherwise, if the user has not been in possession of a token tk_{tp-1}, he/she must execute protocol $\mathfrak{G}_{WS-Adj}'$ with respect to $\mathcal{L}_{i,tp}^\diamond \cup \partial_{i,tp}^\diamond$ and $\mathcal{U}_{i,tp}^\diamond \cup \eth_{i,tp}^{\diamond,*}$ in normal lane authentication. In the end of both authentication, the user will achieve a new express lane token tk_{tp} with respect to the list $\mathcal{L}_{i,tp}^\diamond$. The normal lane authentication and express lane authentication are described in the following.

Normal Lane Authentication. The user parses each list as $\mathcal{L}_i^\diamond = \mathcal{L}_{i,tp}^\diamond \cup \partial_{i,tp}^{\diamond,*}$, $\mathcal{U}_i^\diamond = \mathcal{U}_{i,tp}^\diamond \cup \eth_{i,tp}^{\diamond,*}$ and the weighted score as $s_i^\diamond = s_{i,tp}^\diamond + s_{i,\partial_{tp}^*}^\diamond$, $s'_i^\diamond = s'_{i,tp}^\diamond + s'_{i,\eth_{tp}^*}^\diamond$, where $s_{i,tp}^\diamond, s_{i,\partial_{tp}^*}^\diamond, s'_{i,tp}^\diamond, s'_{i,\eth_{tp}^*}^\diamond$ is the weighted-score with respect to list $\mathcal{L}_{i,tp}^\diamond, \partial_{i,tp}^{\diamond,*}, \mathcal{U}_{i,tp}^\diamond, \eth_{i,tp}^{\diamond,*}$ respectively. Let $\bar{s}_{i,tp}^\diamond = s_{i,tp}^\diamond - s'_{i,tp}^\diamond$, $\bar{s}_{i,\partial_{tp}^* \backslash \eth_{tp}^*}^\diamond = s_{i,\partial_{tp}^*}^\diamond - s'_{i,\eth_{tp}^*}^\diamond$ and for $i = 1$ to m computes the commitments:

$$C_x = CMT(x), \quad C_{i,tp}^{\bar{s}^\diamond} = CMT(\bar{s}_{i,tp}^\diamond), \quad C_{i,\partial_{tp}^* \backslash \eth_{tp}^*}^{\bar{s}^\diamond} = CMT(\bar{s}_{i,\partial_{tp}^* \backslash \eth_{tp}^*}^\diamond)$$

$$C_{i,tp}^{n^\diamond} = CMT(n_{i,tp}^\diamond), \quad C_{i,tp}^{l^\diamond} = CMT(l_{i,tp}^\diamond),$$

$$C_{i,\partial_{tp}^*}^{n^\diamond} = CMT(n_{i,\partial_{tp}^*}^\diamond), \quad C_{i,\eth_{tp}^*}^{l^\diamond} = CMT(l_{i,\eth_{tp}^*}^\diamond)$$

where $n_{i,tp}^\diamond = Cnt(x, \mathcal{L}_{i,tp}^\diamond), l_{i,tp}^\diamond = Cnt(x, \mathcal{U}_{i,tp}^\diamond), n_{i,\partial_{tp}^*}^\diamond = Cnt(x, \partial_{i,tp}^{\diamond,*}), l_{i,\eth_{tp}^*}^\diamond = Cnt(x, \eth_{i,tp}^{\diamond,*})$. The user also picks a random value b and computes a ticket $\tau = (b, t = H_0(b||sid)^x)$. Then the user sends $(C_x, \{C_{i,tp}^{\bar{s}^\diamond}, C_{i,\partial_{tp}^* \backslash \eth_{tp}^*}^{\bar{s}^\diamond}, C_{i,tp}^{n^\diamond}, C_{i,tp}^{l^\diamond}, C_{i,\partial_{tp}^*}^{n^\diamond}, C_{i,\eth_{tp}^*}^{l^\diamond}\}_{i=1}^m, \tau)$, along with a proof Π to convince that two properties mentioned above are met. The proof Π is constructed as follows:

- **(Property 1)**
  - Execute protocol $\mathfrak{G}_{Sig}(C_x)$ to assure the SP that the user holds a valid credential (A, e, x, y).
  - Execute protocol $\mathfrak{G}_x(C_x, t, H_0(b||sid))$ to assure the SP that the second component of ticket is formed correctly.
- **(Property 2)**
  - For $i = 1$ to m, execute protocol $\mathfrak{G}'_{WS-Adj}(C_x, C_{i,tp}^{\bar{s}^\diamond}, 1, 1, C_{i,tp}^{n^\diamond}, C_{i,tp}^{l^\diamond}, \mathcal{L}_{i,tp}^\diamond, \mathcal{U}_{i,tp}^\diamond, \mathcal{D}_i^\diamond)$ to assure the SP that all $C_{i,tp}^{\bar{s}^\diamond}, C_{i,tp}^{n^\diamond}, C_{i,tp}^{l^\diamond}$ are correctly formed.
  - For $i = 1$ to m, execute protocol $\mathfrak{G}'_{WS-Adj}(C_x, C_{i,\partial_{tp}^* \backslash \eth_{tp}^*}^{\bar{s}^\diamond}, C_{i,tp}^{n^\diamond}, C_{i,tp}^{l^\diamond}, C_{i,\partial_{tp}^*}^{c^\diamond}, C_{i,\eth_{tp}^*}^{d^\diamond}, \partial_{i,tp}^{\diamond,*}, \eth_{i,tp}^{\diamond,*}, \mathcal{D}_i^\diamond)$ to assure the SP all $C_{i,\partial_{tp}^* \backslash \eth_{tp}^*}^{\bar{s}^\diamond}, C_{i,\partial_{tp}^*}^{c^\diamond}, C_{i,\eth_{tp}^*}^{d^\diamond}$ are correctly formed.
  - Given above, it can be proved that the reputation of each category committed in $C_i = \dfrac{C_{i,tp}^{\bar{s}^+} C_{i,\partial_{tp}^* \backslash \eth_{tp}^*}^{\bar{s}^+}}{C_{i,tp}^{\bar{s}^-} C_{i,\partial_{tp}^* \backslash \eth_{tp}^*}^{\bar{s}^-}}$ ($1 \leq i \leq m$) is computed correctly.
  - Execute protocol $\mathfrak{G}_{Pol}(C_1, C_2, ..., C_m)$ to ensure the SP the Pol evaluates to 1 with respect to m categories of reputation values committed in $(C_1, C_2, ..., C_m)$.

If the proof Π is a valid proof, the SP issues a signature σ_x on values $(tp+1, x, \bar{s}_{1,tp}^+, n_{1,tp}^+, l_{1,tp}^+, \bar{s}_{1,tp}^-, n_{1,tp}^-, l_{1,tp}^-, ..., \bar{s}_{m,tp}^+, n_{m,tp}^+, l_{m,tp}^+, \bar{s}_{m,tp}^-, n_{m,tp}^-, l_{m,tp}^-)$ by executing protocol $\mathfrak{G}_{Iss}(C_{tp+1}, C_x, C_{1,tp}^{\bar{s}^+}, C_{1,tp}^{n^+}, C_{1,tp}^{l^+}, C_{1,tp}^{\bar{s}^-}, C_{1,tp}^{n^-}, C_{1,tp}^{l^-}, ..., C_{m,tp}^{\bar{s}^+}, C_{m,tp}^{n^+}, C_{m,tp}^{l^+}, C_{m,tp}^{\bar{s}^-}, C_{m,tp}^{n^-}, C_{m,tp}^{l^-})$ with the user. The user stores $(\sigma_x, tp+1, \bar{s}_{1,tp}^+, n_{1,tp}^+, l_{1,tp}^+, \bar{s}_{1,tp}^-, n_{1,tp}^-, l_{1,tp}^-, ..., \bar{s}_{m,tp}^+, n_{m,tp}^+, l_{m,tp}^+, \bar{s}_{m,tp}^-, n_{m,tp}^-, l_{m,tp}^-)$ as her express pass tk_{pd}.

Express Lane Authentication. The user parses each list as $\mathcal{L}_i^\diamond = \mathcal{L}_{i,tp-1}^\diamond \cup \eth_{i,tp-1}^{\diamond} \cup \eth_{i,tp}^{\diamond,*}$, $\mathcal{U}_i^\diamond = \mathcal{U}_{i,tp-1}^\diamond \cup \eth_{i,tp-1}^{\diamond} \cup \eth_{i,tp}^{\diamond,*}$ and the weighted score as $s_i^\diamond = s_{i,tp-1}^\diamond + s_{i,\eth_{tp-1}}^\diamond + s_{i,\eth_{tp}^*}^\diamond$, $s'_i^\diamond = s'_{i,tp-1}^\diamond + s'_{i,\eth_{tp-1}}^\diamond + s'_{i,\eth_{tp}^*}^\diamond$ respectively. Let $\bar{s}_{i,tp-1}^\diamond = s_{i,tp-1}^\diamond - s'_{i,tp-1}^\diamond$, $\bar{s}_{i,\eth_{tp-1}\backslash\eth_{tp-1}}^\diamond = s_{i,\eth_{tp-1}}^\diamond - s'_{i,\eth_{tp-1}}^\diamond$ and $\bar{s}_{i,\eth_{tp}^*\backslash\eth_{tp}^*}^\diamond = s_{i,\eth_{tp}^*}^\diamond - s'_{i,\eth_{tp}^*}^\diamond$. Let $\mathcal{L}_{i,tp}^\diamond = \mathcal{L}_{i,tp-1}^\diamond \cup \eth_{i,tp-1}^{\diamond}$ and $\mathcal{U}_{i,tp}^\diamond = \mathcal{U}_{i,tp-1}^\diamond \cup \eth_{i,tp-1}^{\diamond}$. For $i = 1$ to m, the user computes the commitments:

$$C_x = CMT(x), \quad C_{i,tp-1}^{\bar{s}^\diamond} = CMT(\bar{s}_{i,tp-1}^\diamond),$$

$$C_{i,\eth_{tp-1}\backslash\eth_{tp-1}}^{\bar{s}^\diamond} = CMT(\bar{s}_{i,\eth_{tp-1}\backslash\eth_{tp-1}}^\diamond), \quad C_{i,\eth_{tp}^*\backslash\eth_{tp}^*}^{\bar{s}^\diamond} = CMT(\bar{s}_{i,\eth_{tp}^*\backslash\eth_{tp}^*}^\diamond),$$

$$C_{i,tp-1}^{n^\diamond} = CMT(n_{i,tp-1}^\diamond), \quad C_{i,tp-1}^{l^\diamond} = CMT(l_{i,tp-1}^\diamond),$$

$$C_{i,\eth tp-1}^{n^\diamond} = CMT(n_{i,\eth tp-1}^\diamond), \quad C_{i,\eth tp-1}^{l^\diamond} = CMT(l_{i,\eth tp-1}^\diamond),$$

$$C_{i,\eth_{tp}^*}^{n^\diamond} = CMT(n_{i,\eth_{tp}^*}^\diamond), \quad C_{i,\eth_{tp}^*}^{l^\diamond} = CMT(l_{i,\eth_{tp}^*}^\diamond)$$

where $n_{i,tp-1/\eth tp-1/\eth_{tp}^*}^\diamond = Cnt(x, \mathcal{L}_{i,tp-1}^\diamond/\eth_{i,tp-1}^{\diamond}/\eth_{i,tp}^{\diamond,*})$, $l_{i,tp-1/\eth tp-1/\eth_{tp}^*}^\diamond = Cnt(x, \mathcal{U}_{i,tp-1}^\diamond/\eth_{i,tp-1}^{\diamond}/\eth_{i,tp}^{\diamond,*})$. The user also picks a random value b and computes a ticket $\tau = (b, t = H_0(b\|sid)^x)$. Then the user sends $(C_x, \{C_{i,tp-1}^{\bar{s}^\diamond}, C_{i,\eth_{tp-1}\backslash\eth_{tp-1}}^{\bar{s}^\diamond}, C_{i,\eth_{tp}^*\backslash\eth_{tp}^*}^{\bar{s}^\diamond}, C_{i,tp-1}^{n^\diamond}, C_{i,tp-1}^{l^\diamond}, C_{i,\eth tp-1}^{n^\diamond}, C_{i,\eth tp-1}^{l^\diamond}, C_{i,\eth_{tp}^*}^{n^\diamond}, C_{i,\eth_{tp}^*}^{l^\diamond}\}_{i=1}^m, \tau)$, along with a proof Π to convince that two properties mentioned above are met. The proof Π is constructed as follows:

- (**Property 1**) The same as normal lane.
- (**Property 2**)
  - Execute protocol $\mathfrak{G}_{Sig}(C_{tp}, C_x, C_{1,tp-1}^{\bar{s}^+}, C_{1,tp-1}^{n^+}, C_{1,tp-1}^{l^+}, C_{1,tp-1}^{\bar{s}^-}, C_{1,tp-1}^{n^-},$ $C_{1,tp-1}^{l^-}, \ldots, C_{m,tp-1}^{\bar{s}^+}, C_{m,tp-1}^{n^+}, C_{m,tp-1}^{l^+}, C_{m,tp-1}^{\bar{s}^-}, C_{m,tp-1}^{n^-}, C_{m,tp-1}^{l^-})$ to assure SP that the user holds an express pass tk_{tp-1}, which in turns to convince that $C_{i,tp-1}^{\bar{s}^\diamond}, C_{i,tp-1}^{n^\diamond}, C_{i,tp-1}^{l^\diamond}$ for $1 \le i \le m$ are correctly formed.
  - For $i = 1$ to m, execute protocol $\mathfrak{G}'_{WS-Adj}(C_x, C_{i,\eth_{tp-1}\backslash\eth_{tp-1}}^{\bar{s}^\diamond}, C_{i,tp-1}^{n^\diamond},$ $C_{i,tp-1}^{l^\diamond}, C_{i,\eth_{tp-1}}^{n^\diamond}, C_{i,\eth_{tp-1}}^{l^\diamond}, \eth_{i,tp-1}^{\diamond}, \eth_{i,tp-1}^{\diamond}, \mathcal{D}_i^\diamond)$ to assure the SP all $C_{i,\eth_{tp-1}\backslash\eth_{tp-1}}^{\bar{s}^\diamond}, C_{i,\eth_{tp-1}}^{n^\diamond}, C_{i,\eth_{tp-1}}^{l^\diamond}$ are correctly formed.
  - Given above, it can be asserted that $C_{i,tp}^{n^\diamond} = C_{i,tp-1}^{n^\diamond} C_{i,\eth_{tp-1}}^{n^\diamond}$ and $C_{i,tp}^{l^\diamond} = C_{i,tp-1}^{l^\diamond} C_{i,\eth_{tp-1}}^{l^\diamond}$ are correctly computed and formed.
  - For $i = 1$ to m, execute protocol $\mathfrak{G}'_{WS-Adj}(C_x, C_{i,\eth_{tp}^*\backslash\eth_{tp}^*}^{\bar{s}^\diamond}, C_{i,tp}^{n^\diamond}, C_{i,tp}^{l^\diamond},$ $C_{i,\eth_{tp}^*}^{n^\diamond}, C_{i,\eth_{tp}^*}^{l^\diamond}, \eth_{i,tp}^{\diamond,*}, \eth_{i,tp}^{\diamond,*}, \mathcal{D}_i^\diamond)$ to assure the SP all $C_{i,\eth_{tp}^*\backslash\eth_{tp}^*}^{\bar{s}^\diamond}, C_{i,\eth_{tp}^*}^{n^\diamond}, C_{i,\eth_{tp}^*}^{l^\diamond}$ are correctly formed.
  - Given above all, it can be proved that the reputation of each category committed in $C_i = \dfrac{C_{i,tp-1}^{\bar{s}^+} C_{i,\eth_{tp-1}\backslash\eth_{tp-1}}^{\bar{s}^+} C_{i,\eth_{tp}^*\backslash\eth_{tp}^*}^{\bar{s}^+}}{C_{i,tp-1}^{\bar{s}^-} C_{i,\eth_{tp-1}\backslash\eth_{tp-1}}^{\bar{s}^-} C_{i,\eth_{tp}^*\backslash\eth_{tp}^*}^{\bar{s}^-}}$ $(1 \le i \le m)$ are computed correctly.

- Execute protocol $\mathfrak{G}_{Pol}(C_1, C_2, ..., C_m)$ to ensure the SP the *Pol* evaluates to 1 with respect to m categories of reputation values committed in $(C_1, C_2, ..., C_m)$.

Given $C_{i,tp}^{\bar{s}^\diamond} = C_{i,tp-1}^{\bar{s}^\diamond} C_{i,\partial_{tp-1}\backslash\eth_{tp-1}}^{\bar{s}^\diamond}$, the new express pass tk_{pd} can be computed as the normal lane authentication if the proof Π is a valid proof.

List Management. Additionally, we add an *unblacklisting* operation *Unblacklist*$(\mathcal{L}, (\tau, s), \mathcal{U})$, which appends a tuple $(\tau, s) \in$ *blacklist/meritlist* $\mathcal{L}$ to corresponding *unblacklist/demeritlist* $\mathcal{U}$.

4.4   Security Goals and Analysis

Security Goals. We informally define the security goals of ExBLACR. As described in [15], a violation of any one goal in the following may have a significant effect on user privacy or the ability to blacklist abusive users. In other words, if an anonymous blacklisting system holds all of the goals, then it satisfies the properties we desire.

1. *Correctness:* An honest SP will always accept any authentication from a non-revoked user, if the protocols are generated correctly.
2. *Revocability(Authenticity):* In the presence of dishonest SPs and users, a user can successfully authenticate to an honest SP only if the user satisfies the authentication policy. Otherwise, the user has been revoked.
3. *Revocation Auditability:* Prior to authentication, a user must have the ability to check her revocation status in the SP.
4. *Backward Anonymity:* An attacker, who has controlled GM and some dishonest SPs and users, cannot determine an honest user's identity of an authentication transaction.
5. *Unlinkability:* An attacker, who has controlled GM and some dishonest SPs and users, cannot link two distinct authentications belonging to an honest user.
6. *Non-frameability:* With overwhelming probability, an attacker with the ability of controlling the GM and some dishonest SPs and users, cannot prevent an honest user who satisfies the authentication policy from authenticating successfully to an honest SP.
7. *Mis-authentication Resistance:* With overwhelming probability, an unregistered user cannot successfully authenticate to an honest SP.

Note that the notions of *revocation auditability, backward anonymity, unlinkability* are also called as *anonymity* in BLACR [5].

Security Analysis. ExBLACR achieves these security goals as BLACR except for some addition. We describe the security analysis in the appendix A.

5   Evaluation

5.1   Complexity Analysis

Let K be the size of revocation window and Δ_L be the numbers of entries added to blacklist since previous authentication in PEREA/PERM. Let $|\mathcal{U}| = U$ and $L = |\mathcal{L}|$ in BLACR/ExBLACR.

As showed in Table 1, generating the proof takes $O(K\Delta_L)$ times for the user in PEREA-Naughtiness as each of K witnesses must be updated Δ_L times and takes $O(K)$ times in PERM as the transaction identifiers in K windows must be decided whether they have be judged. Verifying the proof in PEREA-Naughtiness/PERM for SP takes only $O(K)$ times. Comparing with BLACR, the computation complexity of ExBLACR-Normal/ExBLACR-Express is $O(L) + O(U)$ / $O(|\partial_{tp-1}|+|\partial_{tp}^*|)+O(|\eth_{tp-1}|+|\eth_{tp}^*|)$ respectively since the user additionally proves that if each of U / $|\partial_{tp-1}| + |\partial_{tp}^*|$ entries in $\mathcal{U}$ is belong to him/her or not. Similarly, the communication complexity of ExBLACR is increasing since the user must additionally downloads/uploads the list $\mathcal{U}$ or a portion of $\mathcal{U}$.

Note that it is reasonable to assume that very few of entries in the $\mathcal{L}$ should be unblacklisted (added to the $\mathcal{U} \in \mathcal{L}$), thus $U << L$. That is why we claim that the time complexity of ExBLACR remains same order of magnitude with BLACR except constant factor is a little higher in the beginning.

5.2   Efficiency Analysis

Compared with BLACR, the main factor to affect the efficiency of ExBLACR is that ExBLACR has to additionally prove whether the current ticket is a member of list $\mathcal{U}$. It seems that the efficiency of ExBLACR will be significantly affected if the size of list $\mathcal{U}$ is large. Objectively speaking, controversial behaviors, which is required to be unblacklisted, occupy a very small percentage in the blacklist. We think that five percent of the total is a reasonable proportion, which means the size of $\mathcal{U}$ is small enough that it can not have a significant impact to the efficiency. Based on this understanding, the efficiency of ExBLACR-Normal is close to the efficiency of BLACR-Normal.

The situation of ExBLACR-Express would be more complex since it may take place that $|\Delta_L| \leq |\Delta_U|$ in time period tp ($\Delta_L = \partial_{tp-1} \cup \partial_{tp}^*$, $\Delta_U = \eth_{tp-1} \cup \eth_{tp}^*$). Nonetheless, the amount of these situations occur in a whole execution are at

Table 1. Complexity analysis of authentication

Scheme	Communication		Computation	
	Downlink	Uplink	User(Prove)	SP(Verify)
PEREA-Naughtiness	$O(L)$	$O(K)$	$O(K\Delta_L)$	$O(K)$
PERM	$O(L)$	$O(K)$	$O(K)$	$O(K)$
BLACR-Normal	$O(L)$	$O(L)$	$O(L)$	$O(L)$
BLACR-Express	$O(|\partial_{tp}^*|)$	$O(|\partial_{tp-1}| + |\partial_{tp}^*|)$	$O(|\partial_{tp-1}| + |\partial_{tp}^*|)$	$O(|\partial_{tp-1}| + |\partial_{tp}^*|)$
ExBLACR-Normal	$O(L) + O(U)$	$O(L) + O(U)$	$O(L) + O(U)$	$O(L) + O(U)$
ExBLACR-Express	$O(|\partial_{tp}^*|) + O(|\eth_{tp}^*|)$	$O(|\partial_{tp-1}| + |\partial_{tp}^*|)+$ $O(|\eth_{tp-1}| + |\eth_{tp}^*|)$	$O(|\partial_{tp-1}| + |\partial_{tp}^*|)+$ $O(|\eth_{tp-1}| + |\eth_{tp}^*|)$	$O(|\partial_{tp-1}| + |\partial_{tp}^*|)+$ $O(|\eth_{tp-1}| + |\eth_{tp}^*|)$

most one or more due to the rarity of total entries in the $\mathcal{U}$. From a global perspective, the overall efficiency of the ExBLACR-Express is not significantly affected.

6   Conclusions

In this paper, we presented ExBLACR, which not only preserves the same anonymous authentication functionalities of BLACR but also extends the BLACR with the functionality of *unblacklisting* when BLACR employs express lane authentication. Furthermore, we found it would be under the threat of replay attack when users are permitted to use express lane token. We fixed this flaw by introducing a timestamp when the SP generates an authentication lane token. Additionally, we pointed out that compared with BLACR, the efficiency of ExBLACR is not significantly reduced in that the size of *unblacklist/demeritlist* $\mathcal{U}$ is much less than the size of *blacklist/meritlist* $\mathcal{L}$.

Acknowledgments. The research presented in this paper is supported by the National Grand Fundamental Research 973 Program of China under Grant No. 2013CB338003 and the National Natural Science Foundation of China under Grant Nos. 91118006, 61202414. We also thank the anonymous reviewers for their comments.

References

1. Abbott, R.S., van der Horst, T.W., Seamons, K.E.: CPG: Closed Pseudonymous Groups. In: Proceedings of WPES 2008, pp. 55–64. ACM (2008)
2. Au, M.H., Susilo, W., Mu, Y.: Constant-size dynamic k-TAA. In: De Prisco, R., Yung, M. (eds.) SCN 2006. LNCS, vol. 4116, pp. 111–125. Springer, Heidelberg (2006)
3. Au, M.H., Tsang, P.P., Kapadia, A.: PEREA: Practical TTP-free revocation of repeatedly misbehaving anonymous users. ACM Transactions on Information and System Security 14(4), 29 (2011)
4. Au, M.H., Tsang, P.P., Kapadia, A., Susilo, W.: BLACR: TTP-Free Blacklistable Anonymous Credentials with Reputation. Technical Report TR695, Indiana University Bloomington (2011)
5. Au, M.H., Kapadia, A., Susilo, W.: BLACR: TTP-free blacklistable anonymous credentials with reputation. In: Proceedings of NDSS 2012, ISOC (2012)
6. Au, M.H., Kapadia, A.: PERM: Practical reputation-based blacklisting without TTPs. In: Proceedings of CCS 2012, pp. 929–940. ACM (2012)
7. Brickell, E., Li, J.: Enhanced Privacy ID: A Direct Anonymous Attestation Scheme with Enhanced Revocation Capabilities. IEEE Transactions on Dependable and Secure Computing 9(3), 345–360 (2012)
8. Camenisch, J.L., Stadler, M.A.: Efficient group signature schemes for large groups (extended abstract). In: Kaliski Jr., B.S. (ed.) CRYPTO 1997. LNCS, vol. 1294, pp. 410–424. Springer, Heidelberg (1997)
9. Chaum, D.: Security Without Identification: Transaction Systems to Make Big Brother Obsolete. Communications of the ACM 28(10), 1030–1044 (1985)

10. Chaum, D., van Heyst, E.: Group Signatures. In: Davies, D.W. (ed.) EUROCRYPT 1991. LNCS, vol. 547, pp. 257–265. Springer, Heidelberg (1991)
11. Chen, L.: Access with Pseudonyms. In: Dawson, E.P., Golić, J.D. (eds.) Cryptography: Policy and Algorithms 1995. LNCS, vol. 1029, pp. 232–243. Springer, Heidelberg (1996)
12. Dingledine, R., Mathewson, N., Syverson, P.F.: Tor: The Second-Generation Onion Router. In: Proceedings of USENIX Security 2004, SSYM 2004, vol. 12, p. 21. USENIX (2004)
13. Holt, J.E., Seamons, K.E.: Nym: Practical Pseudonymity for Anonymous Networks. Internet Security Research Lab, BYU, Technical Report 2006-4 (2006)
14. Henry, R., Henry, K., Goldberg, I.: Making a Nymbler Nymble using VERBS. In: Atallah, M.J., Hopper, N.J. (eds.) PETS 2010. LNCS, vol. 6205, pp. 111–129. Springer, Heidelberg (2010)
15. Henry, R., Goldberg, I.: Formalizing anonymous blacklisting systems. In: Proceedings of IEEE S&P, pp. 81–95 (2011)
16. Henry, R., Goldberg, I.: Thinking Inside the BLAC Box: Smarter protocols Faster Anonymous Blacklisting. In: Proceedings of WPES 2013, pp. 71–82. ACM (2013)
17. Li, J., Li, N., Xue, R.: Universal Accumulators with Efficient Nonmembership Proofs. In: Katz, J., Yung, M. (eds.) ACNS 2007. LNCS, vol. 4521, pp. 253–269. Springer, Heidelberg (2007)
18. Lin, Z., Hopper, N.: Jack: Scalable Accumulator-based Nymble System. In: Proceedings of WPES 2010, pp. 53–62. ACM (2010)
19. Lofgren, P., Hopper, N.: BNymble: More Anonymous Blacklisting at Almost No Cost (A Short Paper). In: Danezis, G. (ed.) FC 2011. LNCS, vol. 7035, pp. 268–275. Springer, Heidelberg (2012)
20. Lofgren, P., Hopper, N.: FAUST: Efficient, TTP-Free Abuse Prevention by Anonymous Whitelisting. In: Proceedings of the Workshop on Privacy in the Electronic Society (WPES 2011), pp. 125–130. ACM (2011)
21. Lysyanskaya, A.: Pseudonym Systems, Master's thesis. Department of Electrical Engineering and Computer Science. MIT (1999)
22. Pedersen, T.P.: Non-interactive and information-theoretic secure verifiable secret sharing. In: Feigenbaum, J. (ed.) CRYPTO 1991. LNCS, vol. 576, pp. 129–140. Springer, Heidelberg (1992)
23. Peng, K., Bao, F.: Vulnerability of a Non-membership Proof Scheme. In: SECRYPT, pp. 419–422. SciTePress (2010)
24. Schwartz, E.J., Brumley, D., McCune, J.M.: A Contractual Anonymity System. In: Proceedings of NDSS 2010, ISOC (2010)
25. Tsang, P.P., Au, M.H., Kapadia, A., Smith, S.W.: Blacklistable Anonymous Credentials: Blocking Misbehaving Users Without TTPs. In: Proceedings of CCS 2007, pp. 72–81. ACM (2007)
26. Tsang, P.P., Au, M.H., Kapadia, A., Smith, S.W.: PEREA: Towards practical TTP-free revocation in anonymous authentication. In: Proceedings of CCS 2008, pp. 333–344. ACM (2008)
27. Tsang, P.P., Au, M.H., Kapadia, A., Smith, S.W.: BLAC: Revoking Repeatedly Misbehaving Anonymous Users without Relying on TTPs. ACM Transactions on Information and System Security (TISSEC) 13(4) (2010)
28. Tsang, P.P., Kapadia, A., Cornelius, C., Smith, S.W.: Nymble: Blocking Misbehaving Users in Anonymizing Networks. IEEE Transactions on Dependable and Secure Computing (TDSC) 8(2), 256–269 (2011)

29. Yu, K.Y., Yuen, T.H., Chow, S.S.M., Yiu, S.M., Hui, L.C.K.: PE(AR)^2: Privacy-Enhanced Anonymous Authentication with Reputation and Revocation. In: Foresti, S., Yung, M., Martinelli, F. (eds.) ESORICS 2012. LNCS, vol. 7459, pp. 679–696. Springer, Heidelberg (2012)

A   Security Analysis

We also use a simulation-based approach to analyze the security goals as [4,5]. We would not like to do the repetitive job in the [5] since we just added a functionality to enable *unblacklisting*. Thus, in the following we just demonstrate the necessary and additive part.

Let ε be the environment, $\mathcal{T}$ be a trusted party. Additively, we define a security model of *unblacklisting* as follow.

- *Unblacklist$(j, \mathcal{L}_i^\diamond, \mathcal{U}_i^\diamond)$.* ε instructs the SP j to alter the list $\mathcal{U}_i^\diamond$ with the tickets from the corresponding *blacklist/meritlist* $\mathcal{L}_i^\diamond$.
    - *Real world.* SP j adds the tickets that will be unblacklisted in the $\mathcal{L}_i^\diamond$ to the corresponding *unblacklist/demeritlist* $\mathcal{U}_i^\diamond$.
    - *Ideal world.* SP j sends the request to $\mathcal{T}$, who checks if the unblacklisted ticket is in the list $\mathcal{L}_i^\diamond$ and replies the result of the check. According to the result, SP j adds the ticket to $\mathcal{U}_i^\diamond$ or reject.

Specifically, ExBLACR is secure if for any real world adversary $\mathcal{A}$ and environment ε, there exists an ideal world simulator $\mathcal{S}$ who has blackbox access to $\mathcal{A}$, such that ε cannot distinguish the situation that it is running in the real world interacting with $\mathcal{A}$ from the situation that it is running in the ideal world interacting with $\mathcal{S}$.

The construction of the ideal world simulator $\mathcal{S}$ is also same as [5], together with additionally simulating the unblacklisting. Whether the GM is honest or not, $\mathcal{S}$ can simulate the unblacklisting as follow.

- *Unblacklist$(j, \mathcal{L}_i^\diamond, \mathcal{U}_i^\diamond)$.*
    - *Representing honest SP.* $\mathcal{S}$ checks if the unblacklisted ticket $\tau \in \mathcal{L}_i^\diamond$ and adds the ticket to the corresponding *unblacklist/demeritlist* $\mathcal{U}_i^\diamond$.
    - *Representing dishonest SP to $\mathcal{T}$.* $\mathcal{S}$ sends the request to $\mathcal{T}$ and waits for the reply whether $\tau \in \mathcal{L}_i^\diamond$ from $\mathcal{T}$. if $\mathcal{T}$ replies that the check is successful, $\mathcal{S}$ adds the ticket to the corresponding *unblacklist/demeritlist* $\mathcal{U}_i^\diamond$.

Based on the construction of simulator $\mathcal{S}$, we can prove that ExBLACR is secure due to the zero-knowledgeness of protocols $\mathfrak{G}_{Iss}$, $\mathfrak{G}_{Sig}$, $\mathfrak{G}_x$, $\mathfrak{G}'_{WS-Adj}$ and $\mathfrak{G}_{Pol}$, as well as the DDH assumption. Note that although protocol $\mathfrak{G}'_{WS-Adj}$ is some different with protocol $\mathfrak{G}_{WS-Adj}$ in the implementation inside, they have the same functionality.

A Semantics-Aware Classification Approach for Data Leakage Prevention

Sultan Alneyadi, Elankayer Sithirasenan, and Vallipuram Muthukkumarasamy

School of Information and Communication Technology
Griffith University, Gold Coast Campus, Australia
sultan.alneyadi2@griffithuni.edu.au,
{e.sithirasenan,v.muthu}@griffith.edu.au

Abstract. Data leakage prevention (DLP) is an emerging subject in the field of information security. It deals with tools working under a central policy, which analyze networked environments to detect sensitive data, prevent unauthorized access to it and block channels associated with data leak. This requires special data classification capabilities to distinguish between sensitive and normal data. Not only this task needs prior knowledge of the sensitive data, but also requires knowledge of potentially evolved and unknown data. Most current DLPs use content-based analysis in order to detect sensitive data. This mainly involves the use of regular expressions and data fingerprinting. Although these content analysis techniques are robust in detecting known unmodified data, they usually become ineffective if the sensitive data is not known before or largely modified. In this paper we study the effectiveness of using N-gram based statistical analysis, fostered by the use of stem words, in classifying documents according to their topics. The results are promising with an overall classification accuracy of 92%. Also we discuss classification deterioration when the text is exposed to multiple spins that simulate data modification.

Keywords: Data leakage prevention, N-grams, category profiles, X-counts.

1   Introduction

Protection of sensitive information from unauthorized disclosure is increasingly achieved through "Data Leakage Prevention Systems" or DLPs. These systems perform various types of analysis, for data in transit, in use and in store. They differ from conventional security controls such as firewalls, VPNs and IDSs in terms of dedication and proactivity. Conventional security controls have less dedication towards the actual data content, as they mainly focus on the metadata (context) such as size, timing, source and destination, rather than the sensitivity of the content. Also, they lack proactive actions as they normally work under predefined rules. This can be a major drawback when working in a rapidly changing environment. DLPs on the other hand mainly focus on the data content, since it is more logical to focus on the protection of the data itself rather than the metadata. Further, the state-of-the-art techniques used in DLPs are based on text statistical analysis and group communication analysis [1]. A typical content-based DLP

W. Susilo and Y. Mu (Eds.): ACISP 2014, LNCS 8544, pp. 413–421, 2014.
© Springer International Publishing Switzerland 2014

works by monitoring sensitive data in their repositories or on the go, mainly by using regular expressions, data fingerprinting and statistical analysis. Regular expressions are normally used under a certain rule like detecting social security numbers and credit card numbers. The problem with DLPs using regular expressions analysis is that they offer limited data protection with high false positive rates [2]. For example, it is an easy task to detect and prevent the leakage of a "project name" through emails, by using a rule that prevents emails containing that specific name from being sent. But it is difficult to prevent the leakage of the project's vast details. Also, if the rule is active, a regular email can be blocked if the same project name is used in another context.

DLPs using data fingerprints have better coverage for sensitive data as they have the ability to detect and prevent the leakage of a whole document or parts of a document. However, traditional fingerprinting can lose track when the sensitive data is altered or modified. This happens because traditional hashes that are used to generate data fingerprints such as MD5 and SHA1 [3] have the property where a tiny change to the data being hashed results in totally different fingerprint. This can lead to data bypassing the DLPs, thus data can be leaked. This problem can be partially solved by using multiple data hashing, where the original data is divided into smaller parts i.e. paragraphs and sentences, and each part is hashed separately [4]. This can ensure that parts of the original data fingerprints are retrievable. But these smaller fingerprints are also susceptible to change and a tiniest change can make the method ineffective. More advanced approaches try to overcome this problem by using similarity digests [5], Rabin fingerprinting [6] and piecewise hashing [7]. However, these solutions can be easily affected by various text obfuscation.

Although not widely used in DLPs, statistical analysis as a technique can work in a fuzzy environment, where the sensitive data is not well structured and the data semantic is distributed over a large corpus. The main advantage of such techniques is the ability to identify sensitive documents even after extreme modification using machine learning algorithms or Bayesian probability. Also, it can use text clustering techniques to construct scattered traces of sensitive data. In our research we focus on using statistical analysis techniques to classify documents into different categories. Our main aim is to distinguish between documents with sensitive information and others, in order to prevent important documents from being leaked. This classification task consists of calculating the distance between frequency-sorted N-grams, produced from documents and corresponding categories. In addition, we investigate the effect of using stemmed N-grams on the overall classification by using well-known Porter stemmer. Moreover, we test the ability of statistical analysis to classify documents under the correct category after exposing documents to a series of spins. Document spinning is conducted to simulate documents alteration, where N-grams are replaced by its synonyms.

This paper is divided as follows: Section 2 discusses related work. Section 3 outlines the stemmed N-gram classification methodology. The experiments are discussed in Section 4. Section 5 gives a detailed analysis of the findings. Section 6 concludes the paper.

2   Related Work

There is little research conducted which addresses the prevention of data leakage through statistical content analysis. Only a few examples are available in the literature like in [8] and [9], where ideas were introduced to quantify and limit the leakage of private data. However, these approaches were based on contextual analysis rather than exact sensitive content analysis. Therefore, the detection and protection of a specific piece of information is not guaranteed. A more dedicated approach was discussed in [10] where a DLP system based on Support Vector Machines (SVM) was used to classify enterprise documents as: Enterprise private, Enterprise public and Non-Enterprise. The processed data was represented by the most frequent binary weighted N-grams, i.e. words, found across all corpora. This approach was able to detect 97% of data leaks with a false-negative rate of 3.0%. One drawback of this method is that the data was classified either as public or private; ignoring more flexible classification levels like top secret, secret and restricted.

Moreover, an approach that uses the advantages of data retrieval functions was presented in [11]. In this paper an extension –Cut Once- to the publically available email client "Mozilla Thunderbird" was introduced. The extension was built with capabilities to recommend trustworthy recipients and predict potential leaks through wrongly addressed emails. The Cut Once extension ranks email addresses intended to receive the new message according to the calculated TFIDF scores. Email address - i.e. contacts- with high scores, indicate existing exchanged messages with similar topics. Lower scores indicate wrong recipients or unrecognised new topic. Unfortunately, the detection of the email leaks was totally subjective, since it was up to the users to select appropriate recipients. Additionally, this approach may introduce high level of false positives, since it requires existing messages in the sent folder.

3   Stemmed N-gram Classification

The classification method introduced in this research is inspired by the benefits of using word frequencies and how they reflect the semantic weight of a document. According to Zipf's law [12], the frequency of a word reflects its importance within a document. This is true when ignoring stop words like *the*, *is*, *in*, *at* etc. Moreover, unlike [13] which uses character N-grams, we use a single word N-gram in our classification. Character N-grams which might include two letters, three letters or more, can affect the semantics of the document by splitting words apart. Moreover, according to studies conducted for more than 20 years the use of a single term (word) gives better classification results than using two words or more [14] [15].

3.1   Stemmed N-gram Profiles Generation

We gathered 360 articles from various online sources like PC magazine, SC magazine etc. These articles represent our dataset and our aim is to classify each document under one of the following six categories: Antivirus, Data Leakage Prevention, Encryption, Firewall, Intrusion Detection Systems and Virtual Private Networks. There are 60 documents assigned to every category and we need to correctly classify all the documents under the correct category to ensure 100% classification accuracy.

In addition, we gathered additional 30 documents to create the category profile. It is not mandatory to gather this number of articles to create a category profile, in fact a single document which contains variety of words and discussing one topic (like a "frequently asked questions" page or a "Wikipedia" article) [13] [10] can produce a suitable category profile. We intentionally picked a large number of articles to create the category profile because we need to make sure that the category profile is comprehensive. It does not matter how big the resulting category profile is, since only the top frequency-sorted N-grams are considered for the distance calculation process. The selection of the optimum category profile size is discussed later section 4. Stop words were also removed from the profiles. According to the Oxford English Corpus (OEC), the most common stop words in the English language are: *the, be, to, of, and, a, in, that, have*, and *I* and they account for 25% of the written English language. Removing these words from the profiles can help in avoiding the excess distance when performing document classification.

The second step in the profiles generation was word stemming. Word stemming is the process of stripping words from their suffix to bring them back to the original root. Not only can this reduces the total number of terms processed by a data classification method but also improves words' representation. Therefore we are using an online stemming tool called *Peter Holme's word stemmer* version 1.1.2 [16], which is based on the famous "snowball" stemming algorithm developed by Dr. M. F. Porter [17]. The mentioned algorithm is designed to recognize terms with common stem, such as (*connect, connected, connecting, connection, connections*). Removing suffix: (*ed, ing, ion*, ions) can result in a single stem *connect*.

3.2   Distance Calculation

After the creation of 360 document profiles and six category profiles representing the six topics, we applied a simple Taxicab geometry to calculate distances and classify documents. This approach was introduced in [13] as calculating "out of place" distance; which is calculating the rank difference between N-grams in the document profile and the corresponding N-grams in the category profiles. The sum of all rank differences plus the total "X-count" values gives the overall distance. X-count refers to the absence of an N-gram in the category profile; therefore this term is denoting the maximum distance which is the total number of N-grams in the document profile. This process is repeated until all N-grams in the document profile are processed. The overall distance is calculated using the following equation: *(X-counts × number of N-grams in Doc)* + *"out of place" distance*. This process is repeated six times for each document and an overall distance is reported. Then a document is classified under the category with the smallest distance. This is discussed in details in [18].

3.3   Document Spinning

There are many reasons why data may be altered or modified including deliberate adversary action or business requirements. In both cases, classical DLPs detection techniques like regular expression and data fingerprinting may face great challenges in identifying sensitive data. It is difficult to predict the type and the amount of change a document might receive to avoid detection; therefore it is hard to simulate document modification scenarios. However, in reality there are some tools used to modify documents and articles in a way that makes them difficult to be recognized. These tools are called *"article spinners"* and they are normally used to avoid plagiarism detection and copy right penalties by replacing words with synonyms.

Table 1. An example of word spintax from category "vpn"

Original Word	Spintax
vpn	vpn
connect	{connect|link|hook up|join|be connected}
network	{network|system|community|multilevel|circle}
server	server
access	{access|entry|accessibility|gain access to|admittance}
secure	{secure|safe|protected|risk-free|safeguarded}
remote	{remote|remote control|distant|rural|out of the way}
internet	{internet|web|world wide web|net|world-wide-web}

To test the reliability of our classification approach, we use *BFSpro* v1.0 spinner available from http://bestfreespinner.com/ to modify our documents. Changing words to their synonyms can change the document's metadata like the size in kilobits and the terms frequency, but the documents' semantics should be kept intact. Table 1 gives an example of spintax of N-grams found in the VPN category.

4   Experiments and Results

4.1   Optimum Category Profile Size

It is important to define an optimum size for the category profiles because using an undefined size will result in unbalanced figures. A document can be classified under a wrong category if the correct category profile is noticeably bigger than the rest. This makes the calculated distance grow exponentially. One option was to use length normalization for the calculated distance; however this will not solve the problem of lower ranked N-grams which lie on the bottom of the category profiles. These low rank N-grams do not reflect the category topic and keeping them will affect the purity of the category profile. Therefore it is better to consider only the top N-grams which are better reflecting the category.

Table 2. Category profile sizes performance in the overall classification

Category Profile Size	Correct Classification	Percentage
25	295	81.94%
50	322	89.44%
75	326	90.55%
100	329	91.39%
125	322	89.44%
150	319	88.61%
175	319	88.61%
200	314	87.22%

We ran our experiments on 360 document profiles using a scale of category profile sizes. This scale includes: 25, 50, 75, 100, 125, 150, 175 and 200 top N-grams in each category. The profile size with the most correct classification was "100" with 91.3% accuracy. Table 2 shows the results of using different profile sizes and the effect on the overall classification. It was noticed that too small category profiles resulted in lower accuracy like size "25" as it scores 81.9%. Also, larger category profiles sizes caused accuracy deterioration like in the case of size "200" scoring 87.2%.

4.2   Overall Classification Using Optimum Category Profile Size

By using the optimum category profile size "100" we examined the overall classification of each category profile. Table 3 shows individual categories scoring and the overall classification results. Categories Antivirus, DLP, IDS and VPN scored classification accuracy of 95% and above. The worst classification result was 75% and it was scored by Encryption category. These results make an overall classification average of 91.39%. Comparing to previous work [15] the proposed method has slight improvement in accuracy of 7%.

Table 3. Overall classification results of 360 documents using category profile size "100"

Categories	AV	DLP	Encrypt.	Firewall	IDS	VPN
Antivirus	57	0	0	2	1	0
DLP	0	59	12	2	0	0
Encryption	0	0	45	0	0	1
Firewall	0	0	2	53	2	1
IDS	3	1	1	3	57	0
VPN	0	0	0	0	0	58
Correct	57	59	45	53	57	58
Percentage	95.0%	98.3%	75.0%	88.3%	95.0%	96.6%
Overall			91.39%			

4.3   Document Spinning

To test the reliability of our classification method against document modification we tested the 360 documents again after multilevel spins. Table 4 shows the classification results after multilevel spinning. The overall classification accuracy was affected by the spinning process. Spinning every possible word resulted in the worst classification, as only 83% of the documents were correctly classified. The minimum spinning level was spinning every forth word, and resulted in 88.3%. Comparing to the overall classification results without document spinning, the most deteriorated classification results were when every possible word was spun.

Table 4. Documents spinning results compared to the non-spun documents

Categories	Every Possible	Every Other	Every 3rd	Every 4th	No Spins
Antivirus	56	56	57	58	57
DLP	57	58	59	59	59
Encryption	36	39	41	39	45
Firewall	52	51	52	53	53
IDS	41	47	50	49	57
VPN	57	57	56	60	58
Total	299	308	315	318	329
Percentage	83.06%	85.56%	87.50%	88.33%	91.39%
Deterioration	8.33%	5.83%	3.89%	3.06%	

8.3% of the correctly classified document could not be classified under the correct category. In conclusion, the deeper the spinning levels the worse the classification will be. However, comparing to fingerprinting or regular expression methods with full or partial data matching the proposed method is more efficient.

5   Analysis

5.1   Precision, Recall and F1 Measures

To evaluate our method we use precision and recall measures in our analysis. Precision is the ratio between correct classifications and the number of all classifications under one category. While, recall is the ratio between correct classifications and the number of desired correct classification. We also use F1 measure, which is the harmonic average of both precision and recall. All the results are shown in Table 5. All the six categories scored a precision higher than 0.8, which means that our method tends to classify relevant documents and ignore non-relevant ones. On the other hand, all the categories' recall scores were above 0.8 except for Encryption, which scored only 0.7. This is because Encryption is a vast topic by itself and it may contain N-grams that are shared among other categories.

Table 5. Precision and recall scores for every category

Category	Precision	Recall
Antivirus	0.950	0.950
DLP	0.808	0.983
Encryption	0.978	0.750
Firewall	0.914	0.883
IDS	0.877	0.950
VPN	1.000	0.967
Average	0.914	0.914

According to results in Table 3, there were 12 documents from category E classified under category D. this makes lower recall results for E and lower precision results for DLP. The average precision and recall scores for the six categories indicate that our method has relatively high accuracy. Precisely, our method scored an average of 0.92 precision and 0.91 recall.

Table 6. F1 measure for every category profile size

Profile Size	25	50	75	100	125	150	175	200
F1 Measure	0.832	0.899	0.912	0.918	0.901	0.893	0.89	0.877

In addition, to view both precision and recall in a harmonic average, we calculated the F1 score and compared the results across the category profile scale. F1 can indicate how good a classification method is by combining the benefits of both the precision and the recall measures. Table 6 shows the F1 measures scored by each category profile. The highest precision and recall was achieved by size "100" category profile. This is an indication that 91.8% of the processed documents were both correctly classified and relevant.

6   Conclusion and Future Work

In this paper we proposed the use of N-gram statistical analysis to classify documents to overcome the drawbacks in DLPs' analysis techniques such as data fingerprinting and regular expression. We showed that using word stemming along with fixed category profile sizes can improve the overall classification comparing with previous works [13] [15]. We also studied the effects of data modification on the overall classification and showed that even with extreme modification our proposed method can provide acceptable accuracy. As a future we propose using term weighting methods which can be more flexible than raw frequency used in this research.

References

[1] Raman, P., Kayacık, H.G., Somayaji, A.: Understanding Data Leak Prevention. In: 6th Annual Symposium on Information Assurance (ASIA 2011), p. 27 (2011)

[2] Mogull, R.: Understanding and Selecting a Data Loss Prevention Solution, https://securosis.com/assets/library/reports/DLP-Whitepaper.pdf

[3] Shapira, Y., Shapira, B., Shabtai, A.: Content-based data leakage detection using extended fingerprinting. arXiv preprint arXiv:1302.2028 (2013)

[4] Kantor, A., Antebi, L., Kirsch, Y., Bialik, U.: Methods for document-to-template matching for data-leak prevention. USA Patent US20100254615 A1 (2009)

[5] Roussev, V.: Data fingerprinting with similarity digests. In: Chow, K.-P., Shenoi, S. (eds.) Advances in Digital Forensics VI. IFIPAICT, vol. 337, pp. 207–226. Springer, Heidelberg (2010)

[6] Shu, X., Yao, D. D.: Data leak detection as a service. In: Keromytis, A.D., Di Pietro, R. (eds.) SecureComm 2012. LNICST, vol. 106, pp. 222–240. Springer, Heidelberg (2013)

[7] Kornblum, J.: Identifying almost identical files using context triggered piecewise hashing. Digital Investigation 3, 91–97 (2006)

[8] Borders, K., Prakash, A.: Quantifying information leaks in outbound web traffic. In: 30th IEEE Symposium 2009 Security and Privacy, pp. 129–140 (2009)

[9] Clark, D., Hunt, S., Malacaria, P.: Quantitative analysis of the leakage of confidential data. Electronic Notes in Theoretical Computer Science 59 (2002)

[10] Hart, M., Manadhata, P., Johnson, R.: Text classification for data loss prevention. In: Fischer-Hübner, S., Hopper, N. (eds.) PETS 2011. LNCS, vol. 6794, pp. 18–37. Springer, Heidelberg (2011)

[11] Carvalho, V.R., Balasubramanyan, R., Cohen, W.W.: Information Leaks and Suggestions: A Case Study using Mozilla Thunderbird. In: Proc. of 6th Conf. on Email and Antispam (2009)

[12] Zipf, G.K.: Human behavior and the principle of least effort. Addison Wesley, Massachusetts (1949)

[13] Cavnar, W.B., Trenkle, J.M.: N-gram-based text categorization. Presented at the Ann Arbor MI (1994)

[14] Salton, G., Buckley, C.: Term-weighting approaches in automatic text retrieval. Information Processing & Management 24, 513–523 (1988)

[15] Alneyadi, S., Sithirasenan, E., Muthukkumarasamy, V.: Word N-gram Based Classification for Data Leakage Prevention. In: TrustCom, Melbourne (2013)

[16] Holme, P.: Peter Holme's word stemmer (2011), http://holme.se/stem/

[17] Porter, M.F.: An algorithm for suffix stripping. Program: Electronic Library and Information Systems 14, 130–137 (1980)

[18] Alneyadi, S., Sithirasenan, E., Muthukkumarasamy, V.: Adaptable N-gram Classification Model for Data Leakage Prevention. Presented at the ICSPCS, Gold Coast, Australia(2013)

Route 66: Passively Breaking All GSM Channels

Philip S. Vejre and Andrey Bogdanov

Technical University of Denmark

Abstract. The A5/2 stream cipher used for encryption in the GSM mobile phone standard has previously been shown to have serious weaknesses. Due to a lack of key separation and flaws in the security protocols, these vulnerabilities can also compromise the stronger GSM ciphers A5/1 and A5/3. Despite GSM's huge impact in the field, only a small selection of its channels have been analyzed. In this paper, we perform a complete practical-complexity, ciphertext-only cryptanalysis of all 66 encoded GSM channels. Moreover, we present a new passive attack which recovers the encryption key by exploiting the location updating procedure of the GSM protocol. This update is performed automatically even when the phone is not actively used. Interestingly, the attack potentially enables eavesdropping of future calls.

1 Introduction

The first standard for digital mobile phone communication, *GSM* (Global System for Mobile Communication), was introduced in the late 1980s. GSM brought cryptographic security to mobile communication with the aim of a security level equivalent to that of wired telephony. The purpose was twofold: protect the confidentially of messages (through encryption), and protect the network from unauthorized access (through authentication). In 2008, GSM had 3 billion connections worldwide [1].

GSM uses 66 communication channels with error-correction encoding and a single one without. The purpose of each channel varies, as does the amount of data carried and the preprocessing techniques used. The result of the preprocessing, however, is sent to the same encryption unit, independent of the channel type [2]. One of four encryption ciphers is used in GSM: A5/0 (no encryption), A5/1, A5/2, or A5/3. A5/2 was deployed in Europe due to export restrictions [3]. A5/1 and A5/2 had secret designs, but they were both reverse engineered in 1999 [4]. In 2002, A5/3 was added to the standard. This cipher is based on the peer-reviewed block cipher KASUMI, and its design was published.

Shortly after the reverse engineering of A5/2, several known-plaintext attacks were presented [5,6]. In 2007 Barkan, Biham, and Keller [3][7] presented a *ciphertext-only* attack on A5/2 which utilizes that error correction in GSM is applied before encryption. The attack recovers the encryption key K, has a complexity of 2^{44} XOR operations, and precomputations are used to make the real-time part of the attack instant. Additionally, several attacks on A5/1 and A5/3 have been presented [8,9,10,11,12].

W. Susilo and Y. Mu (Eds.): ACISP 2014, LNCS 8544, pp. 422–429, 2014.

These results show that the GSM standard is rather insecure. Nevertheless, the standard is still widely used. Due to a lack of *key separation* and sometimes *key renewal*, even breaking the weaker A5/2 can compromise communication encrypted with A5/1 and A5/3. Hence, it is still of interest to find more efficient, practical attacks against A5/2 that do not use lengthy precomputations or specialized hardware [13]. Furthermore, previous attacks have only focused on some of the GSM channels, leaving it unclear how efficiently the remaining channels can be attacked.

In this paper we generalize the ciphertext only attack from [3] to a channel encoded with a general linear code. Using M4R (The Method of Four Russians) [14] we improve the complexity of this attack by a factor of 8. We realize this attack in software *without precomputations* and break A5/2 in 12 seconds. Dedicated hardware, such as the design from [13], is much faster, but the cost of such an attack is much higher than ours. While some of the GSM channels have previously been analyzed [3][13], this article presents a full theoretical, ciphertext-only cryptanalysis of all 66 GSM channels which use error correction. The analysis shows that it is possible to attack any type of GSM traffic, and that less than 400 bytes of data collected in under 130 ms is sufficient for most channels.

We present a new ciphertext-only attack on the GSM protocol which passively recovers the A5/2 encryption key, i.e. without the user noticing any activity on the phone. The attack exploits the periodic *location updating procedure* of GSM – a procedure performed automatically without direct user interaction. Due to flaws in the GSM security protocols, the attack allows possible eavesdropping of future calls, and can even compromise the security of the stronger GSM ciphers A5/1 and A5/3 [3][15].

2   Description of A5/2 and GSM

The A5/2 stream cipher takes a 64-bit key K and a 22-bit initialization value f as input and produces a 228-bit keystream S. The internal structure of A5/2 consists of four Linear Feedback Shift Registers of maximal length: R_1, R_2, R_3, and R_4. They have a size of 19, 22, 23, and 17 bits, respectively [3]. If we view an n-bit register as a vector over $\mathbb{F}_2$ (with the LSB first), a single clocking can be described by multiplication with the square matrix

$$L = \begin{pmatrix} t_{n-1} \cdots t_0 \\ I \quad\quad \mathbf{0} \end{pmatrix} , \tag{1}$$

where I is an identity matrix, $\mathbf{0}$ is an all zero column, and $t_i \in \mathbb{F}_2$ is 1 if the i'th bit is tapped and 0 otherwise.

Let x^i be the i'th bit of the bit vector x, with $i = 0$ being the LSB. Denote the clocking matrix of register R_i by L_i. Then the value of the internal state is initialized during the *key setup*, defined for each register by

$$R_i = \sum_{n=0}^{63} (L_i)^{85-n} K_n \oplus \sum_{n=0}^{21} (L_i)^{21-n} f_n \oplus \sigma , \tag{2}$$

where K_n is a vector whose first element is K^n and all other elements are 0 (similarly for f_n), and σ is a vector that sets the values $R_1^{15} = R_2^{16} = R_3^{18} = R_4^{10} = 1$. Thus, we can describe the initial value of each register as

$$R_1 = \left(\alpha^0 \oplus \varphi^0, \ldots, \alpha^{14} \oplus \varphi^{14}, 1, \alpha^{16} \oplus \varphi^{16}, \ldots, \alpha^{18} \oplus \varphi^{18}\right),$$
$$R_2 = \left(\beta^0 \oplus \xi^0, \ldots, \beta^{15} \oplus \xi^{15}, 1, \beta^{17} \oplus \xi^{17}, \ldots, \beta^{21} \oplus \xi^{21}\right),$$
$$R_3 = \left(\gamma^0 \oplus \psi^0, \ldots, \gamma^{17} \oplus \psi^{17}, 1, \gamma^{19} \oplus \psi^{19}, \ldots, \gamma^{22} \oplus \psi^{22}\right),$$
$$R_4 = \left(\delta^0 \oplus \omega^0, \ldots, \delta^9 \oplus \omega^9, 1, \delta^{11} \oplus \omega^{11}, \ldots, \delta^{16} \oplus \omega^{16}\right), \tag{3}$$

where $\alpha^i, \beta^i, \gamma^i, \delta^i \in \text{span}(K^0, \ldots, K^{63})$ and $\varphi^i, \xi^i, \psi^i, \omega^i \in \text{span}(f^0, \ldots, f^{21})$ [13]. Note that these linear combinations are known and are described by (2).

At the start of each cycle of A5/2 the majority $M = maj(R_4^3, R_4^7, R_4^{10})$ is calculated. Then, R_1 is clocked iff $R_4^{10} = M$. Similarly, the clocking of R_2 and R_3 are controlled by R_4^3 and R_4^7, respectively. After this, R_4 is also clocked and a single stream bit s is produced, defined by

$$s = maj\left(R_1^{12}, R_1^{14} \oplus 1, R_1^{15}\right) \oplus maj\left(R_2^9, R_2^{13}, R_2^{16} \oplus 1\right)$$
$$\oplus maj\left(R_3^{13} \oplus 1, R_3^{16}, R_3^{18}\right) \oplus R_1^{18} \oplus R_2^{21} \oplus R_3^{22}. \tag{4}$$

The first 99 generated bits are discarded, and the following 228 bits are used as the keystream which is XOR'ed with the plaintext. The first 114 bits are used to encrypt the downlink, and the last 114 bits are used to encrypt the uplink.

Communication in the GSM standard is split into 114 bit blocks, referred to as a *frame*. Each frame has assigned a publicly known *frame number* [16]. Using the frame number as the initialization value f, each frame is encrypted by A5/2 as described above [15]. Before encryption, the raw communication is subject to error correction and interleaving. The error correction in GSM is done via a convolutional encoder [2]. Each GSM channel has an individual encoder which takes n-bit blocks as input and produces m-bit output blocks. After $i + 1$ input blocks have been encoded, the $i + 1$ coded blocks are *interleaved* with each other, producing $j + 1$ 114-bit frames. The frames are then encrypted with $j + 1$ different A5/2 keystreams and transmitted. The full expression for the ciphertext blocks $C_0, \ldots, C_j$ therefore becomes

$$\begin{pmatrix} C_0 \\ \vdots \\ C_j \end{pmatrix} = I_N \mathcal{G} \begin{pmatrix} D_0 \\ \vdots \\ D_i \end{pmatrix} \oplus \begin{pmatrix} S_0 \\ \vdots \\ S_j \end{pmatrix}, \tag{5}$$

where $D_0, \ldots, D_i$ are the input blocks, $\mathcal{G}$ is the generator matrix for the code, I_N is a permutation matrix describing the interleaving, and $S_0, \cdots, S_j$ are keystreams belonging to different frame numbers.

We can describe the values of the registers in the i'th cycle of A5/2 as

$$R_1^{(i)} = \left(A_i^0 \oplus \Phi_i^0, \ldots, A_i^{18} \oplus \Phi_i^{18}\right), \quad R_2^{(i)} = \left(B_i^0 \oplus \Xi_i^0, \ldots, B_i^{21} \oplus \Xi_i^{21}\right),$$
$$R_3^{(i)} = \left(\Gamma_i^0 \oplus \Psi_i^0, \ldots, \Gamma_i^{22} \oplus \Psi_i^{22}\right), \quad R_4^{(i)} = \left(\Delta_i^0 \oplus \Omega_i^0, \ldots, \Delta_i^{16} \oplus \Omega_i^{16}\right). \tag{6}$$

Here, $A_i^j \in \text{span}(\alpha^k \mid k \neq 15)$ and $\Phi_i^j \in \text{span}(\varphi^k, 1 \mid k \neq 15)$. The remaining variables are defined similarly. For Δ_i^j and Ω_i^j these linear combinations are known, since R_4 is always regularly clocked, so $R_4^{(i)} = (L_4)^i R_4$. The other linear combinations, however, depend on δ^j and ω^j, and therefore on K and f. Using this, the i'th bit of the stream S can be described similarly to the expression in (4), where $R_1^{12} = A_i^{12} \oplus \Phi_i^{12}$, etc. Since the majority function is quadratic, we can rewrite this as a more general quadratic equation over α, β, and γ:

$$S^i = \sum_{\substack{0 \leq m,n \leq 18 \\ m,n \neq 15}} a_{m,n} \alpha^m \alpha^n \oplus \sum_{\substack{0 \leq m,n \leq 21 \\ m,n \neq 16}} b_{m,n} \beta^m \beta^n \oplus \sum_{\substack{0 \leq m,n \leq 22 \\ m,n \neq 18}} c_{m,n} \gamma^m \gamma^n \oplus d \ , \quad (7)$$

for some $a_{m,n}, b_{m,n}, c_{m,n}, d \in \mathbb{F}_2$ which depend on K and f. The coefficients $a_{m,n}$, $b_{m,n}$, and $c_{m,n}$ depend on how the three registers are clocked. Since this depends on the majority function, these coefficients must therefore be at least quadratic terms in the bits of K, and (7) is at least quartic in the bits K.

3   Attacking All GSM Channels

The idea of the attack is to determine the α, β, and γ variables, and use their known linear expressions over the bits of K, to fully determine K [3]. Recall that the value of R_4 right after the key setup can be described by (3). Since we know f, we also know the value of each ω variable. We now guess the value of the δ variables, thus fully determining $R_4^{(i)}$ for any i. Since R_4 determines when the other three registers are clocked, we now also know the linear combinations that define A, B, and Γ, and the exact values of Φ, Ξ, and Ψ. Thus, for any cycle i of A5/2, the stream bit S^i can be expressed using only known linear combinations of α, β, and γ, i.e. we can determine the coefficients of (7).

Now, let $\mathcal{H}$ be the parity check matrix for the generator matrix $\mathcal{G}$. Since I_N^{-1} exists and $\mathcal{H}\mathcal{G} = 0$, we can rewrite (5) as

$$\mathcal{H} I_N^{-1} \begin{pmatrix} C_0 \\ \vdots \\ C_j \end{pmatrix} = \mathcal{H} I_N^{-1} \begin{pmatrix} S_0 \\ \vdots \\ S_j \end{pmatrix} \ . \quad (8)$$

Thus, we have a linear system of equations over the bits of $S_0, \ldots, S_j$. Expressing these bits as quadratic equations using (7), we get a quadratic system of equations over the α, β, and γ variables. Note here that even though we consider streams from different frames, we are still dealing with the same α, β, and γ variables, as these depend only on K. The quadratic system of equations defining each stream will, however, be different, since the Φ, Ξ, and Ψ variables depend on f.

We proceed by solving this quadratic system via *linearization*. From (7) we see that we get a linear system of equations over 655 variables plus a constant. In order to have enough equations to solve the system, we need to consider an appropriate number of frames. Thus, the number j in (8) is determined by how many equations we get from each frame, which in turn depends on the encoder. Note, however, that it is enough to solve the original 61 α, β, and γ variables. Once this is done, we can solve (2) for the bits of K. It is interesting to note that this attack on A5/2 would not work if the convolutional encoding had been performed *after* the encryption.

We need to guess the value of the 16 δ variables, and so we need to make 2^{16} guesses, and solve a linear system of equations for each guess. Using M4R presented in [14], each system can be solved with a complexity of $n^3/\log(n)$. The complexity of the attack is therefore approximately 2^{41} XOR operations, making it 8 times faster than the attack in [3].

We implemented the attack on the TCH/HS channel in software. The multithreaded implementation was written in C++ and tested on a desktop with a quad core processor clocked to 4 GHz. 12 ciphertext frames were required to recover the key in 12.08 seconds on this channel with a success rate of 100%.

In theory the complexity of generating the equation systems is negligible. In practice, however, this part of the attack contributes to about half of the running time, even though we use specialized techniques to generate the equation systems quickly. Hence, the equation generator is an obvious target for improvements.

If the encoder for a single input block is defined by an $m \times n$ matrix $\mathcal{G}$, then $\mathcal{H}$ is an $(m - n) \times m$ matrix. Therefore, for each frame we get $m - n$ equations. Although the equations from one frame are linearly independent, equations from different frames need not be. While analyzing the TCH/HS and SACCH channels we found that 360 linearly independent equations were always enough to recover K. We estimate that about 600 (not necessarily linearly independent) equations should be enough to recover K for any channel. Based on this estimate, we have made a complete theoretical cryptanalysis of all GSM channels, which can be found in Table 1. The table shows the number of frames j required to recover K, and the time needed to acquire j consecutive frames. It is important to remember, however, that the frames used for the attack need not be consecutive. Indeed, we could mix frames from different channels, as long as we can set up enough equations.

The fastest channels to attack (in terms of time taken to acquire data) are the SCH, CTSBCH-SB, CTSARCH and CSCH channels. The channel that has the largest number of required frames is the PDTCH/MCS-4 channel, which needs 76 ciphertext frames for the downlink and 60 frames for the uplink. The reason for this is that we can only extract equations from the extra header data this channel uses.

As explained above, our estimate of 600 equations might be conservative for most channels. In [3] the SACCH channel (and similar channels) was attacked using only 8 frames, TCH/EFS and TCH/FS were attacked using only 16 frames in [13], and we have attacked TCH/HS using only 12 frames. On the other hand, properties of a specific channel might require more than 600 equations. Indeed, our findings suggest that the more frames we use, the fewer linearly independent equations are added per frame. Therefore, it might be hard to gather sufficient data if the number of equations per input block is low to begin with.

Table 1. Overview of attack details for all 66 GSM channels. The no. of input/output blocks are denoted by i and j, respectively.

Channel name	Eqns/block	i	j	No. of eqns	Time to acquire [ms]
TCH/EFS					
TCH/FS	189	4	20	756	92.3
TCH/HS	107	6	14	642	64.6
TCH/AFS12.12	198	4	20	792	92.3
TCH/AFS10.2	238	3	16	714	73.8
TCH/AFS7.95	283	3	16	849	73.8
TCH/AFS7.4	294	3	16	882	73.8
TCH/AFS6.7	308	2	12	616	55.4
TCH/AFS5.9	324	2	12	648	55.4
TCH/AFS5.15	339	2	12	678	55.4
TCH/AFS4.75	347	2	12	694	55.4
TCH/AHS7.95	59	11	24	649	110.8
TCH/AHS7.4	62	10	22	620	101.5
TCH/AHS6.7	72	9	20	648	92.3
TCH/AHS5.9	80	8	18	640	83.1
TCH/AHS5.15	91	7	16	637	73.8
TCH/AHS4.75	99	7	16	693	73.8
E-TCH/F43.2	492	2	26	984	120
E-TCH/F32.0	626	1	22	626	101.5
E-TCH/F28.8	682	1	22	682	101.5
TCH/F9.6 & H4.8	212	3	30	636	138.5
SCH					
CTSBCH-SB	78	8	8	624	36.9
PRACH					
CPRACH	36	17	16	612	73.8
PDTCH/MCS-1[1]	208/217	3	12	624/651	55.4
PDTCH/MCS-2[1]	160/169	4	16	640/676	73.8
PDTCH/MCS-3[1]	88/97	7	28	616/679	129.2
PDTCH/MCS-4[1]	32/41	19/15	76/60	608/615	350.8/276.9
PDTCH/MCS-5[1]	846/871	1	?[2]	846/871	?[2]
PDTCH/MCS-6[1]	703/727	1	?[2]	703/727	?[2]
PDTCH/MCS-7[1]	367/394	2	?[2]	734/788	?[2]
PDTCH/MCS-8[1]	175/202	4/3	?[2]	700/606	?[2]
PDTCH/MCS-9[1]	79/106	8/6	?[2]	632/636	?[2]
PDTCH/CS-2	162	4	16	648	73.8
PDTCH/CS-3	118	6	24	708	110.8
PDTCH/CS-4	No convolutional codes are applied				
FACCH/F	228	3	16	684	73.8
FACCH/H	228	3	14	684	64.6
RACH	36	17	17	612	78
SACCH[3]	228	3	12	684	55.4
TCH/F2.4	380	2	12	760	55.4
TCH/F14.4	162	4	34	648	156.9
TCH/F4.8 & H2.4	304	2	26	608	120
CTSARCH					
CSCH	78	8	8	624	36.9

[1] The numbers specify upload/download variants of the channels.
[2] Due to unclear specifications in [2], we could not determine how many ciphertext frames are needed for the attack.
[3] Also includes similar channels: E-FACCH/F, SDCCH/F, BCCH, PCH, AGCH, CBCH, CTSPCH, CTSAGCH, PACCH, PBCCH, PAGCH, PPCH, PNCH, PTCCH, CPAGCH, CPBCCH, CPNCH, CPPCH, and PDTCH/CS-1.

4   Passive Attack on the GSM Location Update

While results for the SACCH and SDCCH are known [3], our results for the FACCH/F and FACCH/H channels are new. These results allow us to present a new attack that exploits the GSM *location updating procedure* to recover K.

There are two ways for the network to identify a certain phone: the International Mobile Subscriber Identity (IMSI) and the Temporary Mobile Subscriber Identity (TMSI). The IMSI is the unique identification of a phone on the network. In order to transmit the IMSI as infrequently as possible, the TMSI is used, which is an identification specific to the phone's current physical location. The network can recover the IMSI by using the current TMSI and the Location Area Identifier (LAI) of the phone's current location. Because of this, the TMSI needs to be updated every time to phone physically moves. This is done via the location updating procedure [17]. A normal location update is triggered when the phone physically moves, and a periodic location update is triggered when a timer on the phone expires. Periodic updates can be turned off, but usually the timer holds a value between 6 minutes and 25.5 hours.

The location updating procedure happens in six stages. In the first stage, *connection establishment*, the phone requests and is assigned a channel. Here, two messages are transmitted on the RACH channel [17, p. 227]. During the remaining stages, all messages are transmitted on the main DCCH, which is either the SACCH, the SDCCH, or one of the FACCHs [17, p. 38]. During the next stage, the *service request* stage, the phone starts the location updating procedure with a *location updating request* message. This message contains the current LAI and TMSI.

The next two stages, *authentication* and *cipher mode setting*, are optional [15]. If the stages are performed, the phone is first authenticated to the network, and a cipher for encryption is agreed upon. No matter which cipher is chosen, the encryption happens under the same key K. The cipher mode setting stage is ended with a *cipher mode complete* message, which is encrypted. After this message, all future messages are encrypted. For more details on these two stages, see [3]. If these two stages are not performed the network relies on the fact that the phone knows the K of the last conversation, implicitly authenticating the phone via its ability to read encrypted messages. Note that it is not a guarantee that K is different from conversation to conversation [3].

The *location update* stage itself now starts. First, the network sends an encrypted *location updating accept* message, which contains the new TSMI and LAI. The phone then updates its SIM card with the new information and sends a *TSMI reallocation complete* message to the network. More messages can be sent, but we can assume that the network ends the conversation with the *connection release* stage, in which it sends a *channel release* message to the phone.

From the above we see that at least three encrypted blocks are transmitted on the DCCH channel during a successful location update. Assuming A5/2 was used for encryption, we therefore have enough data to recover K, cf. Table 1. This way of recovering K is completely undetectable – all the attacker has to do is wait for a location update to take place. The victim's phone never rings, and there is no suspicious communication or delays. Thanks to the optional authentication and reuse of keys, recovering K from a location update could enable immediate wire-tapping during the next call. If we need to target a specific phone, or if A5/2 was not used for encryption, the attack is still possible using the methods presented in [3]. We stress that even if we need to apply these methods, the attack is still passive in the sense that the victim never sees any activity on the phone or interacts with it – except for physically moving it.

References

1. Association, G.: Brief History of GSM and the GSMA (May 5, 2011), gsmworld.com, http://www.webcitation.org/5yRQRGPgH
2. ETSI: Digital cellular telecommunications system (Phase 2+); Channel coding (GSM 05.03). Technical report, ETSI (1999)
3. Barkan, E., Biham, E., Keller, N.: Instant Ciphertex-Only Cryptanalysis of GSM Encrypted Communication. Journal of Cryptology 21, 392–429 (2008)
4. Briceno, M., Goldberg, I., Wagner, D.: A pedagogical implementation of the GSM A5/1 and A5/2 'voice privacy' encryption algorithms (1999), http://cryptome.org/gsm-a512.htm
5. Goldberg, I., Wagner, D., Green, L.: The (Real-Time) Cryptanalysis of A5/2. Presented at the Rump Session of Crypto 1999 (1999)
6. Petrovic, S., Fster-Sabater, A.: Cryptanalysis of the A5/2 Algorithm. Cryptology ePrint Archive, Report 2000/052 (2000), http://eprint.iacr.org/
7. Barkan, E., Biham, E., Keller, N.: Instant Ciphertext-Only Cryptanalysis of GSM Encrypted Communication. In: Boneh, D. (ed.) CRYPTO 2003. LNCS, vol. 2729, pp. 600–616. Springer, Heidelberg (2003)
8. Golić, J.D.: Cryptanalysis of Alleged A5 Stream Cipher. In: Fumy, W. (ed.) EUROCRYPT 1997. LNCS, vol. 1233, pp. 239–255. Springer, Heidelberg (1997)
9. Barkan, E., Biham, E.: Conditional Estimators: An Effective Attack on A5/1. In: Preneel, B., Tavares, S. (eds.) SAC 2005. LNCS, vol. 3897, pp. 1–19. Springer, Heidelberg (2006)
10. Biham, E., Dunkelman, O.: Cryptanalysis of the A5/1 GSM Stream Cipher. In: Preneel, B., Tavares, S. (eds.) SAC 2005. LNCS, vol. 3897, pp. 1–19. Springer, Heidelberg (2006)
11. Biryukov, A., Shamir, A., Wagner, D.: Real Time Cryptanalysis of A5/1 on a PC. In: Schneier, B. (ed.) FSE 2000. LNCS, vol. 1978, p. 1. Springer, Heidelberg (2001)
12. Dunkelman, O., Keller, N., Shamir, A.: A Practical-time Related-key Attack on the KASUMI Cryptosystem Used in GSM and 3G Telephony. In: Rabin, T. (ed.) CRYPTO 2010. LNCS, vol. 6223, pp. 393–410. Springer, Heidelberg (2010)
13. Bogdanov, A., Eisenbarth, T., Rupp, A.: A Hardware-Assisted Realtime Attack on A5/2 Without Precomputations. In: Paillier, P., Verbauwhede, I. (eds.) CHES 2007. LNCS, vol. 4727, pp. 394–412. Springer, Heidelberg (2007)
14. Albrecht, M.R., Pernet, C.: Efficient Dense Gaussian Elimination over the Finite Field with Two Elements. arXiv:1111.6549v1 (November 2011)
15. ETSI: Digital cellular telecommunications system (Phase 2+); Security related network functions (GSM 03.20). Technical report, ETSI (1998)
16. ETSI: Digital cellular telecommunications system (Phase 2+); Physical layer on the radio path; General description (GSM 05.01). Technical report, ETSI (1997)
17. ETSI: Digital cellular telecommunications system (Phase 2+); Mobile radio interface layer 3 specification (GSM 04.08). Technical report, ETSI (1998)

An Analysis of Tracking Settings in Blackberry 10 and Windows Phone 8 Smartphones

Yogachandran Rahulamathavan[1], Veelasha Moonsamy[2], Lynn Batten[2],
Su Shunliang[3], and Muttukrishnan Rajarajan[1]

[1] School of Engineering and Mathematical Sciences, City University London,
London, U.K.
{yogachandran.rahulamathavan.1,r.muttukrishnan}@city.ac.uk
[2] School of Information Technology, Deakin University,
Melbourne, Australia
{v.moonsamy@research.deakin.edu.au,lynn.batten@deakin.edu.au}
[3] Multimedia Information Technology, City University of Hong Kong,
Kowloon, Hong Kong
{shunlsu2-c@my.cityu.edu.hk}

Abstract. The use of tracking settings in smartphones facilitates the provision of tailored services to users by allowing service providers access to unique identifiers stored on the smartphones. In this paper, we investigate the 'tracking off' settings on the `Blackberry 10` and `Windows Phone 8` platforms. To determine if they work as claimed, we set up a test bed suitable for both operating systems to capture traffic between the smartphone and external servers. We dynamically execute a set of similar `Blackberry 10` and `Windows Phone 8` applications, downloaded from their respective official markets. Our results indicate that even if users turn off tracking settings in their smartphones, some applications leak unique identifiers without their knowledge.

1 Introduction

Many service providers offer tailored services to their customers based on data gathered from the users' smartphones. Advertisements embedded within applications can be used to notify users of promotional offers in their nearby surroundings; however, several existing papers have shown that sensitive information such as the device's unique identifier and user's physical location are often leaked via advertising libraries without the device owner's consent [1]. In general, smartphone users are given the option to control the following two tracking services: location services and advertising. There are several papers in the literature analyzing these settings in `Android` and `iOS` based smartphones [2–6]. Some of this work indicates that information can be leaked through advertising.

In this paper, we ask the question: If tracking settings are turned off on `BlackBerry 10` and `Windows Phone 8` smartphones, is it possible that the devices are still tracked? On both of these platforms, to our knowledge, the default options that are provided by the smartphones have not been tested in any prior work. We test them in this paper by addressing the following specific questions:

W. Susilo and Y. Mu (Eds.): ACISP 2014, LNCS 8544, pp. 430–437, 2014.

- Can we verify if applications leak the location information of the smartphone when we turn off the *location services* and *advertising* tracking settings?
- Does any application access the smartphone's unique identifiers when we revoke the application's permission to access information?

The contributions of this work can be summarized as follows:

1. We implement a real-time traffic monitoring platform and demonstrate how to capture communication on Wi-Fi enabled smartphones.
2. We determine how well the tracking settings for *location services* and *advertising* work when they are turned off on a sample of `BlackBerry 10` and `Windows Phone 8` applications.
3. In the event where the settings fail to operate properly, we provide recommendations on how users can ensure that attackers do not compromise communications due to improper implementation[1] of Secure Sockets Layer (SSL) in applications.

The rest of the paper is organized as follows: Section 2 summarizes existing work and Section 3 provides background on tracking services. In Section 4 we explain our experimental work, followed by an analysis of our empirical results in Section 5. In Section 6, we conclude the paper and provide some recommendations.

2   Related Work

2.1   BlackBerry

The `BlackBerry 10` OS offers developers a list of permissions which can allow users to control the resources accessible to the applications once installed on the device. Unlike `Android` [5], many `Blackberry` permissions can be unchecked, prompted or revoked from application permissions settings on the `BlackBerry 10` devices. If an application tries to perform an action for which it does not have the required permission, the user is given a prompt. This often leads users to accept all permissions by default. `BlackBerry` reminds developers to have a highly visible privacy policy of their own, and ensure that they comply with local internet privacy legislation. This frees the `Blackberry` official applications site, BlackBerry App World, of any responsibility for privacy breaches by applications.

2.2   Windows Phone

The permission system on the `Windows Phone` platform bears many similarities to that of the `Android` OS. However, Microsoft's smartphone OS offers about 20 permissions for its application developers to which the users have to grant full access upon installation of the application.

Even though many publications have been written about the `Android` and `iOS` OS, to the best of our knowledge, there is little work in the literature analysing any versions of the `BlackBerry` and `Windows Phone` OS.

---

[1] http://heartbleed.com/

3   Tracking Services

We establish an experiment to determine if turning off tracking service settings actually prevents tracking. If we capture leaked information when the setting is 'off', it is not working as it should. Since no data capture when the setting is 'on' does not necessarily indicate a malfunction, we do not test the 'on' settings. We divide the tracking services into the following two categories: *location services* and *advertising*.

3.1   Tracking Services on BlackBerry 10

Location services can be accessed under the *Settings* option of a `BlackBerry` device. By default, the assumption is that whenever the setting for *location services* is turned off, applications should not have access to the user's location. To verify if this stands true, we monitor access to the following three pieces of information which are unique to the device and its user: (i) Media Access Control (MAC), a 12-character unique device identifier, (ii) Internet Protocol (IP) address and (iii) Global Positioning System (GPS) coordinates.

In order to test whether the tracking setting for *advertising* leaks any information when it is turned off, we monitor the use of two device identifiers that are unique to a `Blackberry` smartphone: (i) International Mobile Equipment Identity (IMEI), a 15-digit identifier and (ii) Hardware Personal Identification Number (PIN), an 8 alphanumeric identifier. These distinct codes are highly sought after by advertising companies for efficient user-profiling and to target advertisements.

3.2   Tracking Services on Windows Phone 8

We follow a similar rationale as described in Section 3.1. To test whether the `Windows Phone` 8 device leaks location-related information when the *location services* setting is turned off, we observe the use of MAC address, IP address and GPS coordinates by installed applications. On the `Windows Phone` platform, users can switch off *Location* under the *Settings* option to deter access to location information.

As for advertising, users do not have any option on the actual device to regulate access to advertisements. Instead, they have to use their Microsoft account and visit the online 'opt out page'[2] to opt out of receiving personalized advertisements and prevent applications from sending unique device identifiers to 3rd parties. We survey the usage of the IMEI and Device Identifier (ID), an alphanumeric string, by installed applications after a user has opted out of communicating this information to external servers.

---

[2] http://tinyurl.com/l2x8dyv

4 Experiment

4.1 Dataset Collection

The experiment was conducted using applications downloaded from the official markets of BlackBerry 10 and Windows Phone 8 OS. To ensure that the experiment was consistent, we only considered applications which were developed by the same developer or the same company for both platforms. Since developer profiles cannot be publicly accessed on the application markets, we manually checked the developer's information for each application for both of the OS before including it in our dataset. Due to this constraint, we conducted our study with a small dataset of 40 BlackBerry and 40 Windows Phone applications.

4.2 Experimental Work

We set up a traffic monitoring test bed, as in [7], which is suitable for capturing information from any device using Wi-Fi connectivity as shown in Fig. 1. We used a BlackBerry Z10 smartphone (contributed by BlackBerry) running on the BlackBerry 10 OS and a Nokia Lumia 520 smartphone running on the Windows Phone 8 OS to test our dataset. The traffic sniffing tool, Mallory, was installed in a VM which was running on Ubuntu version 12.04. The Mallory tool was developed by the firm Intrepidus Group[3] and is capable of capturing traffic packets to and from the smartphones. We chose this tool as it facilitates the interception of SSL traffic and acts as a MiTM proxy to capture packets in real-time communication.

We faced the issue of unstable network connections at the beginning of the experiment, and, because traffic was being relayed through Mallory, we experienced lengthy delays which often resulted in IP addresses being reset. To counter this problem, we set up a dedicated mini Wi-Fi modem which allowed us to connect all our devices on the same network. The VM hosting the Mallory tool was allowed to connect to the Internet. In order to relay traffic between the smartphones and Mallory, with the Blackberry phone, we were able to set up a VPN, while at the time of the experiment, Microsoft had not yet implemented the VPN option on their smartphone OS. To bypass this issue, we used a Wi-Fi USB adapter which allowed us to carry out packet injections. This ensured that Mallory could piggyback on the traffic being sent to and from the Windows Phone 8.

As the smartphones and Mallory both share the same Internet connection, any Internet-based traffic on the smartphones can be captured by Mallory (see Fig. 1). The communication from smartphone to server is referred to as "c2s" and server to smartphone as "s2c"; the Mallory tool captures both. This information is then recorded in an SQL database which was later exported for further analysis. Since the aim of this experiment is to monitor information leaked by the smartphones when tracking services are turned off, we ignored the "s2c" communications and instead focused on the "c2s" ones as they are more likely to

---

[3] http://intrepidusgroup.com/insight/mallory/

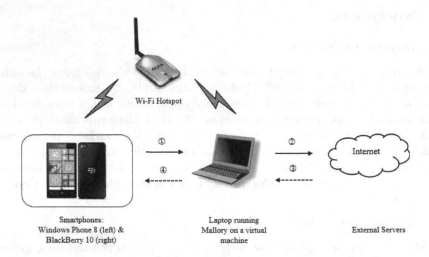

Fig. 1. Overview of Our Experimental Setup

reveal whether the applications on the smartphones are sending out information without the user's knowledge.

As explained in Section 3, we began by turning off all the tracking settings on our experimental devices and then analyzed our dataset by installing one application at a time. Each application was tested for two minutes. During the execution, we dynamically executed the application by checking all its features and clicking on advertisements. Once the execution time was over, we stopped Mallory from recording further traffic and uninstalled the application. We repeated these steps for each of the 40 BlackBerry and 40 Windows Phone applications. Once the experiment was concluded, we exported all traffic logs outside the VM and searched for the keywords mentioned in Section 3.

5   Analysis of Results

5.1   Presentation of Results

For each application in our dataset, we present our empirical results in two parts: *Location Services* and *Advertising*. The results for BlackBerry and Windows Phone are listed in Table 1 where the symbol ✗ means that one or more keyword items were leaked; alternatively, ✓ is placed to demonstrate that the application did not leak any information when tracking settings were turned off.

Recall that in our choice of application, we specifically chose ones for each OS by the same developer and with the same name, therefore appearing to have identical functionality. However, Table 1 indicates that this is not the case. For instance, the 2nd and 23rd applications, namely **Tube Map** and **Poynt** from Table 1 are considered to be *consistent* as the results on both OS are identical. Conversely, the 1st and 3rd applications - **BBC iPlayer** and **Bible**

Table 1. BlackBerry and Windows Phone Applications with Tracking Setting Off (✓ = Not leaked and ✗ = Leaked)

BlackBerry		Application Name	Windows Phone	
Location Services	*Advertising*		*Location Services*	*Advertising*
✓	✓	1.BBC iPlayer	✗	✓
✓	✓	2.Tube Map	✓	✓
✗	✓	3.Bible	✓	✗
✓	✗	4.Carrefour	✓	✓
✓	✓	5.To Do List	✓	✓
✓	✓	6.Combo Pic	✓	✗
✗	✓	7.Copter	✓	✗
✓	✓	8.Jetpack	✓	✓
✓	✓	9.Wizards Choice	✓	✗
✓	✓	10.Economic Times	✓	✓
✗	✓	11.Falldown	✓	✗
✓	✓	12.Real FootBall2013	✓	✓
✓	✓	13.Flashlight	✓	✓
✓	✓	14.Hangman	✓	✗
✓	✓	15.HDFC Bank	✓	✓
✓	✓	16.Kompass	✓	✓
✗	✓	17.Lega De Fulbol	✓	✓
✓	✓	18.Logo Quiz	✓	✗
✓	✓	19.Millionaire	✓	✗
✓	✓	20.Nu NL	✓	✓
✓	✓	21.OK Magazine	✓	✗
✗	✓	22.PGA Tour	✗	✓
✗	✓	23.Poynt	✗	✓
✓	✓	24.QR Code	✓	✓
✓	✓	25.Robotek	✗	✓
✓	✓	26.Skyscanner	✓	✓
✓	✓	27.Texas Holdem P.	✓	✓
✓	✓	28.Top Gear	✓	✓
✓	✗	29.Tuding	✓	✓
✓	✓	30.Tune in Radio	✓	✓
✗	✓	31.Wikipedia	✓	✓
✗	✓	32.WWE	✓	✓
✗	✓	33.XE Currency	✓	✓
✓	✓	34.Avianca	✓	✓
✓	✓	35.Chelsea FC NEWS	✓	✗
✓	✓	36.Daily Express UK	✓	✓
✓	✓	37.USA Today	✓	✓
✓	✓	38.Money Control	✓	✓
✓	✓	39.Toshl Finance	✓	✓
✓	✓	40.Park Mobile	✓	✓

respectively, are *inconsistent* as despite being the same applications executed on two different platforms, the results are different. In fact, there are 18 applications in our dataset that produced *inconsistent* results[4].

We believe there might be several reasons behind this discrepancy. During the experiment, each application was executed for a period of two minutes. Although this time constraint was applied to both BlackBerry and Windows Phone platforms, there is no guarantee that the execution patterns on each OS were identical. Moreover, despite the fact that all the applications in our dataset are available on both the BlackBerry and Windows Phone official application

---

[4] Application numbers 1,3,4,6,7,9,11,14,17-19,21,25,29,31-33,35 from Table 1.

markets and share application developers, we did not verify if the applications also make use of the same third party libraries. Different advertising libraries can appear in several posted versions of the same initial application because the business model of smartphones encourages developers to embed multiple third party libraries in order to increase revenue from advertising.

5.2 Information Leaks When Tracking Setting Is Off

Out of 40 applications executed on the `BlackBerry` platform, 10% (4) leaked either the GPS coordinates or IP address despite the setting for *location services* being off. These 4 applications are also part of the subset of 18 applications which produced *inconsistent* results, as described in Section 5.1. However, the results for *advertising* are far better as only 2 applications, **Carrefour** and **Tuding** leaked information about the Hardware PIN to advertisers when the tracking setting was turned off. It is also worth mentioning that none of the `Blackberry` applications leaked the IMEI or MAC address.

As for the `Windows Phone` platform, 35% (14) leaked information related to either *location services* or *advertising*. Whilst none of the 40 `Windows Phone` applications sent out GPS coordinates, the following four applications leaked either the MAC address or IP address: **BBC iPlayer**, **Robotek**, **PGA Tour** and **Poynt**. Unlike on the `BlackBerry` platform, the last 2 applications do not appear in the subset of 18 applications mentioned in Section 5.1. In terms of *advertising* related information leaked when the tracking setting was off, 10% of the `Windows Phone` applications sent out the Device ID information and the IMEI identifier was not divulged at all.

6 Conclusion

In this paper, we empirically analyzed 40 `Blackberry` and 40 `Windows Phone` applications. We tested whether tracking service settings for *location services* and *advertising* leak information when their tracking is turned off. We found that some applications still leak the user's location and device related information to third parties. Additionally, we observed that if an application does not leak any information on one particular smartphone OS, for instance `BlackBerry`, there is no guarantee that the same application will behave in a similar way on a different platform, (here for example, `Windows Phone`). Finally, we recommend some actions to overcome the issues we highlighted based on our empirical results.

6.1 Recommendations

Application developers earn revenue from in-application advertisements which is why many offer their applications free of charge. Advertising is very important for the smartphone application ecosystem as it is a major factor in the business model of the smartphone platform. Generally, the applications are required to send the smartphone's unique identifiers to advertizing agencies and in return, the application developers earn a revenue for using that agency's advertizing library. Hence, there is a trade-off between convenience and user privacy. Therefore, we recommend the following:

1. Smartphone users should have easy access to adequate functionalities on their devices that will help protect their private information. As such, we recommend that Microsoft implements a setting on their smartphones to allow users to easily opt out of advertising, instead of doing so via the web.
2. Application developers should be obliged to list the names and owners of third party advertising libraries that are used in their applications. Users should be made aware upfront of the advertising companies that have access to their information.
3. Smartphone OS providers should ensure that when *location services* is turned off, no location-related information is revealed to third parties. This could either take the form of an additional check that is conducted when a new application is uploaded on the application market or after the fact, fines could be issued to deter application developers from unethically accessing such information.

References

1. Moonsamy, V., Alazab, M., Batten, L.: Towards an understanding of the impact of advertising on data leaks. International Journal of Security and Networks 7(3), 181–193 (2012)
2. Han, J., Owusu, E., Nguyen, L., Perrig, A., Zhang, J.: ACComplice: Location inference using accelerometers on smartphones. In: Proceedings of the 4th International Conference on Communication Systems and Networks (COMSNETS 2012), Bangalore, India, pp. 1–9 (January 2012)
3. Mann, C., Starostin, A.: A framework for static detection of privacy leaks in android applications. In: Proceedings of the 27th Annual ACM Symposium on Applied Computing (SAC 2012), pp. 1457–1462 (March 2012)
4. Micinski, K., Phelps, P., Foster, J.S.: An Empirical Study of Location Truncation on Android. In: Proceedings of the 2013 Mobile Security Technologies Conference (MoST 2013), San Francisco, CA, pp. 1–10 (May 2013)
5. Shekhar, S., Dietz, M., Wallach, D.: Adsplit: Separating smartphone advertising from applications. In: Proceedings of the 20th USENIX Security Symposium (USENIX Security 2012), Bellevue, USA, pp. 1–15 (August 2012)
6. Zhao, Z., Osono, F.: TrustDroid: Preventing the use of Smartphones for information leaking in corporate networks through the use of static analysis taint tracking. In: Proceedings of the 7th International Conference on Malicious and Unwanted Software (MALWARE 2012), Puerto Rico, USA, pp. 135–143 (October 2012)
7. Moonsamy, V., Batten, L., Shore, M.: Can Smartphone Users Turn Off Tracking Service Settings? In: Proceedings of the 11th International Conference on Advances in Mobile Computing & Multimedia (MoMM 2013), Vienna, Austria, pp. 1–9 (December 2013)

Running Multiple Androids on One ARM Platform

Zhijiao Zhang, Lei Zhang, Yu Chen, and Yuanchun Shi

Department of Computer Science and Technology, Tsinghua University, Beijing, China
{acer.zhang,sosilent.lzh}@gmail.com,
{yuchen,shiyc}@tsinghua.edu.cn

Abstract. Smartphones are widely used nowadays. Many users want to separate work and personal use of smartphones for security and privacy consideration, but it is very inconvenient to carry multiple smartphones. Multi-boot and virtualization are two existing techniques used to solve this problem. In this paper, we present a prototype on which multiple Android instances can time-share one ARM platform by using suspend and resume mechanism. We describe the design and implementation of our prototype and evaluate its performance. The performance result shows that our implementation imposes negligible time overhead, and the switching speed is much faster than the multi-boot approach. We also avoid a huge number of modified code lines, considerable memory occupation and significant performance penalty of the virtualization solution.

Keywords: Android, Mobile Device, Security and Privacy, OS Switching.

1 Introduction

Nowadays, smart mobile devices such as smartphones and tablets are widely used, and mobile users can download more than 700,000 different applications in various online APP stores [1]. Unfortunately, the open environment of mobile device make mobile users be vulnerable to attacks launched by malicious programs. For this reason, some enterprises and government agencies enforce their employees to use a locked OS with preinstalled applications, and it cannot be used for personal purpose. Besides carrying two or more mobile devices to meet the demand for both work use and personal use, an effective way to resolve this problem is to provide multiple OS instances on one device for the mobile user. Virtualization and OS switching are two main approaches to accomplish this task.

Virtualization can offer multiple virtual machines on one physical machine. Generally, a program called hypervisor controls all resources of the physical machine (CPU, memory, disk, bandwidth, etc.) and allocates them among virtual machines. Each virtual machine runs a separate guest OS instance, and they are well isolated; moreover, because the number of virtual machines as well as resources for each virtual machine can be manually profiled, virtualization technology provides a great deal of flexibility and scalability. However, for mobile users, we must consider the available hardware platform in the first place. In smartphone market, the proportion of ARM (Advanced RISC Machines) architecture CPUs is about 90% [2]. Unfortunately, ARM CPUs are not virtualizable, thus paravirtualization technique is used in each

W. Susilo and Y. Mu (Eds.): ACISP 2014, LNCS 8544, pp. 438–445, 2014.
© Springer International Publishing Switzerland 2014

case [3, 4, 5, 12, 13, 14], which requires not only a considerable hypervisor, but a great quantity of modifications to source code of the OS kernel and device driver [5, 6], thus the virtualization layer itself may pose a security risk to the mobile device [11]. Another drawback of virtualization is the intolerable performance degradation. Experiment results show that the average latency of common OS services in paravirtualized Linux running on a virtual machine is twice the value of which in native Linux running on bare hardware [5].

OS switching [9] is derived from Multi-boot [10]. In brief, Multi-boot installs several different OS instances in different disk/flash partitions. A boot loader program runs first when a machine starts up. It requests the user to choose a booting OS and then loads and transfers control to the OS kernel, in turn the kernel initializes the entire system [7]. When the user wants to switch among different OSes, he must exit from the current OS and reboot the machine. Comparing with multi-boot, OS switching not only installs several OS instances on the same machine, but saves the state of the running OS instance. It means that when switching between OS instances, the necessary states of the machine (e.g., CPU, memory, I/O devices) are saved by the current running OS. Then this OS instance suspends and passes control to the incoming OS instance. Next time the user switches back to the former OS instance, all the states saved for it will be resumed, so it can run immediately without a reboot.

The main difference between virtualization and OS switching is that in OS switching, at any time only one OS instance is permitted to run actively, so it has less flexibility. However, the usage model of mobile devices is that at all times only one application can occupy the touch screen and interact with the user [8], so we can make the foreground OS instance as the active OS instance, and let other OS instances wait until the user activates one of them.

Although suspend/resume is not a new technique, as far as we are concerned, this paper is the first to introduce how to implement multiple Androids on one mobile device by this means. The remainder of this paper is structured as follows: Section 2 introduces suspend and resume mechanism of Linux and Android. Section 3 presents design and implementation. Section 4 demonstrates evaluation results. Finally, we summarize this paper with a conclusion in Section 5.

2   Suspend and Resume Mechanism

2.1   Linux Suspend and Resume Mechanism

As a modern operating system, Linux supports suspend and resume mechanism. The main purpose of suspend is to save power. Linux kernel has three suspend states: Standby, Suspend-to-RAM, and Suspend-to-Disk (hibernation) [16]. Standby has the minimal wakeup latency, but it does not save much power, nor does it save system and device states before machine sleeps. Hibernation has minimum power consumption, but it needs a relatively long time to wake-up [18]. Generally, Suspend-to-RAM state has the same time latency as Standby state, and supports saving system states. In this paper, the term *suspend* refers to Suspend-to-RAM state.

Suspend course can be roughly divided into 3 major steps: Firstly, freezing all kernel tasks and user space processes. In this step, OS kernel must save the context of each process, and free unnecessary memory. Secondly, calling all drivers' callback functions. These functions will save some certain information, stop services, and power off the related devices. Finally, saving all registers' contents to RAM and suspending the CPU. Obviously, this part of RAM will be powered on from beginning to end. After these steps, the OS enters in the wait-for-interrupt state.

Resume course is the reverse of suspend course. It is initialed by some pre-defined interrupt or event, and the entire system will return to the state it was before the suspend course started. Figure 1 shows an overview of suspend/resume course of Linux.

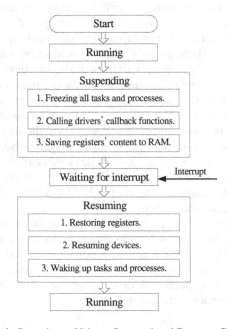

Fig. 1. Overview of Linux Suspend and Resume Course

Though the original purpose of suspend is to pause the entire system and save power, in theory, the state of an OS instance can be detached from the state of the hardware. That means, when an OS instance suspends, the hardware platform can run another OS instance.

2.2   Android Wakelocks

Android is running on top of Linux kernel which is modified from the standard version. Android uses wakelocks to perform power management. Both kernel tasks and user processes can apply for and hold wakelocks. Skipping wakelocks before suspending will lead devices to an uncertain state, so before the OS suspends, it must wait until all wakelocks are released.

3   Design and Implementation

3.1   Design Principle

We must comply with some design principles to meet mobile users' requirements:

1. Security and privacy: We must ensure all OS instances are isolated from each other. That is, any application running on one OS instance cannot access or damage data of other instances. We also need to ensure when an OS instance crashes, other instances can run normally.
2. Small additional overhead: As the main shortage of the mobile device is the limited hardware resources, our implementation cannot add large overhead, and at the same time the response time of the system must be almost unaffected.
3. Software compatibility: The user's applications can run on our platform without any modification; moreover, all applications can read or write data as normal.
4. Fast switch: Our implementation must provide acceptable switching time for the impatient mobile user.

3.2   Implementation

Our implementation is based on an OMAP4460 Pandaboard ES platform (1.2 GHz Dual-core Cortex-A9 CPU, 1 GB RAM, PowerVR SGX540 GPU, DVI-D or HDMI display), running two Linaro Android 12.06 instances (The Android version is 4.0.4). The Linux kernel version is 3.4.0, and we choose u-boot 2012.04 as the boot loader program. We use a 32GB SD card to store OS kernel images, Android file systems and all application files.

In the first place, we modified u-boot, letting it load two kernel images into different RAM blocks which cannot overlap each other. Then we reserved a little of RAM (about 4K), and split the remained memory into two separate parts, each part is about 500MB, which is enough to host kernel and userspace for Android 4.0 [17]. Though the memory used for one OS instance can be used for the other, we let the two OS instances use different memory areas. We have two reasons: One is that frequent occurrence of page faults may lead to a considerable passive impact on the OS's running speed. The other is for security. Because an OS instance can only access the memory area exclusively allocated for it, neither the running OS instance nor the suspending OS instance knows anything about each other.

Afterwards, we changed the suspend process of both OS instances. When switching occurs, the outgoing OS instance will enter the wait-for-interrupt state after the normal steps of suspend course. Normally core0 will be in a low-power state and wait for an interrupt, while other cores will be powered off. We changed the suspend route, lead core0 execute the incoming OS instance's instructions, and there are two situations: If the incoming OS instance has not been started up, the outgoing OS instance will jump to the boot loader program (u-boot), and u-boot will boot up the incoming OS instance. In other cases, the incoming OS instance will have been in suspend state, and core0 will perform its resume course (see Figure 2).

In normal path of the suspend course, it is OS saves context information from registers to SAR (Suspend and Resume) RAM before the CPU is powered off and registers are invalid. This part of RAM will not be powered off. Then in resume course, OS restores registers from SAR RAM. In our implementation, saving context information for the outgoing OS instance will destroy SAR RAM content of the incoming OS instance, so we need copy SAR RAM content (about 4K) to another place before this step. This is why we reserved a part of RAM before.

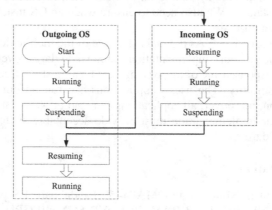

Fig. 2. Running 2 OS instances with Suspend/Resume Mechanism

Though these steps sound very simple, we must consider some problems:

— Firstly, we must think about the influence of MMU. Because each OS kernel uses virtual address and has its own page table, before we jump from one OS instance to the other, we must turn off MMU. Since turning off MMU is also a set of instructions, to ensure the CPU to execute the same section of code before and after turning off MMU, we must create a page table by which the CPU can use physical address to access the right location in RAM. This can be done after the outgoing OS instance has been suspended. Similarly, before the incoming OS instance is resumed, we will turn on MMU and load the new page table address.
— Secondly, influence of multi-core will also be considered. When the CPU suspends the entire system, only one core (it ought to be the core0) will execute relative instructions. It must wait until other cores complete their work, and ensure memory accessing of other cores has been finished. Similarly, when the CPU resumes the system, core0 needs to prepare the context before waking up other cores.
— Thirdly, by default the CPU prefetches a number of instructions before it actually executes them, and before the ARM CPU reaches a branch, it will prefetch instructions either at the branch target or following the branch. This is known as branch prediction [15, 19]. In normal circumstance, branch prediction can reduce CPU circles and enhance execution performance. When OS switching occurs, after we disable the MMU, the CPU should access physical address, but it prefetches instructions in logical address, and the number of prefetched instructions is various dynamically, so we cannot know how many instructions to be discarded. Therefore, we ought to invalidate branch prediction before turning on or off MMU.

4   Evaluation

In this section we present a measurement evaluation. All experiments were performed on the OMAP4460 Pandaboard ES platform (see Section 3). We ran the original Android OS on the platform at first. Then we ran the two modified Android instances (we named them OS1 and OS2) simultaneously on the same platform.

We tested suspend and resume time cost of each OS instance, and compare the results to see the influence of our implementation. Figure 3 and Figure 4 show the result. In each case, we tested for 10 times.

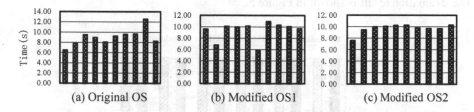

(a) Original OS   (b) Modified OS1   (c) Modified OS2

Fig. 3. Suspend time cost of each OS instance

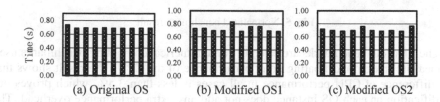

(a) Original OS   (b) Modified OS1   (c) Modified OS2

Fig. 4. Resume time cost of each OS instance

Figure 3 shows that the suspend time in each case varies from 6 seconds to 12 seconds. But in Figure 4, the resume time is almost the same. This is likely due to the influence of Android wakelock. If some task holds a wakelock and doesn't release it in time, the OS will wait before it suspends.

Table 1. shows the average suspend and resume time of each OS instance. Note that we need to choose a booting OS instance manually when running multi-OS instances, so we only calculated average reboot time when running single OS instance.

Table 1. Compare of suspend and resume time

OS instance	Average Suspend time (s)	Average Resume time (s)	Average Reboot time (s)
Original OS	9.00	0.6919	21.64
Modified OS1	9.34	0.7246	
Modified OS2	9.69	0.7084	

From Table 1 we can see that the suspend time cost of the modified OS instances is a little higher than that of the original standard OS instance. It is mainly because we copy the 4k SAR RAM contents to reserved RAM when switching from one OS instance to the other. However, the additional time cost is unnoticeable for the user; besides, there is no obvious difference between resume time cost of the modified OS instances and the standard OS instance. We can also see that the total time cost of suspend and resume course is about 10 seconds. It's an acceptable value comparing to more than 20 seconds which is needed to reboot the entire system.

To see if our implementation will produce performance degradation, we run some benchmarks in each OS instance. There is no other additional workload in each test. The evaluation result is shown in Figure 5.

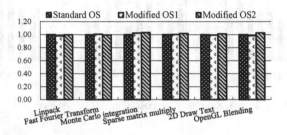

Fig. 5. Normalized benchmark result

The first four benchmarks are scientific and numerical computing benchmarks used to measure integer and floating point performance of the CPU. The result shows that the difference of CPU performance in all cases is less than 3.5%, which proves our modification on each OS instance does not add any extra performance overhead. The 2D Draw Text and 3D OpenGL Blending benchmark result shows that time overheads in all cases are almost the same, which indicates that the modified OS instances can also achieve full graphics acceleration performance.

5   Conclusion

In this paper we propose an approach which supports multiple Androids time-share the same mobile device by using suspend and resume mechanism. Our approach avoids huge performance degradation and considerable source code modification of the virtualization technology, overcomes inflexibility of the multi-boot solution, provides native performance and whole hardware access, and fulfills the security request of the mobile user. We believe multiple OS running on one mobile device is very useful in many scenarios, and our implementation is a good choice for mobile users.

Acknowledgements. This work is supported in part by the Natural Science Foundation of China under Grant No. 61170050, National Science and Technology Major Project of China（2012ZX01039-004）. The authors would also like to thank anonymous reviewers who have helped us to improve the quality of this paper.

References

1. Android (operating system),
   http://en.wikipedia.org/wiki/Android_(operating_system)
2. http://en.wikipedia.org/wiki/ARM_architecture
3. Dall, C., Nieh, J.: KVM for ARM. In: Proceedings of the Ottawa Linux Symposium, Ottawa, Canada (2010)
4. Barr, K., Bungale, P., Deasy, S., Gyuris, V., Hung, P., Newell, C., Tuch, H., Zoppis, B.: The VMware Mobile Virtualization Platform: Is That a Hypervisor in Your Pocket? ACM SIGOPS Operating Systems Review 44, 124–135 (2010)
5. Hwang, J., Suh, S., Heo, S., Park, C., Ryu, J., Park, S., Kim, C.: Xen on ARM: System Virtualization using Xen Hypervisor for ARM-based Secure Mobile Phones. In: Proceedings of the 5th Consumer Communications and Newtork Conference, Las Vegas, NV (January 2008)
6. Xen Hypervisor Project, http://www.xen.org/products/xenhyp.html
7. GNU Grub Project, http://www.gnu.org/software/grub/.
8. Andrus, J., Dall, C., Van't Hof, A., Laadan, O., Nieh, J.: Cells: A Virtual Mobile Smartphone Architecture. In: Proceedings of the 23rd ACM Symposium on Operating Systems Principles (SOSP) (2011)
9. Sun, J., Zhou, D., Longerbeam, S.: Supporting Multiple OSes with OS Switching. In: USENIX Annual Technical Conference, pp. 357–362 (2007)
10. Multi-boot specification,
    http://www.gnu.org/software/grub/manual/multiboot/multiboot.html
11. Keller, E., Szefer, J., Rexford, J., Lee, R.B.: NoHype: Virtualized cloud infrastructure without the virtualization. In: Proceedings of the 37th Annual International Symposium on Computer Architecture, Saint-Malo, France, June 19-23 (2010)
12. Open Kernel Labs. OK: Android,
    http://www.ok-labs.com/products/ok-android
13. Iqbal, A., Sadeque, N., Mutia, R.I.: An Overview of Microkernel, Hypervisor and Microvisor VirtualizationApproaches for Embedded Systems. Technical Report, Lund University, Lund (2009)
14. Bylund, M.: Evaluation of OKL4. Bachelor Thesis in Computer Science, Mlardalens University (2009)
15. OMAP4460 Multimedia Device Silicon Revision 1.x. Technical Reference Manual. Version Q. Texas Instruments (2012), http://www.ti.com/product/omap4460
16. Kaminaga, H.: Improving Linux Startup Time Using Software Resume (and other techniques). In: Linux Symposium (2006)
17. Android 4.0 Compatibility Definition Document,
    http://source.android.com/compatibility/4.0/android-4.0-cdd.pdf
18. Brown, A.L., Wysocki, R.J.: Suspend-to-RAM in Linux. In: Linux Symposium (2008)
19. ARM Architecture Reference Manual,
    http://infocenter.arm.com/help/index.jsp?topic=/com.arm.doc.subset.architecture.reference/index.html

CoChecker: Detecting Capability and Sensitive Data Leaks from Component Chains in Android

Xingmin Cui[1], Da Yu[2], Patrick Chan[1],
Lucas C.K. Hui[1], S.M. Yiu[1,*], and Sihan Qing[2]

[1] Department of Computer Science, The University of Hong Kong,
Pokfulam, Hong Kong
{xmcui,pfchan,hui,smyiu}@cs.hku.hk
[2] School of Software and Microelectronics, Peking University, Beijing, China
dyu@pku.edu.cn, qsihan@ss.pku.edu.cn

Abstract. Studies show that malicious applications can obtain sensitive data from and perform protected operations in a mobile phone using an authorised yet vulnerable application as a deputy (referred to as privilege escalation attack). Thus it is desirable to have a checker that can help developers check whether their applications are vulnerable to these attacks. In this paper, we introduce our tool, CoChecker, to identify the leak paths (chains of components) that would lead to privilege escalation attacks using static taint analysis. We propose to build a call graph to model the execution of multiple entry points in a component and eliminate the false negatives due to the Android's event-driven programming paradigm. We further carry out inter-component communication through intent-tracing and formulate the call graph of the analyzed app. The evaluation of CoChecker on the state-of-the-art test suit Droid-Bench and randomly downloaded apps shows that it is both efficient and effective.

Keywords: Android security, Privilege escalation attack, Static taint analysis.

1 Introduction

The most recent data from IDC shows that in Q4 of 2013 Android made up 78.1% of devices shipped[1]. With Android devices being prevalent, their security becomes a major concern. Android relies on the use of sandbox and permission mechanism to control data access and application execution.

In spite of all kinds of security mechanisms, recent research[2] discovered privilege escalation attack (or confused deputy attack) in Android applications. The idea is that an application with less permissions can gain access to the components of a more privileged application. To prevent this attack, an application must enforce additional checks to protect the permissions it has been granted. However, since most Android application developers are not security experts,

---

* Corresponding author.

W. Susilo and Y. Mu (Eds.): ACISP 2014, LNCS 8544, pp. 446–453, 2014.

there is a need to have a checker that can help them check whether their applications are vulnerable to such kind of attack.

Both dynamic and static analysis have been used to detect privilege leak paths. In dynamic analysis, sink methods are monitored by some hooked functions to track the flow of sensitive data in third-party apps[3] or regulate communications between applications[4][5]. However, these solutions either have limited usage scenario or large overhead to use practically. Static analysis checks the vulnerabilities in Android apps before installation. Examples are ScanDroid[6], DroidChecker[7], CHEX[8], Flowdroid[9], Epicc[10]. But these tools either work on the user side or on the market side. Besides, these tools either do not perform inter-component communication analysis or fail to consider Android's event-driven programming paradigm.

We use static taint analysis to help developers check whether their developed applications are safe. In previous studies, there does not exist a systematic study on classifying leak paths. In this paper, we propose to classify leak paths into two types based on the nature of Android API calls: capability leak paths and sensitive data leak paths. Capability leak paths start from an entry point of the vulnerable app and end at an action call which is protected by permissions. By utilizing this vulnerable app, an unauthorised app can also perform protected actions. Sensitive data leak paths start from retrieving sensitive data by invoking a permission protected data call and end at a sink through which the retrieved data can be leaked to the unauthorised app.

We propose a tool, CoChecker, to automatically identify capability leaks and sensitive data leaks in Android apps. Both types of leak paths can cross multiple components, therefore inter-component communication analysis is essential. CoChecker constructs invoking chains to connect different components in the analyzed app. We propose to construct a call graph to model the execution of multiple entry points in an Android component and get a complete set of tainted variables. We further combine the call graph of each component to formulate the call graph of the analyzed app using the information in the invoking chains. This models the inter-component interactions and enables us to achieve a higher precision of analysis.

2   Analysis Challenges

2.1   Challenge One: Inter-Component Communication Analysis

Analyzing the inter-component communication in an Android app is prerequisite to find all potential leak paths. On one hand, the source and sink methods of a leak path can reside in different components. On the other hand, without parsing the sender and receiver components of an intent, we cannot get the set of components that can be accessed and exploited by external malicious apps.

CoChecker performs inter-component analysis and constructs invoking chains for the analyzed app. An *invoking chain* starts from an entry point of the app (exported components that require no permission from other component to interact with them) and is extended to include all components that are reachable from this entry point using intents. CoChecker only raises an alarm when source and sink methods reside in these components to make sure the leak paths are exploitable. At the beginning CoChecker builds an invoking chain for each entry point of the app and starts the analysis from these entry points. When CoChecker encounters an intent, it will parse the parameters to find the target receiver components and add them to the corresponding invoking chain.

2.2   Challenge Two: Entry Points and Their Order of Execution

Android applications are composed of components whose lifecycle is managed by the Android framework in an event-driven manner. Besides, Android provides Event Listener interfaces for developers to implement and override the callback methods in these interfaces in react to users' UI interaction or system state change (eg. locationUpdate). Therefore unlike traditional Java programs which use a single main method as the entry point, Android components can have many entry points, including Android lifecycle methods and user-defined event handlers. These methods are invoked by the Android framework at runtime and cannot pre-determine their order of execution.

CoChecker adopts static taint analysis to detect leak paths. In taint analysis, we need to get a complete set of tainted variables and check whether these variables can reach the sink methods. If any tainted variables can reach a sink method, an alarm will be raised to indicate a leak. In an Android component, the taint status of the globally accessible variables can be different given different execution sequences of multiple entry points. Therefore, we need to consider the taint status under all possible execution sequences in order to get a safe approximation of the tainted variable set. We propose to construct a call graph for each component to emulate the execution of multiple entry points and get a complete tainted variable list. Details will be given in the system design section.

3   System Design

We provide a tool, CoChecker, to detect capabilities and sensitive data leaks in Android applications. CoChecker aims to help Android application developers better regulate their apps to avoid privilege escalation attacks, therefore we choose the source code as our analysis target.

CoChecker will perform the following procedures: (1)Parse the Manifest file and layout XML file to extract the list of components contained in the app, the entry points to the app, intent-filter list and callbacks registered in the layout file. (2)Construct the abstract syntax tree(AST) of each component and build the control flow graph (CFG) of the methods in each component. In the CFG of each method, nodes represent the statements in this method and edges represent the control flow. (3)By traversing the AST of each component, CoChecker discovers the intents sent by them and builds up the invoking chain. (4)Distinguish the entry points of each component, including the lifecycle methods and user-defined event handlers. (5)Construct the call graph of each component. (6)Construct the call graph of whole app. (7)Traverse the call graph of the app to detect leak paths.

Steps (1) and (2) are trivial. Step (3) has been mentioned in Section 2. Next we will introduce steps (4)-(7) in detail.

3.1 Construction of the Call Graph

The Call Graph of Each Component. CoChecker builds a call graph for each component to model the execution of multiple entry points in this component. The nodes denote the entry points of this component and the edges indicate their order of execution. The call graph is constructed incrementally with the identification of every entry point.

For each component declared in the Manifest file, CoChecker firstly extracts its Abstract Syntax Tree(AST) and constructs the Control Flow Graph (CFG) of each method in it. After that CoChecker traverses the AST of each component to distinguish the lifecycle methods and user-defined event handlers by matching with an input file. This file contains a list of lifecycle methods and Event Listener interfaces (eg. LocationListener, onClickListener, etc) extracted from the Android documentation. When a lifecycle method is found,CoChecker inserts a corresponding node to the call graph according to the pre-defined execution order of lifecycle methods in the Android documentation. CoChecker retrieves a list of user-defined event handlers by looking for the corresponding overridden callback methods declared in the classes which implement the input Event Listener interfaces. These registered callback methods will be invoked by the Android framework when there is UI interaction or system state change. Since their order of execution can be arbitrary, we assume that they can be executed in any order and represent them in parallel between a pair of *ParBegin* and *parEnd* nodes in the call graph when the component is running.

The Call Graph of the Analyzed App. After constructing the call graph of each component, the call graph of the whole app can be easily derived. A component usually starts another component using component interaction methods such as *startActivity*. During the construction of the invoking chain, CoChecker records the location of the interaction methods. By adding an edge pointing from this interaction method to the *Begin* node of the call graph of the invoked component, CoChecker simulates what happens during execution. The call graph of the analyzed app is constructed by traversing all invoking chains and linking the call graphs of related components.

3.2 Taint Propagation and Leak Paths Detection

After constructing the call graph of the checked application, CoChecker traverses the CFG of each method in accordance with their order in the call graph to check whether data can flow from source methods to sink methods. Next we will introduce the taint propagation principle and leak path detection policy in detail.

The taint information at a program point p is a tuple $\{GTV, LTV, CTV, CSink\}$ consisiting of:

GTV :the set of current Tainted Global Variables. This list is effective during the checking of all methods of the current component and is passed on from one method to another. CoChecker raises an alarm and reports a leak path if any variables in this list reach a sink.

LTV: the set of current Tainted Local Variables. It is only effective within the scope of the current method and CoChecker also raises an alarm and reports a leak path if any variables in this list reach a sink.

CTV: the set of Conditional Tainted Variables. It stores the list of variables that may become tainted because of the interference of other methods. Here we consider two situations: if a variable is assigned to the value of a global variable or a parameter, it is put into the *CTV* list because this global variable or parameter may become tainted in other methods and in turn makes this variable tainted. This list is backfilled after collecting the taint status of global variables in methods that may happen before the current method.

CSink: the set of Conditional Sinks. It stores the list of sink methods whose parameters are in the *CTV* list. If any parameters actually get tainted after backfilling the *CTV* list, CoChecker will raise an alarm and report the leak path.

The effect of a method M on the tuple is defined by a transform function **F**.

$$\mathbf{F}\{GTV, LTV, CTV, CSink\} = \{GTV', LTV', CTV', CSink'\} \qquad (1)$$

where:

$$
\begin{aligned}
GTV' &= GTV \cup gen_{G_M} - kill_{G_M}, & CTV' &= gen_{C_M}, \\
LTV' &= gen_{L_M} - kill_{L_M}, & CSink' &= gen_{CSink_M}
\end{aligned}
\qquad (2)
$$

Here gen_{G_M} and $kill_{G_M}$ represent the set of generated and killed global variables in method M while gen_{L_M} and $kill_{L_M}$ represent the set of generated and killed local variables. We differentiate local variables and global variables because one method can only influence the taint status of the global variables in another method. gen_{L_M} and $kill_{L_M}$ are only effective within the scope of M.

We traverse every node in the CFG of method M to calculate the *gen* and *kill* set. In the taint propagation process, we consider assignment statements in the form "$v = expr$" or variable declaration statements in the form "$type\ v = expr$". If *expr* contains source methods or tainted variables, v is added to the gen_{GTV} or gen_{LTV} set depending on it is a global or local variable. Otherwise, if *expr* contains global variables or parameters whose taint status is not determined at the moment, v is added to the gen_{CTV} set. Otherwise, v is added to the *kill* set. We consider an object to be tainted if any of its member attribute is tainted. A set of data is tainted if any of the contained data is tainted. We also consider some pre-set propagation functions such as *Bundle.putString* and *Intent.putExtra*. Whether the caller instance should be put into the *gen* set or *kill* set depends on the taint status of its parameters.

For the nodes between $ParBegin$ and $ParEnd$, the situation is different. Without loss of generality, we assume that there are n user-defined event handlers between a pair of $ParBegin$ and $ParEnd$ nodes. For event handler M_i ($i = 1, ..., n$), all other event handlers may happen before it. Therefore for this parallel part we adopt a two-round checking policy. We use $GTV_{M_{ir}}$ and $GTV_{M_{ir}}'$ to denote the incoming and outgoing set of global tainted variables of method M_i in the r-th round ($r = 1, 2$). Therefore $GTV_{M_{i1}}$ is the GTV list at the exit point of the preceding method. After traversing the CFG of M_i in the first round, we get the set

$$GTV_{M_{i1}}' = GTV_{M_{i1}} \cup gen_{G_{M_i}} - kill_{G_{M_i}} \qquad (3)$$

In order to take into account the set of variables that may become tainted if other event handlers execute first, we introduce a set I, which represents the taint status of global variables after the execution of other event handlers. So:

$$I_i = \bigcup_{j \in [1,n], j \neq i} GTV_{M_{j1}}' \qquad (4)$$

In the second round, at the entry of M_i, $GTV_{M_{i2}} = GTV_{M_{i1}} \cup I_i$. This way we have considered the maxim set of tainted variables before the execution of M_i and reduced the false negatives to the minimum.

During the second round traversal, CoChecker checks the CTV list to backfill the potential tainted variables. Besides, it checks the $CSink$ list to see whether the potential tainted parameters can actually get tainted or not.

For the nodes that have two or more precedent nodes, a similar strategy is adopted. CoChecker backfills the CTV and $CSink$ lists after checking all precedent nodes. In this way, CoChecker ensures the completeness of the tainted variable list and the accuracy of the checking.

4   Implementation and Evaluation

4.1   Implementation

The entire system of CoChecker consists of around 5,000 lines of JAVA code. We designed and implemented our own static taint analysis tool instead of using Soot or WALA because we want to combine the inter-component analysis and build a customised taint analysis tool. The system runs under Linux Ubuntu 13.04 on a computer with Intel Core I5 3.4GHz CPU and 4GB RAM.

4.2   Evaluation

Evaluation on DroidBench. We evaluated our system using 21 test cases in the the state-of-the-art Android analysis benchmark suite DroidBench[11]. These test cases covered Android-specific challenges including callbacks, inter-app communication and lifecycle. Among these 21 test cases, CoChecker found 16 out of 19 leak paths.

10 potential leaks exist in the 12 test cases related to callbacks. CoChecker identified 8 of them with no false positive. The 2 false negatives reside in test case *MethodOverried1* and *RegisterGlobal1*. CoChecker fails to find the leak in *MethodOverride1* because it does not consider method overrides except in pre-extracted interfaces. In *RegisterGlobal1*, both source and sink are in a subclass of Application which are invoked when the application is initially launched. CoChecker fails to detect this leak because it does not parse the *android:name* attribute of the Application tag to find out whether a subclass of Application is defined to customize the Application launch process. CoChecker can be easily adjusted to enclose this situation. CoChecker discovered all of the 3 leak paths in test cases related to inter-app communication. 5 out of 6 leak paths were found by CoChecker among the cases related to Android lifecycle. The false negative is also because CoChecker fails to consider class inheritance.

Evaluation on Downloaded Apps. Apart from the evaluation on Droid-Bench, we also used CoChecker to scan 1123 Android applications downloaded from Android Freeware[12]. The downloaded apk files are first decompiled to JAVA code using dex2jar. Then the configuration files and source files are input into CoChecker. CoChecker finished checking all applications in about an hour. Our tool is efficient because it did not use the Soot or WALA framework which need to convert the input to their intermediate representation. CoChecker raised 117 alarms for potential leak paths among which 84 are capability leak paths and 33 are sensitive data leak paths. For the same test set, DroidChecker[7] only raised 23 alarms among which 8 are true alarms.

We manually analyzed these alarms to search for leak paths. We regard an alarm as a true alarm only when an exploitable leak path is found in the application. For the 84 type 1 alarms, 77 of them are true alarms. For the 33 type 2 alarms, 30 of them are true alarms. We manually analyzed their source files that raise true alarms and confirmed the leak paths identified by CoChecker[1]. For the 10 false alarms, 6 of them are because CoChecker fails to deal with object sensitivity and 4 are caused by nonexistent path that CoChecker mistakenly found. This is resulted from the reverse engineering process.

5   Conclusions and Future Work

In this paper, we aim at checking whether an Android application is vulnerable to privilege escalation attacks by detecting two types of leak paths: capability leak paths and sensitive data leak paths. We rely on static taint analysis to detect these leak paths. We designed and implemented a checker, CoChecker, to automatically detect the leak paths in Android apps. We evaluated our system on the state-of-the-art bench suite DroidBench and 1123 randomly downloaded apps. The result shows CoChecker is effective and efficient.

---

[1] Please refer to our full paper for the sample attacks exploiting the detected leak paths.

For future research, we aim to improve our system to achieve a higher precision by enclosing more properties such as object-sensitivity, point-to analysis, etc. Besides, currently we only checked privilege escalation vulnerabilities caused by Activity, Service and BroadcastReceiver. Operations on Content Providers may also cause privilege escalation problems which need our further exploration.

Acknowlegement. This research is in part supported by the National Natural Science Foundation of China under Grant No. 61170282 and the NSFC/RGC Joint Research Grant (N_HKU 729/13).

References

1. Android and iOS Continue to Dominate the Worldwide Smartphone Market with Android Shipments Just Shy of 800 Million in 2013, According to IDC, http://www.idc.com/getdoc.jsp?containerId=prUS24676414
2. Davi, L., Dmitrienko, A., Sadeghi, A.-R., Winandy, M.: Privilege escalation attacks on android. In: Burmester, M., Tsudik, G., Magliveras, S., Ilić, I. (eds.) ISC 2010. LNCS, vol. 6531, pp. 346–360. Springer, Heidelberg (2011)
3. Enck, W., Gilbert, P., Chun, B.-G., Cox, L.P., Jung, J., McDaniel, P., Sheth, A.N.: TaintDroid: an information-flow tracking system for realtime privacy monitoring on smartphones. In: Proceedings of the 9th USENIX Conference on Operating Systems Design and Implementation (2010)
4. Felt, A.P., Wang, H.J., Moshchuk, A., Hanna, S., Chin, E.: Permission Re-delegation: Attacks and Defenses. In: Proceedings of the 20th USENIX Conference on Security, SEC 2011, San Francisco, CA (2011)
5. Bugiel, S., Davi, L., Dmitrienko, A., Fischer, T., Sadeghi, A.R., Shastry, B.: Towards Taming Privilege-Escalation Attacks on Android. In: 19th Annual Network and Distributed System Security Symposium (NDSS) (2012)
6. Fuchs, A.P., Chaudhuri, A., Foster, J.S.: SCanDroid: Automated security certification of Android applications, Univ. of Maryland (2009) (manuscript), http://www.cs.umd.edu/~avik/projects/scandroidascaa
7. Chan, P.P., Hui, L.C., Yiu, S.-M.: Droidchecker: analyzing android applications for capability leak. In: Proceedings of the Fifth ACM Conference on Security and Privacy in Wireless and Mobile Networks, pp. 125–136 (2012)
8. Felt, A.P., Chin, E., Hanna, S., Song, D., Wagner, D.: Chex: Statically vetting android apps for component hijacking vulnerabilities. In: Proceedings of the 2012 ACM Conference on Computer and Communications Security, CCS 2012, NY, USA (2012)
9. Christian, F., Steven, A., Siegfried, R., Eric, B., Alexandre, B., Jacques, K., Yves le, T., Damien, O., Patrick, M.: Highly Precise Taint Analysis for Android Applications. Ec spride technical report tud-cs-2013-0113 (2013)
10. Octeau, D., McDaniel, P., Jha, S., Bartel, A., Bodden, E., Klein, J.: Jacques and Y.Le Traon: Effective inter-component communication mapping in android with epicc: An essential step towards holistic security analysis. In: Proceedings of the 22nd USENIX Security Symposium (2013)
11. DroidBench, EC SPRIDE, https://github.com/secure-software-engineering/DroidBench
12. Freeware Lover, Best and Free software for Android mobile platform, http://www.freewarelovers.com/android

Integral Zero-Correlation Distinguisher for ARX Block Cipher, with Application to SHACAL-2*

Long Wen and Meiqin Wang**

Key Laboratory of Cryptologic Technology and Information Security,
Ministry of Education, Shandong University, Jinan 250100, China
longwen@mail.sdu.edu.cn, mqwang@sdu.edu.cn

Abstract. At ASIACRYPT'12, Bogdanov et al. revealed the identity of integral distinguishers and zero-correlation linear approximations where the mask consists of two parts: one part should take any non-zero value and the other part should be fixed to zero. For zero-correlation linear approximations of some ARX block ciphers, one bit of input mask usually is fixed to one, which do not conform to zero-correlation linear approximations considered by Bogdanov et al.. Can they also be converted to an integral distinguisher? In this paper, we show that such zero-correlation linear approximations can be transformed to an integral distinguisher too. As an application, we give the attack on SHACAL-2 which is one of the four selected block ciphers by NESSIE. Namely, a attack on 32-round SHACAL-2 is reported. As an integral attack, our attack is much better than the previous integral attack on 28-round SHACAL-2 in terms of the number of rounds. In the classical single-key setting, our attack could break as many rounds as the previous best attack, but with significant improvements in data complexity and memory complexity.

Keywords: zero-correlation, integral, SHACAL-2, ARX block cipher.

1 Introduction

Integral distinguisher is originally proposed by Knudsen as a dedicated attack against Square [7], so it is commonly known as Square attack. Afterwards, variants of integral distinguishers have been proposed, including saturation distinguisher [8] and multiset distinguisher [1]. Integral distinguisher uses sets or multisets of chosen plaintexts where one part is held constant and the other part varies through all possibilities, and as a result the XOR sum of the corresponding sets of ciphertexts is zero.

Zero-correlation linear cryptanalysis proposed by Bogdanov and Rijmen in [2] has its theoretical foundation in the availability of numerous key-independent unbiased linear approximations with correlation zero for many ciphers. And it

---

* This work has been partially supported by 973 Program (No. 2013CB834205), NSFC Project (No. 61133013, 61103237), Program for New Century Excellent Talents in University of China (NCET-13-0350), as well as Interdisciplinary Research Foundation of Shandong University (No. 2012JC018).
** Corresponding author.

W. Susilo and Y. Mu (Eds.): ACISP 2014, LNCS 8544, pp. 454–461, 2014.
© Springer International Publishing Switzerland 2014

has been developed a lot in [3, 4]. At ASIACRYPT'12, Bogdanov et al. revealed fundamental links of integral distinguishers to zero-correlation linear approximations [4]. To be specific, consider a zero-correlation distinguisher for an n-bit block cipher, w.l.o.g suppose the last s-bit of input mask is zero and the last $n - t$-bit of the output mask is zero. The zero-correlation distinguisher is equivalent to an integral distinguisher where fixing the first $n - s$ bits in the input leads to a balanced function when only the first t bits of the output are considered.

However, one bit of input mask of zero-correlation linear approximations for some ARX block ciphers is usually fixed to one. That is the input mask consists of three parts: some bits that can take any value, one bit fixed to 1, and the other bits that are fixed to zero. For example, the zero-correlation linear approximations for TEA, XTEA, HIGHT have such form [3,12]. Apparently, the input mask for this kind of zero-correlation linear approximations does not conform to the style in [4]. It is interesting to see if they can be transformed to an integral distinguisher.

1.1 Our Contributions

Zero-Correlation and Integral Distinguisher for ARX Block Cipher. We show that in ARX block ciphers zero-correlation distinguisher also imply an integral distinguisher. More precisely, we proved in Section 3 that zero-correlation linear approximations $a \to b$ over (part of) n-bit ARX block cipher H' can be converted to an integral distinguisher, where the input mask is consisted of three parts: r bits that can take any value, one bit fixed to 1, and $s = n - r - 1$ bits that are fixed to zero, and the output mask is composed of two parts: t bits that can be any non-zero value and $n - t$ bits fixed to zero. The derived integral distinguisher uses the set where r input bits are fixed as constant and traverse all possible values for one input bit (with mask value 1) and the s input bits (with mask value 0), to compute the XOR sum of t output bits with non-zero mask value, then the obtained XOR sum is zero.

Table 1. Summary of Single-Key Attacks on SHACAL-2

Attack Type	Rounds	Data	Time Ens.	Memory Bytes	Source
Saturation	28	$464 \cdot 2^{32}$CPs	$2^{494.1}$	$2^{45.9}$	[9]
Imp. Diff	30	744 CPs	$2^{495.1}$	$2^{14.5}$	[6]
Diff-Linear	32	$2^{43.4}$CPs	$2^{504.2}$	$2^{48.4}$	[9]
Zero-Integral	**32**	**28CCs**	$\mathbf{2^{508.2}}$	$\mathbf{2^{10.8}}$	Sect. **4.2**

CPs: Chosen Plaintexts, CCs: Chosen Ciphertexts

Integral Zero-Correlation Attack on 32-Round SHACAL-2. SHACAL-2 has received some attention from cryptanalysts in recent years. In the single-key setting, the impossible differential attack on 30 rounds of SHACAL-2 is given in [6], the differential-linear attack on 32 rounds of SHACAL-2 along with the saturation attack on 28 rounds of SHACAL-2 has been proposed in [9].

In this paper, we present integral zero-correlation attack on 32 rounds of SHACAL-2. As an integral attack, our attacks are much better than the previous saturation attack on 28 rounds of SHACAL-2 in terms of the number of rounds. We can break as many as rounds as the previous best attacks, namely 32 rounds, with significantly reduced data complexity and memory complexity, while keeping the time complexity virtually unchanged. The attacks are given in Section 4. Our improvements upon the state-of-the-art cryptanalysis for SHACAL-2 under single-key are summarized in Table 1.

2   Preliminaries

2.1   Notation

- $\neg$: the complement operation
- $\boxplus$: the addition modulo 2^{32} operation
- $\boxminus$: the substraction modulo 2^{32} operation
- $\|$: concatenation of two binary strings
- P, C: 256-bit plaintext and ciphertext, respectively
- A, B, C, D, E, F, G, H: eight 32-bit words, corresponding to eight branches
- P^r: 256-bit input of the rth round, $P^r = A^r \| B^r \| C^r \| D^r \| E^r \| F^r \| G^r \| H^r$
- K^r, W^r: r-th round key and round constant, respectively

2.2   Description of SHACAL-2

SHACAL-2 [5] is a 256-bit block cipher introduced by Handschuch and Naccache and has been selected as one of the four block ciphers by NESSIE. It is composed of 64 rounds and the round function is based on the compression function of the hash function SHA-2 [10]. SHACAL-2 supports variable key length up to 512 bits, yet it should not be used with a key shorter than 128 bits.

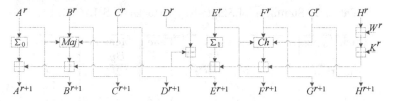

Fig. 1. The r-th round of SHACAL-2

According to the notations in Section 2.1, the 256-bit plaintext P is divided into eight 32-bit words $A^0 \| B^0 \| C^0 \| D^0 \| E^0 \| F^0 \| G^0 \| H^0$ and the output value of the 63th round $A^{64} \| B^{64} \| C^{64} \| D^{64} \| E^{64} \| F^{64} \| G^{64} \| H^{64}$ is the ciphertext C. Figure 1 illustrates the details of the r-th round encryption.

The functions used in the round function are defined as follows, where $S_i(X)$ means the right rotation of 32-bit word X by i-bit position.

$$Ch(X, Y, Z) = (X\&Y) \oplus (\neg X\&Z)$$
$$Maj(X, Y, Z) = (X\&Y) \oplus (X\&Z) \oplus (Y\&Z)$$
$$\textstyle\sum_0(X) = S_2(X) \oplus S_{13}(X) \oplus S_{22}(X)$$
$$\textstyle\sum_1(X) = S_6(X) \oplus S_{11}(X) \oplus S_{25}(X)$$

3   Integral Zero-Correlation Distinguisher for ARX Block Ciphers

3.1   Decomposition of the Target Cipher

Assume that $H : \mathbb{F}_2^n \to \mathbb{F}_2^n$ is (part of) a cipher. To simplify notation and without loss of generality, H could be split into two subfunctions $H : \mathbb{F}_2^r \times \mathbb{F}_2^s \to \mathbb{F}_2^t \times \mathbb{F}_2^u$

$$H(x, y) = \begin{pmatrix} H_1(x, y) \\ H_2(x, y) \end{pmatrix}$$

Furthermore we define function $T_\lambda : \mathbb{F}_2^s \to \mathbb{F}_2^t$ as $T_\lambda(y) = H_1(x, y)$. The function T_λ is the function H when the first r bits of its input are fixed to λ and only the first t bits of the output are taken into account. The decomposition for H is used in [4].

Moreover, for an ARX cipher H', split the inputs into three parts and the outputs into two parts $H' : \mathbb{F}_2^r \times \mathbb{F}_2 \times \mathbb{F}_2^s \to \mathbb{F}_2^t \times \mathbb{F}_2^u$.

$$H'(x, y, z) = \begin{pmatrix} H_1'(x, y, z) \\ H_2'(x, y, z) \end{pmatrix}$$

Function $T_{\lambda\|\lambda'} : \mathbb{F}_2^s \to \mathbb{F}_2^t$ is defined as $T_{\lambda\|\lambda'}(z) = H_1'(\lambda, \lambda', z)$. Function $T_{\lambda\|\lambda'}$ is the function H' when the first r bits and the $(r + 1)$-th bit of its input are fixed to λ and λ' respectively and only the first t bits of the output are considered. We will consider this decomposition for H' in this paper.

3.2   Convert Zero-Correlation to Integral Distinguisher

At ASIACRYPT'12, Bogdanov et al. showed that any zero-correlation linear approximation corresponds to an integral distinguisher. More precisely, consider a zero-correlation distinguisher for an n-bit block cipher where for each non-zero input mask with zeros in s bits and each non-zero output mask with zeros in $n - t$ bits, the corresponding linear approximations have a zero correlation. They prove that the zero-correlation distinguisher is equivalent to an integral distinguisher where fixing the first $n - s$ bits in the input leads to a balanced function when only the first t bits of the output are considered. This conclusion comes from the following proposition.

Proposition 1. *[2, Subsection 3.1] If the input and output linear masks a and b are independent, the approximation $b \diamond H(x) \oplus a \diamond x$ has correlation zero for any $a = (a_1, 0)$ and any $b = (b_1, 0) \neq 0$ (zero-correlation) if and only if the function T_λ is balanced for any λ (integral).*

For ARX ciphers, one bit of input mask of zero-correlation linear approximations is usually fixed to one, i.e. the input mask is consisted of three parts: r bits
that can take any value, one bit fixed to 1, and $s = n - r - 1$ bits that are fixed
to zero. Apparently, such kind of zero-correlation linear approximations do not
conform to the form in [4]. Here we show that such zero-correlation linear approximations imply an integral distinguisher which is concluded in the following
proposition. The proof of Proposition 2 will be shown in the full version of this
paper [11].

Proposition 2. *If the input and output linear masks a and b are independent
and the approximation for H' has correlation zero for any $a = (a_1\|1, 0), a_1 \in \mathbb{F}_2^r$
and any $b = (b_1, 0), b_1 \neq 0, b_1 \in \mathbb{F}_2^t$, the sum of XOR of the function $H_1'(x, y, z)$
is zero for any λ, $\bigoplus_{y\|z} H_1'(\lambda, y, z) = 0$, which means an integral distinguisher.*

4   Integral Zero-Correlation Attack on 32-Round SHACAL-2

4.1   Integral Zero-Correlation Distinguisher for SHACAL-2

If the mask value of a 32-bit word is zero or undetermined for all 32 bits, we simply denote it correspondingly with '0' or '?'. Otherwise, the bit positions having
nonzero or undetermined mask values are listed in the subscripts of '1' or '?', respectively. The mask value of those bits not involved in the subscripts is zero. For
example, $1_{25,22}?_{21-0}$ means a mask value: 0000001001????????????????????????.

According to the propagation property of linear masks, we can construct zero-
correlation linear approximations over 12-round SHACAL-2 as described in Theorem 1.

Theorem 1. *If the input mask is $a = (?, ?, ?, ?, ?, ?, ?, 1_{31}?_{30-0})$ and the output
mask after 12 rounds of decryption for SHACAL-2 is $b = (1_0, 0, 0, 0, 0, 0, 0, 0)$,
then any linear approximation $a \xrightarrow{12r} b$ has correlation zero.*

With Proposition 2, the zero-correlation linear approximations over 12-round
SHACAL-2 can be transformed to an integral distinguisher. We can vary the
most significant bit of H^{12} and fix the other 511 bits of P^{12} as constants,
the XOR sum of the corresponding input bit A_0^0 is zero. The distinguisher
can be further expressed as: for the decryption of 12-round SHACAL-2, de-
crypting 2 ciphertexts $C = (A^{12}, B^{12}, C^{12}, D^{12}, E^{12}, F^{12}, G^{12}, H_{31}^{12}|H_{30-0}^{12})$ and
$C' = (A^{12}, B^{12}, C^{12}, D^{12}, E^{12}, F^{12}, G^{12}, H_{31}^{12} \oplus 1|H_{30-0}^{12})$, then the corresponding
plaintexts have the relation $A_0^0 \oplus A_0'^0 = 0$.

4.2   Key Recovery Attack on 32-Round SHACAL-2

By adding 17 rounds before and appending 3 rounds after the 12-round integral distinguisher of SHACAL-2, we can attack 32-round SHACAL-2. The distinguisher can be summarized as given two message pairs (P, C) and (P', C')

satisfying the condition that the intermediate state value P^{29} and P'^{29} differs only at the most significant bit of H^{28} and H'^{28}, then the XOR of the intermediate value obtained under the right key A_0^{17} and $A_0'^{17}$ is zero, see Figure 2 and Figure 3. To mount the key recovery attack, we start with choosing proper message pairs.

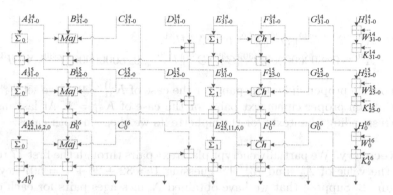

Fig. 2. Partial encryption from 14th round to 16th round

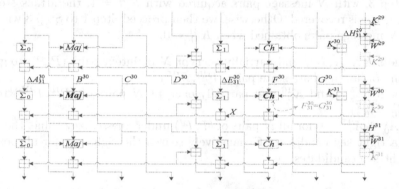

Fig. 3. Last three rounds of the attack on 32-round SHACAL-2

Choose Message Pairs. The modulo addition with subkeys in the last three rounds is equivalently moved, see Figure 3. The single bit nonzero difference between P^{29} and P'^{29} could be regarded as a nonzero difference ΔH_{31}^{29}, which can be guaranteed by only two bits' nonzero differences ΔA_{31}^{30} and ΔE_{31}^{30}. If we randomly choose P^{29} and P'^{29} and try to compute the corresponding ciphertexts, the value of K^{31} needs to be guessed. To scale down the effect of K^{31}, we choose values for $A^{30}, B^{30}, C^{30}, D^{30}, E^{30}, F^{30}, X$ and H^{31}, with which the ciphertext could be computed without guessing any key values, see Figure 3.

For the sake of simplicity, we'd like to eliminate any nonzero difference that might occur between X and X' due to the nonzero difference ΔE_{31}^{30} of $Ch(E^{30}, F^{30}, G^{30})$. As $Ch(E^{30}, F^{30}, G^{30}) = (E^{30} \& F^{30}) \oplus (\neg E^{30} \& G^{30})$, to eliminate the possible output difference of $Ch(E^{30}, F^{30}, G^{30})$, we need to guarantee that $F_{31}^{30} = G_{31}^{30}$. $G^{30} = H^{31} \boxminus K^{31}$, by setting $H^{31} = 0xffffffff$

we can wipe off the effective of borrow bit of modulo subtraction and make sure that $F_{31}^{30} = 1 - K_{31}^{31}$. Thus the value of K_{31}^{31} matters in how we choosing message pairs and we need to choose proper message pairs for the case of $K_{31}^{31} = 0$ and for the case of $K_{31}^{31} = 1$ independently. Generate random values for $A^{30}, B^{30}, C^{30}, D^{30}, E^{30}, F^{30}, X$, set $H^{31} = 0xffffffff$ and set $F_{31}^{30} = 1$, then from Y and Y':

$$Y = A^{30}\|B^{30}\|C^{30}\|D^{30}\|E^{30}\|F^{30}\|X\|H^{31},$$
$$Y' = A^{30} \oplus 0x80000000\|B^{30}\|C^{30}\|D^{30}\|E^{30} \oplus 0x80000000\|F^{30}\|X\|H^{31},$$

we can obtain proper ciphertext pairs for the case of $K_{31}^{31} = 0$. If we set $F_{31}^{30} = 0$, we can obtain proper ciphertext pairs for the case of $K_{31}^{31} = 1$. At last, ask for the corresponding plaintexts for the ciphertexts we chose in both cases.

Key Recovery. We partially encrypt plaintext pairs through the first 17 rounds to get the value of A_0^{17} and $A_0'^{17}$ by guessing $15 * 32 + 26 + 1 = 507$ key bits, see Figure 2. Suppose that we have obtained N messages pairs for each of the two cases ($K_{31}^{31} = 1$ and $K_{31}^{31} = 0$). We firstly proceed the following steps, Step 1 to Step 3, with N message pairs acquired with $K_{31}^{31} = 1$, the attack stops if the right key is recovered. Otherwise, we then proceed Step 1 to Step 3 with the other N message pairs obtained when $K_{31}^{31} = 0$.

1. Guess $K^0, \ldots, K^{14}$ and partially encrypt N plaintext pairs (P, P') to get N pairs of intermediate state pairs (P^{15}, P'^{15}).
2. Guess K_{25-0}^{15} and K_0^{16} and partially encrypt N pairs of (P^{15}, P'^{15}) to get $(A_0^{17}, A_0'^{17})$.
3. If $A_0^{17} \oplus A_0'^{17} = 0$ for all N pairs of (P, P') under guessed key value, then this is a right key candidate. Exhaustively search the right key for all possible right key candidates.

Complexity Estimation. The time complexities of Step 1 and Step 2 are $2^{15*32} \cdot N \cdot 2 \cdot 15/32 \approx N \cdot 2^{479.9}$ and $2^{507} \cdot N \cdot 2 \cdot 2/32 \approx N \cdot 2^{504}$ encryptions, respectively. The time complexity of the exhaustive search phase, Step 3, is about 2^{512-N} encryptions because with N message pairs we can filter out 2^{-N} wrong key guesses. Then, the time complexity of Step 1 to Step 3 is about $N \cdot 2^{479.9} + N \cdot 2^{504} + 2^{512-N}$ encryptions. If we failed to recover the right key after Step 3, we need to re-proceed these steps with the other N message pairs. Thus, in the worst case, the total time complexity of our attack on 32-round SHACAL-2 is about $2 \cdot (N \cdot 2^{479.9} + N \cdot 2^{504} + 2^{512-N})$ encryptions. If we set $N = 7$, then the time complexity of the whole key recovery is about $2^{508.2}$ encryptions and the data complexity is 28 chosen ciphertexts. The memory requirements are about $2 \cdot 7 \cdot 2 \cdot 512/8 \approx 2^{10.8}$ bytes to store (P, C) pairs and intermediate values.

5   Conclusion

In this paper, we extend the work of integral zero-correlation distinguisher for ARX block ciphers. For some ARX block ciphers, zero-correlation linear approximations do not conform to those which have been transformed to an integral distinguisher in [4]. We show that such zero-correlation linear approximations also imply an integral distinguisher. With the zero-correlation integral distinguisher, we improve upon the state-of-the-art cryptanalysis for one NESSIE algorithm SHACAL-2 by reducing attack complexities for the previous attack on the highest number of rounds in the classical single-key setting.

References

1. Biryukov, A., Shamir, A.: Structural Cryptanalysis of SASAS. In: Pfitzmann, B. (ed.) EUROCRYPT 2001. LNCS, vol. 2045, pp. 394–405. Springer, Heidelberg (2001)
2. Bogdanov, A., Rijmen, V.: Linear Hulls with Correlation Zero and Linear Cryptanalysis of Block Ciphers. Designs, Codes and Cryptography 70(3), 369–383 (2014)
3. Bogdanov, A., Wang, M.: Zero Correlation Linear Cryptanalysis with Reduced Data Complexity. In: Canteaut, A. (ed.) FSE 2012. LNCS, vol. 7549, pp. 29–48. Springer, Heidelberg (2012)
4. Bogdanov, A., Leander, G., Nyberg, K., Wang, M.: Integral and Multidimensional Linear Distinguishers with Correlation Zero. In: Wang, X., Sako, K. (eds.) ASIACRYPT 2012. LNCS, vol. 7658, pp. 244–261. Springer, Heidelberg (2012)
5. Handschuh, H., Naccache, D.: SHACAL: A Family of Block Ciphers. Submission to the NESSIE project (2002)
6. Hong, S.H., Kim, J.-S., Kim, G., Sung, J., Lee, C.-H., Lee, S.-J.: Impossible Differential Attack on 30-Round SHACAL-2. In: Johansson, T., Maitra, S. (eds.) INDOCRYPT 2003. LNCS, vol. 2904, pp. 97–106. Springer, Heidelberg (2003)
7. Knudsen, L.R., Wagner, D.: Integral Cryptanalysis. In: Daemen, J., Rijmen, V. (eds.) FSE 2002. LNCS, vol. 2365, pp. 112–127. Springer, Heidelberg (2002)
8. Lucks, S.: The Saturation Attack–A Bait for Twofish. In: Matsui, M. (ed.) FSE 2001. LNCS, vol. 2355, pp. 1–15. Springer, Heidelberg (2002)
9. Shin, Y., Kim, J.-S., Kim, G., Hong, S.H., Lee, S.-J.: Differential-Linear Type Attack on Reduced Rounds of SHACAL-2. In: Wang, H., Pieprzyk, J., Varadharajan, V. (eds.) ACISP 2004. LNCS, vol. 3108, pp. 110–122. Springer, Heidelberg (2004)
10. U.S. Department of Commerce.FIPS 180-2: Secure Hash Standard, Federal Information Processing Standards Publication, N.I.S.T (2002)
11. Wen, L., Wang, M.: Integral Zero-Correlation Distinguisher for ARX Block Cipher, with Application to SHACAL-2. IACR ePrint Archive report (2014)
12. Wen, L., Wang, M., Bogdanov, A., Chen, H.: Multidimensional Zero-Correlation Attacks on Lightweight Block Cipher HIGHT: Improved Cryptanalysis of an ISO Standard. Information Processing Letters 114(6), 322–330 (2014)

Author Index

Alawatugoda, Janaka   258
Alneyadi, Sultan   413
Aoki, Kazumaro   17

Bai, Shi   322
Banik, Subhadeep   34
Batten, Lynn   430
Bogdanov, Andrey   422
Boyd, Colin   258

Chan, Patrick   446
Chen, Xiaofeng   82, 115
Chen, Yu   274, 438
Chu, Xiaobo   397
Cui, Xingmin   446

Datta, Nilanjan   306
Datta, Pratish   98
Deng, Yingpu   148
Ding, Zhaojing   162
Dutta, Ratna   98, 209

Feng, Dengguo   397
Fukumitsu, Masayuki   290
Fukuzawa, Yasuko   226

Galbraith, Steven D.   322
Gu, Haihua   162
Guo, Wei   162

Hasegawa, Shingo   290
Huang, Qiong   274
Hui, Lucas C.K.   446

Isobe, Shuji   290

Jia, Chunfu   115
Jing, Jiwu   354, 370

Khan, Mohammed Shafiul Alam   386
Kogure, Jun   338
Koshiba, Takeshi   338
Kunihiro, Noboru   176

Lei, Lingguang   354
Li, Jin   115
Li, Miao   370
Liu, Jianwei   242
Liu, Liang   82
Liu, Weiran   242
Liu, Zheli   115
Liu, Zongbin   370
Lou, Wenjing   82

Mitchell, Chris J.   386
Moonsamy, Veelasha   430
Moriai, Shiho   17
Mukhopadhyay, Sourav   98
Muthukkumarasamy, Vallipuram   413

Nandi, Mridul   306

Pan, Yanbin   148

Qin, Bo   242
Qin, Yu   397
Qing, Sihan   446

Rahulamathavan, Yogachandran   430
Rajarajan, Muttukrishnan   430
Rao, Y. Sreenivasa   209

Sato, Hisayoshi   226
Sepehrdad, Pouyan   50
Shao, Jianxiong   397
Shi, Yuanchun   438
Shimoyama, Takeshi   338
Shizuya, Hiroki   290
Shunliang, Su   430
Sithirasenan, Elankayer   413
Stebila, Douglas   258
Su, Liangjian   162
Sušil, Petr   50

Taga, Bungo   17
Takayasu, Atsushi   176
Tanaka, Keisuke   66

Vaudenay, Serge   50
Vejre, Philip S.   422

Wang, Meiqin   454
Wang, Mingsheng   131
Wang, Qiongxiao   354
Wang, Weijin   397
Wang, Yanfeng   1
Wang, Yuewu   354
Wang, Yuyu   66
Wei, Jizeng   162
Wen, Long   454
Wu, Qianhong   242
Wu, Shengbao   131
Wu, Wenling   1

Xi, Li   397
Xiang, Ji   370

Yamamoto, Dan   226
Yang, Jun   115
Yasuda, Masaya   338
Yiu, S.M.   446
Yokoyama, Kazuhiro   338
Yu, Da   446

Zhang, Bin   131
Zhang, Lei   438
Zhang, Mingwu   192
Zhang, Qinglong   370
Zhang, Zhijiao   438
Zhang, Zhongwen   354
Zhang, Zongyang   274
Zhong, Xiao   131